500 miles

zou

Okinawa

Io-Jima
(Japan)

Taipei

Nansei (Japan) shoto

Hualien

TAIWAN

P A C I F I C

P H I L I P P I N E

NORTHERN
MARIANA
ISLANDS
(USA)

page
296

Batan
Islands

Babuyan
Islands

Tangatan

S E A

ag

Itagan

Luzon

Dilalongan

page
308

Guam
(USA)

io

PHILIPPINES

nla

Lucena

Naga

O C E A N

mba

Legazpi

ngas

Samar

Masbate

Calbayog

alapan

oro

Panay

Sagay

Tacloban

tay

Iloilo City

Cebu City

Babelthuap

Negros

Butuan

nt

ULU

Pagadian

Mindanao

S E A

mboanga
City

Davao City

General
Santos

PALAU

C E L E B E S

S E A

Manado

Halmahera

Gorontalo

Ternate

Pulau Waigeo

Manokwari

Pulau
Biak

G. Kwoka
2452

Maluku (Moluccas)

Pulau Misool

Pulau
Yapen

Jayapura

Kepulauan
Sula

SERAM SEA

Seram

West Papua
(Irian Jaya)

Puncak Jaya
5030

Mamberamo

Sulawesi

Buru

Ambon

pegunungan Maoke

New PAPUA

A Guinea

PAPUA
NEW
GUINEA

Pulau
Muna

BANDA SEA

Amamapare

Kepulauan
Aru

Digul

E

S

LORES SEA

Wetar

Flores

Pulau Yamdena

Pulau Dolak

Torres Strait

Ende

Dili

EAST
TIMOR

aingapu

Kupang

Timor

A R A F U R A   S E A

Melville
Island

Somerset

Pulau Roti

Bathurst
Island

A U S T R A L I A

Cape York
Peninsula

Darwin   Arnhem Land

INSIGHT GUIDES

SOUTHEAST ASIA

APA PUBLICATIONS

Part of the Langenscheidt Publishing Group

INSIGHT GUIDE
SOUTHEAST asia

Editorial
Project Editor
Heidi Sopinka
Managing Editor
Scott Rutherford
Editorial Director
Brian Bell

Distribution
UK & Ireland
GeoCenter International Ltd
Meridian House, Churchill Way West
Basingstoke, Hampshire RG21 6YR
Fax: (44 1256) 817 988

United States
Langenscheidt Publishers, Inc.
36–36 33rd Street 4th Floor,
Long Island City, NY 11106
Fax: (1 718) 784 0640

Australia
Universal Publishers
1 Waterloo Road
Macquarie Park, NSW 2113
Fax: (61 2) 9888 9074

New Zealand
Hema Maps New Zealand Ltd (HNZ)
Unit D, 24 Ra ORA Drive
East Tamaki, Auckland
Fax: (64 9) 273 6479

Worldwide
Apa Publications GmbH & Co.
Verlag KG (Singapore branch)
38 Joo Koon Road, Singapore 628990
Tel: (65) 6865 1600. Fax: (65) 6861 6438

Printing
Insight Print Services (Pte) Ltd
38 Joo Koon Road, Singapore 628990
Tel: (65) 6865 1600. Fax: (65) 6861 6438

©2007 Apa Publications GmbH & Co.
Verlag KG (Singapore branch)
All Rights Reserved
First Edition 1995
Second Edition 1999
Updated 2007

CONTACTING THE EDITORS
We would appreciate it if readers
would alert us to errors or outdated
information by writing to:
**Insight Guides, P.O. Box 7910,
London se1 1WE, England.
Fax: (44 20) 7403 0290.
insight@apaguide.co.uk**

www.insightguides.com
In North America:
www.insighttravelguides.com

ABOUT THIS BOOK

The first Insight Guide pioneered the use of creative full-colour photography in travel guides in 1970. Since then, we have expanded our range to cater for our readers' need not only for reliable information about their chosen destination but also for a real understanding of that destination. Now, when the Internet can supply inexhaustible – but not always reliable – facts, our books marry text and pictures to provide those much more elusive qualities: knowledge and discernment. To achieve this, we rely heavily on the authority of locally based photographers and writers.

In this, the second edition of *Insight Guide: Southeast Asia*, we journey to eclectic nations and cultures: Thailand, Burma, Laos, Cambodia, Vietnam, the Philippines, Malaysia, Singapore, Indonesia and Brunei. Assembling an overview of Southeast Asia was a formidable task. Fortunately, we had one great advantage: Insight Guides for each nation from which to extract insight on the many cultures, peoples and places.

How to use this book
Insight Guides' proven format of informative and well-written text paired with exciting and evocative

and culture of the country in a series of authoritative essays written by specialists.

◆ The main **Places** section, indicated by a blue bar, provides a full run-down of all the attractions worth seeing. The principal places of interest are cross-referenced by number to maps.

◆ The **Travel Tips** section, with an orange bar, provides a handy point of reference for information on getting around, restaurants, hotels, and more.

The contributors

The second edition was supervised by managing editor **Scott Rutherford**. Enlisted to distil down each existing Insight Guide for this book was Canadian editor and writer **Heidi Sopinka**. Contributing new essays for this edition were writers from Chiang Mai-based CPA, supervised by **Andrew Forbes**, and **Jim Michener**, in Vientiane. The *Insight On* pictorial essays were written by **Clare Griffiths**.

In 2007, the guide was updated by **Jocelyn Lau**, **Low Jat Leng** and the following writers: Yogyakarta-based **Linda Hoffman**, who updated the Indonesia section with the help of **Supardi Asmorobangun** and **Jacky Djokosetio**, as well as **William Ingram** from Threads of Life, a non-profit organisation dedicated to sustaining Indonesia's textile arts; Chiang Mai-based **Joe Cummings**, who updated the Burma section; and **Wan Zainal Abidin**, who updated the Brunei section.

European impression of Ayutthaya in the 1600s.

photography continues throughout this edition of *Insight Guide: Southeast Asia*. The guide is structured to convey a complete understanding of the many countries and their cultures, and to guide readers through the wide-ranging and diverse region's sights and activities.

◆ The **Features** section, indicated by a yellow bar at the top of each page, covers the history

Map Legend

▬▬ ▪▬	International Boundary
▬▪▬	National Park/Reserve
▬ ▬ ▬	Ferry Route
✈ ✈	Airport: International/ Regional
🚌	Bus Station
℗	Parking
❶	Tourist Information
✉	Post Office
✝ ✝ ⳨	Church/Ruins
✝	Monastery
☾	Mosque
✡	Synagogue
🏰 🏚	Castle/Ruins
∴	Archaeological Site
∩	Cave
𝟏	Statue/Monument
★	Place of Interest

The main places of interest in the **Places** chapters are coordinated with a full-colour map: by number with a regional map (e.g. ❶) and by letter with a city map (e.g. Ⓐ). A note at the top of every right-hand page tells you where to find the map.

INSIGHT GUIDE
SOUTHEAST asia

CONTENTS

Rain forest,
Sabah, Malaysia

SOUTHEAST ASIA

One would be challenged to find a region with a more eclectic

mix of people, culture, languages, history and lifestyles

It is not without some coincidence that the nations covered in this Insight Guide – Thailand, Burma, Vietnam, Laos, Cambodia, Malaysia, Philippines, Singapore, Indonesia and Brunei – are members of ASEAN, the Association of Southeast Asian Nations. Since its 1967 founding by Indonesia, Malaysia, Thailand, Singapore and the Philippines, ASEAN has had its ups and downs as the region's countries try to build a common identity and purpose, an admirable but impossible dream.

The withdrawal of the Western colonial powers from Southeast Asia following World War II left a power vacuum. It was clear to Southeast Asia's emerging cadre of leaders that cooperation would make their collective position stronger. But the realities behind the idea of forming an organisation were far from smooth. The climate of the 1960s was a mine field of border disputes, economic competition and differing working styles inherited from the colonial powers. An obvious obstacle was – and forever will be – the great difference in economic structures and levels of development amongst the member nations, a difference even more pronounced following the admission of Burma, Laos and Cambodia to ASEAN in the late 1990s. Consider the differences in per capita income: Singapore's exceeds US$29,000, while Laos' is approximately US$440. Expectations are going to be different, as are goals.

These Southeast Asian countries combined cover 4.5 million sq. km (1.8 million sq. miles), half the size of China and 18 times the size of Great Britain. The region's combined population of 568 million people is just over half that of India's and twice that of the United States. While the numbers are impressive, what can't be quantified and simplified is the simply awesome diversity and complexity of the region's cultures, histories, arts and people. This diversity and complexity, forgetting for the moment any political facet of decision-making, makes an ASEAN of consensus a dream.

Thailand is perhaps the best-known and most-visited Southeast Asian nation amongst Westerners. While the Thai beaches of interest have shifted over the decades, from Pattaya to Phuket to Samui, the architectural delights of Bangkok (although a civil engineer's and city planner's bad dream) and Chiang Mai, along with the diversity of the northern hill-tribe people, persist.

Until the mid 1990s, when modern hotels began punctuating the skyline, Burma's former capital of Yangon seemed a place lost in time. The people changed, but the city's momentum had long ago evaporated. To the north, Mandalay has chimed like music to the Western ear, ever since Rudyard Kipling wrote of its magic. And if

PRECEDING PAGES: a few of Indonesia's volcanoes, Java; temple detail from Vietnam; southern village, Philippines; the holy temples of Bagan, Burma; Kuala Lumpur's glittering skyline. **LEFT:** Vietnamese violin student.

Yangon once seemed stalled in time, Bagan was and always will be frozen in time, its thousands of ancient pagodas peppering the expansive plain as testimonial to the great kings that rose and fell.

Laos and Cambodia, wedged in amongst stronger neighbours, are the region's poorest countries. Laos is increasingly opening up, and Cambodia would like to do so despite its ongoing internal problems. Laos' capital of Vientiane is indubitably Asia's most quiet and laidback capital city, while the ancient capital of Luang Prabang to the north is not only quiet, but adorned with the best of Laos' ancient architecture. Cambodia's historical anchorage lies in Angkor, representative of the great Khmer kingdom that long ruled the region.

Vietnam has the distinction of having been a divided country for much of its modern history. Today, its economy and the people's innate entrepreneurial skills are hobbled by a stagnant leadership fearful of a brave new world of commerce and information. But the Vietnamese are an intensely resourceful people, and travellers to Hanoi, Vietnam's capital, or especially Ho Chi Minh City, the former Saigon, can't help but be impressed by the people's zeal against inertia. On the coast east of Hanoi, Ha Long Bay entrances the visitor with its otherworldly scenery. Midway between Hanoi and Ho Chi Minh, Hue is a place where the artefacts of ancient kings still hold sway over the senses.

Like Burma, Malaysia was once part of the British Empire. Unlike Burma, Malaysia has turned itself into one of the region's most important economies. Graced with a blend of colonial, Islamic and ultramodern architecture, Kuala Lumpur keeps getting higher (though it would have to outdo itself, as the world's tallest twin buildings are already standing in KL) and more congested. Penang, an island off the western coast to the north of Kuala Lumpur, has long lured Westerners with its mix of cluttered Chinese alleys and white-sand beaches. Far to the east on Borneo, the states of Sabah and Sarawak are synonymous with the exotic and adventurous. Wedged in between is Brunei, ruled by a sultan, one of the world's richest persons. At the southern tip of the Malaysian peninsula is Singapore, the city-state governed like a corporation and perhaps the most efficient place on earth.

Indonesia is Southeast Asia's largest country both in size and population. It is also the world's largest Islamic nation. Jakarta is like many Asian cities, a new skyline shiny and electric, with roads below chaotic and claustrophobic. Jakarta is on Java, one of the world's most densely populated places and where some of the region's great ancient empires arose. At the eastern end of Java is Bali, increasingly modern and developed, but still intriguing with its intense self-confidence and pride in its culture and history.

The Philippines is the most unlikely of Asian nations, with nearly five centuries of Spanish and American influence – four centuries in a convent followed by 50 years in Hollywood. It's a Catholic country, an inescapable cast in Manila, where cathedrals rise to rival those of Europe. Yet in the north of Ilocos or the southern islands of the Visayas, the Western textures are well moderated by local ways. ❏

RIGHT: Sukhothai Hindu deity.

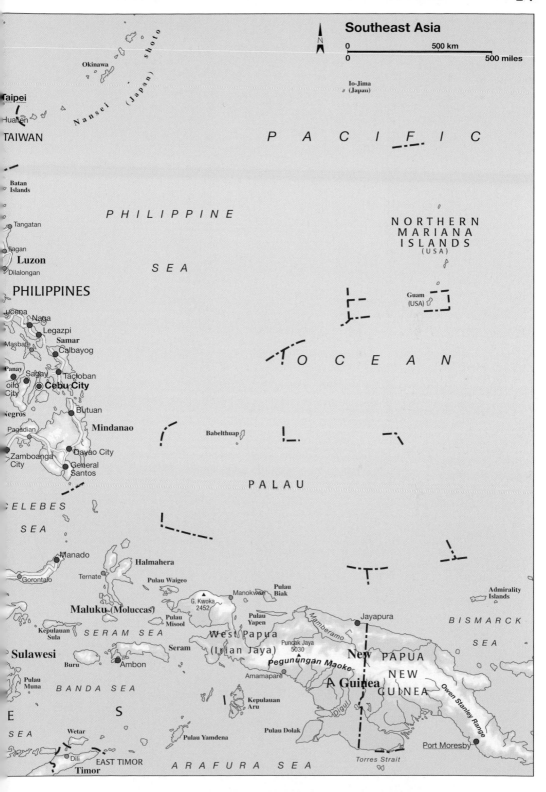

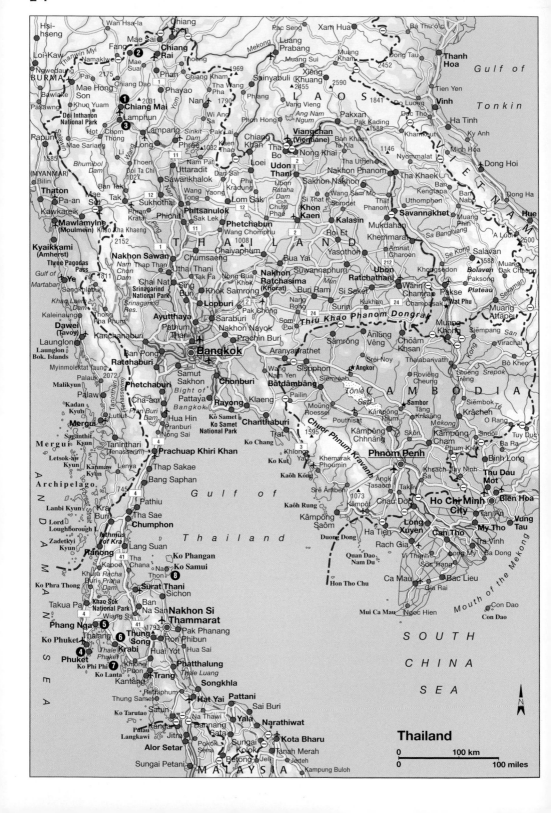

Thailand

0   100 km

0   100 miles

THAILAND

More than any other Southeast Asian country, Thailand has long been identified with the region's uniqueness

L and of the Free. Land of Smiles. The former is a literal translation of the word *Thailand,* the latter a promotional slogan – and a truthful one at that. Beneath their graciousness, the Thais have a strong sense of self and a humanity without subservience. It is this pride in themselves that underlies their sense of identity and their ability to smile at the vicissitudes of life.

Thailand has a population of more than 66 million, and it is nearly the size of Central America, or of France, or twice that of England. Its capital of Bangkok (with a population, at rough estimates, of more than 10 million) lies on the same latitude as Madras, Khartoum, Guatemala City, Guam and Manila.

Lying inland from the apex of the Gulf of Thailand, Bangkok is the country's international gateway, and seat of government, business and the monarchy. Bangkok bears little relation to the rest of the country, mostly a patchwork of rice fields, villages, plantations and forests whose second largest city is just a fraction – perhaps one-fiftieth – the size of Bangkok. The country is commonly divided into four regions: the Central Plains, including Bangkok, and the North, Northeast and South. Each region has its own culture and appeal. When a Thai says "I'm heading upcountry tomorrow," she or he could mean anywhere outside Bangkok's city limits.

Elevations run from sea level along the 2,600-km-long (1,600-mile) coastline to a peak of 2,600 metres (8,500 ft) in the north, a region of hills clad in teak forests and valleys carpeted in rice, fruit trees and vegetables, and bordered by Burma and Laos. The northeast is dominated by the arid Khorat Plateau, where farmers struggle to cultivate rice, tapioca, jute and other cash crops. With strong cultural affinities to neighbouring Laos and Cambodia, the region is rimmed and defined by the Mekong River. In the central plains, monsoon rains transform the landscape into a vast hydroponic basin, which nourishes a sea of rice, the country's staple and an important export.

Through this region flows the Chao Phraya River, carrying produce and people south to Bangkok, washing rich sediment down from the northern hills, and during the monsoon season, further flooding the rice fields. The south runs down a long, narrow arm of land leading to Malaysia. Rubber and palm oil plantations alternate with rice and fruit trees, an area strongly influenced by Malay culture.

Since the East discovered it a millennium ago and the West began trickling in during the 16th century, Thailand has been a powerful magnet for adventurers and entrepreneurs. An abundance of resources, a wealth of natural beauty, stunning architecture and art, and a warm, hospitable people have long proved irresistible.   ❏

PRECEDING PAGES: every Thai male spends time as a Buddhist monk.

Decisive Dates

Pre-Thai civilisation

3600–250 BC: Ban Chiang bronze culture flourishes in northeastern Thailand.

circa 250 BC: Suvannabhumi trading with India.

4th–8th centuries AD: influence of Mon and Khmer empires spreads into Thailand.

9th–13th centuries: Khmer Empire founded at Angkor. Thai peoples migrate southeast from the Dien Bien Phu area of Vietnam into northern Thailand, Burma, and Laos. Lopburi becomes an important provincial capital in Khmer Empire, later tries to become independent.

Sukhothai era

1238: Khmer power wanes. Kingdom of Sukhothai founded under Intaradit.

1281: Chiang Saen kingdom founded in north.

1296: Lanna Kingdom founded at Chiang Mai. Mangrai controls much of northern Thailand and Laos.

1280–1318: Reign of Ramkamhaeng in Sukhothai. Often called Thailand's "Golden Age", the period saw the first attempts to unify the Thai people, the first use of the Thai script, and a flourishing of the arts.

1317–47: Lo Thai reigns at Sukhothai. The slow decline of the Sukhothai kingdom begins.

1438: Sukhothai is now virtually deserted; power shifts to the Kingdom of Ayutthaya, to the south and along the Chao Phraya River.

Kingdom of Ayutthaya

14th century: Area around Ayutthaya settled by representatives of the Chiang Saen kingdom.

1350: City of Ayutthaya founded by Phya U-Thong, who proclaims himself Ramathibodi I. Within a few years he controls the areas encompassed by the kingdoms of Sukhothai and the Khmer empire.

1369: Ramesuan, son of Ramathibodi, becomes king.

1390: Ramesuan captures Chiang Mai.

1393: Ramesuan captures Angkor in Cambodia.

1448–88: Reign of King Trailok, who briefly unites the Lanna (Chiang Mai) and Ayutthaya kingdoms.

1491–1529: Reign of King Ramathibodi II.

1549: First major warfare with Mon Kingdom of Bago.

1569: Burmese capture and loot Ayutthaya.

1590: Naresuan becomes king, throws off Burmese suzerainty. Ayutthaya expands rapidly at the expense of Burmese and Khmer empires and flourishes.

1605–10: Ekatotsarot reigns, begins significant economic ties with European traders and adventurers.

1610–28: Reign of King Songtham. The British arrive and obtain land for a trading factory.

1628–55: Reign of Prasat Thong. Trading concessions expand and regular trade with China and Europe is established.

1656–88: Reign of King Narai. British influence expands. Reputation of Ayutthaya as a magnificent city and a remarkable royal court spreads in Europe.

1678: Constantine Phaulkon arrives at Narai's court and gains great influence; French presence expands.

1688: Narai dies, Phaulkon executed.

1733–58: Reign of King Boromakot. Ayutthaya enters a period of peace, and of arts and literature.

1767: Burmese King Alaungpaya captures and sacks Ayutthaya, destroying four centuries of Thai civilisation. Seven months later General Phya Tak Sin returns and expels the Burmese occupiers. He moves the capital from Ayutthaya to Thonburi, near Bangkok.

Beginning of the Chakri dynasty

1767: Phya Taksin crowned as King Taksin.

1779: Generals Chao Phya Chakri and his brother Chao Phya Sarasin conquer Chiang Mai, expel the Burmese from what is now Thailand and so adding most of the Khmer and Lao kingdoms to the Thai kingdom. The Emerald Buddha brought from Vientiane, Laos, to Thonburi.

1782: The now erratic Taksin is deposed and executed. Chao Phya Chakri is offered the throne, founding the Chakri dynasty and assuming the name Ramathibodi and later Rama I. Capital is moved across the river to the city that becomes known to the west as Bangkok. Under Rama I, the Siamese

Kingdom consolidates and expands its strength. Rama I revives Thai art, religion, and culture.

1809–24: Reign of Rama II; best known for construction of Wat Arun and many other temples and monasteries. Rama II reopens relations with the West, suspended since the time of Narai.

1824–51: Reign of Rama III, who left as his trademark the technique of embedding Chinese porcelain fragments as decorations on temples.

1851: King Mongkut (Rama IV) ascends the throne. He is the first Thai king to understand Western culture and technology. Before becoming king he spends 27 years as a monk, studying Western science.

1868: Chulalongkorn (Rama V) ascends the throne, reigning for the next four decades. Chulalongkorn ends the custom of prostration in royal presence, abolishes slavery, and replaces corvee labour with taxation. Infrastructure, schools, military and government modernised.

1910–25: Reign of Vajiravudh (Rama VI), Oxford-educated and thoroughly Westernised.

1925–32: Reign of Prajadhipok (Rama VII). Economic pressures from Great Depression spur discontent.

End of the absolute monarchy

1932: A coup d'etat ends the absolute monarchy and ushers in a constitutional monarchy.

1939: The name of the country is officially changed from Siam to Thailand, "Land of the Free". King Ananda (Rama VIII) ascends the throne.

1942: Japan invades Thailand with the acquiescence of the military government, but a spirited if small resistance movement thrives.

1946: King Ananda is killed by a mysterious gunshot; Bhumibol Adulyadej (Rama IX) ascends the throne. The royal family becomes a symbol of national unity.

1973–91: Bloody clashes between army and demonstrating students brings down the military government; political and economic blunders brings down the resulting civilian government just 3 years later. Various military-backed and civilian governments come and go for almost 20 years.

1991: Another clash between military and civilians brings the unusual sight of the leaders of both factions kneeling in contrition before the king; as a result, the military leaves government to the civilian politicians.

1992: Thailand begins 5 years of unprecedented economic growth. The face of Bangkok changes rapidly.

1996: King Bhumibol Adulyadej celebrates 50 years on the throne, the world's longest-reigning monarch.

1997: The Thai economy suffers a serious setback during the Asian financial crisis.

2001: Billionaire tycoon Thaksin Shinawatra and his Thai Rak Thai party win the election.

2003: Shinawatra's policies strengthen the economy.

2004: Tsunami claims 8,000 lives along Thailand's Andaman coastline.

2005: Thaksin is re-elected by a large majority despite accusations of corruption.

2006: Results of snap election called by Thaksin are annulled by Thai courts. In September, the Royal Thai Army successfully stages a bloodless coup, deposing Thaksin. Retired general Surayud Chulanont is appointed as interim prime minister in October. ❑

CHAKRI MONARCHY

Since 1782, a single royal dynasty – known as Chakri – has ruled over Thailand.

Rama I (Chakri)	1782–1809
Rama II (Phutthalaetia)	1809–1824
Rama III (Nangklao)	1824–1851
Rama IV (Mongkut)	1851–1868
Rama V (Chulalongkorn)	1868–1910
Rama VI (Vajiravudh)	1910–1925
Rama VII (Prajadhipok)	1925–1935
Rama VIII (Ananda)	1935–1946
Rama IX (Bhumibol)	1946–

LEFT: Ayutthayan general mounts battle elephant.
RIGHT: portrait of King Chulalongkorn, or Rama V.

PEOPLE OF THE HILLS

The tribal people of Thailand make up fewer than one in fifty

of the nation's population, but their way of life continues to lure visitors

Thousands of foreigners annually trek to the tribal people's mountain villages in Thailand. The average Thai, however, views tribal people as foreigners, if not illegal aliens, and thus not entitled to the same rights as Thais. Most tribal immigration – typically from Burma or Laos – has occurred only in the past 100 years. In fact, only in the past decade have significant numbers of tribal people been granted Thai citizenship.

Thailand is home for up to 20 tribes, but there are six principal groups: Karen, Hmong, Mien, Lahu, Lisu and Akha. Living in villages at higher elevations, most hill-tribe farmers practise slash-and-burn, or swidden, agriculture. The ashes at first provide a rich fertiliser, but over the years the process depletes the soil, and unfortunately, today there's no longer much forest left to burn. Villagers used to then move their villages to a new site, but there's no place to move nowadays. With poorer soil and increasingly less of it, villagers sometimes rely on the opium poppy as a cash crop.

Karen

The 320,000 Karen form by far the largest tribe. In Thailand, they comprise two sub-groups, the Sgaw and Pwo, whose dialects are not mutually intelligible. Karens have been settled in Thailand since the 18th century and they are still (illegally) trickling in from Burma, where a Karen rebel army has been fighting the Burmese government for decades. The Karen separatist movement in Burma sometimes makes relations between Burma and Thailand edgy.

Karens were early converts to Christianity when Burma was a British colony, and some Thai Karens are Baptists or Seventh-Day Adventists. All Karens place great emphasis on monogamy, condemn premarital sex, and trace ancestry through the mother. Unlike other Thai tribes, they have long practised lowland wet-rice farming.

OPPOSITE: distinctive headdress of an Akha woman.
RIGHT: antique hill-tribe textile.

Hmong

The most recent arrivals in Thailand, Hmong are the second-largest hill tribe in the country, numbering about 120,000. The majority of them immigrated to Thailand in the 1950s and 1960s, fleeing from the long civil war in Laos. Ever on the alert for communists, the Thai mil-

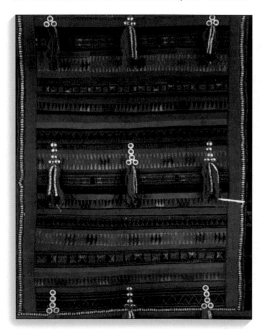

itary then regarded Hmong as subversives, and Hmong relations with Thai officialdom still remain complicated. Ironically, Hmong are renowned for their fierce independence and, in Laos, for anti-communism. Indeed, they were American allies during the Vietnam War.

Opium use is common, kinship is patrilineal, and polygamy is permitted. Like Thai, the Hmong language can be traced to southern China, where 4 million Hmong live today in China's Yunnan Province. Dialects and clothing identify the Hmong: Blue Hmong women wear indigo, pleated skirts and their hair in huge buns. White Hmong women wear white hemp skirts and black turbans.

Mien (Yao)

Like Hmong, most of Thailand's 40,000 Mien (also known as Yao) probably came from Laos, but there are also large numbers in Burma, Vietnam and China's Yunnan Province – not to mention the Lao Mien refugee communities in San Francisco and Seattle. Many Chinese elements, such as ancestor worship and Daoism, are evident in their animistic religious beliefs. Kinship is mostly patrilineal, and polygamy is practised. The Mien

> **NORTHERN HOMES**
>
> With the exception of the Karen, whose range extends down to Kanchanaburi and Tak provinces, most hill tribes in Thailand live in three northern provinces: Chiang Mai, Chiang Rai and Mae Hong Son.

Sheleh – varies only slightly. The Lahu people are skilled makers of baskets and bags, and they are also famous for their hunting prowess. The Lahu dialects are of the Tibeto-Burman group.

Lisu

There are only about 28,000 Lisu. They are easily identified by their penchant for bright colours. Lisu are good silversmiths and make jewellery for the Akha and Lahu. They are regarded by other tribal people as rather sharp business people.

place great emphasis on the peaceful resolution of conflict, which is apparent in their smooth relations with Thais in general. Traditionally, Mien women can be distinguished by their black jackets and trousers, red fur-like collars and large blue or black turbans.

Lahu

Like the Karen, traditional Lahu mix animism with millennial myths, while a good proportion of the 73,000 Lahu are also Christian. Besides the usual opium, corn and rice, Lahu have successfully cultivated chilli peppers as a cash crop. The traditional dress of the four groups – Red Lahu, Black Lahu, Yellow Lahu and Lahu

Animistic beliefs are combined with ancestor worship. Lisu are known to cite reasons for the pre-eminence of their family, clan or village, yet, unlike other tribes, they have an organisation that extends across villages. Lisu are a subgroup of the Kachin, a large minority group in the far north of Burma. Kachin languages are Tibeto-Burman.

Akha

Thailand's 48,000 Akha are the hill-tribe people that most tourists want to see, drawn by the heavy ornate head-dress worn by the women: silver disks festooned with old coins, beads and feathers. And unlike other tribal women, who save their finery for ceremonies, Akha wear this even while working in the fields. Animist beliefs are mixed with ancestor worship; Akha can recite their ancestry back 20 generations. Their language is Tibeto-Burman.

Other minorities

Two other groups, the Shan and Padaung, deserve mention, as their villages are frequent stops on trekking tours. However, strictly speaking, they are not Thai hill tribes.

In their settled communities, rice-growing practices and Theravada Buddhism, the Shan are very similar to Thais. Their language is sim-

years ago, tours from Mae Hong Son would ferry tourists across the border to view Kayan women whose necks had been elongated by layers of heavy brass coils.

Kayan leaders had long discouraged the practice and it had virtually died out. But the tourist attraction was so great that Thai officials allowed three villages to set up west of Mae Hong Son. Many Kayan women have since donned the coils and initiated girls beginning at age five. Tours to view the "giraffe women" have been heavily promoted in Bangkok. Tourists paying to go on these tours are thus directly responsible for the return of this barbaric practice.

ilar to the northern Thai dialect, although not intelligible to central Thai speakers. Many Shan have migrated to Thailand in recent times to escape the upheavals in Burma, but the Shan may have been the first Tai inhabitants of northern Thailand, in the 9th or 10th centuries. The large area of Burma bordering the northern tip of Thailand is the home of 4 million Shan and several armies battling for autonomy.

The Padaung (Kayan) are a Karennic people residing in the southern Shan areas. Until a few

LEFT: Mien resplendent in traditional clothing.
ABOVE: Hmong women are distinguished by costumes of heavy black cotton.

Cultures under threat

The cultures of Thailand's hill tribes are very much in danger of extinction. The chief culprit is not tourism: greater threats are posed by a shortage and loss of land, resettlement, lack of land rights and citizenship, illiteracy, and poor medical care. Official Thai hill-tribe policies have been shaped by the desire to discourage swidden farming and the cultivation of opium. Some of the crop-substitution programmes sponsored by the Thai government, United Nations and foreign governments have been successful, and tribal people now market coffee, tea and fruit. But such projects have not penetrated to many distant villages. ❏

THAILAND'S CUISINE

You bet it can be hot. It can also be cool. There is nothing apathetic about Thai cuisine, which most likely explains its universal appeal

Good food in Thailand is found in fascinating places, from seafood markets to floating restaurants to hawker stalls. Thais take time over their meals, talking and making an entire evening of the affair. Since dishes are typically shared by all, take several friends so that one can order and sample more dishes.

While it's true that there are very spicy regional dishes – certain southern Thai curries are notable – not all Thai food is hot and spicy. Generally, an authentic Thai meal will include at least one very spicy dish, a few that are less hot, and some that are comparatively bland, flavoured with only garlic or herbs.

A THAI APPROACH TO SWEET-TOOTH SATISFACTION

In Thailand, desserts and sweets (*khanom*) come in a bewildering variety – from light concoctions to custards, ice creams and cakes, and an entire category of confections based upon egg yolks cooked in flower-scented syrups. Bananas and coconuts grow everywhere in Thailand, and if they were to be removed from the list of ingredients available to the khanom cook, the entire edifice of Thai dessert cookery would come crashing down.

Anyone walking through a Bangkok market is bound to come across a sweets vendor selling anything from candied fruits to million-calorie custards made from coconut cream, eggs and palm sugar, generally sold in the form of three-inch squares wrapped in banana leaves. Try sampling *sangkhya maphrao awn*, a custard made from coconut cream, palm sugar and eggs, or *khao laam*, a glutinous rice mixed with coconut cream, sugar and either black beans or other goodies. *Kluay khaek* uses bananas sliced lengthwise, dipped in a coconut-and-rice flour batter and then deep-fried until crisp. Many of these sweets are amazingly inventive. You may finish off a rich pudding, for example, before realising that its tantalising flavour came from crisp-fried onions. In buying Thai sweets, picking what looks good is usually disappointment-proof. If nothing else, try a dish of *katih*, a rich and heavenly coconut ice cream.

Traditionally, rice has always been the most important dish in any Thai meal. At the start of the meal, heap some rice onto a plate and then take a spoonful or two of curry. It is considered polite to take only one spoonful at a time, consuming it before ladling another dish onto the rice. Thais eat with the spoon in their right hand and fork in their left, the fork used to push the food onto the spoon for transport to the mouth. Contrary to popular opinion in the west, nurtured in part by experiences in Thai restaurants abroad,

SPOON SHOCK

A surprise to some visitors is that most Thais use a spoon and fork, not the chopsticks regularly found in Thai restaurants located in Europe and North America.

kaeng khiaw waan, employs a hand-ground, cumin-based curry paste braised with coconut milk and chunks of meat (usually chicken or beef) and tiny pea-sized eggplants. *Kaeng phet* is a hotter red version popular with beef or pork. A close relative is *kaeng phanaeng*, a "dry" curry with peanuts added for a creamier texture. Yellow with turmeric, *kaeng karee* is a milder Indian-style curry typically made with chicken and potatoes. Southern-style curries include heavily spiced *kaeng matsaman* (peanuts, potatoes

chopsticks are not used for Thai food, but rather only for Chinese noodle dishes. Also contrary to popular belief, peanut sauce, an "indispensable" addition to nearly every dish in Thai restaurants found in Western countries, is really of Malayan and Indonesian origin and is used in Thailand only for *satay*.

Spicy and hot dishes

Kaeng means curry. The group includes the spiciest of Thai dishes and forms the core of Thai cooking. Thailand's famous green curry,

LEFT: styles of preparation are many, as are tastes.
ABOVE: street-cooked meal in natural packaging.

and either chicken or beef) and the very pungent fish-based *kaeng leuang*. *Kaeng som,* or "sour curry", consists of a chilli-based soup laced with plenty of tamarind juice and *kapi* (shrimp paste), along with pieces of either fish or shrimp.

Among other fiery favourites is *tom yam kung*, a lemongrass-scented broth teeming with shrimp. *Po taek* ("the fisherman's net bursts") is a cousin of *tom yam kung*, containing squid, mussels, crab and fish, and redolent with fresh basil. *Yam* is a hot and spicy salad combining meat or seafood and vegetables. Popular throughout Thailand, it is one of the hottest dishes available.

Mild curries

Tom khaa kai, a thick coconut-milk soup of chicken chunks with lemongrass and galangal (a spicy and fragrant root in the ginger family) is milder than the average Thai dish. *Plaa-meuk thawt kratiam phrik thai* is squid stir-fried with garlic and black pepper. Substitute *muu* (pork) for *plaa-meuk* (squid) if you prefer. Another milder dish is *kaeng juet*, a non-spicy clear broth filled with glass noodles, minced pork, tofu and mushrooms. *Neua phat nam-man hawy* is beef stir-fried in oyster sauce and garnished with chopped shallots and green vegetables.

Regional distinctions

Each of Thailand's four regions has its own cuisine. Northern and northeastern dishes are related to Lao cooking, which is eaten with glutinous rice. Southern food is flavoured with the tastes of Malaysian cooking. Central cuisine corresponds closely to the food in Thai restaurants abroad.

Northern specialties are generally eaten with *khao niaw* or sticky rice, which is kneaded into a ball and dipped into various sauces and curries. *Sai oua* is an oily, spicy pork sausage that epitomises northern cooking. Some of the northern dishes originate from neighbouring Burma, including the egg-noodle dish *khao soi*

and *kaeng hang-lay*, a thick, spicy curry which is not fiery hot. Northeastern food is simple and spicy. Like northern food, it is eaten with sticky rice, which for those who are unused to eating it may weigh heavily on the brain and make one sleepy. *Som-tam* is a northeastern speciality of raw shredded papaya, dried shrimp, lime juice, cherry tomatoes and chillies tossed to become a delectably spicy salad.

Heavily influenced by Malay neighbours below the southern border, southern cuisine combines Muslim tastes with Thai sensibilities. *Khao yam* is a rice salad made with toasted coconut flakes, sliced lemongrass and dried shrimp. *Phat phet sataw* is a stir-fry dish made with *sataw* (which looks like a lima bean but has a slightly bitter yet pleasant flavour), chillies and shrimp. *Khanom jeen* (sieved rice noodles), although found throughout Thailand, is claimed to have originated in the south. It's usually served with *nam ya*, a spicy red-brown gravy made with minced fish and a fragrant root called Chinese key.

Chinese

Most lunch-time meals and dishes are derived from Chinese cuisine, and noodle dishes, a Chinese invention, have been adopted by the Thais. *Kuaytiaw* (rice noodles) served at street-side, open-front shops come in two varieties: wet (with broth) and dry (tossed with condiments to make a noodle salad). When ordering either, specify the wetness by adding the word *nam* (wet) or *haeng* (dry) to the name.

Most Thai Chinese are of Teochew descent, so the typical Thai Chinese restaurant serves Teochew dishes, which bear many similarities to Cantonese cuisine – not surprisingly, as Teochew is a district in Guangdong Province. Typical Teochew dishes found in Thailand include goose doused in soy sauce, and roasted duck with fresh green vegetables. Fruits and teas are integral parts of every meal. Poultry, pork and seafood are essentials, as are a huge variety of fungi and mushrooms. Other Chinese cuisines are also well represented in Thailand. Shanghai food, for example, is typified by dishes that are fried in sesame or soy sauce for a long time, making them sweeter and oilier than other cuisines. ❏

Left: Thai sweets are definitive caloric lodestones.
Right: Thai cuisine uses only fresh produce.

CRAFTS AND CLOTHING OF THE HILL TRIBES

Each hill tribe of Southeast Asia has its own customs, dress, language and beliefs that are reflected in their clothing and crafts.

Textiles and silver jewellery play a very important role in the ceremonial activities of hill-tribe communities. Hill-tribe women define their ethnicity by what they wear, and their choice of clothing and adornment can reveal not only what tribe they are from, but also their social status, age and even where their home town is located. However, the way of life of Thailand's hill-tribe people, for example, is changing as they are slowly assimilated into mainstream Thai society, abandoning many features of their traditional culture. This may be sad for visitors in search of traditional hill-tribe culture, but the process is inevitable and has distinct advantages for these ethnic minorities, since they can now benefit from educational opportunities and medical facilities.

Hill-tribe people began making handicrafts commercially in the mid-1970s when small craft centres were set up in refugee camps. Authentic items are now rare, but expensive high-quality modern crafts can be found in craft shops.

BRASS NECK COILS ▷
Padaung women once wore brass coils around their arms, legs and necks; the tradition has, thankfully, diminished. Some Padaung women still make their living by posing for pictures.

◁ HMONG EMBROIDERY
Women from the Hmong hill tribe used to hand-weave cloth, but today they use ready-made fabrics for their intricately embroidered clothing. The Hmong are skilled in making indigo-dyed batik which is then embroidered with appliquéd layers of geometrically-shaped fabric to make up their skirts.

▽ LISU TEXTILES
Lisu women make distinctive clothing. In the past, the cloth was woven by hand but the Lisu now use machine-made material that they run up on sewing machines.

◁ HMONG COTTONS

Women of the Hmong hill tribe spin cotton into thread with a hand spindle, then weave it on a foot-treadle loom. The cloth is dyed indigo and is then appliquéd and decorated with shells, seeds, silver or buttons and made into clothing for the family. The men make a variety of baskets and other items from wood, bamboo and rattan.

LISU CEREMONIAL WEAR ▷

On special occasions, Lisu men wear turbans and the women don large amounts of hand-crafted silver jewelry, chunky necklaces and colourful tunics with silver buttons. Men of the tribe are skilled blacksmiths. The sale of crafts means they no longer need to grow opium poppies to make a living.

HOW THE KAREN MAKE *IKAT*

The White Karen tribe (above) produce striped warp *ikat* textiles woven on back-strap looms. Ikat is a technique used to pattern cloth that involves the binding of the cloth with fibre or strips of material, so in places it becomes resistant to dyeing.

Before the cloth is dyed, the weft (yarns woven across the width of the fabric) or the warp (lengthwise yarns) is pulled tightly over a frame and then threads are bound tightly together singly or in bunches. The cloth is then dyed several times using different colours. As a result, complex and beautiful patterns are built up with soft, watery edges on the parts of the cloth not completely covered by the binding materials.

The dyeing process is complex, with the dominant colour of the ikat dyed first. Cotton yarns are the most suitable for making warp ikat, and the dyes used to produce these textiles are natural dyes that are easily absorbed by cotton. The most popular colours for warp ikat are indigo and red. Weft ikats use mainly yellow dyes (made from turmeric), diluted indigos and a deep crimson red extracted from the lac insect. Orange, green and purple are created by an overdyeing process.

▽ AKHA HEADDRESS

Married Akha women are famous for their head-dresses decorated with silver coins, which they wear all the time. Unmarried women from the tribe attach small gourds to their head-dresses.

Bangkok

0   500 m
0   500 yds

Ⓢ Skytrain BTS
Ⓜ Metro MRT

BANGKOK

This is one of the most confounding and challenging cities in the world. Amidst its traffic-clogged roads and towering buildings are some of the most exquisite historical edifices anywhere

Map on pages 38–39

At first glance, this metropolis of over 10 million people appears as a bewildering melding of new and old, and of exotic and commonplace and indeterminate, all tossed together into an expansive urban fuss. If Bangkok seems to lack order, it is because it's never had it, save for the royal core of the city, Rattanakosin, where the kings built their palaces and royal temples. Bangkok begins its life on the banks of the Chao Phraya River, the "River of Kings". Although the city is some 400 years old, it became the nation's capital only in 1782, when the royal dynasty that currently reigns in Thailand was established.

Royal Bangkok

The southern side of Thanon Na Phra Lan is lined by the white crenullated walls of the **Wat Phra Kaew** and **Grand Palace** Ⓐ complex (daily 8.30am–3.30pm; entrance fee; tel: 0 2623 5500; www.thailandmuseum.com). The only entrance and exit to the complex is in the middle. On the right are the offices of the Royal Household, to the left is the ticket booth.

The first stop within the palace grounds is Wat Phra Kaew (Temple of the Emerald Buddha), the royal chapel of the Grand Palace. Passing though the gate, you will confront 6-metre-tall (20-ft) demon statues inspired by the *Ramakien*, the Thai version of the Indian epic *Ramayana*. You must walk the glittering length of the *bot* (ordination chapel) to reach its entrance. In front are scattered Chinese-style statues, which function as stand-ins for incense offerings to the Emerald Buddha inside. The 75-cm-tall (30-inch) jadeite statue is perched high on an altar near the opposite wall, clothed and enclosed in a glass case, and shielded by a towering nine-tiered umbrella.

Directly opposite the Grand Palace on the other side of the Chao Phraya River is **Wat Arun** Ⓑ (daily 8.30am–5.30pm; entrance fee; tel: 0 2891 1149), one the river's oldest and most distinctive landmarks, dating back to the Ayutthaya period, before the Thai capital was moved south to Thonburi and later to Bangkok. The temple's 82-metre-high (270-ft) *prang* is bedecked with millions of tiny pieces of Chinese porcelain donated by average Thai citizens.

Exiting from the Grand Palace, turn left on Thanon Maharat and walk south past Thanon Thai Wang, which runs into the Tha Tien river-taxi dock after passing a fresh market surrounded by early 20th-century shophouses.

Turn left (that is, east) onto Soi Chetuphon and head for the gate to **Wat Pho** Ⓒ (daily 8am–6pm; entrance fee; tel: 0 2222 0933), Bangkok's largest and oldest temple, predating the Bangkok dynasty. Its first build-

OPPOSITE: the Phra Si Rattana Chedi at Wat Phra Kaew.
BELOW: the Emerald Buddha.

ings were constructed in the 16th century. Few statues are more impressive than Wat Pho's mammoth **Reclining Buddha**, which occupies the entirety of a long building in the northwestern corner of the extensive palace complex.

A trove of both Thai and Southeast Asian riches, the **National Museum**  (Wed–Sun 9am–4pm except public holidays; entrance fee; tel: 0 2281 2224; www.thailandmuseum.com) comprises a half-dozen old and new buildings. One of oldest is at the rear of the compound, the Wang Na, dating from 1782. This vast palace once extended across to Khlong Lot and up to the Grand Palace. The name refers to the palace of the so-called second king, a deputy king of sorts. When King Chulalongkorn's heir-apparent – the second king – attempted a violent overthrow, Chulalongkorn abolished the office in 1887 and tore down most of the buildings. The Wang Na today is one of the remnants, serving as the National Museum and housing *khon* masks, gold and ceramic pieces, palanquins, weapons, instruments and an elephant riding-seat made from ivory.

Malai, Buddhist flower offerings.

East of the Grand Palace

At the next cross-street, Thanon Ratchabophit, turn right to visit one of the most attractive wats off the beaten tourist path. Before crossing over the canal, however, notice immediately to the north what, yes, appears to be a golden pig lording over a construction site, actually an archaeological excavation. The **Pig Memorial** was built in 1913 as a birthday present from friends to Queen Saowapha, Chulalongkorn's favourite wife, who was born in the Year of the Pig.

Across the bridge, **Wat Ratchabophit**  (daily 8am–6pm; tel: 0 2221 0904; free) is easily recognisable by its distinctive doors, carved in relief with jaunty soldiers wearing European uniforms. Built in 1870 by Rama V (1868–1910), the

BELOW: the Dusit Maha Prasat, in the Grand Palace.

design was intended to meld Western and Thai art forms. The bot's windows and entrance doors are works of art. Inlaid mother-of-pearl depicts the insignias of the five royal ranks.

Continue north up Thanon Fuang Nakhon and turn right at the second corner onto Soi Suthat. Two short blocks on is **Wat Suthat** ❻ (daily 8.30am–5.30pm; entrance fee; tel: 0 2224 9845). Finished during the reign of Rama III, it is noted for its enormous bot, said to be the tallest in Bangkok. The bot doors are among the wonders of Thai art. Carved to a depth of 5 cm (2 inches), they follow the Ayuthayan tradition of floral motifs, with tangled jungle vegetation hiding small animals. Immediately north of Wat Suthat is a giant red and wooden gateway. This is the 200-year-old **Giant Swing** (Sao Ching Cha), once the centrepiece of an annual ceremony honouring the Hindu god Shiva. A bench bearing teams of two to four standing young men was suspended from the crosspiece. When the swing was swung, the men would attempt to catch, with their teeth, a bag of gold suspended from on high.

North of the old royal city

Northward to Dusit, crossing the *khlong* (canal), Thanon Ratchadamnoen turns into a pleasant, tree-lined boulevard that leads to an immense square with a statue of King Chulalongkorn on horseback. To the left of the square lies the spacious **Amporn Gardens**, complete with fountains, trees and an air of grandeur.

At the back of the square is the former **National Assembly** (Parliament) building, built in 1907 by Chulalongkorn. To the east is **Dusit Zoo** ❼ (daily 8.30am–6pm; entrance fee; tel: 0 2281 2000), the city's main animal park and one of the most popular places in Bangkok for family outings. A lake with boats for

Map on pages 38–39

BELOW: Wat Suthat and Giant Swing.

rent is surrounded by an aviary and enclosures containing the exotic wildlife of Asia. Behind the old National Assembly is **Vimanmek ⑪** (daily 9.30am–3.15pm; entrance fee, or free with Grand Palace entrance ticket; tel: 0 2628 6300), billed as the world's largest golden teak building. Vimanmek was built by Chulalongkorn as a residence for his family in what was, in 1900, a suburb of Bangkok. The 100-room home is filled with exquisite European things.

Just past the railway line on the north side of Thanon Si Ayutthaya is a huge leafy set of grounds, belonging to the **Chitralada Palace ⑫** (closed to the public), where the current king and queen live. Surrounded by a moat and high fencing, the grounds include grazing cattle, milk churns and fish ponds.

Beyond the Chitralada compound, on the other side of Thanon Si Ayutthaya, is **Wat Benjamabophit ⑬** (daily 8am–5.30pm; entrance fee; tel: 0 2282 7413), the Marble Temple. The last major temple built in Bangkok, it was started by Rama V in 1900 and was finished 10 years later. Designed by Prince Naris, a half-brother of the king, the temple's features are largely a departure from the traditional style. The most obvious of these must be the enclosed courtyard, the Carrara marble used to cover the main buildings, and the curved, yellow Chinese roof tiles. The bot's principal Buddha image is a replica of the famous Phra Buddha Chinnarat, in Northern Thailand's Phitsanulok. Behind the bot is a gallery holding 51 Buddha images from around Asia.

Stained-glass window, Wat Benjamabophit.

Chinatown

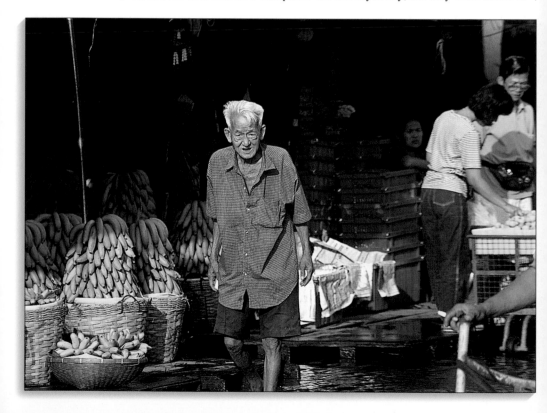

BELOW: morning market scene in Chinatown.

South of the Dusit area, east of the old royal city and on the north side of the winding Chao Phraya, is Bangkok's Chinatown. Chinese merchants originally settled the area that now comprises the old royal city, but they were asked to move to the present **Sampeng Lane**  when construction began on the Grand Palace in the 1780s. In 1863, King Mongkut built Charoen Krung (New Road), the first paved street in Bangkok, and Chinatown soon began to expand northward towards it. Chinatown was followed at Khlong Krung Kasem by a Muslim district that, in turn, was followed by an area occupied by *farang* (Westerners) where the Oriental Hotel now stands on the river's east bank.

The area has had a somewhat rowdy history. What began with mercantile pursuits soon degenerated into a lusty entertainment area. By 1900, alleys led to opium dens and houses whose entrances were marked by green lanterns *(khom khiaw)*. A green-light district functioned like a Western red-light district, and while the lanterns have disappeared, the term *khom khiaw* still signifies a brothel.

Bangrak and Silom

Further south and just east of the Chao Phraya is Bangrak, a vibrant modern district that has risen in just the past three decades. This area has long been a neighbourhood of *farang*, the expat Westerners. Anchoring the western end is the grand **Oriental Hotel**  (www.mandarinoriental.com/bangkok), directly on the bank of the Chao Phraya. From the Oriental, stroll inland, or east, past the gaggle of *tuk-tuk* drivers, long-tail-boat touts and "copy watch" sellers to the end of the *soi*, turn right and you'll soon be at the less exciting end of one of Bangkok's most exciting streets, Thanon Silom, which comes to life at night.

Love it or hate it, and few have any other opinion, the notorious **Patpong**  (actually two streets – Patpong I and Patpong II) at the opposite end of Thanon Silom has an electric, sinful arrogance. It's hard to imagine a starker contrast to the serene temples and palaces and the gracious smiles and *wai* of hotel staff

Map on pages 38–39

BELOW: modern Bangkok at dusk.

Map on pages 38–39

TIP

For outlying trips, excellent highways now lead out of Bangkok in all directions, and what used to be a 3- or 4-hour trip can now be made in just over an hour.

OPPOSITE: garden of Jim Thompson's House Museum.
BELOW: lake, Lumphini Park.

than the raucous touting and outrageous sex shows of Patpong. Nowadays, there seem to be more curious middle-aged couples than die-hard sex tourists.

At the end of Thanon Silom, just east of Patpong, is a huge and busy intersection that can take what seems a good 15 minutes to cross. To the northeast across the intersection lies **Suan Lumphini** Ⓝ (Lumphini Park; open daily 5am–8pm; free), a tranquil and tropical oasis of greenery with boating lakes, open-air gymnasiums and outdoor cafés.

Directly west along Thanon Rama IV is the **Queen Saovabha Memorial Institute** Ⓞ (Mon–Fri 8.30am–4.30pm, Sat–Sun and holidays 8.30am–noon; entrance fee; tel: 0 2252 0161–4), or as it is better known, the **Snake Farm**. Operated by the Thai Red Cross, its primary function is the serious business of producing anti-venom serum to be used on snakebite victims, of which there are many every year throughout the country. The institute, the second oldest of its kind in the world, produces serum from the king cobra, Siamese cobra, Russell's viper, Malayan pit viper and the green pit viper.

Heading north along Thanon Ratchadamri towards the intersection with Thanon Rama I, one passes two of the city's most opulent hotels, The Regent and the Grand Hyatt Erawan. At the intersection, the **Erawan Shrine** Ⓟ (open daily) draws visitors and locals. To improve their fortunes or to pass exams, believers make offerings at a statue of a four-faced deity. Originally erected by the Erawan Hotel, now the Grand Hyatt, to counter a spate of bad luck, the shrine is redolent with incense smoke and jasmine. To repay the god for wishes granted, supplicants place floral garlands or wooden elephants at the god's feet, or hire a resident troupe to perform a traditional dance.

The intersection of Rama I and Phayathai is one of the best areas to shop, especially for those who like a little local colour and chaos. But there are other attractions besides shopping and eating in this area. On Khlong Mahanak at the north end of Soi Kasemsan II is the **Jim Thompson's House Museum** Ⓠ (daily 9am–5pm; entrance fee; tel: 0 2216 7368; www.jimthompsonhouse.com). This Thai-style home comprises six Thai houses acquired throughout the country and joined together by the remarkable American, who revived the Thai silk industry. In 1967, while on a visit to Cameron Highlands in Malaysia, Thompson mysteriously disappeared; despite an extensive search, no trace has ever been found of him. His legacy however lives in the beautiful silk sold at Jim Thompson boutiques in Bangkok.

Outside of Bangkok

The hinterland outside of Bangkok is filled with a rich variety of sights and experiences that can be visited as day-trips or overnighters from the capital. Among the highlights, 80 km (50 miles) north of Bangkok, is the old royal city of **Ayutthaya**, Thailand's capital from 1350 to 1767. The ruined city is immense, comprising several sites that should not be missed.

The nearest hills to Bangkok are in the massive **Khao Yai National Park** (open daily 6am–6pm; tel: 0 4429 7406; entrance fee; www.dnp.go.th), which sprawls across parts of four provinces northeast of the capital. Tigers and elephants call the park home. ❏

CHIANG MAI

In the northern mountains, Chiang Mai is a pleasant northern Thai base from which to explore the many hill tribes and national parks that retain Thailand's more traditional textures

Map on page 24

Despite its increasingly rapid urbanisation, 700-year-old **Chiang Mai ❶** remains prized as a pleasantly cool alternative to the sticky humidity of Bangkok. Situated 300 metres (1,000 ft) above sea level in a broad valley divided by the picturesque 560-km-long (350-mile) **Ping River**, the city reigned for seven centuries as the capital of the Lanna kingdom. In its splendid isolation, Chiang Mai developed a culture quite removed from that of the central plains to the south, with wooden temples of exquisite beauty and a host of unique crafts, including lacquerware, silverwork, wood carvings, ceramics and umbrella-making. Although the hospitality of both the hill tribes and the northern Thais is sometimes strained by the sheer numbers of visitors, the northern people remain more gracious than in many other cities.

Origins

Chiang Mai's story actually begins further north, in the town of Chiang Rai. Its founder and king, Mangrai, ruled a sizable empire that ran as far north as Chiang Saen, on the Mekong River. He founded Chiang Rai in 1281. But when the Mongol ruler Kublai Khan sacked the Burmese kingdom of Bagan in 1287, Mangrai feared that his realm might be threatened and so formed an alliance with the rulers of Sukhothai, then Siam's capital. With his southern boundaries secure, Mangrai captured the old Mon kingdom at Lamphun. To centralise his rule, he established a new base in the Ping River Valley in 1296. This new capital he named Chiang Mai, or New City.

The location was chosen by the auspicious sighting of white deer along with a white mouse with a family of five, all at the same time, or so the story has it. Rather than building on the banks of the Ping, which often floods, he built his city – with the help of 90,000 labourers – half a kilometre to the west, surrounding it with stout brick walls.

Less than a century after Chiang Mai's founding, however, Ayutthaya replaced Sukhothai as the capital of Siam. This new kingdom had its own expansionist dreams and ambitions, including designs on its neighbour to the north. For the next 400 years, there was fierce competition and sometimes open warfare. In the 16th century, Ayutthaya crushed an invasion by Chiang Mai, and Chiang Mai's power waned. To compound its troubles, the region was invaded in the early 1700s by the same Burmese enemy who were laying siege to Ayutthaya.

Although the Burmese were finally defeated, the people of Chiang Mai were so exhausted and discouraged by the constant conflict that they abandoned

OPPOSITE: northern hill-side farming.
BELOW: modern Chiang Mai.

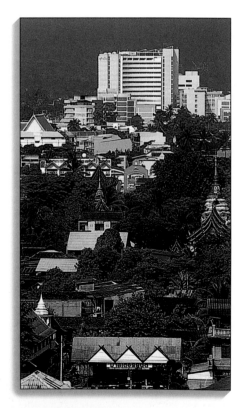

TIP

Be careful on the streets on 13 April, and for several days thereafter. Songkran, the traditional Thai new year, is when people sprinkle water on friends to bless them. In Chiang Mai, especially, it rapidly degenerates into a deluge. Tourists and strangers are not excluded.

BELOW: Wat Chiang Man, first temple built by Mangrai.

the city. It remained deserted until 1796, when the Burmese army was defeated; new nobles began restoring the city to its former prominence. It continued to enjoy autonomy from Bangkok until the railway brought meddling central government administrators. In 1932, following the death of the last king of Chiang Mai, the north was finally fully incorporated into the Thai nation.

Old Chiang Mai

The commercial centres of downtown are along Thanon Thaphae, with numerous hotels, shops and guest houses. Hotels and shops have also sprung up along Thanon Huai Kaeo, which leads out to Doi Suthep.

The city's history begins with **Wat Chiang Man** (daily 9am–5pm; free), which translates as "power of the city". It was the first *wat* to be built by Mangrai, who resided there during the construction of the city in 1296. Located in the northeast part of the old walled city, it is the oldest of Chiang Mai's 300-plus temples. Two ancient, venerated Buddha images are kept in the abbot's quarters and can be seen on request. The first image, Phra Sae Tang Tamani, is a small 10-cm-high (4-inch) crystal Buddha image taken by Mangrai to Chiang Mai from Lamphun, where it had reputedly resided for 600 years. Apart from a short sojourn in Ayutthaya, the image has remained in Chiang Mai ever since. On Songkran in April it is paraded through the streets. The second image, a stone Phra Sila Buddha in bas-relief, is believed to have originated in India around the 8th century. Both statues are said to possess the power to bring rain and to protect the city from fire.

The only other important structure in Wat Chiang Man is Chang Lom, a 15th-century square *chedi* buttressed by rows of stucco elephants.

Imperiously positioned at the head of Thanon Ratchdamnoen is **Wat Phra Singh** (daily 8am–6pm; free), which is noted for three monuments: a library, chedi and the Wihan Lai Kham. The former, a magnificent Lanna-style wooden library on the right side of the compound, is raised on a high base decorated with lovely stucco angels. Behind the main wihan, built in 1925, is a beautiful wooden *bot* (ordination chapel), and behind this, a chedi built by King Pha Yu in 1345 to hold the ashes of his father. Wat Phra Singh's most beautiful building is the small Phra Wihan Lai Kham, to the left of the bot. Built rather late in the Lanna period, in 1811, the wooden building's front wall is decorated in gold flowers on a red lacquer ground. Intricately carved wooden window frames accent the doors.

The interior walls of the Wihan Lai Kham are decorated with murals commissioned by Chao Thammalangka, who ruled over Chiang Mai between 1813 and 1821. Although focusing on the Buddhist stories of Prince Sang Thong (on the north wall) and the Tale of the Heavenly Phoenix (south wall), they also record in fascinating detail aspects of early 19th-century Lanna society and exhibit clear indications of persisting Burmese cultural influence.

Calamity is associated with **Wat Chedi Luang** (daily 8am–6pm; free), built in 1401 to the east of Wat Phra Singh on Thanon Phra Pokklao. A century and a half later, a violent earthquake shook its then 90-metre-high (295-ft) pagoda, reducing its height to 42 metres (140 ft). It was never completely rebuilt, although it has been impressively restored. Even in its damaged state, the colossal monument is majestic. For 84 years the Emerald Buddha, now in Bangkok, was housed here before being moved to Vientiane.

Close to the wat's entrance stands an ancient and tall gum tree. When it falls, says a legend, so will the city. As if serving as counterbalance, the *lak muang,* or

Map on page 24

BELOW LEFT: Wat Suan Dok.
BELOW RIGHT: northern children.

city boundary stone in which the spirit of the city is said to reside, stands near its base. The wihan of **Wat Phan Tao** (daily 8am–6pm; free), adjacent to Wat Chedi Luang, formerly a palace, is a masterpiece of wooden construction. Its doorway is crowned by a beautiful Lanna peacock framed by golden *naga* (serpents).

Located one kilometre northwest of the city walls, **Wat Jet Yot** (daily 8am–6pm) was completed by King Trailokaraja in 1455. It was built as a vague replica of the Mahabodhi Temple in India's Bodhgaya, where Buddha gained enlightenment while spending seven weeks in its gardens. The beautiful stucco angels that decorate its walls are said to bear faces of Trailokaraja's own family. Although similar to a temple in Burma's then-capital of Bagan, it did not stop the Burmese from severely damaging it during their invasion of 1566.

Outside Chiang Mai

A steep series of hairpin curves rises up the flanks of **Doi Suthep** – 15 km (9 miles) northwest of the city – to Chiang Mai's best-loved temple, **Wat Phra That Doi Suthep** (daily 8am–6pm; entrance fee). The site was selected in the mid-1300s by an elephant that was turned loose with a Buddha relic strapped to its back; where it stopped, it was believed, a temple should be built. It not only climbed the slopes of Doi Suthep to this site, it dropped dead here.

The ascending road passes the entrance to the **Huai Kaew Falls**, where a minibus goes to the top. The scenery en route is spectacular, with the road winding its way to a large car park beneath Wat Phra That Doi Suthep. Seven-headed naga undulate down the balustrade of a 290-step stairway that leads from the parking lot to the temple. For the weary, a funicular makes the same ascent for a few baht. Below from the wat, Chiang Mai is spread at one's feet.

Chiang Mai is known for its fine umbrellas.

BELOW: Songkran festival in Chiang Mai.

From the upper terrace, a few more steps lead through the courtyard of the temple itself. In the late afternoon light, there are few sights more stunning than that which greet one at the final step. Emerging from cloisters decorated with murals depicting scenes from the Buddha's life, one's eyes rise to the summit of a 24-metre-high (80-ft) gilded chedi, partially shaded by gilded bronze parasols. The chedi is surrounded by an iron fence with pickets culminating in praying *thevada,* or angels. Appearing in the east and west ends of the compound are two wihan. At dawn, the eastern one shelters chanting nuns in white robes. At sunset, the one on the west holds orange-robed monks chanting their prayers.

From the parking area of Wat Phra That Doi Suthep, a road ascends a further 5 km (3 miles) to **Phuping Palace**, the winter residence of the royal family. Constructed in 1972 and situated at 1,300 metres (4,265 ft), the palace has audience halls, guest houses, dining rooms, kitchens and official suites. It also serves as headquarters for royal agricultural and medical projects carried out among hill tribes and in villages. When the royal family is absent, the public may stroll through the gardens (Sat–Sun and holidays 8.30am–4pm; entrance fee; tel: 0 5321 9932).

Commercialised hill tribes

From the palace entrance, the road continues through pine forests to the commercialised Hmong hill-tribe village of **Doi Pui**. The village has been on the tourist track for some time, but improvements over the past decades have brought material benefits to its inhabitants, including a paved street lined with souvenir stands. It is possible to wander by the houses to glimpse how the people live.

At one time subsistence farmers, the tribespeople have learned that visitors come bearing gifts, and aiming a camera automatically triggers a hand extended

Map
on page
24

BELOW: northern Akha woman feeding cattle.

Map on page 24

TIP

Chiang Mai is best visited during winter, late November through early February, when it is abloom with an astounding variety of beautiful flowers. Numerous resorts in Mae Sa Valley carpet the hillsides with flower gardens, and in February is the Flower Festival.

Buddha image in a niche at Wat Kukut, Lamphun.

for a donation. Hmong are itinerant farmers here, as they are in Burma and Laos. They once depended upon opium cultivation for their livelihoods; despite government efforts to steer them towards more socially acceptable crops, many still cultivate patches deep in the hills. An interesting insight into opium farming is provided by Doi Pui's **Opium Museum**, which describes in detail the process of cultivation and harvest. This Hmong village also offers a tainted example of hill-tribe life, though one doubts it retains much of its original personality.

Once an agricultural region, the **Mae Sa Valley** cultivates a new money-earner – tourism. Waterfalls, working elephant camps, butterfly farms, orchid nurseries and a charming private museum called **Mae Sa House Collection** (with prehistoric artefacts and Sukhothai ceramics, among many things) vie for the visitor's attention. The valley also has quiet resorts along its river.

North of Chiang Mai

To reach the northern town of **Fang ❷**, take Route 107 north from Chiang Mai (beginning at Chang Phuak Gate) towards Chiang Dao. The road passes through rice fields and small villages, then begins to climb past Mae Taeng into the Mae Ping Gorge, which forms the southern end of the Chiang Dao Valley. Ahead, on the left as one follows the river's right bank through scenic countryside, is the massive outline of Chiang Dao mountain.

At the 56-kilometre marker is the **Chiang Dao Elephant Training Centre** (daily 8am–5pm; entrance fee; tel: 0 5329 8553), on the bank of the Mae Nam Ping. Twice daily, a line of elephants walk into the Ping to be bathed by mahout for the amusement of tourists, who reward the baby elephants with bananas. The elephants then move to a dusty arena to demonstrate how to make huge logs seem like toothpicks, picking them up or dragging them with great ease across the teak-shaded open space.

About 60 km (40 miles) from Chiang Mai on Route 107, a dirt road branches left and goes to **Doi Chiang Dao**, which at 2,186 metres (7,175 ft) is Thailand's third-highest peak. A jeep or a trail bike is needed to negotiate this 9-km track, which leads to the Hmong village of Pakkia up the mountain. Entry to the sanctuary is restricted and permission must be obtained from the wildlife headquarters near Wat Pa Bong at the foot of the mountain.

Further north, Route 107 enters the quiet town of **Chiang Dao**, located 70 km (45 miles) from Chiang Mai. At the far end of town, a simple road leads off to the left for 5 km (3 miles) to **Tham Chiang Dao** (daily 8am–5pm; entrance fee; tel: 0 5329 8553), a complex of caves filled with Buddha statuary. In a deeper section is a large, reclining limestone Buddha.

South to Lamphun

The road south from Chiang Mai is one of the most beautiful in northern Thailand. **Lamphun ❸** itself dates back from the mid-6th century and is famed for two old *wat*, attractive women, and young and prolific *lamyai* fruit trees.

To gain the best perspective on Lamphun's **Wat Pra That Haripunchai**, enter through its riverside gate, where large statues of mythical lions guard its portals. Inside the large compound, monks study in a large Buddhist school set amidst monuments and buildings, which date as far back as the late 9th century. A kilometre west of Lamphun's old moat stands **Wat Kukut** (also known as Wat Chama Devi), dating from the 8th century. The temple has a superb pair of unusual chedi. Erected in the early 1200s, the larger chedi consists of five squared tiers, each of which contains three niches. Each niche holds a Buddha statue.

South of Lamphun, beyond Pasang, is the hill-top pilgrimage centre of **Wat Phrabat Tak Pha**, said to protect a footprint of the Buddha. ❏

Thailand's Gems: Crystal Power

Thais have turned a national passion for gems and jewellery into one of the country's largest export industries. Rubies, sapphires and jade are among the best bargains, while gold, silver and diamond products, finished by master craftsmen, are also popular buys.

Rubies, the name given to red, gem-quality corundum stones, vary in shade from pinkish or purplish to the brownish-red found in Thailand, depending upon the stone's chromium and iron content. A really fine ruby can appear to glow like hot coal. Since prehistoric times, rubies have been associated with a range of spiritual and supernatural beliefs. The Burmese thought rubies conferred invulnerability, and that they could foretell danger by loss of colour or brilliance. Most of the rubies in Thailand traditionally originated from the Chanthaburi region, and from the Pailin area of Cambodia, which together account for around two-thirds of the world's supply of rubies. A small number come from Vietnam and parts of Africa.

Thailand's ruby mines were known in early times, with the first known reference coming from a Chinese traveller, Ma Huan, in AD 1408. Now they are close to depletion. At Bo Rai, once the king of Thai ruby-mining towns, abandoned equipment litters the landscape. Where there used to be hundreds of traders, just a few remain. Supplies from the Cambodian side of the border have become sporadic. Rubies from the remote Mogok and Mong Hsu mines in upper Burma, where primitive, back-breaking extraction methods still apply, are relatively rare and highly sought-after for the international market when they get to Thailand.

An important distinction is made between prime-quality unheated stones, most of which come from Mogok, and less valuable heat-treated samples, originating primarily in Mong Hsu. The latter tend to look like bad garnet before treatment, after which they turn into bright-red gems.

Sapphires, also composed of corundum, come in different colours, from the highly-prized rich-blue to orange, green, yellow, pink and colourless varieties. Sapphire was traditionally believed by Buddhists to produce a desire for prayer, to help ward off negative energies, and to promote calm. Thailand's sapphires now come mainly from Sri Lanka, Australia and Africa. Locally mined sapphires in Kanchanaburi and Phrae, and Cambodian stones from the Pailin area, are increasingly limited in number and quality.

In recent years, Thailand has also become a major centre for processing diamonds, catering to a large foreign as well as thriving domestic jewellery.

Shopping for gems and jewellery in Thailand is easy and rewarding, so long as one sticks to reputable stores. (If in doubt, contact the local Tourism Authority of Thailand office for authorised gem and jewellery establishments.) Many scams involving gullible tourists have been reported. They often take the form of an individual with a "special offer", backed up by a convincing story. A polite but firm refusal will deflect the scam. ❑

RIGHT: blue sapphire in hand.

THE SOUTHERN ISLANDS

Map on pages 24, 57

Significant numbers of travellers come to Thailand for its seductive southern islands – Phuket, Samui, Phi Phi. Whether they want to be pampered or find rustic ambience, the islands can satisfy

Thailand's south, a long arm of land sometimes likened to an elephant's trunk, contains 14 provinces and is rich in stunning scenery and unspoiled beaches. In many ways the south is a world far removed from the rest of the country, especially in the deep south near Malaysia. A different climate, religion and type of farming make it unique among Thailand's regions. Groves of rubber trees are more common than fields of rice, and the gilded dome of a Muslim mosque becomes a more familiar sight than the sloping orange roof of a Buddhist temple. Once cut off from the rest of Thailand, the south is easily accessible these days.

The earthquake-generated tsunami at the end of 2004 caused massive damage to life and property along Thailand's Andaman coast. Fortunately, most tourist destinations in the six Andaman provinces were back to near-normal conditions within six months.

Phuket

The undeniable physical beauty of **Phuket ❹** extends beyond its exquisite beaches to its picturesque villages, coconut groves, rubber plantations and forested hills. For centuries Phuket was a backwater. The long road south from Bangkok, the lack of a bridge across the causeway, bad roads on the island itself, and a seeming lack of interest in developing it for recreation meant that it languished in relative isolation for decades despite natural resources of tin, rubber and coconut.

Today, the road from Phang Nga on the mainland crosses the 600-metre (2,000-ft) Thaothep Kasetri Bridge to Phuket, an island about the same size as Singapore. The sojourn to Phuket town, 30 km (20 miles) south along a busy dual carriageway, soon reaches the heart of the island. The crossroads at **Ban Tha Rua ❹** to Surin Beach and Khao Phra Taew National Park is dominated by two bronze statues of female warriors, swords in hands. The pair are sisters: Chan and Muk. In 1785 they led an army of villagers to repel Burmese invaders on Phuket.

Unlike many Thai provincial centres, the town of **Phuket ❸** on the island's southeast coast has a rich identity of its own. The charm of Phuket's old buildings is complemented by the many colourful Chinese shrines around the city. Of note is the brightly painted **Jui Tui Temple** (daily 8am–6pm; free) and the smaller **Put Jaw** (daily 8am–6pm; free) next door, which sit just past the market on Thanon Ranong. Like many similar Chinese shrines elsewhere in Asia, their central altars are dedicated to Kuan Yin

OPPOSITE: southern island fishing, Phang Nga Bay.

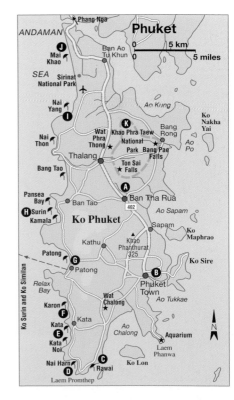

In 1786, Capt. Light sought to secure Phuket for England. Thai claims and England's desire for a more strategic island to guard the Straits of Malacca led Light to drop the plan and found Penang, which became England's primary colony on the Malay peninsula until the founding of Singapore in 1819.

BELOW: offering at a Chinese temple, town of Phuket.

(Guanyin), the goddess of mercy. Jui Tui is the starting point for the five days of colourful and bizarre parades that mark the annual Phuket Vegetarian Festival in October.

Southeast along the coast is **Rawai ©**, whose foreshore is a mass of rocks that lies exposed during low tide, when clam hunters venture out, turning over the stones in search of dinner. Rawai holds one of the island's handful of *chao lay*, or sea gypsy, villages. The sea gypsies, once nomadic fishing families, are skilled fishermen both above and below the water. From a young age, they learn to dive to great depths in search of lobsters, prawns, and crabs, staying below for up to 3 minutes. However, diminishing stocks and environmental and tourism concerns have robbed the sea gypsies of traditional fishing grounds. The most exclusive hotel in the area is **Evason Resort and Spa**, with its own private beach as well as access to an offshore island, **Ko Bon**, for guests.

Phuket's glory, however, lies in its many beautiful beaches, and it has a wealth of them. From Rawai the coastal road continues over the north–south ridge of hills, offering great views for 45 km (28 miles) as far as Ko Phi Phi. Continue south around the tip at **Laem Promthep** to **Nai Harn ©**, one of the island's prettiest beaches. Further north are the smaller and more picturesque bays of **Kata Noi** and **Kata ©**. There is fine snorkelling at the southern end of Kata Noi beach. **Karon Beach ©** is a long quiet strip of sand backed by hotels and restaurants at its top, middle and bottom. Both Karon and Kata boast a growing choice of hotel, dining and watersport facilities. Relax Bay, with its single hotel, **Le Meridien Phuket**, offers some snorkelling along its northwestern rocks.

The most developed beach is **Patong ©**, due west of Phuket town on the opposite side of the island and north of Karon. In the early 1970s, Patong was

little more than a huge banana plantation wedged between the mountains and a wide crescent of sand. The plantation is now a tourist city-by-the-sea, with multi-storey condominiums and hotels rising above night markets, seafood emporiums, beer bars, discos, and tour shops. Dive shops offer trips into the bay or northwest to the **Similan Islands National Marine Park**, considered one of the best diving areas in Asia, with crystal-clear water and ample marine life.

Some 3 km (2 miles) north of Patong, **Kamala Bay** has charming Islamic hamlets with well-kept gardens against a backdrop of forested hills rising to over 500 metres (1,600 ft). Its former tranquillity has been broken at the northern end, where a giant Disney-like theme park has been built, called **Phuket Fantasea** (Fri–Wed 5.30–11.30pm; tel: 0 7638 5333; www.phuket-fantasea.com).

The attractive coastal road north to **Surin Beach ❿** passes mouthwateringly compact **Singh Beach**, its sandy cape hedged by verdant headlands. Larger Surin Beach with its dappled seafood shacks soon gives way to idyllic **Pansea Bay** dominated by two proprietary resorts, the Chedi and the Amanpuri. The long beach at **Bang Tao** is dominated by the immense Laguna Phuket, which shelters five large resorts.

Nai Yang Beach ❶, just south of the airport, is under the jurisdiction of **Sirinat National Park**. There are a few Spartan bungalows for rent in the national park. With a good map it is possible to drive along Phuket's scenic west coast from Nai Yang to the island's southern tip, Prom Thep.

North of Nai Yang is Phuket's longest beach, **Mai Khao ❶**. The beach, 9 km (5½ miles) long, is relatively undeveloped, a haven for beachcombers and the giant sea turtles that come ashore from December through February to lay their eggs. Green forest can be experienced on hikes through **Khao Phra Taew**

Map on page 57

Rua hang yao, *the Thai long-tail boat.*

BELOW: Kata Noi.

National Park ⓚ (daily 6am–6pm; entrance fee). The park is fringed by two pretty waterfalls: Ton Sai on the west, and Bang Bae on the east.

Phang Nga and Krabi

The town of **Phang Nga ❺** is revealed as a lovely, peaceful township left behind in Thailand's development surge. The main objective of any first-time trip here, however, should be to the geological wonderland of **Phang Nga Bay**.

Just before the mouth of Phang Nga River, the boat approaches the base of **Khao Kien** mountain, where a cavern contains primitive paintings depicting human and animal forms. Such cave daubings are quite common in the limestone caves in the area. They were painted by primitive people around 2,000 years ago. The floors of many caves in Phang Nga and Krabi are still scattered with the discarded sea shells of prehistoric people. Tide fluctuations have compromised archaeological evidence. Forty thousand years ago, it was possible to walk to Phi Phi. Five thousand years ago, sea levels were higher than at present.

Ko Ping Kan is perhaps the most spectacular and most-visited of Phang Nga's islands. Behind the beach, the mountain seems to have split in two, the halves leaning against each other. Locals say they are two lovers. This area was the setting of part of a James Bond movie, *The Man with the Golden Gun*.

About 50 km (30 miles) south of Phang Nga, **Thanboke Koranee National Park** (daily 8am–6pm; entrance fee; tel: 0 7568 1071; www.dnp.go.th), near Krabi, is one of the most beautiful in Thailand. The town of **Krabi ❻** itself is a small but bustling service centre built opposite mangrove swamps along the Krabi River. From town, Krabi River mangroves can be explored by renting a long-tail boat, first stopping off to visit the huge cavern inside the Khanab Nam

TIP

From Krabi, visitors can catch long-tail boats sailing out to Railae Beach, with larger ones leaving daily for Ko Phi Phi, and for Ko Lanta from November to May.

BELOW: one of Phang Nga's many caves, and rocky retreat near Krabi.

Map on page 24

twin peaks, which the flank the river. Traditionally, the leaves, bark, fruit and mosses of the surrounding mangroves provided folk cures for the alleviation of lumbago, kidney stones and menstrual pains. The trees also provided a source of weak alcohol and leaves for wrapping tobacco. Two rare bird species inhabit the mangroves: the mangrove pitta and the brown-winged kingfisher.

Note: Areas of Krabi province affected by the 2004 tsunami included Ko Phi Phi, Ao Nang, and Ko Lanta. Ao Nang and Ko Lanta quickly recovered, but some parts of Ko Phi Phi, including the twin beaches of Ao Lo Dalam and Ao Ton Sai, were very badly hit and closed for nearly a year. The reconstruction has been completed and all of Ko Phi Phi's beaches are now open.

Ko Phi Phi

Turquoise waves caress a beach so dazzlingly white, it is almost painful to the eye. The water is so crystalline, colourful fishing boats seem suspended in mid-air. With palm-fringed beaches and lofty limestone mountains as a backdrop, **Ko Phi Phi** ❼ arguably surpasses Phuket as one of the most beautiful islands in Asia. Phi Phi lies equidistant, about 45 km (30 miles), from both Phuket and Krabi. The island is in fact two islands: the smaller **Phi Phi Ley**, a well-preserved craggy limestone monolith similar to the other shrub-covered peaks of Phang Nga Bay, and **Phi Phi Don**, an epicentre of anarchic tourism development with a few remaining unspoiled beaches at its northern tip. Should the diving bug bite, Phi Phi Island has several dive shops where visitors can earn their open water scuba certification.

Ko Samui

Over four million tourists arrive at **Ko Samui** ❽ every year. There are luxury hotels, fancy restaurants, a modern airport, easy transport, a few absolutely chaotic and stressful commercial strips, and the full panoply of water sports and other diversions.

In addition to all the outlets for water sports, in the interior are several waterfalls descending from the heights of **Khao Phlu**, the island's highest point at 635 metres (2,080 ft). Sprinkled elsewhere around the island are a go-kart track, snake farm, butterfly aviary and lots of snooker parlours. The numerous signs for "monkey shows" are opportunities to see pig-tailed macaques engaged in their usual jobs on coconut farms. They twist coconuts from the tree tops, then retrieve and deposit them in burlap bags.

Aside from attendance at the Catholic Church or immigration office, there's no reason to linger among the drab cement blocks of Samui's biggest town, the western port of **Na Thon**. Ferries to Ko Pha Ngan and Ang Thong National Marine Park depart from Na Thon.

Long ago, the original beachcombers and today's tasteful hotels were drawn by a 6-km (4-mile) swathe of soft, silky sand at **Chaweng**, on the eastern coast. The sand at its half-sized southern neighbour, **Lamai**, is slightly lower grade. South of Lamai, the smaller beaches of **Ban Hua Thanon** and **Ban Bangkao** are nothing to write home about, but the coral reef is healthy near the former and the latter is a charming

BELOW: beach on Ko Samui.

Map
on page
24

TIP

Song thaew – small
pickup trucks con-
verted to taxis – serve
Ko Samui. Cheap and
fast, they rarely refuse
a fare and will load up
until passengers are
hanging from the
tailgate and roof.

RIGHT: beach
on Ko Phi Phi.
BELOW: Big Buddha.

Muslim village. From either, make a day trip inland and swim at the two-tiered waterfall at **Na Muang**. On the western side of the island, **Ban Taling Ngam** offers a couple of rather deluxe resort retreats.

Almost the entire northern coast of Ko Samui is occupied by three lovely bays. For panorama, head along the north shore to **Maenam**. The sand is coarser than that of the east, but the 4-km stretch is little developed. East of Maenam, **Bo Phut** is much narrower, but relatively protected. It's a short walk from the little fishing village of Ban Bo Phut. As for **Bangrak** (better known as **Big Buddha Beach**), it's a mystery why anyone stays here unless they enjoy the din from the adjacent road or the jets roaring overhead. Or perhaps it's the view of the indisputably large Buddha statue and its complement of especially garish souvenir shops. Quieter **Choeng Mon**, on the island's northeastern spur, has decent sand and water, and is within quick access of Chaweng's commercial facilities.

Last but not least, located 30 km (20 miles) west of Ko Samui, are the attractions of 41 brilliant isles comprising **Ang Thong National Marine Park** (daily 8am–6pm; entrance fee; tel: 0 7728 6025). Day-long package trips voyage to Ko Wua Talab, park headquarters, and Ko Mae Ko. But these tours allow little time to investigate any more than a viewpoint and a cave on Wua Talab, and the clear, pea-green saltwater lake on Mae Ko. On both islands, the designated swimming spots have negligible coral and fish.

Ko Phangan

If Ko Samui is increasingly the island of package tours and brief vacations, its neighbour 15 km (9 miles) to the north, **Ko Phangan**, is a refuge for backpackers on leisurely world tours and Europeans lazing away winter-long holidays. From the cacophonous southern port town of **Thong Sala**, a ferry port for Ko Samui and Ko Tao, there is a paved 10-km (6-mile) stretch that runs due north to the village of **Chalok Lam**. East of Chalok Lam, the justly prized beach of the moment is **Hat Kuat** (Bottle Beach), accessible only by sea. Probably the quickest way to get there is from Ban Chalok.

Continuing eastward and down the coast, one could well enjoyably argue the merits of **Hat Sadet** (with a waterfall and jumbo rocks bearing the graffiti of Thai royalty) or **Thong Nai Pan Bay**, with wonderful cliff viewpoints, a double-barrelled bay and a coral reef. Eventually you will reach the pretty southern cove of **Hat Thian**, which offers an additional choice of beaches on either side. Pick one and drop anchor.

Just 10 minutes away by long-tail boat is **Hat Rin**, known for its monthly all-night "full-moon" party. The biggest bashes of the year take place in December and January, when leading British DJs fly in with cutting-edge sounds and hordes of young clubbers. There's even a thrice-daily boat connection between Hat Rin and Samui. Nonetheless, the roller-coaster road joining Hat Rin and Thong Sala is now paved and has further opened up the intervening villages and beaches of **Ban Tai** and **Ban Khai**.

An easy stroll up a hill from Ban Tai is **Wat Khao Tham** (daily; entrance fee; www.watkowtahm.org), where Buddhist meditation courses are held. ❑

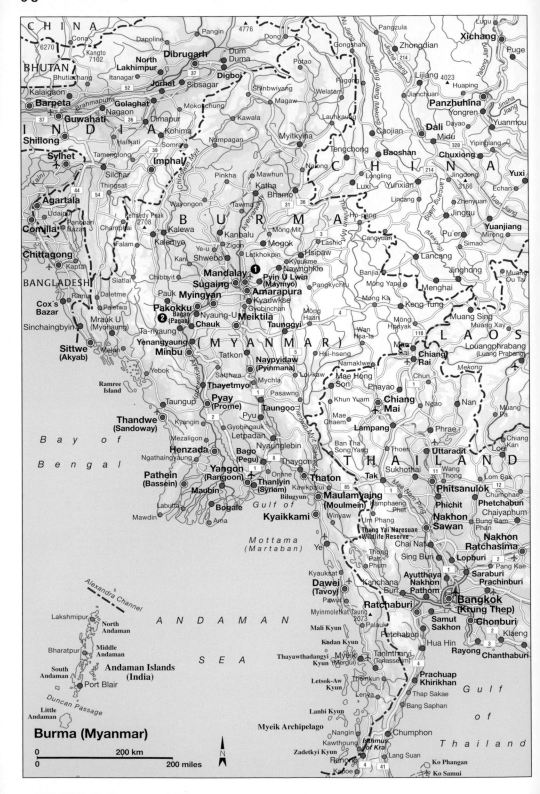

Burma (Myanmar)

0   200 km
0   200 miles

BURMA

Visiting Burma has always been a magical experience
but there is also an ethical dimension

Travellers contemplating a trip to Burma will be aware that it is regarded by a large section of the global community as a pariah because of the human rights abuses of the Burmese people by the ruling military junta. The burning question is this: does visiting Burma endorse the current regime or, in a small way, reduce the country's isolation from the outside world and constrain the junta's actions? Both views have convincing advocates, and informed travellers must make up their own minds.

The essence of Burma lies in its atmosphere, its varied scents and colour, its ambience recalling past ages. That eternal beauty will remain after today's political repression has become part of history, and we hope that keeping this section of the book up to date may play a part in ensuring that the country and its deeply religious and dignified people will not be forgotten or ignored.

Today even the country's place names are contentious. In 1989, the Burmese authorities implemented a series of name changes replacing colonial names with equivalents closer to actual Burmese usage. The most significant alteration was to the English name of the country, changed from the "Union of Burma" to the "Union of Myanmar" (to match the official Burmese name). The same is true with "Rangoon", which became "Yangon", a name given to the city as far back as 1755 by Alaungpaya when he captured and renamed the city of Dagon. The river Irrawaddy is now the Ayeyarwady, the Sittang changed to Sittoung, the Chindwin to Chindwinn, and the Salween to Thanlwin.

Of the cities, Pegu became Bago, Pagan changed to Bagan, Tavoy to Dawei, Prome to Pyay, Moulmein to Mawlamyaing, Maymyo to Pyin-U-Lwin, Magwe to Magway, Bassein to Pathein, Mergui to Myeik, and Sandoway to Thandwe. Tenasserim is now Tanintharyi and Arakan has become Rakhaing. Burmans are now called Bamar, the Karen are called Kayin, and the Arakanese are called Rakhaing. In this book we use the new names, with the old names in parentheses in the first reference of each chapter.

The name of the country, however, will remain Burma and that of the language Burmese, since this is derived from the internationally accepted term "Tibeto-Burman". We have made a distinction between the Bamar (Burman) people, the country's majority ethnic group, and the Burmese, a term that represents all the peoples of Burma. Indigenous terms used are from the Burmese language, except for Pali language words in religious contexts. ❏

PRECEDING PAGES: fishing on Inle Lake, in central Burma; Shwedagon Pagoda in the northern part of Yangon.

Decisive Dates

The early empire

3000–5000 BC: Anyathian culture flourishes in northern Burma.

circa **500 BC:** The Pyus enter the upper part of the Ayeyarwady (Irrawaddy) River basin.

3rd century BC: Mon settle in the Sittoung Valley.

AD 832: Pyu state of Thayekhittaya (Sri Ksetra) founded. Conquest of Pyu capital of Halin by Tai-Shans of Nan-Chao.

9th century AD: The Myanmar people, known as the Bamar, come from the China-Tibet border area, over-

run the Kyaukse plain and establish themselves as a major power in the rice-cultivation region. From Bagan, they control trade routes between China and India.

The Burman dynasties

1057 AD: Anawrahta founds first Burman empire.

1084-1113: Golden Age of Bagan. Under Kyanzittha, the golden age of pagoda-building begins.

1287: Fall of first Burmese empire following Mongol invasion. Mon establish state at Mottama (Martaban).

1364: Inwa (Ava) founded as capital of a Shan-Bamar dynasty in northern Burma.

1369: Mon capital transferred to Bago.

1385–1425: War between the Mon and Shan.

1519: Portuguese establish trade station at Mottama.

1531: Second Burmese Empire established.

1600–13: Portuguese, de Brito, rules at Thanlyin.

1635: Burma capital is moved to Inwa. British, French and Dutch develop trade with Burma.

1752: Mon conquer Inwa, ending the Second Burmese Empire.

1755: Alaungpaya founds new dynasty and Third Burmese Empire at Shwebo.

1767: Burmese conquer Thai capital of Ayutthaya.

1785: King Bodawapaya conquers Rakhaing (Arakan).

Colonial period to World War II

1824–1826: First Anglo-Burmese war; under Treaty of Yandabo, Britain gains the regions around Rakhaing and Tanintharyi (Tenasserium).

1852: Second Anglo-Burmese war; Britain annexes Yangon (Rangoon) and Southern Burma.

1861: King Mindon (1853–78) transfers his court to the new city of Mandalay.

1886: Britain annexes all of Burma.

1886–95: Burmese wage guerrilla warfare against British in northern Burma.

1937: Burma is separated from India.

1939: Communist Party of Burma (CPB) is founded.

1941: Japanese military enters Burma.

1942–45: Most of Burma under Japanese occupation.

1943: Declaration of Burma's independence under the Japanese military.

1945: Burma National Army starts anti-Japanese uprising. Allies reconquer all of Burma.

1947: Aung San-Attlee agreement is signed. Panglong agreement is signed. Constituent assembly elections are held. Aung San and six other members of interim government are assassinated. Constituent assembly adopts new Burmese constitution. Nu-Attlee agreement concluded.

Independence

1948: Burma regains independence as Union of Burma and leaves British Commonwealth. CPB goes underground and civil war begins.

1951: First parliamentary elections in post-independence Burma are held.

1956: Second parliamentary elections.

1958: Ruling party splits into two factions. A caretaker government, headed by General Ne Win, assumes office.

1960: Border agreement and treaty of friendship and non-aggression concluded between Burma and People's Republic of China. U Nu's Pyidaungsu Party wins in parliamentary elections.

1961: Union Parliament makes Buddhism the official state religion.

Military rule

1962: Military coup brings to power the Revolutionary Council (RC) of General Ne Win, who declares the "Burmese Way of Socialism". Burma Socialist Programme Party (BSPP) founded.

1963: Peace talks between the RC and various rebel organisations and groups are held in Yangon.

1964: All legal political parties and organisations except BSPP are banned. Nationalisation of all export trade and commodity distribution is implemented.

1967: Anti-Chinese riots in Yangon.

1969: Former Prime Minister U Nu founds Parliamentary Democracy Party to fight RC from abroad.

1971: First BSPP Congress is held and the Twenty-Year Plan (1974–94) announced. Ne Win's state visit to China marks normalisation of official relations.

1974: New constitution becomes effective, creating the Socialist Republic of the Union of Burma.

1979: Burma withdraws from Non-Aligned Movement.

1987: UN General Assembly approves Least Developed Nation status for Burma.

1988: Major demonstrations at Yangon University campuses. On 26 July, Brigadier-General Sein Lwin elected as BSPP's new chairman and chairman of state council (President of the State). On 3 August, martial law is declared in Yangon. Five days later general strike and demonstrations in Yangon; the army kills many demonstrators. Dr Maung Maung replaces Sein Lwin on 12 August. The largest demonstration in Yangon occurs on 28 August and martial law is lifted there. U Nu sets up League for Democracy and Peace.

SLORC takes power

September 1988: U Nu proclaims "parallel government" with himself as Prime Minister. On 18 September, the military takes power in a coup. State Law and Order Restoration Council (SLORC), headed by General Saw Maung, is formed. Aung Gyi, Tin U and Daw Aung San Suu Kyi found National League for Democracy (NLD). BSPP is now the National Unity Party (NUP).

1989: Rebellious Wa troops capture CPB's headquarters at Panghsang, ending Communist insurgency. The English name of Burma is changed to Myanmar.

1990 While Aung San Suu Kyi is confined under house arrest, general elections are held and the NLD gains over 80 seats in the Assembly.

1991: SLORC refuses to recognise election results till a new constitution is drafted. Daw Aung San Suu Kyi is awarded Nobel Peace Prize while under house arrest.

LEFT: the only portrait of King Mindon, founder of Mandalay. **RIGHT:** General Ne Win, head of the Revolutionary Council in 1963.

1992: The UN Human Rights Commission condemns Burma for serious rights violations. General Saw Maung resigns and is succeeded by General Than Shwe (Vice-Chairman of SLORC), who becomes the new Prime Minister. Burma is readmitted to Non-Aligned Movement. Two decades of martial law and curfew end.

1993: The largest rebel group, Kachin Independence Organisation (KIO), signs a cease-fire agreement with the government, ending a 30-year war. This is followed by agreements with 14 other insurgent groups.

1995: In July, Aung San Suu Kyi is temporarily freed from six years of house arrest but cannot leave Yangon. Soon she is returned to effective house arrest.

1997: SLORC is renamed State Peace and Development Council (SPDC). Burma is admitted to the Association of Southeast Asian Nations (ASEAN).

2002: The UN helps secure Aung San Su Kyi's release from house arrest. General Ne Win, accused of plotting to overthrow the military, dies after a long illness.

2004: The SPDC reconvenes a national convention to write a new constitution. The NLD refuses to participate as Aung San Suu Kyi is barred from it. In October, Khin Nyunt is ousted by Soe Win, a more conservative member of the ruling military junta.

2005: The capital moves from Yangon to Naypyidaw (Pyinmana).

2006: The military regime extends Aung San Suu Kyi's house arrest for another year. ❑

THE BURMESE

The population of Burma is unquestionably a collection of diverse people, its origins found in the cultures of ancient China and Thailand

The Burmese name for the country, Myanmar, implied that the nation is a federation of many peoples. But it is an uneasy federation. "Burma Proper", as it was called by the British and chief settlement area of the Bamar (Burman) majority, is encircled by separate minority states of the Chin, Kachin, Shan, Kayin or Karen, Kayah (Red Karen/Karenni), Mon and Rakhaing (Arakanese). Through the centuries, there have been mistrust, antagonism, and frequent wars among the various groups, and the situation is no different today.

The current administrative divisions were built into Burma's 1948 constitution, which was based on a model devised by the British. During the colonial era, the British, on their favoured principle of "divide and rule", made a distinction between Burma Proper and "Outer Burma", the latter comprising the settlement areas of the ethnic minorities. Burma Proper was placed under the direct rule of British India, but the minorities were left with much greater autonomy under indirect rule. At this time, nearly 250 separate languages and dialects were spoken.

While the Bamar were denied a place in the colonial army, the various minorities were heavily depended upon by the British for their fighting skills. The racial enmity between the Bamars and the minorities festered just beneath the surface until independence was granted in 1948. Since that time, a succession of violent domestic confrontations has played havoc with the nation's hopes of internal peace.

No less than 67 separate indigenous racial groups have been identified in Burma, not including the various Indians, Chinese and Europeans who make the country their home.

Traces of prehistoric people

Long before ancestors of the modern Burmese moved from central Asia and Tibet, prehistoric

people inhabited the area that is now known as Burma. These aborigines eventually moved on toward what is today Indonesia. No trace of them is found in the present-day population of Burma. The Andaman Sea islanders in the Bay of Bengal and the Semang of the Malay Peninsula might be direct descendants.

In historic times, three separate migrations were important in Burma's development.

The first to arrive were the Mon-Khmer people from the arid, wind-swept plains of Central Asia, and it is not difficult to imagine their motivation. Anyone who has seen the mountains of golden rice piled high at harvest time will understand why the first Mon-Khmer kingdom was called Suvannabhumi, or the Golden Land.

Then came the Tibeto-Burman, who pushed the Mon-Khmer people further to the south and east, away from the middle reaches of the Ayeyarwady (Irrawaddy) River. First the Pyu, then the Bamar, moved down the valleys of the

LEFT: monk in the mountains of northern Burma.
RIGHT: old photo of Naga, an animistic people from the mountainous Sagaing Division.

Ayeyarwady and Sittoung (Sittang) rivers, establishing their magnificent empires at Thayekhittaya (Sri Ksetra) and Bagan (Pagan).

Between the 12th and 14th centuries, the Tai (known today in Burma as Shan), a Sino-Tibetan race, began moving south from Yunnan down the river valleys. When they tried to force the Bamar out of the Ayeyarwady Valley, centuries of warfare followed.

Bamar and Mon

There are about 30 million Bamar in Burma today, constituting about 60 percent of the population. As the majority racial group and the pre-

dominant landholder as well as the group holding the reins of the present government, the Bamar bear the brunt of much interracial hostility.

The Buddhist Mon live mainly around the cities of Mawlamyaing (Moulmein) and Bago (Pegu). Before the Bamars came, they were the most powerful group in Burma. In 1995, after decades of armed resistance, they signed a cease-fire agreement with the Burmese army. Today, the Mon – who number just over 1 million – are largely assimilated in the mainstream Burmese culture, although they continue to use their own language and have retained their own sanctioned state within the Burmese union.

Padaung and Wa

Among the smaller minority groups belonging to the Mon-Khmer language family are the Padaung and the Wa. Both groups have gained a certain fame – or notoriety – that far exceeds their meagre numbers.

There are only about 7,000 Padaung, all of whom live in the vicinity of Loikaw, capital of Kayah State. Their "giraffe women" were publicised by various ethnographers of the 19th and 20th centuries. Despite the illusion, the women's necks have not been elongated at all – their collarbones and ribs have been pushed down by the brass coils worn around their necks.

The Wa are the notorious frontier inhabitants of Burma's northeast. About 300,000 Wa live in remote habitats on both sides of the border with China. Until the 1940s, there was little known about them, except that they were head-hunters who offered human skulls as sacrifices to their gods. Most of the Burmese Wa live in the east of the vast Shan State.

Shan

Shan. Siam. Assam. All three geographical names have the same root meaning, an indication of the widespread migration and settlement area of this race. The origins of this ethnonym are unknown, but as a culture their influence in the river valleys of Laos, Thailand and Burma has been vast.

Most of Burma's 4 million Shan are Buddhists who make their homes in valleys and on high plains. Living at an average altitude of 1,000 metres (3,280 ft) above sea level, the Shans are Burma's leading producers of fruit, vegetables and flowers and, over the centuries, they have developed sophisticated irrigation systems in the river valleys.

After the Shan State, the Shan's next largest concentration is in Kachin State, but they can also be found throughout much of Burma.

Kayin, Kayah and Kachin

The Kayin people belong linguistically to the Tibeto-Burman-speaking majority of Burma. There are presently 3 million members of this race living in Burma. Although they have their own separate administrative division – the Kayin (Kawthule) State – only about one-third of the Kayin population lives there.

The Kayah, also known as Red Karen or

Karenni, have the smallest state in Burma in terms of area as well as population. Virtually all members of this ethnic group – about 75,000 – reside here. The Kayah are primarily hill people, making their living by dry cultivation of rice, millet and vegetables.

Kachin State is a real hotch-potch of hill tribes. Throughout this large, mountainous district in the far north, Jinghpaw (Kachin), Shan and Bamar share space with Maru, Lashi, Azi, Lisu, Rawang, Tailon, Taikamti, Tailay, Kadu and

> ## ETHNIC MEDLEY
>
> "In no other area are the races so diverse, or the languages and dialects so numerous…"
>
> C.M. Enriquez
> *Races of Burma* (1933)

a tourist destination, since both sides of the border are inhabited by some of the most colourful people in Southeast Asia.

Rakhaing and Chin

The Rakhaing (Arakanese), who are also known as Rakhine, inhabit Rakhaing State and constitute about 4 percent of the total population. Although closely related to the Bamar, the latter have had their hands full dealing with this coastal race over the two centuries since

Kanang villagers without any recognisable settlement pattern. The label Kachin is sometimes indiscriminately applied to all inhabitants of this state. In fact, the only true Kachin are the Jinghpaw people. Traditionally hilltop dwellers, their lifestyle and social structure are distinctly different from those of the Shan. Animism and sorcery are a part of daily life.

After decades of fighting the government, cross-border trade with China has developed tremendously. The region has great potential as

Rakhaing was annexed by King Bodawpaya.

The Rakhaing are about 75 percent Buddhist and 25 percent Muslim, with the two groups having little to do with each other.

With its exposure to monsoons, Rakhaing gets far more rain and has higher humidity. The entire transportation system is therefore dependent on boats, and cultivated land is always situated close to navigable waters.

The Chin, and related Naga people, make up about 2 percent of Burma's population. They live in the far northwest, spilling over the border into India and Bangladesh. Most Chin are animists who practise slash-and-burn agriculture to grow dry rice. ❑

LEFT: an elderly Kachin woman savours a puff on a local cheroot. **ABOVE:** *thanaka*-bark makeup is a traditional sun-block for Burmese women.

BUDDHA, JAMBUDVIPA AND THE 37 NAT

Religion is a defining element in Burmese life. Buddhism permeates the everyday lives of Burma's people, placing great emphasis on individual achievement

It has often been said that Burma is the most profoundly Buddhist country in the world. That may well be true. But the brand of Buddhism practiced in this isolated land is unique on the face of the globe.

particularly that of the Brahmans. According to the Burmese, the European-Asian continent is called Jambudvipa. It is the southern of four islands situated at the cardinal points surrounding Mount Meru, the centre of the world.

Burmese Buddhism, theoretically, is Theravada or Hinayana Buddhism, that sect of Buddhism adhering most closely to the Buddha's original teaching, and which is the dominant form of Buddhism that is found throughout much of Southeast Asia. It was preceded in Burma, however, by the animistic beliefs of the hill tribes and by the Hindu-Brahmanism of early traders, which has had a profound effect on the cosmological concept of the people.

Burmese cosmology

Strictly speaking, Burmese cosmology is Buddhist cosmology, but it has been shaped by millennia of influences from other cultures,

This southern island is the only place where future Buddhas can be born. This is because Jambudvipa is a place of misery compared to the other abodes of this universe.

There are, in fact, 31 planes of existence on, above, and below Mount Meru. They can be divided into three main groups: the 11 planes of *Kama-Loka*, the realm of the sensuous world; the 16 planes of *Rupa-Loka*, the realm of subtle material matter; and finally, the four planes of *Arupa-Loka*, the realm of formlessness.

ABOVE: a monk rests between periods of meditation in a monastery. **RIGHT:** many popular tattoos represent animistic deities.

King Anawrahta, founder of the First Burmese Empire, devoted his attention to simplifying spiritual beliefs. When he introduced Theravada Buddhism into Upper Burma as the national religion, he was unable to eliminate the animistic beliefs of his people. Despite radical measures, 36 of the countless *nat* survived in the people's daily activities. For the Burmese, these 36 nat serve nearly the same purpose as the saints of the Catholic Church. In both cases they are called upon in times of need. So Anawrahta introduced a 37th figure – Thagyamin – and made him king of the nat. He thereafter tolerated the popular worship of these 37 nat, once it had been established that they were also followers of the Buddha's teachings.

Beatitudes of Buddhism

Theravada Buddhism is recognised as the principal religion of about 80 percent of all Burmese people. While there are significant numbers of Hindus, Muslims, Christians and primitive animists (especially among the northern hill tribes), it is safe to say that over 99 per cent of the Bamar (Burman), Mon, Shan and Palaung are Theravadins.

The division between the Theravada and Mahayana styles, while developing for some

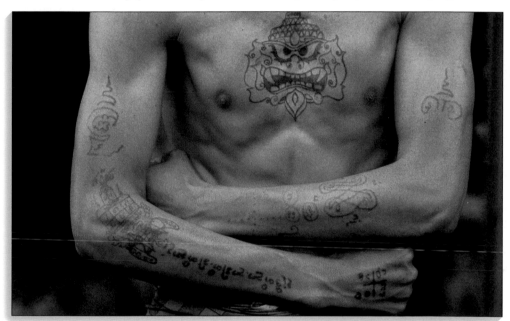

THREE JEWELS, FOUR NOBLE TRUTHS, AND THE EIGHT-FOLD PATH

As there is no true form of worship in the Theravada style of Buddhism, the only true ritual to which both monks and laity submit themselves is the recitation – three times a day – of the "Three Jewels", or the *Triratna*: "I take refuge in the Buddha. I take refuge in the Dhamma. I take refuge in the Sangha."

The formula of the "Three Jewels" offers solace and security. These are needed for strength, if one understands the "Four Noble Truths" expounded upon by Gautama Buddha in his first sermon:

- Life always has in it the element of suffering
- The cause of suffering is desire

- In order to end the suffering, give up desire and give up attachment
- The way to this goal is the Noble Eight-fold Path

The Noble Eight-fold Path consists of right view, right intent, right speech, right conduct, right means of livelihood, right endeavour, right mindfulness, and right meditation. This "path" is normally divided into three areas: view and intent are matters of wisdom; speech, conduct or action, and livelihood are matters of morality; and endeavour, mindfulness, and meditation are matters resulting from true mental discipline.

time, actually occurred in 235 BC when King Ashoka convened the Third Buddhist Synod at Pataliputra, India. The Buddhist elders (Theravada means "the way of the elders") held tight to their literal interpretation of the Buddha's teaching. They were opposed by a group which sought to understand the personality of the historical Buddha, and its relationship to one's salvation. Theravada Buddhism is actually a more conservative, more orthodox, form of the Buddhist thought.

The latter group became known as the Mahayana school. It established itself in Tibet, Nepal, China, Korea, Mongolia, Japan and

Vietnam, where its further development varied greatly from region to region.The Theravada school, meanwhile, has thrived in Sri Lanka, Burma, Thailand, Laos and Cambodia.

No soul

The Buddha denied the existence of a soul. There is no permanence, he explained, for that which one perceives to be "self". Rather, one's essence is forever changing. The idea of rebirth, therefore, is a complicated philosophical question within the structure of Buddhism. When a Buddhist (or any person, for that matter) is reincarnated, it is neither the person nor the soul which is actually reborn. Rather, it is the sum of

one's *karma*, the balance of good and evil deeds. One is reborn as a result of prior existence. A popular metaphor used to explain this transition is that of a candle. Were a person to light one candle from the flame of another, then extinguish the first, it could not be said that the new flame was the same as the previous one. Rather, in fact, its existence would be due to that of the previous flame.

The Noble Eight-fold Path, therefore, does not lead to salvation in the Judeo-Christian sense. By pursuing matters of wisdom, morality and mental discipline, one can hope to make the transition into *nirvana*, which can perhaps best be defined as extinction of suffering, cessation of desire. It is not heaven, nor is it annihilation. It is simply a quality of existence.

The monk

There are no priests in Theravada Buddhism. But the faithful still need a model to follow on the path to salvation. This model is provided by the colourfully clad Southeast Asian monks. In Burma, there are about 800,000 monks. Most of these are students and novices who put on the monk's robe only temporarily; nearly all male Burmese devote a period – from a few weeks to several years – in their lifetime to the monkhood. There are three fundamental rules to which the monk must subscribe. First, the renunciation of all possessions, except eight items: three robes, a razor for shaving, a needle for sewing, a strainer (to ensure that no living thing is swallowed), a belt, and an alms bowl. Second, a vow to injure no living thing and to offend no one. Finally, the vow of complete sexual celibacy. The monk must make his livelihood by seeking alms, setting out two hours before dawn and going door to door. The food received is the monk's only meal of the day.

A young Burmese begins his novitiate at around the age of nine. For the majority of Burmese, the novitiate does not last long. Most have left the monkhood before their 20th birthday. Those who are fully ordained devote their lives to meditation, the study of the Pali scriptures, and the instruction of the laity. ❏

LEFT: the head-shaving part of a young Burmese boy's *shin-pyu*, the initiation as a novice into the order of monks. **RIGHT:** Rangoon monks pause during their daily alms-collection rounds.

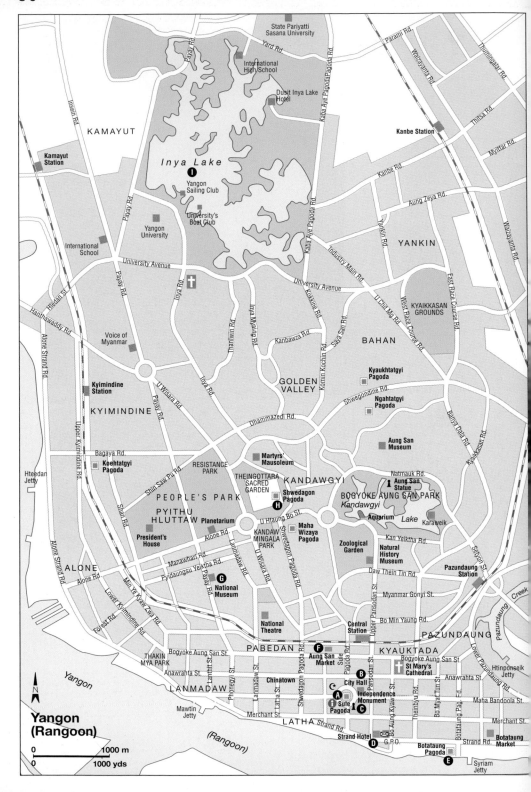

State Pariyatti
Sasana University

Yard Rd.

Parami Rd.

International
High School

Dusit Inya Lake
Hotel

Warizawlanta Rd.

Thumingalar Rd.

KAMAYUT

Kanbe Station

Kamayut
Station

Inya Lake

Myittar Rd.

Kanbe Rd.

Kanbe Rd.

Aung Zeya Rd.

Yankin Rd.

YANKIN

Yangon
Sailing Club

University's
Boat Club

Industry Main Rd.

U Chit Mg Rd.

West Race Course Rd.

East Race Course Rd.

KYAIKKASAN
GROUNDS

International
School

Yangon
University

University Avenue

University Avenue

Warizawlanta Rd.

Hledan St.

Hanthawaddy Rd.

Payay Rd.

Inya Rd.

Thanlwin Rd.

Inya Myaing Rd.

Kokine Rd.

Komin Kochin Rd.

Saya San Rd.

Kanbawza Rd.

BAHAN

Voice of
Myanmar

Alone Strand Rd.

Kyimindine
Station

U Wisara Rd.

Payay Rd.

GOLDEN
VALLEY

Kyaukhtatgyi
Pagoda

Shwegondine Rd.

Ngahtatgyi
Pagoda

Banya Dala Rd.

Kyaikkasan Rd.

KYIMINDINE

Dhammazedi Rd.

Upper Kyimindine Rd.

Hteedan
Jetty

Bagaya Rd.

Koehtatgyi
Pagoda

RESISTANCE
PARK

Martyrs'
Mausoleum

Aung San
Museum

Shin Saw Pu Rd.

THEINGOTTARA
SACRED
GARDEN

KANDAWGYI

Natmauk Rd.

PEOPLE'S PARK

Shwedagon
Pagoda

H

BOGYOKE AUNG SAN PARK

Aung San
Statue

PYITHU
HLUTTAW

Planetarium

U Htaung Bo St.

Kandawgyi

Aquarium

Kandawgyi
Lake

Karaweik

President's
House

KANDAW
MINGALA
PARK

Maha
Wizaya
Pagoda

Zoological
Garden

Natural
History
Museum

Kan Yeiktha Rd.

Sekton Rd.

Pazundaung
Station

Shan Rd.

Alone Rd.

Lanmadaw Rd.

Shwedagon Pagoda Rd.

U Wisara Rd.

ALONE

Manawhari Rd.

Pyidaungsu Yeiktha Rd.

Payay Rd.

National
Museum

G

Daw Thein Tin Rd.

Myanmar Gonyi St.

Bo Min Yaung Rd.

Pazundaung
Creek

Min Ye Kyaw Zwa Rd.

Lower Kyimindine Rd.

Forest Rd.

THAKIN
MYA PARK

National
Theatre

Central
Station

Upper Pansodan St.

PAZUNDAUNG

Bogyoke Aung San St.

PABEDAN

KYAUKTADA

Bogyoke Aung San St.

Htinponseik
Jetty

Anawrahta St.

LANMADAW

Aung San
Market

F

Sule
Pagoda Rd.

Pansodan St.

St Mary's
Cathedral

Anawrahta St.

Lanthit St.

Phongyi St.

Chinatown

Lanmadaw St.

Latha St.

Shwedagon Pagoda Rd.

City Hall

B

Independence
Monument

Theinbyu Rd.

Bo Aung Kyaw St.

Bo Myat Tun Rd.

Maha Bandoola St.

Lower Pazundaung Rd.

A Sule
Pagoda **C**

Merchant St.

Mawtin
Jetty

Merchant St.

LATHA

Strand Rd.

Strand Hotel **D**

G.P.O.

Botataung
Pagoda

Botataung
Market

E

Syriam
Jetty

Yangon

(Rangoon)

N

**Yangon
(Rangoon)**

0   1000 m

0   1000 yds

YANGON (RANGOON)

Map on page 80

Kipling had ogled, Theroux has prophesied. Burma's former capital of Yangon, or Rangoon, continues to evoke lyricism from those who venture among its streets of "dispossessed princes"

I t's been more than 100 years since Kipling sailed up the Yangon River to the Burma's former capital of Yangon (Rangoon), and now, as then, the glistening golden stupa of the Shwedagon Pagoda continues to dominate Yangon's landscape and image as perhaps few other structures do in any other major city of Southeast Asia. The massive pagoda not only is a remarkable architectural achievement, it is also the perfect symbol of a country in which Buddhism pervades every aspect of life. Indeed, it is hard to imagine a more stunning sight than watching the first rays of dawn bounce off the brilliant gold-plated pagoda and reflect in the serene waters of the nearby lake.

But while the Shwedagon Pagoda may dominate Yangon from its post of Singuttara Hill north of the city centre, it is far from the whole show. If you look beyond the ageing British colonial architecture of most of Yangon's buildings, you will find an oddly cosmopolitan city of 19th-century charm, with quiet, tree-lined avenues and a people that are known to be gracious and fun-loving. Even though the city centre around Sule Pagoda is sprouting high-rise buildings, the facelift that is being conducted by the present government has changed little of the appearance of the city, preserving some of the city centre with a bit of the ambience present when the British left in 1948.

Water on three sides

A burgeoning city of 4.6 million people (the population has more than quarupled in three decades), Yangon is surrounded on three sides by water. The Hlaing or Yangon River flows from the Bago (Pegu) Yoma down Yangon's west and south flanks, then continues another 30 km (20 miles) to the Gulf of Mottama (Martaban). To the east of the city is Pazundaung Creek, a tributary of the Hlaing.

To the north are the foothills of the Bago Yoma (Bago Mountain Range). It is here that one finds the Shwedagon *(see page 86)* and the charming lakes artificially created by the British, now the centres of residential districts.

We first hear of "Dagon, the town with the Golden Pagoda" from European travellers in the 16th century. An English merchant, Ralph Fitch, in 1586 described Shwedagon as "the fairest place, as I suppose, that is in the world." But it was the nearby town of Syriam, across the Bago and Hlaing rivers from Dagon, that was the most important European trading colony and Burma's main port well into the 18th century.

King Alaungpaya essentially founded Yangon and started it on its modern path in 1755 when he captured the village of Dagon from the Mon people. He called the settlement Yangon, or "End of Strife",

BELOW: girl with *thanaka* bark paste on her face.

which the British then converted into Rangoon, a name that was carried for over 150 years. With the destruction of Syriam the following year, Yangon assumed its commercial functions. After the British conquered the town in 1824 during the First Anglo-Burmese War, its importance as a trade port flourished. But fire devastated the town in 1841. Then, 11 years later, it was again almost completely destroyed in the Second Anglo-Burmese War.

Exploring Yangon

In the downtown area, amidst the mildewing grey brick government offices erected by the British colonialists, and the gleaming high-rise hotels built by Singaporean investors, is the city's commercial centre, its markets and cinemas. And it is here, especially in the markets, that the true colours of Yangon's diverse population can be seen.

If the Shwedagon is the soul of Yangon, then surely the **Sule Pagoda Ⓐ** is its heart. For centuries it has been the focus of much of the social and religious activity of the city. The British anchored the pagoda as the centre of the urban area when they structured their Victorian street-grid system around it in the mid-19th century. Today, the 48-metre (157-ft) pagoda remains among the taller structures in the city centre, and although the street names have been changed to Burmese from English, the thoroughfares in the central city still intersect at right angles with geometrical symmetry.

The origins of the Sule Pagoda are bound up in the mythical pre-history of Burma. Perhaps the most credible tale is that of two monks who were sent from India as missionaries to Thaton around 230 BC. After some hesitation, the king of Thaton gave them permission to construct a shrine at the foot of Singuttara

TIP

As with all pagodas, visitors to Sule Pagoda should stroll around in a clockwise direction. Sule Pagoda's eight sides are dedicated to the days, planets and animals of the eight cardinal points.

BELOW: colonial architecture, and father and daughter on way to worship.

Hill. In it the monks preserved a hair of the Buddha that they had carried from India. The octagonal structure of Sule Pagoda, which is consistent up to the bell and inverted bowl, clearly indicates its Brahman-Buddhist heritage. During the first centuries of the Christian era, when the influence of Indian merchants and settlers was especially strong, astrology blended with *nat* worship and Buddhist doctrine to create the unique Burmese brand of Buddhism. Even today, Sule Pagoda, whose name and shape document this religious development, is a magnetic centre for astrologers and fortune-tellers.

Colonial remnants

On the northeast corner of Sule Pagoda Road and Maha Bandoola Street, facing Sule Pagoda, is the **Yangon City Hall B**. Built by the British, it is a massive stone structure worth a glance for its colonial architecture with Burmese ornamentation. Note especially the traditional Burmese peacock seal high over the entrance.

On the southeast corner of the intersection is **Maha Bandoola Park**, named after a Burmese general of the First Anglo-Burmese War. In the centre of the park is the **Independence Monument C**, a 46-metre (150-ft) obelisk surrounded by five smaller 9-metre (30-ft) pillars. The monument represents Burma's five former semi-autonomous states – Shan, Kachin, Kayin (Karen), Kayah and Chin – in union with their larger Bamar (Burman) brothers.

On Strand Road is the famous **Strand Hotel D**. By stopping over for the night or even just for a meal, a visitor might turn nostalgic over the British colonial era. Before its substantial and expensive renovation in the mid 1990s, most of the formerly mosquito-infested rooms were cooled by electric paddle fans and serviced

Map on page 80

A cheerful hat pedlar in Yangon.

BELOW: Yangon street in colonial days.

BELOW: Water
Festival, Yangon.

by dribbling water pipes. Indian waiters, however, still hover attentively over every table and every guest in the high-ceilinged restaurant, which now carries a real menu. Since the Beverly Hills-class facelift, rooms are no longer as reasonably priced as they were during the 1980s. Nevertheless, it's worth stepping into the teak-furnished lounge for a cup of tea or bottle of cool beer.

Heading east on Strand Road for several blocks, you'll come to the **Botataung Pagoda ⓔ**. It is said that when eight Indian monks carried some relics of the Buddha here more than 2,000 years ago, 1,000 military officers *(botataung)* formed a guard of honour at the place where the rebuilt pagoda stands today. One of the pagoda's treasures, locked away, is a tooth of the Buddha, which Alaungsithu, a king of Bagan, tried unsuccessfully to acquire from Nan-chao (now China's Yunnan province) in 1115. China gave the relic to Burma in 1960.

At the end of Botataung Pagoda Road is the **Syriam Jetty**. Persons intent on making the 45-minute ferry trip across the river to Syriam should be warned, however, that the Syriam ferry leaves not from this jetty, but from the Htinbonseik Jetty on Pazundaung Creek, some distance east on Monkey Point Road (the eastern extension of Strand Road), then north. On the way you'll pass near the lively **Botataung Market** on the left and a teak mill on the right. Though the ferry crossing is a fascinating experience, there is, for the less adventurous, the Thanlyin bridge across the Bago River that connects Yangon with Syriam and shortens the travelling time considerably.

West and north of the Sule Pagoda is Yangon's market district. Largest of Yangon's markets and a must for every visitor is the **Bogyoke Aung San Market ⓕ** (formerly the Scott Market). At the corner of Sule Pagoda Road and Bogyoke Aung San Street, next to the red-brick Railway Administration

Building with its Moorish arches (one day to be converted into a first-class hotel), you can find under one roof all the consumer goods a Burmese family could possibly need or want. From spices to bicycles, local artefacts to Japanese stereo systems, everything is available here. Before World War II, a large majority of the inhabitants of Yangon were Indian or Chinese. To the south of the Bogyoke Market, off Shwedagon Pagoda Road, are the open-air markets – especially noted for the delicious Chinese soup sold at many of its stalls – and the Thein Gyi Zei, or Indian market. The oft-described "1000 Scents of the Orient" dominate this wholesale fruit-and-vegetable market: red chillies and cinnamon bark, mangosteen and durian, dried fish and seafoods.

The **National Museum** (daily 10am–4pm; entrance fee; tel: 01-282 563) is in a neighbourhood filled with foreign missions. The showpiece of the museum is the Lion's Throne, upon which King Thibaw once sat in his hall of audience at Mandalay Palace. Taken from Mandalay in 1886 after the Third Anglo-Burmese War, the throne and 52 other pieces of royal regalia were carried off by the British. Some items were left behind in the Indian Museum in Calcutta; others were kept in the Victoria and Albert Museum in London. They were returned to Burma as a gesture of goodwill in 1964 after Ne Win's state visit to Britain. The throne, made of wood, is 8 metres (27 ft) high and is inlaid with gold and lacquer work. It is a particularly striking example of the Burmese art of wood carving. Among the other Mandalay Regalia, as they are known, are gem-studded arms, swords, jewellery and serving dishes. Also in the archaeological section of the museum are artefacts from Burma's early history in Beikthano, Thayekhittaya (Sri Ksetra) and Bagan (Pagan). There is an 18th-century bronze cannon, a crocodile-shaped harp and many other items.

The government has prohibited selling betel nuts on the streets with hopes of getting rid of the red stains that still mark many lower sections of the house walls.

BELOW: women sweeping outside Shwedagon Pagoda to gain merit.

Map on page 80

"'There's the old Shway Dagon,' said my companion.... The golden dome said, 'This is Burma, and it will be quite unlike any land you know about.'"

— RUDYARD KIPLING
Letters from the East,
1889

OPPOSITE: part of Shwedagon, 1900.
BELOW: Shwedagon Pagoda.

Shwedagon Pagoda

It has been said there is more gold on the **Shwedagon Pagoda** ❿ (daily 5am–10pm; entrance fee) than in the vaults of the Bank of England. The bell-shaped stupa, soaring nearly 100 metres (330 ft) above its setting on Singuttara Hill, is plated with 8,688 solid-gold slabs. The tip of the stupa is set with 5,448 diamonds and 2,317 rubies, sapphires and topaz. A huge emerald sits in the middle to catch the first and last rays of the sun. All of this is mounted upon a 10-metre-high (33 ft) umbrella (*hti*), built upon seven gold-plated bars and decorated with 1,500 gold and silver bells. The central stupa is surrounded by more than 100 other buildings, including smaller stupas, pavilions and administrative halls.

According to legend, inside the stupa are eight enshrined hairs of Gautama Buddha, as well as relics of three previous Buddhas. While the origins of the pagoda are shrouded in legend, it was definitely well established when Bagan dominated Burma in the 11th century. Queen Shinsawbu, who ruled in the 15th century, is revered today for giving the pagoda its present shape and form. She established the terraces and walls around the stupa, and gave her weight in gold to be beaten into gold leaf and used to plate the stupa. This act has been repeated by many rulers in the course of the pagoda's history.

Much of the pagoda's history is recounted in its bells. For example, a bell weighing 30 tons was plundered in the early 1600s by a Portuguese mercenary intent upon melting it into cannons. As he attempted to ferry the bell across the river, it fell into the water and was never recovered. In the early 1800s, the British tried the same thing, with the same result, though the bell was recovered.

Standing before the stupa (*see photograph, pages 66–7*) is humbling. With a circumference at platform level of 433 metres (1,420 ft), its octagonal base is

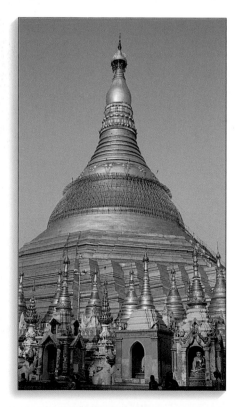

ringed with 64 smaller stupas. Northwest of the main stupa is the Maha Gandha Bell, cast of bronze in 1779 and which the British unsuccessfully tried to carry off. It weighs 23 tons and has a diameter of nearly 2 metres (6½ ft). Behind in the northwest corner of the compound are two Bodhi trees, adorned with flowers and small flags.

The eight enshrined hairs, which Gautama Buddha, close to achieving enlightenment in Bodhgaya, India, plucked from his own head, had an arduous journey to Burma. Half of them were lost to misfortune. When the Burmese king opened the casket containing the hairs, all eight were in place, emitting a brilliant, heavenly light that rose high above the trees. The blind could see, the lame could walk. The earth quaked, and a shower of precious stones rained down.

Northern Yangon

Continuing northeast through the winding residential streets north of the Shwedagon, past the "Rangoon Modern" stucco houses built for Westerners during the colonial era, you'll reach the huge and artificial **Inya Lake** ❶. On the southern shore are the Yangon Arts and Sciences University, with over 10,000 students, and the Myanmar Sailing Club, which sponsors races on the lake. Perhaps the best known structure on the lake is the Inya Lake Hotel, built by the Soviet Union in the early 1960s. ❏

MANDALAY

The city of Mandalay, made famous in Rudyard Kipling's verse, is not only the religious and cultural centre of upper Burma, it is also the economic hub for the entire region

Map on page 68

The capital of Upper Burma is a young city at just one and a half centuries or so. Nostalgia for Burma's last royal capital, enchantment with the myriad of pagodas dotting all corners of the region's landscape, and the warmth and vitality of the indigenous people weave a strong spell around the visitor that seems impossible to escape.

Mandalay ❶, 620 km (400 miles) north of Rangoon, is only 80 metres (260 ft) above sea level. Sprawling across the dry plains of the upper Ayeyarwady (Irrawaddy) River rice-growing district, Mandalay has a population of around 1.2 million people. Scenic beauty and historical tragedy are inextricably meshed in this city. There is the indestructible Mandalay Hill with its kilometre-long covered stairways and remarkable pagodas, and below it are the ruins of the Royal Palace, King Mindon's "Golden City" of ancient prophecy. In the middle of the city is Zegyo Market, centre of trade for all the people of Upper Burma who can be seen there in their colourful national costumes. Skilled artisans and craftsmen are found here, working their age-old wonders with gold and silver, marble and chisel, thread and loom. The sluggish Ayeyarwady flows by with its bustling wharves and flotilla of rice-laden boats.

Mandalay was founded in 1857 by King Mindon to coincide with an ancient Buddhist prophecy. The "Golden City" was formally completed in 1859, and Mindon then shifted his government and an estimated 150,000 people from nearby Amarapura in 1861, dismantling most of the previous palace and taking it with him to to help create the new capital.

The dream of Mandalay was short-lived, however. In November 1885, King Thibaw handed the town over to the British army and went into exile with his queen. Mandalay soon became just another outpost of British colonialism, albeit one crowned by richly furnished palace buildings, which by now had been renamed Fort Dufferin.

The palace structures were almost universally built of teak, and this was their demise. In March 1945, British troops shelled the stronghold, at the time defended by a handful of Japanese and Burmese soldiers. By the time the siege had ended, the interior of the Golden City was in ashes. All that remained intact before part of the palace was reconstructed were the walls and the moat.

Centre of the world

Mindon had built his **Royal Palace** on the model of Brahman-Buddhist cosmology to represent the centre of the world, the fabled Mount Meru. The palace formed a perfect square, with the outer walls facing the four cardinal directions, and the 12 gates, three

LEFT: rain-soaked rice paddies, central Burma.
BELOW: *chinthes* of Mandalay Hill.

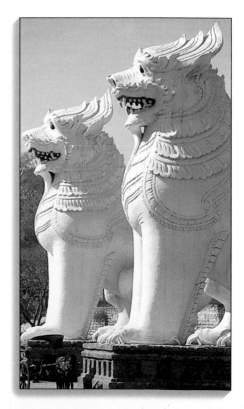

Mandalay's founder, King Mindon.

on each side, are marked with the signs of the zodiac. In the exact centre of the palace was the throne room, called the Lion's Room. The Royal Palace with the Lion's Room and the *pyathat* have been rebuilt.

These days the renovated palace shares the grounds of **Mandalay Fort** (Mon–Fri 8am–6pm) with the army. The grounds and a museum on Mandalay's history are open to the public. A little to the west is a scale model of the ancient palace created by archaeologists. The model indicates the location of all main and secondary buildings within the old palace walls, and it gives a good idea of the "centre of the world" concept. King Mindon's mausoleum is also in the palace grounds.

Mandalay Hill

You might start a visit to Mandalay by climbing famous **Mandalay Hill** (daily 8am–5pm; entrance fee), which rises 240 metres (790 ft) above the surrounding countryside. The slopes of Mandalay Hill are clothed in covered stairways, which contain small temples at regular intervals. There are 1,729 steps to the top, but the walk is not particularly difficult. About halfway up the hill, you'll encounter the first large temple, said to contain three bones of the Buddha.

About two-thirds of the way to the top of the hill stands a gold-plated statue of the Shweyattaw Buddha. His outstretched hand points to the place where the Royal Palace was built. This stance is unique; in all other Buddha images anywhere else in the world, Gautama is in one of the *mudra* positions. The statue was erected before King Mindon laid the first stone of his Golden City and symbolises Gautama Buddha's prophecy.

BELOW: a bronze *dvarapala.*

On the way up the steps, there is also a statue of a woman kneeling in front of the Buddha, offering to him her two severed breasts. According to legend, Sanda Moke Khit was an ogress, but she was so impressed by the Buddha's teachings that she decided to devote the rest of her life to following the Enlightened One. As a sign of humility, she cut off her breasts. The Buddha smiled as he accepted the gift, and the ogress's brother asked why he did so. He replied that Sanda Moke Khit had collected so many merits that in a future life she would be reborn as Min Done (Mindon), king of Mandalay.

At the base of Mandalay Hill's southeast stairway, surrounded by a high wall, is Mindon's **Kuthodaw Pagoda** (daily 8am–5pm; entrance fee). Its central structure, the 30-metre (100-ft) high Maha Lawka Marazein Pagoda, was erected in 1857 and modelled on the Shwezigon Pagoda in Nyaung U, near Bagan (Pagan). Sometimes called the "world's largest book", it was created by a team of 2,400 monks who required almost six months to recite the text. The canons were recorded on the marble slabs by devoted Buddhist scholars, and the letters were originally veneered with gold leaf.

Close to the Kuthodaw are other important pagodas and monasteries. Not far from the south staircase is the **Kyauk-tawgyi Pagoda**. Begun in 1853, the original plan was to model this after the Ananda Temple at Bagan, but the 1866 revolt hampered this and other projects. The building was eventually completed in 1878. The main point of interest here is a huge Buddha figure carved out of a single block of marble

from the Sagyin quarry. This undertaking was of ancient Egyptian proportions: 10,000 men required 13 days to transport the rock from the Ayeyarwady River to the pagoda site. The statue was finally dedicated in 1865, with 20 figures on each side of the image representing the Buddha's 80 disciples. A painting of King Mindon is also contained within the pagoda.

Map on page 68

The **Sandamuni Pagoda** (daily 8am–5pm) was built on the site where King Mindon had his provisional palace during construction of the Mandalay Palace. There are two monasteries located south of the Kuthodaw Pagoda, not far to the east of the palace moat. The **Shwe Nandaw Kyaung** (daily 8am–5pm; entrance fee), at one time part of the royal palace, is the only building from Mindon's Golden City that has survived the ravages of the 19th century.

Beside the Shwe Nandaw lie the remains of the **Atumashi Kyaung** (daily 8am–5pm), which means "Incomparable Monastery". An 1890 fire destroyed the monastery, taking with it four historic sets of the Tipitaka (Buddhist scriptures). This extraordinary masonry-and-teak monastery has been restored according to the original plan.

Maha Muni Pagoda

The most important religious structure in Mandalay is the **Maha Muni (Great Sage) Pagoda** (daily 8am–5pm; entrance fee). It is also called the Rakhaing (Arakan) Pagoda or Payagyi Pagoda. Located about 3 km (2 miles) south of the city centre on the road to Amarapura, this pagoda was built in 1784 by King Bodawpaya and was reconstructed after a fire a century later.

The Maha Muni Buddha figure is almost 4 metres (13 ft) high and is coated with layers of gold leaf several centimetres thick. Except during the rainy sea-

An important trading city on the crossroads of India and China, Mandalay is the centre of Burmese Buddhism and also of Bamar nationalism.

BELOW: Kuthodaw Pagoda.

Map on page 68

The makers of oiled bamboo paper live on 37th Road. This kind of paper, which is placed between layers of gold leaf, is produced by a remarkable 3-year process of soaking, beating flat and drying of bamboo.

In 1890, Rudyard Kipling penned the famous verse:
"On the road to
  Mandalay
Where the flyin'
  fishes play
An' the dawn comes
  up like thunder
outer China 'crost
  the Bay!"
Kipling had never been to Mandalay. If he had been, he might have noticed the complete absence of flying fishes.

OPPOSITE: the fabled Maha Muni.

son, when the Buddha's body is cloaked with robes, you can watch the Buddhist faithful pasting on the thin gold leaf. Only six of the Khmer bronzes have survived the centuries – two *dvarapala* (warriors or temple guardians), three lions, and a three-headed elephant. They are kept in a small building in the Maha Muni Pagoda courtyard. Streets with covered stalls lead up to the Maha Muni Pagoda from all directions, providing the bazaar atmosphere for which Burma was once famous amongst foreigners.

There are four other Buddhist buildings in the vicinity of downtown Mandalay that are definitely worth visiting. Fortunately, the city's grid street plan makes them easy to find. Heading north from the Maha Muni Pagoda, one first encounters the **Shwe In Bin Kyaung**. This monastery, situated to the south of 35th Road, contains very fine 13th-century woodcarvings. At 31st Road and 85th Street stands the **Setkyathiha Pagoda**, rebuilt after being badly damaged in World War II.

Proceeding northward leads to the **Eindawya Pagoda** at 27th Road and 89th Street. The pagoda houses a Buddha figure made of chalcedony (a form of quartz), carried to Burma in 1839 from Bodhgaya, the place in India where Gautama achieved Buddhahood. The pagoda was built in early 1847 by King Pagan Min. Today it has been covered with gold leaf. The oldest pagoda in the city is the **Shwekyimyint Pagoda**, on 24th Road between 82nd and 83rd streets. Erected in 1167 by Prince Minshinsaw, the exiled son of King Alaungsithu of Bagan, it houses a Buddha image consecrated by the prince himself.

A couple of blocks from the Shwe Kyi Myint, at 24th Road and West Moat Road, are the **Cultural Museum Mandalay** (Wed–Sun 10am–4pm; tel: 02-24603). The museum collection extends across many eras of Burmese history. One of its most interesting pictures shows King Thibaw and Queen Supyalat on the eve of their exile. The library is widely noted for its assemblage of important Buddhist documents.

Market centre of the north...

For the Chin of the west, the Kachin of the north, and the Shans of the east, Mandalay is the primary market for goods. And the **Zegyo Market**, located on the west side of the city centre, on 84th Street between 26th and 28th roads, is Mandalay's most important bazaar. The Italian Count Caldrari, first secretary of the Mandalay municipal government, had the Zegyo Market laid out around the Diamond Jubilee Clock, which had been erected in honour of Queen Victoria's 60-year reign. Rebuilt as a new concrete structure, the market still offers visitors a fine opportunity to see Burma's ethnic minorities in their national costumes, and at the same time gives an insight to daily Burmese life.

Part of Mandalay's enchantment comes from its location beside the Ayeyarwady River. At the western end of A Road, which follows the railroad tracks north of the Shwe In Bin Kyaung, one finds the jetties where the ships that ply the "Road to Mandalay" are docked.

...and craftsmen of the south

In the southern part of Mandalay, especially in the precincts of the Maha Muni Pagoda, are the artists' and craftsmen's quarters. Here you can watch as Burmese men, using the same skills and methods as their forefathers, pursue their trade in religious sculpture – Buddha images in all positions, Buddha footprints, lotus-blossom pedestals, or even the occasional Virgin Mary, a reminder of earlier missionary days.

In the area around Mandalay, visitors should make it a point to see other artisans – the silk and cotton weavers of Amarapura; the silversmiths of Ywataung; and the bronze and brass workers from Kyi Thun Kyat. ❑

BAGAN

*One of Asia's most venerable wonders and home of the
temple of omniscience, Bagan is an ancient and
deserted city full of awe-inspiring pagodas*

Map
on page
68

In many respects **Bagan ❷** has changed very little in the past century. It remains the way Sir James Scott saw it, as "Burma's deserted capital on the Irrawaddy, thickly studded with pagodas of all sizes and shapes". It was – and still is – a veritable elephants' graveyard of medieval Burmese culture. There is nowhere, perhaps, a sight so striking as the view across the plain of Bagan (also, Pagan), one ancient red-brick pagoda after another rising above the flat land on the dusty eastern shore of greatest river in Burma.

Between the time of Anawrahta's conquest of Thaton in 1057 and the over-run of Bagan by Kublai Khan's forces in 1287, some 13,000 temples, pagodas, *kyaung* and other religious structures were built on this vast plain. After seven long centuries, just over 4,000 of these remain standing.

There has been a settlement in the region of Bagan since early in the 2nd century AD, when Thamuddarit, a Pyu king, led his followers here. The walls of the city were erected by King Pyinbya in 849, but it was left to King Anawrahta, 42nd ruler of the Bagan dynasty, to usher in the city's age of glory, and to his successor, King Kyanzittha, to perpetuate that glory.

The economic centre of the Bagan plain today is at **Nyaung U**, about 5 km (3 miles) to the north of the walled village of Bagan. There are a few important monuments in the immediate vicinity of Nyaung U, notably the Shwezigon Pagoda, and there are others a few kilometres to the south of Bagan village near Myinkaba. The picturesque Bagan village, once situated around the main temples, was relocated in a controversial military operation in 1990 to clear the principal temple quarter of local habitations. **New Bagan**, as it is called, has now been reconstructed some 8 km (5 miles) south of its original site, close to the village of Thiripyitsaya.

Bagan monuments

All visitors to the **Bagan Archaeological Zone** – which encompasses most of the temple and stupa ruins of note – must pay a US$10 entry fee, which is valid for one's entire visit. Many travellers begin their exploration of the ancient ruins at the **Ananda Temple**, just to the east of the old city wall. This impressive white-washed edifice dominates the view as one approaches Bagan from the north. Considered the masterpiece of Mon architecture, it was completed in 1091. When the great temple was completed, Kyanzittha is said to have been so awe-struck by its unique style that he personally executed the architect by Brahman ritual to assure that the temple could not be duplicated, thereby sealing its permanence and importance. At present, some of the statues in the temple are actually copies because the originals were destroyed by temple thieves.

LEFT: one of Bagan's pagodas.
BELOW: Ananda Temple.

The desecration of temples has been, in fact, a serious problem in Bagan. As far back as mid-16th century, Thohanbwa, Shan King of Inwa (Ava), gave impetus to the temple robbers when he said, "Burma pagodas have nothing to do with religion. They are simply treasure chambers." It was Thohanbwa, in fact, who ordered many of the Bagan pagodas to be plundered in order to fill his own treasure chambers.

The most important time of year at the Ananda Temple is January, when an exuberant festival is held to raise money for the upkeep of the temple. This is a joyous spectacle, and the corridors and vestibules of the temple, normally lined with small stalls, are especially lively.

Temple of omniscience

The centre of Bagan is dominated by the **Thatbyinnyu Temple**, about 500 metres (1,550 ft) to the southwest of the Ananda. Known as the "temple of omniscience", it is the tallest building in Bagan at 61 metres (201 ft). The construction of this temple introduced the idea of placing a smaller "hollow" cube on top of a larger Bamar-style structure, whereas the previous Mon-style temples were of one storey. The centre of the lower cube is solid, serving as a foundation for the upper temple, which houses an eastward-looking Buddha figure.

A short distance north of the Thatbyinnyu is the **Thandawgya**, a huge seated Buddha figure. Six metres (19½ ft) tall, it was erected by Narathihapate in 1284. The Buddha's hands are in the *bhumisparsa* mudra, signifying the moment of enlightenment.

BELOW: Thatbyinnyu Temple and Tally Pagoda.

Close to the bank of the Ayeyarwady River is the 12th-century **Gawdawpalin Temple**, built by King Narapatisithu in Bamar style to resemble the Thatbyinnyu

Map on page 68

Temple. This impressive building suffered more than any other monument in the 1975 earthquake. Just south of the temple is a museum containing displays of Bagan's varied architecture, iconography and religious history. Along the museum verandas are stones collected from the region, bearing inscriptions in various languages – Burmese, Mon, Pyu, Pali, Tamil, Thai and Chinese.

The oldest of the Bamar-style temples, the **Shwegugyi Temple** is a short distance up the road toward Nyaung U. King Alaungsithu had it built in 1131, and it took just seven months to raise, according to the temple history inscribed on two stone slabs within.

Atonement for patricide

Despite his brief tenure as king, Narathu is remembered as the founder of Bagan's largest shrine, the **Dhammayangyi Temple**. Deeply concerned about his *karma* for future lives after having murdered his father, Narathu built the Dhammayangyi to atone for his misdeeds. Today, it is the best-preserved temple in Bagan, with a layout similar to that of the Ananda Temple but lacking the delicate, harmonious touch of its prototype, perhaps reflecting the black cloud that hung over central Burma during Narathu's reign. The Dhammayangyi Temple is over a kilometre (⅔ mile) to the southeast of the city walls towards Minnanthu.

About halfway between the temple and the walled Bagan centre are the **Shwesandaw Pagoda** and the **Shinbinthalyaung**, which houses a reclining Buddha. One of only three religious structures Anawrahta built in Bagan, the Shwesandaw was erected in 1057 upon his victorious return from Thaton. Its stupa enshrines some hairs of the Buddha sent to Anawrahta by the king of Bago. The long, flat building within the walls of the Shwesandaw enclosure

It is said that Narathu oversaw the construction of Dhammayangyi Temple himself, having stone masons executed if a needle could be pushed between the bricks.

BELOW: monks receiving their daily meal.

Shwesandaw Pagoda.

contains the Shinbinthalyaung Reclining Buddha, over 18 metres (60 ft) in length. Created in the 11th century, this Buddha lies with its head facing south to denote a sleeping Buddha (only a dying Buddha's head would point north).

The last Bamar-style temple built in Bagan, the **Htilominlo Temple**, is about 1.5 km (1 mile) northeast of Bagan proper on the road to Nyaung U. King Nantaungmya had this building constructed in 1211 at the place where he was chosen to be king. The Htilominlo Temple is 46 metres (150 ft) high and 43 metres (140 ft) on a side at its base. Four Buddha figures placed on the ground and four more figures on the first floor face the cardinal points. Some of the old murals can still be discerned, as can a number of the friezes. Several old horoscopes, painted to protect the building from damage, can be found on the walls.

Entering Bagan from Nyaung U, the road passes through the **Sarabha Gateway**, the only section of King Pyinbya's 9th-century city wall that is still standing and that has recently been reconstructed. Although the rest of the wall consists of overgrown hillocks strewn with rubble, Bagan's guardian spirits – the Mahagiri *nat* – have their prayer niches in this eastern gateway. The two *nat*, Nga Tin De (Mr Handsome) and his sister Shwemyethna (Golden Face), are called Lords of the Great Mountain because it is believed they made their home on sacred Mount Popa. After Thagyamin, king of the *nat*, they are the most important spirit beings in Burma.

One of the few secular buildings in Bagan that has been preserved over the centuries is the **Pitaka Taik**, King Anawrahta's library. The library is near the Shwegugyi Temple. Across the main road is the **Mahabodhi Temple**. This temple is an exact replica of a structure of the same name in India's Bihar State, built in AD 500 at the site where the Buddha achieved enlightenment. The pyramid-like shape of the temple tower is a kind that was highly favoured during India's Gupta period, and it is quite different from the standard bell-shaped monuments in the rest of Burma.

Of warships and monks

A short distance north of Bagan's Mahabodhi is the **Pebinkyaung Pagoda**, most notable for its conical Singhalese-style stupa. The stupa contains relics mounted on top of the bell-shaped main structure in a square-based relic chamber. The construction of this pagoda in the 12th century confirms that close ties existed between Burma and Sri Lanka, a result of the concern shown by King Anawrahta for the propagation of Theravada Buddhism.

A few steps from the Pebingyaung on the banks of the Ayeyarwady is the **Bupaya Pagoda**. According to tradition, the pagoda was built by the third king of Bagan, Pyusawti (AD 162–243) but it was more likely constructed in the 19th century. As the original Bagan Pagoda, this edifice became the basic model for all pagodas built after it. It has a bulbous shape, similar in some ways to the Tibetan *chorte,* and it is built on rows of crenellated walls overlooking the river. Because of the way it stands out on the banks, it is used as a navigation aid by boats. On the pagoda grounds, beneath a pavilion with a nine-gabled roof, is an altar to Mondaing, *nat* of storms.

The **Mimalaung Kyaung Temple**, near the old city's south gate, was erected in 1174. The small, square temple is characterised by multiple roofs and a tall spiral pagoda that stands on a 4-metre (13-ft) high plinth intended to protect it from destruction by fire and floods. The temple's creator, Narapatisithu, is noted in Bagan's history for the manner in which he acceded to the throne in 1173. His brother, King Naratheinka, had stolen his wife and made her queen while Narapatisithu was on a foreign campaign. The wronged sibling returned to Bagan with 80 of his most trusted men, murdered his brother and ensconced himself on the throne. His wife, Veluvati, was spared and remained queen.

Just to the east of this temple is the **Pahtothamya Temple**, dating from before Anawrahta's reign. King Taungthugyi (931–64), also known as Nyaung U Sawrahan, is said to have built the temple to look like those at Thaton. No temple ruins have ever been unearthed at Thaton to allow comparison, however, and the architectural style of this temple has been proven to be that of the 11th century.

To the east is the **Nathlaung Kyaung Temple**, a perfect example of the religious tolerance that prevailed in Bagan during the so-called Era of the Temple Builders. It is thought to have been constructed by Taungthugyi in 931 – more than a century before Theravada Buddhism was introduced from Thaton – and was dedicated to the Hindu god Vishnu. Immediately to the north, the **Ngakywenadaung Pagoda** is much like the Pahtothamya Temple attributed to King Taungthugyi in the 10th century. A bulbous structure on a circular base, it stands 13 metres (43 ft) high.

A short distance south of walled Bagan is the **Mingalazedi Pagoda**, the last of the great stupas erected during the Era of the Temple Builders. Six years in construction, it represents the pinnacle of Bamar pagoda architecture. The terraces are adorned with large terracotta tiles depicting scenes from the *Jataka*.

Map on page 68

BELOW: Bagan's temples with balloons overhead.

Map
on page
68

TIP

Those travelling during
the second week of the
Burmese month of
Nadaw (November/
December) can witness
Buddhist pilgrims
converging for the
festival at Shwezigon
Pagoda.

RIGHT: young
monks.
BELOW: guardian
nat of the arts.

To Nyaung U and beyond

About 1.5 km (1 mile) down the road from Bagan proper, towards the regional centre of Nyaung U and almost directly opposite the Htilominlo Temple, lies the **Upali Thein**, or Hall of Ordination. Named after the monk Upali, it was erected in the first half of the 13th century. The Upali Thein was renovated during the reign of the Konbaung dynasty in the late 1700s; during the renovation, its walls and ceilings were decorated with beautiful frescoes representing the 28 previous Buddhas, as well as scenes from the life of Gautama. Sadly, the plaster came off the walls during the 1975 earthquake, and most of the fresco work was destroyed.

Near the village of Wetkyi-in are the **Gubyauknge Temple**, notable for the fine stucco work on its exterior walls, and the **Wetkyi-in Gubyaukgyi Temple**, a short distance further east. The Kubyaukgyi dates from the early 13th century, and it has a pyramidal spire very similar to that of the Mahabodhi. Inside are some of Bagan's finest frescoes of the *Jataka* tales.

A short distance west of Nyaung U village is the **Kyanzittha Cave**, a cave temple that served as monks' lodgings. Although its name points to Kyanzittha as its creator, it probably dates from Anawrahta's reign. The long, dark corridors are embellished with frescoes from the 11th, 12th and 13th centuries; some of the later paintings even depict the Mongols who occupied Bagan after 1287.

The **Shwezigon Pagoda**, a short walk north of the cave temple, is the prototype for all Burmese stupas built after the rule of Anawrahta. It was built as the most important reliquary shrine in Bagan, a centre of prayer and reflection for the new Theravada faith that Anawrahta was establishing in Bagan.

Cave temples

There are several cave temples to the east of Nyaung U. Just one kilometre (⅔ mile) to the southeast of the town are the caves at **Thamiwhet** and **Hmyathat**, formed by the excavation of hillsides during the 12th and 13th centuries. Their purpose was to give monks a cool place to live and meditate, a refuge from the scorching heat of central Burma.

About 3 km (2 miles) upstream from Nyaung U, standing on the ledge of a cliff overlooking the Ayeyarwady, is the **Kyaukgu Temple**. The structure could be described as an ideal cave temple – the manner in which it is built into the hill-side gives the impression that a small stupa stands on top of the temple, when it actually rests on a pillar. The Kyaukgu's ground floor dates from the 11th century.

Minnanthu temples

The village of Minnanthu is located about 5 km (3 miles) southeast of Bagan proper. There is a large number of temple ruins in the vicinity, but few of major significance. One of the largest is the **Sulamani Temple**, not in Minnanthu itself but about halfway between the village and Bagan. Immediately to the north of the Minnanthu village is the **Lemyethna Temple**, built by Naratheinhka's minister-in-chief, remembering a poem written by his predecessor and namesake, Ananthathurya. ❑

LAOS AND CAMBODIA

Long forgotten by the travellers of the world, both Laos and
Cambodia are slowly emerging as challenging adventures

Together, Laos and Cambodia form the little-known hinterland of Indochina. In the colonial period they were considered back-waters by the French, who concentrated on exploiting the resources of Vietnam – the third and dominant country in French Indochina. During the long years of warfare that followed independence they were once again considered backwaters, and this view of them continued, though they were hardly forgotten by the military strategists of both sides. Communist Vietnam used the Ho Chi Minh trail through Laos to re-supply its forces in the south, while the United States waged a viciously destructive "Secret War" against the North Vietnamese Army and its Lao allies, the Pathet Lao.

Meanwhile sleepy Cambodia was similarly sucked into the quagmire. Used as a base sanctuary by the Vietnamese Communists, it was secretly – and illegally – carpet-bombed by the US Air Force. The consequences of Communist victory in 1975 were far more terrible for the Cambodians, "liberated" by the auto-genocidal Khmer Rouge, than for the Lao people. Nevertheless, for almost the next two decades, both countries experienced impoverishment and isolation from the outside world.

Nowadays all this is changing fast. Both Laos and Cambodia have opened their doors to the international community and, in particular, to overseas visitors. The governments in both Vientiane and Phnom Penh see tourism and its related industries as a way to accelerate national development and assure a more prosperous future.

There are other good reasons for linking Laos and Cambodia. Each carries the scars of the Indochina Wars, and there are areas in both countries that must remain off limits to travellers until mines and other detritus of past battles have been cleared. Both have a long tradition of Indic culture as well as being culturally related through Theravada Buddhism and long years of interaction with neighbouring Thailand. Each is startlingly beautiful, populated by generous and friendly people, and both have benefited from the French culinary tradition – as Cambodia's King Sihanouk once put it: "I am an anti-colonialist, but if one must be colonised it is better to be colonised by gourmets."

Today Laos and Cambodia are free, independent members of ASEAN and stand on the verge of development and prosperity as the 21st century unfolds. There has never been a better time to visit them. ❑

PRECEDING PAGES: That Luang, Vientiane; a traditional dancer's hands.

Decisive Dates

A great kingdom rises and falls

2000 BC–AD 500: Development of an early pottery and bronze culture, based on wet rice cultivation and associated with the Ban Chiang culture, in the central Mekong Valley.

AD 802: Jayavarman II claims independence from Javanese control and sows the initial seeds of the Khmer/Angkor empire by declaring himself the first *davaraja*, or god-king.

1050: Khmer empire is weakened by internal fights.

1131–50: Suryavarman II reigns over the Khmer

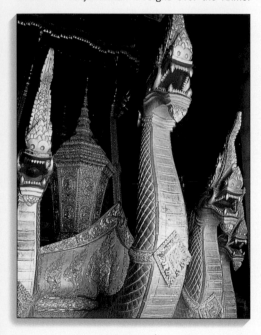

empire and builds Angkor Wat. The Khmer empire is strengthened and now includes most of Thailand, Laos, and southern Vietnam.

1200s: Khmer empire is in decline.

1279: The Sukhothai kingdom in Siam is founded by Ramkamhaeng; parts of Laos, including Vientiane, come under Sukhothai control for a short time.

1349: Fa Ngum begins coalescing townships into the Lan Xang kingdom, establishing his capital at Xieng-dong Xiengthong (Luang Prabang).

1353–73: Reign of Fa Ngum over the Lan Xang empire.

1373–1547: Successors of Fa Ngum continue to rule Lan Xang, fighting wars against Burma and Siam.

1431: Angkor is abandoned, and Cambodia becomes part of the Sukhothai kingdom.

1574–78: Lan Xang is subsumed by Burma.

1633–90: Reign of King Souligna Vongsa, a high point and "golden era" in Laotian culture.

1690–1713: Succession struggles for the throne of the Lan Xang empire. In 1713, the Lan Xang empire is divided into smaller kingdoms of Luang Prabang, Vientiane, and Champasak.

1778: Siam takes control of Luang Prabang, Vientiane, and Champasak.

France introduces itself

1867–87: A French expedition up the Mekong River reaches Luang Prabang. Siam must now deal with France, which already controls Vietnam.

1890: French colonial rule of Laos begins; a treaty is concluded in 1893 between France and Siam that acknowledges French control over Mekong territory.

1930: France officially designates Laos as a French colony. Communist Party of Indochina is founded.

1940–45: All Lao territories west of the Mekong are given to Thailand; Laos is occupied by Japan in 1945. Lao Issara (Free Lao) guerrillas take control of Vientiane and establish a provisional government.

1946: King Sisavang Vong is deposed and France reoccupies Laos. Sisavang Vong declared king-in-exile by Lao Issara government, exiled in Thailand.

1947: Laos becomes a constitutional monarchy. Elections are held for the National Assembly. Prince Souvannarath forms the government of Kingdom of Laos.

1949: Laos is granted limited self-government within the French Union. The Lao Issara government, in exile, is dissolved, but some members join the Pathet Lao.

1950: United States and Britain recognise Laos and Cambodia as part of the French Union. The Pathet Lao form a "resistance government".

Independence from France

1953: Laos and Cambodia gain independence from France, but France retains control of military affairs.

1954: Geneva Conference on Indochina establishes armistice in Cambodia, Laos and Vietnam.

1955: Laos is admitted to the United Nations.

1956: Pathet Lao set up the Lao Patriotic Front (LPF).

1957: First Lao coalition government is formed under Prince Souvanna Phouma.

1959: Northern Laos erupts in fighting with communist insurgency, with possible North Vietnamese involvement. Lao King Sisavang Vong dies; Savang Vatthana takes the throne and rules until 1975.

1960: A provisional government is formed in Laos after an army coup attempt. A coup d'état topples the rightist government; a counter-coup group led by the army declares martial law. Phoumi Nosavan captures

Vientiane, and the Soviets begin an airlift to Pathet Lao troops. Prince Norodom Sihanouk is elected head of state in Cambodia.

1961–62: Heavy fighting breaks out between Soviet- and Western-backed factions in Laos. Another Geneva Conference on Laos establishes a peace amongst the various factions. A second coalition government is formed, but civil war resumes.

1964: North Vietnamese troops expand the Ho Chi Minh Trail through Lao territory. The Lao coalition government collapses.

1968: Fighting intensifies between Pathet Lao and the Royal Lao Army.

1970: Cambodian Prince Sihanouk is deposed in a right-wing coup led by Lt-Gen. Lon Nol, who aligns himself with the U.S. Sihanouk forms a Cambodian government in exile, supported by the Khmer Rouge.

1972: Lao People's Party changes its name to Lao People's Revolutionary Party, which it retains today.

1973: The Laotian government and Pathet Lao sign the Vientiane Agreement that establishes ceasefire.

1974: A third coalition government in Laos takes office by royal decree.

Communist victories

1975: Communist victory in Vietnam. The Lao People's Democratic Republic (LPDR) is proclaimed, and Souphanouvong is its first president. Khmer Rouge forces led by Pol Pot take Phnom Penh, and "Year Zero" begins in Cambodia. Millions die in the Khmer Rouge's "social engineering".

1977: A treaty of friendship and cooperation between Laos and Vietnam is signed.

1978: Vietnam invades Cambodia, taking Phnom Penh at the beginning of 1979. The Khmer Rouge regroup in the countryside.

1988: First Lao elections since 1975 are held at the district and provincial levels.

1989: National elections in Laos are held for delegates to the first Supreme People's Assembly. The last Vietnamese troops leave Laos. In Cambodia, Vietnamese forces withdraw. The nation's name is changed back to Cambodia; fighting continues between anti-government forces, nominally led by exiled Prince Sihanouk, and the Phnom Penh government.

Steady Laos, chaotic Cambodia

1991: Souphanouvong retires as president of Laos. A new constitution is adopted; Kaysone Phomvihan becomes president. A UN accord brings an unsteady

peace to Cambodia; Sihanouk returns to the country.

1992: In Laos, Phomvihan dies and is replaced as president by Nouhak Phoumsavan.

1993: UN-sponsored elections result in a coalition government with two prime ministers: Hun Sen and Prince Ranariddh. They fail to get along.

1994: The Friendship Bridge between Thailand and Laos opens.

1995: Prince Souphanouvong dies.

1997: Fighting between factions in Phnom Penh; co-prime minister Prince Ranariddh is exiled. Pol Pot is denounced by the Khmer Rouge and sentenced to house arrest. Laos joins ASEAN.

1998: Pol Pot dies in the jungle. Elections leave Hun

Sen in power. Khamtay Siphandon becomes president.

1999: Cambodia joins ASEAN. Laos moves closer to Thailand as Vietnamese influence diminishes.

2003: Gradual transition to market economy continues.

2004: Hun Sen is re-elected by parliament. King Sihanouk abdicates and Norodom Sihamoni is elected by a nine-member Throne Council as successor.

2005: A war crimes tribunal to try surviving Khmer Rouge leaders receives UN approval. In Laos, the World Bank approves loans for the Nam Theun 2 hydroelectric dam project.

2006: In Laos, Choummaly Sayasone takes over as leader of the ruling communist party in March and succeeds Khamtay Siphandon as president. ❑

OPPOSITE: royal urn, at Wat Xieng Thong, Luang Prabang. **ABOVE:** upper gallery of Angkor Wat.

PEOPLE OF THE MEKONG

Nestled as they are amidst various cultures, some often more powerful, it is no surprise that Laos and, to a lesser degree, Cambodia are comprised of many peoples

Some political scientists say Laos is an unnatural nation. There is an element of truth in this view: there are dozens of ethnic groups dotting the country, and ethnic culture is highly segmented and extremely complex in Laos. Still, travellers will find the Lao, of whatever persuasion, most accommodating and friendly.

It might be said that charm and friendliness is Laos' most exportable commodity. One former expat, Judy Rantala, a retired social worker who lived in Laos during the mid-1970s, expressed this sentiment best in her book, *Laos*: "In my admittedly short visit I found among the Lao people what endeared me to them years ago and in fact is validated by everyone I know who has ever lived in Laos: the people continue to be peace-loving, non-confrontational, generous and friendly. They have a capacity to adapt and to avoid becoming bitter or disillusioned or discouraged. Their buoyant sense of humour and sense of self-worth are as strong as I remember. I hope they can – I hope they will – preserve the freshness of spirit which makes this often overlooked small country a treasure-pot of human dignity and grace."

Over 75 percent of the population of Laos are subsistence farmers. Most villages are far from roads or other transportation links, and less than 20 percent of its 5.8 million people live in towns or cities. Laos is one of the world's poorest countries, with a per-capita income of about US$400 annually. The population density is quite low for Asia: around 20 people per square kilometre.

There are over 60 ethnic peoples in Laos, divided into three major groupings: Lao Soung, the upland Lao of the mountainous regions and comprising less than 20 percent of the population; Lao Theung, about a quarter of Laos' population and living on the slopes of mountains; and Lao Loum, the lowlanders and the politically dominant and most numerous group, with over half of the population. The Lao Loum originally derived from southern China and are ethnic cousins of Thais in northeastern Thailand. Today they dominate the fertile plains of the Mekong River basin. The Lao Theung, of Mon-Khmer heritage, were nomadic people and today practise slash-and-burn agriculture.

The Lao Soung are newcomers to Laos, arriving from China and Burma in the 1700s and inhabiting the high mountain regions. Hmong and Mien (Yao) hill tribes, also found in northern Thailand, are Lao Soung.

Cambodia's population of 13.7 million is dominated by Khmer – nearly 90 percent of the country's people – with substantial numbers of Vietnamese and Chinese, along with small numbers of ethnic minority groups, the largest of which are the Cham, a Muslim people. Other groups include Lao, Shan and Thai. Historically, the Khmer culture has been considerably influenced by the once great kingdoms centred in Java and India.

LEFT: young girl offers alms to monks.
RIGHT: harvesting the rice.

Village life

The village is the most important economic and political unit. Among some tribes there are well defined territories claimed by the village. Generally, these are associations to safeguard the village's farming, fishing and hunting rights, rather than political units.

Traditional houses are made of natural jungle products. Bamboo is the most popular building material, split for studs and rafters, or plaited for walls and roofs. Where bamboo is unavailable or impractical, thatch or other available varieties of wood may be utilised. Houses are generally on stilts, with the floor of the house

local beliefs about evil spirits. Just as many of the villages erect protective devices against malevolent spirits, so do individuals. Since evil spirits are thought to be able to approach the village from only one direction, the house may be built with doors and windows on the opposite side of the house, so that the spirits will not be able to enter. In addition to this style of house construction, many tribal houses employ additional means to ward off evil spirits or to appease them in case it has not been sufficiently frightened. A structure typical of many animistic villages is that of the spirit house. The village spirit house may be dedicated to the

above the ground. Raising the house on stilts not only provides protection from wild animals and the moist ground during the rainy season, but also creates a space below the house for storage, animal pens, children's play, or as a shady area out of the hot sun.

Some of the Montagnards in south Laos and northeast Cambodia utilise longhouses up to 100 metres in length. These provide living quarters for a number of families – more than a hundred people may live in a single longhouse. Normally the inhabitants of the individual longhouses are related, and so are members of an extended patrilineal or matrilineal family.

Most houses are erected in harmony with

spirit of the village, or there may be numerous spirit houses erected by individual households of the village. The latter are usually quite small, from just a few inches to perhaps a metre in length and width. Regardless of the size, these houses have great significance.

Another ritualistic feature of some tribal villages is the sacrifice pole. While individual sacrifices of chickens and pigs to the spirits require only small temporary sacrificial poles, water-buffalo sacrifices require a larger pole or post. The heavy sacrificial post may be located in the centre of the village, near the village burial grounds or in some other prominent place. These poles may be simple or elaborate.

Social structures

Because of the religious influence of sorcerers, they also exercise both political and economic authority. Their positions as religious leaders and communicators with the supernatural world make them members of the community elite, possessing an aura of influence and importance exceeding that of most religious figures in Western civilisation.

Family structure will vary greatly from tribe to tribe. In some tribes, parents choose marriage partners for their children based upon alliances or economic factors.

LAO LINGUISTICS

Lao contains 28 vowels, 33 consonants, and 6 tones. Also spoken in parts of Thailand and Cambodia, Lao has borrowed from the Indian Sanskrit and Pali.

determined by whether the family is patrilineal (after the father's family) or matrilineal (after the mother's family). Customs pertaining to divorce vary widely between tribes. However, in spite of the many differences, the family plays a central role in tribal life throughout the two countries.

Except for some limited wet-rice farming, the major means of farming among the tribespeople is the slash-and-burn method, or swidden farming, in which bushes, vines and trees in a chosen area are cut down,

dren based upon alliances or economic factors. Others allow the male to choose his own bride with the encouragement and support of the clan. A few tribes are so structured that the girl or her mother makes the choice of groom. Some tribes require dowries of the husband, others dowries of the wife, while some have none at all. Marriages usually require an intermediary, as a buffer when dowry bargaining becomes serious.

When children are born, their names will be

LEFT: young hill-tribe boy, and fishing on the Mekong River, Vientiane. **ABOVE:** irrigating the field, and retaining the traditional dance through practice.

allowed to dry, and then burned. Crops such as mountain rice, millet, corn, pumpkin, squash, and manioc are planted. After the fields have been used for one to three years, they are abandoned and new fields slashed and burned. Harvesting is shared by men and women, with children joining in as soon as they are old enough. Children are also responsible for looking after cattle and buffalo, and for the caring of younger siblings. Those too feeble or old for heavy labour perform lighter tasks, like making bows and arrows or baskets. Because crafts primarily serve the practical needs of daily life, most tribes have not developed residual arts and crafts. ❏

ARCHITECTURE

While the domestic architecture of Laos and Cambodia is typically practical and simple, structures of religious and royal importance are amongst the world's finest

As is the case in most of Southeast Asia, the buildings of Laos and Cambodia were traditionally built of wood, generally in plentiful supply throughout the region. As such, relatively few truly venerable structures remain standing in their original form. Notable exceptions include, of course, the stone temples of Angkor and similar buildings erected under royal patronage.

Many of the area's temples have been frequently reconstructed over the centuries, permitting some observations regarding local styles and construction methods. Inevitably, any brief look at the architecture of these two countries centres on buildings of religious or royal significance. Domestic architecture is on the whole simple and practical, though often borrowing forms and certain adornments from temple structures.

In Laos, the main architectural influences are obviously Buddhist and Thai. Just as in neighbouring Thailand, certain regional variations are distinguishable.

The predominant styles are conveniently referred to as Vientiane and Luang Prabang. While the former shares several features with central Thai styles, the latter is akin to styles found in northern Thailand. A third style, referred to as Xieng Khuang, after the central province of the same name, is now sadly less in evidence, as the province was so heavily bombed during the CIA secret war from 1968 to 1975. A few examples remain in Luang Prabang, however.

Temple architecture

The basic layout of a Lao temple follows the pattern of Theravada *wat* throughout Southeast Asia. The most important structure is the *ubosot*, known in Lao as the *sim*. This is the building where new monks are ordained.

Subsidiary structures include the *viharn,* where Buddha images are housed, a *haw trai,* or scripture library, and various *thaat,* or stupas. The larger of these *thaat* are said to contain relics of the Buddha; smaller ones – *thaat*

kaduk, or bone stupas – contain ashes of the long deceased.

It is perhaps the *thaat* which most distinguishes a truly Lao temple. The archetypal shape is that of That Luang in Vientiane, a four-cornered pillar curving in and then out before tapering away at the top. Stupas of other shapes

generally indicate Thai or Khmer influence. The principal exception, and a genuine oddity, is the hemispherical That Mak Mo, or Watermelon Stupa, in Luang Prabang.

It is in the *sim* that regional differences are most identifiable. The typical Vientiane-style sim is a tall rectangular brick building of narrow aspect covered in stucco. The roof is sharply sloped and high-peaked, generally with an odd number of tiers and supported by tall, thick pillars at the front and rear. The whole is raised on a high, multi-level pediment with a veranda at front, and sometimes at the back. In some cases, a terrace runs all the way around, after the Bangkok fashion. A staircase leads up to the veranda, often guarded by carved *naga* or *nyak* (mythical giants). The edges of the roof, in common with other styles of Lao temple, normally have a fringe of carved repeating flame motifs, with large hooks, known as *jao faa*, pointing to the sky at the corners. The main doors are usually of heavy carved wood. Often, shading the front veranda, high up, is an intricately carved wooden panel depicting mythical creatures against a background of intertwined foliage, testament to the skill of local artisans.

Perhaps the most splendid example of the style is Wat Xieng Thong, which also has magnificently carved shutters, showing scenes from the local variant of the Indian epic classic *Ramayana*, *Pha Lak Pha Lam*.

The most distinctive feature of the few remaining Xieng Khuang-style temples is the single-tiered roof, unusual in Lao temples. Like that of a Luang Prabang-style *sim*, the roof sweeps low, but for structural reasons the cantilevered roof supports are far more prominent, giving the

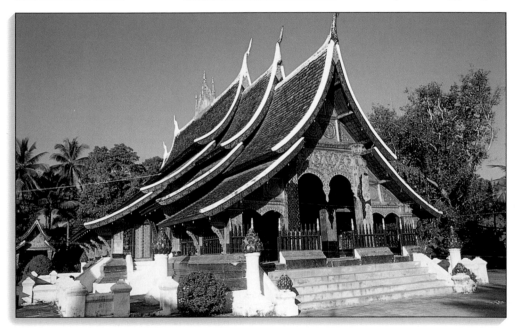

A Luang Prabang-style sim has a far more modest plinth. Like its northern Thai counterparts, the layered roofs slope more gently and often come almost to the ground. The supporting pillars vary in height to support the various roof layers, and are normally slightly tapered towards the top, as they were traditionally made from stout tree trunks.

Much of the elegant yet subdued sparkle of Luang Prabang comes from the gold leaf that so often adorns the local temple doors and walls.

LEFT: the distinctive *thaat* of Vientiane's That Luang, representative of Lao temple stupa.
ABOVE: Wat Xieng Thong, Luang Prabang.

building a pentagonal shape when viewed from the front. The pediment, stepped after the Vientiane-style but usually not so high, is curved, lending the whole a touch of grace.

Limited principally to the difficult-to-access province of Sainyabuli, there is a fourth style of Buddhist temple in Laos, that of the Thai Lu, an ethnic minority from Yunnan's Sipsongpanna. These temples are rather squat in appearance, with low whitewashed walls and small windows. The roof is of two or three tiers, the lower of which slopes towards the front and back as well as the sides. Steps leading up to the main doors often have thick-set *naga* balustrades. The *thaat* of such temples are generally octagonal, gilded and, especially at festival times, bedecked in swaths of Thai Lu fabric, replete with beads and pieces of foil. These temples are very different from the Lao norm.

Colonial influences

The coming of the French in the late 19th century led to some distinctively colonial-style architecture in the main cities of the country, principally Luang Prabang and Vientiane. Many of these buildings were torn down or left to crumble after Lao independence, yet some fine examples still remain along the wide boulevards of Vientiane. Most are solid brick structures

with shuttered windows and tiled roofs, reminiscent of French provincial buildings. Particularly noteworthy is the restored Bibliothèque Nationale opposite Nam Phu fountain.

Grander examples include the Presidential Palace in Vientiane, and the former Royal Palace in Luang Prabang, now a museum. The latter exhibits a pleasing blend of French style and Lao motif. The former, for obvious reasons, is not open to the public, and its splendour can only be glanced from behind the guarded gates.

Lao architecture under the Communists tended towards dull functionalism. Many of the buildings of this era can still be seen, particu-

larly at some of the major road intersections in Vientiane's city centre. These buildings, at their worst, can inspire a sense of jaded, weary depression on the most serenely tropical evening. Wander southeast along the river from the Lane Xang Hotel – until recently Vientiane's premiere hotel, and itself hardly a vision of elegance – and glance to the left at the dull, grey, egg-carton school to see why socialism was such a misfit, and failure, in the country.

Happily, in recent years there has been increasingly more freedom and inventiveness in Lao building design. Traditional Lao forms have been rediscovered and blended with the functional into original and pleasing structures.

Cambodian architecture

Unlike Laos, Cambodia hasn't yet been in a position to make present-day architecture a high-priority issue. For the time being, the story of Cambodian architecture reaches its apogee in the Angkor period between the 9th and 13th centuries. More recent buildings of interest include the Royal Palace in Phnom Penh, together with some French colonial structures in that city.

Several centuries before Jayavarman II (802–850) proclaimed himself *devaraja,* or "god-king", Cambodia and southern Vietnam, known to the Chinese successively as Funan then Chenla, were highly Indianised states as a result of trade with South Asia. Architectural relics from Chenla, some of which can still be seen in present-day Cambodia, are typically square, sometimes octagonal, brick towers standing on stepped pedestals, showing distinct Indian influence and also more local invention.

From the beginning, Angkorean art and architecture were inspired by Chenla temples, and indirectly by Hinduism. Buildings were erected in honour of Shiva and, less often, Vishnu. The temples represent Mount Meru, home of the gods of Indian mythology. The central tower, a blunt tower, is the peak of the mountain, which is surrounded by walls representing the earth, and moats or lakes symbolising the oceans.

In many Angkor complexes, the latter cleverly and conveniently served a practical purpose as part of the complex irrigation and water supply system. ❑

LEFT: colonial architecture, now a restaurant in Vientiane. **RIGHT:** detail of temple door.

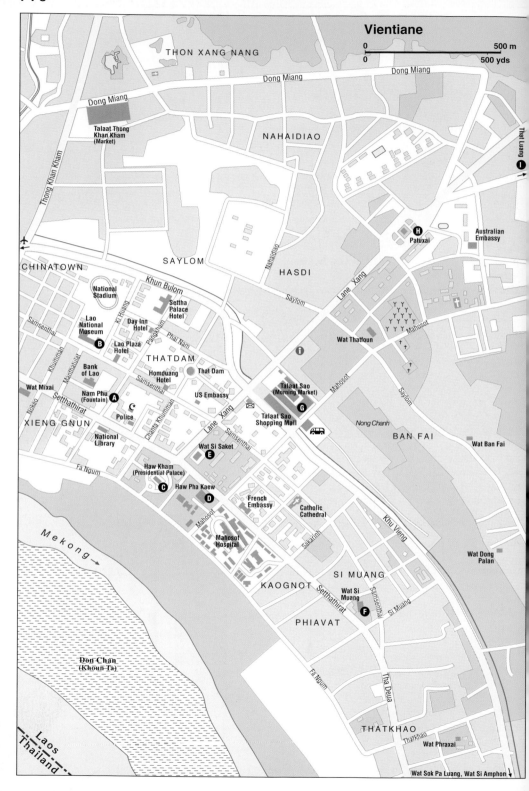

Vientiane

0 — 500 m
0 — 500 yds

THON XANG NANG

Dong Miang
Dong Miang

NAHAIDIAO

Thong Khan Kham

Dong Miang

Talaat Thong
Khan Kham
(Market)

SAYLOM

HASDI

Saylom

I

Patuxai **H**

Australian
Embassy

Lane Xang

CHINATOWN

Khun Bulom

National
Stadium

Settha
Palace
Hotel

Day Inn
Hotel

Wat Thatfoun

Samsenthai

Lao National
Museum **B**

Ki Huang

Pangkham

Phai Nam

Mahosot

Khunnian

Lao Plaza
Hotel

THATDAM

Manthathilat

Bank
of Lao

Homduang
Hotel

That Dam

Talaat Sao
(Morning Market)

Mahosot

i

Setthathirat

Wat Mixai

Samsenthai

Chanta Khumman

US Embassy

Lane Xang

G

Saylom

Nam Phu
(Fountain) **A**

Talaat Sao
Shopping Mall

Nong Chanh

BAN FAI

Nokeo

Police

XIENG GNUN

National
Library

Wat Si Saket **E**

Samsenthai

Wat Ban Fai

Fa Ngum

Haw Kham
(Presidential Palace)

C

Haw Pha Kaew

D

French
Embassy

Catholic
Cathedral

Khu Vieng

M e k o n g →

Mahosot

Mahosot
Hospital

Sakarinh

Wat Dong
Palan

SI MUANG

KAOGNOT

Setthathirat

Wat Si
Muang

Samsenthai

Si Muang

F

Don Chan
(Khoun Ta)

PHIAVAT

Fa Ngum

Tha Deua

THATKHAO

Thatkhao

Wat Phraxai

Laos
Thailand

Wat Sok Pa Luang, Wat Si Amphon ↓

VIENTIANE

*Long closed to tourism after the Pathet Lao takeover,
the capital of Laos is now open for business. Exceedingly low-rise
and low-key, Vientiane is compact enough to negotiate on foot*

Map
on page
118

Lethargic and crescent-shaped, Vientiane reclines on the left bank of the Mekong River. It is about midway between the Chinese and Cambodian borders with Laos, and about midway between Hanoi and Bangkok. Thus, it is not without foreign influences. It is a city that is not quite a city, at least by the frantic standards of other Asian capitals. Traffic is light, and one can even safely cross the main boulevards on foot without fear of death.

In the mid 1500s, Vientiane was the fortified capital of the Lan Xang kingdom, ruled by Setthathirat. Within the city were a palace and two *wat*, or temples: That Luang and Wat Phra Kaew, which at the time was the home for the venerable Emerald Buddha, originally from the Chiang Rai area and now in Bangkok within a wat of the same name. The royal city was called the City of Sandalwood, or Vieng Chan, a name still used today.

The Emerald Buddha remained in Vientiane for over two centuries, until 1778, when the Thai army, led by Gen. Chakri, who would later become the first king in the still-ruling Chakri dynasty, retrieved it and returned the diminutive jade statue to Thai possession. In the early 1800s, Vientiane was sacked by the Siamese again; most of the city was completely destroyed.

With a population of half a million, Vientiane is home today to a little over 10 percent of the country's population. It is a manageable city for the most part, walkable in the downtown districts, and cheap transport to outlying sights such as That Luang is easy to find. Bicycles are completely useful and appropriate, and cheap to rent. The city's architecture is modestly eclectic and low-rise, reflecting both French colonial and generically modern influences.

Central Vientiane

As Vientiane has no central plaza for orientation, locals and visitors alike often use **Nam Phu** Ⓐ, a waterfountain circle on Thanon Setthathirath, as a reference, as it is strategically placed among an assortment of travel agencies, airline offices, bakeries, restaurants, *tuk-tuk* (taxi) stands, guest houses and hotels. Less than a decade ago, hardly any of these commercial establishments existed, as the ruling Pathet Lao had closed the country to tourism in 1975, indirectly preserving the Laotian capital in a time warp.

To the north of Nam Phu, on Thanon Samsenthai, one of two main east–west arteries in the city, is the **Lao National Museum** Ⓑ (daily 8am–noon and 1–4pm; entrance fee). Built in 1925, this elegant structure was once the French governor's resident, and was used by the Lao government as an administrative building before being converted into a museum in

BELOW: mailbox in Vientiane.

1985. The permanent exhibition provides a selective history of Laos' struggle for independence, leaving out major details like the heavy Vietnamese involvement in the "revolution". But it is filled with interesting artefacts from the war, particularly the weapons, clothing and supplies of key revolutionary figures. Just north is the **National Stadium**, and to the east is the **Lao Plaza Hotel**, one of the grandest hotels in Vientiane or anywhere else in Laos, for that matter.

Just a couple of minutes' walk south of Nam Phu is the **Mekong River**, one of those classically mighty rivers that lures travellers like moths to light. A dike parallels the Mekong for several kilometres, and almost all of it is walkable. A small road, Quai Fa Ngum, parallels both river and dike. The dike is actually the old town wall, and its purpose was twofold: a line of defence from ill-intentioned outsiders and protection from rising waters of the Mekong. Recent excavations along the river's banks have revealed ancient artefacts, especially pottery.

The perspective from the path on the dike along the river is a century old. Little has changed if one squints hard enough, but the part of Quai Fa Ngum near the central downtown area is lined by renovated buildings, and between the road and river are numerous but simple outdoor cafes on stilts, popular meeting places for both locals and foreigners. The river itself, especially when it is low, is a time capsule – naked children swim, grandmothers spin silk under houses, women on verandas nurse babies, husbands sip *lao-lao* and talk.

East of Nam Phu is the **Presidential Palace** ❻ (Haw Kham), once the royal palace and today closed to the public. Adjacent is **Haw Pha Kaew** ❼ (daily 8am–noon and 1–4pm; entrance fee), the royal temple of King Setthathirat, who built it in 1565 to house the Emerald Buddha. Destroyed by the Thais in 1827, the wat was rebuilt after World War II. The wat contains a gilded throne,

BELOW: view of downtown from Patuxai.

Khmer Buddhist stelae and bronze frog drums belonging to the royal family.

On the northern side of Thanon Setthathirath is **Wat Si Saket** Ⓔ (daily 8am–noon and 1–4pm; entrance fee), dating from 1818. Established as a monastery, the wat is perhaps the only structure that was not destroyed by the Thais in 1827. The interior walls surrounding its central *sim* are filled with small niches containing more than 2,000 miniature silver and ceramic Buddha images, most of them dating from the 16th to 19th centuries.

Further east is **Wat Si Muang** Ⓕ (daily; free), the most active temple in Vientiane because it houses the village pillar, or *lak muang*, the cornerstone that houses the city's protective deity. When the temple was dedicated, a pit was dug and, so the legend goes, a virgin was sacrificed at its bottom when the pillar was dropped in, a harbinger of good luck to the capital's citizens.

Beginning at the Presidential Palace, a major boulevard, Lan Xang, heads northeast past **Talat Sao** Ⓖ (daily 6am–6pm), the morning market and probably the country's best, to the rather overwhelming **Monument Anousavari** Ⓗ, officially known as **Patuxai** (Victory Gate). Finished in 1969 in memory of those killed in war prior to the Communist takeover of Laos, it offers a panaromic view of the capital (daily 8am–4.30pm; entrance fee).

Past Patuxai and on high ground 3 km (2 miles) from downtown sits stately 16th-century **That Luang** Ⓘ (daily 8am–noon and 1–4pm; entrance fee). Herein lies a relic of the Buddha, a breastbone. Like the downtown temples, That Luang has been rebuilt several times. Representing a miniature Mount Meru, the mythical peak, and some 45 metres (150 ft) tall, it is painted gold and dazzles eyes year-round. Flanked on two sides by smaller temples, it sees scant monkish activity except on holidays, especially during the annual That Luang

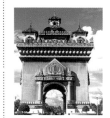

Patuxai, also known as Monument Anousavari.

BELOW: Buddhist ceremony in That Luang.

Map on page 118

Map on page 118

TIP

Up close, That Luang may not meet every traveller's expectations of a sacred monument. It seems to be constructed of painted concrete. Still, it is highly revered.

RIGHT: boat on the Mekong. **BELOW:** herbs in bottles.

festival. Then watch out. Everybody shows up from miles around. The whole hilltop assumes a carnival air, and festivities begin with vendors selling tickets to see a two-headed water buffalo and end two weeks later with a fireworks display second to none in all Laos. Yet people do visit That Luang year-round. Women seeking merit on their journey to Nirvana bring flowers and balls of rice to its ancient gates at dawn. Art students take up position under nearby flame trees to sketch it. Lao and foreigners alike visit its spacious if stark interior. But when it is festival time, those wanting a good position in That Luang's interior show up before sunrise. The remainder sit on straw mats, the crowd extending out several hundred metres. To be Lao is to be devout, and also to be lucky – monks sell lottery tickets immediately outside That Luang's main entrance on festival days.

Wax-paper castles adorned with fake money are carried on poles atop shoulders into the complex the day before the main festival day. These castles are made by families from all over town seeking to gain merit. That evening, people holding candles circle the temple three times in an age-old tradition. The next day is a solemn one as the patriarch speaks. Then everyone wanders away, and temple life returns to pastoral normality.

Beyond Vientiane

There is plenty to do in a day using Vientiane as a hub. The most exotic day-trip, perhaps, is to **Phu Khao Khuai** (Water Buffalo Mountain), a pine-forested plateau surrounded by 2,000-metre (5,500 ft) peaks. Here, nature rules. Butterflies, big as an open hand, dart and hover among blossoms hidden in high grass everywhere. One of the country's National Biodiversity Conservation Areas, it is said to be full of local wildlife, including elephants, black bears, tigers and clouded leopards. The second most exotic day-trip is to the waterfall at **Taat Leuk**.

The trek through the sea-of-a-forest to the waterfall west of Thabok requires a rugged vehicle, but the horizontal and vertical zig-zagging course from Thabok to the waterfall is well marked. The falls are almost as big as the famous Khon Phapheng Falls in Champassak province. Taat Luek remains as pristine as the day the Lao spirits got together in revelry and made it. The banks of the Nam Leuk leading to and from Taat Leuk are camouflaged by jungle and make it impossible to do much hiking. But perhaps this adds to Taat Leuk's charm and enchantment – one can sit in the cool shade for hours.

Another splendid day-trip is to **Ban Thalet** and the lake at **Nam Ngum**. The dam creating the lake provides electrical power to much of Laos, and Laos exports significant amounts to neighbouring Thailand. Small restaurants overlook the blue-green water, and the setting is almost European due to so many alpine-like peaks surrounding the lake. Nam Ngum itself is dotted with picturesque islands, one or two of which offer guesthouses. To the north of the lake is **Vang Vieng**, noted for its scenery of limestone formations, especially caves, and waterfalls. Hmong and Mien (Yao) people inhabit the area, and the caves are part of their mythology. ❑

LUANG PRABANG

*The temples and culture of Luang Prabang, capital of Laos
and seat of the monarchy until the 16th century, have been so
well preserved that the city is now a World Heritage Site*

or centuries prior to its founding, the area around **Luang Prabang ❶** played host to various Thai-Lao principalities in the valleys of the Mekong, Khan, Ou and Xeuang rivers. It was in 1353, though, that King Fa Ngum consolidated the first Lao kingdom, Lan Xang (One Million Elephants), on the site of present-day Luang Prabang. The city was known as Xawa, possibly a local form of Java, but it was renamed Meuang Xieng Thong (Gold City District). A little later, King Fa Ngum received the gift of a Sinhalese Buddha image called Pha Bang from the Khmer sovereign, from which the city's modern name derives.

In 1545, King Phothisarat moved the capital of the Lan Xang kingdom to Vientiane, but Luang Prabang remained the royal heart of the kingdom. After the collapse of Lan Xang in 1694, an independent kingdom was established in Luang Prabang, which co-existed with kingdoms based in Vientiane and Champasak further south. At various times forced to pay tribute to the Thais, the Vietnamese, and most recently the French, kings ruled Luang Prabang until the monarchy was officially dissolved by the Pathet Lao in 1975. The last king and queen were imprisoned in a cave in the northeast of the country, where it is thought they perished some time in the 1980s. An official statement on this has never been issued.

Luang Prabang's royal legacy, although a story of decline, combines with its splendid natural setting at the confluence of the Mekong and Khan rivers to create one of the most intriguing and magical cities in Asia. The city is crowded with old temples and dominated by the 100-metre-high (330 ft) rocky outcrop, Phu Si. In 1995, Luang Prabang was added to UNESCO's World Heritage List.

Palace and temples

In the centre of Luang Prabang, between Phu Si and the Mekong, is the **Royal Palace Museum** (Haw Kham; Wed–Mon 8–11.30am and 1.30–4pm; entrance fee), which offers an insight into the history of the region. The palace was constructed early in the 20th century (commencing in 1904) as the residence of King Sisavang Vong, in a pleasing mix of classical Lao and French styles, cruciform in layout, and mounted on a multi-tiered platform.

In a room at the front of the building is the museum's prize piece, the famed Pha Bang Buddha image. The 83-cm-tall (33-inch) image, in the *mudra* attitude of Abhayamudra, or "dispelling fear", is almost pure gold and weighs around 50 kg (110 lb). Legend holds that the image originated in Sri Lanka in the first century AD, before being presented to the Khmers and later to King Fa Ngum. The image was

LEFT: Buddha image, Wat Chieng Thong. **BELOW:** royal palace.

twice seized by the Siamese in 1779 and 1827 before finally being restored to Laos by Thailand's King Mongkut in 1867. In the same room are several beautifully embroidered silk screens and impressive engraved elephant tusks. The rest of the museum houses a fairly substantial collection of regalia, portraits, diplomatic gifts and art treasures. Interesting are the varied friezes, murals and mosaics throughout.

Across the road to the west of the Royal Palace is **Wat Mai Suwanna-phumaham** (daily 8am–5pm; entrance fee). Dating from the early 19th century, this temple was for some time the residence of the Sangkhalat, the Supreme Patriarch of Buddhism in Laos. The *sim*, or ordination hall, is wooden, with a five-tiered roof in classic Luang Prabang style. The main attraction here is the stunningly gilded walls of the front veranda, the designs of which recount scenes from the epic *Ramayana* and the *Jataka* stories. For the first half of the 20th century, the Pha Bang was housed here, and it is still put on display here during the Lao New Year celebrations. Within the temple compounds are two long boats, in their own shelter, that play their part, too, at New Year.

On the other side of Thanon Sisavangong rises Mount Phu Si, a sheer rock with wooded sides. At the foot is the derelict **Wat Paa Huak** (daily 6.30am–6.30pm; entrance fee), which despite its abandonment contains very well-preserved 19th-century murals showing Mekong scenes. From this temple, 328 steps wind up Phu Si to **That Chom Si** on the summit, which has an impressive gilded stupa in classical Lao form. The summit also offers fine views of Luang Prabang and surrounding mountains.

The path continues down the other side of Phu Si, past an anti-aircraft gun to **Wat Tham Phu Si**, a cave shrine housing a Buddha image of wide girth in the

BELOW: overlooking Luang Prabang and river.

Map on page 106

style known locally as Pha Kachai. Close by the main road is **Wat Pha Phutthabaat**, a temple containing a 3-metre-long (10-ft) Buddha footprint and originally constructed in the late 14th century. There is another Buddha footprint temple, **Wat Pha Baat Tai**, behind Talat Sao, the fresh produce market in the southern part of town. This wat is more modern and decidedly garish, and it shows distinct Vietnamese Buddhist influence. It is a fine place from where to watch the Mekong slip by.

Heading north along Thanon Sisavangong, from the foot of Phu Si towards the confluence of the Nam Khan and the Mekong, takes one past a string of glittering temples, interspersed with evocative colonial buildings. **Wat Paa Phai** (Bamboo Forest Temple) on the left is noteworthy for its century-old fresco and carved wooden facade depicting secular Lao scenes. Further along the street, also on the left, is **Wat Saen** (One Hundred Thousand Temple; daily; free), the name of which refers to the value of the donation with which it was constructed. This temple is noticeably different in style from most others in Luang Prabang, and the trained temple-eye will immediately identify it as heavily Thai-influenced. The *sim*, built in 1718, has been restored twice in the 20th century.

The most renowned temple

Close to the tip of the peninsula, on the banks of the Mekong and reminding the visitor of the importance of river transport in Laos, is Luang Prabang's most renowned temple, **Wat Xieng Thong** (Golden City Monastery; daily 6am–6pm; entrance fee). This temple, which epitomises in its low sweeping roofs the classic Luang Prabang style of temple architecture, was built in 1560 by King Sai Setthathirat and was patronised by the monarchy right up until 1975. Inside the

BELOW: carving windows.

sim, the eight thick supporting pillars, richly stencilled in gold, guide the eye to the serene golden Buddha images at the rear, and upwards to the roof that is covered in *dhamma* wheels. On the outside of the *sim*, at the back, is an elaborate mosaic of the tree of life set against a deep red background. Throughout, the combination of splendid gold and deep red lend this temple a captivatingly regal atmosphere.

Adjacent to the *sim* is a smaller building, dubbed by the French **La Chapelle Rouge** or Red Chapel, containing a unique reclining Buddha figure. What makes the image so unusual are the Lao proportions, especially the robe curling outwards at the ankles, and the graceful position of the hand supporting the head. This figure was displayed at the Paris exhibition in 1931, but happily it returned to Luang Prabang in 1964 after several decades in Vientiane. The Red Chapel itself is exquisitely decorated. On the outside of the rear wall is a mosaic showing rural Lao village life, executed in the 1950s to celebrate two and a half millennia since the Buddha's attainment of *nirvana*. Also in the Xieng Thong compound are various monk's quarters, reliquary stupas and a boat shelter. Close to the east gate is a building housing the royal funeral carriage.

Another temple of note is **Wat Wisunalat** (daily 6.30am–5pm; entrance fee), also known as **Wat Vixoun**. Built by King Wisunalat in 1513, this is the oldest temple in the city still in use. The *sim*, rebuilt in 1898 under the inspiration of the original wooden structure destroyed by fire in 1887, is unique in style, with a front roof sloping down over the terrace. Sketches by Louis Delaporte of the original building exist from the 1860s, confirming what a later visitor wrote: "Wat Wisunalat is shaped like a boat, the same shape that orientals give to their coffins. The wooden walls are sculpted with extreme refinement and delicacy."

Temple mural detail.

BELOW: Wat Wisunalat.

Although the wood has gone, the builders who performed the restoration attempted to capture the shapes of the original wood in the stucco work. Inside is an impressive collection of Buddhist sculpture. In the temple grounds is the That Pathum, or Lotus Stupa, which is affectionately referred to as That Mak Mo, or Watermelon Stupa. It is just as distinctive as the temple itself. The stupa is over 30 metres (100 ft) high and was constructed in 1504, at which time it was filled with small, precious Buddha images. Many of these were stolen by marauders from Yunnan, in China, in the 19th century, but the rest are now safely on display in the Royal Palace museum.

Next to Wat Wisunalat is the peaceful **Wat Aham** (daily 6.30am–5pm; entrance fee), formerly – before Wat Mai took the honour – the residence of the Supreme Patriarch of Buddhism in Laos. The temple's red façade combines with striking green yak temple guardians and mildewed stupas to provide an atmosphere of extreme tranquillity. The temple rarely has many visitors, other than those quietly making offerings at an important shrine at the base of the two large, old pipal trees.

Beyond Luang Prabang

In fact, the city possesses far more notable temples than are indicated here. A few kilometres to the southeast of town is a forest retreat, **Wat Paa Phon Phao** (daily 8–10am and 1–4.30pm; free), with a three-storey pagoda replete with an external terrace near the top that affords excellent views of the surrounding country side. The chedi is a popular destination for locals and visitors alike.

Across the river from the centre of the city, in Xieng Maen District, are no less than four more temples set in beautiful surroundings, one of which, **Wat Tham**

Map on page 106

BELOW: Hmong new year celebrations.

Map
on page
106

Xieng Maen, is situated in a 100-metre-deep (300-ft) cave. This is generally kept locked, but the keys are held at nearby Wat Long Khun, the former retreat of kings awaiting coronation. Boats transport people across the river to this side from a jetty behind the Royal Palace.

A short distance to the east of the city, about 4 km (2½ miles) beyond the airport, is the Thai Lü village of **Ban Phanom**, renowned as a silk- and cotton-weaving village. On weekends, a small market is set up for those interested in seeing the full range of fabrics produced. However, villagers are willing – sometimes too willing – to show off their goods at any time. All weaving is done by hand on traditional looms, a fascinating process to watch.

In the vicinity, a few kilometres along the river, is the **Tomb of Henri Mouhot**, the French explorer who took the credit for "discovering" Angkor Wat in 1860. He died of malaria in Luang Prabang in 1861, although his tomb was abandoned and not discovered till 1990.

A two-hour, 25-km (15-mile) journey by long-tail boat upriver from Luang Prabang is the confluence of the Mekong and the Nam Ou. Opposite the mouth of the Nam Ou, in the side of a limestone cliff, are the **Pak Ou Caves** (daily; entrance fee). It is said King Sai Setthathirat discovered these two caves in the 16th century, and they have been venerated ever since. Both are full of Buddha images, some of considerable age. The lower of the two caves, **Tham Ting**, is easily accessible from the river. The upper cave, **Tham Phum**, is reached by a staircase and is much deeper, requiring a torch for full exploration. There is a pleasant shelter between the two caves, an ideal spot for a picnic lunch.

On the way to Pak Ou, boats will stop by request at **Ban Xang Hai**, the jar-maker village and named after the village's former main industry. Archaeologists digging around the village have unearthed jars dating back more than 2,000 years. Today, jars abound, but they are made elsewhere, and the village devotes itself to producing *lao-lao*, the local moonshine rice-wine. Opposite, at **Ban Thin Hong** and close to Pak Ou village, excavations have uncovered even older artefacts – tools, pottery and fabrics – around 8,000 years old. The site hasn't yet been properly developed.

RIGHT: taking aim with a slingshot.
BELOW: bicycles on the move.

Trails and waterfalls

There are several waterfalls in the vicinity of Luang Prabang that can make for attractive half-day or day excursions, perhaps combined with stops in some of the villages along the way. About 30 km (20 miles) south of town are the multi-tiered falls of **Kuang Si**, replete with interesting limestone formations and crystal-clear pools. Food vendors keep most of the local visitors at the lower level of the falls, which can be very crowded on holidays. There is a second pool and waterfall up a trail to the left of the lower cascade that makes for good swimming, and it is generally quieter. The trail continues to the top of the falls, though after rain it can be hazardously slippy.

The falls at **Taat Sae**, also south of town, are closer to the city, and hence more crowded at weekends. The falls here have more pools and shorter drops. They can be reached by boat from the delightful village of Ban Aen on the Nam Khan river. ❏

ANGKOR

Maps on pages 106, 134

The cities and palaces of ancient Europe were diminutive in both size and detail compared with those of Angkor. Still, until a century ago, the ruins of Angkor were hidden by the overgrowth of jungle

Revealed to the West only by its fortuitous "discovery" in 1860, **Angkor ❷** was the capital of a powerful kingdom whose rulers boasted in their inscriptions that it had "for its moat the Ocean, and for its boundaries China, the Suksma Kamrata [apparently western tribal names], and the territory of Champa [southern Vietnam]". This Khmer state arose on the foundations of other pre-Angkorian, "Indianised" Cambodian states, referred to in old Chinese records as Funan and Chenla. The Angkor period is conventionally considered to have begun in AD 802 with the reign of King Jayavarman II, lasting until 1431, when the capital was abandoned.

The Khmer kings and others of the ruling classes left many inscriptions, hundreds of which have been found and interpreted. These have granted us some insight into royal, religious and administrative questions, and permitted the occasional glimpse into other levels of life as well. The sophisticated and immensely alluring sculpture of the Khmer, which in some large temple bas reliefs can measure hundreds of metres, also provides us with a most revealing archive about this ancient people and their way of life. Art and architecture changed in style over the long period of the existence of the cities in the Angkor region, and fairly sophisticated dating is now possible. Much of the art is, of course, regally oriented, dream-like in its splendour and other worldliness. But the overwhelming impact of the Khmer is best summed up by Angkor Wat, the world's largest religious structure, covering some 80 hectares (200 acres), or by the splendid royal temple called the Bayon. On its towers, the serenely smiling face of the god-king as the Bodhisattva Avalokiteshvara is represented on a gigantic scale.

Khmer architecture

Not unlike the ancient Egyptians, the Khmers are quintessentially identified by their fabulous architecture. Just as Egypt is instantly associated with pyramids and temples, so the Khmer are recognised by the truly staggering achievement of their splendid temples. Some are Buddhist, and others are Hindu, dedicated to their kings and the cult of the *devarajas*, or god-kings. The Khmers aspired to represent no less than the Hindu universe in miniature, centred on the mythical Mount Meru, the main tower of the edifices, with the sanctuary facing east and surrounded by the continents. The outer ocean is represented by the moat, often usefully linking into the city's extensive hydraulic system. Simpler, earlier temples evolved into the later classical form, with five peaks for the central "mountain" and outer courts and towers.

Bas relief depicting apsara, or divine dancers.

Khmer architectural efforts culminated in Angkor Wat, but the Angkor area altogether includes well over a hundred temples. The latest NASA surveys, in 1998, revealed that there is much more to find, including a temple northwest of Angkor. It is said to be as big as a football stadium and to date from before the ninth century, and is thus very important for the study of Angkor's origins.

Surrounding the temples was once a city of wooden structures, including everything from royal palaces carved in fantastic detail, down to the most temporary market shelter. All this has vanished, except on the bas reliefs, leaving the temples isolated from their original setting and amidst the ever encroaching jungle.

OPPOSITE: Angkor Wat at twilight.

The tremendous efforts involved in erecting these structures depended on a strong state machinery administering an extensive human-power resource. An elaborate hydraulic system had to be maintained, with a network of canals and dikes serving the reservoirs. A break-down of the delicate balance of resources, food supplies and administration doubtless eventually caused the collapse of the system. But while it was maintained, the Khmer architects, craftsmen and builders, under the command of the kings who ordered their labours, were able to produce structures that are recognised world masterpieces.

Historical outline

TIP

When visiting Angkor Wat, stay on the well used paths, as there are mines on some outlying tracks.

The Angkor period commenced with the reign of Jayavarman II (AD 802–850), who established himself in the region at various centres, building temples at Mount Kulen, 40 km (25 miles) northeast of Angkor, and also at Roluos, situated to the southeast of Angkor. Jayavarman's monarchy evoked the concept of the *chakravatin*, the universal monarch, and the *devaraja*, or god-king. The royal temple was regarded as Shiva's dwelling place, the holy mountain.

Internal struggles consumed the eras of several rulers until Suryavarman II took the throne in 1113, reigning until 1150. It was he who built Angkor Wat. In his time, the Khmer frontiers remained extended, embracing a substantial area of what is now Thailand. Suryavarman's religious inclinations favoured Vishnu, as represented at Angkor Wat.

In 1177, a Cham invasion – perhaps sparked by Khmer raids into Cham territory – caused widespread destruction at Angkor, until repelled by Jayavarman VII, the last of the great Khmer kings. Jayavarman fought to regain the ravaged city of Angkor Thom, and then freed the rest of the empire after killing

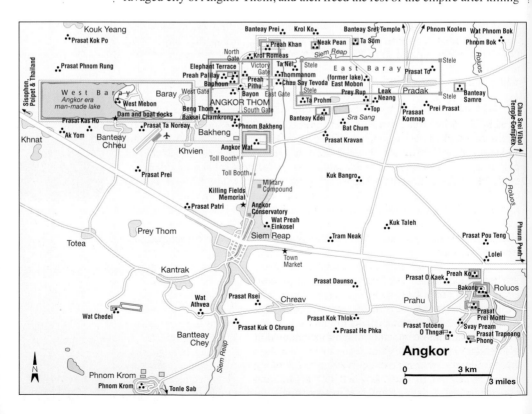

the king of the Cham. Jayavarman was a Mahayana Buddhist, perhaps in reaction to the discredit that the Cham defeat had brought to the divine incarnations of Shiva or Vishnu who had ruled the Khmer so long. His reign saw tremendous building activity in the area. This was the swansong of the Khmer monarchy. In 1431, weakened and unable to maintain themselves in the face of the strong monarchy established at Ayutthaya in Thailand (which had already captured Angkor once in 1389), the kings of Angkor are supposed to have retreated to a new capital at Phnom Penh. Alternatively, it has been proposed that another line of kings installed themselves near Phnom Penh, and that some sort of monarchy continued at Angkor. But slowly Angkor became a ghost city, some of it taken over by the jungle, some parts occupied by monks.

Map on page 134

Apsaras reflected the perfect image of female beauty. Heaven was their abode, and they lived mainly to have sex with heroes and even holy men.

Angkor Wat

Seven kilometres (4 mi) north of **Siem Reap**, the nearest town and where most of the hotels are located, the moated temple of **Angkor Wat** occupies an area of almost 2 square kilometres (500 acres). It was built by King Suryavarman II as a microcosmic representation of the celestial world. Every aspect of the structure possesses meaning on a religious and metaphorical level. The king was identified as the god Vishnu, the deity honoured here, and Angkor Wat seems to have been both a royal temple and a mausoleum.

The temple is immensely imposing, the world of the gods seemingly floating on the waters of the 190-metre-long (625-ft) moat. The pillared galleries and towers bestow an impressive breadth, height, and mass, while the incredibly lavish carvings and bas reliefs fill every corner with information about the heavenly world. As a construction project alone, the effort involved is awe-inspiring.

BELOW: bas relief at a gate to Angkor.

A stone causeway approaches the temple, or *wat*, from the west, and an earthen one from the east. Within the moat, the temple "island" is walled, with four gates; the western gate is the main entrance. The triple-towered porch measures 235 metres (770 ft) in width, and is elaborately decorated, with the figures of the divine dancing girls, the *apsaras*, prominent.

A massive statue of Vishnu stands to the south, holding the deity's various attributes in its eight arms. From the porch, an avenue nearly 500 metres (1,600 ft) long, flanked by *naga* serpents, leads past two so-called library buildings and two pools to another walled area, the central temple approached by a staircase from a cruciform terrace. Inside this inner area, around the temple and completely enclosing it, is a gallery or cloister accessible from doorways on either side of an entrance pavilion. The cloister houses the tremendous series of bas reliefs 2 metres (6½ ft) high, for which Angkor is so famous. The carved reliefs represent stories from the *Ramayana*, the Indian epic account of Rama's search for his wife, Sita, snatched away by a demon king of Lanka, and the great battle described in the *Mahabharata*. There are also scenes of the king and his court, and a magnificent depiction of a military parade, the different contingents and their leaders named in accompanying inscriptions. Finally, scenes of heaven and hell shown what the good can expect *(apsaras)*, and the bad (various tortures).

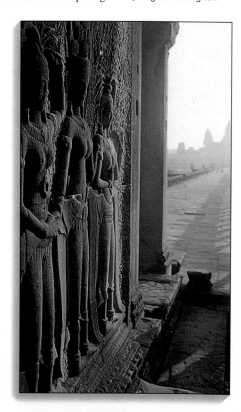

Map
on page
134

*Angkor Thom was
much larger than the
whole of ancient
Rome, and it was
surrounded by a
moat 100 metres
wide and over 10 km
(6 miles) long.*

OPPOSITE: stone
image, Bayon.
BELOW: temple
detail.

Within this gallery, at a higher level, is another gallery with stone-mullioned windows, linked to the outer gallery by a cruciform cloister and the flanking galleries. Here in the "Gallery of a Thousand Buddhas" were once kept the images that pious Cambodians had dedicated to the temple. Finally, inside the second gallery with its four corner towers, presumably shrines, lies the main temple, the golden mountain of Jambudvipa, the abode of the gods. Raised high on a stepped platform, accessible by staircases, another gallery with four corner towers encloses the central great tower, to which it is also linked by four axial galleries. A great statue of Vishnu, representing the king, was enshrined here, the focus of this huge effort.

Angkor Thom and the Bayon

The inner royal city of Angkor, **Angkor Thom**, already occupied by such monuments as the Phimeanakas and the Baphuon, was restored after the Cham invasion by Jayavarman VII. The huge quadrangle, 3 km (2 miles) on each side, is delineated by a broad moat and defended by a wall 8 metres (26 ft) high, with gates sculpted with mythical figures and huge faces.

The temple in the centre of Angkor Thom, called the **Bayon**, makes an extraordinary impression with its numerous towers sculpted with over 200 large faces of King Jayavarman VII as Boddhisattva Avalokiteshvara. Directly north of the Bayon, facing the town's central square, is **Elephant Terrace**, sculpted with a frieze of elephants. This 350-metre-long (1,150-ft) monument may have had some relation to the royal apartments.

The Bayon temple, not dedicated to one deity but more like a national pantheon to all the Khmer deities, is constructed on three levels. With the plethora of towers, set rather close together, the temple gives a rather crowded impression. The first enclosure is surrounded by a magnificent set of bas reliefs, 1,200 metres (4,000 ft) of them, depicting battles by sea and land with the Chams, royal scenes and processions, and other tableaux, with a good deal of information about local life and fauna as well. The carving is incredibly detailed. The second level also has bas reliefs, now much damaged. The third level represents the world mountain, with shrines for the Buddha, Shiva, Vishnu and others.

The temples of the Roluos group, built at the former capital, Hariharalaya, are interesting as precursors to the greater monuments of Angkor. **Preah Ko**, dedicated by King Indravarman in AD 880 to his ancestors, is characterised by six towers built of brick on a stone terrace guarded by lion figures. The remains of some of the elaborate stucco work that would once have covered the brickwork illustrates the fine level to which this technique had been brought.

Bakong was also built by Indravarman as his state temple, dedicated to Shiva. It is a representation of Meru as a five-tiered pyramid platform surrounded by towers constructed of brick with stone plinths, doorways and lintels. Some stucco work survives. The pyramid, topped with a tower and with smaller shrines standing on the level below, rises within an enclosure, surrounded by a moat representing the ocean. ❑

ANCIENT ARTEFACTS OF SOUTHEAST ASIA

Southeast Asia's ancient culture drew its inspiration from diverse religious and artistic influences, leaving the world one of its richest inheritances

The ancient artefacts found in Southeast Asia reveal a wealth of information about the history, traditions, social organisations and religious beliefs of the region. Since early times, the cultural traditions of the region have blended with those of India and China as traders from these countries came to exploit the rich supply of gold and spices. The gradual infusion of the powerful Hindu-Buddhist cultural traditions of India through *vaisyas* (Indian merchants) and *brahmanas* (religious men) resulted in the so-called "Indianisation" of Southeast Asia. This process only took place in areas that had direct contact with India; northern Vietnam, for example, was under Chinese influence and was not affected. This is not to say that the artistic culture of the Indianised kingdoms was not innovative and extraordinary. Indian themes and designs only provided a base for the indigenous people to develop their artistic styles, and it is their genius that is reflected in the artefacts and superlative architecture created at that time.

THE SOUTHEAST ASIAN INNOVATION DEBATE

Bronzeware dating from 3600 BC found in Ban Chiang, in northeast Thailand, has revealed that bronze technology was probably transferred from Thailand to China, not the other way round. This find is significant to the on-going argument that the region was a centre of innovation rather than merely a receptacle of outside influences.

△ **ELEPHANT CAVES, BALI**
Goa Gajah, the Elephant Caves, date back to the 11th century. The sculpted face of the cave has links to Tantric Buddhism or perhaps Bhairavite Siwaism.

▷ **THUNDER-DRUM**
A 7th-century bronze thunder-drum made in Vietnam by the Dong Son. Thunder-drums produce a huge volume of sound and were used to bring on the monsoon thunder.

◁ **BUDDHIST INFLUENCES**
By the end of the 15th century, Theravaha Buddhism was the dominant religion across much of Southeast Asia's mainland.

△ **EARLY CLASSIC JAVANESE**
This beautiful 9th-century *bodhisattva* (goddess) at Candi Sari, Java, shows a strong Indian influence.

▽ **PREHISTORIC THAILAND**
Some of the pottery unearthed at Ban Chiang, Thailand, is believed to be 4,500 to 5,700 years old.

△ **EAST JAVANESE PERIOD**
A *candi* depicted in the reliefs of Candi Panataran Java, the most important *candi* of the East Javanese Period (11th–15th century).

▽ **HINDU CARVINGS**
The Hindu god Indra mounts his elephant, Erawan, in a relief at Myohaung's Htukkan-thein Pagoda, in Burma.

△ **CHAMPA KINGDOM**
These stone dancers in Da Nang, Vietnam, were carved by the Cham, creators of some of the finest Vietnamese art.

THE PLUNDERING OF BOROBUDUR

Borobudur is one of the most impressive monuments ever created by people. It was built around AD 800 when the Sailendra dynasty of central Java was at the height of its artistic and military power, taking 75 years to complete. It probably fell into neglect by about AD 1000. It was completely overgrown and suffering from earthquake damage when it was rediscovered in 1814 by a military engineer serving under Thomas Stamford Raffles.

In the years that followed, Borobudur was uncovered to the elements and to people, enduring almost a century of decay, plunder and abuse, during which thousands of stones were "borrowed" by people living nearby. Scores of priceless sculptures ended up as garden decorations in the homes of the rich and powerful. Typical of the attitude of Dutch officials at the time was the presentation, in 1896, of eight cart-loads of Borobudur souvenirs to visiting King Chulalongkorn of Thailand, including 30 relief panels and five Buddha statues. Many of these and other irreplaceable works of Indo-Javanese art ended up in private collections, residing now in private museums worldwide, a process replicated region-wide.

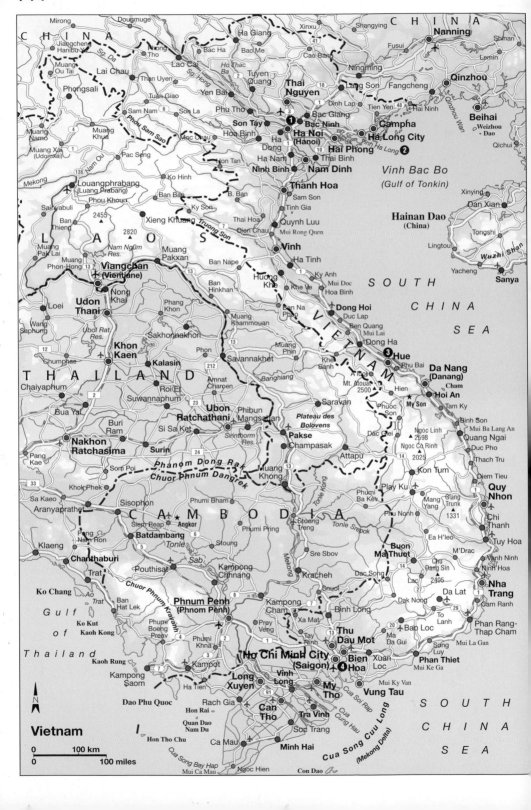

Vietnam

VIETNAM

Vietnamese remind travellers that Vietnam is a nation,

not a war. It's a nation with a heritage as rich as any

In the early 1400s, the Chinese invaded Vietnam, one of many such invasions over the centuries. The Chinese were soundly defeated by the Vietnamese. Le Loi, emperor of Vietnam, might have had the Chinese prisoners killed. He chose otherwise. Le Loi apologised to the Chinese court for defeating its army, made peace with China, and provided the defeated Chinese troops with horses and ships for their return north. Le Loi knew that, although momentarily defeated, China would never disappear.

Indeed, the presence of its leviathan neighbour to the north has, perhaps more than anything else, sculpted the nature of the Vietnamese mind. Centuries of fending off China's invasions, while at the same time not making China too angry, has given Vietnamese a pragmatism, a patience, and a solid sense of national identity. Vietnamese are highly educated and literate (over 90 percent), and they have an open desire to learn from others, and to admit mistakes.

About the size of Germany or Arizona, Vietnam challenges the best of travellers. After decades of war, and with an economy that was subsequently throttled, the country's infrastructure – or lack of it – can test the most hardened traveller's patience. But Vietnam is truly one of those destinations where the inconveniences pale beside the remarkable, and where the beauty of its 83.6 million people and culture seduce all.

Northern Vietnam is anchored by Hanoi, an ancient city established nearly 1,000 years ago. This political capital clings to the rhetoric of a socialist system while at the same time embracing a government-controlled capitalism. The restored villas and façades of the French colonial era give the city an ambience not found elsewhere in Asia.

Southward, following the historical movement of the Viet people, the traveller finds a chain of coastal provinces washed by the South China Sea. In the old imperial city of Hue, an overwhelming sense of the past pervades its older streets. The antiquities don't end here. In the lands of the ancient kingdom of Champa are decaying sanctuaries, temples and towers that testify to the conquest by the Viet people from the north.

Then there is Ho Chi Minh City. Often still called Saigon, it is reviving its long-time image as a proverbial hustling and bustling city of people on the make and on the go. Where Hanoi is quiet, Ho Chi Minh City screams. Where Hue has a subtle and refined beauty, Ho Chi Minh City grabs you by the lapels and shakes. If Hanoi is a city of earth tones, Ho Chi Minh City is neon, all lit up in gaudy lights. ❏

PRECEDING PAGES: river boat on the Mekong; descendants of Hue's royal family.

Decisive Dates

Beginnings

2879 BC: Legendary founding of the Van Lang Kingdom by the first Hung king.

2879–258 BC: Hung dynasty.

1800–1400 BC: Phung Nguyen culture, the Early Bronze Age.

210 BC: Kingdom of Au Lac established. Chinese general Chao Tuo founds Nan Yueh (Nam Viet).

111 BC–938 AD: Chinese rule in the north.

AD 39: Trung sisters lead a rebellion against Chinese.

AD 43: Trung sisters' rebellion is crushed by the Chi-

nese General Ma Yuan, and subsequently, the Viet people are placed under direct Chinese administration.

100–600: Indian traders establish enclaves along the Southern coast and the Funan (Oc Eo) civilization in the Mekong Delta grows.

200: The kingdom of Lam Ap (later called Champa) rises in central and southern Vietnam.

939–967: Ngo dynasty.

968–980: Dinh dynasty.

970–975: Dinh Bo Linh gains Chinese recognition of Nam Viet's independence by establishing a triputary relationship with China's Song dynasty.

980–1009: Tien Le conquer northern Champa.

1010: Hanoi established.

1009–1225: Ly dynasty.

1225–1400: Tran dynasty. Mongol invaders are beaten back in 1257 and 1285.

1400–1407: Ho dynasty.

1407–1428: Chinese Occupation.

1428–1776: Le dynasty.

1471: Le Thang Tong crushes the Kingdom of Champa.

Division and reunification

1543: The Le Dynasty occupies the country's southern capital after a series of fierce battles. The southern court is founded near Thanh Hoa.

1592: The death of Mac dynasty's last king, Mac Mau Hop, ends the war.

1672: Lord Trinh consents to partition the country at the Linh River.

1771–1802: Tay Son Uprising.

1792–1883: Nguyen dynasty.

1802–1820: Viet Nam is united under Gia Long and the capital moves to Hue.

1862: Treaty of Saigon cedes three southern provinces to the French.

1885: French forces acquire Annam and Cochin.

1893: Emperor Ham Nghi and Phan Dinh Phung organise a royalist movement and stage an unsuccessful uprising at Ha Tinh.

1907: Eastward Movement is established by Phan Boi Chau and Cuong De. French authorities discover the scheme and negotiate with Japan to extradite all Vietnamese students.

1919: Nguyen Ai Quoc (later known as Ho Chi Minh) attempts to present a programme for Vietnamese rights and sovereignty at the Versailles Peace conference but is turned away.

1921: Ho Chi Minh joins French Communist Party as founding member.

1924: Ho Chi Minh attends the Fifth Congress of the Communist International (Comintern).

1930: Ho Chi Minh successfully rallies several Communist groups and becomes the founder of the Indochinese Communist Party.

World War II and after

1939: World War II begins.

1940: Japan overthrows the French but allows the Vichy government to remain in Vietnam while Japan retains military and economic control.

1942–43: Ho Chi Minh imprisoned in China.

1943: Ho Chi Minh is released and recognised as the chief of the Viet Minh.

1945: The Japanese surrender to the Allies. The Viet Minh commence the August revolution, gaining effective control over much of Vietnam. On 2 September, Ho Chi Minh declares Vietnam's independence in Hanoi.

1946: Ho Chi Minh visits Paris during negotiations with France; hostilities follow violation of agreements.
1951: Ho unites various factions and announces the formation of the Workers Party (Lao Dong).

North-South divide

1954: French defeated at Dien Bien Phu on 7 May. The Geneva Accord divides Vietnam at the 17th parallel. South Vietnam is led by Prime Minister Ngo Dinh Diem, and North Vietnam under the Communist Ho Chi Minh.
1955: Diem refuses to hold general elections. Start of Second Indochina War. Direct United States aid to South Vietnam begins.
1959: Group 559 established to infiltrate South Vietnam via the Ho Chi Minh Trail.
1960: National Liberation Front of South Vietnam (NLF) is formed. During the 1960s, the southern Communist movement – the Viet Cong – grows stronger.
1962: United States military personnel in Vietnam total about 3,200.
1963: Ngo Dinh Diem, president of South Vietnam, is overthrown and assassinated.
1965: United States begin bombing military targets in North Vietnam. First United States ground combat troops land in Vietnam at Danang.
1968: My Lai massacre. Tet Offensive includes a raid on the American Embassy that stunned the United States. Peace negotiations begin in Paris.
1969: Ho Chi Minh dies aged 79.
1973: Paris Peace Agreement aims to put an end to hostilities. The last United States troops depart from Vietnam in March.
1975: In April, North Vietnamese troops enter Saigon. The South Vietnamese government surrenders.

A unified Vietnam

1976: Vietnam is officially reunified.
1977: Vietnam is admitted to the United Nations.
1978: Cambodian border troops launch cross-border attacks into southern Vietnam, resulting in the Ba Chuc massacre. Vietnam retaliates and the Cambodian government of Pol Pot is overthrown. Vietnam also signs friendship treaty with the Soviet Union.
1979: China retaliates by invading Vietnam. After 17 days, Chinese forces withdraw.

Economic shifts

1986: Sixth Party Congress. Programme of socio-economic renovation called *doi moi* is launched.

LEFT: traditional theme of simple pleasures.
RIGHT: the legendary Ho Chi Minh in the 1950s.

1987: Law on Foreign Investment is passed.
1988: New contract system is implemented to encourage Vietnamese farmers to cultivate their land. Rice production experiences an immediate upsurge.
1989: Vietnamese troops leave Cambodia.
1990: Vietnam adopts a new course in foreign affairs and peace talks in China take place. Diplomatic relations established with the European Union.
1991: China relations normalised. Soviets discontinue aid.
1994: Trade embargo lifted by the United States.
1995: Diplomatic ties are restored with the US, and a US embassy opens in Hanoi. Vietnam is admitted to the Association of Southeast Asian Nations (ASEAN).

1997: Many Asian investors in Vietnam are affected in the wake of the Asian financial crisis.
2000: Bill Clinton pays a three-day official visit.
2001: Trade agreement with the US ratified in December, normalising the trade status between them.
2002: National Assembly elections return a victory for the ruling Communist Party. President Tran Duc Luong and Prime Minister Phan Van Khai are both reappointed for their second terms.
2003: New laws and streamlined government agencies attract more foreign investment to the country.
2006: The president, head of state, and National Assembly chairman are replaced by younger leaders.
2007: Vietnam is finally accepted as member of the World Trade Organization after 12 years of talks. ❑

THE VIETNAMESE

Like much of Southeast Asia's population, the people of Vietnam are of diverse backgrounds, giving the country a colourful heritage that enchants today

Who are the people of Vietnam? Although most of the population of 83.6 million lists as its ethnicity Kinh, the accepted term for the native race, in reality most Vietnamese have evolved from a mixture of races and ethnicities over thousands of years. That mixture is quite naturally the result of repeated invasions from outside Vietnam, particularly from China, and continual migrations within Vietnam, commonly from north to south.

In Vietnam today, the Viet, or Kinh, in fact form the majority of the people, representing about 87 percent of the population. But there are also dozens of distinct minority groups, including the Cham and Khmer of the south, two groups whose own kingdoms were long ago vanquished by invading Vietnamese from the north.

The Vietnamese

Studies of folk songs from the hill region of northern Vietnam and from the coastal area in the northern part of central Vietnam affirm that the Vietnamese originated in the north's Red River Delta. These agricultural, fishing and hunting people were probably animistic.

Their traditional forms of dress, although unique to the region of Indochina, is found in certain Oceanic islands.

Throughout monsoon Asia, which includes northern Vietnam, a shared culture existed from a very early era, as evidenced by its tools, vocabulary and certain essential rites and traditions, such as the blackening of teeth, water festivals, bronze drums, kites, tattooing, betel nut and *cajeput*, pole houses, cock-fighting and mulberry cultivation. Remains of five races have been found in Vietnam: Melanesians, Indonesians, Negritos, Australoids and Mongoloids. The most predominant of these were the Indonesians and Mongoloids.

Studies on the origins of the Vietnamese show that the people who settled on the Indochinese peninsula and its bordering regions

LEFT: elderly woman at northern market.
RIGHT: the young Duy Tan, emperor of Annam.

came from several places: China, the high plateaus of Central Asia, and islands in the South Pacific. Thus, Vietnam can be considered a proverbial melting pot into which major Asiatic and Oceanic migrations converged. Two major Viet emigrations from the coastal and southern provinces of the Chinese empire added

to this population. The first occurred during the 5th century BC, at the fall of the Viet kingdom of the lower Yangtze River valley, and the second, during the 3rd century BC, when the Au, or Au Tay, from Guangxi, invaded northern Vietnam.

Ethnic minorities

More than 50 ethnic minorities inhabit the mountainous regions that cover almost two-thirds of Vietnam. (In the 1990s, a small tribe of fewer than 100 members was found in a northern province, a tribe distinct from previously identified ethnic groups.) The 1.7 million Chinese, or Hoa, constitute an important minority group, many of whom remain loyal to the traditions of their country of origin and mostly settling in Cho Lon, a large commercial centre near Ho Chi Minh City in the south.

The ethnic minorities living in the mountainous regions in central and southern Vietnam form another important group. Called Montagnards by the French, these tribes include Muong, Ra De, Jarai, Banhar and Sedang living in the high plateaus of the west. Totalling around 1.5 million people, they have always opposed foreign influence and only recently have begun to integrate into the national life.

The Cham and Khmer number around 1.2 million. The Chams inhabit the Phan Rang and

Phan Thiet regions, while Khmer are found in the Mekong Delta. The Chams possessed a brilliant culture that lasted for more than a thousand years. Its vestiges can still be seen in the ruins of the Poh Nagar temple and the shrines and Buddhist monasteries at Dong Duong, and in the large scale irrigation systems, temples and towers of central Vietnam.

Today, some Cham preserve their customs, language and script with a religion that is a modified form of Hinduism. Others are Muslim.

In the north

The highlands and midland regions of northern Vietnam are home to many ethnic minori-

ties and diverse tribes, including the Tay, who number over 1.5 million and are found in village groups in the provinces of Cao Bang, Lang Son, Bac Thai, Quang Ninh, Ha Giang, and Tuyen Quang, and in the Dien Bien Phu region.

The villages, or ban, of the Tay are located in valleys near flowing water, where they build their traditional houses, usually on stilts. They cultivate rice, soybeans, cinnamon, tea, tobacco, cotton, indigo, fruit trees and bamboo on the mountainsides above the village. The influence of Viet culture is evident in their dialect and customs, which distinguish them from the other Tay-Tai speaking groups.

The Nung, in many aspects similar to the Tay, share the same language, culture and customs, and often live together in the same villages, where they are referred to as Tay Nung. Numbering about 875,000, they live in Cao Bang and Lang Son provinces.

There are more than 1.3 million Tai living along the Red River, in the northwest of Vietnam, often together with other ethnic minorities. Their bamboo or wooden stilt houses are constructed in two distinctly different styles. The Black Tai build homes shaped like tortoise shells, while the White Tai construct dwellings of a rectangular form.

The San Chi, numbering more than 150,000, live in village groups mainly in Ha Giang, Tuyen Quang and Bac Thai provinces, but they are also found in certain regions of Lao Cai, Yen Bai, Vinh Phu, Ha Bac and Quang Ninh provinces. They are of the Tay-Tai language group and arrived from China at the beginning of the 19th century. The Giai, also of the Tay-Tai language group, number about 51,000 and emigrated from China about 200 years ago. Their villages are often built very close to those of the Tay, Nung and Tai.

The Lao number about 12,000 and belong to the Tay-Tai language group. They are actually closer to the Tai minority then their Laotian namesakes across the border. Their homes are built on stilts in the form of a tortoise shell, like those of the Black Tai. Their traditional costume also resembles that of the Tai.

The Lu belong to the Tay-Tai language group. They number around 5,000 and are found in the Phong Tho and Sin Ho districts of Lai Chau Province, in well arranged villages of 40 to 60 dwellings. They arrived from China and occupied the Dien Bien Phu area as part of the Bach Y settlement in the first century AD.

The Hmong, who number about 900,000, are found in villages known as *giao* throughout the highlands of eleven provinces. Due to their wars with the feudal Chinese, they emigrated to Vietnam from the southern Chinese kingdom of Bach Viet at the end of the 18th and beginning of the 19th centuries. Once they reached Vietnam, they settled in northwestern provinces. As skilled artisans, the Hmong produce a variety of items, including handwoven indigo-dyed

> ### RECORDED HISTORY
> For centuries, the Dao people have used adopted Chinese characters to record their genealogies, rhymes, folk tales, fables and popular songs.

the slash-and-burn method. This form of agriculture has become less sustainable as population density increases.

The Dao are extremely skilled artisans. They make their own paper, used primarily for writing family genealogies, official documents and religious books. The women plant cotton, which they weave, dye with indigo, and embroider.

Central highlands

The Jarai, or Gia Rai, are located in the provinces of Gia Lai, Kon Tum, and Dak Lak,

cloth, paper, silver jewellery, leather goods, baskets, and embroidery. The Hmong have no written language. Their legends, songs, folklore and proverbs have been passed down from one generation to the next through the spoken word.

The Dao first arrived from China in the 18th century. Belonging to the Hmong-Dao language group, the Dao number about 630,000 and are found in the middle and lower regions of Thanh Hoa Province, living in large villages or small isolated hamlets, cultivating rice using

---

LEFT: portrait of a Muong woman.
ABOVE: Dao woman with her children, and a 19th-century photograph of Meo tribeswomen.

and in the north of Phu Khanh. They belong to the Malay-Polynesian language group and arrived in the Tay Nguyen Highlands from the coast a little less than 2,000 years ago. They live a sedentary lifestyle in villages known as *ploi*, or sometimes *bon*. Jarai villages, with at least 50 homes, are built around a central *nga rong*, or communal house.

The community of the Jarai ethnic group is composed of small matriarchal families, with each family an economically-independent unit within the entire village. A council of elders, with a chief as head, directs village matters. The chief is responsible for all the village's communal activities. ❏

LITERATURE

Literature and poetry are long-honoured traditions of the Vietnamese,
who find in both an aesthetic and historical foundation to their character

Writers and poets have always occupied a place of high esteem in Vietnamese society. A seemingly endless wealth of oral storytelling traditions, consisting of myths, songs, legends, folk and fairy tales, constitutes Vietnam's most ancient literature. Later, as the society developed, there were scholars, Bud-

literature, which introduced new ways of expressing ideas – and reflected rising nationalist feelings in Vietnam.

During the 20th-century wars for Vietnamese independence from outside powers, northern writers confined themselves mainly to stories meant to unify the people and to inspire the

dhist monks, kings and court ministers – many of whom were also talented writers and poets – who wrote down their thoughts and related epics using adopted Chinese characters (*chu nho*). This literature was greatly influenced by Confucianism and Buddhism.

Even more poems and literary works were undertaken with the advent of *chu nom*, a complicated script based on chu nho. However, the Vietnamese found the romanised alphabet, introduced by foreign missionaries, to be a more accessible means of communicating than the foreboding need to use thousands of different ideograms. Indeed, Vietnamese literary prose and poetry were influenced by European

population during difficult times. Communist Party cadres strictly controlled publishing after the end of the Vietnam War in 1975, and even today, government censors must approve writings before their publication.

The publication in the early 1990s of *The Sorrow of War*, by a Vietnamese war veteran from the North under the pseudonym of Bao Ninh, was the first war novel to confront the gruesome realities of war and the psychological effects upon surviving soldiers. Another writer, Duong Thu Huong, has had her works translated, and her writing includes thinly veiled criticism of government and party officials. For a time, she was imprisoned for crimes against the state.

Today, writers with reputations for criticism are presumed to be under close surveillance. Despite the appearance of a new period of openness, Party leaders have warned at gatherings of writers that they must focus on ideas that are of a benefit to the nation. An improved economy and increased contact with the outside world have meant that interest in literature, always intense in Vietnam, has declined somewhat. Still, for a poor nation, literacy is high at over 90 percent – it's common for people to read for pleasure.

ment, attitude or mood. The subtleties and nuances are sophisticated and aesthetic.

Vietnamese poetry falls into two major categories: *ca dao*, a popular folk song, oral in origin but collected and transcribed in written form; and *tho van*, literary poetry written by kings, scholars, Buddhist monks, mandarins, Daoist recluses, dissidents, feminists, revolutionaries – even the die-hard Marxists. Poetry has become such an important medium that present-day political slogans must be written in verse to be effective.

> ### POETIC CULTIVATION
>
> Vietnamese follow the declaration by Confucius that "personal cultivation begins with poetry, is made firm by the rule of decorum and is perfected by music."

Poetry

Above all else, poetry dominates the Vietnamese arts. The language of Vietnam is a natural tool for poetry, as each of its syllables can be pronounced in six tones to convey six meanings. By combining these tones and modulating certain words, a sentence turns into a verse and plain speech becomes a song.

Another group of words made up of repeated syllables can cast a discreet shade on the meaning, conjuring up a particular colour, movement

The Tale of Kieu

Nearly every Vietnamese reads and remembers a few chapters of a 3,254-verse story published 200 years ago called *The Tale of Kieu*. Pupils begin studying it in the sixth grade.

Kieu was written by one of Vietnam's most esteemed forefathers, Nguyen Du, and is now considered the cultural bible and window to the soul of the Vietnamese people. One may wonder how *Kieu* came to occupy its special position in Vietnamese literature. Why is the complex tale of a woman's personal misfortunes regarded by a whole people as the perfect expression of their essential nature, of their national soul? After all, the protagonist Kieu,

LEFT: Bao Ninh, author of *The Sorrow of War*.
ABOVE: those who passed the official exams became men of letters and members of officialdom.

though beautiful and talented, is forced into selling herself by unfortunate circumstances.

Regardless of age, gender, geography or ideology, to the Vietnamese the epic of Kieu is the heart and mind of their nation.

Born in the village of Nghi Xuan, in northern Vietnam's Ha Tinh Province, Nguyen Du came from an old aristocratic family of mandarins and scholars. His father was prime minister in the Thang Long (now Hanoi) court of Emperor Le. He grew up in a country, under the nominal rule of the Le dynasty, torn by civil war. After Gia Long, a descendant of the southern Nguyen warlords, defeated the Tay Son brothers and was

declared emperor, Nguyen Du became an official of several northern provinces, distinguishing himself as an honest and able administrator. In 1806, at the age of 41, he was summoned to the capital of Hue to serve as high chancellor.

Having reunited Vietnam, Gia Long faced the problem of national security, foremost of which meant establishing diplomatic relations with China. All Vietnamese envoys to China were chosen from the cream of Vietnamese *literati*, as it was by intellectual, rather than military, might that Vietnam sought to impress China. So Nguyen Du, already recognised as a great poet, was a natural choice to be emissary. After five years in China, he returned and

devoted most of his time to literary pursuits until his death at the age of 53 in 1820.

A literary school founded in 1979 to train writers was named after Nguyen Du, over the objections of government officials who preferred to name the school after a war hero.

What makes *The Tale of Kieu* as relevant today as it was two centuries ago is Nguyen Du's ability and courage to lay bare the whole spectrum of society. The vices and virtues, ugliness and beauty, nobility and trickery, all entangled in a seemingly hopeless tragic comedy, reflect the true face of Vietnam. Kieu also personifies the inherent contradiction faced by the Vietnamese.

"Within the span of a hundred years of human existence, what a bitter struggle is waged between talent and fate", lament the opening lines. And, in the conclusion, Nguyen Du writes, "When one is endowed with talent, do not rely upon it".

The perplexing paradox

Deep in their hearts and behind their gracious modesty, the Vietnamese know they are not lacking in talent, *tai*. At the same time, they do not understand why this tai, which has helped them win their independence against formidable foreign invasions and enabled them to develop a respectable culture and civilisation, has failed to bring them lasting peace and enduring prosperity. Unable to solve this paradox, most believe they are *oan*, a word meaning wronged and which appears throughout *Kieu*. The Vietnamese, like Kieu, see themselves as victims of fate, punished for crimes they are not aware they have committed.

Even Vietnamese who fled the country after the war ended in the 1970s turn to the tales of Kieu for comfort, especially in the cultural isolation of a new land and language. Huynh Sanh Thong, a Vietnamese scholar at Yale University who translated *Kieu* into English, wrote in his introduction that immigrants "know most of its lines by heart, and when they recite them out loud, they speak their mother tongue at its finest. To the extent that the poem implies something at the very core of the Vietnamese experience, it addresses them intimately as victims, as refugees, as survivors." ❑

LEFT: the Temple of Literature in Hanoi.
RIGHT: page of Latin-Annamese text.

Language

I n the Vietnamese language, the word for natural disaster is *thien tai*, from Chinese. The word for cheese is *pho mat*, from the French *fromage*. There are also sounds and words from English and Russian. Thousands of words in the contemporary Vietnamese language – as much as 70 percent of the language – comes from Chinese, a reflection of the centuries of non-too-harmonious relations between Vietnam and its massive neighbour to the north, including the influence of Chinese literature.

There is a touch of French, with words that entered the lexicon first during the colonial period of the 18th and 19th centuries, and well into the 20th century. A dab of English was left by the Americans during the Vietnam War, and subsequent years of fraternisation with the former Soviet Union introduced Russian. In fact, expressions and nomenclature indicating 20th-century technology and ideas are often expressed with French, English and Russian words. The newest foreign linguistic invasion – that of consumerism – is represented by Japanese. The word most commonly used to refer to a two-wheeled motorised vehicle, for example, is *honda*.

Variations: Distinct dialects within Vietnam reveal strong regional identities, as well. Often northerners and southerners confess they cannot understand each other. Foreigners might need two translators, one to translate the foreign language into Vietnamese, another to translate the Vietnamese into another dialect. Some letters of the alphabet are pronounced differently, and the vocabularies of northerners and southerners contain distinct words. Even the syntax is different. In addition to Vietnamese, the country's many ethnic minorities speak their own distinct languages and dialects. In the Mekong Delta, for example, so many people speak the Khmer of Cambodia that local television has a Khmer-language broadcast.

The majority Kinh people and the 53 ethnic minority groups derive from three great language families, the Austo-Asiatic, the Austronesian and Sino-Tibetan.

Written Vietnamese: Chinese influence during the first centuries of Vietnam's history led to the extensive use of Chinese characters known as *chu nho*, which replaced an ancient written script of Indian origin, preserved and used today only by the Muong minority.

After independence in the 10th century, scholars realised the necessity and advantages of developing a separate written Vietnamese language. Several tentative attempts were made to modify the characters of Chinese, but it was two 13th-century poets, Nguyen Thuyen and Nguyen Si Co, who first wrote extensively in *chu nom*. In the following centuries, many poems, stories and encyclopaedia were written in *chu nom*. The golden age of literature during the 18th century was the era of *truyen* or long narrative poems, such as *The Tale of Kieu*, as well as satirical stories attacking the ruling elite, feminist poems and historical works.

Today, however, Vietnam has a romanised alphabet, thanks to a French Jesuit missionary, Alexan-

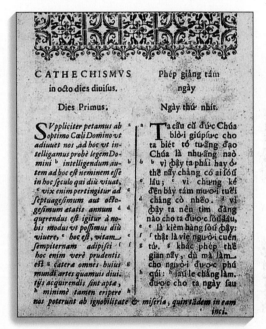

dre de Rhodes, who developed a script called *quoc ngu* in 1651.

Quoc ngu was, at first, used only by the Catholic Church and the colonial administration, gaining widespread popularity only in the early part of the 20th century. The study of *quoc ngu* became compulsory in secondary schools in 1906, and two years later, the royal court in Hue ordered a new curriculum, entirely in quoc ngu. It became the national written language in 1919.

Now, only scholars use the traditional calligraphic chu nom to decipher ancient carvings and writings. And during holidays, such as the lunar new year (Tet), people buy scrolls written in Chinese characters for their homes. ❏

A FEAST OF FRUITS

There is a sizeable range of fruits in Southeast Asia, many of which may be unfamiliar. As well as bananas and pineapples, there are brilliantly coloured and strangely shaped fruits for the adventurous

In Asia, people love food, and during the afternoon they snack on an incredible variety of fruits. For visitors who are in need of a boost, fruit can be a great source of refreshment and energy. Traditional fruit sellers have glass-fronted carts stacked with blocks of ice and pealed pieces of seasonal fruits. Choose a selection of what you want to eat and the vendor will pop it into a bag for you along with a toothpick for spearing the slices. Some fruits, like pineapple, are eaten with a little salt and ground chilli, a twist of which is supplied separately. Don't be afraid of this combination – the natural sweetness of the pineapple is enhanced by this bitter condiment, surprisingly enough.

One of the best ways to cool down is to drink a delicious fruit juice. Another favourite drink is fruit juice blended with ice, what Westerners might call a fruit "smoothie". You can have syrup mixed in to sweeten your juice or salt added (as the Thais like it) to bring out the flavour of the fruit.

CONTROVERSIAL DURIAN

People either love or hate durian. Ask any visitor to those Southeast Asian countries where durians are popular (nearly all) to recall the first time they came across it and they will describe, in detail, its "perfume". To most foreigners the durian's odour is repugnant, but for the Asian the fruit commands the utmost respect, even if most hotels prohibit them in hotel rooms. (Signs are often posted near elevators.)

According to devotees, the rewards of eating durian far outweigh any objections to its smell. The only way to enter the great durian debate is to try it for yourself. If you can't face eating the fruit *au naturel* there is durian cake, ice-cream and chewing gum.

◁ **JACKFRUIT**
The ripe, rich yellow sections of the jackfruit are waxy-textured and semi-sweet. When green they are used in curries, and the flowers and young shoots are eaten in salads.

RAMBUTAN ▷
The hairy rambutan (*rambut* means hair in Malay) is a close relative of the lychee, and its translucent, sweet flesh has a similar taste. There is a technique to squeezing it open to avoid squirting yourself with its juices.

▽ **STAR FRUIT**
This sweet, yellow fruit is native to India. It has a thin waxy skin with a crisp texture and sweet-tart juice. It can be found in fruit salads or can be candied and eaten as a confection. The unripe fruit is bright green and is sometimes added to dishes that require an acidic taste.

△ CUSTARD APPLE

The custard apple looks like a small, light green hand-grenade and can be pulled apart by hand. The pulp is soft, often mushy, very sweet and very tasty. It is best to eat it with a spoon.

▽ MANGOSTEEN

Thais believe durian requires the cool, refreshing sweet taste of the mangosteen as a chaser. See if you can guess how many sections your mangosteen has before you break it open.

THAILAND'S GROWING CONCERN

Farming and fishing have always been at the centre of Thai life. Despite rapid industrialisation, this is still the case. Thailand is self-sufficient in food, and agribusiness is an important pillar of the Thai economy, claiming nearly a quarter of GDP and making Thailand the main net food exporter in Asia. Thailand is the world's leading exporter of canned pineapple and has big overseas markets in canned logans and rambutans.

Fruit production is expected to increase as available land and labour resources dwindle and farmers switch from producing staple crops, such as rice and cassava, to cash crops like soya beans, fruits, sugar cane and rubber. Large fruit farmers are starting to process their products before they reach the consumer, and many are now applying for loans to invest in equipment to dry and freeze their produce. Although some of this produce will be sold to Thailand's neighbours, much of it will end up in the snack food departments of Japanese supermarkets – Japanese businesses have already set up factories in Thailand to process fruits, vegetables and nuts for their home market.

◁ DURIAN

The most expensive of Asian fruits has mushy flesh that tastes good with sticky rice and coconut milk. Ignore the smell and you will be rewarded.

JAPANESE PEAR ▷

This crunchy and slightly dry fruit is usually eaten raw. Its semi-sweet flavour can be enhanced by dipping it into slightly salted water.

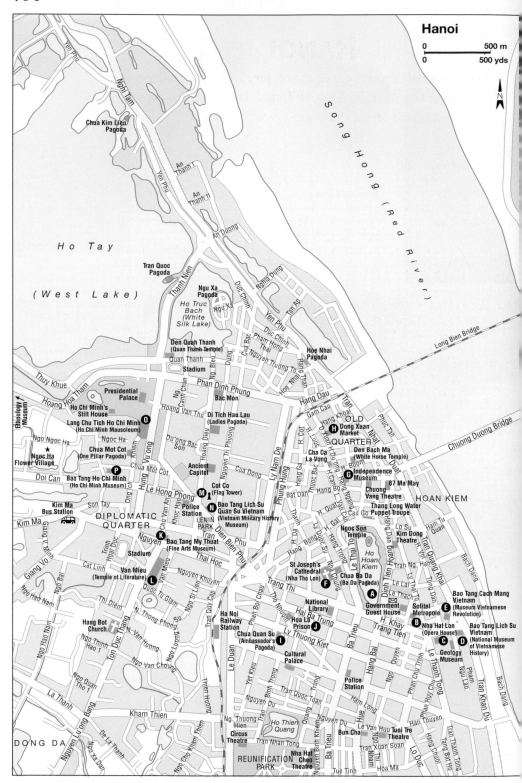

Hanoi

| 0 | 500 m |
| 0 | 500 yds |

Song Hong (Red River)

Ho Tay

(West Lake)

Chua Kim Lien
Pagoda

Yen Phu

Nghi Tam

An Thanh I

An Thanh II

Yen Phu

An Duong

Thanh Nien

Tran Quoc
Pagoda

Ngu Xa
Pagoda

Ho Truc
Bach
(White
Silk Lake)

Ngu Xa

Duc Chinh

Nghia Dung

Tran Ap

Yen Phu

Long Bien Bridge

Den Quah Thanh
(Quan Thanh Temple)

Quan Thanh

Stadium

Cua Bac

Pham Hong
Thai

Nguyen Truong To

Hoe Nhai
Pagoda

Hoe Nhai

Gam Cau

Hang Dau

Hang Khoai

Phuc Tan

Hang Than

OLD
QUARTER

Chuong Duong Bridge

Thuy Khue

Hoang Hoa Tham

Presidential
Palace

Ho Chi Minh's
Stilt House

Lang Chu Tich Ho Chi Minh
(Ho Chi Minh Mausoleum)

Chua Mot Cot
(One Pillar Pagoda)

Bao Tang Ho Chi Minh
(Ho Chi Minh Museum)

Ethnology
Museum

Ngoc Ha

Ngo Ngoc Ha

★
Ngoc Ha
Flower Village

Doi Can

Hong

Vu Vong

Le Hong Phong

Hung

Chua Mot Cot

Phan Dinh Phung

Bac Mon

Hoang Van Thu

Di Tich Hau Lau
(Ladies Pagoda)

Ngo Cam Chan

Ngo
Cam Chan

Nguyen Bieu

Dung

Cua Bac

Duong Bac
Son

Hoang Dieu

Chua Dong

Nguyen Tri Phuong

Cua Dong

Ancient
Capitol

Cot Co
(Flag Tower)

M

Police
Station

LENIN
PARK

N

Bao Tang Lich Su
Quan Su Vietnam
(Vietnam Military History
Museum)

Ly Nam De

Phung Hung

Bat Dan

Hang Ga

Hang Bac

Hang Can

Hang Bo

H. Quat

Cha Ca
La Vong

Den Bach Ma
(White Horse Temple)

Dong Xuan
Market

H

H. Cot

Nha

Hang

G

Independence
Museum

87 Ma May

Chuong
Vang Theatre

Thang Long Water
Puppet Troupe

HOAN KIEM

Lo Su

Cau Go

Gia Ngu

Lan Ong

Lo Su

Ham Tu
Quan

Bach Dang

O

P

Kim Ma
Bus Station

🚌

DIPLOMATIC
QUARTER

Kim Ma

Son Tay

Ong Ich Kiem

Khuc Van Hoan

Dien Bien Phu

Tran
Phu

Le Hong Phong

Nguyen

K

Bao Tang My Thuat
(Fine Arts Museum)

Stadium

Van Mieu
(Temple of Literature)

L

Trinh
Hoai Duc

Cat Linh

Giang Vo

Ngo Hao Nam

Kim Ma

Giang Vo

La Thanh

Nguyen Luong Bang

Van Mieu

Nguyen Khuyen

Quoc Tu Giam

N. Thong Phong

Ngo Si Lien

Ton Duc Thang

Ngo Van Chuong

Ngo Quan
Tho

Ngo Thinh
Hao 1

Ngo Hao Nam

Thi Diem

Ha Noi
Railway
Station

Le Duan

Yet Kieu

Xa Dan

De La Thanh

Kham Thien

Ngo
Cho Kham Thien

Ngo Thuong
Hien

Ho Thien
Quang

Nguyen Du

Circus
Theatre

REUNIFICATION
PARK

Nha Hat
Cheo Theatre

Tran Nhan Tong

Tue Tinh

Hang Bot
Church

Hang Bong

Ha Ba Trung

Phan Boi Chau

Tho Nhuom

Quang Trung

Trang Thi

National
Library

St Joseph's
Cathedral
(Nha Tho Lon)

F

Chua Ba Da
(Ba Da Pagoda)

A

Government
Guest House

Ngoc Son
Temple

Ho
Hoan
Kiem

Le Thai To

Dinh Tien Hoang

Le Thach

Le Lai

Le Lai

Le Thach

Trang Tien

B

Sotitel
Metropole

E

Bao Tang Cach Mang
Vietnam
(Museum Vietnamese
Revolution)

Nha Hat Lon
(Opera House)

C

D

Bao Tang Lich Su
Vietnam
(National Museum
of Vietnamese
History)

Geology
Museum

Phan Chu Trinh

Pham Ngu Lao

Tong Dan

Kim Dong
Theatre

Tran Quang Khai

Tran Ng. Hanh

Trang Thi

Hai Ba Trung

Ly Thuong Kiet

Tran Hung Dao

Hoa Lo
Prison

J

Chua Quan Su
(Ambassador's
Pagoda)

I

Cultural
Palace

Ly Thuong Kiet

H. Khay

Tran Quoc Toan

Nguyen Du

Ba Trieu

Hang Bai

Ham Long

Ngo Hue

Le Van Huu

Hoa Ma

Tuoi Tre
Theatre

Tran Xuan Soan

Lo Duc

Tran Khanh Du

Tran Thanh Tong

Hang Chuoi

Hang Thuyen

Pham Ngu Lao

Nguyen Binh Khiem

Binh Trong

Trung Trac

Trung Nhi

Police
Station

Bun Cha

Bach Dang

DONG DA

Phat Loc

HANOI

Vietnam's capital city may not be the country's most dynamic city –
Ho Chi Minh City leads by far – but Hanoi retains an ambience in
architecture and layout that recalls the earlier French years

Map
on pages
144, 158

Today, with a population of over 3 million, Hanoi ❶, the political and cultural capital of Vietnam, extends more than 2,000 sq. km (800 sq. miles) in size. New buildings in the city centre around Hoan Kiem Lake are restricted to six floors, which leaves Hanoi's original character very much intact, preserved in its traditional pagodas and temples, colonial architecture, tree-lined streets and lakes. The soul of this ancient Thang Long city rests in the old town centre, which dates from the 15th century.

The city centre comprises four districts: Hoan Kiem (Restored Sword), Hai Ba Trung (Two Trung Sisters), Dong Da (where King Quang Trung defeated the Manchu invasion in 1789) and Ba Dinh. It also incorporates 11 integrated suburban districts *(quan)*. In the northwest, the city is bordered by Ho Tay, or West Lake. West of Hanoi, hills extend up to the 1,200-metre (4,000-ft) summit of Mt Ba, 65 km (40 miles) from the city.

Hanoi is accessible from the north by three bridges: Long Bien, Chuong Duong, and the newest, Thang Long, a modern span changing into a four-lane highway to Noi Bai Airport. The 1,682-metre-long (5,520-ft) **Long Bien Bridge** was built by the French and opened in 1902 by Governor-General Doumer, after whom it was originally named. It suffered some damage from American bombing during the Vietnam War, but it was continually repaired. Until 1983, all northbound road and rail traffic passed over it. These days, it is reserved for cyclists, pedestrians and trains.

In the centre of Hanoi

In the very heart of the old town of Hanoi lies **Ho Hoan Kiem** ❹, or Lake of the Restored Sword. Legend has it that in the 15th century, King Le Thai To was given a magic sword by a tortoise that lived in the lake. He used the sword to drive the Chinese from the country, but later the tortoise is said to have snatched the sword from his hand and disappeared into the lake. Near the middle of the lake is a small, 18th-century tower, Thap Rua, or Tortoise Tower.

To the east of Hoan Kiem Lake, behind the main Post Office on Ly Thai To Street, is the **Government Guest House**, a compound with a hotel in the back and an ornate French colonial building, painted yellow with green trim, in front. It was once the palace of the French governor of Tonkin. Today, Vietnamese officials meet visiting foreign dignitaries here.

Across the street from the State Guest House is the venerable **Sofitel Metropole Hotel** ❸, built in 1901 during the French colonial times. Not far from the Metropole is the **Opera House** ❻ (Nha Hat Lon), or the Municipal Theatre, and one of Hanoi's landmarks.

BELOW: Government Guest House.

Legends are woven into Hanoi's history. In 1010, according to one legend, King Ly Thai To founded the city after seeing an auspicious golden dragon rise from the area. He named the city Thang Long, or Ascending Dragon.

Behind the Municipal Theatre, the **National Museum of Vietnamese History** ❿ (Bao Tang Lich Su Vietnam; Tues–Sun 8–11.30am and 1.30–4.30pm; tel: 04-825 1384; entrance fee) is housed in a hybrid-Indochinese style building. The museum opened in 1910, was rebuilt in 1926, and reopened in 1932. Exhibits displayed here cover Vietnam's fascinating and complex history. Nearby, the **Revolutionary Museum** ❼ (Bao Tang Cach Mang; Tues–Sun 8–11.45am and 1.30–4.15pm; tel: 04-825 4151; entrance fee) on Tong Dan Street documents the struggles of the Vietnamese people from ancient times up until 1975.

On the west side of the lake is **Nha Tho Street** (Church Street). Once the property of the Catholic Diocese, it is now lined with upmarket shops and bistros. Facing it is **St Joseph's Cathedral** ❺ (Nha Tho Lon; daily 8–noon, 2–5pm), consecrated on Christmas night in 1886. A narrow passageway next to 5 Nha Tho, leads to the **Ba Da Pagoda** (Chua Ba Da). This charming pagoda was built in the 15th century after the discovery of a stone statue of a woman during the construction of the Thang Long citadel. The statue, which was thought to have magical powers, disappeared and has since been replaced by a wooden replica.

On Ly Quoc Su Street, to the right of the cathedral, is the small **Ly Trieu Quoc Su Pagoda** (Chua Ly Trieu Quoc Su), also known as the Pagoda of Confucius (Chua Kong). It contains some attractive wooden statues. The Bach Ma Temple on Hang Buom Street is dedicated to the deity Bach Ma. Originally built during the 9th century, it was reconstructed in the 18th and 19th centuries.

In a small house on Hang Ngang Street is the **Independence Museum** ❼. Here, Ho Chi Minh wrote Vietnam's declaration of independence, which borrows considerably from America's own declaration, and it was where communist revolutionaries met in secret.

BELOW: art shop, and the St. Joseph's Cathedral.

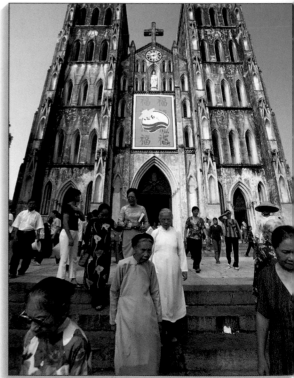

The area around the busy **Dong Xuan Market** in the northern part of the so-called Old Quarter is an interesting place to explore. The market is a good place to find cheap clothing and kitchenware, and in the surrounding streets farmers squat on the pavement selling their produce to passers-by. Southeast of sthe market, at **87 Ma May Street**, is a restored 19-century antique house (daily 8.30am–5.30pm; entrance fee).

Southwest of the lake, several blocks away on Quan Su Street, is **Ambassadors' Pagoda** ❶ (Chua Quan Su). In the 17th century, the site was a house that accommodated visiting foreign ambassadors and envoys from other Buddhist countries. Two blocks away was the infamous **Hoa Lo Prison** ❶ (daily 8–11.30am, 1.30–4.30pm; entrance fee), dubbed the "Hanoi Hilton". The main gate and front portion of the prison have been preserved as a museum. Across the street is the Hanoi People's Court. To the south of the prison and the Quan Su pagoda is a small, lovely lake, Ho Thien Quang, where visitors can rent paddle boats. Across the street is an entrance to **Reunification Park**, and to its right, Hanoi's circus.

The old French Quarter

West from the centre of town is the old French quarter, now the diplomatic area of Hanoi. Here, the old villas house foreign embassies and government offices on quiet, tree-lined streets. The **Fine Arts Museum** ❶ (Bao Tang My Thuat; Tues, Thur, Fri, Sun 8.30am–5pm, Wed and Sat 8.30am–9pm; tel: 04-846 3084; entrance fee), at 66 Nguyen Thai Hoc Street, features an extensive collection of artefacts. Exhibits cover some of Vietnam's ethnic minorities and history. On display are beautiful wooden statues of Buddha from the 18th century, Dong Son bronze drums and other Vietnamese art, both ancient and contemporary.

Map on page 158

TIP

Check out Hanoi's oldest and most fascinating markets: 19–12 Market (Cho 19–12), along Ly Thuong Kiet Street. Its two covered lanes of stalls running through to the next street are crammed with fresh and live produce, dry goods, food stalls, kitchenware and clothes.

BELOW: street flower vendor.

Map
on page
158

Nearby, across the street, is the **Temple of Literature** (Van Mieu; summer daily 7.30am–5.30pm; winter daily 7.30am–5pm; entrance fee). Built in 1070 under the reign of King Ly Thai Tong, the temple is dedicated to Confucius. In 1076, the temple was adjoined by the School of the Elite of the Nation (Quoc Tu Giam), Vietnam's first national university. The large temple enclosure is divided into five walled courtyards. After passing through the temple gate and the first two courtyards, one arrives at the Pavilion of the Constellation of Literature (Khue Van Cac), where the men of letters used to recite their poems. Through the Great Wall Gate (Dai Thanh Mon), an open courtyard surrounds a large central pool known as the Well of Heavenly Clarity (Thien Quang Tinh).

To the north nearby, on Dien Bien Phu Street, is one of the symbols of Hanoi, **Cot Co** ⓜ, the flag tower. Built in 1812 under the Nguyen dynasty as part of the Hanoi citadel, the hexagonal 33.4-metre (110-ft) tower is more or less all that remains of the citadel, which now houses the military. Next to it, **Vietnam Military History Museum** ⓝ (Bao Tang Lich Su Quan Su; Tues–Thur, Sat–Sun 8–11.30am, 1–4.30pm; entrance fee) chronicles Vietnam's battles for independence and unification against the French and American patrons of the former South Vietnam. Across the street is a small, triangular-shaped park with a statue of Lenin. About 100 metres (328 ft) past the flag tower, right on Hoang Dieu Street is a small archaeological dig, **Hanoi Ancient Capital** (Tues–Sun 8–11.30am and 2–4.30pm), and the original city gates. Across the street at No. 30, shrouded by trees, is the home of General Vo Nguyen Giap, now in his 90s.

Excavations at 18 Hoang Dieu to construct government buildings have unearthed an astounding range of artefacts from Hanoi's past. The site is not yet open to the public; across the street is **Ladies Pagoda** (Di Tich Hau Lau). At the corner of Hoang Dieu and Phan Dinh Phung is the North Gate (Bac Mon). From the tower above the gate you can look into the military grounds.

One block west of Hang Dieu looms the imposing and impressive structure of **Ho Chi Minh Mausoleum** ⓞ (Lang Chu Tich Ho Chi Minh; Apr–Oct Tues–Thur 7.30–10.30am, Sat–Sun 7.30–11am; Nov–Mar Tues–Thur 8–11am, Sat–Sun 8–11.30am; free), in Ba Dinh Square. Ho's embalmed corpse lies in a glass casket in this monumental tomb – contrary to his wish to be cremated. It was from this square that Ho Chi Minh read his declaration of independence speech on 2 September 1945. Nearby is the unique **One Pillar Pagoda** (Chua Mot Cot). Built in 1049 under the Ly dynasty, this beautiful wooden pagoda rests on a single stone pillar rising out of a lotus pool. The small Dien Huu Pagoda shares this lovely setting.

Behind the park with the pagodas is the **Ho Chi Minh Museum** ⓟ (Bao Tang Ho Chi Minh; daily 8–11.30am and 2–4pm except Mon and Fri afternoons; entrance fee; tel: 04-846 3752). A massive concrete structure, the museum has some rather bizarre exhibits, but it presents a thorough history of Ho's life.

Ho Truc Bach

From Ba Dinh Square, where the National Assembly building is located across from the mausoleum, and where there is a war memorial, head north towards **White Silk Lake** (Ho Truc Bach). This was the ancient site of Lord Trinh's summer palace, which became a harem where he detained his wayward concubines. This lake derives its name from the fine white silk the concubines were forced to weave for the princesses of ancient Vietnam. Villas, hotels and restaurants have now sprung up around the lake.

Nearby, the ornate temple of **Quan Thanh** (Den Quan Thanh) beside the lake was originally built during the Ly dynasty (1010–1225). It houses a huge bronze bell and an enormous, four-ton bronze statue of Tran Vu, guardian deity of the north, to whom the temple is dedicated. ❏

Mausoleum of
Ho Chi Minh.

OPPOSITE: a
Vietnamese dinner.

HA LONG AND HUE

*Along Vietnam's Pacific coast are two of Southeast Asia's most
spectacular cultural and geographical wonders, mystical
Ha Long Bay and the ancient city of Hue*

Map
on page
144

Heading east from **Hanoi** eventually leads to white-sand beaches washed by **Bien Dong**, or the South China Sea (which remains the focus of contention between Vietnam and China, as both claim rights to the sea and to the archipelago offshore, possibly rich in oil reserves). Before reaching the coast, the road passes through the relatively flat province of Hai Hung, famous for its beautiful orchards. Fruit from Hai Hung, especially longan and lychee, is reputedly the best in northern Vietnam.

Vinh Ha Long

No trip to northern Vietnam would be complete without a trip to Quang Ninh Province, 165 km (100 miles) from Hanoi. This province shares a common border with China in the north, and harbours one of the wonders of the world, with probably the most stunning scenery in Vietnam: **Ha Long Bay ❷** (Vinh Ha Long). The bay's tranquil beauty encompasses 1,500 sq km (560 sq miles) dotted with well over 3,000 limestone islands, many of them not named. Bizarre rock sculptures jutting dramatically from the sea and numerous grottoes have created an enchanted, timeless world, immortalised in the 1992 French film, *Indochine*; Ha Long Bay has been twice designated a UNESCO World Heritage Site: first in 1994 for its natural scenic beauty, and again in 2000 for its great biological interest.

Ha Long Bay's awesome scenery looks the stuff of legends – which it is. Ha Long means "Descending Dragon", originating from the myth that a celestial dragon once flung herself headlong into the sea, her swishing tail digging deep valleys and crevices in the mainland. As she descended into the sea, these filled with water, creating the bay. According to another legend, the Jade Emperor ordered a dragon to halt an invasion by sea from the north. The dragon spewed out jade and jewels which upon hitting the sea turned into wondrous islands and karst formations, creating a natural fortress against enemy ships. The dragon was so enchanted by her creations that she decided to stay in the bay. To this day, local fishermen claim to see the shape of a dragon-like creature in the waters.

Throughout history, Ha Long Bay was the downfall of many marauding invaders. General Ngo Quyen defeated Chinese forces in 938 by embedding hundreds of iron tipped stakes in the Bach Dang River, then luring the fleet upstream in high tide. He then attacked as the tide turned, driving the Chinese downstream and onto the exposed stakes. Incredibly, four centuries later, in 1288, Kublai Khan fell for the same ruse, this time masterminded by General Tran Hung Dao.

OPPOSITE: Ha Long Bay sunset. **BELOW:** collecting salt.

The best time to visit Ha Long is in warmer weather from April to October as you can swim off the boat and relax on sundecks. However, during the typhoon season which peaks in August, boats may cancel due to bad weather. Between January and March, the weather can be cool and drizzly but the swirling mists that swaddle the magnificent limestone outcrops lend an ethereal beauty to it.

BELOW: picture perfect Halong Bay.

Islands and Grottoes

Legends aside, geologists believe that the karst outcrops were formed by a giant limestone sea bed, eroding until only pinnacles remained behind. Locals named them after the shapes they resemble: teapot, toad, elephant's foot, etc. Over the centuries, elements within the rock slowly dissolved by rain formed hundreds of bizarre-shaped grottoes; around 15 are now open to the public.

Boats usually visit a couple of caves en route. The most well known is found on the island nearest to Ha Long City – **Grotto of Wooden Stakes** (Hang Dau Go), where General Tran Hung Dao amassed hundreds of stakes prior to his 1288 victory. On the same island, **Grotto of the Heavenly Palace** (Hang Thien Cung) has some impressive stalactites and stalagmites, as does **Surprise Grotto** (Hang Sung Sot) on an island further south. **Hang Hanh** is a tunnel cave that extends for 2 km (11 miles); access by sampan is strictly regulated by tides. **Three Tunnel Lake** (Ho Ba Ham), a shallow lagoon surrounded by limestone walls on **Dau Bo Island**, can only be reached by navigating three low tunnels at low tide.

Cat Ba Island, the largest in Ha Long Bay at 354 sq. km (136 sq. miles), offers spectacular, rugged landscape – forested limestone peaks, offshore coral reefs, coastal mangrove and freshwater swamps, lakes and waterfalls. Almost half the island and adjacent waters are a national park, with diverse flora and fauna. You can trek through here, cruise through **Lan Ha Bay** or Halong Bay itself. Although the island is dotted with a few villages, Cat Ba town is the main settlement – some boats dock in the fishing harbour, where mini-hotels and basic tourist services are located. Although tourism plays an increasingly dominant role, Cat Ba is still a fishing community.

Many tourist boats spend one or two nights here, or visit the national park.

Despite Cat Ba Island being overrun in the summer with numerous tourist boats in the vicinity, Ha Long Bay is still a peaceful spot. However, several tour companies now sail further east into **Bai Tu Long Bay** in search of more solitude. Bai Tu Long's little-frequented islands such as **Quan Lan Island** – with sweeping deserted beaches and welcoming fishing communities – are now the area's worst kept secret.

A boat trip on the bay is best organised from Hanoi, where numerous tour companies *(see text box below)* offer a variety of tours to suit every interest and budget. These range from one-day trips with a 4-hour cruise, to five-day adventures including luxurious onboard accommodation. Kayaking trips, with a night or two spent on one of the islands, have become an ideal way to see the smaller grottoes and bays. All boats depart daily from Bai Chay in Ha Long City.

A short ferry ride away from Bai Chay, the coal-mining town of Hon Gai has a museum (Tue–Wed and Fri–Sat 8–11.30am, 1.30–4.30pm); it features various archaeological and ethnic artefacts, and a history of the town's coal miners.

Hue, city of kings

The ancient imperial city of the Nguyen kings, **Hue** ❸ is located 12 km (7 miles) from the coast, midway between Hanoi and Ho Chi Minh City on a narrow stretch of land in Thua Thien Hue Province, which borders Laos in the west. The first noble to reach Hue was Lord Nguyen Hoang (1524–1613), in the spring of 1601. He found a particularly good location to build a capital and erected the Phu Xuan Citadel.

Nguyen Hoang also built the **Celestial Lady Pagoda** (Chua Thien Mu), which remains intact on the left bank of the Perfume River, said to be named after a type of fragrant plant that grows near its origins. The seven tiers of the temple's octagonal tower each represent a different reincarnation of Buddha. The main temple, Dai Hung, is in an attractive garden of ornamental shrubs and trees.

BELOW: waiting for boats, Ha Long Bay.

SAILING ON HA LONG BAY

The best way to appreciate Halong Bay is by boat. Every Hanoi tour operator arranges one- to four-day tours of the bay, with transfers, meals and accommodation on a boat. Valiant efforts have been made to regulate the boats and ticketing systems. Complaints of being held hostage by boat captains are no longer heard of, but booking a tour with an agency in Hanoi is still more convenient and recommended. Boats depart from Bai Chay, some 165km (102 miles) east of Hanoi by road. For those with limited time, there are one-day tours with roughly four hours cruising, but this is not worthwhile given the three-hour road journey to Bai Chay.

Most tour operators use standard engine-powered wooden boats with dormitory-style cabins. Luxury junk boats, with top-notch dining, large sundecks and en-suite cabins, are also available. Handspan (tel: 04-933 2375–7, www.handspan.com) operates the most economical trips on board its comfortable *Dragon's Pearl* junk with 18 cabins. Buffalo Tours (tel: 04-828 0702; www.buffalotours.com) operates the mid-priced *Jewel of the Bay* luxury junk with five cabins. Emeraude Classic Cruises (tel: 04-934 0888; www.emeraude-cruises.com) runs the most expensive luxury cruises on a replica paddle steamer.

Nguyen Hoang was the first in an uninterrupted succession of 10 feudal lords to rule over the area of Hue until 1802. That year, after quelling the Tay Son uprising, the 10th Nguyen lord proclaimed himself Emperor Gia Long and founded the Nguyen dynasty, which would last for 143 years, until 1945. But just 33 years into the dynasty's reign, the French invaded Hue. A quick succession of emperors graced the throne. The anti-French demonstrations and strikes of the colonial era were followed by the Japanese occupation in 1940 and the abdication of Bao Dai in 1945, the last Nguyen emperor, in August that year.

The relative peace that reigned after 1954, when Hue became part of South Vietnam following the country's division into two parts, was shattered under Ngo Dinh Diem's regime. Repressive anti-Buddhist propaganda sparked off a series of demonstrations and protest suicides by Buddhist monks in 1963.

Always an important cultural, intellectual and historical city, Hue remains one of Vietnam's main attractions. The charm of this timeless old city lies not only in its historical and architectural value, but also in the natural beauty of its location along the banks of the Perfume River.

Chinese motif, 17th-century building.

The Imperial City

The **Imperial City** (Dai Noi; daily 7am–5.30pm; entrance fee) of Hue is made up of three walled enclosures. The Hoang Thanh (Yellow Enclosure) and the Tu Cam Thanh (Forbidden Purple City) are enclosed within the Kinh Thanh (exterior enclosure). Stone, bricks and earth were used to build the exterior wall, which measured 8 metres (26 ft) high and 20 metres (65 ft) thick, built during the reign of Emperor Gia Long. The Yellow Enclosure is the middle wall enclosing the imperial city and its palaces, temples and flower gardens. Through the

BELOW: guardian at Thien Mu Pagoda, and part of Thien Mu Pagoda.

Ngo Mon (Noon Gate), walk across the Golden Water Bridge, which at one time was reserved for the emperor. It leads to the **Palace of Supreme Harmony** (Dien Thai Hoa), the most important palace in the imperial city. Here, the emperor received local dignitaries and foreign diplomats, and the royal court also organised important ceremonies here. Built in 1805 during Gia Long's reign, the palace was renovated first by Min Mang in 1834 and later by Khai Dinh in 1924. Today it stands in excellent condition, its ceilings and beams decorated in red lacquer and gold inlay.

The temples within the enclosure are dedicated to various lords: the temple of **Trieu Mieu** to Nguyen Kim; the **Thai Mieu** to Nguyen Hoang and his successors; the **Phung Tien** temple to the emperors of the reigning dynasty; and the **Hung Mieu** to Nguyen Phuc Lan, emperor Gia Long's father. The well-preserved **The Mieu** is dedicated to the sovereigns of the Nguyen dynasty, and houses the shrines of seven Nguyen emperors plus monuments to the revolutionary emperors Han Nghi, Thanh Thai and Duy Tan, added in 1959.

In front of the temple, completely undamaged, is the magnificent **Pavilion of Splendour** (Hien Lam Cac), with the nine dynastic urns, known as Cuu Dinh, lined up before it. The **Dien Tho** palace, built by emperor Gia Long in 1804, served as the Queen Mother's residence. Beyond the Palace of Supreme Harmony, the **Forbidden Purple City** (Tu Cam Thanh) was reserved solely for the emperor and the royal family. This area was extensively damaged during the Tet Offensive of 1968, but it is undergoing continuing renovation. The main building in the enclosure is the **Palace of Celestial Perfection** (Can Thanh). The other once-grand palace, Can Chanh, was where the emperor used to receive dignitaries. Sadly, it is now in ruins.

Map on page 144

The urns in the Pavilion of Splendour, cast in 1822 during Minh Mang's reign, are decorated with motifs of the sun, moon, clouds, birds, animals, dragons, mountains, rivers, and historic events. Hundreds of artisans from all over Vietnam were involved.

BELOW: river view from Thien Mu.

Map
on page
144

TIP

Minh Mang's tomb can be reached by hiring a small motor-boat from any of the local owners opposite the Perfume River Hotel. Alternatively, take a car to Ban Viet village. From there, hire a boat across the Perfume River.

RIGHT: tomb of Tu Duc.
BELOW: entrance to Khai Dinh's tomb.

Another world lies beyond the walls of the citadel, which is surrounded in the south and east by Hue's commercial area. This is confined mainly to the area around the arched Trang Tien Bridge, which spans the Perfume River, and the Gia Hoi Bridge. Both bridges lend their names to the areas surrounding them. Located in Phu Cat, with its mainly Chinese and Minh Huong (Vietnamese-Chinese) population, is the lively **Dong Ba Market**, which has been around since the beginning of the 20th century.

The **Museum of Royal Fine Arts** at 3 Le Truc (Tues–Sat 7am–5pm; entrance fee), built in 1845 under Emperor Thieu Tri, houses treasures bequeathed by the royal family and nobility. Across the street, the **Hue Provincial Museum** (daily 7am–5pm; entrance fee) was opened in 1975 and renovated in 2005. It houses archaeological artefacts from the Champa and Sa Huynh epochs in the central building. To the left and right are museums of the first (French) and second (American) Indochina wars. Missiles, tanks and other weaponry guard the courtyard.

Royal tombs and pagodas

Unlike the other dynasties, the Nguyen dynasty did not bury its members in their native village, Gia Mieu, in Thanh Hoa Province. Instead, their imperial tombs lie scattered on the hillsides on either side of the Perfumed River, to the west of Hue. Although the dynasty had 13 kings, only seven of them reigned until their deaths. And only they are laid to rest in this valley of kings. Behind and on either side of the temple are the houses built for the king's concubines, servants and soldiers who guarded the royal tomb. The emperor's body is laid in a concealed place (*bao thanh*), enclosed by high walls behind securely locked metal doors. To reach the tombs, head southwards from Hue.

Minh Mang's Tomb is located where the Ta Trach and Huu Trach tributaries of the Perfume River meet. Its construction was begun a year before his death, in 1840, and was finished by his successor Thieu Tri in 1843. The setting is at its best in mid March, when the Trung Minh and Tan Nguyet lakes blossom with a mass of beautiful lotus flowers.

Tu Duc's Tomb, 8 km (5 miles) southwest of Hue, can be reached by a very pleasant cycle ride through pine forests and lush hills. The mausoleum construction, begun in 1864, took three years to complete. **Thieu Tri's Tomb** is located nearby. Thieu Tri, Minh Mang's son, was the third Nguyen emperor from 1841 to 1847.

Khai Dinh's Tomb is completely different from any of the other Nguyen tombs. If anything, it resembles a European castle, its architecture a blend of the oriental and occidental. A grandiose dragon staircase leads up to the first courtyard, from where further stairs lead to a courtyard lined with stone statues of elephants, horses, civil and military mandarins.

Gia Long's Tomb, 16 km (10 miles) from Hue on a hillside, is somewhat inaccessible by road. However, a more pleasant way to reach the tomb is by boat. The tomb, began in 1814, was completed a year after the emperor's death in 1820. Despite incurring damage during the Vietnam War, the wild beauty of the site, with its mountain backdrop of Thien Tho, makes the effort to get there well worthwhile. ❑

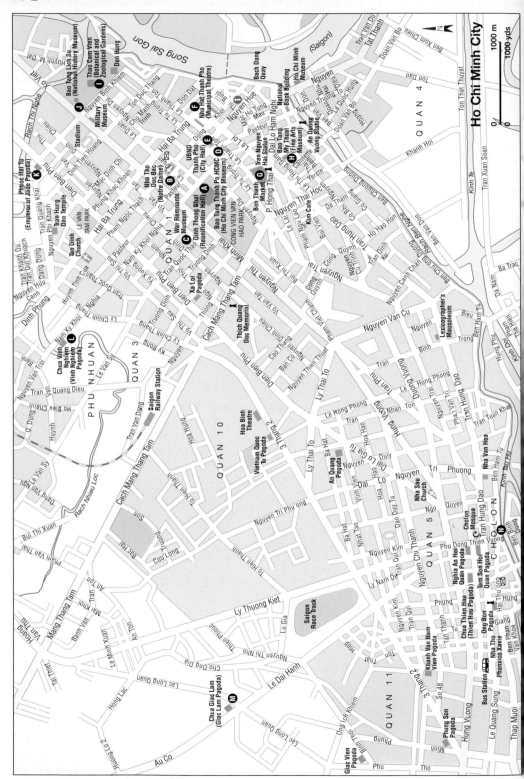

Ho Chi Minh City

Thao Cam Vien (Botanical and Zoological Gardens)
Den Hung
Bao Tang Lich Su (National History Museum)
Bach Dang Quay
Ho Chi Minh Museum
Military Museum
Nha Hat Thanh Pho (Municipal Theatre)
Nguyen Hue
National Bank Building
Stadium
An Duong Vuong Statue
Bao Tang My Thuat (Fine Arts Museum)
Phuoc Hai Tu (Emperor of Jade Pagoda)
Nha Tho Duc Bac (Notre Dame)
UBND Thanh Pho (City Hall)
Tran Hung Dao Temple
War Remnants Museum
Dinh Thong Nhat (Reunification Hall)
Bao Tang Thanh Po HCMC (Ho Chi Minh City Museum)
Tan Dinh Church
Ben Thanh Market
Lexicographer's Mausoleum
Xa Loi Pagoda
Chua Vinh Nghiem (Vinh Nghiem Pagoda)
Thich Quang Duc Memorial
Saigon Railway Station
Hoa Binh Theatre
Vietnam Quoc Tu Pagoda
An Quang Pagoda
Nha Sau Church
Cholon Mosque
Nghia An Hoi Quan Pagoda
Tam Son Hoi Quan Pagoda
Khanh Van Nam Vien Pagoda
Chua Thien Hau (Thien Hau Pagoda)
Ong Bon Pagoda
Nha Tho Phanxico Xavie
Bus Station
Saigon Race Track
Phung Son Pagoda
Chua Giac Lam (Giac Lam Pagoda)
Giac Vien Pagoda

QUAN 1
QUAN 3
QUAN 4
QUAN 5
QUAN 10
QUAN 11
PHU NHUAN
CHOLON

Song Sai Gon (Saigon)

HO CHI MINH CITY

*Once known as Saigon – and still called so by many residents –
and once the capital of the former South Vietnam, this southern
city is the entrepreneurial centre of Vietnam today*

Map
on pages
144, 172

Built on the site of an ancient Khmer city, **Ho Chi Minh City ❹** was a thinly populated area of forests, swamps and lakes until the 17th century. By the end of the 18th century, the area had become an important trading centre within the region. Different theories expound on the origins of the name "Saigon" – what Ho Chi Minh City was called before the Communists changed the official name of the city. The name Saigon is still used by many people, even in official or public capacities. The river coursing through the city remains the Saigon River, for example, and the state-owned tour company is Saigon Tourism. Some say the name derives from the former name Sai Con, a transcription of the Khmer words *prei kor* (kapok-tree forest), or *prei nokor* (the forest of the kingdom), in reference to the Cambodian viceroy's residence, which was located in the region of present-day Cholon.

In the 19th century, southern Vietnam continued to prosper. In 1859, the French captured Saigon and it became the capital of the French colony of Cochinchina a couple of years later. The French filled in the ancient canals, drained marshlands, built roads, laid out streets and quarters, and planted trees. The city developed rapidly, acquiring something of the character of a French provincial town, served by two steam-powered trams.

After the division of the country in 1954 into North Vietnam and South Vietnam, Saigon became the capital of the Republic of South Vietnam, until it fell to the Communists in April of 1975. The revolutionary authorities renamed it Ho Chi Minh City, after the founder of the modern Vietnamese state. Ho Chi Minh was, of course, anathema to supporters of the southern regime that lost the war. To many of its 7 million inhabitants, the city remains Saigon.

The modern city

Today, 50 km (30 miles) inland from the coast, Vietnam's largest city and river port sprawls across an area of 2,000 sq. km (760 sq. miles) on the banks of the Saigon River. The French presence still remains in this southern city, lingering not only in the minds of the older generation but physically in the legacy of colonial architecture, and in the long, tree-lined avenues, streets and highways they left behind.

Prominently located in the city's District *(Quan)* 1 is a building that symbolises, to the Communists, the decadence of the Saigon regime. The former Presidential Palace of South Vietnam is now called **Reunification Hall ❹** (Dinh Thong Nhat; daily 7.30– 11am, 1–4pm; entrance fee). Surrounded by extensive gardens, this large and modern edifice rests on the site of the former French governor's residence, the

BELOW: city street.

Interior of the former Presidential Palace, now known as Reunification Hall.

BELOW: Communist tank entering the Presidential Palace in 1975.

Norodom Palace, which dated back to 1868. After the Geneva Agreement put an end to French occupation, the new president of South Vietnam, Ngo Dinh Diem, installed himself in the palace and called it Independence Palace. In 1962, the palace was bombed by two South Vietnamese air force officers and a new building was erected to replace the damaged structure. The present building was designed by Ngo Viet Thu, a Paris-trained Vietnamese architect, and completed in 1966.

The left wing of the palace was damaged by another renegade South Vietnamese pilot in early 1975, and before the month was out, on 30 April, tanks from the Communist forces crashed through the palace's front wrought-iron gates and overthrew the South Vietnamese government.

Today, the former palace can be visited as a museum, with everything left much as it was in April 1975 when South Vietnam ceased to exist. The ground floor includes the banquet room, the state chamber, and the cabinet room, which was used for the daily military briefings during the period leading up to the overthrow of the South Vietnamese government. In back of the palace is Cong Vien Van Hao Park, a nice and shady green spot. In front, Le Duan is bordered by a large park shaded with trees.

Further down Le Duan is the **Cathedral of Notre Dame** ❸ (Nha Tho Duc Bac; daily 8–11am, 2–5pm), with two bell towers, standing in the square across from the post office. Construction of this cathedral began in 1877, and it was consecrated in 1880. A statue of the Virgin Mary stands in front of the cathedral, looking down Dong Khoi Street.

Across the street, the main **Post Office** (daily 6am–9.30pm) at 2 Cong Xa Paris, with its gingerbread facade, has been repainted and repaired but retains its

old tile floors, wooden writing tables and benches, and a map of Saigon in 1892.

The former War Crimes Exhibition, now the **War Remnants Museum** ●
(Bao Tang Chung Tich Chien Tranh; 7.30am–noon and 1.30–5pm; entrance
fee) occupies the former U.S. Information Agency building on Vo Van Tan
Street, near Reunification Hall. Among items on display here are American
tanks, infantry weapons, photographs of war atrocities committed by the Americans, and the original French guillotine brought to Vietnam in the 20th century,
which saw a lot of use during the colonial period. Graphic pictures of deformed
children illustrate the effects of chemical defoliants such as Agent Orange.
Although a visit here is likely to be distressing, it is a sobering reminder of the
human cost of war and is a must-see for many visitors.

The **Ho Chi Minh City Museum** ● (Bao Tang Thanh Pho HCMC, daily
8–11.30am and 1–4.30pm; entrance fee), one block east from Reunification
Hall on Ly Tu Trong Street, is found in a white neoclassical structure once
known as Gia Long Palace. The walls of the former ballrooms of this colonial
edifice are now hung with pictures of the war, and there are displays of the flat-
bottomed boats in which Viet Cong soldiers hid guns.

A network of reinforced concrete bunkers stretching all the way to the Reunification Hall lies beneath the building. Within this underground network were
living areas and a meeting hall. It was here that President Diem and his brother
hid in the early 1960s just before they fled to a church in Cholon, where they
were captured and subsequently shot.

If Reunification Hall is a symbol of the former South Vietnam regime, then
the **City Hall** ● (UBND Thanh Pho), at the top of Nguyen Hue Street, is the
symbol of the French colonial era. It was finished in 1908 after almost 16 years

Map on page 172

BELOW: Notre
Dame, and city hall.

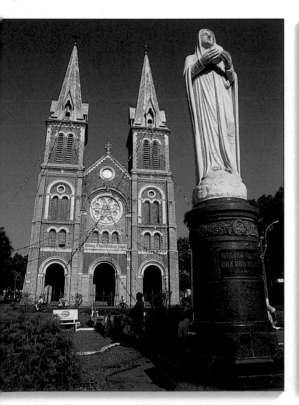

of ferment over its style and situation. Its ornate facade and equally ornate interior, complete with crystal chandeliers and wall-size murals, is now the headquarters of the Ho Chi Minh City People's Committee. Illuminated at night, the building is a lure for insect-hungry geckos.

Across the street, near the **Rex Hotel**, there is a plaza with a statue of Ho Chi Minh in his role as favourite uncle to all children. The plaza is crowded on weekend nights with young people, parents with children, and touts.

Nguyen Hue is a broad boulevard lined with fancy hotels and upscale restaurants. This area of town buzzes with energy, especially at night. At the corner of Le Loi, there is another plaza with a fountain that is crowded with a carnival-like atmosphere into the evenings. Near the end of Le Loi is the **Municipal Theatre F** (Nha Hat Thanh Pho), which faces Dong Khoi Street between the Caravelle and the Continental hotels. The theatre was originally built in 1899 for opera, but was used as the fortress headquarters of the South Vietnam National Assembly. These days, it serves its original purpose, and every week, a different program is on show there – anything from traditional Vietnamese theatre to acrobatics, gymnastics and disco music.

At the junction of Ham Nghi, Le Loi and Tran Hung Dao boulevards, in the centre of town, is the busy **Ben Thanh Market G**. The market covers over 11,000 sq. metres (120,000 sq. ft) and was opened in 1914. Here is an amazing collection of produce, meat, foods, CD players, televisions, cameras, calculators, refrigerators, fans, jeans and leather bags, all imported. At the back of the market, small food stalls serve a wide variety of local dishes and snacks. Not far from the Ben Thanh Market, down Duc Chinh Street, is the **Fine Arts Museum H** (Bao Tang My Thuat; Tues–Sun 9am–4.45pm; entrance fee), housed in a grand

Map on page 172

colonial-era building. Displays include ancient and contemporary Vietnamese art, porcelain and sculpture.

The **Mariamman Hindu Temple**, three blocks from the Ben Thanh Market and on Truong Dinh Street, was built at the end of the 19th century and caters to the city's small population of Hindu Tamils.

At the end of Le Duan, the **Botanical and Zoological Gardens ❶** (Thao Cam Vien) provides a welcome alternative to the noisy chaos of the streets and constitutes the most peaceful place in Ho Chi Minh City. The attractive gardens were established in 1864 by two Frenchmen – one a botanist, the other a veterinarian – as one of the first projects the French embarked upon after they established their new colony. The zoological section has been refurbished and houses birds, tigers, elephants, crocodiles and other indigenous species in cages built during the colonial era.

National History Museum ❿ (Bao Tang Lich Su; Tues–Sun 8–11am and 1.30–4.30pm; entrance fee), located to the left of the entrance of the botanical gardens, was built by the French in 1927. It documents the evolution of Vietnam's various cultures, from the Dong Son Bronze Age civilisation through to the Funan civilisation, the Chams and the Khmers. Among its exhibits are many stone and bronze relics, stelae, bronze drums, Cham art and ceramics, and a display of the traditional costumes of ethnic minorities. Behind the building, on the third floor, is a research library with an interesting and quite extensive collection of books from the French era. To the right of the entrance is the Den Hung, a temple dedicated to the ancestors of Hung Vuong, founding king of Vietnam.

The small Sino-Vietnamese **Emperor of Jade Pagoda ⓚ** (Phuoc Hai Tu), at 73 Mai Thi Luu, dates from 1909. It was built by Cantonese Buddhists and is

BELOW:
a popular intersection with Rex Hotel and the City Hall.

Map on page 172

one of the city's most colourful pagodas. The elaborately-robed and Daoist Jade Emperor surveys the main sanctuary. Just to his left is the triple-headed, 18-armed statue of Phat Mau Chau De, mother of the Buddhas of the Middle, North, East, West and South. A door off to the left of the Jade Emperor's chamber leads to the Hall of Ten Hells, where carved wooden panels portray, in no uncertain detail, the fate that awaits those sentenced to the diverse torments found in the 10 regions of hell.

The Buddhist **Vinh Nghiem Pagoda** ❶ (Chua Vinh Nghiem) at 339 Nguyen Van Troi, District 3, is the largest of the pagodas in the city. Built with aid from the Japanese Friendship Association, this Japanese-style pagoda was begun in 1964 and finished in 1973. The temple's screen and large bell were made in Japan. The bell, a gift from Japanese Buddhists, was presented during the Vietnam War as the embodiment of a prayer for an early end to the conflict. The large three-storey funeral tower behind the main temple holds ceramic burial urns containing the ashes of the dead.

The **Giac Lam Pagoda** ⓜ (Chua Giac Lam) on the western outskirts of the city and thought to be the oldest pagoda in the city, dates from the end of the 17th century. Carved wooden pillars within the main building bear gilded inscriptions in old Vietnamese *nom* characters, which have also been used on the red tablets that record the biographies of the monks of previous generations, whose portraits adorn the left wall. The pagoda houses many beautifully carved jackwood statues.

Cholon

Ho Chi Minh City's Chinatown, **Cholon** ⓝ, was formerly a separate city, but it is now in the Ho Chi Minh City's District 5, thanks to the outward growth of the suburbs. Cholon remains a thriving commercial centre in its own right. With a population of over 1 million Hoas – Vietnamese of Chinese origin – Cholon has come a long way since 1864, when it was home to just 6,000 Chinese, mostly shopkeepers or traders, 200 Indians and 40,000 Vietnamese. Today, countless small family businesses operate in this noisy and bustling Chinatown.

Two interesting temples can be visited on Nguyen Trai Street, near Cholon. At number 710 is the richly-decorated **Thien Hau Pagoda**, or Chua Thien Hau (Heavenly Lady), more commonly known as Chua Ba (Women's Pagoda). This Chinese pagoda, dedicated to the Goddess Protector of Sailors, was built by Cantonese Buddhists at the end of the 18th century. The temple is frequented mainly by women, who bring their offerings to the altar of the Heavenly Lady. Among the other altars is one dedicated to the protection of women and newborn babies, and yet another to sterile women or mothers who have no sons.

The smaller **Ha Chuong Pagoda** (Chua Ha Chuong), at number 802, contains several wooden sculptures and statues, including a statue of the god of happiness and an altar for sterile women.

A large and elegant mosque, built in 1935, on Dong Du Street serves the city's Islamic community. Only a handful of Indian Muslims remain, since most fled the country after 1975. ❑

RIGHT: fountain of Reunification Hall, and Le Duan Boulevard.
BELOW: dockside, Saigon River.

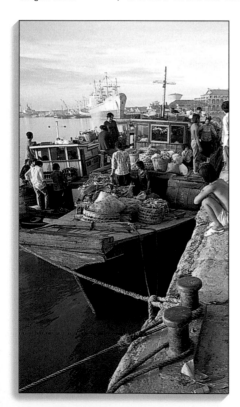

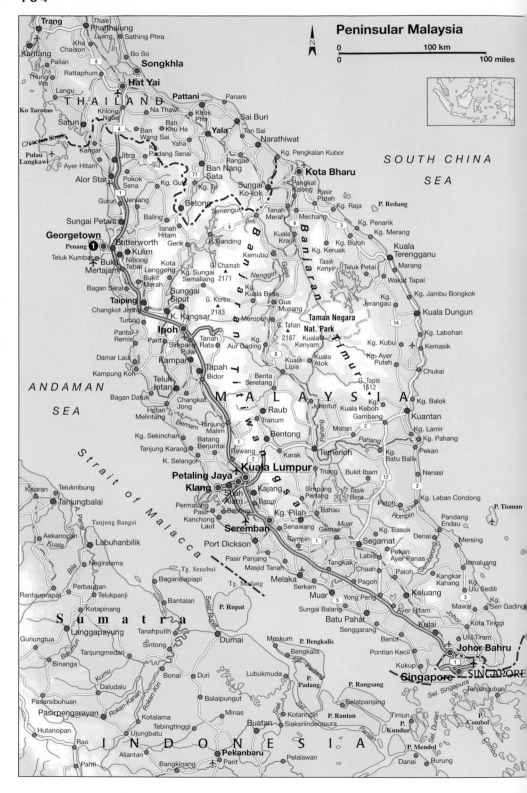

Peninsular Malaysia

MALAYSIA

Once the anchor of the British Empire in Southeast Asia,
Malaysia has an especially independent identity

Over the centuries, Malaysia has been open to millions of visitors from all over the globe, and its people have changed, absorbed and adapted customs and traditions from far-flung countries to suit the Malaysian way of life. Travel brochures romantically depict Malaysia's way of life as a land of beaches with coconut palms and sands as fine as flour, lost idyllic islands and amazing coral reefs.

On the other hand, the pages of Somerset Maugham's short stories paint vivid mental pictures of colonial bungalows set in the heart of a rubber plantation, with tea served on the verandah by a young Malay boy, while the Indian *punkah wallah* moves the fan into action to keep the *orang putih* (white man) cool in the heat of the tropics. Another portrayal of Malaysia lies between the covers of naturalist Alfred Russel Wallace's *Malay Archipelago*, allowing us to imagine ancient jungles screaming with monkeys, brimming with butterflies, and hiding legendary animals such as the most intelligent of primates (next to humans), the orang-utan.

Situated in the middle of Southeast Asia, with a land area of 329,000 sq. km (127,000 sq. miles), Malaysia is about the size of Japan, but with only a fraction of the population – at over 26 million compared to Japan's 127 million. Peninsular Malaysia accounts for 40 percent of the land area and 86 percent of the population. The East Malaysian states of Sabah and Sarawak are separated from the peninsula by 640 km (400 miles) of the South China Sea, but each of the 13 states has a charm and character of its own. Malay and indigenous tribes make up over half the population, while Chinese, Indians and others also come under the broad spectrum that is covered by the term "Malaysian".

Since independence in 1957, Malaysia has faced a series of economic and political pitfalls and triumphs. Perhaps the biggest achievement is a complete transformation of the Malaysian economy from almost total dependence on raw commodities, such as rubber and tin, to a broad manufacturing base.

Kuala Lumpur possesses the world's tallest buildings and orderly traffic snarls to rival Manhattan's. But beneath this modernity are Chinese shophouses and a palpable colonial residue. The island of Penang, once the British Empire's most important Southeast Asian outpost, is a bit complicated to define easily, for its sandy beaches and cluttered, old-feeling urban centre don't fit in the same descriptive breath. And Sarawak and Sabah, on the island of Borneo, which Malaysia shares with Indonesia, are breathtaking in both their biological diversity and grandeur and in the reckless way many of the natural resources, especially wood, have been exploited. ❑

PRECEDING PAGES: spinning tops on the peninsular east coast; taking a break in front of the colonial-era Sultan Abdul Samad Building in Kuala Lumpur.

Decisive Dates

The early centuries

38,000 BC: Remains of people found in Sarawak, on Borneo, date back 400 centuries.

2500 BC: Proto-Malays spread south from Yunnan area in China.

300 BC: Earliest signs of Bronze and Iron Age cultures in Malaysia.

200 BC: Start of trading contacts with India and China.

100 BC–AD 200: Emergence of trading kingdoms in the Isthmus of Kra.

AD 500–800: Development of local trading polities

with Hindu-Buddhist orientation on Bujang Valley and in northern Perak.

1290: First Muslim states begin to develop in northern Sumatra.

The rise of Malacca

1400: Foundation of Malacca.

1403–10: Malacca comes under protection of imperial China.

1409: Emperor of China sends Admiral Zheng Ho to Malacca to proclaim it a city and kingdom.

1445: Malacca becomes a sultanate.

1450: Expansion of Malaccan "empire".

1509: The first Portuguese arrive at Malacca.

1511: Malacca falls to the Portuguese.

1511–1699: Empire of Johor under the Malacca line.

1528: Sultan Muzaffar Shah establishes the Perak Kingdom.

1641: The Dutch take Malacca from the Portuguese; start of Dutch dominance in area.

1699: Assassination of Sultan Mahmud of Johor at Kota Tinggi.

1699–1819: Empire of Johor, mostly at Riau, under Bendahara line.

1699–1784: Period of Minangkabau-Bugis struggle for domination of the Straits of Malacca.

1722: First ruler of Terengganu Kingdom installed.

1784: Death of Raja Haji at Malacca; Dutch break Bugis power in area.

1786: British occupy Penang.

1812: Death of Sultan Mahmud Shah, last ruler of united Johor-Riau kingdom.

Colonial Malaya

1819: British occupy Singapore.

1824: Anglo-Dutch Treaty; Malacca is peacefully ceded to the British.

1826: British treaty with Bangkok limits the spread of Thai influence on the Malay Peninsula.

1831–32: The Naning War.

1840s: The importance of tin increases, bringing an influx of Chinese tin miners to the western coast.

1841: James Brooke established as Rajah of Sarawak.

1846: British annex the island of Labuan.

1858–68: Civil war in Pahang.

1866: Start of Selangor civil war.

1874: Start of British intervention and control in Perak, Selangor and Sungei Ujung.

1875–76: The Perak War.

1881: British North Borneo Chartered Company establishes a centre in North Borneo (what is present-day Sabah).

1891–95: Pahang Rebellion.

1895–1905: Mat Salleh Rebellion. The introduction of new taxes had earlier created general discontent, and Mat Salleh gathers many supporters in his revolt against the North Borneo Company. (Today, he is still regarded as one of Sabah's most famous heroes.)

1896: Treaty of Federation – the Federated Malay States (FMS) are created.

1909: Treaty of Bangkok transfers four northern Malay states from Thai to British control.

1914: Johor brought under British control.

1914–18: World War I.

1920–41: British adopt decentralisation policy in FMS; early signs of a Malay nationalism opposing British rule begin to surface.

Malaya, Merdeka, Malaysia

1941–45: Japanese conquest and occupation.

1945: British reoccupy Malaysia.

1946: Malayan Union Scheme introduced and anti-Malayan Union Movement; formation of UMNO; formation of MIC; Sarawak and British North Borneo become Crown colonies.

1948: Malayan Union Scheme abandoned; Federation of Malaya inaugurated. State of emergency declared by government.

1954: Large numbers of Communist guerrillas are killed. Many more surrender in 1958, and the few remaining guerrillas retreat deep into the jungle.

1955: With the Communists largely eliminated, Malayans begin to clamour for independence.

1956: Tunku leads a delegation to London to negotiate for independence.

1957: Malaya becomes independent, and the Union Jack is lowered for the last time.

1960: The state of emergency ends.

Post-independence

1960: Formation of the Association of Southeast Asia (ASA) with the Philippines and Thailand.

1961: Tunku proposes a political association – called Malaysia – that would include Malaya, Singapore, North Borneo, Sarawak and Brunei.

1963: Creation of Malaysia.

1963–66: Confrontation with Indonesia, which intensifies its "Crush Malaysia" campaign. In 1966, Soekarno is ousted from power in Indonesia; the new Indonesian government, led by Soeharto, is not keen to continue the confrontation, and a peace agreement brings the conflict to an end. The Philippines drops its claim on Sabah and recognises Malaysia.

1965: Singapore leaves Federation and becomes an independent nation.

1969: Riots in the wake of the general elections on 13 May are the result of simmering racial tension between Malays and Chinese. Violent outbreaks, mainly in Kuala Lumpur, kill hundreds of people and destroy a considerable amount of property.

1970: Start of the New Economic Policy (NEP), established to encourage a fairer distribution of wealth among the races.

1981: Malaysia's fourth prime minister, Dato' Seri Dr Mahathir Mohamad, takes office.

1983: Constitutional crisis involving the position of Malaysia's hereditary rulers.

LEFT: Sultan Abu Bakar of Johor.

RIGHT: Tun Dr Mahathir Mohamad, Malaysia's Prime Minister for over two decades.

1987: UMNO racked by power struggle between Mahathir Mohamad and Tengku Razaleigh Hamzah.

1988: Deregistration of UMNO; formation of UMNO *Baru* (New UMNO) by Mahathir Mohamad.

1989: Communist Party of Malaysia abandons its 41-year armed struggle to overthrow the government.

1990: General elections – the ruling coalition retains its two-third majority in Parliament.

1990s: National car project, Proton, leads the move to transform Malaysia into a fully developed nation.

1996: Malaysia launches its first satellite.

1997: Petronas Twin Towers completed. During the Asian financial crisis, currency control laws are imposed to stop the free fall of the ringgit.

1998: Kuala Lumpur is the first Asian city to host the Commonwealth Games. The arrest of deputy prime minister Anwar Ibrahim provokes a political crisis.

1999: Mahathir is re-elected with a comfortable majority, although the Islamic Party (PAS) gains ground. Anwar Ibrahim is jailed on charges of corruption.

2001: Poor US economy stymies Malaysia's growth.

2003: Mahathir retires and Abdullah Ahmad Badawi is appointed as the new Prime Minister.

2004: In a ringing endorsement for the moderate and consensus-seeking Abdullah Badawi, the ruling Barisan coalition wins the elections by a landslide victory, with PAS-controlled Terengganu returned to the government.

2005 The ringgit is unpegged from the US dollar. ❏

THE MALAYSIANS

Islam, colonialism and the Orang Asli provide the threads for the multi-ethnic and interwoven culture of the Malaysian people, not all of who are Malay

The traveller in Malaysia will encounter warm and engaging people, their lifestyles embedded with rich yet culturally diverse traditions. First there are the Orang Asli, the indigenous people of Malaysia who have managed to retain some of their centuries-old roots. Those who followed, the Malays, built upon traditions of the soil and ocean, but embraced influences from elsewhere as well. And because of its rich resources and strategic location, Malaysia attracted still others, including Indians, Chinese, and Europeans.

Orang Asli

The Malay term *orang asli* means "original people" and covers three more or less distinct groups and a score or more of separate tribes. Orang Asli has become a convenient term for explaining those groups of people who do not belong to the three predominant races found on peninsular Malaysia. Of the estimated 90,000 Orang Asli, 60 percent are jungle dwellers, while the other 40 percent are coastal peoples, many of them dependent upon fishing.

The Negritos mostly inhabit the northeast and northwest, and are the only truly nomadic tribes of the Orang Asli. Practising little or no cultivation, the Negrito tribes pride themselves on their mobility, and possessions are thought only to be a hindrance to their lifestyle.

The Senoi are thought to have common ancestors with the hill tribes of northern Cambodia and Vietnam, arriving in present-day Malaysia between 6,000 and 8,000 years ago.

The last group of Orang Asli were the latest group to arrive, no earlier than 4,000 years ago. Many of this group have a distinct resemblance to the Malays, not surprising as modern Malays have a common ancestry with many of them.

Malays

The Malays, long linked to the land, are known as *Bumiputra*, or Sons of the Soil. Although the rift between the farm and the city generally

---

LEFT: Muslim girls. **RIGHT:** Orang Asli family.

widens as years go by, it does not threaten the strong unity the Malays derive from a common faith. The laws of Islam immediately set a Malay apart from non-Malay Malaysians. With ample food and a warm climate, life in the more isolated villages remained the same for centuries. Today, little has changed, for the most

part, as the Malay *kampung* remain peaceful enclaves where the simplicity of an uncluttered life is still cherished.

Intermarriage between races is uncommon, though Muslim foreigners are accepted, keeping the Malay-Muslim cultural identity distinctly separate. In the home of the Malay family, traditional customs are observed daily. The village mosque summons the faithful to prayer several times a day, often interrupting evening television programmes that are now an everyday part of kampung family life.

Muslims in Malaysia are subject to enforceable religious laws, such as that a Muslim woman can't be alone with a non-related male.

Indians

Indians began visiting Malaysia 2,000 years ago following rumours of fortune in a land their ancestors knew as Suvarnadvipa, the fabled "golden peninsula". Tamil blood even flows through the royal lineage dating back to 13th-century Melaka (Malacca), where the first sultanate grew up. But it was not until the 19th century that Indians arrived and stayed in large numbers, employed mainly as rubber tappers or other plantation labourers. Most came from southern India, and approximately 80 percent were Tamil and Hindu, with smaller numbers of Sikh, Bengali, Keralan, Telugu and Parsi.

import and export companies would seem to make the numbers far greater.

Mainland China remains important to the Chinese, but until recently, Malaysian Chinese were forbidden by the Malaysian government to return to mainland China for fear of Communist intrusions. But the older generations regularly sent financial help to relatives in China, while others saved their money to return and die on their home soil.

The Chinese in Malaysia are defined by their history of hardship and pioneering, as well as the three important Chinese ethical threads: Confucianism, Daoism and Buddhism. Even if

Malaysian Indians still maintain strong home ties with their former villages, sometimes even taking wives in India and bringing them back to live in Malaysia.

The greatest cultural influence was brought over by the southern Indians, leaving a rich and colourful stamp on Malaysian life: bright silk saris, Tamil movies, the indomitable prevalence of the Hindu faith, and banana-leaf curries have added further diversity to Malaysian culture.

Chinese

The Chinese population makes up 25 percent of the country's total, yet its presence in and control of major industries such as rubber, tin and

converted to Islam or Christianity, this background is deeply rooted. Consequently, many of traditional Chinese festivals and rites are regularly and openly celebrated in Malaysia.

Peranakans

The colourful Peranakan culture was first established when Chinese trade missions established a port in Malacca in the early 1400s. Intercultural relationships and marriages were naturally forged between traders and local Malay women, as well as between Malacca's sultans and the Chinese Ming-dynasty emperors. Subsequent generations of Chinese-Malays were known as Straits Chinese, or Peranakans, which in Malay means "born here". When the Dutch colonists moved out in the early 1800s, more Chinese immigrants moved in, thus diluting Malay blood in the Peranakans, so that later generations were almost completely Chinese.

Eurasians

When the sultanate of Malacca fell to Portuguese invaders in 1511, the new rulers sought to establish control by encouraging Portuguese soldiers to marry local women. As can be expected, a strong Eurasian community grew up with loyalty to Portugal through its ties of blood and the Catholic religion. Eurasians are proudly protective of their unique cuisine, and often continue to speak Cristao, a medieval dialect once spoken in southwestern Portugal, but now used only in parts of Malaysia which have long-entrenched Eurasian populations.

In neighbouring Singapore to the south, both Eurasians and Peranakans make up part of the population, Eurasians in smaller numbers.

LEFT: Indian newsstand vendors are common in urban areas; Peranakan culture in Malacca.
ABOVE: Dayak woman, Sarawak.

People of Sabah and Sarawak

The two easternmost states of Sabah and Sarawak, situated in the northern part of the island of Borneo, which Malaysia shares with Indonesia, have the most diverse racial groups of all Malaysia. Most of them are of Mongoloid extract and moved here some time ago from Kalimantan (Indonesian Borneo). They generally live in the interior along jungle rivers, although some also live near the coastal regions, while others with some formal education have found

LONGHOUSE STAYS

Most tribes, especially the Iban, are extremely hospitable and guests are welcomed with a glass of strong *tuak* (rice wine) before being offered a bed.

work in towns, commercial centres and in industries throughout Malaysia.

The majority of the indigenous tribes have traditions and ways of living in common, but each group has some unique belief or activity that sets it apart from the rest. Most of the rural peoples of Sabah and Sarawak live in long-houses, large buildings that house the entire community under one roof, and may contain up to 60 families or more.

Borneo was once known for its headhunters. However, in the head-hunting days, taking the heads of one's enemies only occurred when the community was suffering some plague. Head-hunting was outlawed in the early 20th century. ❑

NATURAL HISTORY

*More than two-thirds of peninsular and Bornean Malaysia is jungle. The green
cover begins at the edge of the sea and climbs to the highest point of land*

The rain forests in this region are the oldest in the world, making those in Africa and South America seem adolescent in comparison. While creeping ice ages were swelling and shrinking across the northern hemisphere, the Malaysian jungles had lain undisturbed for an estimated 130 million years. Some of the

in Malaysia is the elegant hibiscus, the country's national flower. The world's largest flower, the *Rafflesia*, is unique to Southeast Asia. The entire plant of Rafflesia consists of just the flowerhead, which can measure up to 1 metre (3 ft) across and weigh up to 9 kilograms (20 lbs). A parasite, it sucks food from the roots

most unique and diverse species of animal and plant life evolved here, and some of the most primitive and remote tribes still inhabit this jungle world, living much like their ancestors did a thousand years ago.

The Malaysian jungles, on the peninsula and in particular on Malaysian Borneo, have generated much scientific interest and continue to do so. The diversity in flora and fauna is truly staggering. In Malaysia, for example, there are over 15,000 species of flowering plants, including 2,000 trees, 200 palms and 3,000 species of orchids, the most exotic of flowers, as well as beautiful highland roses rivalling their English counterparts. The most prominent flower

of the *Cissus liana*, a tree, and starts life as a red bulb. The Rafflesia grows in size and finally bursts open, revealing its pink, red and white interior. The Rafflesia's intensely smelly glory (to attract pollinating insects) lasts only a week, after which it shrivels up into the moist jungle earth from where it was born.

Another world's first is the towering *tualang* tree, tallest of all tropical trees. It can reach up to 80 metres (260 ft) in height and more than 3 metres (10 ft) in girth. The famous pitcher plants can be seen everywhere on the slopes of Mount Kinabalu in the state of Sabah, on Borneo, their honeyed jaws stretched open waiting for a careless insect to drop in.

Malaysia's jungles also hold thousands of species from the animal kingdom, many of which are unique to the region, while others were introduced from elsewhere in Asia.

Almost 300 species of mammals live here, including tigers, elephants, sleek civit cats *(musang)*, rhinoceros (though sadly, their numbers are greatly diminishing), black-and-white tapirs, leopards, honey bears, and two kinds of deer – the *sambar* and the barking deer *(kijang)*, with its dog-like call. Malaysia is

RUBBER GAMBLE

In Malaysia, the rubber tree once took up more than three-quarters of all developed land. The plant was originally viewed with great scepticism by coffee planters, but rubber is now a major export item.

Whether venturing into the jungle or not, you will be sure to see anywhere in Malaysia some of the 736 species of birds, and quite a few of the 150,000 species of insects. Of the over 1,000 species of butterfly in Malaysia, the king of them is the Rajah Brooke's birdwing – the national butterfly – with its emerald markings on jet-black wings. There are over a hundred more other breathtakingly vivid butterflies, as well as magnificent moths. They are best seen at butterfly farms, which can be found

also home to the region's tiny mousedeer (which is not technically a deer at all), wild forest cattle *(seladang)*, the scaly anteater *(pangolin)*, the badger-like *binturong* with its prehensile tail, and many kinds of gibbons and monkeys, including the quaint and slow loris with its sad eyes and lethargic manner. Borneo is also the home of the extraordinary orangutan ("forest man" in Malay), treated like another tribe by the jungle peoples, and the proboscis monkey, the male of the species parading its pendulous nose.

LEFT: strangling fig provides sculptural form. **ABOVE:** a familiar sight in Malaysia – working the rice fields.

throughout the country, especially in insect-abundant Cameron Highlands.

Along the coastline, there are extensive areas of mud swamps and mangroves. Behind the mangroves are the lowland dipterocarp forests, which extend up to an altitude of 600 metres (2,000 ft). Trees grow to majestic heights of 80 metres (262 ft) or more, with the first branches 20 metres (65 ft) above ground. This is called the triple canopy forest. Commercially, this region is the most important; from here comes timber, Malaysia's main natural export. Recently, efforts have been made to control timber exploitation so that Malaysia's jungle will assure the industry a green future.

The next level of forest is mostly oak and chestnut, and above 1,500 metres (5,000 ft), it becomes a kind of never-never land with elfin forests consisting of small gnarled trees, 3 to 5 metres (10–16 ft) high, covered with folds of hanging mosses and lichen. The highland forests, for the most part, are left untouched and unlogged as catchment areas, ensuring the fertility of the soil.

With conservation gaining importance in Malaysia, the government has set aside tracts of land as national parks or game reserves where strict hunting laws are enforced. This state of affairs has come a long way from the days

when animals were killed, not just for food, but also for their skins, horns or feathers.

Agricultural lands

As far as the eye can see, the lush green vegetation of the tropics smothers the landscape. Yet, contrary to its looks, Malaysia is not suited to agriculture.

Unlike the Nile River Basin or the Ganges Valley, where seasonal rains flooding the land bring new fertile soil, the torrential downpours in Malaysia wash away the thin but valuable topsoil. In many places, only red mud remains. Erosion is one of Malaysia's oldest problems. Geologists believe that the Malay peninsula and

Borneo were once a single rugged land mass, joined together and running the entire length of the Indonesian and Malayan archipelago. For millennia, sun, wind, and torrential rains reduced the mountains to hillocks and outcrops. Precious soils were washed into the sea, and fingers of land became cut off by subsidence and erosion. This meticulous work of nature continues today.

Still, despite the shifting landscape and annual monsoon rain, Malaysia's early settlers were basically food growers. As far back as AD 500, crops such as sugar cane, bananas, pepper and coconuts were grown for export, while rice was introduced to these lands over 1,000 years ago. Traditionally, both men and women were involved in the cultivation of this crop – the staple food and prime source of income for the rural Malay. The tempo of *kampung* life has quickened with the introduction of double cropping, using hybrids of rice that reap a second crop each year.

Tides upon the sea

Almost completely surrounded by water, Malaysia was where the regional monsoons met, and where the tides of the Indian Ocean and the South China Sea flowed together into the Strait of Malacca. Seafaring merchants, explorers, adventurers and pirates, seeking the wealth of the Malayan and Indonesian archipelago, stopped along these coasts to wait for the winds to change in their favour. Malaysia was the halfway point to this interchange, linking China to India and India to the Moluccas.

Piracy on the high seas was a widespread, lucrative and once-honourable profession, attracting merchants, noblemen, tribes-people and fishermen alike. For centuries, sailors trembled at the thought of passing unarmed through Malaysian waters at night. (It's still a problem.)

Much of the coast is surrounded by coral reefs of vivid colours, and creatures both beautiful and curious find their home here. The east coast has found profitable possibilities for its long stretches of beach and coral islands, as tourists, eager for sunshine and palm-fringed coral sands, flock to the coconut-sheltered beach huts and developed holiday resorts all along the coast. ❑

LEFT: a butterfly rests on a hibiscus.
RIGHT: orang-utan hanging on in the jungle.

SOUTHEAST ASIAN WILDLIFE

Southeast Asia is home to spectacular endemic animals, ranging from bizarre-looking hornbills to Komodo dragons and the huge Atlas moth

Southeast Asia's wildlife form part of the Indo-Malayan realm, a zoological and geographical zone comprising most of tropical Asia. Several animal species are unique to Southeast Asia, and in some cases entire sub-families and even orders are confined to this area. Distinct species include leaf monkeys, gibbons and flying lemurs. Only one family of bird is restricted to this realm, the leaf birds and ioras.

The region has rich reptilian and amphibian fauna, with many species of lizards (including geckos and the Komodo dragon, the world's largest lizard), colourful and numerous poisonous snakes, crocodiles, and turtles. Marine life is abundant and thrives in the region's rich coral reefs. Birds include colourful kingfishers, the maleo (an exotic megapode that buries its eggs in communal mounds), magnificent argus pheasants, and emerald ground-dwelling pittas.

ENDANGERED SPECIES

The rate of species loss – plants and animals – is probably greater today than in any other time in human history. Humans pose the greatest threat to endangered species through the destruction of habitat, hunting and poaching, and the illegal trade in live animals on the endangered list. Visitors should avoid buying gifts made from animal products.

◁ **ASIAN TIGER**
Only 5,000 to 7,500 tigers exist today. In the past 50 years the Bali and Javan sub-species of tiger have become extinct, largely through hunting.

△ **BANTENG BULL**
The mainly nocturnal Banteng is one of two species of regional wild cattle. Today, it can be found in the Baluran National Park in Java.

△ ATLAS MOTH

The night-flying, richly patterned, dark-brown Atlas moth may span as much as 25cm (14 in) and is one of the largest moth species in the world.

△ MANTIS

Not an exotic plant, but an exotic insect, the flower mantis uses its camouflage to fool predators and to catch prey.

THE VANISHING ORANG-UTAN

Wild orang-utans once ranged in much of Southeast Asia, but today they are found only in Borneo and Sumatra. The present population is estimated to be less than 30,000 – half that of a decade ago. Habitat destruction by logging and cash-cropping is the greatest threat to their survival. It is estimated that 80 percent of the forest in Indonesia may be logged by 2010. The international trade in orang-utans has declined, but demand for orang-utans as pets continues, particularly in Indonesia. It is estimated that five to six animals (often mothers) die for every orang-utan – often an infant – that is traded. The death of adult females increases the risk of extinction.

▽ JAVAN RHINO

The Javan Rhinoceros is the world's rarest large mammal. Fifty animals can be found on the Ujung Kulon peninsula in western Java.

△ ASIAN ELEPHANT

Since 1990, the population of the Asian elephant has declined by 97 percent. Today there are less than 30,000 elephants in Asia.

▽ GREEN TURTLE

Adult green turtles weigh up to 180kg (400lb). Females lay about 80 eggs in the sand. The eggs take about 50 days to incubate.

▷ WRINKLED HORNBILL

The rare wrinkled hornbill is found in coastal and lowland forests. It has a bark, often of two notes, and flies in small flocks.

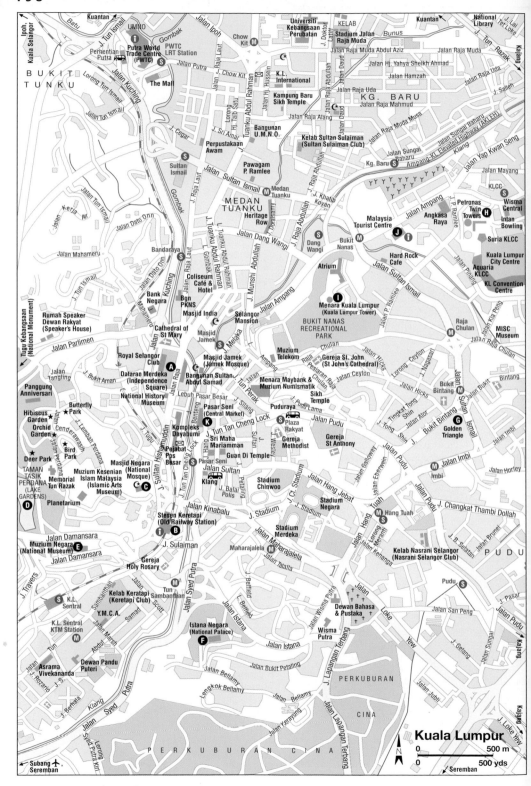

Kuala Lumpur

KUALA LUMPUR

Map on page 198

A mining outpost just a century ago and now the capital of Malaysia with a population of 1½ million, Kuala Lumpur is certainly a big city – and has the world's two tallest buildings

To the newcomer, Kuala Lumpur – or "KL" as it is popularly known – is a fascinating mixture of old and new, increasingly so with the completion of the world's tallest buildings in downtown KL, in 1997. Mosques of Mughal design, elaborate Chinese temples and crowded shophouses, Hindu temples with towering gates, and Indian restaurants and regal remnants of the shipshape British order – all set the colourful scene of multi-ethnic activity.

A century and a half ago, Kuala Lumpur was a precise representation of what its name means in Malay: "muddy river mouth". At that time, a group of tin prospectors, financed by the local Malay chief, journeyed upriver to the confluence of the less-than-crystal-clear waters of the Klang and Gombak rivers. Today, it is the seat of government for Malaysia, with its own administration headed by a minister of cabinet rank. Over the past decade, the skyline of the city has changed beyond all recognition as new high-rise buildings continue their upward thrust.

City centre

If you cross the Gombak and Klang rivers, you will come to the old city centre for British colonial rule, with its Mughal-style administrative buildings that are still important today. The Old City Hall and a British colonial club face **Dataran Merdeka** Ⓐ (Independence Square). Casting its shadow on the Padang is the imposing **Bangunan Sultan Abdul Samad** (Sultan Abdul Samad Building). Once the core of colonial KL, this building was the colonial secretariat headquarters. It now houses the High Court. It was the first building to be built in Mughal style, a trend brought to Malaysia by two architects, A.C. Norman and A.B. Hubback. Both men had spent some time in India, and they deemed that an architectural style featuring Mughal and Arabic motifs would best suit a predominantly Muslim country, apparently ignoring the fact that the Malays already had a very highly developed and practical building style of their own.

Until the opening of the National Mosque after independence, the **Masjid Jamek** (Jamek Mosque; open Sat–Thur 8.30am–12.30pm and 2.30–4pm, Fri 8.30–11am and 2.30–4pm; tel: 03-2691 2829) was the principal Muslim centre for prayer in the city. There are other buildings in the area around the Padang built in Mughal style, and which have influenced more recent edifices since.

Along the same side of the river but further down from the Dataran Merdeka – connected to the Central Market (*see page 202*) and the central business district by a pedestrian bridge – is the towering white **Kompleks Dayabumi**. Below this complex are shops

BELOW: Zouk dance club in the shadows of the Petronas Twin Towers.

Meticulously designed to meet Victorian standards, the construction of the KL Railway Station was actually held up because the design failed to meet British specifications that the station roof must support one metre of snow.

and restaurants, and the equally impressive **Pejabat Pos Besar** (General Post Office). Beyond these modern buildings on Jalan Sultan Hishamuddin lies the old **Stesen Keretapi** B (Railway Station). To arrive by rail on the Eastern & Oriental Express in Kuala Lumpur is a fantastic experience, as turrets, spires, minarets and Arabic arches greet the eye in every direction. Inside, the design is that of many large Victorian railway stations in England. Opposite the station is the **Bangunan KTM** (KTM Building), headquarters of Malaysian Railways, featuring a pastiche of architectural elements, from Mughal-style minarets to large Gothic-style windows and ancient Greek columns.

Up the road from this Victorian enclave is the **Masjid Negara** C (National Mosque; open Mon–Thur 10am–noon and 2–4pm, Fri for Muslims attending prayers only, Sat, Sun and holidays 9am–noon and 2–6.30pm; tel: 03-2693 7784). Completed in 1965, the jagged 18-point-star roof and the 70-metre-tall (240 ft) minaret catch the eye. The 18 points of the star represent the 13 states of Malaysia and the five pillars of Islam. Its Grand Hall – busiest on Fridays – can accommodate 8,000 worshippers. On the roof are 48 smaller domes, their design and number inspired by the great mosque in Mecca. Set within 5 hectares (13 acres) of fine gardens, the mosque is an impressive building with cool marbled halls, long galleries, and reflecting pools outside in the courtyard.

The best-known and most popular of KL's parks is **Taman Tasik Perdana** D or the Lake Gardens (daily 24 hours; free), comprising 104 hectares (257 acres) of undulating green with magnificent trees and flowering plants. At the heart of the gardens is the lake, Tasik Perdana. Early in the morning and in the evening, joggers run past picnickers, senior citizens perform *tai chi* routines and lovers rendezvous here. It is also a great place to watch KL families at play.

BELOW: the Sultan Abdul Samad Building houses the Supreme Court.

For a taste of wildlife, the **Bird Park** (daily 9am–6pm; entrance fee; tel: 03-2272 1010)and **Butterfly Park** (daily 9am–5pm; entrance fee; tel: 03-2693 4799) house local and foreign species in forested enclosures. The **Planetarium** (Tues–Sun 9.30am–4.15pm; entrance fee; tel: 03-2273 5484)sits in a carefully thought-out garden. It has a 36-cm (14-inch) telescope, a theatre, and the Arianne IV space engine used to launch Malaysia's first satellite, the Measat I. Other attractions in the gardens include an orchid garden and deer park. Within and around the park are several interesting buildings.

Map on page 198

On a smaller hill but in an imposing position is the **National Monument** (Tugu Kebangsaan), erected to commemorate those who died in the struggle against the Communist insurgency in the 1950s. At the edge of the gardens, on an incline on Jalan Damansara and facing Jalan Travers, is the **Muzium Negara** ❺ (National Museum; daily 9am–6pm; entrance fee; tel: 03-2282 6255; www. jmm.gov.my). The building is modelled after Kedah's Balai Besar, a 19th-century Thai-influenced audience hall for sultans. It has galleries on local material culture, natural history, and arts and crafts.

At the National Palace, yellow is the colour for royalty, and only kings may walk on the welcoming yellow carpet, while politicians and visiting dignitaries tread on the red one.

Palaces, towers and mansions

In the southern part of Kuala Lumpur is the **Istana Negara** ❻ (National Palace), the official residence of the king. Once the town house of a wealthy Chinese businessman, it was converted into a palace for the king, a position that is rotated amongst the regional sultans. Beyond the National Palace and further south along Jalan Lapangan Terbang is a small road, Jalan Kerayong, that climbs a steep hill. Follow it to find yourself near the Chinese cemeteries, with a commanding view over the city. On this hill stands the largest Buddhist temple in KL, completed in 1985, the **Thean Hou Temple** (daily 9am–9pm; tel: 03-2274 7088). It was built by several Chinese multimillionaires who, it is said, each donated one pillar. It is known that the cost of the temple was phenomenal, but the exact figure remains a secret.

BELOW: National Monument.

The fulcrum of modern consumer life in Malaysia is the intersection of Jalan Sultan Ismail and Jalan Bukit Bintang, an area of expensive shops, high-class restaurants, and international hotels and sophisticated nightlife. It is often called the **Golden Triangle** ❼. You will find a number of large shopping malls in this area: Sungai Wang Plaza and the adjacent Bukit Bintang Plaza offer more than 500 shops, including some of the best bookstores in KL; Imbi Plaza concentrates on computers and software; KL Plaza has fashion accessory shops and electronic outlets; flashy green Lot 10 has European designer boutiques and Isetan.

The city's most striking landmark is the world's tallest pair of buildings, the **Petronas Twin Towers** ❽, two identical towers that are linked midway up by a skybridge. The towers reach a numerically auspicious 88 storeys above the traffic-congested streets and make up part of a larger development called the **Kuala Lumpur City Centre** (KLCC) which includes the huge Suria KLCC shopping mall, an excellent concert hall, KL Convention Centre and the sprawling KLCC Park.

Visitors can ascend to the towers' skybridge on the 42nd floor, but for a higher view try the **Menara**

Map on page 198

Kuala Lumpur ❶ (daily 9am–10pm; entrance fee; tel: 03-2020 5444; www. menarakl.com.my), a 421-metre (1,380-ft) telecom-and-tourism tower built in 1995, and one of the highest such structures in the world.

Historic Jalan Ampang presents a very different aspect of urban architecture – a row of old tin miners' mansions that have been well preserved despite the tropical weather. The tin empire gave mine-owners the money to build lavish mansions, and these were generally built along Jalan Ampang itself. The best preserved of these mansions is Dewan Tunku Abdul Rahman, built in 1935 by a wealthy Chinese tin mogul and rubber planter named Eu Tong Sen. In the late 1980s it was refurbished and commissioned as the **Malaysia Tourism Centre ❷** (MTC; Mon–Fri 7.30am–5.30pm, tourist info desk daily 7am–10pm; tel: 03-2163 3667; www.mtc.gov.my).

Chinatown and other districts

Chinatown lies within the boundaries of Jalan Sultan, Jalan Tun HS Lee and along Jalan Petaling. The area is bustling with good eateries and exotic oddities, including jewellers and goldsmiths, casket and basket makers, dry-goods shops, pet shops, optical houses, and herbalists. Near here is the **Central Market ⓚ** (daily 10am–10pm; tel: 03-2274 9966). A former fruit-and-vegetable market, this Art Deco showpiece was saved from demolition by conservation-minded architects, who eventually won an award for their restoration and renovation efforts. It is now one of the city's most popular tourist stops, with art exhibitions, performances, restaurants, and souvenir shops purveying everything from batik scarfs to portraits done on the spot. There is often an event or exhibition happening – if you're lucky you could catch a *wayang kulit* (shadow puppet) performance or *bangsawan* (traditional Malay theatre) production in full swing.

RIGHT: night market in Kuala Lumpur. **BELOW:** shopping centre.

Besides Chinatown, there are several other districts in which it is pleasant to stroll and enjoy the sights. Northward from the Padang lies another area of interesting shops. The main road here is **Jalan Tuanku Abdul Rahman**, named after the first king of the Federation of Malaysia. To the locals this road is often referred to as Batu Road. The street leads off the Padang; all along it lie shops, both old and new, as well as modern department stores, cheap hotels and many *kedai makan*, or eating stalls.

The **Coliseum Cinema**, built in the 1920s and one of KL's first, lies halfway down this road, and the **Coliseum Café and Hotel** (daily 8am–10pm; tel: 03-2692 6270) next door is the most famous bar and restaurant in town, serving customers for more than 60 years. Off Batu Road where the Dataran Merdeka ends is Jalan Melayu, interesting for its Indian shops.

Beyond Jalan Melayu is **Jalan Masjid India**, whose mosque sits on the same spot where one of the town's first mosques used to be. The road leads to what was formerly the red-light district and is now a thriving commercial area of shops, restaurants and hotels where Indian silks, flowery saris and glittering handmade jewellery are the order of the day. After 6pm every day, portable kitchens with tables and chairs take over the street under the stars, offering tasty, spicy food. ❑

PENANG

It's a place with a colourful past, mysterious back alleys,
palm-shrouded beaches and a stimulating cuisine.
No wonder that it has lured visitors for centuries

Map on page 184

One of the most famous islands in Asia, **Penang ❶** is perhaps the best-known tourist destination in Malaysia. Since 1985, it has been connected to the mainland by the Penang Bridge, which has become a modern symbol of the island. It costs more than the ferry, but the 7-km (4½-mile) drive affords exhilarating views of the harbour, and you have the satisfaction of knowing that you have just driven over one of the longer bridges in the world.

Although once under the dominion of the Sultan of Kedah, 285 sq-km (115 sq-mile) Penang has always been on its own. Until the British came, it was largely deserted despite its strategic position. To encourage trade and commerce, the British made the island a free port; no taxes were levied on either imports or exports. This strategy worked, and in eight years the population increased to 8,000, comprising a diverse grouping of immigrants – Chinese, Indians and Bugis, among others.

Georgetown, named by the British after King George III of Great Britain, is also known by the Malays as Tanjung (or Headland) and is unmistakably a Chinese town. It has one of the most unusual waterfronts in Asia, what locals call the Clan Piers. It consists of villages built on stilts over the sea. As predominantly as the port is Chinese, the countryside beyond Georgetown is Malay, and the entrepreneurial fuss nearly disappears.

No visit should end without sampling the lip-smacking delights of the local cuisine: Indian curry to Malay *nasi* (rice), to Chinese *bah kut teh* (pork ribs in herbal soup). Much of the best food is found at unfashionable roadside stalls and cramped coffee shops in the old parts of Georgetown, especially along Gurney Drive and Jalan Burma.

Old Georgetown

Originally, **Fort Cornwallis** was a wooden structure. In the early 1800s, it was rebuilt with convict labour. Today, the old fort still stands, but its precincts have been converted into a public park and playground. Next to Fort Cornwallis lie the **Padang** (town green) and the **Esplanade** (Jalan Tun Syed Sheh Barakhbah), which is the heart of old historical Georgetown. Handsome 19th-century colonial buildings stand at one end of the Padang, serving as government offices. At the other end, near the entrance to Fort Cornwallis, traffic circles the **Clock Tower**, presented to Penang by a rich Chinese *towkay* in commemoration of Queen Victoria's Diamond Jubilee.

The dignified **St George's Church**, built in 1818 on nearby Lebuh Farquhar, draws much attention as the oldest Anglican church in Southeast Asia. At the **Penang State Museum and Art Gallery** (Sat–Thur 9am–5pm; free; tel: 04-261 3144), on the other side of

LEFT: sunset at Batu Ferringhi. **BELOW:** travelling salesman in Georgetown.

the street, visitors can peer into a Chinese bridal chamber created in the lavish style of the 19th century, or see a jewelled *keris*, the dagger Malays used for protection. The gallery displays batik paintings, oils, graphics and Chinese ink drawings. Further west along the waterfront is the stark white **Eastern & Oriental Hotel** (www.e-o-hotel.com), established in the late 19th century. It reopened in 2001 after renovation, and it once again looks set to stake its claim as one of Asia's grand hotels.

Jalan Penang (better known as Penang Road) is the main shopping bazaar, and it ends in the towering air-conditioned KOMTAR shopping complex, situated at the top of a bus station, which also houses a tourist information centre and a Malaysia Airlines office. Take a ride up its circular tower for a bird's eye view of the city (entrance fee).

Take a walk through **Pasar Chowrasta** (Chowrasta Market), between Lebuh Campbell and Jalan Chowrasta. A wet market with the customary wet market pong, it has a section facing Penang Road that offers the Penang specialities of local biscuits and preserved nutmeg and mango prepared in a wide variety of styles. On Lebuh Tamil is the row of *nasi kandar* (mixed curry rice) stalls whose food is reputed to be the best in the country.

Typical Malaysian institutions are the *pasar minggu* or *pasar malam*, the weekly market or night market. These are temporary markets that spring up in the street or an open space in the evenings or on the weekends. In Penang, they are called *pasar malam* and move from location to location every two weeks. The areas, wherever they might be, are well lit, and the bargains range from tiny trinkets to cheap Kelantan batik sarongs and plastic sandals and slippers. People-watching is especially enjoyable here.

Rooftop patterns in Chinatown.

BELOW: municipal building evokes memories of colonial splendour.

Chinese heritage

Many of the Chinese immigrants arriving in Malaysia a hundred years ago fell under the "protection" and control of one of the clan associations, whose functions were not unlike those of medieval European guilds. The ancestral halls of these clan associations – such as the Khoo, Ong, Tan and Cheah – are called *kongsi* and are scattered all over town. The most impressive is the clan hall built by the Khoo Kongsi. The **Khoo Kongsi** (daily 9am–5pm; entrance fee; tel: 04-261 4609; www.khookongsi.com.my) stands at the junction of Jalan Masjid Kapitan Keling and Lebuh Acheh. Designed to capture the splendour of an imperial palace, it has a seven-tiered pavilion, "dragon" pillars and hand-painted walls engraved with the Khoo rose emblem. The original design was so ambitious that conservative Khoo clansmen cautioned against it, lest the emperor of China be offended. After eight years, the building was completed in 1902; but on the first night after it was finished, the roof mysteriously caught fire. Clan members interpreted this as a sign that even the deities considered the Khoo Kongsi too palatial for a clan house and rebuilt it on a more modest scale. Following a renovation that was completed in 2001 by traditional crasftsmen, the clanhouse has been restored to its former splendour.

Of all the Chinese temples, Penang's oldest is the **Kuan Yin Temple** (daily) in Lebuh Masjid Kapitan Keling, which is also the most humble and the most crowded. A Buddhist deity who refused to enter Nirvana as long as there was injustice on earth, Kuan Yin (Guanyin) typically personifies mercy, and is one of the most popular deities in the traditional Chinese pantheon of gods and goddesses. Set nearby, in direct contrast, is the Moorish-style **Kapitan Keling Mosque** (daily), built in 1800 and the state's oldest mosque. The variety of

Map on page 184

BELOW: Wat Chaya-mangkalaram.

Buddhist worship in Penang is so striking as to make sightseeing a new experience in every temple. One can enter the gigantic meditation hall at **Wat Chayamangkalaram** (daily 6am–5.30pm) and find a workman polishing the left cheek of the 32-metre-long (100-ft) Reclining Buddha, the third-largest statue of its kind in the world.

High above the bustle of Georgetown on a hilltop at **Ayer Hitam**, a few kilometres from downtown, looms the **Kek Lok Si** or Temple of Paradise (daily 9am–6pm). This temple is one of the largest Buddhist temple complexes in Malaysia and one of the largest to be found in the region.

The **Waterfall Gardens**, also known as the **Botanical Gardens** (daily 5am–8pm; free; tel: 04-227 0428), is situated about 3 km (2 miles) due northeast from Penang Hill. This mature and beautifully cultivated showcase of tropical plants has cascading waterfalls over 100 metres (330 ft) high.

Batu Maung, a fishing village on the southeast tip of the island about 3 km from the Bayan Lepas Airport, houses a shrine marking the sacred 85-cm (33-inch) footprint in stone, believed to be that of Admiral Cheng Ho, the Chinese Columbus who explored not only Asia but all the way to the east coast of Africa. On **Pulau Langkawi**, 100 km (60 miles) to the north, is a similar footprint said to belong to the admiral. The two are believed to be a pair and anyone who lights joss sticks and places them in the urns beside the footprint will have good luck and great fortune.

To the north

The road skirts around the southern end of the island and turns north. The scenery changes from flat rice land to rolling hills. Here, spice plantations of pepper, clove and nutmeg lured Arab, Spanish, Portuguese and other Western traders to this part of the world long ago. At **Titi Kerawang**, there are waterfalls and a serene view of the Indian Ocean.

Although the waters are not as clear as on the eastern coast of the Malay peninsula, the beaches of Penang are still quite seductive. On the island's north shore, luxury hotels cluster around the beach at **Batu Ferringhi**. The whole range of eateries can be found here, from air-conditioned steak and seafood restaurants to hawker stalls under winking fairy lights.

Also on the north coast is **Teluk Bahang**, a fine beach. Nearby is the **Tropical Spice Garden** (open daily 9am–6pm; entrance fee; tel: 04-881 1797; www.tropicalspicegarden.com), with more than 500 specimens of flora from all over the tropical world. Further along the same road is the **Penang Butterfly Farm** (daily 9am–5.30pm; entrance fee; tel: 04-885 1253; www.butterfly-insect.com), where some of the loveliest butterflies and most awesome insects of Malaysia are bred and displayed. A couple of minutes down the road is a 100-hectare (250-acre) **Forest Recreation Park and Museum** (daily 9am–5pm; entrance fee). To get a taste of the "real" jungle, head for the 37-hectare (92-acre) **Bukit Mertajam Recreational Park**, about 18 km (11 miles) from the Penang Bridge. It has numerous walking trails for trekkers and rest huts when you tire. ❏

Map on page 184

TIP

The Penang Bird Park is a lush garden with over 200 species of tropical birds from around the world, housed in a huge walk-in aviary and geodesic domes.

RIGHT: Penang Bridge. **BELOW:** Kek Lok Si, the Temple of Paradise.

SABAH AND SARAWAK

These sprawling states have hit the world's headlines because of their severe ecological problems. The problems remain, but so do fascinating remnants of ancient cultures

Map
on page
212

Sabah and Sarawak, two Malaysian states not on the main peninsula, cover the northwestern coast and northern tip of the world's third-largest island, commonly known as Borneo. Malaysia shares Borneo with Indonesia, whose part of the island is called Kalimantan. Together, Sabah and Sarawak bridge 1,000 km (600 miles) of sea to join the Malay peninsula as a federated nation. Although their population accounts for just 15 percent of the country's 21 million people, the land area is larger than the other 11 states combined.

Long a sanctuary of rainforest, unique fauna, and indigenous tribes of people, Borneo's ecosystems have suffered considerably in the past decade, first with extensive logging – much of it going to Japan as chopsticks and plywood – that denuded thousands of hectares, and in the late 1990s by extensive and highly destructive fires that burned out of control for months at a time. These fires, more often than not on the Indonesian side and lit by farmers seeking to clear land, clouded the air of Southeast Asia.

Sabah: Kota Kinabalu

The capital of Sabah, **Kota Kinabalu ❶**, is a sprawling, relaxed town on the west coast of the state. Within the past decade, the town has mushroomed with some of the most striking buildings in all Malaysia, as befits the capital of one of Malaysia's fastest-growing states, making the city a blend of ultramodern structures and old Chinese shophouses. Amongst the most impressive of these buildings, to the north of the city at the end of Likas Bay, is the gleaming tower of the Sabah Foundation, an institution created out of the timber royalties of the state. The monumental **Sabah Mosque** is also worth a visit to see its fine contemporary Islamic architecture. Nearby is the **Sabah Museum** (Sat–Thur 9am–5pm; entrance fee; tel: 088 253 199), built in the longhouse style of the Rungus and Murut tribes. The museum has a wealth of historical and tribal treasures, as well as a good section on Sabah's fascinating flora and fauna. One of the most striking exhibits is a collection of 10 life-size traditional houses set in the museum gardens, each depicting the architecture of a different ethnic group. The complex also has a science centre with an exhibition on the oil and petroleum industry, and an art gallery.

South of town, off the road leading to the airport, is the famous beach at **Tanjung Aru**. The sea here is clear, the sand is clean and the coastal food stalls and restaurants offer delicious local seafood. Offshore is the **Tunku Abdul Rahman Park**, one of the most picturesque marine reserves in Southeast Asia. The park headquarters is on **Pulau Gaya**, the largest and most historically significant of the islands.

OPPOSITE: Mount Kinabalu. **BELOW:** atop Low's Peak.

Beyond Kota Kinabalu

Everyone in Malaysia knows about the mysterious **Gunung Kinabalu ❷**, Southeast Asia's highest peak at 4,093 metres (13,428 ft). To get to the top, one does not need to spend days cutting through tropical rainforest before reaching the granite slopes, unlike the first ascent of the mountain. Well-laid trails with steps and rails made of wood help today's climber ascend and descend the mountain in just two days. Accommodation is available both at the park headquarters and on the mountain slopes. Besides the mountain, **Kinabalu National Park** (daily 7am–10pm; entrance fee; tel: 088-889 098) contains a treasure of other natural features, including a unique rainforest, a myriad of bird species, and Poring Hot Springs, which is found on the eastern side of the mountain.

Sipadan's marine wealth makes it a coveted destination for divers.

Semporna is best known as the departure point for **Pulau Sipadan ❸**, Malaysia's only true oceanic island rising up 600 metres (2,000 ft) from the seabed. The marine life of Sipadan has been hailed by both Worldwide Fund for Nature and late Jacques Cousteau as among the best in the world. All resort operations have been relocated to preserve this world-class diving spot.

In **Sandakan ❹**, in its heyday the boom town of northeastern Sabah, people called the logs bobbing in the Sulu Sea "floating money". Logs floated down the Segama River from timber forests into the hands of Chinese entrepreneurs. So prosperous was Sandakan that at one time many thought it would become another Hong Kong, but the speed of the region's deforestation has shattered that dream.

Sandakan is most famous for the **Sepilok Orangutan Rehabilitation Centre** (daily 8am–4.30pm, feeding times 10am and 3pm; entrance fee; tel: 089-531 180), a 20-minute drive westward from town. The centre helps orang-utans who have lived in captivity or been orphaned to adjust gradually for a return to the wild.

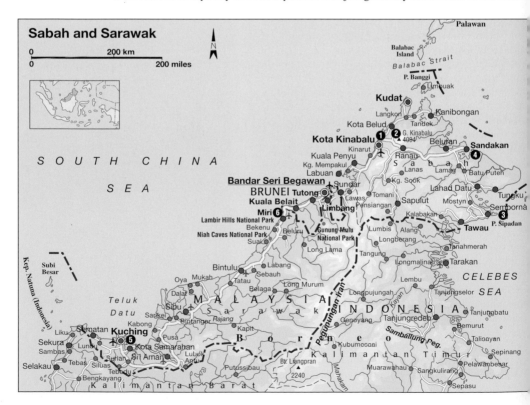

Sabah and Sarawak

0 ⊢——————⊣ 200 km
0 ⊢——————⊣ 200 miles

Pulau Selingaan is the largest of three islands within the confines of **Turtle Islands National Park**, off the coast of Sandakan. The other two islands within the national park are Pulau Bakkungan and Pulau Gulisaan. Green and hawks-bill turtles come here to lay eggs nearly every night of the year, but the best time to watch is between July and September.

Another excursion that can be undertaken from Sandakan is a cruise up the **Kinabatangan River**. After crossing Sandakan Bay, the first stage of the journey is dominated by mangrove swamps and twisting waterways. The Kinabatangan and its tributaries are famed as the home of the long-nosed, pot-bellied proboscis monkey, and wild elephants can also be seen here.

Sarawak

The name of Sarawak still evokes romance rather than reality. White Rajahs and Borneo headhunters ring more nostalgic bells than 125,000 sq. km (48,000 sq. miles) of hills, jungle and swampland located just north of the equator. The days of the reign of the White Rajahs and head-hunting have now passed, it can be noted with certainty. Sarawak became a member of the Federation of Malaysia in 1963, and traces of colonialism soon began to disappear.

With colonialism's end, some of the old serenity went, too, accelerated by the advent of the oil industry, Kuala Lumpur's interest in developing the state, and in the logging disputes of recent decades.

Sarawak's capital city, **Kuching ❺**, is suffused with memories, especially the many colonial buildings that have withstood the march of 20th-century progress. Charles Brooke's Astana, built in 1870 for the newly married rajah, still stands, although it has undergone several renovations since. Kuching's courthouse is

Map on page 212

BELOW: Sarawak River, and traditional design.

Map on page 212

Sarawak's national parks are home to some of the rarest orchid species in the world.

RIGHT: the Pinnacles of Gunung Mulu National Park.
BELOW: Kuching waterfront.

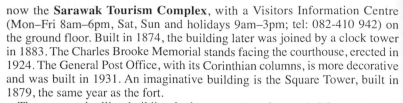

now the **Sarawak Tourism Complex**, with a Visitors Information Centre (Mon–Fri 8am–6pm, Sat, Sun and holidays 9am–3pm; tel: 082-410 942) on the ground floor. Built in 1874, the building later was joined by a clock tower in 1883. The Charles Brooke Memorial stands facing the courthouse, erected in 1924. The General Post Office, with its Corinthian columns, is more decorative and was built in 1931. An imaginative building is the Square Tower, built in 1879, the same year as the fort.

The most enthralling building is the marvellous **Sarawak Museum** (daily 9am–6pm; tel: 082-244 232; free), set in lush grounds between Jalan McDougall and Jalan Tun Haji Openg. Alfred Russel Wallace, the naturalist and co-founder of the theory of evolution along with Charles Darwin, spent many years in Borneo and became a particular friend of Rajah Charles Brooke. With Wallace's encouragement, Brooke built the museum to house a permanent exhibition of native arts and crafts, as well as specimens from Wallace's extensive collection, many of which Wallace shot and preserved himself while exploring the jungle.

Where to relax

Outside of the urban pull, sun worshippers, beach lovers and golfers head for **Damai Beach**, just 30 minutes by road from downtown Kuching. Nearby, the fishing village of **Santubong** is also worth a visit. Between the 9th and 13th centuries, it was an important trading centre. Ancient rock carvings of Hindu and Buddhist influence have been discovered around the river delta here. Nearby is the state's popular attraction, the **Sarawak Cultural Village** (daily 9am–5.30pm; entrance fee; tel: 082-846 411; www.scv.com.my), which spreads across 6 hectares (15 acres) of jungle at the foot of Santubong Mountain. It features authentic dwellings of the six main cultural groups.

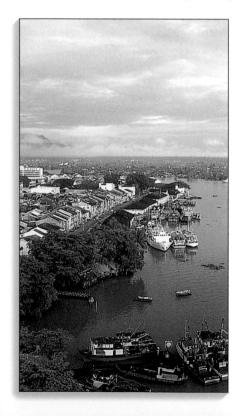

In **Miri ❻**, northward and near the Brunei border, there are a couple of side-trips that attract many to Sarawak. The **Lambir Hills National Park** (headquarters open daily 8am–12.30pm and 1.30–5.15pm; entrance fee; tel: 085-434 184; www.sarawak forestry.com), just south of Miri, makes a pleasant excursion. The park's highlights are waterfalls with natural swimming pools and a climb up Bukit Lambir.

With more to offer, is **Niah Caves National Park** (headquarters open daily 8am–12.30pm and 1.30–5.15pm; entrance fee; tel: 085-434 184; www.sarawak forestry.com). Haematite paintings in the Niah Caves, featuring stick figures with strange little boat-like objects along with other discoveries, revealed that people once living here worked with instruments made from bone and shell, made pottery, cut stone adzes, and carved wooden coffins and burial boats. To many, these discoveries were as significant as the unearthing of Java Man.

Twenty minutes by plane from Miri is the UNESCO World Heritage Site of **Gunung Mulu National Park** (entrance fee; tel: 085-433 561; www.sarawak forestry.com, an inland expanse of diverse terrain and vegetation with unique cave systems and offer limestone features, including the spectacular Pinnacles. Accommodation ranges from simple lodges to a deluxe resort, not to mention longhouse stays. ❏

BRUNEI

*A tiny Islamic sultanate on Borneo, Brunei is one of the
world's smallest countries and one of its wealthiest*

The Sultanate of Brunei, officially known as Negara Brunei Darussalam (in Malay, "Abode of Peace"), is the only country to remain a sovereign entity in the Malay archipelago throughout its contemporary history. Historically, Brunei endured takeover attempts by more powerful sultanates, kept Spanish *conquistadores* and the Dutch East India Company at bay, resisted the territorial ambitions of the White Rajahs of Sarawak, and quelled an attempt in the 1960s to merge the tiny country into a much larger Malaysia.

Today, Brunei is a bit of an anachronism – one of the few nations in the world ruled by an absolute monarch, Sultan Haji Hassanal Bolkiah Mu'izzaddin Waddaulah, the 29th ruler in a long-surviving dynasty and perhaps the world's richest man. He is also the country's prime minister, defence minister and finance minister.

Oil money has transformed once sleepy Brunei into a thriving modern nation. The population of about 379,400 enjoys a per capita income of over US$18,600 a year, one of the highest in the region. The gross domestic product exceeds US$5.5 billion per year. The government has no foreign debt; treasury reserves are said to be more than US$15 billion.

Bruneians have all benefited from their oil wealth. Nearly a quarter of the government budget is spent on education and social services, and Brunei has more than 95 percent literacy among its young people. Many tropical diseases have been completely eliminated. Life expectancy is high and infant mortality is low.

The population is about 67 percent Malay, 15 percent Chinese and the remainder comprises various indigenous Dayak people and Europeans. Islam is the official religion and the creed of two-thirds of the people, but there are also sizeable communities of Buddhists and Christians.

Geographically one of the world's smallest nations, Brunei has just 5,770 sq. km (2,228 sq. miles) of land – about twice the size of Luxembourg or the American state of Rhode Island. It is bounded on the north by the South China Sea and on three sides by the Malaysian state of Sarawak, which actually divides Brunei into two parts. Over 70 percent of Brunei is still forested by primary jungle that has never been logged.

Unique as it is, Brunei is a mixture of modern and ancient influences, and at the same time it is a model of careful and well managed development. ❑

PRECEDING PAGES: an illuminated Omar Ali Saifuddin Mosque; aerial view of Bandar Seri Begawan. **LEFT:** Bruneian kids on the block.

BANDAR SERI BEGAWAN AND BEYOND

Islam and oil money are the two factors that demarcate this compact nation on Borneo, with few travellers making their way to Brunei

With only 60,000 people, Bandar Seri Begawan feels more like a small town than a capital city. It takes no more than 15 minutes to walk from one side of the central city to the other, even if people prefer their cars to walking. Oil money has transformed B.S.B. (as it is commonly known) into a modern if exceedingly compact city of skyscrapers and shopping malls.

The **Sultan Omar Ali Saifuddien Mosque** dominates the downtown skyline. Built in 1958, its Arabic architecture features numerous arches, towers, columns, onion domes and minarets. The great golden dome rises to a height of 50 metres (170 ft), towering above the adjoining lagoon with a replica of a 16th-century royal barge. It is open daily except Thursdays and Fridays.

Northwest of the mosque, obscured by modern office buildings and flats, is the old **Istana Darussalam**. This wooden structure, a classic example of local architecture, was the royal palace of Brunei until the 1960s.

At the junction of Jalan Stoney and Jalan Sultan is the **Royal Regalia Building** (Sat–Thur 8.30am–5pm, Fri 9–11.30am and 2.30–5pm; free; tel: 223 8258). On view inside are the royal chariot, bejeweled crowns and

BELOW: Istana Nurul Iman, the sultan's official residence.

ceremonial armoury. A gallery documents the constitutional history of the nation. Next door is the **Brunei History Centre**, a research facility with an exhibition gallery (Mon–Thur, Sat 8am–12.15pm and 1.30–4.30pm; free; tel: 224 0166; www.history-centre.gov.bn) that traces the genealogy of Brunei's sultans and the country's history.

Across the road is the **Lapau** (Royal Ceremonial Hall), which is used for important state occasions presided over by His Majesty the Sultan and Yang Di-Pertuan of Brunei Darussalam. Through the garden is the **Dewan Majlis** (Parliament House). Nearby, at the intersection of Jalan Sungai Kianggeh and Jalan Elizabeth II, is a Taoist temple where Chinese Bruneians worship. Opposite is the *tamu* or open market, where one can shop for tropical produce or just wander among the stalls, which are open from dawn to dusk.

Along a two-block stretch of Jalan Sultan that runs up from the waterfront are banks, embassies, airline offices, travel agents and shops. The pier opposite the road is the best jumping-off point for exploring the river. From the roof of the multi-storey car park on Jalan Cator there's a fine (and free) view over the city, the Brunei River and the vast water-village. On Jalan MacArthur near the waterfront is the Yayasan Sultan Haji Hassanal Bolkiah, the largest one-stop commercial and shopping centre in downtown B.S.B.

Kampong Ayer, a riverine community built on stilts above the Brunei River, dates from the 15th century. It is home to 30,000 people – half the population of B.S.B. Yet don't think life in this village is not modern simply because it's built over water. There are mosques and schools, cafes and grocery stores, police posts and fire stations, and even gas stations that cater to boats. The water-villagers park their cars on land and get about in water-taxis.

Map on page 223

Although it's now one of the world's smallest nations, Brunei's rule during the 16th century extended over a vast area, including most of the northwest coast of Borneo and many southern Philippine islands.

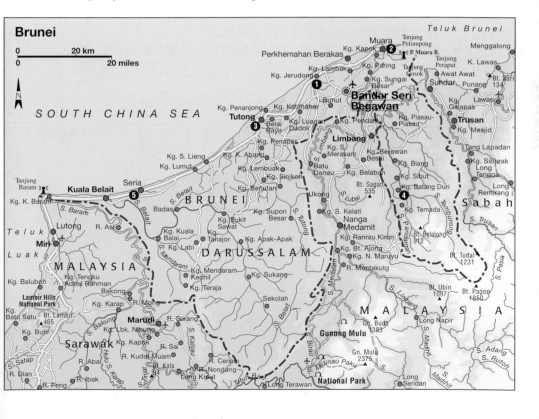

The Malay Muslim Monarchy

L ittle is known about the early history of Brunei, but recent archeological finds have determined that local inhabitants engaged in trade with China and other parts of mainland Asia as early as the 6th century AD.

During the 10th century, the area that is now Brunei was a Buddhist kingdom, part of the Srivijaya Empire of Sumatra. Later it became part of the Hindu Majapahit Empire of Java. By the 14th century, Brunei was a powerful seafaring state with a sultan based on Kota Batu on the Brunei River. Sharif Ali, a descendant of the Prophet Mohammed, came to Brunei at the start of the 15th century. Soon the sultan and most of his subjects converted to Islam, the foundation of a strong religious and cultural tradition that has endured to this day.

The remnants of Ferdinand Magellan's fleet weighed anchor in Brunei in 1521 as the first Europeans to visit the sultanate. In the century that followed, other Spanish and Portuguese mariners explored the coast of Borneo. The Spanish made an attempt to conquer the sultanate, but instead had to settle upon dominance over the Philippines, including lands once ruled by Brunei.

Brunei's first permanent contact with Europe came at the end of the 16th century, when a trading relationship was established with the Dutch East India Company. Brunei remained independent while Indonesia was absorbed into the Dutch colonial empire. The sultanate remained a power to be reckoned with until the arrival of the British in the 19th century.

Although James Brooke became Rajah of Sarawak as a result of helping the Sultan of Brunei, he spent much of his energy chipping away at the power of the sultanate. Brooke's political manoeuvring and superior firepower forced the sultan into ceding large tracts of Brunei. To preserve his nation from being completely swallowed up by Sarawak, the sultan asked for Britain protection in 1888. The first British resident arrived in 1906 to advise the sultan on all matters except those pertaining to customs and religion.

The history of Brunei took a sudden and dramatic turn for the better in 1929 with the discovery of oil at Seria. Thirty years later, the nation achieved full internal self-rule, although Britain continued to administer its foreign affairs and defence. The first off-shore oil deposits were found in 1963.

Despite intense pressure, Brunei refused to become part of the Federation of Malaysia. Sultan Sir Omar Ali Saifuddien – the father of the present ruler – chose to keep Brunei under direct British protection. Sultan Omar abdicated in 1967 in favour of his 21-year-old eldest son, the Sandhurst-educated Prince Muda Hassanal Bolkiah, who became the 29th and current Sultan of Brunei.

In 1979, His Majesty the Sultan signed a treaty with Britain that set forth a five-year timetable for full independence. On 1 January 1984, the sultanate became the sovereign nation of Brunei Darussalam. Today, Brunei has established itself as an important independent nation with memberships in the the United Nations, Association of South East Asian Nations (ASEAN) and the Organization of Islamic Conference (OIC). ❑

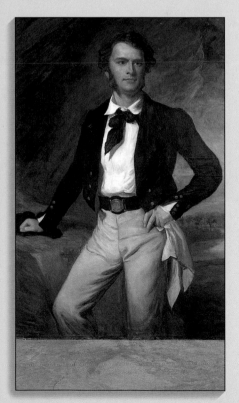

The portion of Kampong Ayer around the golden mosque and across Sungai Kedayam is easily explored on foot along rickety wooden walkways and bridges. But to see the full extent of the water-village, take the river cruise.

The modern **Supreme Court** building sits next to the water as you cross the bridge, while on the right is a hill with an ancient Muslim cemetery and the modern RIPAS Hospital, reputedly among the best in Borneo. In the same area is Brunei's largest mosque, the **Jame' Asr Hassanal Bolkiah**, known also as the Kiarong Mosque. It has landscaped gardens, golden domes, and fountains. It was built to commemorate the sultan's 25th year of reign.

Continuing on, you come to the capital's wet market in Gadong, where housewives buy their seafood, meat, fruits and vegetables. At dusk, the open-air carpark area adjacent to the wet market is transformed into a bustling food market that stays open till late. On Fridays and Sundays the same area becomes a horticultural market, packing in botanical enthusiasts from near and far. A fast-growing district, Gadong has become a busy and popular office and shopping district with restaurants and department stores too.

The impressive 1,788-room **Istana Nurul Iman**, home of the Sultan, is at Jalan Tutong. During the annual Hari Raya Aidilfitri festivities, it is open to the public. Visitors can enjoy a buffet meal before meeting the royal family members. At other times, view the world's largest residential palace from the riverbank park, **Taman Persiaran Damuan**.

At the **Brunei Arts and Handicrafts Training Centre** (Sat–Thur 8am–5pm, Fri 8–11.30am and 2–5pm; free; tel: 224 0676) in Jalan Residency, young artisans make silverware, brassware, baskets and brocade. Two specialties are miniature cannons and *keris*, the Malay dagger.

Map on page 223

The Sultan of Brunei is often said to be the world's richest man. But Bruneians generally have benefited from the oil boom: average incomes are the among the highest in Southeast Asia.

OPPOSITE: James Brooke. **BELOW:** water taxis.

Map on page 223

Five km (3 miles) east of B.S.B is **Kota Batu**, where the superb **Brunei Museum** (Sun–Thur 9am–5pm, Fri 9–11.30am and 2.30–5pm, Sat 9.45am–5pm; tel: 224 4545) has exhibits of natural history, native customs and dress, and the oil industry in Brunei. Its Islamic gallery has a collection of illuminated Korans, pottery, weapons, carpets, brass and glass from the sultan's private collection.

Down the hill, the galleries of the **Malay Technology Museum** (Sat–Mon, Wed–Thur 9.30am–5pm, Fri 9–11.30am and 2.30–5pm; free) show the traditional crafts and technology of the land-dwelling Malays, the water-village people and the Dayak tribes. The adjacent Archaeology Park has the remains of Kota Batu, the old capital of Brunei, and the tomb of Sultan Bolkiah, the "Singing Admiral" who extended his realm into the southern Philippines during Brunei's golden age.

Brunei is the most Islamic country in Southeast Asia. In 1991, the sale of alcohol was banned and stricter dress codes have since been introduced.

Jerudong ❶ town is about 25 km (15 miles) from B.S.B. This town has a polo field and club, royal stables and sports facilities. Its chief lure is **Jerudong Park Playground**; a public amusement garden with fun rides available at a nominal fee. Nearby, the 450-acre (182-hectare) premier Empire Hotel and Country Club (tel: 241 8888) faces the South China Sea. Fifteen minutes by car from B.S.B., via Jalan Berakas, is the site of the **National Stadium and International Conventional Centre**.

Beyond B.S.B.

RIGHT: Omar Ali Saifuddien Mosque. **BELOW:** Chinese temple.

Brunei has fine, unspoiled beaches along the northern coast. **Muara Beach ❷**, 27 km (17 miles) northeast of the capital, is near the main port where freighters and cruise liners dock. **Meragang** or Crocodile Beach is on the coastal road 7 km (4 miles) from Muara. **Serasa Beach**, about 10 minutes from Muara, has a watersports complex. **Pantai Seri Kenangan Beach**, 50 km (30 miles) west of the city near Tutong ❸, has the open ocean on one side and a lagoon on the other. **Tasek Merimbun**, Brunei's largest lake, is over an hour's drive from B.S.B., in Tutong district.

The Brunei government actively promotes eco-tourism. Tour agencies organise trips to **Pulau Selirong**, a 2,570-hectare (6,350-acre) island some 45 minutes from Muara, with a 2-km wooden walkway and nature observation tower. The mangrove islands at the mouth of the Brunei River harbour the rare proboscis monkey, crocodiles and birds.

Across Brunei Bay is Temburong District's main town, **Bangar**, a jumping-off point for visiting Iban and Murut longhouses. The park at **Batang Duri ❹**, about 16 km (10 miles) away, offers walks and swimming. Within the **Batu Apoi Forest Reserve**, the Field Studies Centre near Kuala Belalong specialises in research on lowland tropical forest, while the 50,000-hectare (120,000-acre) **Ulu Temburong National Park** has a walkway through the forest canopy for examining tree-top life. It also offers Brunei's highest peak, Bukit Pagon, rising above 1,800 metres (5,900 ft).

The Seria oils fields, 90 km (50 miles) from B.S.B., is where the original Shell well that struck the first oil was drilled, in 1929. This oil strike ignited Brunei's economic growth for the next half century. Near **Seria ❺**, on the road leading out to Labi, is **Sungei Liang Forest Park**, a small jungle reserve offering nature trails and recreational facilities. ❑

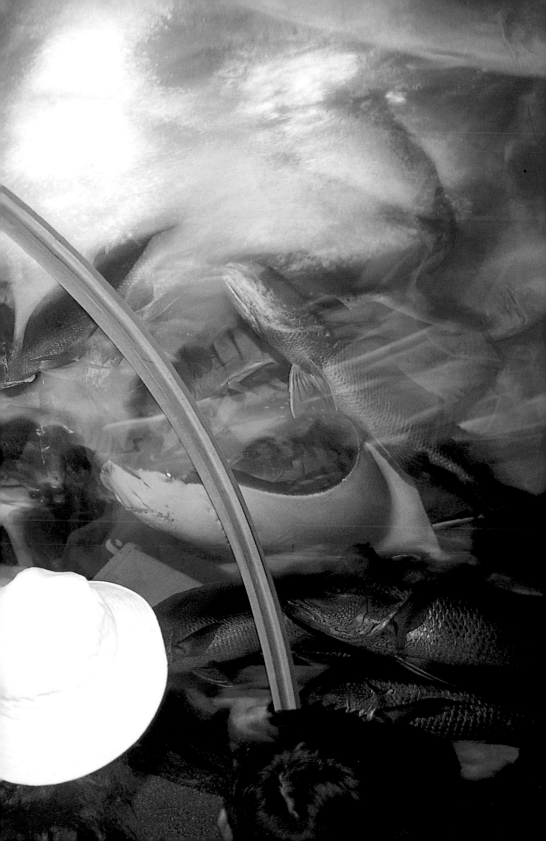

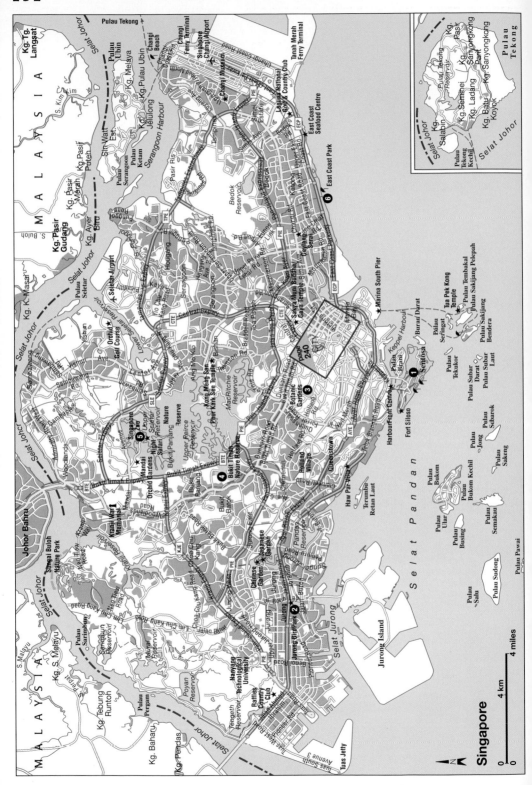

Singapore

SINGAPORE

The island's small size has allowed the government to manage

Singapore as one might operate a modern corporation

Minutes after landing at the stunningly efficient Changi Airport, the visitor is whisked down a wide highway lined with glorious tropical palms and bright bougainvillaea, and mile after mile of housing blocks, with probably the highest rate of home ownership in the world. Offshore, ships from all over the globe wait their turn in the world's busiest container port.

On a map of nearly any scale, the island of Singapore is just a dot at the tip of the Malay Peninsula. Despite well founded fears for its survival as an independent entity, the tiny 699 sq-km (267 sq-mile) island has blossomed into one of Asia's most successful economies. Its success has gone far beyond what Sir Stamford Raffles, its founder, envisioned when he bought the island from its Malay ruler in 1819 and set up as a trading post. From a sleepy Malay village, Singapore grew rapidly, drawing immigrants from China, India, Europe and neighbouring Malaya and Indonesia.

After independence from the British crown in 1965, the driving force behind Singapore's success was Lee Kuan Yew, who as Prime Minister (until 1990) led Singaporeans into a high-tech awakening and the second-highest standard of living in Asia, after Japan. Massive public housing projects and the establishment of educational facilities were initial priorities. Economic stability achieved through cooperation between unions and employers and an efficient infrastructure made Singapore attractive to multinationals. Indeed, some compare Singapore's style of governing to that of a corporation.

Singapore's population of 4.48 million, of which 3.6 million are Singapore residents. Of the resident population, 75 percent are Chinese, 14 percent Malays, 9 percent Indians, and 2 percent are from other ethnic groups. The non-resident population includes a sizeable number of expat employees of multinational corporations as well as unskilled labourers. In deference to the original settlers, Malay is the national language, but the *lingua franca* is English. Nearly every Singaporean is bilingual. English, Chinese, Malay and Tamil are official languages.

Asian and Western culture and values meet and mix in this cosmopolitan city. But Confucian precepts still temper ideals of personal freedom. Society and public discourse are kept on a tight rein, with fines for jaywalking, littering and other social misdemeanours. The result, however, is an uncommonly clean and efficient city, with probably the cleanest streets outside Switzerland. ❏

PRECEDING PAGES: walk-through aquarium at Sentosa; CBD skyline overlooking Singapore River.

Decisive Dates

The early years

2nd century AD: Sabara, a trading emporium, is identified in Ptolemy's *Geographic Huphegesis* as being at the southern tip of the "Golden Chersonese", possibly Singapore.

3rd century: Chinese said to have given the name Pa-luo-chung to the island.

1200s: Settlement called Tamasek reported on Singapore Island.

1300s: A settlement called Singapura is formed by Sultan Iskander Shah.

1330: Small settlement discovered by Chinese explorer and named Pancur. Singapore was probably founded around the middle of the 13th century by the Javanese Srivijayan empire.

14–18th centuries: Siam (modern-day Thailand), followed by Java's Majapahit empire, seizes the small island but shows little practical interest in it. At the beginning of the 16th century, the Portuguese capture Malacca, to the north, then an important centre in east–west trade. In the 17th century, the island of Singapore is settled by about 100 Orang Lauts, or sea nomads. At the end of the 18th century, the British and the British East India Company open a trading post in Penang and take Malacca from the Dutch, who dominate the region at the time.

British colonial rule

1819: Sir Thomas Stamford Raffles arrives in Singapore. His conviction is that the island, located at the crossroads of the South China Sea, will one day become important. The main items of trade are tea and silk from China, timber from Malaya, and spices from Indonesia.

1822: Raffles arrives from Bencoolen in October, declares principle of free trade in November.

1823: Raffles issues regulations outlawing gambling and slavery. Raffles leaves Singapore in June.

1824: The British agree to withdraw from Indonesia, in return for which the Dutch recognise British rights over Singapore. The Sultan cedes Singapore in perpetuity to the British.

1826: The trading stations at Penang, Malacca and Singapore are named the Straits Settlements, under the control of British India.

1839: First ship built in Singapore is launched.

1846: Chinese Funeral riots. First major secret society trouble in Singapore begins.

1851: Straits Settlements placed directly under the rule of the Governor-General of India.

1867: Straits Settlements become a Crown Colony, controlled by the Colonial Office in London.

late 1800s: The Suez Canal opens and the number of ships calling in at Singapore increases. Trade flourishes. John Ridley, director of the Botanical Gardens in Singapore, succeeds in growing a rubber tree. The Malaysian peninsula and Singapore develop into the world's main rubber producers.

World wars

1911: Population of Singapore grows to 250,000 and the census records 48 races on the island, speaking 54 languages.

1920s: The Great Depression's reverberations are felt in Singapore as the prices of commodities such as rubber collapse. But Singapore, even in its relative poverty, is secure – it is the greatest naval base of the British empire east of Suez.

1923: Singapore is linked to Malaysia by a causeway.

1941: Japan invades Malaysia, landing at Kota Bahru. Singapore is bombed on 8 December.

1942: British troops on Singapore surrender to Japan, whose troops surprise the British by coming down the Malay peninsula on bicycles. The Japanese rename Singapore as *Syonan*, "Light of the South". Under their occupation many civilians, particularly the Chinese, are killed or suffer unspeakable hardships.

1945: The Japanese three-and-a-half years' rule ends in August, with the landing of the Allied troops. The British make Singapore a Crown Colony.

Independence and federation

1948: The British allow a limited form of elections to the legislative council. A bill proscribing Pan-Malaya Federation of the Trade Unions is introduced in Malaysia. Emergency declared in June. Malayan Democratic Union dissolved.

1950: Lee Kuan Yew addresses Malayan Forum in London in January. Lee Kuan Yew and Goh Keng Swee return to Singapore in August.

1951: Legislative Council Election. Singapore formally proclaimed a city with a royal charter.

1955: Rendel Commission granted by the British leads to elections and David Marshall becomes chief minister. A legislative council consisting of 32 members, 25 of whom are elected, is established. The Labour Front have a majority, but the PAP (People's Action Party) forms a powerful opposition.

1956: PAP Central Executive Committee election in which Communists decline to run occurs in July. Chinese student riots; leftist PAP leaders are arrested.

1958: A constitutional agreement for partial independence for Singapore is finally signed in London.

1959: PAP wins general election with 43 of 51 seats, and 53 percent of the popular vote. Lee Kuan Yew becomes the country's first Prime Minister and Singapore is declared a state.

1962: Commission on colonialism rejects criticism of referendum.

1963: Malaysia agreement signed in London. The people of Malaya, Sarawak, North Borneo (now Sabah) and Singapore vote to form the Federation of Malaysia. Malaysia forms with Singapore as a component. PAP wins Singapore general election.

1964: PAP wins only one seat in Malaysian general election. Communal riots.

The Republic of Singapore

1965: PAP wins Hong Lim constituency's by-election. Singapore leaves the Federation of Malaysia and becomes an independent sovereign nation. Singapore joins the United Nations and the Commonwealth.

1966: Bukit Merah constituency by-election won by PAP against an independent. Chua Chu Kang, Crawford and Paya Lebar constituencies by-elections won by PAP uncontested.

1967: Singapore, Malaysia, Thailand, Indonesia, the Philippines and Brunei form a political and economic union, ASEAN (Association of Southeast Asian Nations. **1968:** PAP sweeps first Parliamentary general election, winning all 58 seats.

LEFT: Sir Thomas Stamford Raffles.
RIGHT: former Prime Minister Lee Kuan Yew.

1970–89: The PAP continues to dominate parliament.

1971: British Far East Command ceases.

1972: PAP wins all seats in general election.

1974: Combined Japanese Red Army and Popular Front for the Liberation of Palestine terrorists attack Shell Oil refinery at Pulau Bukom and take hostages.

1981: In a by-election, J.B. Jeyaratnam of the Workers' Party wins the first seat to be held by a member of an opposition party.

1984: PAP loses two of 79 seats in general election, its first loss of a seat in a general election since 1964.

1990: Goh Chok Tong takes over as Prime Minister.

1996: As a result of a decision by the OECD, Singapore is no longer regarded as a "developing nation".

1999: The economy makes a dramatic recovery after the 1997 Asian crisis. S.R. Nathan is elected President.

2001: PAP wins 75 percent of the votes in the general elections. The economy takes a tumble in the face of the US and global economic slowdown.

2003: Outbreak of Severe Acute Respiratory Syndrome (SARS) quickly controlled.

2004: Lee Hsien Loong takes over as prime minister. Goh Chok Tong continues as senior minister and Lee Kuan Yew, minister mentor.

2005: The green light is given to legalise casino gambling and to the building of two "integrated resorts", mega entertainment and leisure complexes.

2006: The PAP wins 82 of 84 seats in the general elections. ❑

THE SINGAPOREANS

The island is a proverbial melting pot of cultures, and it is this diversity that

gives the famously structured city-state its distinctive character

Today, the Chinese make up about 75 percent of the resident population in Singapore. For centuries, Chinese junks roamed the neighbouring seas. A Buddhist pilgrim named Fa-Hsien passed through the Straits of Malacca from Ceylon in AD 414. A trader called Wang Ta-Yuan later visited in 1349 when Singapore was a swampy outpost named Temasek. He reported finding Chinese in residence in the area even then.

When Sir Stamford Raffles hoisted a Union Jack ashore and founded modern Singapore in 1819, Chinese planters, pirates, fishermen and traders were already installed. Five years after the colony was established, Singapore had 3,000 Chinese and more were arriving weekly.

The Straits Chinese began settling in the Malay Peninsula and Riau islands more than 400 years ago in order to take advantage of the rich trade along the Straits of Malacca. Straits Chinese culture is often called by a different name, Peranakan, and the people themselves are sometimes called Babas and Nonyas.

After centuries of melding, a hybrid Straits Chinese culture developed with its own distinct language, architecture, cuisine and clothing. Their *lingua franca* is Malay, but an idiosyncratic version of Malay. Peranakan food is unique in its lavish use of spices and shrimp paste for cooking and can be readily found all over the island.

Shortly after Singapore was founded, junks started bringing waves of immigrants from coastal areas of southern and eastern China. Some of the largest groups comprised Hokkien Chinese from southern Fujian province. These hardy Chinese were usually traders and businessmen, largely the roots of today's Hokkien population that account for two-fifths of the Chinese in Singapore. Other Chinese came in numbers, speaking distinct dialects, cooking different foods and engaged in other work. The Chinese had fled from mainland China and the

despotic Qing dynasty. They took on the back-breaking jobs that no one else wanted to do.

Today's Singapore has a curious mixture of the new and old Chinese, broadly labelled "English-educated" or "Chinese educated". The latter tend more towards Chinese chauvinism and strong links to their heritage, respond-

ing more slowly to the new Singaporean identity. They sometimes look upon English-educated Chinese with shades of the contempt that their great ancestors held for barbarians not of the Middle Kingdom. The English-educated frequently perceive them, in return, as being conservative and unprogressive.

The Malays

Like the Chinese and Indians, Singapore's Malays are largely descendants of immigrants, although their arrival most certainly predates that of the other races. Today they make up 14 percent of Singapore's resident population. Despite Singapore's Chinese influence, its

LEFT: Singapore's children reflect Indian, Chinese, Malay and European heritage. **RIGHT:** Muslim women wear a head shawl when praying.

Malay origins are enshrined in the symbolic trappings of statehood – the national anthem is sung in Malay, the national language is Malay and the island's first president after independence was a Malay.

Islam, followed closely by Malays, calls for hours of prayer and study of the Koran. The gentle drone of the *muezzin* echoes above traffic junctions from the lofty minarets of the Sultan Mosque – the centre of Islam in Singapore. The village mosque, lies

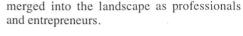

INDIAN NAMESAKE

Ever since early settlers borrowed the Sanskrit words *Singha Pura* (Lion City) in the naming of the island, Singapore's society has continued to draw heavily from the Indian subcontinent.

at the heart of every Malay neighbourhood.

Historically, the Malay community has been socio-economically weaker than the Chinese and Indians. This is partly because of its rural roots and partly due to Malay education, which closely follows a religious syllabus and has a reputation of lagging behind the English school system. The government, aware of these problems, set up a self-help organisation called Mendaki to promote the progress of the Malay community. Today, Malay youths are successfully entering the mainstream, slowly improving the negative perceptions attached to their community. Having imbibed the government's ambitious approach, a good number have

merged into the landscape as professionals and entrepreneurs.

The Indians

The aroma of incense and freshly pounded curry floats over several square kilometres of Little India. Sixty percent of Singapore's Indians are Tamils, from the eastern part of southern India, and approximately 20 percent Malayalis Hindus from the Kerala state on the other side of the subcontinent. The rest are Bengalis, Punjabis, and others – among whom one finds a colourful mixture of Hindus, Buddhists, Christians, Sikhs and the Parsis, a small yet close-knit community. A minority of just 9 percent of Singapore's population, Indians nevertheless influence every aspect of life.

Much of the classical Indian culture has survived in Singapore, from old-style recipes to dance, art and literature. The casual traveller wanting a three-day taste of India might well find the taxi fare to Little India a better investment than a plane ticket to India.

Eurasians and others

The Eurasians are a mixture from two continents. Some are half English, others part Dutch, many part Portuguese. Many of them are also partly Filipino, Chinese, Malay, Indian, Sri Lankan or Thai. Less than 1 percent of Singaporeans are Eurasians, and most trace their roots back to colonial times, when the Portuguese, Dutch and English married local women.

With its policy of attracting "foreign talent" to its shores, Singapore plays host to a significant number of foreigners, many of whom have acquired permanent residency status. Many work in white-collar professions, primarily the IT and finance industries. Also in the local workforce are Filipinos, Indonesians, Thai, Burmese, Sri Lankans and South Indians who work in construction and environment maintainence as well as women who work as live-in domestic maids. They mainly take on the work that younger Singaporeans shun, and unfortunately, are marginalised in Singapore's affluent society. ❑

LEFT: Eurasians are a blend of cultures and races.
RIGHT: most Singaporeans are Chinese, reflected in the Chinese traditions such as *tai chi.*

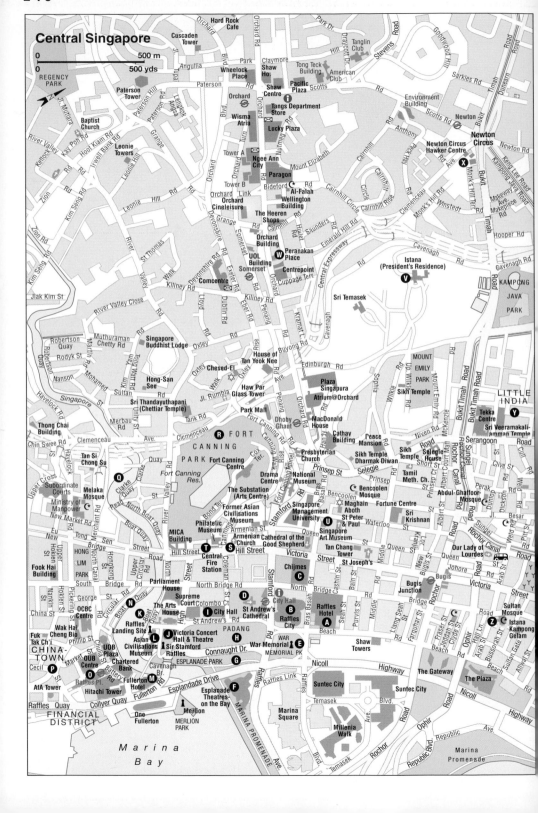

Central Singapore

0 _____ 500 m
0 _____ 500 yds

SINGAPORE

Straddling the equator, this burgeoning city-state, despite being a tiny dot on the map, has made a reputation for itself as one of the most meticulously constructed societies in the world

Map on page 240

More than 170 years after Raffles first set foot in Singapore, the island is still governed from the colonial nucleus he established along the bank of the Singapore River. As well as being the hub of government, the old colonial district is also the location of Singapore's most famous landmark. Nearly everyone who comes to Singapore ends up at **Raffles Hotel Ⓐ** at one point or another – usually to try the world famous Singapore Sling, a cocktail invented at Raffles in 1915 at the Long Bar. Opened in 1887 by the Sarkies brothers, Raffles has seen its fair share of kings and queens, presidents and prime ministers, movie actors and lions of literature, as well as millions of ordinary people who are attracted to this paragon of tropical elegance and style.

Towering beside the hotel is a silver monolith called **Raffles City Ⓑ**, one of the island's largest retail, office and hotel complexes and a busy hub of the Mass Rapid Transit (MRT) network. Next door is **Swissôtel The Stamford**, the world's tallest hotel, with panoramic views offered from its penthouse restaurant at the top. Across the street from Raffles City is **Chijmes Ⓒ**, a former Catholic convent and church dating back to 1860, but now restored into a pleasant hub of restaurants, bars and boutiques. South of Raffles City across Stamford Road is the graceful spire of **St Andrew's Cathedral Ⓓ** (open daily 9am–10pm). The church, built by Indian convict labour, owes its sparkling white surface to a plaster made of egg white, egg shell, lime, sugar, coconut husk and water. The cathedral, in the style of an early Gothic abbey, was consecrated in 1862.

East of Raffles City across Beach Road is the **War Memorial Park Ⓔ**, dedicated to civilians who suffered and died in Singapore at the hands of the Japanese during World War II. On the opposite side of the park are two huge developments on reclaimed land that was once part of the sea. One is a massive convention, hotel and shopping development, called **Suntec City** and the other is **Marina Square**, a huge mall with hundreds of shops.

A world-class arts centre

South of Marina Square along Marina Bay is the prickly hedgehog-like outline of **The Esplanade – Theatres on the Bay Ⓕ** (tel: 6828 8222; www. esplanade.com), a S$600-million performing arts centre with equally grandiose dreams of establishing itself as a cultural landmark akin to Australia's Sydney Opera House. Housing a concert hall, theatre, an open-air amphitheatre, practice studios, outdoor spaces for informal performances and sculpted gardens, its distinctive facade of sharp-edged metal sunshades has been likened to the thorny shell of the

BELOW:
The Esplanade – Theatres on the Bay.

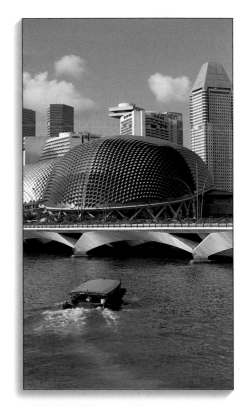

durian fruit. From this vantage point are expansive views of Singapore's CBD skyline with the statue of the water-spewing **Merlion** in the distance, the half-fish, half-lion creature that is associated with Singapore's mythical past.

Across Esplanade Drive is **Esplanade Park**  with its tree-lined **Queen Elizabeth Walk**, formerly a seafront promenade where colonial-day Europeans spent their leisure time strolling or playing cricket. West of the park across Connaught Drive is an expanse of green called the **Padang** ❶ ("field" in Malay), a frequent venue of Singapore's annual National Day celebrations on 9 August. Flanking the Padang are two of Singapore's oldest leisure clubs, **Singapore Recreation Club** (1883) and the **Singapore Cricket Club** (1852) – the former newly rebuilt on its original site.

Facing the Padang is **City Hall** ❶, completed in 1929 with a facade of Greek columns and a grand staircase. It was on these steps that Lord Louis Mountbatten accepted the surrender of Singapore by the Japanese General Itagaki on 12 September 1945. Lee Kuan Yew declared Singapore's independence from Britain on the same spot 14 years later, in 1959. Next door is the former **Supreme Court**, built in 1927 with its stout Corinthian columns and green dome. Across Parliament Place is **The Arts House** (tel: 6332 6900; www. theartshouse.com.sg), a performing arts centre housed in an 1820s-structure, formerly the old Parliament House. Beside this is the new **Parliament House**, completed in 1999. The colonial structure to the east is **Victoria Concert Hall and Theatre** ❶, built in the 1880s to commemorate Queen Victoria's Diamond Jubilee, now venues for opera, ballet and classical music. An 1887 bronze statue of Stamford Raffles graces the front of the theatre, a replica of which is found at the **Raffles' Landing Site** ❶ along the edge of the Singapore River.

BELOW: Victoria Concert Hall and Theatre, a cultural haven in the city.

This is claimed to be the very spot where the founder of modern Singapore stepped ashore on 28 January 1819.

Map on page 240

To its left is the stately **Asian Civilisations Museum** ⓛ (Mon 1–7pm, Tues–Thur and Sat–Sun 9am–7pm, Fri 9am–9pm; entrance fee; tel: 6332 2982; www.acm.org.sg), a beautiful restored neoclassical building that dates back to 1854 and formerly used as government offices. The museum displays a fine collection on the civilisations of East, Southeast, South and West Asia.

From here, cross the 1910 **Cavenagh Bridge** to get to Singapore's former General Post Office. This grand Palladian-style building has been restored to its current glory as the five-star **Fullerton Hotel** ⓜ. Originally built in 1928 and named after Robert Fullerton, the first governor of the Straits Settlements, the building is a wonderful example of the neoclassical style that once dominated the district. Enter by the massive revolving door and see the central atrium, created by punching out several floors and the old ceiling.

For a study in architectural contrast, take the underpass beneath the Fullerton Hotel to the glass-and-steel **One Fullerton** structure, a new restaurant and nightlife hub by the waterfront. There are swanky restaurants and bars, most with floor-to-ceiling windows offering magnificent views of **Marina Bay**.

On the other side of the Singapore River is **Boat Quay** ⓝ, an area of historic interest that has become something of a yuppie enclave. Dozens of Victorian-era shophouses have been restored and transformed into trendy bars and restaurants with outdoor seating.

The core of "Singapore Inc" runs along the waterfront from south of Boat Quay to Keppel Road. The commercial area once centred on **Raffles Place** ⓞ, which has been transformed into an open-air plaza with an MRT station below. Singapore's tallest skyscrapers are centred here: **OUB Centre**, **OUB Plaza** and **Republic Plaza**, all of which reach a height of 280 metres (920 ft), the maximum allowed by civil aviation rules.

Chinatown

It may seem strange to have a **Chinatown** ⓟ in a place that's over 75 percent Chinese, but this can be traced back to Raffles, who subdivided his new town into various districts in the early 1820s.

The heart of Chinatown is an area off South Bridge Road that embraces Pagoda, Temple and Trengganu streets. Begin your exploration in Pagoda Street, where the **Chinatown Heritage Centre** (Mon–Thur 9am–8pm, Fri–Sun 9am–9pm; tel: 6325 2878; entrance fee; www.chinatownheritage.com.sg) is located in the conservation shophouse at No. 48. It showcases the area's cultural heritage and includes a re-creation of the cramped living conditions of early residents.

In the evenings, Pagoda, Trengganu and Sago streets are closed off to traffic and transformed into the lively **Chinatown Night Market** (Sun–Thur 5–11pm, Fri–Sat 5pm–1am). With over 200 stalls selling both traditional Chinese goods like calligraphy, masks and lanterns as well as contemporary items like funky jewellery and bags, the market deserves a leisurely trawl. Another good place to shop in the neighbourhood is **Chinatown Point**, at the corner of New Bridge Road

BELOW:
Raffles' Landing Site and surrounding skyscrapers.

and Cross Street, with its shops selling arts, crafts, souvenirs and antiques.

One of the most curious things about Chinatown is that it harbours some of the island's best Hindu and Muslim shrines. Towering above the shophouses are the brightly painted figures adorning the *gopuram* (tower) at the entrance of the **Sri Mariamman Temple** (daily 7am–8.30pm) on South Bridge Road, the oldest Hindu shrine in Singapore. Brightly clad devotees perform *pujas* amid gaudy statues and vivid ceiling frescoes. Built in the 1820s, this is the site of Thimiti – the fire walking festival – when the faithful work themselves into a trance and walk over burning embers to fulfil their vows to the goddess Droba-Devi. A block away is the **Jamae Mosque** (daily 9.30am–6pm), with its pagoda-like minarets rarely seen in mosque architecture and reflecting strong Chinese influence.

Telok Ayer Street once ran along the waterfront, but today the road is blocked from the sea by a wall of gleaming skyscrapers. It was here that seafarers and immigrants from China's Fujian Province set up a joss house in gratitude for their safe arrival after their long sea voyage from China in the early 1820s. The little joss house eventually became **Thian Hock Keng Temple** (daily 7.30am–5.30pm), the Temple of Heavenly Happiness dedicated to Ma Chu Po, Goddess of the Sea, who reputedly calms the ocean waters and rescues those in danger of drowning.

Further along the road is **Nagore Durgha Shrine**, also called Masjid Chulia. Currently closed for renovations, the mosque, built by Muslims from southern India in 1830, is another example of the ethnic and religious variety in Chinatown.

Upstream along the Singapore River, **Clarke Quay ❻** – bounded by River Valley Road, Tan Tye Place and North Boat Quay – with restored 19-century warehouses now home to dining and nightlife establishments. North of Clarke

Sri Mariamman Temple, on South Bridge Road.

BELOW: Chinatown calligrapher, a disappearing trade.

Quay is historic **Fort Canning Park** . Once known as Bukit Larangan (Forbidden Hill), in the early years of Singapore's history, this strategic location was the site of grand palaces protected by walls and swamps. In 1860, the British built a fort atop the hill, from where dawn, noon and dusk were announced each day by way of cannon fire.

At the base of the hill, at the junction of Coleman and Hill streets, is the **Armenian Church** ❺ (daily 9am–6pm), also called St Gregory the Illuminator. Built in 1835, this exquisite church is the oldest in Singapore. A cemetery in the church grounds is the final resting place of some eminent Singaporeans, among them Agnes Joaquim (1864–99), after whom Singapore's national flower, Vanda Miss Joaquim, is named. At No. 62 Hill Street is another architectural gem of a building, the old red and white **Central Fire Station** ❼, headquarters of the Singapore Fire Brigade, which was completed in 1909. On the ground level is the **Civil Defence Heritage Gallery** (Tues–Sun 10am–5pm; tel: 6332 5642) where a gleaming red fire engine from 1905 occupies pride of place.

Down Hill Street and left into Stamford Road leads to the **National Museum of Singapore** (daily 10am–6pm; entrance fee; tel: 6332 5642; www.national museum.sg). Reopened in late 2006 after a three-year renovation, it has reinvented itself as a hip space to learn about history with interactive displays and lifestyle programmes. Look out for the Singapore History Gallery with 11 national treasures, from the Singapore Stone, a rock with inscriptions dating back to the 10th century, to 14th-century Majapahit gold ornaments. At nearby Bras Basah Road, the **Singapore Art Museum** ❶ (Mon–Sun 10am–7pm, Fri 10am–9pm; tel: 6332 3222; entrance fee, Fri 6–9pm free; www.singart.com), with rotating exhibits covering Singaporean, Asian and Western artists.

Hell money is burned for the well-being of Chinese ancestors.

BELOW: the Armenian Church was built in 1835.

Orchard Road and environs

The de facto heart of modern Singapore is **Orchard Road**, which begins just north of the Raffles Hotel area. Plaza Singapura and Park Mall are the first of the big shopping centres that have given Orchard Road its international reputation. Near Plaza Singapura is the **Istana** , the official workplace and expansive residence of Singapore's president. The palace and its lavish garden are strictly off-limits to the public, except on National Day and certain public holidays, when the gates are thrown open to curious sightseers. The Istana was built in 1869 on the grounds of an old nutmeg plantation, and it served as the residence of the British governor until the island became self-governing in 1959.

Northwards on Orchard Road are the famous shopping centres that inspired one commentator to call Singapore the world's largest shopping centre with immigration controls. Near the Centrepoint mall is the charming **Peranakan Place** ⓦ, a complex of six Peranakan-style terrace houses that have been transformed into a commercial hub. This area was once settled by the Peranakan people, or Straits-born Chinese, a unique culture that evolved through intermarriage between Chinese migrants and local Malay women in the 19th century. Take a walk behind Peranakan Place to **Emerald Hill**, where there are some lovely old restored homes that once belonged to wealthy Peranakan families.

Intersecting Orchard Road is Scotts Road, where there are more shopping malls and luxury hotels like the Grand Hyatt and Goodwood Park Hotel.

Little India

A walk down Scotts Road leads to **Newton Circus Hawker Centre** ⓧ, where one can sample the local fare for which Singapore is so famous for, and very cheaply too. Not far from here is **Serangoon Road**, where the visitor is plunged into a replica of the Asian subcontinent, with undulating music punctuated by car horns and bicycle bells, women drifting gracefully along in vivid *saris* and the pungent aromas of spices. **Little India** ⓨ is filled with interesting religious sights – not just Hindu temples, but shrines representing the entire spectrum of Singapore's various faiths. Tucked away on Dunlop Street is the lovely old **Abdul Gafoor Mosque** (daily 9am–6pm), with its courtyard and small houses for Malay and Indian worshippers.

Hindus congregate at the **Sri Veeramakaliamman Temple** (daily 8am–noon and 4–9pm), dedicated to Kali, Shiva's consort, who epitomises the struggle against evil. She is shown ripping a hapless victim apart. Kali's sons – Ganesh, the elephant god, and Murugan, the child god – are depicted with her at the side of the temple. Further up Serangoon Road, the great *gopuram* (tower) of the **Sri Srinivasa Perumal Temple** (daily 6.30am–noon and 5–9pm) is visible, showing the different incarnations of Vishnu. The annual Thaipusam procession sets off from here. Devotees, their tongues and cheeks pierced by great metal skewers supporting *kavadi* (cage-like constructions decorated with wire and peacock feathers) make their way to the **Sri Thandayuthapani Temple** (better known as Chettiar Temple) in Tank Road. This is done in gratitude or supplication to Lord Murugan.

BELOW: Sri Srinivasa Perumal Temple.

Race Course Road may have lost its horses, but the street is now renowned for its banana-leaf curry restaurants. Down the street are a few Chinese temples. **Leong San See Temple** (daily 6am–5.30pm), dedicated to Kuan Yin, is richly carved and ornately decorated. At the back is a spacious courtyard and numerous ancestral tablets. Over the road is the stunning **Sakya Muni Buddha Gaya Temple**, also known as the Temple of 1,000 Lights (daily 8am–4.45pm), where a 15-metre-high (50-ft) Buddha sits in a halo of light, atop a base depicting scenes from the life of Prince Siddharta Gautama.

At the very heart of the nearby Beach Road district is **Istana Kampung Gelam**, the old royal palace built in the early 1840s by Sultan Ali Iskandar Shah. Arab traders – together with Bugis, Javanese, Sumatrans, Malays and people from the Riau islands – eventually settled in the area, transforming Kampung Glam into a commercial hub, especially the stretch along Arab Street, which still draws those looking for bargains. The **Malay Heritage Centre** (Mon 1–6pm, Tues–Sun 10am–6pm; entrance fee; tel: 6391 0450; www.malayheritage.org.sg) in the compound has interesting displays tracing the history and heritage of Malays. Dominating the neighbourhood is the golden bulk of **Sultan Mosque ❷** (Sat–Thur 9am–1pm and 2–4pm, Fri 2.30–4pm), the largest mosque in Singapore and where the *muezzin* calls the faithful to prayer five times a day, the women to their enclave located upstairs, the men to the mosque's main prayer hall.

Sentosa and the West Coast

Buried in the city and its shopping centres, it's easy to forget that Singapore is in the tropics, so take the opportunity to enjoy a little island hopping. The most accessible island is **Sentosa ❶** (entrance fee; tel: 1800-736 8672; www.sen

Map on pages 240, 232

TIP

During Ramadan – the fasting month for Muslims based on a lunar calendar – the area around the Sultan Mosque is festooned with bright lights and bustling activity at night, after the fast is broken at sundown.

BELOW: beachfront, Sentosa island.

Map on page 232

The Botanic Gardens are famous for its orchid collection.

RIGHT: much of old Singapore is undergoing renovation.
BELOW: bird life in the city.

tosa.com.sg), which has become a major resort and recreation area over the past few years, after its previous life as a military base. A cable car stretches from the **HarbourFront Centre**, on Telok Blangah Road, to Sentosa, or one can reach the island via MRT to HarbourFront station, followed by a bus or Sentosa Express ride. Its name may mean "Island of Tranquillity", but Sentosa is now a lively theme park that has become more of a giant amusement ride than a quiet island retreat. Still, on a quiet weekday, it may be possible to relax on its fine sandy beaches and soak up the sun.

Flora and fauna retreats

Western Singapore embraces both industrial areas such as Jurong and Tuas and a major recreation zone that includes some of Singapore's top green spaces and theme parks, such as the **Jurong BirdPark ❷** (daily 9am–6pm; entrance fee; tel: 6265 0022; www.birdpark.com.sg). Scarlet ibis welcome visitors at the entrance of this 20-hectare (50-acre) park, which is home to 8,000 birds of 600 different species from all over the world.

The lovely **Botanic Gardens ❸** (daily 5am–midnight; free; tel: 6471 7361; www.sbg.org.sg) near Tanglin Road have been in bloom for over a century, although its lineage can be traced back to the 1820s, when Sir Stamford Raffles planted an experimental spice garden near his bungalow. Its orchid gardens are not to be missed. For less manicured flora and fauna, jungle walks weave in all directions throughout the **Bukit Timah Nature Reserve ❹** (daily 8.30am–6.30pm; free), about 12 km (8 miles) from the city centre. The thick tropical vegetation resembles the entire scenery of Singapore when Raffles first arrived. This 164-hectare (405-acre) park has a rich collection of local wildlife, including long-tailed macaque monkeys, flying lemurs, tropical squirrels, civet cats and brilliant forest birds.

The **Singapore Zoo ❺** (daily 8.30am–6pm; tel: 6269 3411; entrance fee; www.zoo.com.sg) at Mandai Lake Road, regarded as one of the best zoos in the world, has the finest wildlife collection in Southeast Asia. The place bills itself as an "open zoo" – few of the animals are in cages or behind bars. Among the rare or endangered species are the Komodo dragon (the world's largest lizard), Malay tapir, clouded leopard, Sumatran tiger, Bawean hog deer and the largest group of orang-utans in captivity. For a different perspective, consider the unique **Night Safari** (daily 6pm–midnight; tel: 6269 3411; entrance fee; www.nightsafari.com.sg), where nocturnal animals can be observed outside under special lighting.

East Coast

Visitors have their first experience of Singapore while travelling into the city from **Changi Airport** along the east coast, with sandy beaches on one side of the coastal highway, and luxury condominium blocks on the other. The east coast is packed on weekends as Singaporeans escape to the beach, but during the week the beach is virtually deserted. **East Coast Park ❻** stretches for more than 10 km (6 miles) along the coast between Marina Bay and the airport, fringed with casuarinas, coconut palms and flowering trees. ❑

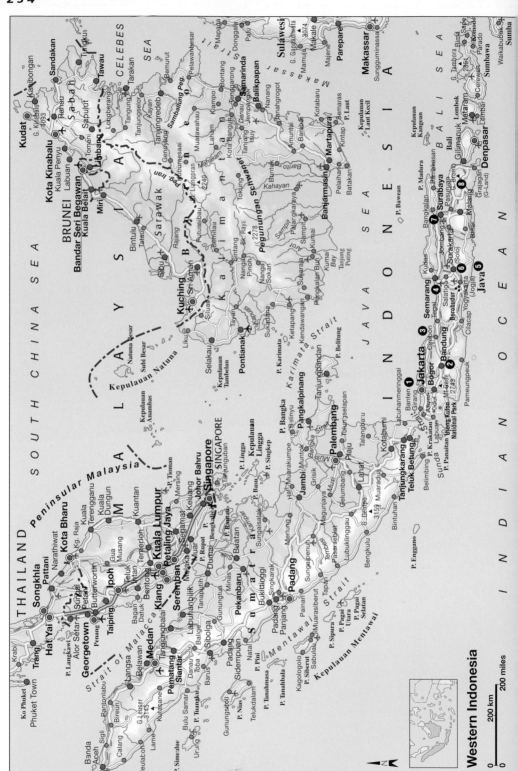

Western Indonesia

0   200 km

0   200 miles

INDONESIA

An immense nation extending one-eighth of the world's circumference, Indonesia is Asia's most diverse country

Indonesia is one of the very few nations on earth to span such a broad spectrum of world history and human civilisation – from its ancient Hindu-Javanese temples to Bali's modern luxury resorts, and from the stone-age lifestyle in Papua (Irian Jaya) to the immense metropolis that is Jakarta. The country's motto, *Bhinneka Tunggallka*, or Unity in Diversity, is no mere slogan. The population of nearly 220 million people is derived from 300 ethnic groups who speak over 250 (some sources say as many as 500) distinct languages. The common element is Bahasa Indonesia, the national language, which is very similar to Malay.

Almost 90 percent of the people are Muslims, with a significant Christian population. There are also smaller numbers of Hindus, Buddhists and Confucians. In most cases, particularly in the rural areas, these beliefs are augmented by indigenous, centuries-old animistic traditions. The fourth most populous nation in the world, Indonesia straddles two geographically defined racial groups, the Asians to the west and the Melanesians in the east. The majority are Asians. Over the centuries, mostly through commerce and trade, Indians, Arabs and Europeans have mingled with the indigenous people. The largest non-indigenous ethnic group is the Chinese, who control nearly three-quarters of the nation's wealth while comprising only 5 percent of the population.

Indonesia's people are unevenly distributed across the archipelago with more than half living in Java and Bali alone, which cover only 7 percent of the total land area. With more than 120 million people living in Java, the demands on its land and resources are considerable. As a result, the government relocated landless people from Java to the more remote provinces. But the programme's success was elusive and caused friction between the locals and migrants. This and East Timor's independence in 1999 added to the push for greater autonomy in the other provinces, whose populations were unhappy that Jakarta continued to drain local resources.

After Soeharto's fall in 1998, regional autonomy was granted. The governments under the presidents who followed – B.J. Habibie, Abdurrahman Wahid and Megawati Sukarnoputri – struggled to cope with political infighting, corruption, religious tensions and a weak economy.

The current president, Susilo Bambang Yudhoyono, who was elected into presidency in 2004, has his hands full fighting corruption, rejuvenating the economy and tackling the multitude of other issues that come with leading a fledgling democracy. However, at least some of his efforts were internationally recognised when he was nominated for the 2006 Nobel Peace Prize for the Aceh truce, which ended almost 30 years of fighting in Nanggroe Aceh Darussalam, northern Sumatra. ❑

PRECEDING PAGES: planting rice, Lombok; Welcome Statue, Jakarta.

Decisive Dates

Prehistoric years

1.7 million years ago: Hominids live in Java.
250,000 years ago: Solo Man, the distinct evolutionary descendent of *Homo erectus*, inhabit central Java.
40,000 years ago: Fossil records of modern humans *(Homo sapiens)* found in Indonesia.
5000 BC: Austronesian peoples begin moving into Indonesia from the Philippines.
500 BC–AD 500: Dong Son Bronze Age. Decorative styles of this period influence many Indonesian arts and spread with bronze-casting techniques.

Indianised kingdoms

AD 400: Hindu kingdoms of Tarumanegara (West Java) and Kutai (East Kalimantan) emerge.
850: Sanjaya (early Mataram) and rival Buddhist Sailendran dynasties merge through marriage. Sanjaya seizes control of central Java. The Sailendrans flee to Srivijaya in southern Sumatra.
860–1000: The golden age of Srivijaya.
910: Political centre of Java moves to East Java; rise of Hindu kingdoms on Bali.
914–1080: First-known Hindu kingdoms.

Singasari and Majapahit

1222: Ken Arok founds Singasari dynasty.
1275: Arok controls vital maritime trade from Sririvijaya.

1292: Civil war in Singasari; Mongol invasion joins Wijaya against Jayakatwang, Arok's successor.
1294: Wijaya founds the Majapahit kingdom, the most powerful in Indonesian history.
1297: Sultan Malik Saleh of Pasai rules as the first-known Muslim king.
1389: Majapahit's decline begins.
1429: Majapahit loses control of the western Java Sea and the straits to Islamic Melaka.
15th century: Majapahit and Kediri are conquered by the new Islamic state, Demak, on Java's north coast. The entire Hindu-Javanese aristocracy moves to Bali.
Early 16th century: Two Islamic sultanates in Java are established: Banten and Cirebon.
1552–70: Banten rises as an independent state.

Dutch colonial years

Early 17th century: Senopati founds second Mataram kingdom; Dutch ships arrive. Both contest the sovereignty of Java.
1602–03: The Dutch form the United Dutch East Indies Company (VOC) and establish a trading post in Banten.
1611: The Dutch establish a trading post in Jayakarta (Jakarta).
1619: The Dutch take over Jayakarta and rename it Batavia.
1613–46: Mataram expands rapidly under Sultan Agung (Imogiri), who unsuccessfully attacks Batavia, enraging the Dutch.
1671: Agung's successor, Mangkurat I, rebels against the Dutch who help suppress the rebellion and enthrone Mangkurat II, who shifts the Mataram capital to Kartasura, west of Surakarta.
1740–55: A major conflict originates in Batavia. The Dutch acquire the right to collect tolls throughout Mataram. A new capital at Surakarta is established.
1755: Another war of succession ensues, leading to the partition of Mataram into two major courts: Surakarta and Yogyakarta.
1757: The Dutch create a minor principality dependent on Surakarta, Mangkunegaran.
1767–77: The VOC fights a bitter campaign to conquer eastern Java, resulting in the demise of the last Hinduised kingdom in Java, Blambangan.
1799–1800: The VOC is dissolved and the Dutch assume control.

Resistance and repression

1811–16: Brief period of English rule under Thomas Stamford Raffles.
1812: The Dutch create another minor principality dependent on Yogyakarta, Pakualaman.

1813: Raffles abolishes the sultanates of Banten and Cirebon.

1817: Raffles authors the monumental *History of Java.*

1825–30: Diponegoro, a charismatic prince of the Yogyakarta Sultanate, leads the cataclysmic Java War against the Dutch. Raffles deposes the sultan; Diponegoro is sent into exile in Sulawesi, where he dies.

1830: In an attempt to remedy government debt, the Dutch introduce a land tax payable by labour or land uco known as the "Cultivation System".

1843–50: As a result of the Cultivation System, serious famines occur in Cirebon (1843) and in central Java, 250,000 people die (1850).

National awakening

1908: Indonesians attending Dutch schools begin to form regional student organisations; new national consciousness takes shape.

1910: Indonesian Communist movement founded.

1910–30: Turbulent period of strikes, violence and organised rebellions.

1927: Sukarno tries to unite nationalists, Muslims and Marxists into a single mass movement. He is imprisoned and later exiled.

1928: Second all-Indies student conference; the motto "one nation, one language, one land" is proclaimed.

World War II and independence

1942–44: Japanese invade Indonesia and promise independence.

1945: Japan surrenders. Sukarno and Muhammad Hatta declare Indonesia's independence. The Dutch resume control; war for independence breaks out.

1949: The Dutch acknowledge Indonesia's independence under pressure from the United Nations.

Late 1950s: A Communist insurgency prompts Sukarno to declare martial law. Sukarno resurrects the "revolutionary" constitution of 1945.

Sukarno and Soeharto years

1960: Sukarno dissolves parliament; his anti-colonial sentiments become more militant.

1963: Confrontation with newly independent Malaysia reveals Sukarno's brand of militant nationalism.

1965: After a failed Communist coup, the Chinese are the focus of anti-Communist attacks. Up to 500,000 people are killed.

1966: Sukarno is persuaded to sign over powers to his protégé, Soeharto, who takes over presidency. Until 1998, he is re-elected 6 times.

LEFT: wife of Ken Arok depicted as a goddess.
RIGHT: Sukarno and Soeharto, early 1960s.

1975–76: Indonesian troops invade East Timor after the Portuguese leave and annex it.

1996: East Timor independence activists Jose Ramos Horta and Bishop Belo win the Nobel Peace Prize.

1997: The rupiah crashes, banks collapse and foreign debt surges during the Asian economic crisis.

1998: Soeharto refuses to reform economy; riots over rising prices and corruption mount. Soeharto is forced to resign amid mass student uprising; vice-president B.J. Habibie takes over as Indonesia's third president.

Contemporary Indonesia

1999: East Timor votes for independence. Indonesia's first democratic elections in 40 years are held;

Abdurrahman Wahid becomes the country's fourth president.

2001: Wahid is impeached and resigns. Megawati Sukarnoputri becomes the fifth president.

2004: First direct presidential election is held; Susilo Bambang Yudhoyono is elected. An 8.9-magnitude earthquake off Sumatra's coast causes a tsunami that kills more than 160,000 people in Indonesia, mostly in Aceh province.

2005: Aceh peace accord signed, ending nearly 30 years of fighting in Nanggroe Aceh Darussalam.

2006: Yudhoyono is nominated for the Nobel Peace Prize for the Aceh peace deal. A 6.3-magnitude earthquake near Yogyakarta kills nearly 6,000 people and leaves hundreds of thousands homeless. ❑

INDONESIA'S PEOPLE

Indonesia is the world's fourth most populous nation, encompassing an astonishing diversity of peoples and cultures

For one travelling the length of Indonesia, the complexity and diversity of peoples, languages, customs and cultures found in the Indonesian archipelago are truly astounding, and thoroughly embracing. Living here are 300 distinct ethnic groups, each with its own cultural identity, who together speak a total of more than 250 (some sources say up to 500) mutually unintelligible languages, but all sharing the official Bahasa Indonesia as a common tongue.

Anyone travelling widely in Indonesia soon recognises the enormous physical differences of people from one end of the archipelago to the other – differences in pigmentation, stature and physiognomy. To explain this range of racial types, scholars once postulated a theory of wave migrations. According to this theory, various Indonesian groups arrived from the Asian mainland in a series of discrete but massive migratory waves, each separated by a period of several centuries. The wave theory, however, has lost considerable currency in recent years.

Migratory theories

The first wave of migrants, it was thought, were the primitive dark-skinned, wiry-haired negritos – people of pygmy stature who today inhabit remote forest enclaves on the Malay peninsula, in the Andaman Islands north of Sumatra, and on several of the Philippine islands. It has commonly been suggested that the negritos somehow migrated the length of the Eurasian continent, from Africa, eons ago.

The second wave, too, were thought to have arrived from Africa or perhaps India. These peoples were dubbed the Australoids, and are the Melanesian inhabitants of New Guinea, including Papua (Irian Jaya), and Australia. The third wave, proto-Malays, were thought to have migrated from China by way of Indochina.

The last wave, the deutero-Malays, were described as pure Mongoloids, hence related to and much resembling the Chinese. These

LEFT: Dayak woman with child and family wealth.
RIGHT: a Javanese soldier of yesteryear.

peoples today inhabit the plains and coastal regions of all the major islands, and many developed large hierarchical kingdoms, attaining a level of pre-modern civilisation comparable to that found anywhere in the world.

The existence of *Homo erectus* (Java Man) fossils in Indonesia – million-year-old remains

of one of our earliest ancestors – suggests that the so-called negrito and Australoid people, with their skin pigmentation, actually evolved partially or wholly in the tropical rain forests of Southeast Asia, just as the light-skinned Mongoloid types evolved in the cold temperate regions of east and central Asia. Of course, during the last Ice Ages, when land bridges linked the major islands of the Sunda shelf to the mainland, these peoples circulated freely and even crossed the oceans, populating Australia by about 50,000 years ago.

The wave theory of coordinated, coherent mass movements seems unlikely for a number of reasons. In a fragmented region like the Indonesia archipelago, village and tribal groups have always been constantly on the move, at least in historic times, dissolving and absorbing each other as they go.

Many experts offer that perhaps it is more realistic, therefore, to imagine a situation in which small groups of Mongoloid hunters, gatherers and cultivators percolated into the region slowly, absorbing and replacing the original Australoid inhabitants over a period of many millennia.

Linguistic babel

Indonesians speak such a variety of different languages that the

> ### SETTLED STABILITY
> Great linguistic diversity has often been interpreted as indicating that an area has been settled and stable for a long period of time.

cultural patterns found in Indonesia: *ladang* and *sawah*. Ladang agriculture, also referred to by the Old English word swidden and by the descriptive expression slash-and-burn, is practised in forested terrains, generally outside of Java and Bali. The ladang farmer utilises fire as a tool, along with axe and bush knife, to clear a forest plot. By carefully timing the burn immediately to precede the onset of rains, the farmer simultaneously fertilises and weeds the land. While these semi-nomadic swidden farmers now comprise less than a tenth

exact number would largely depend upon an arbitrary definition of what constitutes a distinct language, as opposed to a dialect. Most estimates place the total above 250, only a handful of which have been adequately studied. Languages such as Javanese, Balinese and Bahasa Indonesia (the national language, which derives from a literary dialect of Malay) are closely related, belonging to the Malayo-Polynesian branch of the Austronesian language family, but they are as different from one another as are French and Spanish.

Cultural distinctions

One important distinction when considering Indonesia's people focuses on the two main agri-

of Indonesia's total population, they are scattered throughout more than two-thirds of the nation's land area. Although it may seem that this practice in Sumatra, Java and Borneo causes Indonesia's annual uncontrollable fires that send clouds of haze over most of Southeast Asia for months, it is actually the clearing of forests by palm oil plantations that is the culprit.

Most Indonesians, by contrast, inhabit the narrow plains and coastal regions of the major islands, where the principal farming method is sawah, or wet-rice paddy cultivation. In fact, 60 percent of Indonesia's population of 220 million live on Java and Bali, which between them comprise only 7 percent of Indonesia's land. Here, the average rural population densities can soar as high as 2,000 people per sq. km (5,000 per sq. mile) – by far the world's highest population density, which has caused the government to relocate Javanese and Balinese to less-populated provinces.

Sawah cultivation is a labour-intensive form of agriculture that can be successfully practised only under the special conditions of rich soil and adequate water, but one that seems capable of producing seemingly limitless quantities of food. The farmers who plant wet-rice paddies actually reshape their environment over a period of many generations, clearing the land,

As might be expected, the sawah societies of Java and Bali are strikingly different from the ladang communities of the outer islands. The Javanese, for example, put great emphasis on cooperation and social attitudes. Village deliberations are concluded not by majority or autocratic rule, but by a consensus of elders or esteemed individuals. *Rukun,* or harmony, is the primary goal, achieved through knowing one's place within society.

Time, balance and harmony

A favourite expression in Indonesia is *jam karet,* which translates, literally, as rubber time.

terracing, levelling and diking the plots, and constructing elaborate irrigation systems. As a result, this system has both required and rewarded a high degree of social cooperation. Particularly in Java and Bali, populous villages have long been linked with towns – economically and culturally – through a hierarchically defined framework that has coordinated labour to maintain the fragile irrigation works. Until resorts began replacing rice fields, the food surpluses produced by these villages permitted an urban opulence.

LEFT: faces of Bali and Java. **ABOVE:** West Timorese, and working on a tea plantation, Java.

Rarely does a social event or a meeting start exactly at the appointed hour; time can be stretched to suit the occasion.

The notion of balance and harmony is also important in personal contacts. Great respect and deference are shown to superiors and elders, and there are distinct speech levels that are used according to the status of the person. These fine social divisions may hark back to the Hindu caste system, yet another example of Indonesia's Indian heritage.

Finally, to lose face, to be made ashamed *(malu)* is something to be avoided, and for this reason Indonesians often suggest that something can be done when they know it cannot. ❑

TEXTILES

Indonesia's centuries-old textile traditions are unsurpassed,
both for their aesthetic value and cultural importance

From the charming wax-resist batiks of Java to the exquisite *songket* silks of Sumatra, to the anthropomorphic and zoomorphic patterns on tie-and-dye *ikats* from across the archipelago, Indonesia's traditional textile arts exhibit unparalleled diversity.

Such richness is the heritage of migration and two millennia of trade. By the 14th century,

the north coast of Java. *Pesisir* batiks still reflect these cultural identities, combining designs including the mythical Chinese phoenix, elaborate flora and Arabic calligraphy.

Symbolism and identity

The distinctive textile traditions of Indonesia's many ethnic and linguistic groups share many

Indian textiles were the dominant barter goods, with the brilliant silk, double-*ikat*, sari-length *patola* cloths from Gujarat prized above all else by the sultans and clan leaders who controlled access to the spice trade.

Rich influences from Chinese and Indian cloths were captured in the motifs of many Indonesian textiles. Lozenges and rhomboids from Dong Son (200 BC) bronze drums, dragon motifs on pottery from the Ming Dynasty (AD 1368–1644) and the eight-pointed flower (*chabadi bhat* – "flowering basket") motif from Indian *patola* exemplify these influences. In some areas trade led to the development of multicultural settlements, such as the *pesisir* on

common functions while conveying locally important symbolism. On Savu Island the motifs on a woman's warp *ikat* sarong are determined by her clan and subgroup, and tell a potential suitor whether he may marry her. Among the Lamaholot people from the islands east of Flores, continuous-warp *ikat* cloths bearing clan motifs must be given by the bride's family to the groom's. In Sumba, textiles are exchanged at funerals where dozens of cloths may also be used to wrap the corpse. The motifs on these cloths identify the soul to ancestral guides. The *tomina* (traditional healer) in Toraja, Sulawesi, can prescribe a remedy for illness by reading meaning from the stylised black-on-white representations of buffaloes, landscapes and people on a family's hand-drawn *ma'a* cloth. The *palepai* supplementary-weft wall hangings of Lampung in southern Sumatra, which depict large ships full of people and animals, invoke the support of ancestral spirits during important ceremonies, as do the beaded boats on the *lawo butu* ceremonial warp *ikat* sarongs of Ngada in Central Flores. The double-*ikat* cloths of Tenganan Pegeringsingan in Bali are called *geringsing* (literally "against sickness") and draw their protective power from motifs said to have been a gift from the Hindu god Indra.

Respect for and worship of ancestors is often central to the continuity of such traditions. Women weave the motifs to both invoke the support of their ancestors and avoid their ire. Rituals are still performed when collecting dye plants, warping a loom and during weaving. The intention of the weaver, along with the act of replicating centuries-old clan motifs, results in textiles imbued with power.

Batik

Batik is Indonesia's most renowned textile, especially Javanese batik which is regarded as the world's finest. In the technique, dye-resistant wax is applied to the cloth to prevent the dye from penetrating certain areas, thus resulting in a pattern in the negative. This can be done by using a *tulis* (literally "to write") or a *cap* (stamp).

The first step of the *tulis* method is to draw a design on a piece of cloth using a *canting*, a small copper cup with a spout through which melted wax flows. Areas not to be coloured in the first dyeing are covered with wax on both the front and the back of the fabric. The cloth is then immersed in dye and then dried. For the second dyeing, the old wax is first scraped off or removed by boiling the fabric in water. New wax is then applied onto the previously dyed areas to prevent them from taking on the new colour. Dyeing and drying follow, and the process is repeated as many times as there are number of colours on the cloth.

The *cap* method uses a metal printing block

made from thin strips of copper and wire soldered to an open frame. The stamp is first dipped into heated wax before it is pressed firmly onto the cloth. The advent of batik *cap* revitalised the industry in the 1890s, making cloths affordable to all and creating an export trade from Java to the outer islands.

FABRICATED CURRENCY

On many of Indonesia's islands, textiles were required in dowries, and small squares of cloth were used as currency.

Lurik and ikat

References in old Javanese Hindu inscriptions (AD 851–82) mention striped and checked textiles that are today known as *lurik*. In Bali, such textiles are

called *keling* and remain ritually important. Each motif on *lurik* and *keling* cloths is defined by a specific palette and organisation of stripes. Ancient rice-paste-resist patterns on *lurik* textiles were probably the first Javanese batiks, but batik only began to develop the beautiful complexity that made it famous after the 17th-century invention of the *canting* tool.

Lurik probably predates tie-and-dye *ikat* textiles, though the origin of the latter is unclear. The word *ikat* derives from the Malay verb "to knot". The process, when performed on the lengthwise warp threads of a cloth, involves a frame onto which the warp is strung in a mock-up of the final cloth. Threads are arranged into

LEFT: symbolic *hinggi ikat* textiles are used as dowry gifts and in funeral rituals in Sumba.
ABOVE: handwoven *lurik* textiles.

bundles, and sections of these bundles are bound with palm fibre or plastic raffia in a resist pattern. Only exposed areas of thread are coloured when the warp is dyed. By untying and retying sections of *ikat* before continuing with a different dye, the dyer can create complex variations of hue and saturation. Warp *ikat* is found across eastern Indonesia, Kalimantan and Sulawesi. Weft *ikat*, whose crosswise threads are dyed instead, is made in Bali and Sumatra. For double-*ikat*, which is made in the Balinese village of Tenganan Pegeringsingan, both the warp and weft threads are dyed so that the colours of each exactly coincide in the woven cloth.

most. Weaving is done as the agricultural cycle allows and when household chores permit.

Weaving the future

In the past textile arts were entirely women's work. Today men sketch designs and do *ikat* work when the art has moved to higher production levels, and help to collect dye plants. As demand for natural-dye textiles grows, entire weaving communities will need to cultivate dye plants, and establish sustainable harvesting for what is gathered from the wild if extinction of key local species is not to occur.

Today, more than ever before, traditional

Where synthetic dyes are used, the process of dyeing and weaving an *ikat* may take several weeks. When natural dyes are employed on cotton, it could take months or years. While indigo dyeing with the legume *Indigofera tinctoria* is a wet-season activity, the most time-consuming part of natural-dye work is the dry-season mordant process, without which the red dye from the root bark of trees in the Morinda family will not adhere to the thread.

Once the desired colours have been achieved, traditional weaving utilises a backstrap loom, so called because the loom is held in tension by a strap across the weaver's lower back. Most weavers are mothers and farmers first and foremost. Weaving is done as the agricultural cycle

weavers struggle to maintain their textile culture while generating a reliable income from their work. The local market for synthetic-dyed cloth provides essential basic income, though at a narrow profit margin. A growing international market that is sensitive to the weavers' needs and supports the weaving of high-quality textiles can provide important incentives that sustain the art at their highest aesthetic and cultural levels. ❏

ABOVE: tying off thread before dying in the *ikat* process.
RIGHT: *geringsing* cloth, a double-*ikat* weave found in only three places in the world, including Bali, where it is considered to be a sacred cloth.

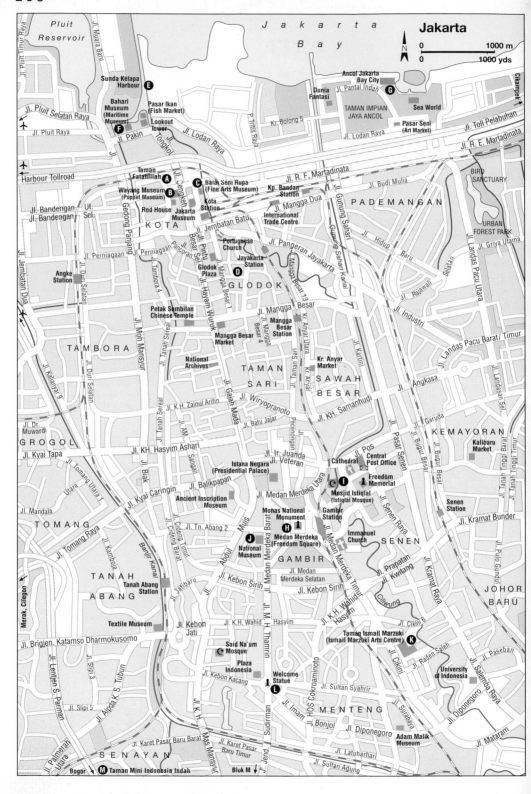

JAKARTA

Don't look for rustic charm in the huge sprawling metropolis of the capital city. Jakarta dwellers are proud of the cultural and intellectual life in this ever-changing, chaotic capital

Map on page 266

Capital of the world's fourth most populous nation and home to more than 15 million Indonesians (not counting sub-district populations), Jakarta is a metropolis that verges on the chaotic. Every day, thousands of vehicles crowd into the busy Thamrin-Sudirman corridor during rush hour, causing traffic jams that can last several hours. Downtown is peppered with high-rise apartments, which are luring an increasing number of young executives to choose integrated living, working and shopping in one tower rather than facing the rigours of traffic each day. Throughout Jakarta, shopping and entertainment areas such as the busy Glodok and Blok M throb with neon signs and modern malls with luxury-brand boutiques, hypermarkets, entertainment centres, restaurants and international five-star hotels. In Kemang, a middle-class suburb in the south, expatriates and Indonesians frequent trendy eateries, while in the north, Kelapa Gading is home to many wealthy families.

Much of Jakarta today is hardly reconisable from a decade ago. Yet there are other parts of the city that seem frozen in time. In some residential districts, large houses stand alongside *kampung* (village) dwellings imparting something of a rustic atmosphere.

Jakarta is located at the mouth of the Ciliwung River, on the site of a pepper-trading port that flourished here in the 16th century. In 1618, the architect of the Dutch empire in the Indies, Jan Pieterszoon Coen, ordered construction of a new town: Batavia. Under the Dutch East India Company (VOC), Batavia at first prospered, but then it began to decline as official corruption, decreasing market prices and frequent epidemics of malaria, cholera and typhoid took their toll. In the 19th century, the old city was demolished to provide building materials for a new one a couple of kilometres to the south, around what is Medan Merdeka (Freedom Square) today.

During the brief Japanese occupation of World War II, Batavia was renamed Jakarta (Djakarta), quickly transforming into a city of more than 1 million people. Since then, Jakarta has been the unrivalled political and economic centre of Indonesia.

Old Batavia

Known as **Kota**, the area of the old town of Batavia came to life in the 1620s as a tiny, walled town modelled after Amsterdam. Most of the original settlement – Old Batavia – was demolished at the beginning of the 19th century. Only the town square area survived. It was restored and renamed **Taman Fatahillah** Ⓐ. On the north side of the square is Si Jagur, an old cannon regarded by many as a fertility

BELOW: early map of Batavia Harbour, late 1780s.

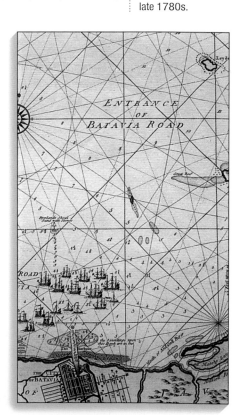

symbol. Surrounding colonial edifices have been converted into museums. The **Wayang Museum**  **B** (Puppet Museum; Tues–Sun 9am–3pm; entrance fee; tel: 021-692 9560) on the western side of the square, displays puppets from all over Indonesia. There is also a collection of *topeng* (masks) and tombstones of several early Dutch governors are on display.

The **Museum Seni Rupa** **C** (Fine Arts Museum; Tues–Sun 9am–3pm; entrance fee; tel: 021-692 6090) on the east side of Taman Fatahillah is housed in the former Court of Justice building, completed in 1879. The museum has mediocre collections of paintings and sculptures by modern Indonesian artists, and an exhibition of rare porcelains.

Behind the Wayang Museum are two Dutch houses dating from the 18th century. The first, across the canal and to the left, is a solid red-brick townhouse (Jalan Kali Besar Barat No. 11) that was built around 1730 by the soon-to-be governor-general. The design, and particularly the fine Chinese-style woodwork, is typical of old Batavian residences. Three doors to the left stands the only other house from the same period, now the offices of a bank. Several blocks to the north along the fetid and polluted canal, an old red wooden drawbridge straddles the canal, recalling the days when Batavia was laced with waterways.

Jakarta's Chinatown, **Glodok** **D**, is adjacent to the old European quarter. Glodok is primarily known for its shops with the best prices for electronics and construction supplies in town. In 2000, the 35-year ban against the public use of Chinese characters was lifted, and today Glodok is the site of festive *Imlek* (Chinese Lunar New Year) celebrations.

To the north lies the old spice trading harbour, **Sunda Kelapa Harbour** **E**, with a mile-long wharf in use since 1817. Early morning is the best time to

BELOW: on the site of Jayakarta, the new town, Batavia, sported features of Amsterdam.

walk along the 2-km (1¼-mile) wharf among the ships' prows and gangways and witness one of the world's last remaining commercial sailing fleets. Filled with the romance of a bygone era, watch the unloading of cargo from the majestic wooden *pinisi* schooners built by the seafaring Bugis people of South Sulawesi.

The area around Sunda Kelapa is rich in history, and the best way to survey it is on foot. Near the river stands a 19th-century **Lookout Tower** (Uitkik), constructed by the Dutch upon the site of the original customs house (Pabean) of Jayakarta. This is where traders once rendered their gifts and tribute to the local ruler in return for the privilege of trading here.

Behind the tower stands a long, two-storey structure dating from VOC times, now the **Museum Bahari ❻** (Maritime Museum; Jalan Pasar Ikan No. 1; Tues–Fri 9am–3pm, Sat–Sun 9am–2pm; entrance fee; tel: 021-669 3406). This former warehouse was erected by the Dutch in 1652 and was used for many years to store coffee, tea and Indian cloth. Inside are displays of traditional sailing craft from all corners of the Indonesian archipelago, as well as some old maps and photographs of Batavia. Down a narrow lane and around a corner behind the museum lies **Pasar Ikan**, the fish market, beyond which are numerous stalls selling nautical gear.

Further east along the waterfront is a giant seaside recreation area called **Ancol Jakarta Bay City ❼** (daily 24 hours; entrance fee; 021-6471 0591). Once swampland, it now features beachfront hotels, a golf course, bowling alley, arts and crafts market, and swimming pools. There are also several theme parks in the area, including **Sea World** (daily 9am–6pm; entrance fee; tel: 021-641 0080) and **Dunia Fantasi** (daily 9am–8pm; entrance fee; tel: 021-6471 2000), Indonesia's only real amusement park complete with roller

Map on page 266

BELOW: vessels at Sunda Kelapa.

coasters and a Ferris wheel. Thousands of Indonesians converge here on the weekends and holidays.

Ferries to some of the 600 offshore islands, known collectively as **Kepulauan Seribu** (Thousand Islands), leave from Ancol Marina. The closer islands are a popular escape for residents of Jakarta on weekends. **Bidadari (Angel) Island Resort** (tel: 021-6471 0048) offers cottages, a restaurant, children's playground and water sports. It is covered by rare flora and fauna, such as the *elang bondol* (hawk), which is Jakarta's mascot.

Central Jakarta

A circumnavigation of central Jakarta begins at the top of **Monas** (National Monument; Tues–Sun 9am–3pm; entrance fee), a 137-metre-tall (450-ft) marble obelisk set in the centre of **Medan Merdeka ⓗ** (Freedom Square). The monument is surmounted by an observation deck and a 14-metre (45-ft) bronze flame sheathed in 33 kg (73 lbs) of gold. It was commissioned by Sukarno and completed in 1961 – a combination Olympic flame and Washington Monument with the phallic overtones of an ancient Hindu-Javanese *lingga*. A high-speed elevator rises to the observation deck, where on a clear day there is a fabulous 360-degree view of Jakarta. There is a museum in the basement, with dioramas that show the history of Indonesia's struggle for independence from the Dutch. In the auditorium, visitors can hear the voice of Sukarno reading the proclamation of independence.

East of Medan Merdeka is the imposing white marble **Mesjid Istiqlal ⓘ** (Sat–Thur except prayer times and holy days), with its massive dome and rakish minarets, on Jalan Veteran. The largest mosque in Southeast Asia, it was

A page from an ancient edition of the Koran, Islam's holy book.

BELOW:
Monas, at Medan Merdeka, and an exhibit at the National Museum.

built on the former site of the Dutch Benteng (Fort) Noordwijk. During the Islamic Ramadan fasting period, the mosques are filled to capacity.

Map on page 266

On the west side of Medan Merdeka lies one of Indonesia's great cultural treasures, the excellent **National Museum ❶** (Tues–Thurs and Sun 8.30am–2.30pm, Fri 8.30–11.30am, Sat 8.30am–1.30pm; tel: 021-381 1551; entrance fee). Opened in 1868 by the Batavian Society for Arts and Sciences – the first scholarly organisation in colonial Asia, founded in 1778 – the museum houses enormously valuable collections of antiquities, books and ethnographic artifacts acquired by the Dutch during the 19th and early 20th centuries. The objects exhibited are fascinating; you could take hours to view the Hindu-Javanese stone statuary, prehistoric bronze wares and Chinese porcelain. The star collection, however, is housed in the Treasure Room – a stupendous hoard of royal Indonesian heirlooms. Southeast of the square, a short ride down Jalan Cikini, are two other noteworthy attractions. **Taman Ismail Marzuki** (TIM) ❶ (Ismail Marzuki Arts Centre; daily 8:30am–5pm, tel: 021-3193 7325; call for performance and exhibition schedules) is a multifaceted cultural centre that presents a continuing bill of drama, dance and music from around the Indonesian archipelago. Nearby, **Jalan Surabaya** is the city's so-called "antique street", with dozens of stalls selling everything from wayang puppets to vintage ship fittings. Be aware that most of it is brand new.

Hail a cab and cruise west across the upper-class Menteng residential area to the **Welcome Statue ❶**, a busy roundabout with a statue of two waving youths and a fountain. Jalan Thamrin, lined with shopping malls and office buildings, runs north and south here, turning into Jalan Sudirman a few more blocks south. The roundabout fountain is an urban anchor of Jakarta, built by

BELOW: the bronze Welcome Statue is one of several grand monuments which dot the city.

Map on page 266

Sukarno in the early 1960s. At the roundabout is the new Grand Indonesia, a hotel attached to a mega multistorey shopping and entertainment complex. Across the street is the ritzy Grand Hyatt perched atop one of Jakarta's many fine, well-stocked malls, **Plaza Indonesia**.

Adjacent to the Sultan Hotel is the **Jakarta Convention Centre**. Everything from art exhibits and cultural events to rock concerts is held here. Further south on Jalan Sudirman, behind the Senayan sports field, home to national soccer games, are five more upscale shopping malls, the newest of which is **Senayan City**, anchored by a Denbenhams department store.

South Jakarta

Blok M is where Jakarta's middle class does much of its shopping. The area bustles with street stalls, hundreds of shops and half a dozen modern shopping malls, including two giant shopping centres: **Blok M Plaza** and **Blok M Mall**. This is also the home of the **Pasaraya** department store, recommended for souvenir shopping.

Take a drive through the nearby residential neighbourhoods like Pondok Indah or Cipete to see how wealthy Indonesians and many expatriates live. **Pondak Indah Mall** is one of Jakarta's busiest malls.

Still heading south about 15 km (9 miles) from the centre of the city is the **Ragunan Zoo** (daily 7am–5pm; entrance fee; tel: 021-789 0613). With a pleasant, relaxed atmosphere set in a tropical garden park, there are over 3,000 animals, most of them indigenous to Indonesia. This may be your only chance to see the infamous Komodo dragon, along with orang-utans and Sumatran tigers.

Just off the super highway leading south to Bogor is a theme park called **Taman Mini-Indonesia Indah** Ⓜ (Beautiful Indonesia-in-Miniature Park; Tues–Sun 8am–5pm; entrance fee). It is worth a visit for the fine bird park if nothing else. Encompassing nearly 100 hectares (250 acres), Taman Mini has 26 main pavilions, one for each of Indonesia's original provinces. More pavilions to represent seven new provinces are planned. The former East Timor pavilion is being converted to a Timor Leste museum. The pavilions have been constructed using authentic materials and workmanship to exhibit a traditional style of architecture from each province. Inside are displays of handicrafts, traditional costumes, musical instruments and artifacts indigenous to the regions. They are clustered around a lake containing islands that make up a three-dimensional relief map of the Indonesian archipelago.

The park contains at least 30 other attractions, including an orchid garden, IMAX cinema, cable-car ride, transport museum, swimming pool, and the splendid **Museum Indonesia** (Tues–Sun 8am–5pm; entrance fee; tel: 021-840 9246), a three-storey Balinese palace filled with Indonesia's cultural arts. The most recent addition is the **Museum Purna Bhakti Pertiwi** (Presidential Palace Museum; Tues–Sun 8am–5pm; entrance fee; tel: 021-840 1687) established by the late First Lady Ibu Tien Soeharto as a showcase for the family's private collection of antiques, art and many diplomatic gifts. ❑

OPPOSITE: Jakarta at night. **BELOW:** West Sumatran wedding clothes, Taman Mini.

JAVA

Although it covers only 6 percent of Indonesia's land area,
Java is Indonesia's most populous island and
its political and economic centre

Map
on page
254

J ava has much to offer to the intrepid traveller, from rich and complex ancient cultures and cool mountain retreats to magnificent volcanoes and stormy southern seas. It also has large areas of pristine forests and verdant rice fields. Of Indonesia's six UNESCO World Heritage sites, four are in Java: Borobudur, Pramabanan and Sangiran, the Java Man site, all in central Java, and Ujung Kulon National Park in West Java.

Java is Indonesia's most populated island. The Javanese constitute about two-thirds of the total population and originate from the fertile plains of central and eastern Java, plus much of the island's northern coast. In Jakarta, the native tribe is the Betawi while in western Java, the inhabitants are mainly Sundanese except for a small pocket of Badui who still adhere to age-old traditions without modern conveniences. Madura and the adjoining coast of eastern Java are home to the Madurese people. Near Gunung Bromo is Java's last enclave of Hindus, the Tenggerese. The trading ports of the northern coast also harbour Chinese, Arabs and Europeans, as well as people from other Indonesian islands.

Beyond Jakarta: western Java

Western Java may be roughly divided into two distinct regions: the Parahyangan (Abode of the Gods) or volcanic highlands centred around the provincial capital, Bandung, and the northern coastal plain. The coast is much more mixed, having absorbed a multitude of immigrants and influences via its trading ports for many centuries.

A quick getaway from Jakarta is a jaunt to Java's sandy and secluded west coast beaches. Stop along the way at **Banten Girang ❶**, lying north of Serang city. One of the most vibrant towns in Asia in the 16th century, it was razed by the Dutch in 1808, and today, it is a tiny fishing village straddling a tidal creek. But there are the ruins of two massive palaces and a Dutch fortress, plus an interesting old mosque, with its adjacent museum, and a Chinese temple. Twenty km (12 miles) further south is **Carita Beach**, a popular weekend retreat for Jakartans that offers seaside bungalows, swimming, sailing, diving and dining. This palm-fringed coast is famous for its views of the volcanic **Krakatau** islands.

Only two hours from Jakarta via a new toll road, the highland city **Bandung ❷** offers a cool alternative. There is an abundance of Dutch colonial, art-deco architecture, including the magnificent **Gedung Sate**, a skewer-shaped building of impressive Indo-European architecture. You can also browse factory outlet shops along Jalan Cihampelas and check out

LEFT: colonial Dutch architecture, Banten.
BELOW: misty montane forest.

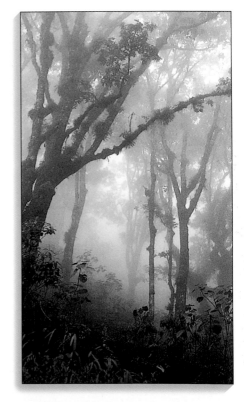

the famed "Java Man" at the Geological Museum on Jalan Diponegoro. The town has a hilly contour, which adds to its character.

Java's northern coastal ports were once the busiest and richest towns on the island. In **Cirebon ❸**, the **Keraton Kasepuhan** (Palace of the Elder Brother), built in 1678, sits on the site of the 15th-century Pakungwati palace of Cirebon's earlier Hindu rulers. Just next to the palace stands the **Grand Mosque**, or Masjid Agung, constructed around 1500. Cirebon is known for its unique batik featuring Chinese-inspired patterns such as *mega mendung* (meaning "cloudy sky").

Javanese mountains.

About 310 km (195 miles) to the east, **Semarang ❹** stretches from steeply rising foothills across a narrow coastal plain. Known during old Islamic times for its skilled shipwrights, Semarang today is the commercial hub and provincial capital of Central Java. Relics of the past bear witness to the presence of a large population of Dutch traders and officials, and a generous sprinkling of affluent Chinese merchants. **Gereja Blenduk**, the old Dutch church on Jalan Suprapto downtown, with its copper-clad dome and Greek cross floor plan, was consecrated in 1753 and stands at the centre of the town's 18th-century European commercial district. Semarang's most interesting district, however, is **Pecinan**, its Chinatown – a grid of narrow lanes tucked away in the centre of the city, reached by walking due south from the old church along Jalan Suari to Jalan Pekojan. Here, some old townhouses retain the distinctive Nanyang style of elaborately carved doors and shutters.

Yogyakarta (Jogja) and historic sites

BELOW: colourful Cirebon boats.

The green crescent of fertile rice lands that blankets Gunung Merapi's southern flanks – with historic Yogyakarta as its focal point – is today inhabited by over 11 million Javanese, with at least 3 million urban residents. Rural population densities here soar above 1,000 people per sq. km (2,500 per sq. mile), and in some areas, a square kilometre feeds an astounding 2,000 people with labour-intensive farming.

Although it was founded only in 1755, sprawling **Yogyakarta ❺** (locally called Jogja) is situated at the very core of an ancient region known as Mataram, site of the first great central-Javanese empires. From the 8th until the early 10th centuries, this fertile and sloping plain was ruled by a succession of Indianised kings – the builders of Borobudur, Prambanan and dozens of other elaborate stone monuments. In about AD 900, however, these rulers suddenly and inexplicably shifted their capital to eastern Java, and for more than six centuries thereafter, Mataram was deserted.

The first stop for all visitors to Jogja is the **Keraton**, the Sultan's Palace (Sat–Thur 8am–1pm; Fri 8–11am; entrance fee; tel: 0274-373 177), a 200-year-old palace complex that stands at the very heart of the city. According to traditional cosmological beliefs, the Keraton is literally the "navel" or central "spike" of the universe, anchoring the temporal world and communicating with the mystical realm of powerful deities. In this scheme of things, the Keraton is both the capital of the kingdom and the hub of the cosmos. It houses not only the sultan and his family, but also the powerful dynastic regalia (*pusaka*), private meditation and ceremonial chambers, a magnificent throne hall, several audience and performance pavilions, a mosque, an immense royal garden, stables, barracks, an armaments foundry and two parade grounds planted with sacred banyan trees. All of this is in a carefully conceived complex of walled compounds, narrow lanes and massive gateways, and bounded by a fortified outer wall measuring 2 km (1½ miles) on every side.

Construction of Yogyakarta's Keraton began in 1755 and continued for almost 40 years. Today, only the innermost compound is considered part of the Keraton proper, while the maze of lanes and lesser compounds, the mosque and the two vast squares have been integrated into the city. Long sections of the outermost wall *(benteng)* still stand, however, and many if not most of the residences inside are still owned and occupied by members of the royal family.

There is much else to see within the Keraton, including the museum, ancient gamelan sets, two great gateways and several spacious courtyards. Behind and just west of the Keraton stand the ruins of the opulent and architecturally ingenious royal pleasure garden, **Taman Sari** (Sat–Thur 8am–1pm; Fri 8–11am; entrance fee). Dutch representatives to the sultan's court marvelled at its construction: a large artificial lake, underground and underwater passageways, meditational retreats, a series of sunken bathing pools, and an imposing two-storey mansion of European design.

Main street, Jogja

Jogja's main thoroughfare, **Jalan Malioboro**, begins directly in front of the royal audience pavilion, at the front of the palace, and ends at a phallic *lingga* some 2 km (1½ miles) to the north, a shrine dedicated to the local guardian

Map on page 254

BELOW: Dutch colonial buildings, downtown Jogja.

spirit, Kyai Jaga. It was laid out by Hamengkubuwono I as a ceremonial boulevard for colourful state processions, and also as a symbolic meridian along which to orient his domain. Today, Jalan Malioboro is a busy avenue lined with shops and souvenir stalls, teeming with vehicles, horse-drawn carriages and pedicabs; it's primarily a shopping district, but also an area of historical and cultural interest. Begin at the north town square *(alun-alun utara)* and stroll up this latter-day processional, stopping first at the **Sono Budoyo Museum** (open Tues–Thur 9am–2pm, Fri 8–11am, Sat 8am–1pm; entrance fee; tel: 0274-376 775) on the northwestern side of the square. It was opened in 1935 by the Java Institute, a cultural foundation of wealthy Javanese and Dutch art patrons, and today houses important collections of prehistoric artefacts, Hindu-Buddhist bronzes, *wayang* puppets, dance costumes and traditional Javanese weapons.

Face full of character, Jogja.

Proceed northward from the square through the main gates and out across Jogja's main intersection. Immediately ahead on the right stands the old Dutch garrison, **Benteng Budaya** (Fort Vredeburgh; open Tues-Thur 8.30am–2pm, Fri 8.30–11am, Sat–Sun 8.30am–noon; entrance fee; tel: 0274-586 934), now a cultural centre, hosting art exhibitions and performances. Opposite it on the left stands the former Dutch Resident's mansion. Used during the revolution as the presidential palace, it is now the State Guest House. Farther along on the right, past the fort, is the huge enclosed central market, **Pasar Beringharjo**, a rabbit warren of small stalls frequented by housewives and souvenir shoppers.

BELOW:
Keraton guard in a *lurik* coat.

Jogja also has some other not-to-be-missed art galleries and museums, including **Affandi Museum** (Jalan Laksda Adi Sucipto; entrance fee; tel: 0274-562 593; www.affandi.org), with the work of Jogja's most famous artist; and **Cemeti Art House** (Jalan D.I. Panjaitan No. 41; free; tel: 0274-371 015) and **Jogja Gallery** (Jalan Pekapalan No. 7; entrance fee; tel: 0274-716 1188; www.jogja-gallery.com), both specialising in contemporary art.

Ancient monuments

A leisurely one-hour drive leads to the steps of fabled **Borobudur** (daily 6am–sunset; entrance fee; multilingual licensed guides available), 40 km (25 miles) northwest of Jogja. This huge stupa, the world's largest Buddhist monument, was built during the Sailendra dynasty, between AD 778 and 856, 300 years before Angkor Wat and 200 years before Notre Dame. Yet, within little more than a century of its completion, Borobudur and all of central Java were abandoned. At about this time, neighbouring Gunung Merapi erupted violently, and some theorised that volcanic ash from that eruption concealed Borobudur for centuries.

It is estimated that 30,000 stonecutters and sculptors, 15,000 carriers and thousands more masons worked for 20 to 75 years to build the monument. Seen from the air, Borobudur forms a mandala. Seen from a distance on the ground, it is a stupa or reliquary, a model of the cosmos in three vertical parts: a square base supporting a hemispheric body and a crowning spire. As one approaches along the traditional pilgrimage route from the east and then ascends the terraced monument, circumambulating each terrace clockwise in succession, every relief and carving contributes to the whole.

About 100 km (60 miles) northeast of Borobudur at **Dieng Plateau** are the oldest temples in central Java, dating back to the late 7th century. Eight temples named after the heroes of the Hindu *Mahabharata* epic stand amid brightly coloured sulphur springs and bubbling mudholes.

East of Jogja is a volcanic plain littered with ancient ruins. Because these *candi* (temples) are considered by the Javanese of central Java to be royal mausoleums, this region is known by them as the Valley of the Kings. In the centre of the plain, 17 km (10 miles) from Jogja, lies the **Prambanan temple complex** (daily 6am–sunset; entrance fee). Completed around AD 856 to commemorate an important military victory, it was deserted within a few years and eventually collapsed. The original restoration of the central temple began in 1937 and was finally completed in 1953. Further restoration on all the temples continues today.

Ancient temple at Prambanan.

Nature at its finest

Jogja is bounded by forest-covered hills, volcanoes and plantations on the north and by the Indian Ocean on the south. Its location lends itself to almost every outdoor pastime imaginable. Enquire about adventure tours and outdoor activities at your accommodation or travel agents.

Most of the southern beaches have lava sand and stormy seas. The most famous is **Parangtritis**, a black-sand stretch where ceremonies are held to appease Ratu Kidul, the goddess of the south sea, who is said to beckon people to her subsea castle. At **Kukup**, with white sand and a swimming lagoon, fishermen sell their daily catch, which can be cooked to customers' specifications on the spot.

Twenty-two km (14 miles) southeast of Jogja, the limestone hills of **Gunung Kidul**, with its many subterranean chambers, is suitable for caving. The incred-

BELOW: Borobudur.

Map
on page
254

ible and highly volatile 2,910-metre (9,550-ft) **Gunung Merapi** (Fire Mountain) constantly belches lava and steam, but hikes up the mountain are possible and popular. Treks, beginning from **Kaliurang**, a hill town 25 km (16 miles) north of Jogja, leave in the pre-dawn hours and reach the top in time for glimpses of the glowing lava at sunrise. Treks are also available from **Ratu Boko** temple near Prambanan.

Bicycling through villages and the countryside puts visitors in close contact with the soul of Java – its hardworking farmers, fishermen and craftsmen. Several villages have been designated *desa wisatas* (tourist villages) and offer homestays, simple meals and activities such as batik and Indonesian-language courses and guided trekking.

Morning rounds.

BELOW:
gamelan musicians.

Surakarta (Solo)

The quiet, old court city, **Surakarta ❻** (more commonly known as Solo), lies just an hour east of Jogja by car. The main attraction, a functioning 18th-century palace called the **Keraton Kasunanan** (Sat–Thur 8.30am–1pm; entrance fee; tel: 0271-41243), was constructed between 1743 and 1746 on the banks of the mighty Benagawan Solo River. The **Keraton Museum** was established in 1963 and contains ancient Hindu-Javanese bronzes, traditional weapons, and coaches dating back to the 1740s. Dance rehearsals at the Keraton take place in the front pavilion within the palace, Bangsal Smorokoto, every Sunday at 10am.

About 1 km (½ mile) northwest of the main palace is **Puro Mangkunegaran** (Sat–Thur 9am–2pm, Fri 9am–12.30pm; entrance fee; tel: 0271-44946), established by another branch of the royal family in 1866. The *pendopo* (pavilion) is the largest in central Java and has four gamelan orchestras. Weekly music and

dance rehearsals are held here every Wednesday at 10am. The museum houses the private collections of Mankunegara IV: dance ornaments, *topeng* (masks), jewellery, ancient Javanese and Chinese coins, bronze figures, and a superb set of ceremonial *keris* blades.

Performances of *wayang orang*, a folk version of the courtly dance-dramas, are held nightly at **Taman Hiburan Rakyat (THR) Sriwedari** at Jalan Slamet Riyadi No. 275 (tel: 0271-711 435). Just west of the Keraton is **Pasar Klewer**, where visitors can browse and bargain for souvenirs and Solo batiks.

Surabaya and eastern Java

With over 400 years of colourful history, **Surabaya ⑦**, East Java's provincial capital, was the largest and most important seaport in the archipelago until the turn of the 20th century. Today it ranks second after Jakarta's Tanjung Priok.

In the centre of the town is the wonderfully refurbished **Mandarin Oriental Hotel Majapahit**, built nearly a century ago in the tradition of the Strand in Yangon, Burma, and the Raffles in Singapore. It is worth visiting for its combination of colonial elegance and art deco trimmings.

On Jalan Selompretan stands Surabaya's oldest Chinese shrine, the 18th-century **Hok An Kiong Temple**, built entirely of wood by native Chinese craftsmen. Chinatown is also known for **Kya-Kya**, a street pedestrianised at night, with hawker stalls and open-air dining. Near the Kali Mas canal on Jalan Kalisosok is the **House of Sampoerna** (Mon–Fri 8am–4pm, Sat 8am–8pm; free), a restored Dutch building housing a museum, gift shop and café. Visitors can see the rolling, cutting, packing and wrapping of *kretek* (clove cigarettes). Nearby is **Sunan Ampel**, the lively Arab quarters with shops selling Muslim clothes, prayer beads and other wares.

The delightful mountain resort **Tretes**, 55 km (35 miles) south of Surabaya, is an excellent base for exploration of eastern Java's ancient Majapahit monuments at **Trowulan**. **Malang** is another pleasant highland town, a 2-hour drive south of Surabaya. In the vicinity are three temples, **Candi Singosari**, **Candi Jago** and **Candi Panataran**. The latter is East Java's only sizeable temple complex, built between AD 1197 and 1454. On the southern coast of the **Alas Purwo National Park** is one of the world's most extreme surfing areas, **G-Land**. **Gunung Ijen**, also within the Alas Purwo National Park, has a haunting sulphuric crater lake.

The steep slopes of the active volcanoes of eastern Java have been the home of the primarily Hindu Tenggerese people for several centuries. In the twelfth month of the Tenggerese calendar is the colourful Kasada festival. Villagers bring offerings to the holy volcano, Bromo, asking their god for protection and blessings. **Gunung Bromo ⑧** itself is a squat volcanic cone inside a gigantic caldera. Trekkers ascend the mountain on foot or horseback (arrange with a travel agent) in the early morning hours to position themselves on the volcanic lip at dawn. The light of the rising sun illuminates the fog-filled caldera, and on clear mornings, the cone of **Gunung Semeru**, Java's highest volcano, looms to the south. ❏

Map on page 204-5

TIP

Most visitors, eager to escape Surabaya's heat, head for the inviting hills to the south of the city, including delightful Malang town. Check out the exquisite antiques, art, and unique rooms at Hotel Tugu Malang.

BELOW: Mt Bromo.

BALI

Map on page 285

Everyone knows Bali, even if they don't know that it's part of Indonesia. Intense commercialisation has changed the southern part of the island, but elsewhere the magical ambience remains

Bali is, first and foremost, a masterpiece of nature formed by an east-to-west range of volcanoes and dominated by two towering peaks, Gunung Batur and Gunung Agung. The Balinese have done much to turn the natural blessings to their advantage. All but the steepest land has been painstakingly terraced over the centuries with rice paddies that hug the volcanic slopes like steps. Each watery patch is efficiently irrigated through an elaborate system of aqueducts, dams and sluices regulated since ancient times by village agricultural cooperatives called *subak*.

The land repays these efforts with abundant harvests, which in turn give the people extra time and energy to devote to their renowned cultural pursuits, the arts and religious obligations.

Abundant harvests are attributed to the goddess of rice and fertility, Dewi Sri. Her symbol is the *cili,* two triangles connected in the form of a shapely woman. Divine spirits dwell in the lofty mountains; dark and inimitable forces lurk in the seas. The human's rightful place is the middle ground between these two extremes, and each home, village and kingdom in Bali has traditionally been aligned along this mountain–sea axis.

LEFT: temple's *kala*-head gateway.
BELOW: Sanur beach.

Isolation and confrontation

Bali was settled and civilised relatively early, as evidenced by stone megaliths like Gunung Kawi. Around a thousand years ago, Bali became a vassal of the great Hindu empires of eastern Java. Yet Balinese culture developed a sophisticated persona all its own. Bali was united in 1550 under an independent ruler, and for two generations, Bali experienced a cultural golden age in which an elaborate ceremonial life, and also the arts, flourished.

Due to their traditional fear of the sea and suspicion of foreigners, the Balinese lived in virtual isolation from the rest of the world until the early 20th century. Throughout this period, its traditions of dance, music, painting, sculpture, poetry, drama and architecture were refined and elaborated, ostensibly for the benefit of Bali's numerous gods.

Throughout the 19th century, the Dutch, under the guise of seeking treaties of friendship and commerce, attempted to establish sovereignty over the island. Their incursions culminated in horrific mass suicides (*puputan*) in 1906, in which Balinese kings and courtiers threw themselves on *keris* knives, or ran headlong into Dutch gunfire rather than face the humiliation of surrender. But Bali has always been adept in absorbing influences from the outside, while retaining, if not strengthening, its local cultural touchstones.

Southern Bali

As the focus for Bali's tourism, commerce and government, the south is by far the island's busiest region. But don't be deceived by the area's development. The south's temple festivals are legendary for the intensity of their trance dances and the earthiness of their rituals. Denpasar's palace ceremonies rank among the most regal on the island, and Kuta establishments host highly professional dance performances nightly. During Nyepi (Hindu Day of Silence), thousands of villagers, arrayed in their ceremonial finery, flood the southern shores of Kuta bearing offerings of food for the *melis* purification rites.

South of the **Ngurah Rai International Airport ❾**, the island's only international airport, a bulbous peninsula fans out to form **Bukit Badung**. The western and southern shorelines are rimmed with sharp, jutting cliffs, and until the early 1990s there was nothing but scarcely populated dry land. Today, **Jimbaran** and further south in **Bukit**, as the area is popularly known, are home to luxury resorts, villas and Bali's largest golf course. Bukit is also the site of the region's most illustrious temple, **Pura Luhur Uluwatu ❿**, or Temple Above the Headstone (daily daylight hours; entrance fee). Giant sea turtles swim in the ocean 300 metres (1,000 ft) below the temple's cliff-top perch.

Nusa Dua ⓫, an extensive planned-resort area on the northeastern coast of Bukit Badung, has superb beaches that give way to **Benoa**'s mangroves. Benoa Harbour is the island's busiest seaport housing fishing boats, inter-island ships and catamarans taking tourists to nearby **Nusa Lembongan** and **Penida** for diving.

Whereas Nusa Dua caters to more upmarket visitors, **Kuta ⓬** is a kind of cluttered, traffic-packed tinseltown with a cosmopolitan feel, especially during peak season (August–September and December–January). Its natural

Chosen by the Balinese saint Pedanda Sakti Wawu Rawuh as the "stage" for his moksa *reunion with the godhead, Pura Luhur Uluwatu is unrivaled for sheer grandeur of location.*

BELOW: net fishing, and the cliffs at Uluwatu temple.

attractions are a broad beach, pounding surf and sunsets. Inland from the beach, Kuta is packed with pubs, bars, restaurants, surf shops, travel agents and inexpensive hotels. Kuta merges north into the more sedate **Legian**. Still further north is decidedly hip **Seminyak**, which, like Kuta and Legian, has a wide sandy beach and thundering surf but without the crowds. There are a handful of upmarket hotels and a large number of good restaurants and bars. Past the Oberoi Bali hotel is the small but key temple **Pura Dalem Petitenget**, the Temple of the Awesome Box (daily daylight hours; donation). Many ceremonies are held at this temple named for the box of betel-chewing ingredients left behind by the Javanese Hindu priest Dang Hyang Nirartha, who came to Bali from Java following the rise of Islam in the 16th century. The main road now extends to **Kerobokan** and then west to **Canggu**, a black-sand beach. Both Kerobokan and Canggu are quickly filling with villas and more restaurants.

The road from Canggu ends at **Pura Tanah Lot ⑬**, or Temple of the Land in the Sea (daily daylight hours; entrance fee). Perched on a large rock just offshore, it was founded by Dang Hyang Nirartha. To the northwest of the temple is an open stage where regular *Ramayana* and *kecak* dance performances are held right after visitors enjoy the famous sunset backdrop over the temple.

On the eastern coast is **Sanur ⑭**, a relatively quiet cluster of hotels and restaurants, with a good beach and water-sports facilities. Of interest in Sanur is **Museum Le Mayeur** (Sun–Thur 8am–3pm, Fri 8am–1pm; entrance fee; tel: 0361-286 201) on the beach north of the Inna Grand Bali Beach Hotel. It exhibits the works of the Belgian painter Jean Le Mayeur de Mepres (1880–1958), who moved to Bali in 1932. All of his paintings depict his wife, Ni Polok, a renowned *legong* dancer.

Map on page 285

TIP

For insight into Balinese performing arts, visitors can observe dance and music classes in progress at ISSI (formerly STSI), Jalan Nusa Indah in Denpasar.

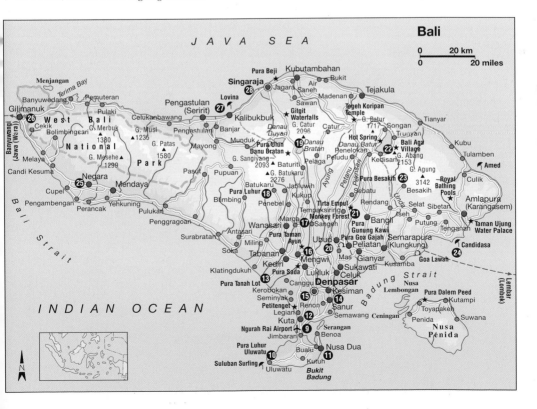

Denpasar

Denpasar ⑮ is a metropolis of more than 400,000 people. Its main square was the scene of the horrific mass suicide in 1906, when almost the entire royal house of Denpasar rushed headlong into blazing Dutch guns. Successive governments have erected monuments commemorating the event. East of the square stands the town's main temple, **Pura Jagatnatha** (daily daylight hours; donation), with a figurine of Tintya, the almighty godhead, glinting from high on the temple's central shrine. **Museum Bali** (Tues–Sun 8am–5pm; entrance fee; tel: 0361-222 860) next door houses a fine collection of archaeological artefacts and examples of Balinese craftsmanship. At the centre of town is **Pasar Badung**, a four-storey building housing Bali's largest traditional market.

Central Bali

One of the most important temples between Denpasar and Ubud is **Pura Sada** (daily daylight hours; donation) in **Kapal**. Dating from the 12th century, it has 64 stone seats resembling megalithic ancestral shrines that are believed to commemorate loyal warriors who fell in battle. Just down the road, **Tabanan**, with its spectacular terraced rice fields, is an ideal place for all-terrain vehicle and four-wheel-drive adventures, cycling, and trekking. Past Kapal, a turn-off toward the mountains leads to **Mengwi** ⑯, a few kilometres north of Kapal. In 1634, the Raja of Mengwi built a magnificent garden temple, **Pura Taman Ayun** (daily daylight hours; entrance fee). The temple's spacious compound is surrounded by a moat and is adjacent to a lotus lake. In the surrounding pavilions, priests recite their Vedantic incantations.

Northeast at **Sangeh** ⑰ is one of Bali's two famed monkey forests. According

BELOW:
Pura Taman Ayun.

to Balinese versions of the *Ramayana* epic, this is where Hanuman's army landed when the monkey king lifted the sacred mountain, Mahameru, and broke it apart in order to crush Rawana. A moss-covered temple lies deep within the jungle.

North of Tabanan is one of Bali's most venerated temples, **Pura Luhur Batukaru** ⓲ (daily daylight hours; entrance fee), on the slopes of 2,278- metre (7,474-ft) Gunung Batukaru. At **Danau Bratan** ⓳, a lake on the road crest to the north shore and a water source for surrounding farmlands, is **Pura Ulun Danu Bratan** (daily daylight hours; entrance fee), which honours Dewi Danu, goddess of the lake.

Map on page 285

Pura Luhur Batukaru is a pura taman, or a temple with a garden pond maintained by a king. Rituals here include veneration of lakes and blessings for irrigation water.

Ubud

Ubud ⓴ and its 15-km (9-mile) radius form Bali's artistic epicentre. **Sukawati**, halfway between Denpasar and Ubud, was once an important kingdom and a centre for Chinese traders during the Dalem dynasty period. A phalanx of shops and a market now conceal the grand Puri Sukawati palace. **Pasar Seni Art Market** in Sukawati is the island's largest art centre offering just about everything from paintings to sculptures. Further north is **Mas**, a village of master carvers. In former times, woodcarvers worked only on religious or royal projects, but now they primarily produce decorative works for export.

Artists have thrived in Ubud since the 1930s when local aristocrat Cokorda Sukawati, German painter Walter Spies and Dutch artist Rudolf Bonnet formed the Pita Maha Art Society. Many of the finest works of the early Pita Maha years are exhibited in **Museum Puri Lukisan** (daily 8am–4pm; entrance fee; tel: 0361-975 136; www.mpl-ubud.com) on Jalan Raya Ubud. **Neka Art Museum** (Mon–Sat 9am–5pm, Sun noon–5pm; tel: 0361-975 074; www.museumneka.com), west of downtown, also has a superb collection of Balinese art.

In the past decade, three other great art museums have been established in Ubud. **Agung Rai Museum of Art** (daily 9am–5pm; entrance fee; tel: 0361-975 742 ; www.armamuseum.com), on Jalan Pengosekan, displays works by famous artists, including the only paintings in Bali by the Javanese artist Raden Saleh. **Museum Rudana** (Mon–Sat 9am–5pm, Sun noon–5pm; tel: 0361-975 779; www.museumrudana.com), at No. 44 Jalan Cok Rai Pudak, has traditional and contemporary Balinese art, and the **Blanco Renaissance Museum** (daily 9am–5pm; entrance fee; tel: 0361-975 502; www.blancobali.com) in Campuan, established by the late flamboyant Spanish-born artist Don Antonio Blanco and his Balinese wife Ni Ronji, features the artist's drawings and paintings.

Pura Penataran Sasih (Lunar Governance), in **Pejeng**, east of Ubud, contains Indonesia's most important bronze-age antiquity: the 2,000-year-old Moon of Pejeng drum. Shaped like an hourglass, beautifully etched, and over 3 metres (10 ft) long, it is the largest drum in the world to be cast as a single piece. According to Balinese legend, it fell from the sky, but the discovery of an ancient, similarly shaped stone mould in Bali proves that sophisticated bronze-casting techniques were known here from an early time.

Pura Gunung Kawi ㉑ is a complex of stone-hewn candi (temples) and monks' cells reached by descend-

BELOW: painter at the Rudana Museum.

ing a long, steep stairway through a stone arch into a watery canyon. The Balinese refer to their religion as Agama Tirta, the religion of the waters. It's not surprising then that a pilgrimage to the **Pura Tirta Empul** spring at **Tampaksiring**, 2 km (1½ miles) upstream from Gunung Kawi, is an essential part of every major Balinese ceremony and ritual. Further north, in the old Gunung Batur crater, is **Danau Batur ㉒**. Here, **Pura Ulun Danu Batur** is one of two major *subak* (irrigation society) temples on Bali. Nearby **Trunyan** village is the home of the Bali Aga, a tribe that has remained separated from modern Bali for over 600 years.

The waters of Tampaksiring are believed to have magical curative and restorative powers.

Eastern Bali

Going from southern Bali to the north and the east is now much faster with the completion of Bypass Ida Bagus Mantra, dubbed Sunset Road as it parallels the beach from Denpasar up to Kusamba, between Klungkung and Amlapura. Several kilometres after **Kusamba**, at the foot of a rocky escarpment, is the cave temple of **Pura Goa Lawah** (daily 7am–6pm; entrance fee), one of the nine great temples of Bali. About 15 km (9 miles) past Goa Lawah, a side road to the right leads to picturesque **Padangbai** harbour town. This is where the Lombok ferry departs and where cruise ships anchor.

The mountain road north from Klungkung, now known as **Semarapura**, climbs along some of Bali's most spectacular rice terraces, passing through several villages on the way until the road ends at the island's holiest spot, **Pura Besakih ㉓** (daily 8am–6pm; entrance fee). With the massive **Gunung Agung** peak as their backdrop, the broad, stepped granite terraces and slender, pointed black pagodas of this 60-temple complex are a fitting residence for the gods. The first record of Besakih's existence is an inscription dating from AD 1007. From

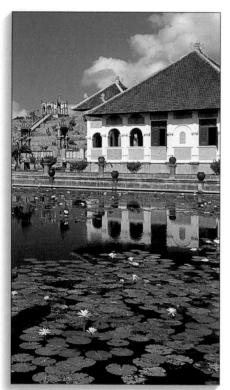

BELOW: the floating pavilion at Taman Ujung.

at least the 15th century – when Pura Besakih was designated as the sanctuary of the deified ancestors of the Gelgel god-kings and their very extended family – this has been the "mother" temple for the entire island.

Candidasa ㉔ is a perfect base for exploring **Tenganan**, home to a pre-Hindu Bali Aga tribe. Located several kilometres inland in an area of lush bamboo forests and mystical banyan trees, it was for some reason never assimilated to the island's Hindu-Balinese culture, and thus it has retained its own traditions of architecture, kinship, government, religion, dance and music, supplying the rest of the island with several valuable items, notably the double-ikat *geringsing* fabrics, some of which are considered to be sacred.

Twenty-five kilometres (16 miles) farther east, the road crosses a wide lava bed and enters **Amlapura**, a medium-size town formerly known as Karangasem and once the capital of Bali's "cultured king". **Puri Kanginan**, the palace where the last raja was born, is an eclectic creation reflecting strong influences of his European education and of his Chinese architect Tung.

During his tenure, King Anak Agung Anglurah Ketut Karangasem, a self-educated architect, built three royal bathing pools. The most adored one is **Taman Ujung** (daily 8am–5pm; entrance fee). Victim of many earthquakes, Taman Ujung was completely refurbished in 2004 under the supervision of UNESCO to its original splendour as a floating royal summer house.

Northern and western Bali

The drive along the southwestern coast is splendidly uncongested after the traffic chaos of southern Bali. There are excellent black-sand beaches along the way. The district capital **Negara** ㉕, near the island's westernmost coast, is famed for its buffalo races between July and October, introduced from eastern Java and Madura less than a century ago.

At the western extreme of Bali is **Gilimanuk** ㉖, a rather nondescript town with frequent ferries to eastern Java. Just before Gilimanuk is **Cekik**, headquarters for the **Bali Barat National Park** (West Bali National Park; headquarters open Mon–Thur 8am–2pm, Fri 8–11am, Sat 8am–1pm; tel: 0365-61060). Trekking permits and guides (required) are available at Cekik and at the Visitor Centre in Labahan Lalang. **Menjangan Island**, in the west end of the park, offers Bali's best scuba diving.

The north coast is peppered with quiet villages and agriculture fields. **Pemuteran**, an emerging resort area not far from Menjangan, is a secluded beachside destination offering endless snorkelling and diving excursions. The culture of the north is different in several ways: the language is less refined, the music more allegro, and the temple ornamentation more fanciful. The towns comprising **Lovina** ㉗ offer countless bungalows for travellers seeking an alternative to the overdeveloped southern part of the island. Lovina offers snorkelling and excursions to catch glimpses of dolphins as the sun rises.

Further on, **Singaraja** ㉘, a port city and the capital of Bali under the Dutch, has sizeable communities of Chinese and Muslims. From Penulisan, the winding road seems to drop straight out of the sky, flattening out several kilometers before **Kubutambahan** village on the coast. ❑

Map on page 285

The nearly extinct Bali starling is protected within Bali Barat National Park.

BELOW: fishing boats at Lovina Beach.

BALI BEACH ACTIVITIES

As well as surf, sand and sun, beaches offer impromptu shopping, outdoor massage and a variety of sports

Bali's beaches are unfortunately not blessed with the archetypal white sands and gin-clear aquamarine waters that one associates with tropical island havens. Many of its beaches are black or grey sand due to the volcanic origins of the island. The only true white sand beaches are found at Nusa Dua, Tanjung Benoa, and to a lesser degree at Sanur. Jimbaran, Kuta, Legian and Seminyak on the southwest coast have grey sand beaches but make up for it with their thundering surf, fabulous mango-streaked sunsets and a broad, flat expanse of beach that is perfect for long walks and beachside sports like volleyball, frisbee and even soccer.

The beaches at Kuta and Legian, especially, are a hive of activity with people in various stages of undress sunning, swimming and surfing while all the time warding off pesky beach vendors. Although you will see young Balinese playing at the beaches, the older ones generally stay away except when they perform traditional cleansing rituals there, as most Balinese regard the sea as the preserve of demons.

△ **KITE FLYING**
Kite flying on Sanur beach. Vendors sell colourful, handmade kites in the shape of birds and sail boats. There's a kite festival every July on Padanggalak beach, next to Sanur. Some kites are so large that it takes several men to launch them.

▽ **SURFING**
Surfer on Kuta beach and a dive instructor at Pulau Menjangan. The breaks and barrels off the south coast attract surfers from around the world, while the coral reefs around Pulau Menjangan in northwestern Bali teem with rich aquatic life.

△ PARASAILING

Parasailing at Nusa Dua. A speedboat launches an eager participant attached to a colourful parachute for an exciting and exhilarating ride high above the water and a unique bird's eye view of the beach. Strong, waiting arms will wait to safely catch the parasailer when it is time to descend.

◁ HAIR BRAIDING

Hair braiding at Kuta beach. Women roam the beach looking for willing customers. Once a price is agreed, nimble fingers will skilfully braid thin cornrows of hair into artistic patterns across the head, threading colourful beads onto the ends of the strands. This can take nearly an hour, so remember to protect yourself from the sun or have it done under the shade of a tree.

▽ FISHING

Fishing at Nusa Lembongan. Special boats and yachts take visitors for a day of fishing in the waters near one of Bali's southeastern offshore islands. Longer liveaboard expeditions to fishing sites further afield can be arranged by chartering a vessel that includes fishing gear, the services of a cook and accommodation on board.

△ HORSEBACK RIDING

Horseback riding on the beach at Seminyak. The lonely coast beyond Kuta and Legian beaches, stretching into Seminyak and Canggu, has long, flat expanses of smooth sand which are great for relaxed horseback rides. Small, gentle ponies can be hired, and guided training for novices is available. Experienced riders will enjoy the freedom of galloping near the shoreline with waves rolling in and breaking at the horses' hoofs.

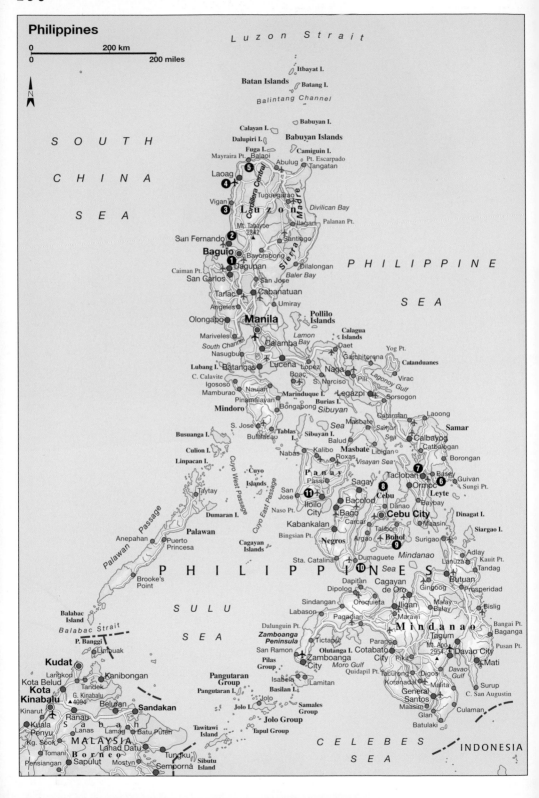

Philippines

0 200 km
0 200 miles

N

Luzon Strait

SOUTH CHINA SEA

Itbayat I.
Batan Islands
Batang I.
Balintang Channel

Calayan I.
Babuyan I.
Dalupiri I.
Babuyan Islands
Camiguin I.
Fuga I.
Mayraira Pt. Balaoi
Abulug
Pt. Escarpado
Tangatan
Laoag ❹ ❺
Cordillera Central
Tuguegarao
Vigan ❸
Luzon
Ilagan
Divilican Bay
Mt. Tabayoc
2842 ▲
Palanan Pt.
San Fernando ❷
Santiago
Bayombong
Baguio
❶ Dagupan
Dilalongan
Caiman Pt.
Sierra Madre
Baler Bay
San Carlos
San Jose
PHILIPPINE

SEA

Tarlac
Cabanatuan
Angeles
Umiray
Olongapo
Pollilo Islands
Mariveles
Manila
Lamon Bay
Calagua Islands
Calamba
Daet
Garchitorena
Nasugbu
Lubang I.
Batangas
Lucena
Lopez
Naga
Pili
Catanduanes
C. Calavite
Igososo
Naujan
Boac
S. Narciso
Virac
Mamburao
Pinamalayan
Marinduque I.
Legazpi
Sorsogon
Mindoro
Bongabong
Burias I.
Sibuyan
Catarman
Laoong
S. Jose
Tablas
Sibuyan Sea
Masbate
Samar
Calbayog
Samar
Busuanga I.
Bulalacao
Balud
Libigan
Catbalogan
Culion I.
Sibuyan I.
Roxas
Borongan
Linpacan I.
Nabas
Kalibo
Visayan Sea
❼ Basey
Guivan
Taytay
Cuyo Islands
Passi
Panay
Sagay
Tacloban ❻
Sungi Pt.
Cuyo West Passage
San Jose
❽ Cebu
Ormoc
Leyte
Dumaran I.
Naso Pt.
Iloilo City ❶❶
Bacolod
Danao
Baybay
Palawan
Bago
Cebu City
Dinagat I.
Anepahan
Cagayan Islands
Kabankalan
Carcar
Siargao I.
Puerto Princesa
Bingsian Pt.
Negros
Talibon
Bohol ❾
Surigao
Brooke's Point
Sta. Catalina
Argao
Mindanao
Adlay
Dumaguete ❶⓿
Sea
Kauit Pt.
Balabac Island
Dapitan
Tandag
SULU
Dipolog
Cagayan de Oro
Gingoog
Butuan
Prosperidad
Balabac Strait
Sindangan
Oroquieta
Bislig
P. Banggi
Labason
Pagadian
Iligan
Malay Balay
Bangai Pt.
SEA
Dalunguin Pt.
Marawi
Baganga
Zamboanga Peninsula
Tictapul
Parang
Mindanao
Kudat
San Ramon
Cotabato City
Mt. Apo
2954 ▲
Pikit
Tagum
Pusan Pt.
Kota Belud
Pilas Group
Zamboanga City
Moro Gulf
Quidapil Pt.
Tacurong
Davao City
Kota Kinabalu
Langkon
Kanibongan
Pangutaran Group
Isabela
Lamitan
Digos
Davao Gulf
Mati
Kinarut
Tandek
Pangutaran I.
Basilan I.
Koronadal
Malita
Kuala Penyu
G. Kinabalu
▲4094
Beluran
Sandakan
Jolo I.
Samales Group
General Santos
Surup
C. San Augustin
Kg. Sook
Ranau
Jolo Group
Maasim
Kanu
Lanas
Lamag
Batu Puteh
Jolo Group
Glan
Culaman
Pensiangan
Tomani
Batu Datu
Tungku
Tawitawi Island
Tapul Group
Batulaki
Sapulut
Mostyn
Semporna
Sibutu Island
CELEBES
SEA
INDONESIA
MALAYSIA
Borneo
Sabah

PHILIPPINES

Spanish and American influence over four centuries has made this intriguing archipelago Asia's unexpected surprise

They lie like lovely gems atop Asia's continental shelf, these 7,107 islands, straddling where two tectonic plates collide to create islands with fluid names like Luzon, Mindoro, Palawan and Sulu. Only a couple thousand of these islands can be considered inhabited by the 90 million Filipinos, or as they call themselves, Pinoy, who represent 111 different linguistic, cultural and racial groups. Their national languages are Pilipino, based on Tagalog, a dialect of the Tagalog people of southern Luzon, and English.

Geographically, the Philippines is a sprawl of half-drowned mountains, part of a great cordillera extending from Japan south to Indonesia. The nation's archipelago stretches 1,840 km (1,140 miles) north to south, spanning 1,100 km (690 miles) at its widest.

This archipelago was born from powerful forces – great tectonic pressures pushing islands upwards and mighty volcanoes depositing their ash to enrich plains nurtured by monsoon rains. The first humans to see this land walked here during the ice ages, when seas were hundreds of metres lower. Later, after the ocean once again flooded the land bridges, waves of colonisers came from Borneo in seagoing *barangay* to settle the coastal areas, pushing the earlier arrivals into the mountains. Nearly everything that the Malay people brought has lasted, including language, custom and culture. To this foundation the endowments of the Spanish and Americans have been added. Three centuries in a convent followed by 50 years in Hollywood, goes the old saying.

Manila, the in-your-face capital, is the usual starting point for most journeys in the Philippines. The traveller leaving Europe or North America for the first time finds the city immensely intimidating in its chaos and frantic energy. Worry not, for aside from the predictable scam artists and the like, it is a city with merit for the traveller. It is an old city, with a history that lingers in its architecture: Malacañang Palace, the inner city of Intramuros, the statues and boulevards.

Manila is on the southern end of Luzon, the largest island, and on the northern end of the archipelago. Northward out of Manila leads into the lofty highlands of Baguio and beyond, or along the western coast of Ilocos. This is the land of immense cascading rice terraces, stretching away beyond the horizon.

South of Luzon are the Visayas, a gathering of variously shaped islands that can keep travellers engaged for years. Central to the Visayas is the island, and city, of Cebu. This is not only the gateway to resorts and coral reefs, it is an entrepreneurial city, noted within and outside the Philippines as the nation's place to do efficient business – but also famous for its guitars. ❏

PRECEDING PAGES: Mt Mayon, southern Luzon, has erupted nearly 50 times since 1616; wedding at San Augustin Church, Intramuros, Manila.

Decisive Dates

Early days

Pre-history: Migrants cross land bridge from Asian mainland and settle archipelago.

AD 900: Chinese establish coastal trading posts over the next 300 years.

1400: Muslim clergy start to bring Islam to the Philippines from Malaya.

1494: The Treaty of Tordesillas is signed between Portugal and Spain, dividing much of the world between the two colonial powers. Everything to the east of a line 370 leagues west of the Cape Verde Islands

belongs to Portugal, while everything to the west belongs to Spain.

Early colonial intrusions

1521: Magellan lands on Cebu, claims region for Spain. Lapu Lapu (Rajah Cilapulapu), in defending the island from the Spaniards, slays Magellan, thus driving expedition from Islands.

1543: Ruy de Villabos sails from Mexico to Mindanao and names archipelago after Crown Prince Felipe II.

1565: Miguel Lopez de Legazpi sails from Mexico and gains a foothold in Cebu.

1571: Legazpi builds walled Spanish city of Intramuros. Intramuros is menaced from the outset by enemies: Japanese *wako*, Dutch fleets, Chinese

pirates and disgruntled Filipinos. The core of modern Manila begins to form outside of Intramuros.

1762: Late in the year, as a minor episode in the Seven Years' War with Spain, Intramuros is seized by England's General William Draper.

1764: End of the British occupation.

Rise of nationalism

1872: Uprising in Cavite. Spain executes Filipino priests Jose Burgos, Mariano Gomez and Jacinto Zamora, who continue to be martyrs today.

1892: Jose Rizal returns from Europe. Andres Bonifacio founds the Katipunan.

1896: Spanish colonists imprison and kill hundreds of Filipinos in Manila. Bonifacio and the Katipunan launch the Philippine revolution. Emilio Aguinaldo and rebel forces capture Cavite, south of Manila. Colonial authorities execute Rizal.

1898: The United States goes to war with Spain, and wins. Treaty between the US and Spain grants the US authority over the Philippines, along with Puerto Rico and Guam.

1899: War breaks out between the US and the Philippines. Aguinaldo is inaugurated as president of the first Philippine republic in 1899.

1901: Aguinaldo captured after guerrilla war of resistance and swears allegiance to the US. Scattered resistance continues throughout the decade.

1916: The US Congress authorises the gradual independence of the Philippines.

1935: Quezon elected president. The Philippines is made an American commonwealth with the promise of independence in 1945; but World War II intervenes. General Douglas MacArthur takes charge of the Philippines' defence against Japan.

World War II

1941: On 22 December, Japanese land on Luzon.

1942: Japan takes Manila. Quezon proposes and Roosevelt rejects Philippine neutrality. MacArthur retreats to Australia. *Hukbalahap (Huk)* established with PKP member Luis Taruc in command. Quezon and Osmena flee to the United States, where they establish a government in exile.

1943: Japanese install puppet republic with Jose Laurel as president. The Japanese rule over the country is exceedingly brutal.

1944: Quezon dies. MacArthur and Osmena land in Leyte, beginning the Allied effort to retake the Philippine archipelago from the Japanese.

1945: The Allies recapture Manila, declared an "open city" by the Allies and thus subject to unlimited bombardment. Much of the city is destroyed.

Problems and opportunities

1946: Roxas defeats Osmena for presidency. On 4 July, the Philippines proclaims independence.

1951: US-Philippine mutual defence treaty signed.

1965: Ferdinand Marcos defeats Macapagal in his bid for re-election to the presidency.

1969: Ferdinand Marcos becomes the first Philippines president to be re-elected.

1970: Peso devaluation fuels price increases, food shortages, unemployment and unrest. Radical students and others stage a series of anti-Marcos, anti-US demonstrations. American senators accuse the Philippines of misusing funds supplied for Philippine forces in Vietnam. Marcos threatens to impose martial law.

1972–81: Martial law imposed by Marcos, who rules with an iron fist during this period, erecting monuments to himself and accumulating a vast fortune. His wife, Imelda, dominates Manila government.

1981: Martial law lifted but Marcos keeps power to rule by decree. Marcos re-elected in contest boycotted by opposition.

1983: Leading opposition leader Benito Aquino returns to Manila from exile in the US, is assassinated on arrival at the Manila airport. Circumstances point to government involvement.

1984: Legislative elections held. "Parliament of the street" holds frequent anti-Marcos demonstrations. Spiralling economic crises.

1985: General Fabian C. Ver and 25 others charged with slaying Aquino, but are acquitted. Marcos announces snap election. Over a million people petition Cory Aquino, widow of the assassinated Aquino, to run against Marcos. Aquino agrees.

1986: Violence escalates before the elections, at least 30 killed on election day. Election rigging enrages Filipinos, and millions join in uprising against Marcos regime. On 26 February, the Marcoses flee. Aquino, elected to the presidency, orders release of political prisoners. First two anti-Aquino coup attempts foiled (Aquino would survive 7 coup attempts in all). New constitution drafted. Labour leader Rolando Olalia murdered. Ceasefire with the New People's Army (NPA).

1987: Ceasefire breaks down, and the military kills 13 peasant demonstrators near presidential palace. Public ratifies constitution after third military mutiny put down. Concern grows about renewed human rights abuses. Pro-Aquino forces win majorities in House and Senate elections. Another bloody coup attempt fails. Activist Lean Alejandro murdered.

1988: Provincial elections. The US agrees to pay $481 million a year for use of American military bases in the Philippines. Marcoses indicted by a US grand jury for fraud and embezzlement.

1989: Ferdinand Marcos dies in Hawaii. Coup attempt splits military; government calls on the US for air support of Aquino government.

1990: Cabinet revamped. Negotiations start on status of American military bases.

1991: Bilateral posturing regarding the US bases ends abruptly with the dramatic eruption of Mount Pinatubo. Americans simply pack up and leave.

1992: Fidel Ramos, Aquino's defence minister and a strong ally who backed her during coup attempts, wins presidential election. His pragmatic leadership and problem-solving defy traditional perceptions of inept Filipino government. Foreign investors return.

1998: Joseph Estrada is elected president.

2000: Estrada is impeached for bribery, betrayal of public trust and violation of the constitution.

2001: Estrada is ousted from office against his will and Gloria Macapagal Arroyo, his vice-president, takes over.

2002: US military joins the Philippines in large-scale exercises in southern Philippines to rescue kidnapped foreign hostages.

2004: Arroyo wins the presidential elections. The peso hits an all-time low. ❑

LEFT: Spanish expedition leaders Villabos, Legazpi and Magellan are fancifully juxtaposed in an old engraving. **RIGHT:** former president Fidel Ramos tends to important matters.

FILIPINO WAYS

From Christian fervour to ancestral worship, and from clans to mountain tribes,
the richness of Filipino culture creates one of Asia's most vibrant societies

Filipinos have a justifiable reputation as one of the most hospitable people in the world, especially in rural areas where traditional attitudes still survive. Clans are the rule of survival, and are both the main strength and source of corruption in Filipino society. They operate as custodians of common experiences (many old families religiously keep family trees), and as the memory of geographical and racial origins. Clans also act as disciplinary mechanisms, employment agencies and informal social security systems.

Perhaps the crowning glory of local sociology is the Filipino expression that one anthropologist has traced to a linguistic root in *Bahala na*, or "leave it to God". This is a typical Filipino reaction to crises and insoluble problems. Development experts have often decried Bahala na as passive and fatalist, the sole factor in the delayed maturity of the Filipino nation. Others, however, praise its philosophical origins.

Filipina and friar

The image of today's Filipina emerged from a checkered history. It is no longer well remembered, but the majority of the Philippines' early tribes relied on the woman to perform their most sacred rites. *Catalonan* to the Tagalog, *baliana* to the Bicolano, *managanito* to the Pangasinense, *babaylan* to the Bisaya – the priestess healed with herbs, exorcised those who were devil-possessed and, receiving the spirits in trance, guided her tribe or clan through crucial junctures of communal life.

There is no cause for wonder, then, that women furiously fought the Europeans' arrival. Feeling the cornerstone of tribal life threatened, priestesses of Cagayan, Pangasinan and the Visayas let out one long wail of incantation against the conqueror. As Catholic missionaries cursed them for being agents of the devil, the priestesses moved their tribes to poison the cowled strangers, burn their Christian altars,

and all else failing, flee to thick forest and higher if not safer ground.

The Filipina who stayed behind to be Christianised proved to be the colonist's delight. She traded and parlayed with the white man, often helping him pacify war-like neighbouring tribes. Here began the special relationship between friar and Filipina. Once daughter and consort to proud and free men, she became an adopted waif to be cast in the Castellan mould. The friar who was father figure to whole villages fancied her a naive child, tenderheartedly teaching her his alphabet. He gave her only enough to keep her serving and worshipful, withholding higher education from her eager grasp until as late as the 19th century.

It was a relatively easy thing to declare political independence. It has been a totally different matter coping with the loose ends of colonial thinking. Under two kinds of white rule, the relationship between the sexes in the Philippines has lived through severe imbalances, giv-

LEFT: Filipinas in traditional dress of the Philippines.
RIGHT: young Filipina.

ing it both comedy and tragedy. The Spaniard moulded the Filipina to an Old World charm. The American touched her ambitions to the quick, kindling a fire that still smoulders today. Yet society continues to remind the Filipina of her former status as a friar ward. She cannot draw up or sign contracts without her husband's consent, and her adultery is more stiffly punished than his.

Religion

Kinship was the glue of early Filipino society, and in no time at all, the souls of departed

> **INCREDIBLE ICONS**
>
> All over the Philippines, at least 50 icons of the Virgin Mary and the Holy Child are surrounded with wondrous stories of miracles.

The difference can be seen today in the oldest churches of the country, particularly in the Tagalog provinces, and in Cagayan, Ilocos, Cebu and Panay islands.

Propaganda was part and parcel of the missionary kit. Friars made sure that every important event in the lives of their flock was attributed to divine intervention. Thus Mary and her son (along with the various patron saints of particular places) became the agents for fire prevention, earthquake-proofing (especially of churches), the

ancestors, the spirits of nature, and not a few mythical monsters were replaced by (and in many cases, incorporated within) an extended Christian family that consisted of both the human and the divine.

Depending on the temperamental and cultural quirks of the settlement, emphasis varied between either Mother, the Virgin Mary, or the Child Jesus. In the shrines and churches of Luzon, where women's equality with men had long ago extended into roles of power as priestesses, Mary became the standard-bearer of Catholicism. In the Visayas of Queen Juana, where children to this day are indulged in extended childhood, the Santo Niño was king.

countering of spells to outside invasions by the Dutch, British, Muslim, Portuguese and Chinese, as well as deities of rain, fertility and the entire range of human needs and concerns.

In the same tradition, there is hardly a Catholic home without its own enshrined Virgin and Child, usually near the master bedroom. Just a generation ago, it was a standard practice to affix a *Maria* or a *Jesus Maria* to a Filipino child's given name.

Ethnic and minority groups

Of the Philippine population, now just under 90 million, some 10 percent are classified as cultural or ethnic minorities. Most of these people live outside the cultural mainstream of lowland Filipino Christians. They comprise the most diverse and exotic population of the nation, with the vast majority of these minorities, some 60 percent, made up of various Muslim groups living on the southern islands of Mindanao and the Sulu Archipelago.

The remaining peoples, who are mostly animists, inhabit the mountain provinces of northern and central Luzon, and the highland plains, rain forests and the isolated seashores of Mindanao and Palawan. These people often live as they have for generations, but are also accessible to outsiders.

There are five major ethnic groups spread across the Cordillera highlands of northern Luzon: Ibaloi, Kankana-ey, Ifugao, Kalinga and Apayao. Other indigenous groups of northern Luzon include the Bontoc and Tingguian.

These are the unconquered people of the north who have evolved robust indigenous cultures and traditions in highland seclusion, far removed from lowland colonial history. These mountain tribes live sedentary lives based upon a highly developed agricultural economy. They worship tribal ancestors or spirits of nature, and

---

LEFT: a ritual cult practice on Mt. Banahaw, south of Manila. **ABOVE:** Ifugao elder, northern Luzon.

turn a suspicious face upon the "intruders" from the lowlands.

Cordillera is home to various tribes, including the gold- and copper-mining Ibaloi and the mountain people of Kankana-ey. Probably the best-known people of the mountains, the Kankana-ey combine American missionary teaching with their ancestral religion.

The Ifugao of the eastern and central Cordillera are the master architects of the most famous rice terraces in the world. The Ifugao rice terraces, first constructed between 2,000 and 3,000 years ago, cover over 260 sq km (100 sq. miles) of steep mountain slopes in Ifugao Province.

Muslims

Considered as a whole, the Muslims of the south constitute the largest cultural minority of the Philippines. The Muslims, also known as Moros and equally known as fiercely independent and combative, are classified into five major groups: Tausug, Maranao, Maguindanao, Samal and Badjao.

Another unique cultural group, living on Basilan Island south of Zamboanga amidst the Sulu Islands, are the Yakan. They are of partial Polynesian origin, with mixed Muslim and animistic beliefs. They are the most superb textile weavers of the southern archipelago.

The non-Muslim ethnic tribes of the Mindanao highlands are the least studied of the Philippine cultural minorities, and among the most highly costumed and colourful. There are over 10 tribes living in relative isolation in the Mindanao interior, including the Tiruray, the Bagobo and the Subannon.

The debatable Tasaday

The cave-dwelling Tasaday of southern Mindanao have been the focus of furious anthropological debate since their so-called discovery in 1971. They were portrayed as a stone-age tribe of some two dozen people living in harmony with nature, with no prior contact to the outside world. However, many anthropologists consider the Tasaday a hoax of the Marcos regime. They argue that the tribe's habitat cannot support their hunter-gatherer existence; the Tasaday language is closely related to the nearby Manobo tribe; and that no trash heaps, showing long-term occupation, have been found anywhere near their caves. ❑

FIESTAS AND FESTIVALS

Splashes of colour, raucous laughter, and an air of insouciance can be found at
any Filipino celebration – and celebrations are a Filipino speciality

The present textures of the Filipino fiesta comes from the wisdom of old Spanish friars, who were disturbed by early symptoms of forced – and seemingly incomplete – conversion of Filipinos to Catholicism. When natural calamities and tribal enemies threatened the life of Christian settlements, the friars took

10 Bornean lords escaping religious tyranny in the south fled northward with their followers. Upon their arrival in Panay, they sought rights to this island and struck an accord with the local king. Later, the peace pact was reinforced by a lavish harvest feast prepared by the Bornean immigrants for their Ati neighbours. Ever eager

the opportunity to lead everyone to the church in quest of a "miracle". The guardian spirits of traditional harvest feasts were slowly replaced by Christian saints, and as summer heat rose in the blood, friars would scurry through their memories of Spain for songs, dances and colours to woo a musical people in the worship of the Virgin Mary.

January

Kalibo's Ati-Atihan festival, held during the third week of January, is the Philippines' most famous fiesta. *Ati-Atihan* means "making like Atis", and refers to the black Negrito aborigines, the original inhabitants of Panay. In 1212,

to please, the Borneans enlivened up the welcome with gongs and cymbals, smeared soot on their faces and started dancing in the streets in merry imitation of their Ati guests. The Christ-child figure of Santo Niño was introduced in later years, when the Borneans successfully fought off marauding Muslim attackers.

February

The giant ring road encircling Metro Manila, Epifanio de los Santos Avenue, or EDSA, was the focus for the February 1986 revolution that toppled former dictator Ferdinand Marcos without violence or bloodshed. Despite their fears, hundreds of thousands of Filipinos converged on this road of resistance to form a protective human wall. Since then, Filipinos have celebrated the EDSA People's Power anniversary with moving church masses, stage shows, dancing, displays, singing and fireworks.

March

During Holy Week, there are colourful Easter celebrations throughout the Philippines. The heart-shaped island of Marinduque especially turns into a stage for a unique spectacle: the Moriones festival and the re-

In the late 1960s, a Manila-based oil company, in a flash of public relations genius, launched a search for a so-called Jeepney King.

Amid the typical hoopla of a local Filipino fiesta, jeepney drivers from all over the archipelago compete in contests designed to test their judgement and reflexes on the road and steadiness at the wheel, not to mention a showy parade of wondrous and unique jeepneys.

> ### MAY FLOWERS
>
> *Sampaguita, ilang-ilang* and hibiscus surround the month-long May tributo to the Queen of Heaven, or the Virgin Mary.

May

The first of May is an important day throughout the Philip-

enactment of the ancient Biblical legend of Longinus and his miracle. On Good Friday, Christ's resurrection is then dramatically re-enacted.

April

Filipino, jeepneys have for years served as the country's most important mode of transport. They were originally a solution to the problem of what to do with army jeeps abandoned by American soldiers at the end of World War II.

LEFT: fire-breathing during Ati-Atihan, and fiesta clown. **ABOVE:** mask used in Marindugue's Moriones festival during Holy Week.

pines, as it marks the beginning of a merry month of flowers, dainty maidens in pretty gowns and the Queen of the Philippine festivals, the Santacruzan, or Queen of Heaven. The Santacruzan is a Spanish legacy that commemorates the search for the True Cross of Christ.

June

At the centrepiece of any Filipino fiesta table, the *lechon*, or whole roast pig, is king. So revered is the aroma of this succulent dish that the people of Balayan and Batangas provinces have highlighted the feast of their patron saint, St John, with a tribute to the golden-red and crispy lechon.

July

A colourful procession highlights the festival of Santa Ana Kahimonan Abayan, held on 27 July in the northern Mindanao city of Butuan. In earlier times, human-eating crocodiles infested the Agusan River, biting, so to speak, into the townpeople's life.

Faced with a common enemy, the townspeople implored their patron saint Santa Ana to give them bountiful harvests and safe passage over the river. Santa Ana heard their prayers and destroyed the creatures.

Today, the river-people honour their patron saint by staging a waterborne high mass. Hun-

dreds of boats strung with multicoloured bunting and festooned with decorations are linked side by side to form a long platform spanning the river.

August

Four-metre-high (14-ft) papier-mâché *gigantes* strut through the Quezon town of Lucban representing Juan Cruz, a farmer, his wife and their two children. During the month of August, a full-blown fiesta is dedicated to these symbolic, fun-loving gigantes.

Heightening the fun is the *toro*, an enormous papier-mâché bull brightly painted red and rigged with firecrackers. Throughout the parade, the enormous bull scampers around the town plaza, scattering spectators as fireworks inside are ignited.

September

The religious observance surrounding one September festival involves the ritual transfer, known as the *translucion*, of the statue of Our Lady of Peñafrancia to the Metropolitan Cathedral. Devotees travel by any means to catch a glimpse of her at the festival in Naga. A nine-day *novena* is then held before the statue is returned to her shrine down the Bicol River.

October

The Masskara festival was first conceived in 1980 to add colour and gaiety to the Negros city of Bacolod's celebration of its Charter Day anniversary, on 19 October. *Masskara* is coined from two words: *mass*, meaning crowd or many, and the Spanish word *cara*, or face; thus the double meaning for "mask" and "many faces". The symbol of the festival – a smiling mask – was adopted by the organisers to dramatise the Negrense's happy spirit, despite periodic economic downturns in the sugar industry.

November

Built in the 16th century, Manila's Intramuros district is a stellar example of a medieval fortress town. In November is a festival of regal revelry, when the walled city relives its colonial golden age. The underlying theme of the varied activities, including a choral competition, is the traditions observed during the Spanish colonial period.

December

This month is host to the Christmas lantern festival. Three days before Christmas, at sunset, lanterns glow like phantasmagorical stars along the streets, illuminating the night. Townspeople dance through the streets to the beat of a lively brass band, the air cool and filled with the sound of Christmas carols. The lanterns, or *parols* as they are known, are specimens of pyrotechnic splendour, representing the synergistic endeavour of every town barrio. On the 22nd, the lanterns go on parade accompanied by music, feasting and dancing. ❑

LEFT: Christmas lantern of San Fernando.
RIGHT: painted "warriors" for the Pintados fiesta, Leyte.

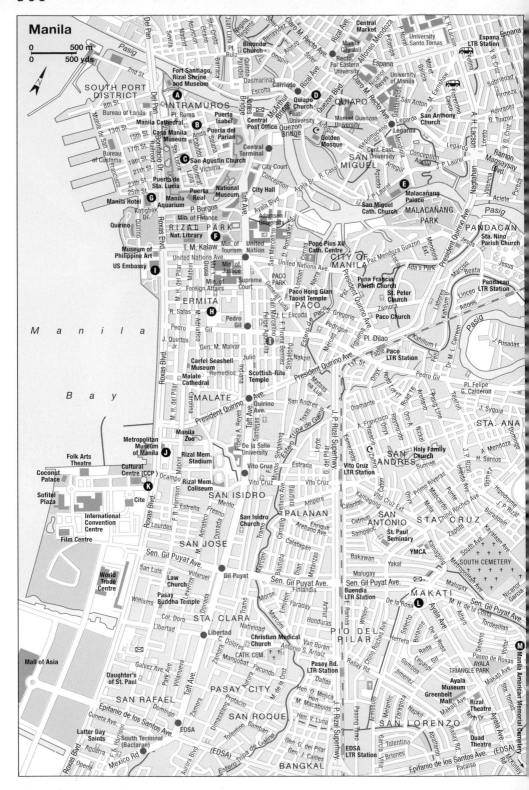

Manila

0 — 500 m
0 — 500 yds

SOUTH PORT DISTRICT

INTRAMUROS

Fort Santiago, Rizal Shrine and Museum

Manila Cathedral

Casa Manila Museum

Puerta Isabel
Puerta del Parian

San Agustin Church

Bureau of Lands

Bureau of Customs

Puerta de Sta. Lucia
Puerta Real

Manila Hotel
Manila Aquarium

Quirino

Museum of Philippine Art
US Embassy

RIZAL PARK
Nat. Library

Min. of Finance

T. M. Kalaw

Min. of Tourism
Min. of Justice

ERMITA

Min. of Foreign Affairs

Carfel Seashell Museum
Malate Cathedral

MALATE

Manila Zoo

Metropolitan Museum of Manila

Rizal Mem. Stadium

De la Salle University

Folk Arts Theatre

Coconut Palace
Sofitel Plaza

Cultural Centre (CCP)

Cite

Rizal Mem. Coliseum

SAN ISIDRO

International Convention Centre

Film Centre

San Isidro Church

PALANAN

World Trade Centre

SAN JOSE

Law Church

Pasay Buddha Temple

STA. CLARA

Mall of Asia

Christian Medical Church

Daughter's of St. Paul

CATH. CEM.

Pasay Rd. LTR Station

SAN RAFAEL

PASAY CITY

Latter Day Saints

South Terminal (Baclaran)

SAN ROQUE

BANGKAL

National Museum

City Hall

Central Terminal

City Court

Adamson University

Supreme Court

PACO PARK

Pedro Gil

Scottish-Rite Temple

Quirino Ave.

Vito Cruz

San Isidro Church

SAN JOSE

Gil Puyat

Sen. Gil Puyat Ave.

Christian Medical Church

INTRAMUROS

Manila Cathedral

Jones Bridge

MacArthur Bridge

Central Post Office

Quiapo Church

QUIAPO

Central Market

Manila City Jail

Far Eastern University

University Santo Tomas

University of Manila

Golden Mosque

SAN MIGUEL

Quezon Bridge

Malacañang Palace

San Miguel Cath. Church

MALACAÑANG PARK

Espana LTR Station

San Anthony Church

Ramon Magsaysay Blvd.

PANDACAN

Sta. Nino Parish Church

Pandacan LTR Station

CITY OF MANILA

Pope Pius XII Cath. Centre

United Nation

United Nations Ave.

PACO

Pena Francia Parish Church
St. Peter Church

Paco Church

Paco Hong Gian Taoist Temple

Pl. Dilao

Paco LTR Station

President Quirino Ave.

STA. ANA

Holy Family Church

SAN ANDRES

Vito Cruz LTR Station

SAN ANTONIO

St. Paul Seminary

YMCA

SOUTH CEMETERY

SOUTH CEMETERY

Buendia LTR Station

MAKATI

Sen. Gil Puyat Ave.

PIO DEL PILAR

Manila American Memorial Cemetery

AYALA TRIANGLE PARK

Ayala Museum
Greenbelt Mall

Rizal Theatre

Quad Theatre

SAN LORENZO

EDSA LTR Station

Epifanio de los Santos Ave. (EDSA)

STA. CRUZ

Manila Bay

MANILA

Over the years, the legacies of different eras in Manila have melded with contemporary demands, holding this capital city of the Philippines in a heady flux of never-ending motion

Map on page 308

O f course, Manila is not the Philippines, although countless visitors leave Manila with what they think is an image of the Philippines: happily Westernised Asians on the move and in the know, flashing their best hospitality smiles. It is a shallow impression, and false, too. To go beyond the facade for a deeper understanding of Philippine people and history, start in Old Manila, the centre of the archipelago.

What is commonly called Metro Manila is bisected by the **Pasig River**, so that most city areas are known as either north or south of the Pasig. The Spanish conquistador Miguel Lopez de Legazpi arrived in the area in 1571. After a battle, he took over the ruins of the ruler's fortress at the mouth of the Pasig. According to legend, the ruler, Sulayman, razed his palace at his impending defeat to Legazpi. Legazpi founded Spanish Manila that same year, beginning construction of a medieval fortified town that was to become Spain's most durable monument in Asia, Intramuros.

Intramuros

The city fortress, which stands today and was an expanded version of the original Fort Santiago, was defended by moats and walls 10 metres (30 ft) thick with well positioned batteries. It was called **Intramuros** or "Within the Walls". **Fort Santiago ⓐ** (daily 8am–6pm; entrance fee) is near where the Pasig empties itself into Manila Bay. On this site four centuries ago stood the bamboo fortress of Rajah Sulayman, the young warrior who ruled the palisaded city state of about 2,000 inhabitants before losing it to Legazpi. Four gates connected Intramuros to the outlying boroughs, where lived the *indios* (as the Spaniards called the natives), *mestizos*, Chinese, Indians and other foreigners, including a number of Spanish commoners. Trade and commerce flourished to such an extent in these suburbs that they soon outstripped the city proper in area and population.

Though Intramuros is a far cry from the bustling Spanish city it once was, it has come a long way from the ravages of wartime. Once a jumble of broken buildings, portions of the old city have been restored, including the *Ayuntamiento* (Municipal Hall), once the grandest structure here. Part of the continuing restoration plan is to replicate eight houses to illustrate different styles of local architecture. A few are already open to the public, including the splendid **Casa Manila** (Tues–Sun 9am–6pm; entrance fee), a restored Spanish merchant's house from the late 1800s.

From Fort Santiago, cross over to the **Manila Cathedral ⓑ**, an imposing Romanesque structure. A

BELOW: Casa Manila, Intramuros.

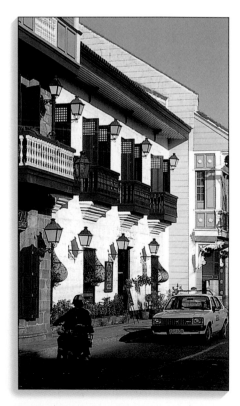

plaque on its facade tells of a phoenix-like cycle that holds true for most old churches in the country: a relentless history beginning in 1571 of construction and reconstruction after the repeated ravages of fire, typhoon, earthquakes and war.

Fronting the cathedral is **Plaza Roma**, where bullfighters imported from Spain performed in the 18th century. Colonial soldiers once drilled in the plaza, originally called Plaza de Armas. Later the Spanish rechristened it Plaza Mayor when it became the government centre in Intramuros. It was also briefly known as Plaza McKinley during the American occupation at the end of World War II.

At this point, facing Manila Cathedral, imagine the former Intramuros laid out as a rough pentagon or triangle. The perimeter measured nearly 4.5 km (3 miles). Following Legazpi's blueprint for the capital, succeeding Spanish governors constructed 18 churches and chapels, convents, schools, a hospital, publishing house, university (as early as 1611), palaces for the governor-general and the archbishop, soldiers' barracks, and houses for the assorted elite.

From Plaza Roma, walk down General Luna Street, past the western side of the cathedral, for four blocks to the intersection of General Luna Street and Calle Real. Here, incongruous Chinese *fu* dogs carved of granite guard the entrance to the courtyard of **San Agustin Church Ⓖ** (daily 8am–noon, 1–6pm; entrance fee), the only structure in Intramuros not bombed in World War II.

The church facade is notable for its combination of styles – Doric lower columns and Corinthian upper columns – and the evident absence of its original left tower, victim to the violent earthquakes of 1863 and 1889. The remarkable main door is carved out of a Philippine hardwood called *molave*, and it is divided into four panels depicting Augustinian symbols and the figures of St Augustine and his mother, Santa Monica.

The Spanish called Manila the Noble and Ever Loyal City – El Insigne y Siempre Leal Ciudad.

BELOW:
overview of old Manila, with Rizal Park on the left.

From San Agustin Church, there are several options. Turn right at Calle Real and prowl the remains of Intramuros until reaching Muralla Street. Here, follow the walls or pass through one of the restored gates leading back to the Pasig River, or to a plaza, **Liwasang Bonifacio**. On this busy square is a statue of the revolutionary leader Andres Bonifacio, with the **Central Post Office** just to the north.

Between these two landmarks is a system of overpasses and underpasses handling, at all hours, the great bulk of Manila's traffic. The left lane leads to Jones Bridge, the centre lane to MacArthur Bridge, and the right one to Quezon Bridge. These three bridges are the major passageways across the river, leading to the half of Manila north of the Pasig.

Quiapo

The area north of the Pasig includes the district of Quiapo. Recto Avenue is marked by a stretch of small shops selling new and second-hand schoolbooks for the university belt, an area that begins right after Recto Avenue's juncture with Quezon Boulevard. Quiapo is saturated with colleges, offering degrees in just about everything. Turning left at Quezon Boulevard leads to **Central Market**, really more of a textile emporium, and eventually to España, which leads to the vast residential and governmental area of Quezon City.

Turning right at Quezon Boulevard from Recto Avenue will end up at **Quiapo Church ⏺**. The area beside the church is the terminal for most public road transport plying north–south routes of the metropolis. A frenzied quarter, it has long been considered the heart (some say the armpit) of downtown Manila. Close to where Recto Avenue becomes Mendiola Street is the **San Sabastion Church**, reputedly the only prefabricated steel church in the world.

Map on page 308

TIP

Just next to the post office, beneath MacArthur Bridge, board the Metro Ferry and chug along the Pasig River to Guadeloupe, near Makati, glimpsing river life, old buildings and Malacañang Palace.

BELOW: Manila kids.

Mendiola Street leads to **Malacañang Palace** **E**, formerly the office and residence of Philippine presidents. It now houses the **Malacañang Museum** (Mon–Fri 9am–4pm by appointment made at least one week in advance only; entrance fee; tel: 02-736 4662; www.op.gov.ph/museum). Originally a country estate owned by a Spanish nobleman, Malacañang became the summer residence of Spanish governor-generals in the middle 1800s. Since Independence Day in 1946, ten Filipino chief executives have set up shop in the Presidential Palace, including Ferdinand Marcos. His successor after the People's Revolution, Corazon Aquino, broke with tradition by choosing to operate from the adjacent Guest House. Joseph Estrada, in contrast, fully entrenched himself in Malacañang.

Mother and child.

Rizal Park

Formerly known as Luneta (Little Moon, for its crescent shape), **Rizal Park** **F** is a large rectangular field broken up into three sections, with an elevated strolling ground bounded by Roxas Boulevard and ending at the sea wall facing Manila Bay. On the harbour end is the legendary **Manila Hotel** **G**, once the most exclusive address in the Pacific.

At the central portion of Rizal Park is **Rizal Monument**, a memorial to the national hero and the object of much wreath-laying by visiting dignitaries. Under 24-hour guard, the regular drill manoeuvres of the sentries are an attraction in themselves. Behind the monument is a series of plaques on which are inscribed Rizal's poem *Mi Ultimo Adios (My Last Farewell)* in the original Spanish and in various translations. A marble slab marks the spot where Rizal met his martyr's death by firing squad, while an obelisk stands on the site of the earlier executions of three Filipino priests.

BELOW: jeepney colours, and Malacañang Palace.

This central section of the park, where the Rizal Monument is located, is bordered by Roxas Boulevard to the west, T.M. Kalaw Street to the south, M. Orosa Street to the east, and Padre Burgos Street to the north. Close to the Burgos side are the Japanese and Chinese gardens, and an orchidarium, all of which charge token fees for entrance. On this side, too, is the city planetarium, where an interesting audiovisual show is conducted twice a day for a nominal charge.

The eastern side of the park is bounded by Taft Avenue, one of the major arteries cutting through Manila south of the river. Burgos Street, on the park's northern side, leads past the Old Congress Building, which once housed the Philippine Senate and still houses the **National Museum** (Tues–Sun 9am–5pm; tel: 02-527 1207). Northward is Manila City Hall, and beyond, Liwasang Bonifacio, from where the three bridges noted earlier lead to north of the Pasig River.

Ermita

From Taft, turn right at any of the perpendicular streets beginning with United Nations Avenue; this will lead to **Ermita ❽**, an unusual district in many respects. Its tourist-belt reputation is built on the strength of its proximity to Rizal Park, the seawall along Manila Bay, and a number of government buildings, such as the Department of Justice on Padre Faura Street. Consequently, many hotels and lodging houses exist in the area, in turn attracting a conglomeration of eateries, nightspots, boutiques, antique shops, handicraft and curio stalls, and travel agency offices.

Legend has it that around 1590, a Mexican secular and hermit made the small seaside village his retreat. Four years later, an Augustinian priest founded the hermitage dedicated to Nuestra Señora de Guia, and the label *Ermita* ("her-

Map on page 308

BELOW: Manila Bay sunset from Roxas Boulevard.

Map on page 308

Jeepneys are a novel form of Philippine transport.

RIGHT: Manila's Coconut Palace.
BELOW: Makati by night.

mitage") has stuck ever since. By the 19th century, the district had become an aristocratic suburb, together with the adjacent district of **Malate** further south.

Ermita offers diverse nightspots featuring Filipino folk singers, rock bands, and jazz groups. Here, still, another facet of the Ermita spirit may be glimpsed – the bohemian lifestyle of its younger and well educated residents made up of artists, writers, musicians and dancers.

Roxas Boulevard

Parallelling Manila Bay and Ermita is Roxas Boulevard and its seawall fronting the bay. The seawall begins where the sprawling grounds of the **US Embassy ❶** – hard to miss with the long lines of visa seekers outside – end. Along President Quirino Avenue on the landward side is a government complex that includes the Manila Hospital, the **Metropolitan Museum of Manila ❷** (Mon–Sat 10am–6pm; tel: 02-521 1517; entrance fee; www.metmuseum.ph) and the Central Bank of the Philippines. Behind the hospital are the **Manila Zoological and Botanical Gardens** (daily 7am–6pm; entrance fee; tel: 02-525 8157).

Past the Navy Headquarters and on the seaward side of Roxas Boulevard is the immense **Cultural Centre of the Philippines ❸** (tel: 02-832 1125–39; www.culturalcenter.gov.ph), the centrepiece of a spit of reclaimed land called CCP complex. The main building houses two theatres and two art galleries, and a museum and library. In the northwest corner is a former Marcos guesthouse, the **Coconut Palace** (Tues–Sun 9–11.30am, 1–4.30pm; tel: 02-832 0223; entrance fee), built entirely of indigenous materials like narra and molave hardwoods in addition to coconut wood and husks. The palace is available for private functions, often hosting lavish parties for Manila's rich and famous. It is best to call in advance to avoid a private event.

Makati

From NAIA Avenue, take a short bus or taxi ride to **Makati ❹** via Epifanio de los Santos Avenue (EDSA), Makati's main east–west boulevard and focus of the 1986 People's Power demonstrations. Makati's main north–south street, Ayala Avenue, has been dubbed the Philippine Wall Street, as it is the financial hub of the Philippines. On Makati Avenue is the **Ayala Museum** (Tues–Fri 9am–6pm, Sat–Sun 10am–7pm; entrance fee; tel: 02-757 7117). It has an outstanding archive and a permanent exhibit of dioramas portraying significant episodes in Philippine history, and detailed replicas of ships that have plied Philippine waters.

From Ayala Avenue's end at the EDSA, cross the highway to **Forbes Park**, a swanky housing area built by the wealthy Ayala family. Forbes Park's McKinley Road leads to the Manila Polo Club and to the **Fort Bonifacio Global City** development with the **Fort Bonifacio Entertainment Center**. Nearby **Serendra** has fashionable bars, restaurants and good shopping.

Nearby is the **Manila American Memorial Cemetery ❺** (daily 6.30am–5pm), where the remains of 17,000 Allied dead rest below seemingly endless rows of white crosses. The Libingan ng Mga Bayani (Graveyard of Heroes) is close by with its eternal flame burning by the Tomb of the Unknown Soldier. ❑

NORTH TO ILOCOS

The northwestern part of Luzon island, far beyond the congestion of Manila, embraces misty highlands and rocky coastline, and also tribal people who retain their traditions

There is a rugged symmetry to Ilocos that sets it, and its people, apart from others in the Philippines. Perched on a narrow ledge along the rugged northwest, the coast rises from the South China Sea to rocky bluffs and rolling sand dunes. Behind it, a slim, arable strip of land is tucked under the towering Cordillera Mountains. In this narrow confine lie the Ilocano provinces of La Union, Ilocos Sur (South), and Ilocos Norte (North).

Sometime after the first century, waves of migration swelled out of Borneo to crest along the Philippine coast. Late-comers to the archipelago, the immigrants were pushed ever northward along the coast by those who had come earlier. By the time they reached the northwestern coast, there was no where else to go but ashore. The migrants flooded into the hundreds of coves along the jagged coast and shifted up onto the narrow plains. With superior numbers and metal weapons, the immigrants pushed the region's indigenous tribes, who had lived here for centuries, high into the bordering mountains. The people became known for the coves (*looc*) around which they built their communities (*ylocos*).

The conquistador Juan de Salcedo landed in Vigan, Ilocos Sur, in the late 16th century. Soon, the Spanish introduced corn, cocoa, tobacco and, of course, Christianity. Chapels were built alongside the garrisons, schools were organised, and soon the missions were pulling converts into the town square. Compulsory native labour and hired Chinese masons and artisans soon resulted in Spain's most lasting landmarks in the Ilocos – the churches, like the grand old cathedral of Vigan. Fascinating architectural specimens, nicknamed "earthquake baroque" by Filipino historians, they were built as much to dramatise the power of the Old World god as to withstand natural disasters. Indeed, the 17th and 18th centuries saw a flowering of baroque that filtered into the Philippines.

LEFT: churchyard basketball.
BELOW: Spanish baroque church, Bantay.

Baguio and environs

Leaving the flat plains of Pangasinan, the National Highway begins to climb over the rolling hills of southern Ilocos. The first province along the way is La Union. It was carved out of Pangasinan, Ilocos Sur and the Cordilleras by royal decree in 1854. Entering La Union, the sea begins to glint behind the palms, where creamy sand beaches await.

At **Agoo-Damortis National Seashore Park** in Lingayen Gulf, near **Agoo** the sands are nearly black because of the iron deposits. The Shrine of Our Lady of Charity, in the baroque-style Agoo basilica, attracts visitors on a Good Friday, when patron saints are paraded through the streets. The Museo de Iloko, in the old Presidencia of Agoo, houses artefacts of Ilocos culture.

Inland from Agoo is the famous highland town of **Baguio ❶**, more or less the gateway to Luzon's highlands if coming north from the Manila area. By road it's four hours from Manila; by plane, just an hour. Nestled atop a 1,500-metre-high (5,000-ft) plateau, Baguio's cool climate and pine-clad hills have long lured visitors. Baguio was severely damaged by an earthquake in 1990, but little evidence of the quake is visible today.

Baguio is not noted for any tourist hot-spots, but rather for a sense of leisure that the environs nurture in both Filipinos and foreigners. Baguio seduces with cool air, clean parks, lovely gardens, quaint churches, and a variety of restaurants and hotels. The main avenue for the easy life is Session Road, with its gamut of bookstores, bakeries, Indian bazaars, coffee houses, Chinese restaurants, pizza parlours, and antique stores.

Catholic relic in wood.

Back along the coast and a few kilometres inland sits **Naguilian**, the *basi*-making capital of the Ilocos. Basi, the local Ilocano wine, is a fermented sugarcane concoction, coloured with *duhat* bark.

San Fernando ❷ produces bursts of sound and an array of colours on market day: loud gourd hats from up north, burnished earthenware from San Juan, and bright blankets from Bangar line the stalls and shops. Overlooking it all is a dragon-encrusted Chinese temple, Macho. Six km (4 miles) north of San Fernando, along Monalisa Beach, runs some of the best surf in Ilocos.

Bacnotan to Bangar

BELOW: the women of Ilocos are known to smoke what must be the world's largest cigars.

In **Bacnotan**, local silk production can be seen at the state university. In the mountains to the east, around **Bagulin**, trails along the Bagulin-Naguilian River offer some trekking opportunities. The century-old church of St Catherine, in

Luna, houses an image of Our Lady of Namacpacan, the patroness of Ilocano travellers. **Bangar**, on the northern border of La Union Province, is a blanket-weaving centre, where the best woven blankets and handcrafted bolos in the region are made.

Map on page 296

Ilocos Sur

Ilocos Sur Province twists along the coast as the narrowest province in Ilocos. In some places, the Cordilleras range extends right down to water's edge. Because the land is ill-suited for agriculture, most people in Ilocos Sur have turned to trade and handicrafts, and each town in the region seems to have its own specialty. In San Esteban, there is a quarry from which mortars and grindstones are made. San Vicente, Vigan and San Ildefonso specialise in woodcarving, importing their raw material from the mountain provinces. Skilled silversmiths work in Bantay. Other towns make saddles, mats, brooms and hats. Sisal and hemp-fibre weaving are household industries everywhere.

The first town in Ilocos Sur along the National Highway is **Tagudin**, where a sundial built by the Spanish in 1848 sits in front of the Municipal Hall. The next town, **San Esteban**, has a round, stone watch tower built by the Spanish to keep lookout for Moro pirates, and Apatot Beach.

The small burg of **Santa Maria** has a centuries-old church nestled atop a hill, which served as a fortress during the 1986 revolution and now stands as a national landmark. Near Santa Maria is Pinsal Falls, a favourite setting for many films, and where the legendary footprints of the Ilocano giant, Angalo, can be seen. **Santa** has a small picturesque church with a pure-white facade and slight greenish tint standing by the sea.

BELOW: Vigan's quiet ambiance, and piling into a jeepney.

Map on page 296

TIP

In Currimao it is worth stopping for the old abandoned tobacco warehouses at the port – vestiges of the great tobacco monopoly once dominating the region.

Nipa-hut smile.

OPPOSITE: Catholic church in Luzon's mountains.

Vigan

A living repository of Spanish architecture and Filipino culture, **Vigan ❸** was the third Spanish city to be built in the Philippines, in 1572, following the first in Cebu and the second, Intramuros, in what is now Manila. The **Cathedral of St Paul**, built in 1641, is the centre of Vigan. Stretching out in front of St Paul's is Plaza Salcedo, an elliptical plaza with the Salcedo Monument and a towering bell tower. Across the plaza to the west is the **Ayala Museum** (Tues–Sat 8.30–11.30am, 1.30–4.30pm; entrance fee), also called the Burgos House.

Probably the best attractions in Vigan are the old ancestral houses in the former Mestizo District, known as **Vigan Heritage Village**, south of St Paul's along Mena Crisologo Street. Each building in the district has been lovingly preserved, and many now house antique shops, bakeries, and craft shops. Other Vigan attractions include the **Crisologo Memorial Museum** (Sun–Fri 8.30–11.30am and 1.30–4.30pm; free) on Liberation Boulevard. Stop at RG Potter, at the southwest end of Liberation Avenue, where the famous Ilocano jars, or *burnay*, are made for storing vinegar and basil. Walk back into the kiln area to see one of the best examples of a Chinese dragon kiln anywhere in the world.

Outside of Vigan, the church in **Bantay** features Philippine earthquake baroque with Gothic influences. Its belfry, a few metres away from the church, was used as a lookout for Moro pirates. Further north, in **Magsingal**, the Museum of Ilocano Culture and Artifacts has a collection of early trade porcelains, neolithic tools, weaponry, baskets, and old Ilocano beadwear.

Ilocos Norte

Unlike its poorer cousin to the south, Ilocos Norte stands rich in timber, minerals, fisheries, and agriculture. Garlic is the principle cash crop, and it gives the province its flavour and aroma. It also did not economically hurt that the Philippines' longest-serving president, Ferdinand Marcos, was an Ilocano Norte.

The first town in Ilocos Norte is **Badoc**. Exhibited at **Luna House** (Tues–Sat, 9am–5pm; donation) are reproductions of a renowned 19th-century Filipino painter, Juan Luna. The Badoc Church is also worth a visit.

Past Badoc, at the kilometre-460 junction, turn left for **Currimao**. From Currimao, take the side road to **Paoay**. The church here is a real stunner and perhaps the most famous in Ilocos. It is a successful hybrid creation wedding the strong features of "earthquake baroque" (such as massive lateral buttresses) with an exotic Asian quality, reminiscent of Javanese temples. Built of coral blocks at the turn of the 18th century, its bell tower served as a observation post during the Philippine revolution and was used by guerrillas during the Japanese occupation. Paoay Church has been declared a UNESCO World Heritage Site. Not far from the town is Lake Paoay where loom weaving is a major activity, producing textiles with ethnic Ilocano designs.

South of **San Nicolas**, back down the National Highway in **Batac**, is the mausoleum of Ferdinand Marcos and the house in which he grew up. Across the bridge from San Nicolas is the capital of Ilocos Norte, **Laoag ❹**, the Sunshine City. St William's Cathedral, dating back to the 16th century, is another notable example of earthquake baroque.

Further north, **Pagudpud** on Bangui Bay has some of the best coral reefs in the archipelago. The reef is virtually untouched and swarms with countless tropical fish. The beaches here are some of the finest in the Philippines.

Balaoi ❺ is the last town in Ilocos Norte before passing into Cagayan Province. The town sits on the eastern side of the northernmost point of Luzon and overlooks Paseleng Bay. Along the shore of Paseleng Bay is what some consider one of the best hideaway resorts in the islands, Saud Beach Resort. ❑

THE VISAYAS

Six major islands and other fringe groups of isles parade together in a series of idyllic images – the calm waters, shimmering coves, rocky coasts and palm-fringed beaches that are the Visayas

Map on page 296

Hanging like a necklace of uneven beads strung together by various geographic threads, the islands of the Visayas lend themselves to the sort of languid exploration that is perhaps more identifiable with the South Pacific. People from Luzon, when asked about these southern islands, generally point out the slower pace, the seductive lilt to the Visayan speech, and perhaps, chauvinistically, the sensuousness of the women.

In 1521, Ferdinand Magellan anchored off the tiny island of Homonhon in Leyte Gulf. He had sailed up through the Canigao Channel to the island of Cebu, where he Christianised the local rajah and 500 of his followers. A minor rajah of Mactan – a flat, muddy island where Cebu's international airport now stands – stood in rebellion to the rajah of Cebu and his new foreign guests. Now known to all Filipinos as Lapu Lapu, Rajah Cilapulapu (the *ci* simply means, "the") defended his island with some 2,000 warriors against 48 armour-clad Spaniards shortly after their arrival. During the battle that raged for just over an hour, Magellan was slain.

LEFT: Cebu is known for quality guitars.
BELOW: Visayan beach.

Samar

This large island lies opposite the southern tip of Luzon and can easily be reached from Manila via the National Highway. The first landfall of Samar is the town of **Allen** with its nearby hot springs. The main roads wind along the northern coast to **Catarman**, capital of Northern Samar Province. Several interesting waterfalls are found in the interior of this part of the island, but reaching them requires considerable hiking through roadless terrain.

In the southwest corner of the island is the San Juanico Bridge, the longest in the Philippines and linking Samar to the adjacent island of Leyte. Near the approach to the bridge is **Basey ❻**, known for Sohotan Caves, Sohotan Natural Bridge, and **Sohotan National Park**. Basey is also the home of mat weavers whose designs have become popular items in the markets of Tacloban, on Leyte across the bridge.

Leyte

Trading centre of the eastern Visayas is **Tacloban ❼**, the capital of Leyte Province. The Capitol Building features the scene of Gen. Douglas MacArthur's historic landing on Leyte in 1945. In the centre of town is an attractive Spanish-style museum and shrine, the Santo Niño Shrine, housing Imelda Marcos' collection of statues of the infant Jesus. (Leyte is her home province.) The island has several fine beaches on its western coast, notably Agta Beach in Almeria and

TIP

Ferries cross the
Surigao Strait from
Maasin – Leyte's
provincial capital –
southeasterly to
Lipanta Point, in
Suriagao del Norte,
from where the
highway proceeds
across Mindanao.

Banderrahan Beach in Naval. The town of **Caibiran**, on the eastern coast, has the spring-fed San Bernardo pool and the falls of Tumalistis, once claimed as having the sweetest water in the world.

From Tacloban, the National Highway follows the eastern coastline southward past Palo and **Tolosa**, the home-town of Imelda Marcos, where a visit to her former grand residence should not be missed. Past Abuyog, the road veers west and crosses Leyte's Central Cordillera Mountains to the town of Baybay.

The road then follows the western coastline to southern Leyte's provincial capital of **Maasin**.

Cebu

On the island of Cebu, the oldest city in the Philippines, **Cebu ❽**, is the commercial and education centre of the Visayas, and the hub of air and sea travel throughout southern Philippines. Cebu is a busy capital, second in commercial activity only to Manila, but considerably more entrepreneurial than Manila.

On Juan Luna Street is **Santo Niño Basilica and Musuem** (open on request; free), built in 1565 to house the country's oldest religious relic, the Image of the Holy Child Jesus, presented by Magellan to Queen Juana of Cebu on her conversion to Christianity.

As the oldest Spanish settlement in the country, Cebu has plenty of spots that depict its rich colonial heritage. The foremost is the newly refurbished **Fort San Pedro** (daily 7am–10pm; entrance fee), a Spanish fort built in the early 1700s to repel the attacks of Muslim raiders. Close to the fort runs Colon Street, the oldest street in the country, situated within the Parian district, which was Cebu's original Chinatown. A piece of a wooden crucifix left by Magellan in

BELOW: Daoist
temple, Cebu.

1521 commemorates the archipelago's first encounter with the West. Magellan's cross is Cebu's most important historical landmark. The **Magellan's Marker**, erected in 1886, marks the spot where he was slain on Mactan's shore, while the **Lapu Lapu Monument** stands at the plaza fronting the Lapulapu City Hall.

Cebu is well-known for its pristine, sun-drenched white beaches and year-round tropical climate. The coastal waters off Cebu offer fantastic scuba-diving sites. Among them are **Mactan Island**, the Olango Islands and Moalboal, all of which have complete facilities and international-standard accommodations. On the southwest coast, **Moalboal** is a haven for scuba diving enthusiasts as well as budget travellers.

For many travellers, Cebu means handcrafted guitars and ukeleles made of soft jackfruit wood. The guitar-making industry is centred in Maribago and Abuno on Mactan.

Bohol

A 20-minute flight southeast of Cebu's airport is **Bohol ❾**, which is one of the largest coconut-growing areas in the country. Miguel Lopez de Legazpi, the Spanish conqueror and coloniser of the Philippines, anchored briefly near the island in 1563 and is said to have sealed a blood pact with a chieftain, Sikatuna.

For its relatively small size, Bohol has much to offer in history and natural attractions. A good road system traverses the island. The coastline is marked by picturesque coves and clean, white-sand beaches, most of them a short ride from **Tagbilaran**, the provincial capital and Bohol's main port of entry. Seven km (4 miles) from Tagbilaran is Baclayon Church, built by Jesuits in 1727. Also known as the Church of La Purisima Concepcion (Immaculate Conception),

Map on page 296

Surfing instructor.

BELOW: Chocolate Hills, Bohol.

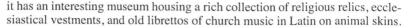

Map on page 296

A recent theory of dubious merit purports that Filipino faith healers are descendants of the kahuna, *the ancient healers of old Tahiti and Hawaii. The shamans are said to have had the ability to dematerialise tissues and bones and to rematerialise them in perfect order.*

RIGHT: Boracay.
BELOW: Ati-Atihan, Panay.

it has an interesting museum housing a rich collection of religious relics, ecclesiastical vestments, and old librettos of church music in Latin on animal skins.

But what remains Bohol's most famous attraction, with which in fact the island has become synonymous, is a unique panorama in the vicinity of **Carmen**, a town 55 km (34 miles) northeast of Tagbilaran in Bohol's central regions. Here, several hundred haycock hills – formed by limestone, shale, and sandstone – rise some 30 metres (100 ft) above the flat terrain. These are the **Chocolate Hills**, so-called for the confectionery-like spectacle they present at the height of summer, when their sparse grass cover turns dry and brown.

Negros

The capital of Negros Oriental (Eastern Negros) Province, **Dumaguete** is a small university town built around the Protestant-run Silliman University. Offshore is **Siquijor Island**, accessible by an hour's fast ferry from Dumaguete. This small island has long been considered the centre of sorcery in the southern Philippines. There are some 50 *mananambal*, or folk healer-sorcerers, on the tiny island. They are classified as "white" or "black" sorcerers, depending upon the nature of their abilities and intents.

Dominating the northwest shore is **Bacolod,** the capital of Negros Occidental (Western Negros) Province. Its points of interest do not go beyond several fine antique collections, ceramic shops, and weaving centres producing principally *hablon* fabric – a textile originally developed in Bacolod and much in vogue in the 1960s.

A few minutes' drive north is **Silay**, small and sleepy, but with several interesting old houses recalling the Castilian past. A bit further north is Victorias Milling Company, reputedly the largest sugar-cane mill and refinery in the world. Within the Vicmico compound is St Joseph, the workers' chapel noted for its psychedelic mosaic made from pop bottles depicting an angry Jesus and saints as Filipinos in native dress. It is still sometimes referred to as the Chapel of the Angry Christ.

Panay

From Bacolod, it's a two-hour ferry ride to **Iloilo** ⑪ on Panay Island. By the river's mouth is **Fort San Pedro**, originally built in 1616 with earthworks and wooden palisades, and transformed into a stone fort in 1738. In 1937 the fort became the quarters for the Philippine Army. The fort has since been turned into a promenade area, popular in the early evening. The **Museo ng Iloilo** (Iloilo Museum; Mon–Fri 9am–noon and 1–5pm; entrance fee) on Bonifacio Drive showcases prehistoric artifacts from the many burial sites excavated on Panay, including gold-leaf masks for the dead, seashell jewellery, and other ornaments worn by pre-Spanish islanders.

The district of **Molo**, 3 km (2 miles) from the city centre, has a Gothic-Renaissance church completed in the 1800s and the Asilo de Molo, an orphanage where little girls hand-embroider church vestments. Panaderia de Molo (Molo Bakery), the oldest bakery in the South is a favourite. Biscuits and breads are packed in tins for convenient take-home gifts. ❑

Boracay

In an archipelago of over 7,000 islands, there's bound to be one island that really stands out. Boracay, in the Visayas off Panay Island, is shaped like a slender butterfly drawn in sugar-fine white sand.

It was first "discovered" back in the 1960s, when beachcombers went looking for its rare *puka* shells. By the 1970s, Boracay was on the must list of every intrepid adventurer in Asia. They came in small numbers at first, staying in the *nipa* huts along White Beach for a couple of dollars a night.

But like every other magical spot – with a pristine environment and an increasing cachet amongst backpack travellers – the word spread. By the 1980s, the adventurers had become the hordes, and boutique resorts sprang up all along White Beach. It was still a journey to reach, as it remains today, but that was part of the draw.

Today, Boracay has moved way up-market. Since the mid 1980s, it has attracted the well-heeled of Europe, America and Asia, as well as Filipinos, who have lately begun to outnumber the foreign visitors. The sight greeting arrivals is nothing but spectacular: a gentle sea, the whitest of white beaches, and tall palms swaying in the breeze.

And yet, not all seems well in paradise. The resorts, restaurants and bars that had sprung up to serve the tourists were found to have been dumping their sewage into the sea. In 1997, the Philippine Department of Health declared the waters around Boracay to be severely polluted. The waters are now regularly monitored. If bacteria levels are within an acceptable range blue flags are raised along the beach.

Still, new arrivals continue to stake out a stretch of white sand beneath Boracay's special sun. Meanwhile, the locals in *maong* pants and T-shirts quietly serve the outsiders' needs.

Visitors can hire sailboats, kiteboards and windsurfing boards at any of the score of rental shops that have sprung up along White Beach. There is also an endless array of other watersports, such as jet skiing, parasailing, snorkelling and scuba diving. Little horses wait above the beach for those who have always dreamed of riding along the sands. For those who still feel the need for exploration, bicycles are available to explore the tiny island, 8 km long by 3 km wide (5 miles by 2 miles). Thirty minutes of pedalling leads through the corn and cassava fields to fishing villages that have been there for, well, nearly forever. Yap-ak village on the northern end is where everyone heads for puka shells.

Accommodation can be found everywhere nowadays. There're still some basic nipa huts, but it's mostly resorts that splatter the beach now. It has gotten so crowded that resorts are even springing up along the less spectacular eastern coast. Boracay dining, which was once simple but good island fare, now ranges from haute Filipino to haute French, with Indonesian, Thai, Italian, Swiss, and even English food available.

Getting there is not quite the adventure it once was. Fly from Manila to Caticlan and take the 15-minute boat ride to Boracay, or fly to Kalibo, take a jeepney or van (2–3 hrs) to Caticlan, and then make the crossing. ❑

INSIGHT GUIDES
Travel Tips

CONTENTS

Getting Acquainted

The Place

Situation In the South China Sea, bordered by Malaysia on the south, Burma to the west, Laos across the Mekong River to the northeast and Cambodia to the east.

Area 514,000 sq. km (198,455 sq. miles), nearly the size of France or twice as large as England, with 2,600 km (1,600 miles) of coastline.

Population 66 million, of whom 75 percent are Thai and 11 percent Chinese.

Capital Bangkok.

Time Zone 7 hours ahead of Greenwich Mean Time (GMT), so New York is 12 hours, Los Angeles 15 hours and London 7 hours behind, Australia 3 hours ahead.

Currency Baht.

Weights and Measures Metric.

Electricity 220 volts, with flat-pronged or round-pronged plugs.

International Dialling Code 66.

Climate

There are three seasons: hot, rainy and cool. But for most tourists, Thailand has only one season: hot. To make things worse, it drops only a few degrees during the night and is accompanied 24 hours by humidity above 70 percent. Only air-conditioning makes Bangkok and other towns tolerable during the hot season. The countryside is cooler, but the northern regions can be hotter in March/April than Bangkok.

Hot season (March to mid-June), 28°–38°C (82°–100°F).

Rainy season (June to October), 24°–32°C (75°–90°F).

Cool season (November to February), 18°–32°C (65°–90°F), but with less humidity.

Economy

Nearly half of Thailand's 66 million people are farmers. Thailand is the world leader in the export of tapioca, rice, rubber, canned pineapple, and is a top-ranked exporter of sugar, maize and tin. Increasingly, Thailand is turning to manufacturing, especially in clothing, machinery and electronics.

Government

Thailand is a constitutional monarchy headed by His Majesty King Bhumibol. Although he no longer rules as did the absolute monarchs of previous centuries, he can influence important decisions merely by a word or two. He is still regarded as one of the three pillars of the society – monarchy, religion and the nation. This concept is represented in the five-banded national flag: the outer red bands symbolising the nation; the inner white bands the purity of Buddhism; and the thick blue band at the centre representing the monarchy.

The king's dedication over many years to improving farmers' lands

Public Holidays

1 January New Year's Day
February full moon* Magha Puja
6 April Chakri Day
13–15 April Songkran (Thai New Year)
1 May Labour Day
5 May Coronation Day
May* Ploughing Ceremony
May full moon* Visakha Puja
July full moon* Asalaha Puja
July* Khao Phansa
12 August Queen's Birthday
23 October Chulalongkorn Day
5 December King's Birthday
10 December Constitution Day
31 December New Year's Eve

Chinese New Year in January/February is not an official public holiday, but many businesses are closed for several days.
* Variable

and yields, and her Majesty Queen Sirikit and others' promotion of the interests of poorer Thais have gained the royal family genuine respect. Photographs of the king and queen hang in nearly every home, shop and office.

The government is defined by a constitution and its enabling ordinances, although numerous military coups have temporarily suspended constitutional law over the years. Thirty-two prime ministers, 54 governments and 16 constitutions have governed Thailand since the promulgation of its first charter in 1932. An interim constitution was issued following the military coup of September 2006, and once a civilian government is reinstated, a new permanent charter will be created.

The legislative branch is the National Assembly, consisting of two houses, a 200-member Senate and a 500-member House of Representatives. Following the issuance of the "people's constitution" of 1997, members of the Senate are elected by popular vote; previously they were appointed by the prime minister. The house of representatives comprises 500 members from all walks of life.

The executive branch is represented by a prime minister, who must be an elected member of parliament. He is selected by a single party or coalition of parties and rules through a cabinet of ministers. They implement their programmes through the very powerful civil service.

Business Hours

Government offices 8.30am–4.30pm Monday to Friday.
Offices 8am or 8.30am–5.30pm Monday to Friday. Some open 8.30am–noon on Saturday
Banks 8.30am–3.30pm Monday to Friday, but many operate money-changing kiosks open until 8pm daily.
Shops 10am to 8–10pm.
Restaurants 11am–11pm, except for night markets, 6pm–5am.
Coffee shops Most close at midnight; some stay open 24 hours.

Planning the Trip

Visas & Passports

Travellers should check visa regulations at a Thai embassy or consulate or on the Ministry of Foreign Affairs website at www.mfa.go.th before starting their journey. All foreign nationals entering Thailand must have valid passports. At the airport, nationals from most countries will be granted a free tourist visa valid up to 30 days, provided that they have a fully paid ticket out of Thailand. Tourist visas allowing for a 60-day stay may also be issued in advance of arrival.

Visas can be extended before they expire at immigration offices in Bangkok and other cities.

Visitors wishing to leave Thailand and return before their visas expire can apply for a re-entry permit before departure. An exit visa is not required.

Tourist Information

Tourism Authority of Thailand's (www.tourismthailand.org) overseas offices are at the following locations:

● **Australia**
Suite 20.02, Level 20, 56 Pitt Street, Sydney.
Tel: 02-9247 7549.
● **United Kingdom**
3rd Floor, Brook House, 98–99 Jermyn Street, London SWIY GEE.
Tel: 207-925 2511
● **United States**
304 Park Avenue South 8th Floor, NY 10010.
Tel: 212-219 4655.
611 North Larchmont Boulevard, 1st Floor, Los Angeles, CA
Tel: 323-461 9814

Immigration offices are located at:
Bangkok: 507 Soi Puan Plu, Thanon Sathorn Tai; Mon–Fri 8.30am–4.30pm; tel: 0 2287 3101–10; www.immigration.go.th.
Chiangmai: 71 Airport Road, Thanon Suthep, Amphoe Muang; tel: 0 5327 7510.
Phuket: Thanon Kalim Beach; tel: 0 7634 0477.

Customs

The Thai government prohibits the import of drugs, dangerous chemicals, pornography, firearms and ammunition. Attempting to smuggle heroin or other hard drugs may be punishable by death.

Foreign guests are allowed to import, without tax, 200 cigarettes, and one litre of wine or spirits.

For more details, check the **Thai Customs Department** website at www.customs.go.th, or call 1164.

Health

Malaria is still very dangerous in some regions of Thailand, mainly along the Burmese and Cambodian borders. Mosquitoes in several areas are resistant to many brands of anti-malarial drugs, so seek advice on medication from a tropical institute before your departure. Should you contract malaria, there is a network of malaria centres and hospitals throughout Thailand. The most dangerous form appears disguised as a heavy cold, so if you have flu symptoms, see a doctor at once.

Dengue fever, a mosquito-borne disease for which there is no vaccination or chemical prophylaxis, is relatively common in rural areas during the rainy season. The best prevention is the use of repellent during the daytime.

Aids is not confined to "high risk" sections of the population in Thailand. You're at risk from casual sex if you don't use condoms.

Establishments catering to foreigners are generally careful with food and drink preparation. But although Bangkok water is clean when it leaves the modern filtration plant, the pipes are less than new, so it may still be safer to drink bottled water or soft drinks.

Money Matters

The Thai baht is the national currency, and is divided into 100 satang. Banknote denominations include 1,000 (grey), 500 (purple), 100 (red), 50 (blue), and 20 (green). There are 10-baht coins (brass centre with a silver rim), 5-baht coins (eight-sided silver pieces), 1-baht coins (small silver), and two small coins of 50 and 25 satang (both are brass-coloured).

Thailand has a sophisticated banking system with representation by the major banks of most foreign countries. Money is best imported in cash or traveller's cheques and converted into baht. There is no minimum requirement on the amount of money that must be converted. Foreign tourists may freely bring in foreign banknotes or other types of foreign exchange. For travellers leaving Thailand, the maximum amount permitted to be taken out in Thai currency without prior authorisation is 50,000 baht.

Both cash and traveller's cheques can be changed in hundreds of bank branches; rates are more favourable for traveller's cheques than for cash. Hotels generally give poor exchange rates.

Most banks now have 24-hour ATM machines outside where cash (in baht only) can be withdrawn with credit or debit cards. Note, however, that some banks only accept ATM cards linked directly to Thai bank accounts; for those with ATM cards on the Plus or Cirrus networks who wish to withdraw funds directly from their home bank accounts, Bangkok Bank, Kasikorn Bank and Siam Commercial Bank are good bets. Occasionally an ATM card may not work at one machine – simply try another branch.

Credit cards are widely accepted throughout Bangkok and in larger cities. In smaller provincial destinations, it is better to check that plastic is accepted, and not to count on using cards.

What to Bring/Wear

Lip balm and moisturisers are needed in the north during the cool season. Sunglasses, sunblock and hats are essential. Clothes should be light and loose. Open shoes (sandals during the height of the rainy season, when some Bangkok streets get flooded) and sleeveless dresses for women or short-sleeved shirts for men are appropriate. A sweatshirt or fleece is needed for nights in the north. In general, Thailand lacks the formal dress code of Hong Kong or Tokyo. Casual but neat and clean clothes are suitable for most occasions.

One exception is the clothing code for Buddhist temples and Muslim mosques. Shorts are taboo for both women and men, and improperly dressed and unkempt visitors will be turned away.

Getting There

BY AIR

Bangkok is a gateway between east and west and a transport hub for Southeast Asia served by major airlines. In addition to Bangkok, Thailand has five other international airports: Chiang Mai, Phuket, Hat Yai, Samui and Sukhothai.

Thai Airways International (THAI; www.thaiairways.com) flies to more than 60 cities worldwide. **Bangkok Airways** (www.bangkokair.com), **AirAsia** (www.airasia.com) and **Orient Thai** (www.orient-thai.com) operate routes between major tourism centres in Thailand and Asian cities. A direct flight (such as on British Airways, EVA Airways, Qantas and THAI) from the UK and Europe takes about 12 hours. From the west coast of the US, it takes about 18 hours (not including transit time) and involves a connection in North Asia – Japan, Korea or Taiwan. The east coast route via Europe takes about 19 hours. THAI operates the only non-stop flight from New York to Bangkok. From Australia and New Zealand, the flight is about 9 hours.

BY SEA

Star Cruises (www.starcruises.com) operates luxury cruises around the Asia-Pacific. Its various cruises around Southeast Asia , which set off from Singapore, call at Bangkok, Hua Hin, Phuket and Ko Samui.

BY RAIL

Trains operated by the **State Railways of Thailand** (tel: 0 2222 0175; www.railway.co.th) are clean, cheap and reliable, albeit slow. There arc only two entry points into Thailand, both from Malaysia on the southern Thai border.

A daily train, the *International Express*, leaves Butterworth, the port opposite Malaysia's Penang Island, at 1.15pm and arrives in Bangkok at 8.30am the next morning. There are second-class cars with seats which are made into upper and lower sleeping berths at night. There are also air-conditioned first-class sleepers and dining cars. Trains leave Bangkok's Hualamphong Station daily at 2.45pm for the return journey to Malaysia.

BY ROAD

Malaysia provides the main road access into Thailand, with crossings near Betong and Sungai Kolok. It is possible to cross from Laos into Nong Khai via the Friendship Bridge, or by river ferry into Chiang Khong. From Cambodia, visitors can cross at Poipet into Aranyaprathet.

Arrive in Style

The Eastern & Oriental Express is Asia's most exclusive travel experience. Travelling between Singapore, Kuala Lumpur and Bangkok, the 22-carriage train with its distinctive green-and-cream livery passes through spectacular scenery. It's expensive but classy. www.orient-express.com

Practical Tips

Media

PRESS

There are two national English-language dailies, *Bangkok Post* and *The Nation*. The *Asian Wall Street Journal* and *International Herald Tribune* are printed in Bangkok. Newsstands in major hotel gift shops carry air-freighted, and therefore expensive, editions of British, French, American, German and Italian newspapers. Newsagents on Soi 3 (Soi Nana Neua), Thanon Sukhumvit, Bangkok also offer Arabic newspapers.

In addition, check out *Metro and Farang*, two local monthly magazines which feature interesting writing; book, film and restaurant rcviews; shopping information; and a calendar of Bangkok events, including sport, health and kids' activities. Several pages in each magazine are also devoted to Phuket and Samui.

In Pattaya, the weekly *Pattaya*

Tipping

Tipping is not a custom in Thailand, although it is becoming more prevalent. A service charge of 10 percent is generally included in restaurant bills and is divided among the staff. A bit extra for the waitress would not go unappreciated.

Do not tip taxi or *tuk-tuk* drivers unless the traffic has been particularly bad; 10 baht would suffice for a journey costing over 60 baht. Hotel bellmen and room porters are becoming used to being tipped in urban centres but will not hover with hand extended.

Mail contains local news and features, as well as information on events, special offers and new facilities and services in the area. The related *Chiangmai Mail* does the same for Chiang Mai and the north.

RADIO

AM radio is devoted entirely to Thai-language programmes. FM frequencies include Radio Thailand (92.5 FM) with a variety of English-language programmes, and Chulalongkorn University (101.5) which plays jazz 5pm–6pm and classical music 8pm–10pm. Other popular stations can be found at 90 FM (Thai country music); 104.5 FM (English-speaking DJs playing alternative rock); 105 FM (easy listening with hourly international, local and traffic news); 107 FM (50s–90s hits with hourly CNN broadcasts).

In addition, Voice of America, BBC World Service, Radio Canada, Radio Australia and Radio New Zealand all offer shortwave radio broadcasts in English and Thai. Check newspapers for current frequencies and programme schedules.

TELEVISION

Bangkok has five VHF Thai language television channels. Only one company, UBC, offers cable television services, mostly downloads from regional satellites, including CNN International, BBC World Service HBO and Cinemax.

Postal Services

Thailand has a comprehensive and reliable postal service. Major towns offer regular air mail services, as well as express courier services.

In Bangkok, the General Post Office (GPO), on Thanon Charoen Krung (New Road) between Thanon Surawong and Thanon Si Phraya , tel: 0 2233 1050/9, 0 2235 2834, is open 8am–8pm during the week, and 8am–1pm on weekends and

holidays. (Note that it is easier to conduct business in person, rather than by phone.) A separate building to the right of the main GPO provides telecommunications services around the clock, including telephone, Internet, fax and telex.

Branch post offices are located throughout the country, many staying open until 6pm. Post office kiosks along some of the city's busier streets sell stamps, aerograms and chip small parcels. Hotel reception desks will also send letters and postcards for no extra charge.

COURIER SERVICES

A number of international courier agencies have offices in Bangkok:
DHL, tel: 0 2658 8000
Fedex, tel: 0 2367 3222
TNT, tel: 0 2249 5702
UPS, tel: 0 2712 3300

Telecommunications

TELEPHONES

The country code for Thailand is 66. When calling Thailand from overseas, dial the international access code, then 66 and the 8-digit number (without the preceding 0). To make an international call from Thailand, dial 001 before the country and area codes, then the telephone number. For international call assistance, dial 100.

Prepaid international phone cards (called Thaicard) of 300-, 500- and 1,000-baht value can be used to make international calls. These can be bought at post offices, shops that carry the

Area Codes

Thailand's former area codes have been incorporated into local phone numbers to produce eight-digit numbers throughout the country. A zero must be dialled when making domestic calls. If calling from overseas, drop the prefix zero. Dial 1133 for local directory assistance in English.

Emergencies
● **Police** 191
● **Tourist Police** 1155

Thaicard sign, or the office of the Communications Authority of Thailand in Bangkok, tel: 0 2950 3712; www.cat.or.th.

PUBLIC PHONES

There are many coin- and card-operated telephone booths in the city. Public phones accept 1-, 5- and 10-baht coins and phone cards for local calls in denominations of 50, 100 and 200 baht can be purchased at convenience stores. Most international telephone calls can be dialled direct from anywhere in Thailand. International telephone calls can be placed at the General Post Office (GPO) 24 hours a day. Most provincial capitals have telephone offices at the GPO; hours are generally 7am–11pm.

MOBILE PHONES

Any number that begins with the prefix 08 is a mobile phone number. Just as for fixed-line phones, dial the prefix 0 for all calls made within Thailand but drop the zero when calling from overseas.

Only users of GSM 900 or GSM 1800 mobile phones with international roaming facility can hook up automatically to the local Thai network.

If you're planning to travel in Thailand for any length of time, it's more economical to buy a local SIM card with a stored value from a mobile phone shop. You will be assigned a local number and local calls to and from the phone will be at local rates.

INTERNET

Internet cafés can now be found on almost every street in Bangkok, and even the least developed provinces have Internet services.

All major hotels in Thailand offer broadband Internet services, and wireless surf zones (WiFi) are also a growing trend in hotels and café outlets such as Starbucks.

Medical Services

HOSPITALS

First-class hotels in Bangkok, Chiang Mai and Phuket have doctors on call for medical emergencies. The hospitals in these three destinations are the equivalent of those in any major western city. Most small towns have clinics which treat minor ailments and accidents.

Bangkok
BNH Hospital, 9/1 Thanon Convent, tel: 0 2686 2700, www.bnhhospital.com.
Samitivej Hospital, 133 Soi 49, Thanon Sukhumvit, tel: 0 2711 8000; www.samitivej.co.th.
Thai Nakharin Hospital, 345 Thanon Bang Na Trat, tel: 0 2361 2712/61.

Chiang Mai
Chiang Mai Maharaj Hospital, 110 Thanon Suthep, tel: 0 5322 1122, 0 5322 1075; www.med.cmu.ac.th.
Chiang Mai Ram Hospital, 8 Thanon Bunruangrit, tel: 0 5322 4850; www.chiangmairam.com.
McCormick Hospital, Thanon Kaew Nawarat, tel: 0 5326 2200; www.mccormick.in.th.

Embassies in Bangkok

Australia: 37 Thanon Sathorn Tai; tel: 0 2287 2680.
Canada: No. 990, 15th Floor, Abdulrahim Place, Thanon Rama IV, Bangrak; tel: 0 2636 0540.
New Zealand, M Thai Tower, 14th Floor, All Seasons Place, 87 Thanon Witthayu; tel: 0 2254 2530.
United Kingdom: 1031 Thanon Witthayu; tel: 0 2305 8333.
United States: 120/122 Thanon Witthayu; tel: 0 2205 4000.

Phuket
Bangkok Phuket Hospital, 2/1 Thanon Hongyok Utit, Phuket, tel: 0 7625 4425. Emergencies: ext. 1060; www.phukethospital.com.
Patong-Kathu Hospital, Thanon Sawatdirak, Patong Beach, tel: 0 7634 0444.
Phuket International Hospital, Thanon Chalermprakiat, Ror 9, Phuket, tel: 0 7624 9400. Emergencies: 0 7621 0936.

MEDICAL CLINICS

For minor problems, there are numerous clinics in all major towns and cities. In Bangkok, the **British Dispensary**, at 109 Thanon Sukhumvit (between Soi 3 and 5), tel: 0 2252 9179, has British doctors on its staff.

In Chiang Mai, go to **Loi Kroh Clinic** on Thanon Loi Kroh, tel: 0 5327 1571. Most international hotels also have an on-premises clinic or doctor on call.

Tourist Information

The **Tourism Authority of Thailand** (tourist hotline: 1672; www.tourismthailand.org) offers brochures, maps and videos of the country's attractions.
● **Bangkok**
Head Office, 1600 Thanon New Phetchaburi, Makkasan, Rachathewi, tel: 0 2250 5500; 4 Thanon Ratchadamnoen Nok, tel: 0 2283 1500; Suvarnabhumi Airport Domestic Arrival Floor and International Arrival Floor, tel: 0 2132 1888.
● **Chiang Mai**
105/1 Thanon Chiang Mai–Lamphun, tel: 0 5324 8604, 0 5324 1466.
● **Pattaya**
609 Moo 10 Thanon Pratamnak, Banglamung, Chonburi, tel: 0 3842 7667.
● **Phuket**
73–75 Thanon Phuket; tel: 0 7621 2213, 0 7621 1036.

Getting Around

On Arrival

SUVARNABHUMI AIRPORT

Bangkok's international airport, **Suvarnabhumi** (tel: 0 2132 1888; www.airportthai.co.th), lies approximately 30 km (19 miles) east of the capital and is linked to the city by a system of elevated highways. Road travel to most parts of Bangkok averages 45 minutes.

Limousine Service
Airport Associate Co Ltd (tel: 0 2962 7190; www.airporttaxithai.com) operates a limousine service to Bangkok city: 600–1,100 baht by Mercedes Benz sedan, 700–1,500 baht by mini-van. Its limousine service to Pattaya costs 2,360 baht and 2,960 baht by Mercedes Benz sedan and mini-van respectively.
Thai Airways Limos (tel: 0 2130 0056; www.thaiairways.com) has a premium service (using Mercedes Benz E220) to downtown for 1,500 baht, or a regular service (Mercedes Benz 200) for 800 baht.

Airport Bus
A special express bus service operates from the airport to four areas of Bangkok: **route AE-1** goes to the Thanon Silom area; **route AE-2** goes to Banglamphu; **route AE-3** goes to Soi Nana; and **route AE-4** ends at Hualamphong Railway Station. Detailed maps of the routes are available at the bus counter. Buses run daily every 15 minutes from 5.30am to 12.30am and tickets cost 150 baht.

Taxis
Operating 24 hours daily, all taxis officially serving the airport are air-

Bangkok Taxi Talk

Thai taxi drivers are not renowned for their fluency in English, so it's often wise to have your destination written in Thai to hand to the driver.

Note that in Bangkok, Wireless Road, base of many embassies, a large hotel and several banks, is more commonly known by its Thai name, Thanon Witthayu. Similarly, Thanon Sathorn, a main thoroughfare divided into north and south which runs between Lumphini Park and the river, is often referred to as Sathorn Neua (north) and Sathorn Tai (south).

---

conditioned and metered. Arrange for a taxi at one of the taxi desks located on Level 1 of the arrival hall. Alternatively, take the express shuttle bus to the Public Transportation Center's taxi stand.

At the arrival hall's taxi desk, a receipt will be issued, with the licence plate number of the taxi and your destination in Thai written on it. At the end of your trip, pay what is on the meter plus a 50 baht airport surcharge. If the driver uses the expressway (with your consent), toll fees of 60 baht (20 baht for the first toll booth and 40 baht for the second) also apply.

Depending on traffic, an average fare from the airport to the city centre is around 300 baht (excluding toll fees and airport surcharge).

DON MUANG AIRPORT

In March 2007, the old **Don Muang** airport, 23 km (14 miles) north of Bangkok, reopened. A large number of domestic services have relocated there from Suvarnabhumi, including many of THAI's flights and all domestic flights of Nok Air and Orient Thai.

If making a flight connection between Suvarnabhumi and Don Muang airports, be sure to allow for sufficient time as taxi travel time between the two airports could take up to 1½ hours.

CHIANG MAI AIRPORT

Chiang Mai's airport is a 15-minute drive from the city centre. There is no bus service, visitors should choose between one of the following services:

Taxis: If you have not made arrangements with your hotel to pick you up, airport taxis are available for the 15–20 minute ride to the city for 100 baht.

Minibus: Thai Airways International operates a minibus between its town office on Thanon Phra Pokklao and the airport (but not vice versa).

PHUKET AIRPORT

Travelling to Phuket Town from the airport takes about 45 minutes, while Patong Beach can be reached in around half an hour.

Taxis: Airport taxis and limousines can be hired at the arrival hall at set rates. Prices start at 200–400 baht for the nearby northern beaches, rising to 550–750 baht for other locations

Minibus: Tickets for these 8-seaters are sold next to the limousine booths. The fare starts from 900 baht.

Airport Bus: Tickets for the airport bus to Phuket Town or to the beaches can be bought on board or from designated booths in the arrival hall. The fare is about 300 baht. A larger airport bus, route 8411, also runs daily between the airport and town.

By Air

The domestic arm of **Thai Airways International** (THAI: www.thaiairways.com) operates a network of daily flights to 11 of Thailand's major towns aboard a fleet of 737s and Airbuses. THAI offers a "Discover Thailand" visitor's pass, allowing four domestic flights, for about US$250. Certain conditions apply, notably that this pass must be purchased outside Thailand. Contact a TAT office for further details (see page 333).

In addition, **Bangkok Airways** (www.bangkokair.com) flies from Bangkok to several domestic destinations daily, including Sukhothai, Chiang Mai, Ko Samui and Phuket. It also connects the capital city to other cities in the region, including Phnom Penh and Siem Reap in Cambodia, Pakse in Laos, and Shenzhen in China.

Other airlines offering domestic services, often at lower fares than either THAI or Bangkok Airways, include **AirAsia** (www.airasia.com), **Nok Air** (www.nokair.com), and **Orient Thai** (www.orient-thai.com).

Note that if you are planning a trip to the tropical island of Ko Samui from Bangkok, you will save much travelling time if you go by air, a journey of less than two hours; the same trip by road and boat may take as long as 14 hours.

By Rail

The **State Railways of Thailand** (www.srt.or.th) operates three principal routes from Hualamphong Railway Station. The **northern** route passes through Ayutthaya, Phitsanulok, Lampang and terminates at Chiang Mai. The **upper northeastern** route passes through Ayutthaya, Saraburi, Nakhon Ratchasima, Khon Kaen, Udon Thani and terminates at Nong Khai, with a lower northeastern branch from Nakhon Ratchasima to Ubon Ratchathani. The eastern route goes due east from Bangkok to Aranyaprathet on the Thai–Cambodian border. The **southern** route crosses the Rama VI bridge and calls at Nakhon Pathom, Phetchaburi, Hua Hin and Chumphon. It branches at Hat Yai, one branch running southwest through Betong and on down the western coast of Malaysia to Singapore. The **southeastern** branch goes via Pattani and Yala to the Thai border opposite the Malaysian town of Kota Bharu.

A shorter spur line leaves **Bangkok Noi** station, in Thonburi, on the western bank of the Chao Phraya River, for Nakhon Pathom and Kanchanaburi in western Thailand. There is also a short route leaving Bangkok Noi that travels west along the rim of the Gulf of Thailand to Samut Sakhon and then on to Samut Songkhram.

Express and rapid services on the main lines offer first-class, air-conditioned or second-class, fan-cooled cars with sleeping cabins or berths and dining cars. There are also special air-conditioned express day coaches that travel to key towns along the main lines.

Reservations can be made at the station or with any travel agent within 30 days prior to departure.

In Bangkok, details from **Hualamphong Station:** Thanon Rama IV. Tel: 0 2233 7010, 0 2233 7020 (information), 0 2223 3762, 0 2224 7788, 0 2225 6964 (reservations), fax: 0 2225 6068. **Bangkok Noi (Thonburi) Station,** Thanon Arun Amarin (near Siriraj Hospital). Tel: 0 2225 0300.

By Road

Bus services are reliable, frequent and very affordable to most destinations in Thailand. Rest stops are regular, and in some cases refreshments are available.

Fan-cooled buses, painted orange, are the slowest since they make stops in every village along the way. For short distances, they can be an entertaining means of travel, particularly in the cool season when the fan and the open windows make the trip reasonably comfortable.

Blue air-conditioned buses are generally a faster, more comfortable way to travel. VIP buses are available on some of the longer routes; these usually have larger seats, more leg room and toilets.

Bus Stations

For bus and coach journeys to destinations outside of Bangkok,

Guard Your Bags!

Pocket-picking and bag-slashing are not uncommon on Bangkok buses. Keep your wallet in a front pocket and your bag in front of you at all times.

the major terminals are:
Eastern, Thanon Sukhumvit, opposite Soi 63 (Soi Ekkamai). Tel: 0 2391 2504, 0 2391 8097. Departures for Pattaya, Rayong, Chanthaburi.
Northern and Northeastern, Moh Chit Mai, Thanon Kamphaeng Phet 2. Tel: 0 2936 2853–7. Departures for Ayutthaya, Lopburi, Nakhon Ratchasima, Chiang Mai.
Southern, Thanon Boromrat Chonnani, Thonburi. Tel: 0 2435 1199, 0 2434 5557. Departures for Nakhon Pathom, Kanchanaburi, Phuket, Surat Thani.

To reach a small town from a large one, or to get around on some of the islands, songthaew (meaning two benches), pick-up trucks with benches along either side of the bed, function as taxis.

Public Transport

BANGKOK

Taxi, Tuk-Tuk and Motorcycle

All car taxis in Bangkok are metered, air-conditioned and reliable, but the drivers' command of English is usually minimal.

Make sure your taxi driver turns on the meter before you begin your journey The basic fare at flagfall is 35 baht, after which the fare increases in increments according to time

Bangkok's Waterways

Chao Phraya River express boats (tel: 0 2623 6143; www.chao phrayaboat.co.th) run regular routes at 15- to 20-minute intervals along the Chao Phraya River, between Tha Nonthaburi pier in the north and Tha Wat Rajsingkorn near Krungthep Bridge in the south. The service runs

and/or distance. Taxi drivers do not charge you an extra fee for baggage stowage or extra passengers, and tipping isn't necessary (though much appreciated).

Occasionally a driver will try to negotiate a flat fare from you instead of turning on his meter. Sometimes the fare quoted amounts to thievery; you will nearly always get a better rate from a metered taxi. Note that any trips made along the expressway ("highway" to some drivers) will involve an additional toll of 30–70 baht, which you will be expected to pay. Also, most taxi drivers do not maintain a ready supply of small change; it's best not to offer anything larger than a 100-baht note in payment of fare.

If the English fluency of taxi drivers is limited, that of tuk-tuk (also called samlor, meaning three wheels) drivers is even less. Tuk-tuks are the brightly coloured three-wheeled taxis whose nickname comes from the noise their two-cycle engines make. They are fun for short trips, but choose a taxi for longer journeys. A tuk-tuk driver on an open stretch of road can seldom resist racing, and the resultant journey can be a hair-raising experience. For very short trips, the fare is 20 baht.

As the traffic situation worsens in Bangkok, motorcycle taxis have proliferated; their drivers wear single-colour vests. Passengers are required to wear helmets on the major roads, but the drivers do not always supply them. In the case of an accident, not a rare occurrence, the driver will likely not hold any insurance. In spite of the risks, this

from 6am to 7.55pm. The fares are collected on board.

Ferries also cross the river at dozens of points and are very cheap. They begin operating at 6am and stop at 10pm or later.

It is also possible to catch a long-tail taxi to many points along the Chao Phraya or the canals.

means of travel is worth trying when the streets are jammed.

Bus and Minibus

Bus transport in Bangkok is very cheap but can also be equally arduous, time-consuming and confusing. Municipal and private operators all come under the charge of the **Bangkok Mass Transit Authority** (tel: 0 2246 0973; www.bmta.co.th).

With little English signage and few conductors or drivers speaking English, boarding the right bus is an exercise in frustration. There are four types of public buses: microbus, Euro II bus, air-conditioned and non-air-conditioned "ordinary".

Skytrain & MRTA

The Bangkok Transit System (BTS), or **Skytrain** (tel: 0 2617 7340, www.bts.co.th), is the perfect way to beat the city's traffic congestion. Trains arrive every three-to-five minutes, and no journey exceeds 30 minutes. Single-trip fares range between 10 baht and 40 baht. Tourists may buy the unlimited ride 1-day Pass (100 baht) or the 30-day Adult Pass (250 baht: 10 rides; 300 baht: 15 rides and 540 baht: 30 rides).

The Skytrain consists of two lines: the **Sukhumvit Line** runs from On Nut along Thanon Sukhumvit to Siam Square, Thanon Phayathai, Victory Monument and Mo Chit. The **Silom Line** extends from Saphan Taksin through Silom's business district, Siam Square and ends at the National Stadium. The two lines cross at Siam Square.

A 20-km (13-mile) underground subway system, operated by the **Metropolitan Rapid Transit Authority** (MRTA; tel: 0 2617 5744, www.mrta.co.th), opened in 2004 with 18 stations extending from Hualamphong Railway Station to Bang Sue. The line intersects the BTS Skytrain routes near the Asoke and Mo Chit Skytrain stations.

The air-conditioned trains are frequent (2–4 minutes peak, 4–6 minutes off-peak). Fares range between 14 baht to 36 baht. Coin-sized plastic tokens are used, and tourists may buy the unlimited ride 1-day Pass (150 baht), 3-day Pass (300 baht) or stored-value Adult Card (200 baht).

CHIANG MAI

Bus: Chiang Mai has red *songthaew* that carry passengers almost anywhere within the town for 10 baht per person per trip. There is also a single air-con "pink bus" line that runs along main streets, 10 baht per person regardless of distance.

Tuk-tuk: They charge according to distance, starting at 20 baht. You must bargain for the price before you get in.

Samlor. These pedal trishaws charge 10 baht for short distances. Bargain before you board.

PHUKET

Bus: Wooden buses ply regular routes from the market to the beaches. They depart every 30 minutes between 8am and 6pm between Phuket town market and all beaches except Rawai and Nai Harn. Buses to Rawai and Nai Harn leave from the traffic circle on Thanon Bangkok. Flag one down along the beach roads; 15–20 baht per person.

Tuk-tuk: The small cramped *tuk-tuks* function as taxis, and they'll go anywhere. Barter your fare before getting on. For example, Patong to Karon, 120 baht, Patong to airport, 300 baht. Within town, 10–20 baht.

Motorcycle taxi: 10–20 baht per ride. A convenient if dangerous way to get around.

LIMOUSINE

Most major hotels operate air-conditioned limousine services. Although the prices are at least twice those of ordinary taxis, they offer English-speaking drivers and door-to-door service.

RENTAL CAR

Thailand has a good road system with over 50,000 km (31,000 miles) of paved highways. Road signs are in both Thai and English. An international driver's license is required.

Driving on a narrow and busy road can be terrifying; right of way is generally determined by size. It is not unusual for a bus to overtake a truck despite that the oncoming lane is filled with vehicles. It is little wonder that, when collisions occur, several dozen lives are often lost. In addition, many of the long-distance drivers consume pep pills and have the throttle to the floor because they are getting paid for beating schedules. You are strongly advised to avoid driving at night.

Avis, Hertz, Budget and numerous local agencies offer cars with and without drivers, and with insurance coverage for Bangkok and upcountry trips. A deposit is usually required except with credit cards.

In the provinces, agencies can be found in major towns like Chiang Mai, Pattaya and Phuket. These also rent four-wheel-drive jeeps and minibuses. When renting a jeep, read the fine print carefully and be aware that you are liable for all damages to the vehicle. Ask for first-class insurance, which covers both you and the other vehicle involved in a collision.

Motorcycle Rental

Motorcycles can be rented in Chiang Mai, Pattaya and Phuket (just about everywhere, in fact) for economical rates. Remember that when you rent a motorcycle, you must surrender your passport for the duration.

Motorcycles range in size from 100cc to giant 750cc models. The majority are 100cc step-through bikes. Rental outlets can be found along beach roads and main roads in each town.

It is not uncommon for rental bikes to be stolen; lock them up when not in use, and only park them in areas with supervision.

Where to Stay

Thailand's hotels and guesthouses are equal to the very best anywhere in the world. The facilities in the first-class hotels may include as many as six or more different restaurants serving Western and Asian cuisines, coffee shops, swimming pools, fitness centres, business centres, shopping arcades, and cable and satellite television.

Expect the level of service to be second to none. It is not surprising, therefore, that top hotels like the Oriental and the Shangri-La in Bangkok, the Amanpuri in Phuket, and the Four Seasons in Chiang Mai are consistently voted among the best in the world. Even budget and inexpensive hotels will invariably have a swimming pool and more than one food outlet.

In first-class hotels add 10 percent service charge and 7 percent value-added tax to the prices. It is acceptable to bargain, especially during the low season (May–October).

Price Guide

A general guide for a standard double room, excluding taxes.
$$$$ = above US$150
$$$ = US$100–150
$$ = US$50–100
$ = under US$50

Hotel Listings

BANGKOK

Amari Watergate
847 Thanon Phetchaburi, Pratunam
Tel: 0 2653 9000
www.amari.com/watergate
This large tower has been refurbished within. Excellent facilities, including a great gym and the basement Americana pub Henry J. Beans. Located across from Pratunam Market and the main shopping district around Central World Plaza. The closest Skytrain station is Chit Lom, although not within walking distance. **$$$$**

Bangkok Marriot Resort and Spa
257 Thanon Charoen Nakhon
Tel: 0 2476 0022
www.marriott.com
A resort hotel with the conveniences of nearby downtown. Located on the western side of the Chao Phraya River. The warren of streets nearby offers a glimpse of old Bangkok life. **$$$$**

Dusit Thani
946 Thanon Rama IV
Tel: 0 2236 9999
www.dusit.com
Bangkok's first high-rise hotel. Adjacent to major banks and businesses on Thanon Silom. Views of Bangkok from the rooftop restaurant are excellent. Close to the Patpong nightlife scene. **$$$$**

Four Seasons Hotel Bangkok
155 Thanon Ratchadamri
Tel: 0 2251 6127
www.fourseasons.com/bangkok
High luxury in the heart of the city. With music and tea in the lobby lounge, there are echoes of the old Orient. The best hotel pool in Bangkok. **$$$$**

Grand Hyatt Erawan
494 Thanon Ratchadamri
Tel: 0 2254 1234
www.bangkok.grand.hyatt.com
On a major intersection and close to the famous Erawan Shrine, one of the best known religious symbols in Bangkok. Just adjacent are major shopping malls. The hotel has a good mix of restaurants and high standards of service. **$$$$**

Millennium Hilton Bangkok
123 Thanon Charoennakhon
Tel: 0 2442 2000
www.bangkok.hilton.com
This swish Hilton on the Thonburi side has a stylish modern Asian interior designed by Tony Chi. All rooms have expansive windows with river views. Spa, four restaurants and two bars, plus complimentary shuttle boat service. **$$$$**

The Oriental
48 Oriental Avenue
Tel: 0 2659 9000
www.mandarin-oriental.com/bangkok
A visit is a must, even if it is only to have a drink on the river terrace or afternoon tea in the Author's Lounge. The Oriental is part of the history of East meeting West. Repeatedly voted one of the world's best hotels. **$$$$**

The Peninsula Bangkok
333 Thanon Charoennakorn
Tel: 0 2861 2888
www.peninsula.com
Standing on the Thonburi side of the Chao Phraya River, this hotel – one of the finest in the world – has the city's nicest river views. Stylishly contemporary but still Asian in character, it has some of the best dining options in the city. Free shuttle boats to Tha Sathorn pier opposite and the Saphan Taksin Skytrain station. **$$$$**

Shangri-La
89 Soi Wat Suan Plu,
Thanon Charoen Krung
Tel: 0 2236 7777
www.shangri-la.com
With 799 spacious guest rooms, recently refurbished and all facing the river, the Shangri-La is the largest of the five-star hotels located on the river, and consistently ranks among the top five hotels in Asia. Restaurants, particularly Angelini's and the Maenam Terrace barbecue, are top notch. **$$$$**

Sofitel Silom
188 Thanon Silom
Tel: 0 2238 1991
www.sofitel.com
This 38-storey hotel located in the quieter part of busy Thanon Silom is only a short walk to Chong Nonsi Skytrain station. Stylishly refurbished to a chic modern style, it caters to both business and leisure travellers. Wine bar V9 has stunning city views from its 37th-floor perch while one floor above is the excellent Shanghai 38 Chinese restaurant. **$$$$**

The Sukhothai Bangkok
13/3 Thanon Sathorn Tai
Tel: 0 2287 0222
www.sukhothai.com
This stunning contemporary Asian

hotel draws architectural inspiration from the ancient Thai kingdom of the same name. One of the top five hotels in Bangkok, this class act has well-appointed rooms, the excellent La Scala Italian restaurant and the chic Zuk Bar, tropical gardens and a reflecting pool. **$$$$**

Emporium Suites
622 Thanon Sukhumvit (Soi 24)
Tel: 0 2664 9999
www.emporiumsuites.com
Conveniically located above the upmarket Emporium shopping mall and close to the Phrom Pong BTS station, this stylish service apartment complex offers a range of accommodation options – from studio and one-bedroom suites to 3-bedroom apartments. Ideal for long-term stays. **$$$**

Novotel Bangkok
Siam Square Soi 6
Tel: 0 2255 6888
www.accorhotels-asia.com
Located in the middle of Siam Square, a busy shopping area with a huge variety of shops, cinemas and eating places. **$$$**

Landmark
138 Thanon Sukhumvit
Tel: 0 2254 0404
www.landmarkbangkok.com
Good location, with easy access to Nana Skytrain station and the girly bar enclave of Nana Entertainment Plaza. Geared toward the business traveller with a busy business centre. Attached to a plaza with a few shops and eateries. **$$$**

Shanghai Inn
479–481 Thanon Yaowaraj
Tel: 0 2678 0101
www.shanghai-inn.com
A classy boutique hotel in a part of town often written off as lacking in any decent lodgings. The rooms have lovely over-the-top Chinoise-inspired furnishings, four-poster beds and bright colours. Free Internet and a spa on site. **$$$**

Arun Residence
38 Soi Pratoo Nok Yoong,
Thanon Maharat
Tel. 0 2221 9158
www.arunresidence.com
This tiny boutique hotel housed in an old Sino-Portuguese mansion along a residential street just off Thanon

Maharat is a gem of a find. It perches on the banks of the Chao Phraya River and offers views of Wat Arun. Its French-Thai restaurant Deck is perfect for a sunset cocktail and dinner afterwards. **$$**

Asia Bangkok
296 Thanon Phayathai
Tel: 0 2215 0808
www.asiahotel.co.th
Great location for shopping with Siam Square, Siam Discovery Centre and the Central World Plaza all close. Good facilities include a sauna and health club plus a Brazilian restaurant. **$$**

Atlanta
78 Thanon Sukhumvit Soi 2
Tel: 0 2252 1650
www.theatlantahotel.bizland.com
Well located for shopping and night entertainment. One of Bangkok's oldest and most respected establishments. Good value for money. **$$**

CHIANG MAI

Four Seasons Chiang Mai
Thanon Mae Rim-Samoeng
Tel: 0 5329 8181
www.fourseasons.com
This is the most luxurious accommodation in northern Thailand. The "Modern Lanna" pavilion-style rooms are set amid rice fields that are still worked. A true world-class resort. Plan early if you want to stay here during the high season. **$$$$**

The Rachamankha
6 Thanon Ratchamankha
Tel: 0 5390 4111
www.rachamankha.com
Tucked away in a narrow lane behind Wat Phra Singh, this architect-owned hotel is laid out like a 16th-century Lanna temple compound and furnished with antiques from the owner's collection, including ceramics unearthed during construction of the hotel. **$$$$**

Amari Rincome
1 Thanon Nimmanhemin
Tel: 0 5322 1130
www.amari.com/rincome
One of the oldest and best-known hotels in Chiang Mai. A low-rise

hotel that offers a quiet ambience, good restaurants and a superb swimming pool. **$$–$$$**

D2hotel
100–101 Thanon Chang Khlan
Tel: 0 5399 9999
www.d2hotels.com
The D2 is Chiang Mai's most stylish contemporary-style hotel. Ultra-chic and functional rooms are well laid out and come with plasma-screen TVs and high-speed Internet. Its Moxie restaurant is one of the city's best hotel eateries. Facilities include a spa/fitness centre and a minimalist-style bar featuring innovative cocktails. **$$–$$$**

PHUKET

Dusit Laguna
390 Thanon Srisoontorn, Bang Thao
Tel: 0 7632 4324
www.dusit.com
This five-star resort reflects its Thai heritage, apparent in its decor, staff costumes and the acclaimed Ruen Thai restaurant. **$$$$**

Katathani Phuket Beach Resort
Kata Noi
Tel: 0 7633 0124–6
www.katathani.com
A four-star property with 433 rooms, located on quiet Kata Noi where guests get pretty much the run of the stunning beach. Four swimming pools and full facilities. Five restaurants, serving seafood, German, Brazilian, Italian and Asian fare. **$$$$**

Mom Tri's Boathouse
182 Thanon Kaktanod, Kata Beach
Tel: 0 7633 0015–7
www.boathousephuket.com
Situated on the quiet end of Kata, this small and elegant beachfront hotel prides itself on attentive and personalised service. Famous for the sophisticated Boathouse Wine & Grill restaurant and its wine list. **$$$$**

Royal Phuket City Hotel
154 Thanon Phang Nga, Phuket Town
Tel: 0 7623 3333
www.royalphuketcity.com
Grand high-rise with marbled lobby and 251 nicely appointed rooms. Pool, fitness centre and spa. **$$$**

Where to Eat

What to Eat

Anyone who has tried Thai cuisine knows that it is one of the best in the world. The astonishing variety of flavours and textures ensures a wealth of dining experiences and provides an excellent excuse for a visit to Thailand. For homesick palates, the country's foreign restaurants are also among the finest and least expensive in Asia.

Curries are usually made with coconut milk, and although most are spicy, they can be made bland on request. Among the fiery favourites are *kaeng khiaw-wan* (a hot green curry with chicken or beef) and *kaeng phet* (a red curry with beef or seafood). Another spicy special is *tom yam kung* (piquant soup with shrimp).

Among the non-spicy dishes are: *tom kha kai* (spicy coconut milk soup with chicken), *thawt krathiam phrik thai* (pork or seafood fried with garlic and black pepper), *nua phat nam-man hawy* (beef in oyster sauce), *muu phat priaw wan* (sweet and sour pork), and *haw mok thalay* (a seafood mousse). Thais also make luscious sweets from coconut milk, tapioca and fruits. Some of the best are sold by sidewalk vendors. A plate of fresh Thai fruit is a delicious dessert.

The following restaurants are recommended as much for their atmosphere as for their superb food. Most restaurants close at 10pm; most hotel coffee shops at midnight. You can probably be seated without a reservation but to be sure, telephone beforehand. In the Bangkok section the station mentioned in the address line of some of the restaurants refers to the nearest 'Skytrain' station.

Restaurant Listings

BANGKOK

Baan Khanitha
69 Thanon Sathorn Tai
Tel: 0 2675 4200
Having outgrown its home on Soi Ruam Rudee, this well-known place moved to a much larger location in Sathorn. Tasty foreigner-friendly flavours, ranging from Chiang Mai sausage and spicy salads to various curries, such as red duck with grapes. Second outlet at 36/1 Thanon Sukhumvit Soi 23; tel: 0 2258 4181). **$–$$**

Cabbages & Condoms
10 Thanon Sukhumvit Soi 12
Tel: 0 2229 4610
Renowned for its family planning promotion, this two-storey restaurant with mainly outdoor seating has a pleasant ambience and decent Thai standards. **$–$$**

Le Lys
104 Narathiwat Soi 7
Tel: 0 2677 5709
Charming restaurant in a homey interior, *a la* a French bistro. The Thai-French owners serve tamarind-flavoured soups (*tom som* with stuffed squid) and delicious baby clams in curry sauce. Outdoor seating available. **$**

Shangrila Yaowarat
306 Thanon Yaowarat
Tel: 0 2224 5933
Busy Cantonese place with casual cafe-style *dim sum* lunches, and more formal dinners. Menu includes drunken chicken with jellyfish, smoked pigeon, and fresh seafood. Or choose from displays of roasted duck, *dim sum* and freshly baked pasties. **$$**

Supatra River House
266 Soi Wat Rakhang
Thanon Arun-Amarin, Siriraj
Tel: 0 2411 0305

Restaurant Price Guide

A general guide for dinner for two people, excluding beverages:
$$$ = above US$30
$$ = US$20–30
$ = under US$20

www.supatrariverhouse.com
Former home of owners Patravadi Mechudhon (of Patravadi Theatre fame) and her sister. Decent Thai cuisine is served on the riverbank terrace. On Friday and Saturday, traditional music and dance accompanies your dinner. Take the express boat to Tha Maharaj pier and transfer to the opposite bank on Supatra's complimentary shuttle boat service. **$$–$$$**

Tamarind Café
Thanon Sukhumvit Soi 20
Tel: 0 2663 7421
www.tamarind-cafe.com
A haven for art-loving vegetarians, this stylish café holds photography exhibitions and has a flair for European–Asian flavours. Tapas-style starters include tabouleh, falafel coated in sesame seeds and Thai crispy mushrooms with a mild chilli dip. Follow up with vegetable gratin and coconut cream pie. **$–$$**

Zanotti
Ground Floor, Saladaeng Colonnade, 21/2 Soi Saladaeng
Tel: 0 2636 0002
www.zanotti-ristorante. com
Homey Italian fare from the Piedmont and Tuscany regions, including more than 20 pasta dishes and seafood and steaks charcoal-grilled over orange wood from Chiang Mai. Good selection of wines by the glass. **$$$**

CHIANG MAI

The Gallery
25–29 Thanon Charoenrat
Tel: 0 5324 8601/2
Superb Thai cuisine in an old Chinese merchant's house and garden on the river. To get to the terrace restaurant you walk through a very stylish art gallery. **$$**

Old Chiang Mai Cultural Centre
185/3 Thanon Wualai
Tel: 0 5320 2993-5
Typical northern Thai *kantoke* dinner with cultural programme of Lanna and hill-tribe dances and music. Food is served at low tables called *kantoke* and consists of northern Thai favourites such as *nam prik ong* (spicy minced pork

and tomato) and *gaeng hanglay* (pork curry with ginger). **$$**

Riverside Bar and Restaurant
9–11 Thanon Charoenrat
Tel: 0 5324 3239
www.theriversidechiangmai.com
Noisy but lively restaurant with live music and good Thai and European fare. Beautiful sunset views over the Ping River. **$**

PHUKET

Baan Rim Pa
233 Thanon Prabaramee
Patong Beach
Tel: 0 7634 0789
Baan Rim Pa is probably Phuket's best Thai restaurant. In addition to excellent cuisine, it offers elegant decor and cliff-top views. Essential to reserve. **$$$**

Mom Tri's Boathouse Wine and Grill
182 Thanon Kata
Tel: 0 7633 0015
www.boathousephuket.com
An award-winning restaurant serving superb Thai, European and seafood dishes on a terrace overlooking the beach. Extensive wine list and set menus available. **$$$**

Salvatores
15–17 Thanon Rasada
Tel: 0 7622 958
www.salvatoresrestaurant.com
Voted Thailand's best Italian restaurant by *Tatler Thailand*. The gnocchi with lamb sauce, homemade ice cream and fresh ground Italian coffee are popular. Reservations recommended. **$$–$$$**

Savoey Seafood
136 Thanon Thaweewong
Tel: 0 7634 1174
Impossible to miss with its prime beachfront location and elaborate outdoor displays of fresh fish and huge "Phuket lobsters". Seafood is cooked to your liking – fried, grilled or steamed with Thai herbs. **$$**

On the Rock
Marina Phuket Resort, Karon Beach
Tel: 0 7633 0625
As the name suggests, this restaurant is perched on the rocks overlooking Karon Bay. It specialises in Thai and European seafood dishes of superb quality. **$$**

Culture

General

Modern pop culture seems to have gained ascendancy over traditional Thai arts, despite government support for Thai arts and performers. Foreign culture is promoted by the respective country cultural organisations, but little is done to attract foreign performers in the manner of, say, Hong Kong's Art Centre and the annual Hong Kong Arts Festival.

The many museums in Bangkok and in major towns around the country are devoted to preserving the past and contain some superb specimens. Exhibitions of modern art are arranged by private gallery owners, foreign cultural centres, or corporate patrons, usually banks.

Museums

BANGKOK

The **National Museum** on Thanon Na Phra That (Wed–Sun 9am–4pm; entrance fee; tel: 0 2224 1333), next to Sanam Luang in the heart of the old royal city, is a repository of archaeological finds, Buddha images, old royal regalia, ceramics and art objects (usually Buddhist) from neighbouring countries. The walls of the Buddhaisawan Chapel in the museum grounds are covered in some of the finest Buddhist murals in Thailand.

The National Museum offers free two-hour guided tours, in a number of languages, of Buddhist and other art. Tours start at 9.30am. For information call at 0 2215 8173.

Almost every urban centre in Thailand has a branch of the National Museum.

CHIANG MAI

]The **National Museum**, near Wat Jet Yot on Highway 11, tel: 0 5322 1308. Collections of Sawankhalok china and Buddha images are highlights.

The **Tribal Research Museum**, at Ratchamangkala Park, Mae Rim, tel: 0 5321 0872. A small ethnographical museum with costumes and implements of hill tribes on display.

Theatres

The **National Theatre** presents Thai works and, occasionally, big-name foreign ensembles like the New York Philharmonic. For more experimental works, Thai or foreign, look to the **Thailand Cultural Centre** (tel: 0 2247 0028, fax: 0 2245 7747; www.thaiculturalcenter.com). The Centre, which is a gift of the government of Japan, is located on Thanon Ratchadapisek north of central Bangkok. Its three stages present everything from pianists to puppets. See the newspapers for announcements.

It is also possible to find Chinese opera performed as part of funeral entertainment or during the Vegetarian Festival each September in Chinatown. Performances are normally not announced, but are an unexpected surprise one stumbles across in back alleys.

Likay, the village version of the great *lakhon* and *khon* dance/ dramas of the palace, was once staple fare at temple fairs, but most of the fairs have faded away in the city and are found only in rural areas. Performances of *kae bon*, an offshoot of *khon*, can be seen at Lak Muang, where successful supplicants pay a troupe to perform for gods of the heavens and angels of the city.

Traditional puppet theatre is best represented by **Joe Louis Theatre** (Suan Lum Night Bazaar, 1875 Thanon Rama IV, tel: 0 2252 9683; www.joelouis-theater.com), which stages a *hun lakhon lek* puppet show, inspired by local folk tales and the Ramakien, nightly (7.30pm).

Contemporary Thai theatre can be enjoyed at **Patravadi Theatre** (69/1 Soi Wat Rakhang, Thanon Arun Amarin, Thonburi, tel: 0 2412 7287; www.patravaditheatre.com).

Concerts

The Fine Arts Department offers concerts of Thai music and dance/drama at the **National Theatre** (tel: 0 2221 0171). At 2pm on Saturdays, Thai classical dance is presented at the auditorium of the **Public Relations Building** on Ratchadamnoen Klang Avenue, opposite the Royal Hotel.

Concerts of European music and dance are now regular events. The Bangkok Symphony Orchestra and groups from western countries give frequent concerts. See *Bangkok Post*'s Sunday magazine.

Art Galleries

The **National Gallery** is located to the north of the National Museum in Bangkok, across the approach to the Phra Pinklao Bridge at 4 Thanon Chao Fa (Wed–Sun 9am–4pm; entrance fee; tel: 0 2281 2224). The gallery displays works by Thai artists and offers frequent film shows. Exhibitions of paintings, sculpture, ceramics, photographs and weaving are numerous.

Silpakorn University, opposite the Grand Palace on Thanon Na Phra Lan, is the country's premier fine arts college. It frequently stages exhibitions of students' work. Other promoters of Thai art and photography are the British Council, the Goethe Institut and Alliance Française.

Art galleries seem more interested in selling mass market works than in promoting experimental art; but one, **Visual Dhamma**, takes an active role in ensuring that talented artists exhibit their works. It is interested primarily in a new school of Thai art which attempts to re-interpret Buddhist themes. It is located at 44/28 Soi 21 (Soi Asoke), Thanon Sukhumvit. Tel: 0 2258 5879.

Shopping

General

Whatever part of your budget you have allocated for shopping, double it or regret it. The widest range of handicraft items is found in Bangkok and Chiang Mai.

Value Added Tax: Non-Thai visitors to Thailand are entitled to reclaim the 7 percent VAT charged on goods and services purchased from stores displaying the "VAT Refund for Tourists" sign. Ask sales staff for the details. Claims are made before departure at any of the six international airports.

What to Buy

REAL/FAKE ANTIQUES

Wood, bronze, terracotta and stone statues from all Thailand and Burma can be found in Bangkok and Chiang Mai. There are religious figures and characters from classical literature, carved wooden angels, mythical animals and more. Most fake antiques passed off as real are crafted in Chiang Mai and surrounding villages.

Export Permits

The **Fine Arts Department** (tel: 0 2226 1661) prohibits the export of all Thai Buddha images, images of other deities and fragments (hands or heads) of images dating from before the 18th century.

All antiques and art objects, regardless of type or age, must be registered with the Fine Arts Department. The shop will usually do this for you. If you decide to handle it yourself, take the piece to the Fine Arts Department at the National Museum on Thanon Na Phra That, together with two

Thailand's Nightlife

For years, Thailand has enjoyed a lusty reputation as a centre for sex of every persuasion and interest. But times and clienteles have changed. The American GIs of the 1960s and the German and Japanese sex tourists of the 1970s and 80s have been replaced by upmarket tourists, usually couples. While there has been no diminution in massage parlours and bars, there has been an increase in activities for the new breed of travellers.

Nightlife

Jazz clubs, discos and open-air restaurants are the most popular form of nocturnal entertainment in towns. The queen of nighttime activities in Bangkok is shopping, with night markets along Sukhumvit and Silom roads. Even in that wrinkled old harlot of a street, Patpong, vendors' tables choke the street, drawing more patrons than the bars, with their counterfeit watches, shirts and tapes. The change has rubbed off on the bars as well. Many of Patpong's bars have metamorphosed into discos.

The scene is essentially the same in Chiang Mai, where the night bazaar on Thanon Chang Klan attracts more tourists than the bars along Thanon Loi Kroh.

In Phuket, "barbeers" (a bar which serves beer) line the streets of Patong beach's Soi Bangla and similar areas of Karon and Kata.

Massages

"Traditional Thai Massage" and "Ancient Thai Massage" are therapeutic according to age-old traditions. The best place for this is at Wat Pho. "Special" massages are sexual. Punters pick a woman from behind a one-way mirror and spend the next hour getting a bath and whatever else they arrange.

Shoppers' Map

Nancy Chandler's *Map of Bangkok*, available in bookstores and hotels, is an invaluable reference for shoppers. It is the best map for pointing you in the direction of the top shopping areas, restaurants and sights.

postcard-sized photos of it. The export fee ranges between 50 and 200 baht depending on the antiquity of the piece.

Fake antiques do not require export permits, but airport customs officials are not art experts and may mistake it for a genuine piece. If it looks authentic, clear it at the Fine Arts Department to avoid problems later.

BASKETS

Thailand's abundant bamboo, wicker and grasses are transformed into lamps, storage boxes, tables, colourful mats, handbags, letter holders, tissue boxes and slippers. Wicker and bamboo are turned into storage lockers with brass fittings and furniture to fill the house.

Yan lipao, a thin, sturdy grass, is woven into delicate patterns to create purses and bags for formal occasions. Although expensive, the bags retain their beauty for years.

CERAMICS

Best known among the distinctive Thai ceramics is the jade green celadon, which is distinguished by its finely glazed surface. Statues, lamps, ashtrays and other items are also produced in dark green, brown and cobalt blue hues.

Modelled on its Chinese cousin, blue-and-white porcelain includes pots, lamp bases, household items and figurines. Quality varies according to the skill of the artist, and of the firing and glazing.

Bencharong (meaning five colours) describes a style of porcelain derived from 16th-century Chinese art.

Normally reserved for bowls, containers and fine chinaware, its classic pattern features a small religious figure surrounded by intricate floral designs, usually green, blue, yellow, rose and black.

DECORATIVE ARTS

Lacquerware comes in two styles: the gleaming gold-and-black variety normally seen on temple shutters, and the matte red type with black and/or green details, which originated in northern Thailand and Burma. The range includes ornate containers and trays, wooden figurines, woven bamboo baskets and Burmese-inspired Buddhist manuscripts. Pieces may also be bejewelled with tiny glass mosaics and gilded ornaments.

Black lacquer is also the base into which shaped bits of mother-of-pearl are pressed. Scenes from religious or classical literature are rendered on presentation trays, containers and plaques.

GEMS AND JEWELLERY

Thailand is one of the world's exporters of cut rubies and sapphires. Customers should patronise only those shops that display the trade's official emblem: a gold ring mounted with a ruby.

Thailand is now regarded as the world's leading cutter of gemstones, the "Bangkok cut" rapidly becoming one of the most popular. Artisans set the stones in gold and silver to create jewellery and bejeweled containers. Light green Burmese jade (jadeite) is carved into jewellery as well as into art objects.

Phuket produces international standard natural, cultured Mob (teardrop) and artificial pearls. Costume jewellery is a major Thai business.

HILL-TRIBE CRAFTS

Northern hill tribes produce brightly coloured needlepoint in a variety of

geometric and floral patterns. These are sold as produced, or else incorporated into shirts, coats, bags, pillowcases and other items.

Hill-tribe silver work is valued less for its silver content (which is low) than for its intricate work and imagination.

METAL ART OBJECTS

Silver and gold are pounded into jewellery, boxes and other decorative pieces, many set with gems. Tin, mined near Phuket, is the prime ingredient in pewterware, of which Thailand is a major producer. Items range from clocks and steins to egg cups and figurines.

Thai Silk and Fabrics

● **Silk** is perhaps Thailand's internationally best-known craft. First brought to world attention by American entrepreneur Jim Thompson, Thai silk has enjoyed enduring popularity and is on the shopping list of many visitors. Sold in a wide variety of colours, it is characterised by the tiny nubs which, like embossings, rise from its surface – and, of course, by its smooth silkiness.

Unlike sheer Indian silks and shiny Chinese patterned silks, Thai silk is a thick cloth that lends itself to clothes, curtains and upholstery, but is also used to cover purses, tissue boxes and picture frames.

Mutmee is a silk from the northeast of Thailand and whose colours are sombre and muted. A form of tie-dyed cloth, it is sold both in lengths and as finished clothing or accessories.

● **Batik** Southern Thailand is a batik centre and offers ready-made clothes and batik paintings.

● **Wall hangings** Burmese in origin and style, *kalaga* wall hangings are popular. The figures are stuffed with *kapok* to make them stand out in relief.

Getting Acquainted

The Place

Situation In the Indian Ocean, bordering Thailand and Laos to the east, Bangladesh to the west and India and China to the north.
Area 671,000 sq. km (260,000 sq. miles).
Capital Naypyidaw (Pyinmana).
Population 54 million.
Highest Point Hkakabo Razi (5,889 m/19,320 ft) is the highest mountain in Southeast Asia.
Time Zone 6.5 hours ahead of Greenwich Meridian Time (GMT), so New York is 11.5 hours, Los Angeles 14.5 hours and London 6.5 hours behind, Australia 2.5 hours ahead. Bangkok is half an hour behind.
Currency Kyat (pronounced *chat*).
Weights and Measures Imperial.
Electricity 230 volts, using three-pin plugs, but the power supply is intermittent and unreliable.
International Dialling Code 95.

National Flag

The Burmese national flag is red in colour with a dark blue canton in the top left corner. Within the blue field are a white pinion and ears of paddy rice, surrounded by 14 white stars. The pinion represents industry, the rice symbolises agriculture, and the stars correspond to the 14 administrative states and divisions of Burma. The three colours of the flag represent decisiveness (red), purity and virtue (white) and peace and integrity (blue). The state flag was adopted in 1974.

Climate

Like all countries in South and Southeast Asia's monsoonal region, Burma's year is divided into three seasons. The rains begin in May, and are most intense between June and August. The central inland is drier than other parts of the country, but is subject to much rain during this time.

In October, the rains let up. The ensuing winter "cool season" (November through to February) is the most pleasant time to visit Burma. The average mean temperature along the Ayeyarwady plain, from Yangon to Mandalay, is 21–28°C (70–82°F), although in the mountains on the north and east, the temperature can drop below freezing and snow can fall.

During the months of March and April, Burma has its "dry season". Temperatures in the central plain, particularly around Bagan (Pagan), can climb to 45°C (113°F).

Annual rainfall along the rain-shadow coasts of Rakhine (Arakan) and Tanintharyi (Tenasserim) ranges from 300 to 500 cm (120 to 200 in). The Ayeyarwady Delta gets about 150 to 200 cm (60 to 78 in), while the central Burma region, between Mandalay and Bagan and the surrounding areas, averages 50–100 cm (20–40 in) of rain each year. In the far north, the melting snows of the Himalayan foothills keep rivers fed with water.

The People

Burma has seven minority-dominated states: Rakhaing (Arakan), Chin, Kachin, Kayin (Karen), Kayah (Red Karen/Karenni), Mon and Shan. There are seven divisions populated mainly by Bamar (Burman): Ayeyarwady (Irrawaddy), Magway (Magwe), Mandalay, Bago (Pegu), Yangon (Rangoon), Sagaing and Tanintharyi. Eighty percent of the population live in the country and 20 percent in towns. Population density is 46.9 per sq. km (123 per sq. miles). Annual growth rate is around 1.95

Public Holidays

All offices are closed on the following days:
● **4 January** Independence Day commemorates the date in 1948 that Burma left the British Commonwealth and became a sovereign independent nation.
● **12 February** Union Day marks the date in 1947 that Aung San concluded an agreement with Burma's ethnic minorities at Panglong in the Shan State.

The Union of Myanmar (Burma) flag, which has been carried by runners to each of Burma's state capitals, is returned to Yangon amid the roar of hundreds of thousands of people from all over the nation.
● **2 March** Peasants' Day honours the farming population.
● **27 March** Resistance (*Tatmadaw*) Day commemorates the World War II struggle against Japan. It is celebrated with parades and fireworks. Ironically, Burma spent most of the war on the Japanese side fighting Allied forces, but switched allegiance in early 1945.
● **1 May Workers'/May Day** The working people's holiday.

● **19 July** Martyrs' Day is a memorial to Burma's founding father, Aung San, and his cabinet who were assassinated in 1947. Ceremonies take place at the Martyrs' Mausoleum, Yangon.
Non-Buddhist religious holidays: Minority groups celebrate holidays not on the Burmese calendar: the Hindu festival *Dewali* in October, the Islamic observance of *Bakri Idd* with changing dates, the Christian holidays of Christmas and Easter, and the Kayin (Karen) New Year Festival on or about 1 January.

Business Hours

- **Government offices/post offices** 9.30am–4.30pm Monday to Friday, 9.30am–12.30pm Saturday.
- **Banks** 10am–2pm weekdays.
- **General Post Office** 7.30am–6pm Monday to Friday.
- **Myanmar Travels & Tours** information counter 8.30am–5pm seven days a week.
- **Restaurants** Most close by 10pm, although some tea and coffee shops will stay open later.

percent. Life expectancy is 60 years for men and 64 for women; the infant mortality rate is 51 per 1,000.

Economy

Burma's gross national product is around US$83 billion, a per capita GNP of US$1,800. It is growing by about 2.5 percent per annum. The national labour force numbers 28 million, of whom 70 percent are employed in agriculture and 7 percent in industry.

Government

In 1990 the first free elections were held in 30 years, and Nobel laureate Aung San Suu Kyi's NLD (National League for Democracy) won by a large majority. The military-led "State Peace and Development Council" (SLORC) responded by raiding NLD headquarters and arresting key members. Since then, SLORC has been fighting a war of attrition with the NLD. Several attempts have since been made to adopt a new constitution for the Union of Myanmar (in Burmese, Myanmar Naing-Ngan). In 1997 SLORC transformed itself into the State Peace and Development Council (SPDC).

Planning the Trip

Visas & Passports

Visitors to Burma must present a valid passport and a tourist or business visa obtained at one of Burma's overseas embassies or consulates (*right*). An entry visa for tourists (EVT) is valid for 28 days. These visas can now easily be extended for another four weeks at the Yangon immigration office. It is also possible to obtain a multiple journey entry visa for those operating a business in Burma.

Children above seven years of age, even when included on their parents' passport, must have their own visas.

Independent travel is allowed around Burma, but you may find it easier to travel as part of an organised group, particularly in border areas.

Health

Malaria is a danger in Burma. The risk is highest at altitudes below 1,000 m (3,000 ft) between May and December. Mosquitoes in several areas are resistant to many brands of anti-malaria drugs, so seek advice on medication from a tropical institute before you leave. Many upcountry hotels have mosquito nets, but they're worthless if they have holes in them. It can be a worthwhile investment to carry your own mosquito net and pack mosquito coils to burn while you sleep.

Amoebic dysentery is a danger to those who do not take precautions: under no circumstances should you drink water unless you know it has been boiled; all fruit should be carefully peeled before being eaten,

and no raw vegetables or salads should be eaten.

Health standards in much of Burma are still relatively low, so it is essential to buy private medical insurance before your departure.

Money Matters

Burma's official currency is the kyat (pronounced "chat"). Hotel rooms, air tickets and Myanma Railways tickets are now priced in US dollars, so you'll need to bring enough US currency to cover these expenses. For just about everything else you will have to use kyat.

The official rate of exchange is artificially pegged at about six kyats to US$1. However, no one pays any attention to this rate, and instead use the free market exchange rate – currently between 1,200 to 1,500 kyat for US$1.

Burma has abolished licensed money-changers so your best bet is to buy kyats from hotels, travel agencies or trustworthy shopkeepers. Avoid moneychangers on the street wherever possible, and don't hand over your money before having counted the kyat.

Kyat can be used to pay for meals, souvenirs, tips, bus and car transportation and occasionally (in the outlying districts) for accommodation. But you will still need US dollars to pay for hotel rooms in the main cities, as well as airline and rail tickets.

Embassies Abroad

Visas can be obtained from the following embassies abroad:
- **Australia**
22 Arkana Street
Yarralumla
ACT 2600
Tel: 06-6273 3811.
- **United Kingdom**
19a Charles Street
London W1X 8ER
Tel: 020-7629 6966/499 8841.
- **United States**
2300 S Street NW
Washington DC 20008
Tel: 202-332 9044/5/6.

Tourist Information

There is a limited amount of literature on Burma and no official overseas tourist offices. Burma embassies abroad have brochures and leaflets, and specialist tour operators can supply helpful details, but the best source of information (albeit lacking in brochures) is **Myanmar Travels & Tours** (MTT), which is part of the government tourist board. Though it provides little in the way of brochures, it sells tours and can arrange various types of transport around Burma. Head office: 77–91 Sule Pagoda Road, Yangon, tel: 01-282 075; e-mail: mtt.mht@mptmail.net.mm; www.myanmars.net/mtt.

There is also: **Myanmar Tourism Promotion Board** (MTPB), Traders Hotel, 223 Sule Pagoda Road, Yangon, tel: 01-242 828, ext. 6482, fax: 01-242 800; www.myanmar-tourism.com.

In addition, you may wish to check the following websites:
www.myanmar.com
www.ayezay.com
www.myanmars.net

US dollars are the best currency to have, although some places will accept pounds sterling. Other hard currencies such as the Euro and Japanese yen can only be changed at very disadvantageous rates.

You can draw US dollar advances on your Visa or MasterCard at the Foreign Trade Bank (in Yangon, it's on Barr Street; in Mandalay, on B Road at 82nd Street).

Credit Cards

Visa, American Express and MasterCard are only accepted at Myanmar Travels & Tours, all the major hotels, at airline offices and at the Yangon Duty Free Shop.

What To Wear/Bring

Unless you are conducting business in Yangon, you won't be expected to wear a tie. Long trousers for men and dresses or long skirts for women, lightweight and appropriate for the weather, are the generally accepted mode of dress for Westerners. Quick-drying clothes are a good idea for visits during the rainy season or *Thingyan* ("water festival"). Shorts or mini-skirts are frowned upon by the Burmese. A sweater or jacket should be carried if you plan a visit to the hill stations or Shan Plateau, especially in the cool season. Open shoes, such as sandals, are acceptable, but remember to remove footwear when entering religious institutions.

Sunblock, sunhat and sunglasses are essential.

Getting There

BY AIR

Most of Burma's visitors arrive at Yangon's **Mingaladon Airport**. Situated 19 km (12 miles) northwest of the capital, it is where most scheduled international flights arrive. Others have begun to arrive in Mandalay from Chiang Mai, Thailand. There are plans to make the new **Mandalay International Airport** eventually a regional hub of Indochina. The largest number of international flights connect Yangon and Bangkok. **Thai Airways International** (www.thaiairways.com) and Burma's international carrier, **Myanmar Airways International** (www.maiair.com), each have two roundtrip flights daily. MAI also operates daily flights to Singapore, three flights a week to Hong Kong, two a week to Kuala Lumpur and one per week to Dhaka. **Silk Air** (www.silkair.com) flies daily from Singapore, **Malaysian Airlines** (www.malaysiaairlines.com) has two roundtrip flights from Kuala Lumpur, **Biman Bangladesh** (www.biman air.com) flies once a week from Chittagong via Yangon to Bangkok and back. **Air Mandalay** (www.airmandalay.com), a private domestic airline, operates a biweekly service between Yangon and Chiang Mai. **Air China** (www.airchina.com.cn) has a weekly flight between Yangon and Kunming (Yunnan). **Indian Airlines** (indian-airlines.nic.in) links Yangon with Kolkata and Bangkok twice weekly. Travellers from the US, Australia and Europe probably will find it easiest to reach Burma via Bangkok or Singapore. Over 80 airlines connect these cities with other world capitals.

BY ROAD

Burma's frontiers have long been closed to overland international travel, primarily due to the continuing rebellions by various ethnic groups in the border areas. It is, however, possible to visit Tachilek and Kyaingtong (Kengtung) in Shan State from Mae Sai in northern Thailand. For a day trip the visa is available at the border post. Similarly, the island of Kawthaung (the former Victoria Point) in the Myeik (Mergui) archipelago can be reached from Ranong in southern Thailand. On the Burma-Yunnan frontier border posts have been opened at Lwe-ge from where organised group tours can go to Bhamo, Muse, Namkham and Kunlon. Organised groups are also permitted to continue up to Lashio. The Thai and Burmese governments have constructed a bridge across the Moei River between Mae Sot and Myawaddy but so far travel is still not permitted between the two countries except for the visit to a casino within sight of the bridge. If the present development plan is carried through, it should eventually be possible to travel by car from Singapore through Burma to India or China and on to Europe.

Practical Tips

NEWSPAPERS

The daily English language newspaper is called The *New Light of Myanmar* and is available at newsstands and in all hotels. Western publications can be read at the British and American Libraries in Yangon. The English-language *Myanmar Times* is available online at www.myanmar.com/myanmartimes.

TELEVISION AND RADIO

Television: Myanmar Television (Channel 3) and Myawaddy TV (Channel 6) send telecasts at various times of the day between 7am and 10.30pm to 109 re-transmission stations covering most areas around the country.

Radio: Only radio stations affiliated with the state-owned Radio Myanmar are permitted in Burma. Radio Myanmar and Myawaddy Radio broadcast intermittently between 7am and 9pm daily. Yangon City FM 89 broadcasts news, music and entertainment 8 to 10am and 2 to 6pm daily. Visitors with shortwave radios can also pick up BBC Radio (www.bbc.co.uk) and Voice of America (www.voanews.com). Check their website for the respective shortwave frequencies.

Postal Services

The **Yangon General Post Office**, tel: 01-285 499, is located on Strand Road at the corner of Bo Aung Gyaw Street and is open 7.30am to 6pm Monday to Friday. All other post offices in Burma are open 9.30am to 4.30pm Monday to Friday, and 9.30am to 12.30pm Saturday. They are closed Sunday and public holidays.

The only exception is the Mingaladon (Yangon) Airport mail sorting office, which is open round-the-clock every day for receipt and dispatch of foreign mail and ordinary letters and postcards.

Registered letters can be taken at the airport postal counter only during normal government working hours.

Telecommunications

The country code for Burma is 95, the code for Yangon is 01. Burma has direct satellite links to seven countries: Japan, Hong Kong, Singapore, Thailand, India, UK and Australia. Siemens of Germany has installed additional satellite communication lines that have brought telecommunication connections up to Western standards. International-class hotels offer in-room IDD telephone and fax service to foreign countries.

Call 101 for an overseas or inland booking between 7am to 7pm. The operator will call you when the line is open.

When dialling from outside the country omit the 0 in the area code. IDD (International Direct Dialling) is easily available in major Yangon and Mandalay hotels and at kiosks; costs are based on US$ rates plus a service fee. From the smaller towns it may be possible to call Yangon but not overseas.

If you encounter problems with any of the communications systems, contact the **Myanmar**

Embassies in Yangon

● **Australia**
88 Strand Road.
Tel: 01-251 809/10.
● **United Kingdom**
80 Strand Road.
Tel: 01-256 918.
● **United States**
581 Merchant Street.
Tel: 01-379 880.

Emergency Numbers

The following Yangon numbers can be called in emergencies:
● **Police** 199
● **Fire Brigade** 191
● **Ambulance** 192
● **Immigration** 01 286 434
● **Customs** 01-284 533

Posts and Telecommunications, 43 Bo Aung Gyaw Street, tel: 01-285 499, or the hotline tel: 277 209.

Mobile Phones: There is no international roaming facility for mobile phones in Burma. Visitors to Burma can rent mobile phones by the week or month at rates well above the world market.

Medical Treatment

By Western standards, healthcare provision is still primitive in Burma. The **International sos Clinic**, at the Renaissance Inya Lake Hotel in Yangon (tel: 01-667 879), is the best on offer, or there are reasonable private military hospitals in Yangon, Mandalay and Pathein. For more serious problems, however, you are probably best flying out to Bangkok or Singapore.

For minor problems, pharmacies operate an out-of-hours rota, which should be posted in their windows. **AA Pharmacy**, just north of Sule Pagoda on Sule Pagoda Road (tel: 01-253 231), is open 24 hours.

Security & Crime

Although terrorist attacks are always a possibility in Burma, the country is basically safe and hospitable to tourists. But as in other countries, look after your belongings. Avoid driving at night, too, as highwaymen are not uncommon.

Getting Around

General Conditions

In Burma, it is not the distance that you should concern yourself with but rather the road conditions in the particular area in question. Average speeds achievable on road or rail are well below those in neighbouring countries. Many roads are pot-holed while others are mere dirt tracks.

On Arrival

There are two ways to get from **Mingaladon Airport** to downtown Yangon, a distance of 19 km (12 miles). You have the option of getting a "limousine" (actually just a better-looking taxi) for US$3–5 to anywhere in the city, payable in advance at the counter. Otherwise taxi drivers will besiege you in a bid to drive you into the city. If you book a room through the hotel desk at the airport, transport into town is usually arranged free of charge. On departure, the fare from Yangon to the airport usually can be paid in local currency.

By Air

Four different domestic airlines ply a network of air routes to over 40 localities within Burma. Privately owned **Air Mandalay** (www.airmandalay.com) serves several domestic destinations and offers Western standard service, check-in procedures and flight safety. **Air Bagan** (www.airbagan.com) and **Yangon Airways** (www.yangonair.com) have similar standards. Government-owned **Myanma Airways** has a reputation for unreliable service and a questionable safety record and cannot be recommended.

Air Mandalay, Yangon Airways and Air Bagan tickets can be purchased in Bangkok, or through many travel agents in Yangon or Mandalay. Myanma Airways tickets may only be purchased at offices of Myanma Airways or Myanmar Travels & Tours (see page 348). Air Mandalay, Yangon Airways and Air Bagan tend to keep more strict flight schedules than Myanma Airways, and in-flight service is much better as well.

By River/Sea

Burma's rivers provide more than 8,000 km (5,000 miles) of navigable routes. Shipping is the most important means of transport for people and goods.

Popular River Routes

The most travelled river route for tourists is the part of the Ayeyarwady between Mandalay and Bagan.

A local slowboat leaves Mandalay twice weekly at 5am, arriving in Bagan (Pagan) in 15 hours. You can travel deck class or "first class" but facilities are very basic. Two modern and faster express boats, Shwe Kein Nayi 1 & 2, sail the same route daily except Sunday and Wednesday, leaving at 6am from both Mandalay and Bagan for the 9-hour journey. For all bookings, contact the **Inland Water Transport** office (for foreigners) near the Kaingdan Jetty in Yangon, tel: 01-284 055; and in Mandalay near the Gawein Jetty on 35th Street, tel: 02-36035.

If you have the money to burn, book yourself on the Road to Mandalay (operated by Orient-Express

Official Priority

The Burmese government runs an unofficial but nevertheless rigid priority list which can disrupt flight bookings right up to the last minute. Burmese VIPs, of course, have priority. Behind them, in order, come tour parties, individual foreign visitors, foreign expatriate residents, and – last and least – native residents of Burma.

Buying Air Tickets

Domestic flight schedules of Yangon Airways can be checked at www.yangonair.com; Air Mandalay at www.airmandalay.com, and Air Bagan at www.airbagan.com. Travel agents sometimes sell domestic air tickets below their recommended published fares, but they accept cash payment only, while airlines can accept credit cards.

Trains & Cruises), which sails the Ayeyarwady between Mandalay and Bagan in great splendour. Three-to six-night itineraries spending two to four nights aboard the luxury ship are offered. Contact **Orient-Express Trains & Cruises** in Yangon, tel: 01-229 860, www.orient-express.com.

A smaller cruise boat, the Irrawaddy Princess, runs regularly between Bagan and Mandalay. Contact **Barani Cruise & Trading** in Yangon, tel: 01-220 949; e-mail: barani@cyberway.com.sg.

A third option for the Mandalay-Bagan stretch is on board the Pandaw III, a newly-built river steamer that recalls the experience of river travel during colonial times. Operated by the London-based Irrawaddy Flotilla Company (IFC), the Pandaw III has 39 comfortable cabins with attached bathrooms. There are overnight as well as 2-night cruises from Mandalay to Bagan and vice versa. Contact the **Irrawaddy Flotilla Company** at its Yangon office, tel: 01-244 256 or check its website: www.pandaw.com.

A short popular ferry trip for tourists is the one up the Ayeyarwady from Mandalay to Mingun. Boats leave from Mandalay's B Road Jetty several times daily for the one-hour voyage.

By Train

Myanmar Railways has a network of more than 4,500 km (2,800 miles) of track. Yangon's Central Railway Station is the nation's hub. By day and night, express trains, mail trains and local trains depart on journeys of varying lengths. Most popular are the daily services between Yangon and Mandalay.

Ordinary (second class) and Upper Class (first class) seating is available on all trains. Upper Class seats cost almost three times that of Ordinary Class. Sleepers are not readily available for overnight trips. Foreigners can purchase their tickets through **Myanmar Travels & Tours** *(see page 348)* or at the **railway station**, tel: 01-274 027, advisably 24 hours in advance.

Yangon to Mandalay

For the main train route most often used by tourists, the 716-km (445-mile) **Yangon-Mandalay Line** uses reasonably comfortable Korean and Chinese coaches. This is the country's most acceptable railway and is recommended for the scenes of Burmese village life it offers from its windows. Passengers however must be willing to put up with a little discomfort, and often long delays (the train often arrives in Mandalay four or more hours later than scheduled).

By Road

BUS

Government Buses

Public bus travel aboard government-owned Road Transport Company vehicles tend to be long and tedious. Many roads are poor, vehicles are overcrowded, and in the event a bus breaks down, it can be hours before mechanical assistance becomes available.

Yangon city is served by an extensive network of local buses which connect Yangon with the new satellite towns that were created after 1989.

Private Buses

Several companies run comfortable air-conditioned buses from Yangon to Mandalay, Bagan, Taunggyi/Inle Lake for the approximate equivalent of US$10. These companies operate from one station, the **Highway Bus Centre** at the intersection of Pyay and Station roads, southwest of Mingaladon Airport. Some also maintain ticket offices opposite the Central Railway Station.

Travel from Yangon to other major tourist destinations is overnight and you can choose between several companies. Some travellers prefer bus to train, it's less than a quarter of the price (as you can pay in kyats) and the arrival times are more reliable than that of trains. Regular stops for food and refreshments are also made.

Among the companies providing reliable service and vehicles are: **Leo Express**, tel: 01-249 512; **Shwe Kabar**, tel: 01-243 053.

City Transport

TAXI

Cab drivers wait in front of all the big tourist hotels in Yangon; their vehicles nowadays are second-hand Japanese cars or retired Singapore taxis.

Taxis are not metered although they charge by the trip. Ask at your hotel or guesthouse for the proper fare, which shouldn't exceed US$2 within the city. Rates for a full day's charter run is about US$25 within Yangon; a little more if the driver speaks good English, and about US$30 for a day trip into the countryside (Bago or Thanlyin). Taxis are by far the best way to explore the countryside surrounding Yangon, especially if one is able or willing to share the fare with other passengers.

TRISHAW & OTHER TRANSPORT

Bicycle trishaws (*sai-kaa*) or motorised three-wheelers (*thoun bein*) are the most popular means of getting around the streets of the larger cities – less so in Yangon where taxis have taken over. Easily available and cheap, they take their passengers anywhere they want to go in the city for US$1 or less per trip. For longer trips in the vicinity of Yangon, Mandalay and other large population centres, jeep collectives or "pick-ups" (*kaa*) – similar to the Thai *songthaew* – do yeomen's work carrying large numbers of riders. They don't follow a set schedule; instead, they take off whenever the last seat is taken.

Tour Operators in Yangon

Abercrombie & Kent
64, B-2 Shwe Gon Plaza
Tel: 01-542 949/542 902
Fax: 01-542 992
e-mail: tun@mptmail.net.mm
www.abercrombieandkent.com

Ainda Travel
134/ (14) Anawrahta Street
Tel: 01-660 266
Fax: 01-544 014
e-mail: ainda@mptmail.net.mm

Asian Trails Tour Ltd
73 Pyay Road
Tel: 01-211 212/727 422
Fax: 01-211 670
e-mail: res@asiantrails.com.mm
www.asiantrails.info

Diethelm Travel & Tours
Dusit Inya Lake Resort, 37 Kaba Aye Pagoda Road, Mayangon
Tel: 01-652 905, 652 898
Fax: 01-653 182, 652 907
e-mail: leisure@diethelm.com.mm
www.diethelmtravel.com

Exotissimo
#0303 Sakura Tower
339 Bo Gyoke Aung San Street
Tel: 01-255 266
Fax: 01-255 428
e-mail: myanmar@exotissimo.com
www.exotissimo.com

Golden Land Travel & Tours
Bldg 170, 176, MGW Centre,
6th Floor, Bo Aung Kyaw Street,
Botahtaung
Tel: 01-256 561, 256 581
Fax: 01-283 898
www.goldenland-travel.com

Good News Travels & Tours
380 Bogyoke Aung San Road,
FMI Center, Pabedan
Tel: 01-246 788, 240 378
Fax: 01-240 270
e-mail:
good-news@mptmail.net.mm

Where to Stay

Choosing a Hotel

From a low 25,000 visitors per year in the 1980s, Burma tourism had by 2006 grown to an estimated 250,000 a year. The hotel building boom of the 90s has calmed down somewhat but at any time of year, except December to February, there is usually an excess of rooms available. For the savvy traveller, this may present an opportunity to ask for better rates.

Hotels and guesthouses – many of which are now privately owned – are required to post rates in US dollars, although much lower kyat rates may be available for Burmese nationals. In the case of some of the remaining government-owned hotels, rates can be high compared to those of similar standards offered in the rest of Southeast Asia. With increased competition from the private sector, however, all hotel rates tend to follow what the market can bear.

Hotel Listings

YANGON

The Strand
92 Strand Road
Tel: 01-243 377
Fax: 01-289 880
www.ghmhotels.com
In a class of its own in price, but also in its tasteful décor and appointments. Originally built in 1903 by the Sarkies brothers and completely renovated in 1993, it reflects the epoch of the 1920s and 30s. It has 52 guest rooms including 32 suites, and a business centre. The Strand Grill, an elegant evening restaurant, and the Strand Café serve Burmese, Southeast

Asian and Continental fare. The Strand Bar offers a full range of drinks in a club-like atmosphere. The Strand's restaurants and bar provide rewarding experiences. **$$$$**

Dusit Inya Lake Resort
Kaba Aye Pagoda Road
Tel: 01-662 857
Fax: 01-665 537
inyalake.dusit.com
Built by the Russians in 1961, completely renovated and modernised in 1995, and now owned by a Thai hotel group, the Inya Lake offers a complete range of facilities including a swimming pool, tennis courts, fitness centre, putting green, barber shop, beauty salon and conference facilities. **$$$**

Price Guide

A general guide for a standard double room, excluding taxes.
$$$$ = above US$200
$$$ = US$80–200
$$ = US$20–80
$ = under US$20

The Governor's Residence
35 Taw Win Road
Tel: 01-229 860
Fax: 01-228 260
www.pansea.com
A beautiful 49-room hotel set in spacious grounds. The superb Mandalay Restaurant superb restaurant is known for its French and Asian cuisines. **$$$**

Grand Plaza Parkroyal Yangon
33 Alan Pya Paya Road
Tel: 01-250 388
Fax: 01-252 478
www.yangon.parkroyalhotels.com
Located north of the centre of Yangon and containing 312 rooms, this hotel was recently refurbished and rebranded. The décor features lots of rattan, wood and Burmese art. Along with a business centre, disco/bar, swimming pool and fitness centre there are Chinese and Japanese restaurants. **$$$**

Hotel Nikko Royal Lake Yangon
40 Natmauk Road
Tel: 01-544 500
Fax: 01-544 400

www.nikkoyangon.net
Overlooking Kandawgyi Lake, this 303-room hotel is geared towards the business traveller with facilities that include internet access, business centre and secretarial services. Excellent Japanese restaurant. Swimming pool and fitness centre. **$$$**

The Kandawgyi Palace
Kanyeiktha Road
Tel: 01-249 255
Fax: 01-280 412
www.kandawgyipalace.com
At the lake shore. Located on the site of the former Museum of Natural History and the Orient Boat Club, the Kandawgyi Palace Hotel was renovated in 1996. Facilities include a fitness centre, swimming pool and business centre. **$$$**

Sedona Hotel
1 Kaba Aye Pagoda Road
(near Inya Lake)
Tel: 01-666 900
Fax: 01-666 911
www.sedonamyanmar.com
The Sedona has a business centre, fitness centre with sauna, swimming pool and a lively pub/disco. **$$$**

Traders Hotel
223 Sule Pagoda Road
Tel: 01-242 828
Fax: 01-242 800
www.shangri-la.com
Elegant décor with Oriental touches, four excellent restaurants and bar establishments; business centre with e-mail facility; gym, sauna, pool. Contains 407 rooms. **$$$**

Summit Parkview
350 Ahlone Road
Tel: 01-211 888
Fax: 01-227 995
www.summityangon.com
One of the first modern hotels in Yangon, this hotel contains 140 rooms and serviced apartments. Its facilities include a swimming pool, health club, coffee shop and a shopping arcade. Popular with business travellers and Japanese visitors. Some rooms face Shwedagon Pagoda, which is magnificent at night. **$$–$$$**

Comfort Inn
4 Shwe Lin Street
Tel: 01-533 377

Fax: 01-524 256
Located in spacious grounds which include a putting green.
Comfortable rooms; breakfast included; provides transfers to the airport. **$$**
Thamada Hotel
5 Alan Paya Road
Tel: 01-243 639
Fax: 01-245 001
This older moderate-class hotel is located opposite the Yangon railway station. Popular with both business and leisure travellers. **$$**

MANDALAY

Mandalay Hill Resort
9 Kwin (416B), 10th Street
Tel: 02-35638
Fax: 02-35639
www.mandalayhillresort.com.mm
206 rooms; high-rise hotel at base of Mandalay Hill. Café, restaurant, disco, outdoor performance theatre, large pool, tennis courts. Room rates include breakfast. **$$$**
Sedona Hotel Mandalay
Corner of 26th and 66th streets
Tel: 02-36488
Fax: 02-36499
www.sedonamyanmar.com
247 rooms. Great location opposite southeast corner of Mandalay Palace with view of Mandalay Hill. Easily the best hotel in town; pool, fitness centre, business centre with e-mail facility. **$$$**
Mandalay Swan Hotel
Corner of 26th Road and 68th streets facing Mandalay Palace
Tel: 02-35691
Fax: 02-35677
www.mandalayswanhotel.com
The restored former Mandalay Hotel, with 100 comfortable rooms ranging from economy to suites. Coffee shop, restaurant, pool and tennis courts. MTT travel office on premises. **$$–$$$**
Emerald Land Inn
14th Street between 87th and 88th streets
Tel: 02-39471
Fax: 02-39472
Comfortable hotel in a garden setting located in a residential area northwest of the Mandalay

Palace. Restaurant, bar and pool. **$$**
AD–1 Hotel
Corner of 87th and 28th streets, near the Eindawya Pagoda
Tel: 02-34505
One of the best budget hotels. Clean rooms with fans and showers or with air-conditioning. Breakfast included in the room rate **$**
Royal City Hotel
130, 27th Street between 76th and 77th
Tel: 02-31805
This is a well-run hotel with pleasant economy rooms equipped with TV and phone. A rooftop garden offers views of Mandalay Hill and Mandalay Fort. **$**

BAGAN

Bagan Hotel
Old Bagan
Tel: 61-60317
Fax: 61-60032
www.bagan-hotel.com
108 rooms, on the river near Gawdawpalin Pagoda; new hotel with air-conditioned rooms, satellite TV and IDD telephones. Pretty gardens, good value and well located. **$$$**
Bagan Thande Hotel
Old Bagan
Tel: 61-60025
Fax: 61-60050
www.hotelbaganthande.com
Located near the Archaeological Museum overlooking the river, with 70 rooms and attractive bungalow units. Originally built in 1992 for the Prince of Wales, this hotel also has a dining room and bar. Breakfast included in the room rate. **$$**
Thazin Garden Hotel
22 Thazin Road
Tel: 61-60052
Fax: 01-512 749 (Yangon)
www.thazingardenhotel.com
Charming hotel in a quiet location. Low-rise wood-panelled rooms furnished with Burmese artefacts are located amid well tended gardens. Restaurant serving Burmese and Western fare. Staff are very helpful and go out of their way to make you feel welcome. **$$**

Where to Eat

What to Eat

Due to the economic improvements in Burma's main towns over the last decade it is no longer difficult to find good Burmese food. Good Chinese, Indian and European food is also available at restaurants throughout the country.
Reservations are seldom needed and restaurants, except those located in the larger hotels, tend to close early in the evening. Burmese take their main meal at lunchtime and usually have an early dinner, around 6pm. Below is a categorised list of a few food items and their respective English translations easily available on any Burmese restaurant menu.

Soups
Chin Ye Hin. Spicy fish soup.
Bu Thee Hin Khar. Clear soup with vermicelli and gourd.
Kin Mone Ywet Hin Khar. Clear soup with herbal leaves.

Appetisers
Pa Zun nga paung kyaw. Deep-fried prawns with onions.
Ginn Thoke. Pickled ginger salad with fried condiments.
Nga Paung Kyaw. Deep fried beansprouts with fish.
Ah Kyaw Sone. Selection of deep fried appetisers.

Salads
Pe Thee Thoke. Long bean salad.
Pa Zun Thoke. Prawn salad.
Myin Khwar Ywet Thoke. Herbal leaves salad.
Ngar Phe Thoke. Pounded fish salad.
Kyet Thar Thoke. Burmese chicken salad.

Vegetables
Ah Sone Kyaw. Mixed-fried vegetables.
The Sone Hin. Vegetables in curry sauce.
Kha Yan Thee Hnat. Eggplant curry with shrimps.

Curries
Kyet Tha Hin. Chicken curry.
Wet Tha Hin Lay. Pork curry.
Ah Mae Tha Hnat. Beef curry.
Ngar See Pyan. Fish curry with tomatoes.
Pa Zun Ne Ahloo Hin. Prawn curry and potatoes.

Seafood
Ngar Doke Kha. Red snapper with garlic and parsley.
Pa Zun Oh Kat. Shrimp with chilli.
Nga Su See. Yangon fish fillet.
Mawlamyine Nga Thalauk Paung. Fish steamed in lemongrass, ginger and garlic.

Meat Dishes
Wet Tha A Sat Kyaw. Pork with chillies and onions.
Kyet Tha Cho Chet. Chicken with basil.

Desserts
Rakhine Nget Pyaw Paung. Steamed banana with coconut milk.
Mote Kyar Sae. Sticky rice, lotus seeds and syrup.
Thaku Pyin. Sago with coconut milk.

Restaurant Listings

YANGON

50th Street Bar & Grill
9/13 50th Street, Botataung
Tel: 01-298 096
Colonial atmosphere; popular with the expat community and locals. Serves good pizza and pasta. Bar stays open until late. **$$–$$$**

Aung Thuka
17A 1st Street (between Shwegondine Street and Dhammazedi Road)
A clean, reasonably priced Bamar restaurant. Easy to order as all you have to do is point at the array of cooked food in clay pots to indicate your choice. **$**

Danubyu Daw Sawyi
175/177 29th Street
Tel: 01-275 397
Modern looking restaurant, serving traditional Bamar dishes. Good place to go for breakfast as it serves noodles and other local snacks. **$**

Green Elephant
519A Thirimingalar Road,
off Pyay Road
Tel: 01-531 231
Recommended. Serves very good Bamar food in air-conditioned atmosphere. The pennywort salad is excellent. Popular with both visitors and locals. **$–$$**

Restaurant Price Guide

A general guide for dinner for two person excluding beverage:
$$$ = above US$20
$$ = US$10–20
$ = under US$10

Hla Myanma Htamin Zain
27 5th Street
Simple restaurant offering a wide variety of Bamar and Shan dishes displayed in pots, plus some Chinese and Indian food. **$**

Le Planteur
16 Sawmaha Street
Tel: 01-549 389
Serves very good French-Swiss food with smoked ham and salami. The house punch is excellent. **$$$**

Mandarin Restaurant
125 Mahabandoola Garden
Tel: 01-272 960
Opposite the north end of Mahabandoola Garden, the centrally located Mandarin offers a wide variety of regional Chinese dishes, including a good vegetarian selection. **$**

New Delhi Restaurant
Anawrahta Street between 29th and Shwebontha streets
Tel: 01-275 447
Wide range of North and South Indian dishes available. Excellent *masala dosa*. Longer opening hours than most Indian restaurants. **$**

Strand Grill and Strand Café
Strand Hotel
Tel: 01-243 377

The Grill is one of the most elegant restaurants in Yangon. Both the Grill and the Café have similar menus that offer excellent Burmese dishes, among others. The Grill is open only for dinner while the Café serves lunch and dinner at slightly lower prices too. **$$–$$$**

MANDALAY

Lashio Lay Restaurant
23rd Street between 83rd and 84th streets
Very tasty and spicy Shan food and a few vegetarian dishes. It's easy to order as dishes are on display. **$**

Pyi Gyi Mon Royal Barge
Tel: 02-26779
Replica of the floating Karaweik restaurant in Yangon and located in the southeastern corner of the moat at Mandalay Palace. Mostly Burmese and Chinese dishes and dinner is accompanied by a puppet show. **$–$$**

Sakantha Restaurant
24 72nd Street, between 27th and 28th streets
Tel: 02-21066
The good Bamar food justifies the higher than average prices. Setting is pleasant as its dining room looks out onto a garden. **$–$$**

Too Too
27th Street between 74th and 75th streets
This long-running local restaurant serves traditional Burmese dishes in a rustic but clean atmosphere. **$**

BAGAN

Everqueen Restaurant
Old Bagan
Fine garden setting, but it can be a bit breezy at night. Tucked along a sandy road before the old city gate. Offers good variety of Burmese food, especially fish dishes. **$**

Sarabha Restaurant
Old Bagan
Offers a choice of Bamar, Shan, Thai and Chinese dishes either indoors or outdoors. Great location near the Tharaba Gate. **$–$$**

Culture

Pagodas & Temples

There are two main types of Buddhist monuments in Burma: pagodas and temples.

A pagoda consists of a stupa and its surrounding enclosure. The stupa (known as a *zedi* in Burmese) is a monument of commemoration containing a relic chamber beneath (or sometimes over) the bell-shaped central structure. Burmese stupas are sometimes built on several terraces; these are passages upon which the devotees should walk in a clockwise direction.

The term "temple" is applied to Buddhist structures in Burma only because a more specific terminology does not exist in English. In Theravada Buddhism a temple is not a place of worship of a higher being; the Buddha is not a god, and Theravada Buddhism in its pure form does not recognise any form of divine worship. The temple is instead seen as a place of meditation. The Burmese word is *ku*, derived from the Pali *guba*, which roughly translated means "cave". This word also reflects the cultural heritage of the edifice – these buildings were formerly constructed as artificial caves used

Spirit Worship

Before Burma adopted Buddhism, people worshiped *nat* or spirits (usually in hills, trees and natural features). Though the young generally don't subscribe to this superstitious world, drivers of all ages tie red and white strips of cloth to their car mirrors to protect them from *nats*.

Images of Buddha

Just as temples and pagodas are created in different styles, so are Buddha images. The various body postures and hand and leg positions have symbolic meanings, each of considerable importance to students of Buddhism. These positions, called the *mudra*, are thousands of years old.

by monks where there were no overhanging slopes.

The main feature of a *ku* is that it is dark and cool inside. This feature characterises the Mon-style ("hollow cube") Bagan temples, into which only a little light is able to enter through the perforated stone windows. The Bamar-style ("central pillar") temples are totally different: they were built with huge entrances and two tiers of windows to make the interiors bright and airy.

One can trace the development of the "central pillar" type from the stupas. During festivals, it was the custom to stretch huge awnings from the stupa to the surrounding wall of the enclosure to offer protection from rain and sun. As a result, a covered walkway surrounds the central sanctuary. When this was copied in solid materials, it gave the impression that the upper part of a stupa had been built on the temple roof. The same principle applies to the multi-storeyed Bamar-style temples.

The "hollow cube" type of temples are not actually hollow inside; they may seem to be so, but the majority have a central supporting pillar. From the outside, their pointed, bell-shaped domes resemble Gothic buildings. But the temples of Bagan could not be more different. Instead of spanning the greatest possible space, the Buddhist temple interiors consist of a multitude of walls enclosing narrow passageways and chambers, thereby satisfying the *ku*'s original purpose as a sanctuary for inner peace and meditation. The exteriors of these

temples – white, and invariably decorated with a gold finial – represent Mount Meru and the devout Buddhist's striving for a spiritual goal via the ever-valid *dharma*, or law of life.

Museums

Burma's myriad pagodas and temples are her finest museums. The following have also assembled various items of historical and anthropological interest:

National Museum
Pyay Road and Pyidaungsu Yeiktha Road, Yangon, tel: 01-282 563. It contains the Mandalay Regalia from Burma's last royal court and various artefacts of ancient history. Daily 10am–4pm.
Cultural Museum Mandalay
24th Road and West Moat Road, Mandalay, tel: 02-24603. Contains a variety of memorabilia from many eras of Burmese history, and a fine collection of Buddhist literature.
Bagan Museum
Near Thiripyitsaya Sakura Hotel, Bagan. A good introduction to the images and architectural styles of this ancient city. Daily 9am–4.30pm.
Shan State Cultural Museum
Main Road, Taunggyi. Displays traditional costumes and cultural artefacts of the 30-plus ethnic groups living in the Shan Plateau region. Daily 9.30am–3.30pm.

Theatres

The best place to view a Burmese *pwe* (or traditional ceremonial dance to propitiate the spirits) is at city streets or pagoda grounds at festival times. For those whose visit doesn't coincide with a festival, however, there are two public theatres in Yangon and one in Mandalay that have irregular performances of various types:
Garrison Theatre, U Wisara Road.
Open-Air Theatre, Lanmadaw Road.
Mandalay Marionette, Garden Villa Theatre, 66th Street (between 26th and 27th streets), Mandalay, tel: 02-34446.

Festivals

When the moon waxes full, there is a Burmese celebration, the mood of which varies from season to season: frivolity during the water dousings of the New Year in March/April, solemnity for Buddhist Lent in July, and joyousness during the October Festival of Light.

Thingyan – Changing Over is the year's biggest party *(see below)*.

Day of Buddha *Kason* (April/May) is a month of anticipation, as the annual monsoon could break at any time. On the full moon, the birth, enlightenment and death of the Buddha is celebrated. People join in a procession of musicians and dancers to the local pagoda.

Scriptures Exam During the full moon day of *Nayon* (May/June), after the rains have begun, Burmese students are tested on their knowledge of the *Tipitaka*, the Buddhist scriptures. *Sayadaw* lecture before large crowds, schools operated by monasteries are opened to the public.

Beginning of Lent The monsoon begin season marks the beginning of the Buddhist Lent. On *Dhammasetkya*, the full moon day of *Waso* (June/July), the people celebrate the Buddha's conception, his renunciation of worldly goods, and his first sermon after enlightenment. Those who wish to devote their lives to the Sangha are ordained. During the next three months, members of the Sangha go into retreat for study and meditation.

"Draw-a-Lot" Festival The full moon of *Wagaung* (July/August) is purely a religious time for merit-making. The name of each member of the local Sangha is written on a piece of paper, which is then rolled up and deposited in a large basket. A representative from each household draws a slip of paper from the basket, and the next day provides an elaborate feast for the *pongyi* named on the piece of paper. One layman will have drawn a paper containing the name of the Gautama Buddha. He is the most fortunate of all, because he will have the opportunity to host the Buddha.

Boat Racing Festival By the time of *Tawthalin* (August/September), Burma's rivers are full and flowing and boat races are held in rivers and lakes. At Inle Lake, the Phaung Daw U Festival is held this month or next, with leg-rowing competitions and the voyage of a recreated royal *karaweik* barge.

Festival of Light Buddhist Lent comes to an end with the arrival of the full moon of *Thadingyut* (September/October), indicating the approach of clear blue skies. On this full moon night, the Burmese celebrate the descent of the Buddha and his followers to earth from *Tavatimsa* (heaven) where, according to legend, he travelled to preach the doctrine to his mother. **The Weaving Festival (Kathein)** During *Tazaungmone* (October/November), unmarried girls sit under the full moon in the pagoda grounds, engaged in weaving competitions to make new robes for monks.

Month of temple festivals *Pyatho* (December/January) is when gifts are presented to monks and offerings made for temple upkeep. These are also occasions for merrymaking, lasting three or more days. A bazaar, boat and pony races, magic acts and sideshows, and evening *pwe* performances are commonplace. Burmese culinary delicacies are also offered.

Harvest festival When *Tabodwe* (January/February) arrives, it is time to harvest the paddy and celebrate the harvest festival. After the first harvest is offered to the monastery, elaborate meals are prepared, and Burmese women show off their cooking prowess. The celebration is named *Htamein* after a food offering of rice, sesame, peanuts, ginger and coconut.

Thingyan: Burma's New Year

The year's biggest party is the *Thingyan* Festival in the month of *Tagu* (March/April), when the Burmese celebrate New Year. For 3–4 days (the length of the celebration is determined annually by *ponnas*, or Brahman astrologers), government, farm labour and business come to a virtual standstill.

Thingyan is best known as the Water Throwing Festival. The old year must be washed away and the new anointed with water. No one, Burmese or visitor, is safe from deluges that seem to appear from nowhere out of the hot blue sky.

Celebrations begin when Thagyamin, king of the *nat*, descends to earth to bring blessings for the new year. He also carries two books with him: one bound in gold to record the names of children who have been well-behaved in the past year, and one bound in dog skin with the names of naughty children.

Thagyamin comes riding a winged golden horse and bearing a water jar, symbolic of peace and prosperity in Burma in the coming year. Every house greets him with flowers and palm leaves at their front doors. Guns fire in salute and

music resounds from all corners of the land. Gaily decorated floats parade up and down the streets of the cities and larger towns.

Yet there are times of tranquillity in the midst of this exuberance. All revellers find a quiet moment each day to make offerings at pagodas and at the homes of their elders. Buddha images are given a thorough washing on this holiday by devout elderly women.

In medieval times, *Thingyan* was observed with a public hair-washing by the Burmese king, a ritual purification.

Shopping

Markets & Bazaars

Burma's markets and bazaars are the most interesting, and at the same time the most reasonable, places to shop for native arts and crafts. In Yangon the **Bogyoke Aung San Market** is open 8am–6pm Monday to Saturday. It is the place where most tourists do their last shopping before leaving the country. Some of the shops in the market offering reasonable prices include:

Lacquerware, Daw Chit Khin Lacquerware, Shop 43, East (C) Block.
Jade, Colourful Jade Store, Shop 42, West "D" Arcade.
Mother of Pearl, Myanmar Variety Store, Shop 75, Centre Arcade.
Silverware, William Tan, Shop 33, Main Line. This shop offers beautiful hammered silverware.
  Bazaars and markets thrive in Yangon. There are open-air markets

Where to Buy Gifts

● **Markets** Burma's numerous bazaars and markets, the most popular of which is Yangon's Bogyoke Aung San *(see above)*, are full of gift ideas.
● **Tourist Department Stores** A pricey selection of all types of Burmese handicrafts is always for sale at the tourist stores at 143–144 Sule Pagoda Road in Yangon. Open 10am–4pm Monday to Friday and 10am–1pm Saturday, the stores will accept only foreign exchange.
● **Hotels** There are gift shops at Inya Lake and Strand hotels. Both are open 9.30am–5pm Monday to Saturday.

across Bogyoke Aung San Street from the Bogyoke Market; at the corner of St John's Road and Pyay Road; and east of the Botataung Pagoda. The **Thein Gyi Zay** Indian market is just off Anawrahta Street, and there's a Chinese market at the corner of Maha Bandoola Street and Lanmadaw Road.
  The entrances to the **Shwedagon Pagoda** are also bazaars – of some length, in fact, covering both sides of the stairways. The bazaar at the east entrance is most interesting; among items frequently sold are puppets, drums, masks, toys, brassware and metal goods, including swords. The bazaar at the pagoda's south entrance is notable for wood and ivory carvings.
  Wood carvings are also sold in quantity and quality at the **New Carving Shop**, 20 University Avenue. For other types of artwork, try the **Beik Thano Art Gallery**, 113/3 Kaba Aye Pagoda Road, tel: 01-542 560; **Ivy Art Gallery**, 159 45th Street, tel: 01-297 654; **J's Irrawaddy Dream**, 59 Taw Win Road, tel: 01-221 695; **Myanmar Gallery of Contemporary Art**, 5 Kaba Aye Pagoda Road, tel: 01-548 058; **Orient Art Gallery**, 121E Thanlwin Road, tel: 01-530 830.
  Other markets, including Mandalay's **Zegyo Market**, generally stay open from early morning until dark. The best shopping for lacquerware is in New Bagan, the residential area about 8 km (5 miles) from the archaeological zone.
  There are also night markets that set up after dark. The best are in Yangon's Chinese and Indian quarters, and in Mandalay on 84th Street between 26th and 28th streets.

Other Shops in Yangon

Art
Golden Valley Art Centre, 54D, Golden Valley, tel: 01-513 621.
Traditional Arts and Sculpture Sales Shop, 188–192, East Wing Bogyoke Aung San Market.
  If you are looking for a special

Bargaining

Few prices are seen to be believed in Burma – bargaining is a way of life. Except for at top-of-the-range hotels, restaurants and department stores, you should be able to get a few kyats off the "fixed" price of most things. Even room prices are negotiable. Offer half the asking price, work up, and expect to settle for a bit more than 50 percent. Bartering is also an accepted means of payment in markets: stall holders are all too happy to accept jeans, watches and T-shirts.

producer or distributor, look at the Myanmar Business Directory. Chamber of Commerce, 74-86, Bo Sun Pat Street. Tel: 01-877 103/ 70749.

Antiques
Augustine's Antiques, 23 Attiyar Street, Kamaryut, tel: 01-504 290.

Furniture
Hla Gabar, 166 Maha Bandoola Road, tel: 01-291 311.
Green Elephant, 12 Inya Road, tel: 01-530 263.

Jewellery
Myanmar Silver & Ruby Co. Ltd., 35 Myazabe Street and International Airport Departure Hall, tel: 01-664 900.
Myanmar VES Joint Venture Co. Ltd., 66 Kaba Aye Pagoda Road, tel: 01-661 902.
Golden Owl, Bogyoke Aung San Market, tel: 01-281 863.

Books
Innwa Book Store, 232 Sule Pagoda Road.
Myanmar Book Centre, 477 Pyay Road.
Bagan Bookshop, 100 37th Street.

Longyi
U Chan Special Quality Longyi Ground Floor, Mingala Zay Market, tel: 01-203 066.

Getting Acquainted

The Place

Situation Laos is a landlocked nation bordered by China to the north, Burma (Myanmar) to the northwest, Thailand to the west, Vietnam to the east, and Cambodia to the south.
Area approximately 236,800 sq. km (91,400 sq. miles), dominated by the Mekong River, the 12th longest river in the world.
Population 5.8 million
Language Lao
Religion Theravada Buddhism
Time Zone 7 hours ahead of Greenwich Mean Time (GMT).
Currency kip (but US$ widely used).
Weights and Measures Metric.
Electricity 220 volts at 50Hz, using two-prong flat or round sockets. (adaptors available at major markets in Vientiane).
International Dialling Code 856

Climate

Laos has a tropical monsoon climate. During the summer months, moisture-laden air blows inland from the Indian Ocean and is known as the southwest monsoon, bringing the rainy season.

The rainy season lasts from around May or June to October, followed by a cooler dry season until February, and a hot and dry period in March and April. The average temperature is 28°C (83°F), but in April it can reach 38°C (100°F). In the mountains, temperatures are cold from December to around February, dropping to 15°C (60°F) or even lower. Relative humidity is fairly high, ranging from 90 percent down to 50 percent.

Rainfall varies according to region. The highest amount – 3,700 mm (146 in) annually – was recorded on the Bolaven Plateau in Champasak Province of Laos. Vientiane receives about 1,700 mm (67 in) annually, and Luang Prabang about 1,360 mm (53 in).

Geography

Laos is well endowed with rivers, including a 1,865-km (1,160-mile) portion of the Mekong River, which demarcates western borders with Burma and Thailand. While most of the river is navigable, the Khong Falls prevent direct access to the ocean. Still, cargo boats travel along the Mekong in Laos during most of the year.

In addition to commerce, the Mekong and its tributaries are important sources of fish, a primary source of protein. The alluvial plains and terraces of the Mekong River and its tributaries extend over only 20 percent of the country.

Mountains and plateaus blanket over 70 percent of Laos, leaving around 10 percent of the land suitable for agriculture. Forests cover over half of the country, making timber one of Laos' biggest exports; unfortunately, much of the forested land has decreased significantly since the 70s because of logging and slash-and-burn farming.

Mountains (up to 2,820 metres/9,250 ft high) have long posed impediments to both transport and communications. Those above 500 metres (1,600 ft) are characterised by steep terrain and confined river valleys. Mountains extend across most of Laos' north, except for the plain of Vientiane and the Plain of Jars, in Xiangkhoang Province. On the other hand, some of the southern provinces have large amounts of level land which is used for rice cultivation and livestock.

Economy

Rural and agricultural, Laos is among the world's poorest countries, with average annual income hovering around US$400. Agriculture accounts for a significant portion of both countries' gross domestic product and labour forces. Fishing and forestry are also major sources of revenue. Industrial manufacturing is almost non-existent at present.

The currency, while not convertible outside the country, has been allowed to float according to market forces, largely eliminating a once-thriving black market for the kip.

Business Hours

Normal working hours are 8am–noon and 1pm–4pm Monday to Friday. Government offices, including post offices are not open on Saturday morning. But travel agencies and airline offices open Saturday morning.

Government

The government of the Lao People's Democratic Republic replaced the monarchy of Royal Lao Government in 1975. The National Assembly oversees the judiciary and bureaucratic activities. The president is the head of state and is elected by the National Assembly for a five-year term. The Council of Ministers is the highest executive body and is chaired by the prime minister. The Lao People's Revolutionary Party (LPRP) is the only legal party.

Public Holidays

1 January New Year's Day
6 January Pathet Lao Day
20 January Army Day
8 March Women's Day
22 March People's Party Day
Mid April* Lao New Year
1 May Labour Day
21 May Visakha Puja Day
1 June Children's Day
13 August Lao Issara Day
23 August Liberation Day
7 October Teacher's Day
2 December Lao National Day
* Variable

Planning the Trip

Visas & Passports

To enter Laos you must have a valid passport. Citizens of all countries are also required to apply for an entry tourist visa, except as follows: Brunei Darussalam, Cambodia, Malaysia, Philippines, Singapore, Thailand and Vietnam.

Fifteen-day single-entry tourist visas are issued on arrival at Wattay International Airport in Vientiane, Luang Prabang International Airport, Pakse International Airport, and at the international border checkpoints.

You will need one passport photo and US$30 for the visa application. There is an "overtime" charge of US$1 for entry after 4pm and on weekends. Alternatively, 15- or 30-day tourist visas can be obtained in advance of your trip at a Lao embassy or consulate, or at travel agencies in any major city in Asia.

Visa extensions can be obtained from the Lao Immigration Office in Vientiane, opposite Tala at Sao (Morning Market), tel: 021-212 529. The cost is US$3 per day up to a maximum of 30 days. Tour agencies and guesthouses and some cafés can also arrange visa extensions for a small fee. Overstaying costs US$10 per day.

Customs

The duty-free allowance for each visitor is 1 litre of spirits, 2 litres of wine and 200 cigarettes, 50 cigars or 250g of tobacco.

Antique cultural items such as Buddha images cannot be exported. Officially, purchases of silver or copper items are subject to customs duty – based on their weight.

Health

Tapwater is unsafe for drinking, but purified bottled water is available everywhere. You should also avoid unpeeled fruit, salads and uncooked vegetables.

Malaria is prevalent in Laos, and if planning to travel outside the capital cities, you should take precautionary measures.

It is essential to arrange vaccinations and private medical insurance before departure.

Money Matters

The official currency, the kip, comes in denominations of 5,000, 2,000, 1,000, 500. There are no coins, and notes smaller than 500 have been rendered obsolete. The kip is not convertible outside Laos.

Most major currencies, as well as travellers' cheques in US dollars, pound sterling, and often euro, can be exchanged at banks and money changers in major towns. Credit cards are accepted at a few upmarket hotels, restaurants and shops in Vientiane and Luang Prabang. Cash advances can also be obtained on a VISA/MasterCard in Vientiane. There are some ATMs in Vientiane now, but they may not always be reliable.

What to Wear

Women visitors should avoid clothing that bares the thighs, shoulders or breasts; long trousers, walking shorts and skirts are acceptable, while tank tops, short skirts and running shorts are not. Both men and women should dress conservatively when making a visit to a temple or government office.

Whatever the season, bring lightweight cotton clothing and a light jacket or pullover for cool nights in December and January.

Getting There

BY AIR

There are three international airports in Laos: **Wattay**
International Airport in Vientiane, **Luang Prabang International Airport** in the old capital, and **Pakse International Airport** in Champasak Province. Vientiane is served by international flights from Thailand (Bangkok and Chiang Mai), Vietnam (Ho Chi Minh City and Hanoi), Cambodia (Phnom Penh and Siem Reap), China (Kunming) and Taiwan (Taipei). Most visitors travel via Bangkok, from which there are daily connections to Vientiane and Luang Prabang. It is also possible to fly to Luang Prabang from Chiang Mai.

Many travellers opt to fly from Bangkok to the northeastern Thai town of Udon Thani (for onward travel by road to Vientiane), or to Ubon Ratchathani (for onward travel by road to Pakse in southern Laos).

Lao Airlines (tel: 021-212 051–4; www.laoairlines.com) is the national carrier and provides regular services between Vientiane and several regional destinations. A US$10 airport tax applies for international flight departures from Laos.

BY LAND

There are at least 13 international border checkpoints with Laos. You can obtain a 15-day tourist visa-on-arrival (VOA) at these checkpoints, unless otherwise indicated. As visa regulations may change without prior notice, check with a Lao embassy or consulate, or with a reliable travel agent, before travelling.
From Thailand:
Nongkhai/Vientiane
Mukdahan/Savannakhet
Chiang Khong/Huay Xai
Chong Mek/Vang Tao
Nakhon Phanom/Tha Kaek
Nakasing/Nam Hong (no VOA)
Beung Kan/Paksan (no VOA)
From Vietnam:
Dong Ha/Lao Bao
Cau Treo/Kaew Neua
Nam Xoi/Na Maew
Nam Can/Nam Khan
From China:
Mengla/Boten
From Cambodia:
Voen Kham/Si Phan Don (no VOA)

Practical Tips

Media

The *Bangkok Post* and *The Nation* are both good Thai newspapers in English and are available in many shops and most hotels. International English-language newspapers, such as the *International Herald-Tribune*, *Asian Wall Street Journal*, or the *Financial Times* are often available in major hotels.

The local English-language publications include the weekly *Vientiane Times* and *Sayo*, a monthly business and lifestyle magazine.

Postal Services

The **General Post Office** (GPO) is on the corner of Thanon Khou Vieng and Lane Xang Avenue. It offers postal services and public telephones for local, national and international calls. There is no mail delivery service in Laos; mail is collected from the boxes at the GPO.

For urgent or important mail and packages, most expats use the **Express Mail Service (EMS)**.

Incoming parcels and packets must be inspected by a Customs official. All mail should use the official title of the country: Lao PDR, in preference to Laos.

Telecommunications

TELEPHONES

All major towns are linked by phone, and International Direct Dialling (IDD) is widely available.

International calls can be made at Lao Telecom offices (usually operator-assisted), post offices, or from public phones with IDD facility.

For the latter you will need to purchase a phone card, available at post and telecommunication offices and many shops throughout the country. Fax services are also available at most Lao Telecom offices and many post offices.

To call within the country, dial 0 first, then the provincial area code and number. For international calls, dial 00, the country code, then the area code and number.

MOBILE PHONES

Mobile phone coverage is surprisingly good throughout the country. In addition to Lao Telecom (Laotel; Call Centre tel: 101), a few other local service providers also offer mobile phone services. Visitors with GSM-enabled mobile phones can buy a starter kit from Tango (www.tangolao.com) for US$5, which consists of a SIM card with a local phone number and about 20,000 kip (about US$2) worth of stored value, from which international and local calls and text messages can be made. The credit can be topped up at outlets bearing the "Tango" sign.

Mobile phone numbers usually begin with the prefix 020.

INTERNET

Internet cafés are found all over town in Vientiane, Luang Prabang and Vang Vieng, which receive the highest numbers of travellers, and connections are very good. Costs

Tipping

Tipping is not expected in Laos, except at a few upmarket restaurants in Vientiane and Luang Prabang, where you might leave 10–15 percent if a service charge has not already been added to your bill. Taxi and *tuk-tuk* drivers also do not expect to be tipped, unless the trip was unusually difficult or much longer than originally expected.

are also low in these major towns because of stiff competition, and can be as cheap as 100 kip per minute (about US$0.10). In many of the other provinces, Internet facilities are becoming increasingly available and reliable, but costs are higher in places in which only one or two shops offer Internet-based services. Visual Internet telephony and PC-to-phone services are also well supported. In addition, stored-value pay-as-you-use Internet cards, for use with land lines, can be

Etiquette

The people of Laos are extremely polite and well mannered. Remember that local standards and expectations of efficiency and procedure can be very different from Western perceptions; do be patient.

The traditional form of greeting among Lao people is the *nop*: one's palms are placed together in a position of praying, at chest level, but not touching the body. The higher the hands, the greater the respect. This is accompanied by a slight bow to show respect. The *nop* is a greeting, thanks, expression of regret and goodbye.

As elsewhere in Southeast Asia, the head is thought to be the most sacred part of the body, the soles of the feet the lowliest.

Dress: Visitors should dress modestly, especially near and in pagodas, temples and public places. Shorts should not be worn when visiting pagodas and temples, and all footwear must be taken off when entering them.

Public displays of anger or discontent are considered a weakness and will garner no respect. Similarly, most traditional Asian customs also apply in Laos, including:
• don't touch people, including children, on the head
• don't point your foot at a person
• Buddha images are sacred objects and to be treated with the utmost respect.

purchased from Lao Telecom branches and at some Internet cafés and retail outlets.

Medical Treatment

Standards of healthcare are generally pretty dire by Western standards. But the following reasonable facilities are available in emergencies:
International Clinic, Mahosot Hospital, Setthathirat Road, tel: 021-214 022. Open daily 24 hours.
Australian Embassy Clinic, Phonsay Road, tel: 021-413 603, 511 462. Open Mon, Tues, Thurs, Fri 8.30am–noon and 2–5pm, and Wed 8.30am–noon.

Embassies

Australia: Nehru Street, Wat Phonsay area, Vientiane. Tel: 021-413 610, 413 815.
United States: Bartholomie Road, Ban That Dam, Vientiane. Tel: 021-213 966, 212 581/2.

Tourist Information

Lao National Tourism Authority
Lane Xang Avenue, tel: 021-212 248; www.tourismlaos.gov.la
This government-run tourism office can provide some good information about tours. It is also cooperating with local tour operators on ecotourism tours in the country. See also www.ecotourismlaos.com

Dielthelm Travel
www.diethelmtravel.com
Reputable agent with many years of experience in the region. Has offices in the following locations:
● **Vientiane**
Namphu Circle
Tel: 021-213 833
● **Luang Prabang**
47/2 Sisavangvong Road
Tel: 071-212 277

Useful Websites
www.visit-laos.com
www.laos-travel.net

Getting Around

By Air

Lao Airlines (tel: 021-212 051; www.laoairlines.com) flies to several domestic destinations, and its service has improved in recent years, though schedules still tend to be irregular and dependent on demand and on the weather and visibility. It is not uncommon for flights to be cancelled or delayed. Visitors are advised to confirm their flight reservation prior to travelling even if they have a confirmed ticket, and to arrive at the airport early. All domestic tickets must be purchased using US dollars. Thai baht and other major Western currencies are sometimes accepted, but the exchange rate is not favourable. Kip is not accepted.

The most popular routes are Vientiane–Luang Prabang, Vientiane–Pakse, and Vientiane–Xieng Khuang. The major routes are served by the newer, more reliable and comfortable ATR-725 planes, while the less popular routes are usually served by smaller Chinese-built aircraft.

There is an airport departure tax of 10,000 kip (about US$1) per passenger flying a domestic route.

By Boat

It is possible to take transport up and down the **Mekong River** year-round. Check with a travel agent for up-to-date information.

There are speedboats on the upper reaches of the Mekong that travel from Luang Prabang to northern Thailand, and even to the Chinese border. Bookings can be made in northern Thailand and Luang Prabang. Slow boats travel

the rest of the Mekong from Luang Prabang southward to the Cambodian border.

By Road

The road system in Laos has improved tremendously. The main highway, Route 13, originally built by the French during the colonial period, is now fully paved from Luang Prabang in the north to Savannakhet in the south. However, many roads remain in poor condition. Interprovincial transport by bus and truck is widely available, which makes it possible to visit at least part of every province in Laos.

Regular buses, many air-conditioned, ply Route 13 between Luang Prabang and Savannakhet. For more remote routes, pick-ups or trucks converted into passenger vehicles by the addition of two long wooden benches in the back (*songthaew*) are the most common forms of road transport.

Public Transport

For short trips in towns, stick to *tuk-tuks* and jumbos. The city bus system in Vientiane runs only between the centre of the city and outlying villages. Car taxis in Vientiane can be found in front of major hotels, the Morning Market and at the airport – always agree on the price before you set out.

Private Transport

Perhaps the best way to get around any town in Laos is to hire a bicycle, or, for more ambitious day trips, a motorcycle. Bicycles can be hired for the day from restaurants and guesthouses in towns throughout Laos, and motorcycles can be hired from dealers in Vientiane, Luang Prabang and Savannakhet. Cars, pick-ups and 4WD vehicles are available for hire from private operators in Vientiane.
Asia Vehicle Rental
354 Samsenthai Road, Vientiane
Tel: 021-217 493
www.avr.laopdr.com

Where to Stay

Choosing a Hotel

Accommodation in Laos has improved over the last few years but it is still limited. Good quality hotels are restricted to the capitals and a few major centres. Mid-level accommodation can be found in most areas and is usually quite comfortable. At the lower end, guesthouses are now becoming more common and some of them are really quite good. Hotels that charge more than US$20 per night will have rooms that are air-conditioned and equipped with satellite television and a refrigerator. Hot water is usually available even in the cheaper guesthouses.

Online hotel booking service is available at www.laos-hotel-link.com and www.laos-hotels.com.

Price Guide

A general guide for a standard double room, excluding taxes.
$$$$ = above US$100
$$$ = US$50–100
$$ = US$20–50
$ = under US$20

Hotel Listings

VIENTIANE

Don Chan Palace
6 Ban Piawat, off Fa Ngum Road
Tel: 021-244 288
Fax: 021-244 111
www.donchanpalacelaopdr.com
Located 10 minutes from the airport, this 14-storey five-star hotel commands good views of the Mekong River. All rooms have Internet access and cable TV.
$$$$

Lao Plaza Hotel
63 Samsenthai Road
Tel: 021-218 800
Fax: 021-218 808
www.laoplazahotel.com
Built by the Thai-owned Felix chain, this hotel is located in the centre of the city. Has all the services expected of an international-standard hotel, including a pool, fitness centre and Internet access. $$$$

Settha Palace Hotel
6 Pang Kham Street
Tel: 021-217 581
Fax: 021-217 583
www.setthapalace.com
Built at the turn of the century, this building was magnificently restored as a welcome addition to Vientiane's hotel scene and certainly the most elegant place to stay in town. Offers spacious rooms and suites with private terraces in a graceful colonial-era building. $$$$

Royal Dokmaideng Hotel
Lane Xang Avenue
Tel: 021-214 455
Fax: 021-214 454
www.dokmaidenghotel.laopdr.com
Near the Morning Market on Vientiane's main avenue, the Royal offers a Chinese restaurant and night club (with occasional traditional Lao music and dance performances), a swimming pool and fitness centre. $$$

Anou Hotel
3 Heng Boun Road
Tel: 021-213 360
Fax: 021-213 632
www.anouhotel.laopdr.com
Includes satellite television in all rooms and downstairs there's the Anou Cabaret. Also serves a good lunchtime buffet. $$

Day Inn Hotel
59/3 Pangkham Street
Tel: 021-223 847, 223 848
Fax: 021-222 984
e-mail: dayinn@laotel.com
Popular with UNDP staff on temporary stints in Vientiane, this refurbished colonial structure downtown has a refreshingly light and airy interior, large rooms and an excellent location. $$

Le Parasol Blanc Hotel
263 Sibounheuang Road
Tel: 021-215 090, 216 091
Fax: 021-222 290, 215 444
e-mail: vicogrp@laotel.com
Among the best in this category, the hotel has bungalow-style rooms with beautiful hardwood floors, satellite TV, a swimming pool and shaded garden. A bar and restaurant (with occasional live piano music) serves good French, Lao and Thai food in one of the more charming surroundings in town. $$

LUANG PRABANG

The Grand Luang Prabang
Baan Xiengkeo, Khet Sangkalok
Tel: 071-253 851
Fax: 071-253 027
www.grandluangprabang.com
This beautiful hotel is situated in the grounds of the old Xiengkeo Palace. The palace was once the home of Prince Phetsarath, Lao national hero. All rooms combine the best of the art deco style of the 1920s with modern amenities. $$$

La Residence Phou Vao
Phou Vao Road
Tel: 071-212 530
Fax: 071-212 534
www.pansea.com/laos
On a hilltop just outside Luang Prabang, this hotel was recently refurbished by Pansea, a French hotel company. It has an attractive ambience and a swimming pool. $$$

The Villa Santi Resort
Tel: 071-252 157
Fax: 071-252 158
www.villasantihotel.com
Managed by the same group as the well-known Villa Santi Hotel in Luang Prabang town, this resort 4km (2 miles) south of the town offers 55 charming rooms in a rural setting with mountain views. Also has a swimming pool. $$$

Tum Tum Cheng
50/1 Ban Xieng Thong
Tel: 071-253 262
www.tumtumcheng.com
Personable 10-room guesthouse with ensuite showers. A new guesthouse building with four equally well-furnished fan-cooled rooms, is just around the corner. Friendly husband-and-wife owners. $

Where to Eat

What to Eat

Lao cuisine, like that of neighbouring Southeast Asian countries, revolves around rice. This isn't the long grain rice that Vietnamese, Central Thai and most Westerners are used to eating, however, but *khao niaw*, or glutinous 'sticky rice', deftly rolled into a neat, small ball and eaten with the hand. In Vientiane, the Lao capital, as indeed in all other large towns, long grain rice or *khao jao* is readily available – but *khao niaw* remains the basic staple of the Lao people, and is the single most distinctive feature of Lao cuisine. Another essential is fish sauce or *naam paa*, which is the universal Lao condiment.

This sticky rice is generally accompanied by a selection of dips, parboiled vegetables, salad, soup and various curried meat dishes or fish dishes. The sticky rice is usually served in a woven bamboo container called a *tip khao*. Whilst sticky rice is eaten by hand, long grain rice is always eaten with a spoon and fork.

Popular Lao dishes include *tam som*, a spicy salad made of sliced green papaya mixed with chilli peppers, garlic, tomatoes, ground peanuts, field crab, lime juice and fish sauce. This is often eaten with sticky rice and *ping kai* or grilled chicken. Another standby is *laap*, a

Restaurant Price Guide

A general guide for dinner for two people excluding beverages:
\$\$\$ = above US\$20
\$\$ = US\$10–20
\$ = under US\$10

spicy dish of minced meat, poultry or fish mixed with lime juice, garlic, chilli pepper, onion and mint. Meats used in *laap* are generally cooked, but can also be raw. If you are concerned about this, ask for *laap suk*, or cooked *laap*.

Restaurant Listings

VIENTIANE

Bunmala
Khu Vieng Road
Tel: 021-313 249
Famous among Lao and expats alike for its excellent grilled chicken, duck and fish, papaya salad, sticky rice and fresh beer. **\$**

Dao Fa Bistro
Setthathirat Road
Tel: 021-215 651
Located next to Joma Bakery, this cheerful, modern restaurant serves homemade pasta, pizzas and a good variety of cocktails. **\$\$\$**

KhopChaiDeu Restaurant-Bar
54 Setthathirat Road, next to the Namphu Fountain
Tel/Fax: 021-251 564
www.khopchaideu.com
A lovely outdoor food garden in the grounds of an illuminated (and nicely dilapidated) two-storey French mansion, this place serves a wide range of food, including barbecue dishes, soups, salads and desserts, as well as an economical lunch buffet. In the evenings, a live band plays from 9 to 11pm. **\$\$**

Kua Lao
111 Samsenthai Road
Tel: 021-215 777
An upscale Lao restaurant – which you might say is an oxymoron – offering good Lao and Thai food in a beautiful French colonial mansion. Nightly traditional Lao music and dance performances. **\$\$**

L'Opera
Namphu Circle
Tel: 021-215 099
L'Opera offers excellent Italian food in a romantic setting. The charismatic Italian owner ensures that the service is impeccable and that his favourite opera music is always playing. The restaurant's takeout *gelati* bar is a highlight. **\$\$\$**

Namphu
Namphu Circle
Tel: 021-216 248
One of the oldest high-end establishments in town, the Namphu has a good bar and serves excellent French and German food, and some impressive desserts. Also has a few Lao specialities. **\$\$\$**

Santisouk Restaurant
Nokeo Khumman Road
Tel: 021-215 303
Has been around since the revolution days, and is known for its sizzling steak platters, good breakfasts, and retro atmosphere. Also serves Lao food. Probably the best value French restaurant in town. **\$**

LUANG PRABANG

Luang Prabang Bakery
Sisavangvong Road
Tel: 071-212 617
Café serving good salads, quiches, sandwiches and pastries. **\$\$**

Pak Huoy Mixay
Ban Wat Nong
Savang Vatthana Road
Tel: 071-212 260
Probably the best place in town for Lao specialities, this place serves excellent fresh fish from the Mekong; they also have a barbecue out on the terrace. **\$\$**

Restaurant l'Elephant
Ban Wat Nong
Tel: 071-252 482
An elegant French brasserie situated in the most picturesque part of the old city. A daytime tea salon and a variety of daily specials including vegetarian meals make this many visitors' favourite restaurant in Luang Prabang. **\$\$**

Tum Tum Cheng Restaurant and Cooking School
Sakkarine Road
Tel: 071-252 019
www.tumtumcheng.com
Tastefully decorated, this third Tum Tum Cheng branch in Luang Prabang serves well-prepared Lao and Lao–European food. Cooking classes are also held here; Chef Chandra will show you how to prepare Lao meals and select ingredients. **\$\$**

Getting Acquainted

The Place

Situation Cambodia is bordered by Vietnam, Thailand and Laos and opens into the Gulf of Thailand.
Area about 181,035 sq. km (69,900 sq. miles).
Population 13.7 million.
Language Khmer.
Religions Buddhism, Cham Islam, Christianity.
Time Zone 7 hours ahead of Greenwich Mean Time (GMT).
Currency riel (but US$ widely used).
Weights and Measures Metric.
Electricity 220 volts at 50Hz, using two flat or round-pin plugs (adaptors available at major markets in Phnom Penh). It is a good idea to bring along a torch with you, as temporary power outages are quite common.
International Dialling Codes 855

Climate

Cambodia's climate is based on the annual monsoon cycle. Between May and October the southwest monsoon carries heavy daily rainfall, usually for a few hours in the late afternoon. The northwest monsoon, between November and March, brings somewhat cooler temperatures and lower rainfall. The coolest months are between November and January, though even then temperatures rarely fall below 20° C (68° F). The driest months are January and February, when there is little or no rainfall, and the wettest months are usually September and October. The best time to visit is certainly during the cool season; April, which can be furnace-like, is best avoided.

Geography

Cambodia has 435 km (270 miles) of coastline, including extensive mangrove stands. The central plains cover three-quarters of Cambodia's land mass, while the remaining highlands are mostly densely forested and sparsely populated. About 20 percent of the land is used for agriculture. As with Laos, Cambodia's largest and most important river is the Mekong.

Economy

Rural and agricultural, Cambodia are among the world's poorest countries, with average annual income hovering around US$400. Agriculture accounts for a significant portion of both countries' gross domestic product and labour forces. Fishing and forestry are also major sources of revenue. Industrial manufacturing is not an important part of the economy at present.

Government

The Kingdom of Cambodia is a parliamentary monarchy. The king, who is elected, is the head of state and holds the throne, but he does not have legislative or judicial power. The National Assembly, the only organ to adopt laws, is elected by the people for five years and consists of at least 120 members. The Council of Ministers is the Royal Government and the executive body of the country, controlling the armed forces and in charge of the execution of national policy. It is accountable to the Assembly.

Public Holidays

7 January National Day
14–16 April Cambodian New Year
1 May Labour Day
12 May Vesak Day
13–15 May King's Birthday
31 October King-Father's Birthday
9 November Independence Day

Planning the Trip

Visas & Passports

Your passport should be valid for at least 6 months. An entry visa is also required for citizens of all countries except Malaysia, the Philippines, Singapore and Laos. Single-entry Cambodian tourist visas, valid for 30 days, are issued on arrival at Phnom Penh International Airport and Siem Reap–Angkor International Airport. For details, look up the Cambodian Immigration Department website (www.cambodia-immigration.com).

Tourist e-visas are also available for entry to the two airports. Apply online at http://evisa.mfaic.gov.kh.

Tourist visas can be extended only once, for 30 days, at the Department for Foreigners (Pochentong Road; tel: 012-581 558; e-mail: visa_info@online. com.kh). Some guesthouses and travel agencies in Phnom Penh will also handle visa extensions for a nominal fee. Overstaying your visa will set you back by US$5 per day.

Customs

You are allowed to import 200 cigarettes and 1 litre of alcohol duty-free into Cambodia. It is illegal to take antiquities out of the country.

Health

Tapwater is unsafe for drinking, but purified bottled water is available everywhere in Cambodia.

Malarial mosquitoes are widespread in the countryside, but as long as you are staying close to the tourist areas it should be fine.

As the standard of healthcare is relatively low, it is essential to arrange vaccinations and private medical insurance (preferably covering evacuation in an emergency) before departure.

Money Matters

The local currency is the riel, but the US dollar is widely accepted. For the sake of practicality, most locals are accustomed to rounding the rate down to 4,000 riel during transactions. Carry plenty of small-denomination US dollars; they are far easier to change than larger notes, and have some small riel notes (500 and 1,000) for minor purchases. All major currencies can be changed at the airports and upmarket hotels. Moneychangers can be found around the markets in towns.

Travellers' Cheques & Credit Cards

Travellers' cheques have become easier to encash in well-touristed areas such as Phnom Penh, Siem Reap and Sihanoukville, but they remain difficult to change elsewhere. US dollar cheques are preferable. Credit cards have also become more widely accepted. Most good hotels will accept Visa, JCB, MasterCard, and sometimes AMEX for hotel and restaurant payments. Cash advances on cards are possible in some banks in Phnom Penh, Siem Reap, Battambang and Sihanoukville. Most businesses charge a 2–4 percent fee for credit card usage.

What to Wear/Bring

Clothes should be light and loose, preferably cotton. Open shoes and sleeveless dresses for women or short-sleeved shirts for men are appropriate, but visitors should abide by local ideas of modesty when visiting pagodas, temples and official places. A sweater or sweatshirt is needed for nights. Lip balm and moisturisers are needed just about anytime, as are sunblock, sunglasses and hats. Tampons and sanitary towels can be difficult to obtain in smaller towns.

Getting There

BY AIR

Many international visitors arrive by air at the **Phnom Penh International Airport** or at **Siem Reap–Angkor International Airport**. For more information, call the airport information hotline, tel: 023-890 890, or look up www.cambodia-airports.com.

BY LAND

There are several points of entry into Cambodia by road. From Thailand, the most popular points of entry are at Poipet/Aranyaprathet, Cham Yeam/Hat Lek and O'Smach/Chong Jom.

From Vietnam, you can enter at Bavet/Moc Bai and Kham Samnor/Ving Xuong. From Laos, cross at Dom Kralor/Voeung Kam, but the situation sometimes changes, so check with your consulate or travel agent before travelling.

Tourist Information

Ministry of Tourism
The MOT has a useful website (www.mot.gov.kh) with travel information. Use it as a resource and deal with travel agents directly.

Dielthelm Travel (www.diethelm travel.com) is a reputable agent with many years of experience in the region.
● **Phnom Penh**
No. 65, Street 240
Tel: 023-219 151
● **Siem Reap/Angkor**
House No. 4,
Road No. 6, Phum Taphul
Tel: 023-57524

Useful Websites
The following websites provide useful travel information on travel in Cambodia:
www.visit-mekong.com
www.cambodian-online.com
www.tourismcambodia.com

Practical Tips

Media

The weekly *Phnom Penh Post* reports national news, while the *Cambodia Daily*, *Bangkok Post* and *International Herald Tribune* cover international events. *Cambodge Soir* is a daily newspaper published in French and English.

Postal Services

The main post office in Phnom Penh is located east of Wat Phnom on Street 13, tel: 023-426 832.

A number of international courier agencies are in Phnom Penh:
DHL, tel: 023-427 726
Fedex, tel: 023-216 708
TNT, tel: 023-424 022

Telecommunications

TELEPHONES

For international calls, dial the IDD access code 001 or 007, followed by the country code, then the area/network code and number. For calls within a province, simply dial the six-digit subscriber number. To call a number in another province, dial the provincial area code with the initial 0, followed by the subscriber number.

If calling from overseas, dial Cambodia's country code 855, followed by area/network code (omitting the initial 0) and the number you want.

PUBLIC PHONES

Many public phone booths take phonecards, which can be purchased at post offices and good hotels.

MOBILE PHONES

A most economical way of using your own GSM-enabled mobile phone in Cambodia is to purchase a local SIM card from Mobitel, Samart and Camshin. Mobile phone numbers begin with the prefix 012, 011, 015, 016, 018 or 092.

INTERNET

Internet access at Internet cafés is usually fast and relatively inexpensive. There are many such shops in the major tourist towns.

Medical Treatment

Good hospitals are few and far between in Cambodia, and only a limited range of medicines is available. For major ailments it would be best to go to Bangkok or Singapore.
Calmette Hospital, Monivong Boulevard, Phnom Penh; tel: 023-426 948.
International Dental Clinic, 193 Street 208; tel: 023-212 909.
International SOS Medical & Dental Clinic, 161 Street 51; tel: 023-216 911, mobile tel: 012-816 911.
Raffles Medical Centre, Sofitel Cambodiana, 313 Sisowath Quay, Office No. 3, Ground Floor, Phnom Penh; tel: 023-426 288.

Embassies

Australia/Canada: 11 Street 254, Phnom Penh. tel: 023-213 470.
UK: 27–29 Street 75, Phnom Penh, tel: 023-427 124.
United States: 16 Street 228, Phnom Penh, tel: 023-216 436.

Emergency Numbers

Police Tel: 117 or 023-924 484
Fire Tel: 118 or 023-786 693
Ambulance Tel: 119 or 023-724 891

Getting Around

On Arrival

PHNOM PENH INTERNATIONAL AIRPORT

The airport is 10 km (6 miles) from the centre of Phnom Penh and the journey into town takes around 20 minutes. The average fare to Phnom Penh centre is about US$7 by taxi or US$2 by moto.

SIEM REAP–ANGKOR INTERNATIONAL AIRPORT

The airport is located about 8 km (5 miles) from town. The journey by taxi or moto will take 10–15 minutes. Most hotels and some of the better guesthouses provide airport transfers for guests.

By Air

Siem Reap Airways (www.siemreap airways.com), **Royal Phnom Penh Airways** and **Progress Multitrade Air** (www.pmtair.com) serve Siem Reap, Sihanoukville, Rattanakiri, Mondulkiri, Koh Kong and other cities. Routes and timetables change frequently; check www.cambodia-airports.com. For foreigners, a domestic airport tax of US$6 is levied.

By Boat

Air-conditioned boats ply between Phnom Penh and Siem Reap. The journey takes around 6 hours and usually begins at 7am.
With the improvement of the roads between two cities, however, this mode of transport is fast losing its popularity to air-conditioned

buses, which are cheaper, more comfortable and far quicker.

By Road

Several air-conditioned bus services ply between Phnom Penh and various destinations, including Siem Reap, Sihanoukville, Kampot/Kep, Battambang, Kompong Cham, Kratie and Poipet.
Shorter trips to places such as Udong or Kompong Chhnang can also easily be made by air-conditioned buses. Many bus services depart from the bus terminal near the Central Market.

Public Transport

In Phnom Penh the "cyclo" or pedicab costs a little less than a moto, but is not as quick. Cyclos can be hired by the hour or by the day and are a great way to see the sights (not applicable to Angkor). Agree on a price in advance.
Because car taxis are sometimes hard to find, motorcycle taxis, or "motos", are the best way to get somewhere quickly. Expect to pay 3,000 riel to US$1 for a short journey and US$2 for longer ones. Always agree on the fare beforehand.
Air-conditioned taxis are readily available at the airports. Within Phnom Penh city, they may be hard to find. In Siem Reap, there are plenty of taxis willing to take you around the temples at Angkor for about US$30 for a full day. You may have to pay up to double that to visit the temples further afield.
Share taxis ply between Phnom Penh and all the major towns. The drivers may wait until they have filled the vehicle, sometimes taking up to six or seven passengers, so this is not always comfortable.

Private Transport

Tourists are not allowed to drive their own cars in Phnom Penh and Siem Reap, and must hire a driver. Motorcycle rental is allowed in Phnom Penh, however.
In Sihanoukville, car and motorcycle rentals are permitted.

Where to Stay

Choosing a Hotel

Good accommodation in Cambodia is limited to a few major centres: Phnom Penh, Siem Reap, Sihanoukville (Kompong Som) and Battambang. Phnom Penh offers luxury accommodation at very reasonable prices. Mid-level accommodation options are abundant and are usually quite comfortable. At the lower end, guesthouses are common, and some of them are excellent. A useful hotel booking service is available at www.cambodia-hotels.com.

Price Guide

A general guide for a standard double room, excluding taxes.
$$$$ = above US$100
$$$ = US$50–100
$$ = US$20–50
$ = under US$20

Hotel Listings

PHNOM PENH

Hotel Cambodiana
313 Sisowath Quay
Tel: 023-426 288
Fax: 023-426 290
www.hotelcambodiana.com
A splendid hotel, overlooking the confluence of the Sap, Bassac and Mekong rivers. Contains all the amenities of a top modern hotel. **$$$$**

InterContinental
Regency Square, 296 Mao Tse Toung Boulevard (Issarak Street)
Tel: 023-424 888
Fax: 023-424 885

www.ichotelsgroup.com
A five-star hotel with all the amenities of this world-wide chain. Good business facilities and one of the best Cantonese restaurants in Phnom Penh. **$$$$**

Raffles Hotel Le Royal
92 Rukhak Vithei Daun Penh (off Monivong Boulevard)
Tel: 023-981 888
Fax: 023-981 168
www.phnompenh.raffles.com
Established in 1929 this is a luxury hotel with a history. It has seen a succession of foreign guests including all the top journalists of the Vietnam War and also UN aid workers after the defeat of the Khmer Rouge. All rooms are decorated with traditional Cambodian folk art. **$$$$**

FCC Hotel Phnom Penh
363 Sisowath Quay
Tel: 023-724 014
www.fcccambodia.com
The FCC Hotel has spacious, well-appointed rooms, with verandas overlooking the river. **$$$**

Sunway
1 Street 92, near Wat Phnom
Tel: 023-430 333
Fax: 023-430 339
www.sunway.com.kh
At the heart of old colonial Phnom Penh. Facilities include Jacuzzi, swimming pool and sauna. **$$$**

Goldiana Hotel
10–12 Street 280
Tel: 023-727 085
www.goldiana.com
Excellent mid-range hotel with a fitness centre and swimming pool. **$$**

Renakse Hotel
40 Sothearos Boulevard
Tel: 023-215 701
Fax: 023-722 457
e-mail: renakse-htl@camnet.com.kh
Beautiful French colonial-style hotel located opposite the Royal Palace and close to the riverfront. **$$**

SIEM REAP

Raffles Grand Hotel D'Angkor
1 Vithei Charles de Gaulle
Tel: 063-963 888
Fax: 063-963 168

www.siemreap.raffles.com
This fabulous hotel sits in the centre of Siem Reap opposite King Sihanouk's villa. It was completely refurbished by the Raffles Group and can rightly claim to be one of Southeast Asia's grandest hotels. **$$$$**

Angkor Hotel
Street 6, Phum Sala Kanseng
Tel: 063-964 301
Fax: 063-964 302
www.angkor-hotel-cambodia.com
A resort-style four-star hotel with swimming pool and well located for the Angkor complex. **$$$**

La Residence d'Angkor
River Road
Tel: 063-963 390
Fax: 063-963 911
www.pansea-angkor.com
The French Pansea group specialises in unique properties in historical sites such as Angkor Wat and Luang Prabang, Laos. All rooms are beautifully decorated in teak wood and Khmer cotton. The gardens surround a free-form swimming pool with a fountain. **$$$**

Shinta Mani
Om Khum Street and Street 41
Tel: 063-761 998
Fax: 063-761 999
www.shintamani.com
Charming 18-room property, ideally located in the French quarter in the centre of Siem Reap. Facilities include a spa, swimming pool and restaurant. **$$$**

Sofitel Royal Angkor Golf and Spa Resort
Angkor Wat Road
Tel: 063-964 600
Fax: 063-964 610
www.sofitel.com
A modern low-rise with a cool airy feel. A bit out of town. Beautiful garden and pools plus a variety of restaurants, a bar and an 18-hole golf course. **$$$**

La Noria
Achasvar Street
Tel: 063-984 242
Fax: 063-964 243
www.angkor-lanoria.com
Small but cool and quiet cottages with terraces set in a garden. Amenities include a restaurant and massage centre. **$$**

Where to Eat

What to Eat

Cambodian food draws heavily on the traditions of both its Thai neighbours and Chinese residents. Often referred to as Thai food but without the spiciness. The main national staple is of course rice, but French colonial influence has dictated that the Cambodians eat more bread than any other Southeast Asian country. Because of the country's vast waterways, freshwater fish and prawns are especially popular. Beef, pork, chicken and duck are widely available. Visitors up country will generally find only Cambodian cuisine or eateries serving only the fairly ubiquitous baguette and paté. In towns of any size Chinese food will also be available. In the west of the country Thai food is widespread. Similarly in the east Vietnamese influence is common.

Restaurant Price Guide

A general guide for dinner for two people excluding beverages:
$$$ = above US$20
$$ = US$10–20
$ = under US$10

Restaurant Listings

PHNOM PENH

Baan Thai
2 Street 306 (off Norodom Blvd)
Tel: 023-362 991
A popular restaurant with a good selection of high-quality Thai and Khmer food in a Cambodian-style wooden house. Seating is Thai style, on cushions around low tables. **$$**
Eid Restaurant
327 Sisowath Quay

Tel: 023-367 614
Serves some very good Khmer dishes as well as special Thai dishes prepared by a Thai cook. **$**
Foreign Correspondents Club of Cambodia
363 Sisowath Quay
Tel: 023-210 142
Great setting overlooking the confluence of the rivers. In the early evenings watch the fishermen on the Sap River. Draught beer available and always an interesting international menu. **$$**
Friends
215 Street 13, near the National Museum
Tel: 023-426 748
www.streetfriends.org
This cosy non-profit tapas restaurant is run as part of a programme to teach former street youth useful skills. Very good snacks, salads and fruit shakes, as well as good service at reasonable prices. **$$**
La Croisette
241 Sisowath Quay (Riverfront)
Mobile tel: 012-876 032
Another great riverside location with the emphasis on charcoal grilling. One of the house specialities is "Beef Skewers A La Corsaire", they also serve good breakfasts. **$$**
Malis
136 Norodom Boulevard
Tel: 023-221 022
A highly regarded restaurant with artfully prepared traditional or contemporary Khmer dishes by renowned Cambodian chef Luu Meng, and a full bar with an extensive wine list. Elegant dining environment, either indoors or outdoors in the terrace garden. **$$**
Ponlok
232 Sisowath Quay
Tel: 023-426 051
Overlooks the Sap River. There are two air-conditioned floors and a terrace. An extensive menu with many Khmer specialities. **$$**
Tamarind Bar
31 Street 240
Mobile tel: 012-830 139
An old favourite serving French and Mediterranean dishes in a French colonial building. Choice of indoor, sidewalk or rooftop seating. **$$$**

Veiyo Tonle
237 Sisowath Quay
Mobile tel: 012-847 419
A selection of Khmer dishes plus an array of pizza and pasta dishes. Also some other international favourites on the menu. Overlooks the Sap River. **$$**

SIEM REAP

Abacus
Oum Khun Street
Mobile tel: 012-644 286
Occupying a traditional two-storey Cambodian house, this restaurant and bar serves international cuisine with a good wine selection. Indoor, garden and balcony seating is available. **$$**
The Blue Pumpkin
Old Market area
Tel: 063-963 574
Hugely popular place for its excellent pastas, salads, breads and freshly made ice cream. **$$**
Dead Fish Tower
Sivatha Boulevard
Mobile tel: 012-630 377
Its architecture is as playful as its name suggests. This cool restaurant offers good Khmer and Thai food, and traditional Cambodian music and dance performances at lunch and dinner. **$$**
FCC Angkor
Pokambor Street
Tel: 063-760 283
The sister restaurant of Phnom Penh's famous FCCC. Amid a refined atmosphere, choose from an extensive menu of international and local dishes, and a full bar. **$$**
Little India
Near Old Market, opposite Blue Pumpkin
Mobile tel: 012-652 398
Siem Reap's oldest and best Indian restaurant. Try its delicious homemade breads. **$**
The Red Piano
Near the Old Market
Tel: 063-964 750
One of the most popular places in town for Western and Asian food, and its extensive wine list. Its Guesthouse nearby has stylish rooms with small verandas. **$$**

Getting Acquainted

The Place

Situation A thin 1,600-km strip extending from China down to the Gulf of Thailand.
Area 329,556 sq. km (127,242 sq. miles).
Terrain Variable, from low mountains to the mangrove swamps of the Mekong Delta. 75 percent of the country is mountainous; it has a 3,200-km (1,990-mile) coastline.
Population 83.6 million, one-third of whom are under 15.
Capital Hanoi
Language Vietnamese
Religion Buddhism with Confucian/Taoist influences, Christianity.
Ethnic origins Over 85 percent of the population are Vietnamese (known as Viet or Kinh); 1.7 million Chinese (Hoa); around 140,000 Chams (in the central and south provinces); 1.06 million Khmers (in the south), and over 1.5 million Montagnards (hill tribes in the north and central highlands).
Time zone 7 hours ahead of GMT, so New York is 12 hours, Los Angeles 15 and London 7 hours behind, Australia 3 hours ahead. Note: the sun sets around 5.30pm in winter and 8pm in summer.
Currency Dong (pronounced *dome*).
Weights and Measures Metric
Electricity Mainly 220 volts. Protect your electronic equipment against power surges.
International Dialling Code 84

Economy

Vietnam is essentially an agricultural country, with rice cultivation accounting for 45 percent of the GNP and employing over half of the population. Other

Business Hours

Offices and public services generally open from around 7.30 or 8am and close for lunch at around 11.30pm or noon, opening again around 1.30 or 2pm until 4.30 or 5pm Monday to Friday.
Banks 8am to 4pm Monday to Friday and closed on Saturday and Sunday in Hanoi and Ho Chi Minh City. Banks close for lunch in other cities from 11.30am to 1pm.
Shops are open from 8.30am until late in the evening seven days a week.
Food markets generally close around 5pm.

major crops include tea, coffee, maize, bananas, manioc, cotton, tobacco, coconut and rubber.

Industry represents 32 percent of the country's GNP and occupies 11 percent of the active population. Electricity, steel, cement, cotton fabrics, fish sauce, sea fish, wood, paper and the growing oil exploration and production industry represent Vietnam's major areas of industrial production.

Ho Chi Minh City now has a small oil refinery and has become Vietnam's economic capital, accounting for 30 percent of the national industrial production.

Vietnam's standard of living ranks among the lowest in Southeast Asia. Decades of war had left Vietnam in poor economic shape, but reforms in 1986 stimulated a period of rapid economic growth.

Despite the regional economic crisis in 1997–8, Vietnam's growth has steadily increased at about 6–9 percent per year. The "Miracle of Rice" resulted because of these reforms: from being a rice importer in the mid 1980s, Vietnam became a rice exporter in the early 1990s.

In an effort to revive the ailing economy the country has opened its doors to encourage foreign investment and tourism, while further reform policies have been geared to re-establishing a market economy and encouraging

production in the private sector, agriculture and light industry.

Government

Vietnam has been a socialist republic run by a three-person collective leadership, consisting of the Communist Party general secretary, the prime minister and the president, since the liberation of Saigon in 1975 and the country's subsequent reunification in 1976. Vietnam continues to be organised politically along orthodox communist lines, and the Communist Party is still the dominant political force. Vietnam's domestic policy is shaped primarily by the party and its Secretary General. The Prime Minister presides over drafting of laws and day-to-day governing. The President oversees state policy, the military and police.

The government is nominated by the National Assembly, proposed by the party and theoretically elected by the people.

Climate

Vietnam has a monsoon climate. The south's dry season runs from December to May, with rains May to November. Temperatures rarely fall below 20°C (68°F). The centre is cooler. Along the coast, the "dry" season is March to August, but can be fairly wet. The north's dry season is October to December. The summer months tend to be hot and sticky, with temperatures up to 40°C (104°F). Hanoi's average is 30°C (86°F).

Public Holidays

The most important holiday is Tet, or Lunar New Year (late January/early February). It usually lasts for four days although the preparations begin weeks before, and the effects are felt for weeks after.
Other public holidays include:
1 January New Year's Day
30 April Liberation of Saigon
1 May International Labour Day
2 September National Day

Planning the Trip

Visas & Passports

It used to be incredibly difficult for independent travellers to gain entry to Vietnam, but today it is fairly straightforward. It is possible to get a one-month single entry tourist visa for US$30 in two working days from travel agents in Bangkok or Hong Kong. A 30-day multiple entry visa is about $50. Bangkok is definitely one of the best places in Asia to pick one up and many travel agents offer attractive round-trip flight and visa packages.

Six-month business visas require that your sponsor in Vietnam submit a request to the Ministry of the Interior. This process can take weeks, so make sure you get a head start.

Visa-on-arrival is a misnomer as you must receive approval before you board the plane. You then receive the visa at the border. This is useful if your country does not have a Vietnamese embassy or consulate but is time consuming when you arrive.

You cannot enter Vietnam without a visa but it is easy to obtain an extension in Vietnam. Most tour companies can facilitate this for a fee, however visa policies are continually changing so check early if you need an extension.

Overseas Vietnamese may be granted extensions for as long as six months, but family reasons must be proven. Visa extensions may also be granted for foreigners working in joint-venture offices, foreign representative offices and who have proper visas.

You will be given a copy of your landing card on arrival. This must be handed back at departure.

Customs

When you arrive you have to fill in a form declaring your valuables, including cameras and video cameras. You keep a photocopy of this form to show to Customs on your departure, so it's worth declaring as much as you can just in case you lose your luggage or Customs question anything as you leave. Visitors are allowed to import 400 cigarettes and 1.5 litres of alcohol duty free.

Export of anything of "cultural or historical significance" is forbidden. So if you buy antiques you must apply for an export license, and if you want to take any fakes home it's worth getting them cleared as fakes by the ministry so there is no hassle at Customs.

Health

The only vaccination required is for yellow fever, for travellers coming from Africa. Immunisation against hepatitis (A & B), Japanese encephalitis and tetanus are strongly urged. It is a good idea to consult a doctor a month to six weeks before departing to leave enough time to get the injections.

Malaria is widespread in Vietnam, especially in the Central Highlands and the Mekong Delta. The best protection is prevention. Always sleep under a mosquito net when visiting rural areas, use a strong repellent and wear long sleeves and trousers from dusk to dawn. Mosquitoes in several areas are resistant to many brands of anti-malaria drugs, so seek advice on medication from a tropical institute before you leave.

Do not drink tap water unless it has been boiled and avoid ice in drinks, especially in the country. Imported bottled water is available in most cities, but beware of bottles that are refilled with tap water.

Caution should be taken when eating, because food is often not prepared in sanitary conditions. Doctors advise abstaining from shellfish, especially shrimps. Fruit and vegetables should be peeled before eating; cooking them is a better idea. Avoid mayonnaise and raw eggs, raw vegetables like the herbs and lettuce served with *pho*, the noodle soup, and spring rolls. Eat in restaurants that are crowded. Because most places do not have refrigeration, eat at places where you know food will not be spoilt – if it is crowded, it is a good sign.

Should you have an accident or an emergency health problem in Vietnam, you may want to consider evacuation to Singapore or Bangkok for treatment. Vietnam has no shortage of well trained doctors, but hospital services and supplies are in very short supply. It is essential to take out private medical insurance before you leave.

Money Matters

The dong (pronounced *dome*) currently circulates in bank notes of 500,000, 100,000, 50,000, 20,000, 10,000 and banknotes and coins of 5,000, 2,000, 1,000, 500 and 200 denominations. The 100 dong banknote is quickly disappearing from use. The larger notes are now made of polymer plastic ensuring a longer life span and fewer copies. Care should be taken when exchanging money or receiving change. The 20,000 dong notes and 5,000 notes (both widely used) are the same size and colour (blue) and easily confused.

Vietnam's black market for US dollars isn't what it used to be. The difference between the street rate and the bank rate is very small – if any. Changing money on the street is foolish. Because the dong notes are so similar, you can easily be given the wrong denomination. As the old saying goes, you get what you pay for. Better to stick to a bank or currency exchange booth, of which there are many in all the major cities.

After banking hours, it is possible to change dollars at almost any jewellery or gold shop; sometimes the rate is higher than the bank rate. Look for the shops with a sign *vang* (gold). They are easily identifiable because their signs usually have bright gold-coloured letters.

Dong or Dollars?

Although the government issued a decree that all transactions be conducted in Vietnamese dong, in reality the country still uses a dual-currency system. That is, most purchases can be made in US dollars as well as Vietnamese dong. However, often shops, restaurants and taxi drivers insist on a lower exchange rate when using dollars – such as 15,000 dong to US$1 instead of the current rate of exchange (about 15,980 dong to US$1). To avoid haggling, it is better to carry some Vietnamese dong with you.

One other potential problem is the quality of the notes. Although Vietnamese dong notes are often ripped, faded and crumpled, Vietnamese are reluctant to accept US dollars that are not crisp and new. Before taking US dollars from a bank, you should inspect them to make sure they have no stray marks or tears, or appear old.

Note: the Vietnamese currency is not convertible so you cannot legally bring in or take out dong as a foreigner.

Be prepared to be offered two exchange rates: one for denominations of 50 and 100 USD, a lower rate for smaller denominations. It is better to change larger bills.

Some banks will also exchange Vietnamese dong for other currencies: French francs, German marks, Japanese yen, Australian dollars, for example. But gold shops will not. Better to bring US dollars. Traveller's checks in US dollars are accepted in most banks and in major hotels, but not in shops and smaller hotels and restaurants.

Major credit cards are accepted. Sometimes a high commission – 3 percent is standard – is charged when using them, however. Cash advances can be collected from major credit cards (again with the 3 percent commission) from major banks, including Vietcombank. ATMs can be found in all major cities.

When you arrive in Vietnam, the Customs form requires you to note currency brought into the country if it is worth more than 3,000 US dollars. However, visitors no longer have to account for money exchanged or spent during trips.

What to Wear/Bring

The main thing to consider is the weather, as it can be freezing cold in the mountainous north and at the same time hot and humid on the Central Coast. If you are travelling in the north or the Central Highlands during the winter months definitely bring jeans and a warm coat or sweater. It seems that it is always raining somewhere in Vietnam, so bring lightweight rain gear. Sunblock, sunglasses and hat are also essential.

In the hot months, dress cool but conservatively. Many Vietnamese cannot understand why foreigners insist on wearing shorts and sleeveless tops when they have the money to dress well. For them, appearance is very important, so if you are dealing with an official of any rank make sure you are dressed appropriately.

Imported pharmaceutical drugs are widely available in Hanoi and Ho Chi Minh City, but it is best to bring a small supply of medicine to cope with diarrhoea, dysentery, eye infections, insect bites, fungal infections, and the common cold.

The market economy has blossomed in Hanoi and Ho Chi Minh City so don't worry about running out of something; supermarkets (*sieu thi*) have arrived.

Getting There

BY AIR

The easiest way to get to Vietnam is by air. Hanoi's **Noi Bai Airport** is served by direct flights from Bangkok, Beijing, Berlin, Dubai, Frankfurt, Guangzhou, Hong Kong, Kuala Lumpur, Kunming, Moscow, Paris, Phnom Penh, Seoul, Siem Reap, Singapore, Sydney, Taipei, Tokyo and Vientiane.

Ho Chi Minh City's **Tan Son Nhat Airport** is connected via international flights to Bangkok, Beijing, Busan, Dubai, Frankfurt, Guangzhou, Hong Kong, Kaohsiung, Kuala Lumpur, Macau, Manila, Melbourne, Moscow, Nagoya, Osaka, Paris, Phnom Penh, Seoul, Singapore, Sydney, Taipei, Tokyo, Vienna, Vientiane and Zurich.

There are also direct flights to Danang from Bangkok, Hong Kong and Singapore.

Passengers leaving Vietnam on international flights must pay a departure tax of US$12 (Ho Chi Minh City) and US$14 (Hanoi).

BY SEA

Cruise ships sometimes make stops in Ho Chi Minh City, Ha Long and Hai Phong and Danang as part of South China Sea cruises, but there is no regular service. Anyone considering arriving by sea on a freighter or private vessel should contact the Hanoi immigration office directly to receive authorisation. It is possible to take a ferry from Cambodia at Vinh Xuong (30 km north of Chau Doc) border crossing in the Mekong Delta to Vietnam. There is also a ferry from Ha Long City to Beihai in China.

BY ROAD

It is also possible to enter Vietnam from China (and vice versa) at Dong Da (near Lang Son) and Lao Cai (by road and rail), and Mong Cai (by road only) border crossings.

It's now easy to cross from Laos to Hue or Vinh by the Lao Bao border crossing. It is also possible to enter from Vientiane via Cau Treo and travel on to Hanoi. Frequent minibuses service the Moc Bai border crossing from Ho Chi Minh City to Phnom Penh, Cambodia. Travellers can also enter via Vinh Xuong, located about 30 km (18 miles) north of Chau Doc.

Practical Tips

Media

Outside Hanoi and Ho Chi Minh City, getting your hands on accurate news in Vietnam can be difficult.

Foreign newspapers, including the *International Herald Tribune*, *Bangkok Post*, *The Nation* (from Bangkok), and *The Asian Wall Street Journal* can be purchased in Hanoi and Ho Chi Minh City. Usually you can buy the same day's paper in Ho Chi Minh City and Hanoi.

News magazines such as *Newsweek*, *Time*, *The Economist* and the *Far Eastern Economic Review* are also sold. French newspapers and magazines are readily available, and there are some English-language Vietnamese publications as well. *Vietnam Discovery*, *Vietnam Economic Times* (The Guide), *Vietnam Investment Review* (Timeout) and *Vietnam Heritage Magazine* (Vietnam Airlines in-flight magazine) all have tourist information, maps and listings of restaurants, hotels and services. The daily *Vietnam News*, published in Hanoi, contains official news from the Vietnam News Agency (a government-run service), stories

Tipping & Bargaining

Tipping is not expected, although small gratuities are always welcome. But bargaining is usual (except in department stores and large hotels and restaurants). The impoverished Vietnamese see tourists as fair game for making a dong or two. The rule of thumb is stay friendly and if you reach stalemate remember you're probably haggling over a few cents.

from Reuters, reprints of articles from Vietnamese newspapers, some foreign news and sports scores. News about Vietnam itself tends to be sanitised.

Postal Services

Post offices are open every day from 7am to 8pm. Every city, town and village has one of some sort, and the domestic service is remarkably reliable and fast (unlike for overseas mail). Within the country, mail reaches its destination within three days, sometimes faster. There is also an express mail service for overnight delivery.

Post offices are located at:
Ha Long City Vuon Dao crossroads
Hanoi 75 Dinh Tien Hoang.
Tel: 04-825 2730.
Ho Chi Minh City 2 Cong Xa Paris.
Tel: 08-823 2541.
Hue 8 Hoang Hoa Tham.

COURIER SERVICES

A number of international courier agencies have offices in Vietnam:
DHL, tel: 04-775 3999 (Hanoi), 08-844 6203 (HCMC)
Fedex, tel: 04-8249 054 (Hanoi), 08-8119 055 (HCMC)
UPS, tel: 04-514 2888 (Hanoi), 08-997 2888 (HCMC)

Telecommunications

TELEPHONES

International telephone connections are quite clear from Vietnam but the cost of calling overseas still ranks among the highest in the world. Direct calls can be placed from hotels, post offices and residences. Reverse charges are not allowed for foreigners, however. Expect to pay

Emergency Numbers

- **Fire** 114
- **Information** 1080
- **Medical aid** 115
- **Police** 13

up to US$3 a minute to call the United States, Europe, or Australia. Hotels will add a surcharge that can make calls about US$5 a minute.

When calling a city in Vietnam from overseas, dial the country code 84, followed by the area code but drop the prefix zero. When making a domestic call from one province or city to another in Vietnam, dial the area code first (including the prefix zero). Note: local calls within the same province/city do not require the area code. Many Internet cafés now have Internet-assisted calls at very low rates.

MOBILE PHONES

Most mobile phone users with a roaming facility will be able to hook up with the GSM 900/1800 network that Vietnam uses. The exceptions are users from Japan and the North America (unless they have a tri-band phone). Check with your service provider before leaving.

To save on mobile phone charges, consider using a local prepaid SIM card which will give you a local number to use in Vietnam. These are available at the main post offices and mobile phone shops.

Mobile phone numbers in Vietnam begin with the prefix 090, 091, 095, 098.

INTERNET

Internet cafés abound in Ho Chi Minh City and Hanoi, and costs range from 100–500 dong a minute. Most big hotels in both cities also provide Internet and e-mail services (although fees are much higher than at the cafés). Post offices are another place where you will find public Internet access.

Medical Treatment

HOSPITALS

Medical facilities have dramatically improved in the past few years, especially in the larger cities.

Hanoi
Vietnamese French Hospital, 1 Phuong Mai Street, tel: 04-574 0740, emergencies tel: 04-574 1111; www.hfh.com.vn.

Ho Chi Minh City
Cho Ray Hospital, 201 Nguyen Chi Thanh Street, tel: 08-855 4137.

Ha Long City
Ha Long City Hospital, Gieng Day Area, tel: 033-846 566.

Hai Phong
Hai Phong Viet Tiep Hospital, Nha Thuong, tel: 031-832 721.

Hue
Hue General Hospital, 16D Le Loi, tel: 054-822 325.

MEDICAL CLINICS

Foreign doctors run outpatient clinics, which are probably the best alternative to hospitals for medical care. The ones recommended below are affiliated to emergency evacuation companies:

Hanoi
International SOS, 31 Hai Ba Trung, tel: 04-934 0555 (24 hours); www.internationalsos.com.

Ho Chi Minh City
HCMC Family Medical Practice, 34 Le Duan St. Dist. 1, tel: 08-822 7848 (24 hours); e-mail: hcmc@vietnammedicalpractice.com.

Ha Long City
Medical Clinic, Ha Long Road, tel: 033-846 584.

Hue
Medical Clinic, 73 Dien Bien Phu, tel: 054-746 046.

Tourist Information

Vietnam's tourism industry lags behind other Asian countries. Even in the capital, you won't find official tourist information kiosks giving out impartial free information. The official representative and responsibility for Vietnam's tourism comes under the government-run **Vietnam National Administration of Tourism** (VNAT; www.vietnamtourism.com), which is more involved in new hotels and infrastructure investments than in providing tourist services. State-run "tourist offices" under the VNAT (or local provincial organisations) are merely tour agents who are out to make money and are not geared to Western requirements. For tours and information, go to private-run tour agencies *(see below)*.

Hanoi tourist information, maps and listings are found in English-language magazines: *Vietnam Discovery*, *Vietnam Pathfinder*, *The Guide* (*Vietnam Economic Times* supplement), *Time Out* (*Vietnam Investment Review* supplement) and *Vietnam Heritage* (Vietnam Airlines in-flight magazine).

Call **1080** for a state-run, telephone information service – with English-speaking staff.

Hanoi
Buffalo Tours, 9–13 Hang Muoi; tel: 04-828 0702; www.buffalotours.com

Embassies and Consulates

Australia: 8 Dao Tan Street, Hanoi, tel: 04-831 7755; 5-B Ton Duc Thang, Dist. 1, PO Box 659, CPO Ho Chi Minh City, tel: 08-829 6035; www.vietnam.embassy.gov.au
Canada
31 Hung Vuong, Hanoi, tel: 04-734 5000; 235 Dong Khoi, Dist. 1, Ho Chi Minh City, tel: 08-827 9899; www.vietnam.gc.ca
New Zealand
63 Ly Thai To, Hanoi. tel: 04-824 1481, www.mfat.govt.nz
United Kingdom
31 Hai Ba Trung, Hanoi, tel: 04-936 0500; 25 Le Duan, Dist. 1, Ho Chi Minh City, tel: 08-829 8433; www.uk-vietnam.org
United States
7 Lang Ha. Hanoi, tel: 04-772 1500; 4 Le Duan, Dist. 1, Ho Chi Minh City, tel: 08-822 9433; http://hanoi.usembassy.gov

Handspan Adventure Travel, 80 Ma May, tel: 04-926 0589; www.handspan.com
Sinh Café, 25 Hang Be Street, tel: 04-836 4212; www.sinhcafevn.com.

Ho Chi Minh City
Exotissimo Travel, Saigon Trade Centre; tel: 08-825 1723; www.exotissimo.com
Sinhbalo, 283/20 Pham Ngu Lao, Dist. 1; tel: 08-837 6765; www.sinhbalo.com

Crime & Security

In general, Vietnam is a very safe country to travel in and violent crimes against foreigners are rare. However, there are dangers. In Ho Chi Minh City and Nha Trang, tourists are increasingly becoming the victims of pickpockets, snatch-and-grab thieves, and hotel burglars. Always leave valuables in a hotel safe, and when you must carry cash, put it in a money belt inside your clothes. When walking or travelling in a cyclo, keep one hand firmly on handbags and cameras.

Vietnamese police can be less than friendly. Corruption among them is commonplace due to low wages. Don't get conned into paying a trumped-up fine: if you have genuinely broken the law, they must hand you a fine ticket; if the charge is false, patience, a few calm words and cigarettes usually do the trick. Never take photographs of military sites.

Women should take care when travelling alone, especially at night. Paying a reliable driver extra to wait for you is better than having to find a lift home in a deserted area.

Getting Around

By Air

Flying is by far the best way to travel if you intend only to visit a few cities in Vietnam. A Vietnam Airlines flight from Hanoi to Ho Chi Minh City costs under US$200, whereas the train for the same distance, if you figure in meals for two days, is roughly the same price. Scheduled **Vietnam Airlines** flights (www.vietnamairlines.com) from Ho Chi Minh City serve Buon Me Thuot, Da Lat, Danang, Hai Phong, Hanoi, Hue, Nha Trang, Phu Quoc, Pleiku, Qui Nhon and Rach Gia. From Hanoi there are scheduled flights to Danang, Ho Chi Minh City, Hue, Vinh and Nha Trang.

The major problem with flying is finding space during the busy season before and after Tet.

You can use credit cards to buy airline tickets in Hanoi and Ho Chi Minh City, but in other cities you may be asked to pay cash.

Vietnam Airlines' **Hanoi** office is located at 1 Quang Trung Street, tel: 04-832 0320, and the **Ho Chi Minh City** office at 116 Nguyen Hue, District 1, tel: 08-832 0320.

By Rail

Train travel, operated by **Vietnam Railways** (www.vr.com.vn) in Vietnam, is very slow. The fastest Hanoi–Ho Chi Minh City express train, known as the Reunification Express, covers 1,730 km (1,073 miles) in 30 hours, so if you need to get somewhere fast forget about the train. However, if you want to soak in the Vietnamese countryside leisurely the train has a lot to offer, including mountain passes, ocean views, tunnels, French-era bridges,

and an opportunity to get to know the Vietnamese up close and personal. However, there have been burglaries on board so make sure you secure your bags properly.

There are two express trains every day and berths are reserved fast, so try to make reservations two days in advance. There are also local train services on the Hanoi–Ho Chi Minh City line that serve coastal cities. Lines also run from Hanoi West to Pho Lu, East to Hai Phong and North to Lang Son.

In **Ho Chi Minh City**, the train station is at 1 Nguyen Thong Street, tel: 08-823 0105 (ticket sales daily 7.15–11am and 1–3pm). Book at least 2–3 days in advance for sleepers. In **Hanoi**, go to 120 Le Duan Street, tel: 04-825 3949 (ticket sales daily 7.30–11.30am and 1.30–3.30pm).

By Road

In Hanoi and Ho Chi Minh City it is possible to hire good cars and minivans to go on day trips or week-long excursions. Hiring a driver and vehicle is good value if your travelling party is large enough to spread the cost. Self-drive is not advised.

Modern air-conditioned tour buses travel between all the major towns and cities. Competition among tour companies is fierce and these buses are good value if you don't mind herds of tourists. Local buses are slow and often break down.

City Transport

BICYCLE

In the cities the best way to get around is by bicycle or *cyclo* (trishaw). Bicycles can be rented for as little as US$1 or US$2 per day from tourist cafés in Hanoi and Ho Chi Minh City. If you have a mechanical problem or a tire puncture, don't worry as there are stands set up on practically every street corner where most repairs will cost a few thousand dong.

No trip to Vietnam is complete without a ride in a cyclo. Vietnam

has thousands of waiting cyclo drivers who can be hired by the kilometre or the hour. Expect to pay at least 5,000 dong for a short ride or 40,000 dong for an hour. It is essential to bargain with cyclo drivers. As a rule, halve their first offer and work up.

MOTORCYCLE TAXI

A faster way to get around town in Hanoi and Ho Chi Minh City is a motorcycle taxi, called a *xe om* (pron. *say ome*) or Honda *om*, which literally means "hugging taxi" as passengers grab on to the driver's waist. Fares are actually cheaper than on cyclos, and of course the ride is quicker. Some of the drivers navigate the roads badly, however, so be careful. If a driver seems unsafe, tell him to stop, get off and pay him, then find another driver. Buy a helmet if you decide to use motorcycle taxis. They're available in the markets. Some women travellers have reported problems with *xe om* drivers getting too friendly; be careful late at night, especially.

TAXI

Taxis in Hanoi and Ho Chi Minh City are generally comfortable, with meters and air-conditioning and are generally reasonably priced.

In **Ho Chi Minh City**, **Vinataxis**, tel: 08-811 0888 and **Airport Taxis**, tel: 08-844 6666, provide an efficient metered service. Taxis are seldom found outside these two cities, but old jalopy-style cars are available for hire as taxis in many areas.

BUS

In Hanoi and HCMC there are city buses with defined routes and schedules. Bus maps are difficult to find but signs on the front of the buses are accurate. For 3,000 to 5,000 dong they are another Asian experience, and who knows what you'll find on your trip or where you'll end up.

Where to Stay

Choosing a Hotel

There is a wide range of accommodation to suit every budget and taste, from the five-star luxury hotels and resorts to family run 'mini-hotels'. Service has improved greatly and internet access and business centres are provided by all the major hotels. The relaxation of government control and easing of restrictions has encouraged the building of tourist facilities in most towns. Only at TET (Lunar New Year) or during an international conference are hotel rooms difficult to find. Rates are subject to 10–15 percent government tax.

Price Categories

A general guide for a standard double room, excluding taxes.
$$$$ = above US$150
$$$ = US$100–150
$$ = US$50–100
$ = under US$50

Hotel Listings

HANOI

Melia Hanoi
44B Ly Thuong Kiet Street
Tel: 04-934 3343
www.meliahanoi.com
Located in the business and diplomatic district, this glitzy affair managed by the Spanish Sol and Melia chain of hotels has 306 rooms, restaurants, bar and pool. It even has its own heliport. **$$$$**
Sheraton Hanoi Hotel
11 Xuan Dieu Road
Tel: 04-719 9000
www.sheraton.com/hanoi

Hanoi's newest five-star, the Sheraton overlooks Hanoi's picturesque West Lake to the north of downtown. **$$$$**
Sofitel Metropole Hanoi
15 Ngo Quyen Street
Tel: 04-826 6919
www.sofitel.com
In the summer of 1901, the Grand Hotel Metropole Palace opened its doors. Still an icon in the 21st century it is home to the best French, and Vietnamese fusion restaurants in Hanoi. **$$$$**
Hilton Hanoi Opera
1 Le Thanh Tong Street
Tel: 04-933 0500
www.hilton.co.uk/hanoi
Superb location in an architecturally impressive building which aims to complement the neighbouring French-built Opera House. Excellent range of facilities, including a swimming pool and spa. **$$$–$$$$**
Hanoi Horison Hotel
40 Cat Linh Street
Tel: 04-733 0808
www.swiss-belhotel.com
An imposing five-star hotel that rises somewhat pyramid-like over the skyline. The Horison has 250 very comfortable, attractive rooms. All the usual amenities plus a great health club and swimming pool. **$$$**
Nikko Hotel
84 Tran Nhan Tong
Tel: 04-822 3535
www.hotelnikkohanoi.com.vn
A favourite with Japanese tourists. This elegant hotel has one of the better swimming pools in town, a superb *dim sum* restaurant and the fine Japanese Benkay restaurant. **$$$**
Sofitel Plaza Hanoi
1 Thanh Nien Road
Tel: 04-823 8888
www.sofitel.com
This five-star hotel has 322 rooms commanding pretty lake views. Amenities include an all-weather swimming pool with retractable roof and an all-glass 20th-floor bar. **$$$**
De Syloia Hotel
17A Tran Hung Dao Street
Tel: 04-824 5346
www.desyloia.com
An international-quality hotel, with an excellent restaurant called the

Cay Cau serving fine Vietnamese food and a fitness centre. Airport transfer is available upon request. **$$**
Sunway Hotel
19 Pham Dinh Ho Street
Tel: 04-971 3888
www.sunway-hotel.com/vietnam
The Sunway is a boutique business hotel just south of downtown. **$$**
Moon River Retreat
Bac Cau 3, Ngoc Thuy Village
Long Bien District
Tel: 04-871 1658
Fax: 04-871 3665
New riverside retreat in a tranquil village setting, 5 km (3 miles) from central Hanoi. Features traditional Asian architecture in tropical gardens, with comfortable ensuite guestrooms and a fine-dining restaurant in authentic timber houses. **$$**

HO CHI MINH CITY

Caravelle Hotel
19 Lam Son Square, District 1
Tel: 08-823 4999
www.caravellehotel.com
Extensively renovated but still retains a strong French character. Rooftop affords great views of the city. Easily the best hotel in HCMC. **$$$$**
Sheraton Saigon Hotel
88 Dong Khoi Street, District 1
Tel: 08-827 2828
www.sheraton.com/saigon
Centrally located, the Sheraton is a luxury business hotel. **$$$$**
Continental Hotel
132 Dong Khoi Street
Tel: 08-829 9201
www.continental-saigon.com
The setting for Graham Greene's *The Quiet American*. Refurbished tastefully, the place exudes old world charm and comfort. This is a personal favourite of many visitors to Vietnam. **$$$–$$$$**
Saigon Prince Hotel
63 Nguyen Hue Boulevard
Tel: 08-822 2999
www.duxton.com/ho.htm
Well located in the heart of the city. This modern, spacious hotel complete with fountains and wide, curving staircases attracts mostly

business executives and tour groups. Good Japanese, international and Chinese restaurants. **$$$–$$$$**

Sofitel Plaza Saigon
17 Le Duan Boulevard; District 1
Tel: 08-824 1555
www.sofitel.com
One of the first five-star hotels in the city, the Sofitel is an elegant modern high-rise with tastefully appointed rooms, Western and Asian restaurants, and a rooftop pool offering panoramic city views. **$$$**

Renaissance Riverside Hotel
8–15 Ton Duc Thang Street
Tel: 08-822 0033
The Renaissance holds a commanding position on the city's waterfront, with 349 tastefully furnished rooms and full facilities. **$$**

Bong Sen Hotel
117–123 Dong Khoi Street
Tel: 08-829 1721
www.hotelbongsen.com
85 air conditioned rooms located conveniently in the middle of the central shopping district and in close proximity to a number of excellent Vietnamese and French restaurants. **$$–$$$**

Rex Hotel
141 Nguyen Hue Boulevard
Tel: 08-829 2185
www.rexhotelvietnam.com
A classic, somewhat eccentric hotel with a popular rooftop garden restaurant. That this hotel is still a popular choice has less to do with its garish mix of Eastern and Western decorative styles than with its colourful history. **$$–$$$**

Norfolk Hotel
117 Le Thanh Ton
Tel: 08-829 5368
www.norfolkgroup.com
Centrally located, the Norfolk Hotel is only minutes from landmarks such as Ben Thanh Market and the Opera House. Billing itself as a boutique business hotel, this has a business centre and restaurants. **$$**

HUE

La Residence
5 Le Loi Street
Tel: 054-837 475
www.la-residence-hue.com
This former governor's palace, lying on the the Perfume River, has been restored to its former art deco grandeur. Its Le Parfum Restaurant, which looks out to the Imperial Citadel, serves the finest food in Hue. **$$–$$$**

Saigon Morin Hotel
30 Le Loi
Tel: 054-823 526
www.morinhotel.com.vn
Built in 1901 and renovated in 1998, the Morin is centrally located with excellent service. **$$**

Thanh Noi Hotel
57 Dang Dung Street
Tel: 054-522 478
www.thanhnoihotel.com
Located in the heart of the old city near the citadel, this hotel features 60 rooms, a swimming pool and a garden restaurant offering European and Asian food. **$$**

HA LONG CITY

Halong Dream Hotel
10 Halong Road
Tel: 033-844 288
Fax: 033-944 855
www.halongdreamhotel.com.vn
This four-star hotel is centrally located in Ha Long City and overlooks Ha Long Bay. Its 184 rooms and suites feature satellite television reception, IDD telephone, and central air conditioning with individual temperature control. **$$$**

Halong Plaza Hotel
8 Halong Road
Tel: 033-845 810
www.halongplaza.com
This 12-storey high-rise has 200 rooms and suites with the usual mod cons and bayfront views. Amenities include a fully equipped fitness centre and Thai massage services. Organises tours of Halong Bay with English-speaking guides. **$$$**

Halong P&T Hotel
Halong Road
Tel: 033-844 890
Fax: 033-845 416
On the main road in Ha Long, this hotel is run by its neighbour, the government post office. **$$**

Where to Eat

What to Eat

Vietnamese cuisine reflects long years of cultural exchange with China, Cambodia and France. Rice is the main staple, though bread – especially baguettes introduced by the French – is usually very good. Dishes are usually served at the same time rather than by course, and eaten with long-grain rice, *nuoc mam* (fish sauce), and a range of fresh herbs and vegetables.

Some of the more popular Vietnamese dishes include *Cha gio* or *nem*: small 'spring rolls' of minced pork, prawn, crabmeat, mushrooms and vegetables wrapped in thin rice paper and then fried. *Cha gio* is rolled in a lettuce leaf with fresh mint and other herbs, then dipped in a sweet sauce. *Chao tom* is a northern delicacy: Mashed shrimp is baked on a stick of sugar cane, then eaten with lettuce, cucumber, coriander and mint, and dipped in fish sauce. Another dish eaten in a similar fashion is *cuon diep*, or shrimp, noodles, mint, coriander and pork wrapped in lettuce leaves.

Hue is famous for its vegetarian cuisine and for its *banh khoai*, or 'Hue pancake'. A batter of rice flour and corn is fried with egg to make a pancake, then wrapped around pork or shrimp, onion, bean sprouts and mushrooms. Another Hue speciality is *bun bo*, or fried beef and noodles served with coriander, onion, garlic, cucumber, chilli and tomato paste.

Soups are popular, and generally served with almost every meal. Perhaps the best known of all Vietnamese soup dishes, often eaten for breakfast or as a late night snack, is *pho*, a broth of rice noodles topped with beef or chicken, fresh herbs and onion.

Restaurant Listings

HANOI

Cay Cau
De Syloia Hotel, 17A Tran Hung Dao
Tel: 04-933 1010
Excellent Vietnamese place popular among people in the know. Pomelo salad, crabs in tamarind and pork-stuffed egg plant are all winners. **$$**

Cha Ca La Vong
14 Cha Ca Street
Tel: 04-825 3929
It only serves fried freshwater fish, a Hanoi speciality, and it's truly excellent. There are plenty of other *Cha Ca* restaurants around town, but this is the best. **$$**

Chim Sao
65 Ngo Hue
Tel: 04-976 0633
Whistling Bird has excellent Vietnamese food, traditional décor, art shows and medicinal wines. **$**

Emperor
18B Le Thanh Tong Street
Tel: 04-825 8801
Royal Vietnamese dining in an exquisite setting. **$$$**

Green Tangerine
48 Hang Be Street
Tel: 04-825 1286
In the heart of the old quarter, this serves mouthwatering international fusion and traditional French food with innovative twists. **$$**

Le Beaulieu
Sofitel Metropole, 15 Ngo Quyen
Tel: 04-826 6919
A Vietnamese and mainly French menu. Each morning there is a large breakfast buffet with various freshly baked cakes and breads. **$$$**

Quan An Ngon
18 Phan Boi Chau Street
Tel: 04-942 8162
Successful Saigon venture that has found equal success in Hanoi. Sit in a pretty alfresco villa courtyard and enjoy authentic Vietnamese dishes served from surrounding mock street food stalls. Open all day. **$**

Seasons of Hanoi
95B Quan Thanh
Tel: 04-843 5444
Classic Vietnamese cuisine in a beautiful French-style villa with live traditional music. **$$**

Tandoor
24 Hang Be Street
Tel: 04-824 2252
Located in the Old Quarter near the Hoan Kiem Lake. Excellent North Indian and vegetarian curries. **$$**

HO CHI MINH CITY

Asian Reflections
Caravelle Hotel, 19 Lam Son Square, District 1
Tel: 08-823 4999
Cutting-edge Asian fusion cuisine, plated Western-style. Stylish atmosphere and excellent service. **$$$**

Au Manoir De Khai
251 Dien Bien Phu, District 3
Tel: 08-930 3394
High-class French cuisine in a renovated manor. Advance bookings are essential. **$$$**

Lemon Grass
4 Nguyen Thiep, District 1
Tel: 08-822 0496
Excellent Vietnamese cuisine. You may be serenaded by guitarists playing traditional Vietnamese folk music. **$$–$$$**

Mandarin
11A Ngo Van Nam, District 1
Tel: 08-822 9783
A fabulous selection of traditional Vietnamese cuisine in beautiful surroundings. **$$**

Pho 24
89 Mac Thi Buoi
Tel: 08-825 8325
This popular eatery now has some 30 outlets. Traditional noodle soup is served in a clean, bright setting. **$**

Pomodoro
79 Hai Ba Trung, District 1
Tel: 08-823 8957
The best in Italian dining at this friendly place with wood-fired oven pizzas, great lasagne and daily specials. The owner makes his own wonderful grappa liquer. **$$**

Restaurant Price Guide

A general guide for dinner for two people excluding beverages:
$$$ = above US$20
$$ = US$10–20
$ = under US$10

Culture

Museums

HANOI

Ethnology Museum (Bao Tang Dan Toc Hoc Vietnam), Duong Nguyen Van Huyen. Tel: 04-824 5117, www.vme.org.vn. Tues–Sun 8.30am–5.30pm; entrance fee.

Fine Arts Museum (Bao Tang My Thuat), 66 Nguyen Thai Hoc. Tel: 04-846 5081. Tues, Thur, Fri, Sun 8.30am–5pm, Wed and Sat 8.30am–9pm; entrance fee.

Hoa Lo Prison (Bao Tang Nha Tu Hoa Lo), 1 Hoa Lo. Tel: 04-824 6358. Daily 8–11.30am and 1.30–4.30pm; entrance fee.

Ho Chi Minh Mausoleum (Lang Chu Tich Ho Chi Minh), Ba Dinh Square. Tel: 04-845 5124. Daily except Mon and Fri, about 8–11am; free.

Ho Chi Minh Museum (Bao Tang Ho Chi Minh), 19 Ngoc Ha. Tel: 04-846 3752. Daily except Mon and Fri afternoons, 8–11.30am and 2–4pm; entrance fee.

Ma May House, 87 Ma May. Tel: 04-928 5604. Daily 8.30am–5.30pm; entrance fee.

National Museum of Vietnamese History (Bao Tang Lich Su Vietnam), 1 Trang Tien. Tel: 04-825 3518. Tues–Sun 8–11.30am and 1.30–4.30pm; entrance fee.

Revolutionary Museum (Bao Tang Cach Mang), 216 Tran Quang Khai. Tel: 04-825 4151. Tues–Sun 8–11.45am and 1.30–4.15pm; entrance fee.

Temple of Literature (Van Mieu), Van Mieu Street. Tel: 04-843 3615. Daily 7.30am–5.30pm; entrance fee.

Vietnam Military History Museum (Bao Tang Lich Su Quan Su), 28A Dien Bien Phu. Tel: 04-823 4264. Daily except Mon and Fri, 8–11.30am and 1–4.30pm; entrance fee.

HA LONG

Quang Ninh Museum (Bao Tang Quang Ninh), 165 Nguyen Van Cu. Tues, Wed, Fri, Sat 8–11.30am and 1.30–4.30pm.

HO CHI MINH CITY

Fine Arts Museum (Bao Tang My Thuat), 97A Duc Chinh, Dist. 1. Tel: 08-821 0001. Tues–Sun 9am–4.45pm; entrance fee.
Ho Chi Minh City Museum (Bao Tang Thanh Pho Ho Chi Minh), 65 Ly Tu Trong, Dist. 1. Tel: 08-829 8250. Daily 8–11.30am and 1–4.30pm; entrance fee.
Ho Chi Minh Museum (Bao Tang Ho Chi Minh), 1 Nguyen Tat Thanh St. P12, Dist. 4. Tel: 08-825 5740. Tues–Sun 7.30–11.30am and 1.30–5pm; entrance fee.
Military Museum (officially called the Museum of Ho Chi Minh's Campaign, Bao Tang Chien Dich Ho Chi Minh), 2 Le Duan. Tel: 08-822 4824. Daily except Sat 8–11.30am and 1.30– 4.30pm; entrance fee.
National History Museum (Bao Tang Lich Su), 2 Nguyen Binh Khiem, Dist. 1. Tel: 08-829 8146. Tues–Sun 8–11am, 1.30–4.30pm; entrance fee.
Reunification Hall (Dinh Thong Nhat), 133 Nam Ky Khoi Nghia. Tel: 08-822 3652. Daily 7.30–11am and 1–4pm; entrance fee.
War Remnants Museum (Bao Tang Chung Tich Chien Tranh), 28 Vo Van Tan, Dist. 3. Tel: 08-930 5587. Daily 7.30–noon and 1.30–5pm; entrance fee

HUE

History Museum (Bao Tang Lich Su), 23/8 St. Tel: 054-522 397. Daily except Wed 7.30–11am and 1.30–5pm.
Ho Chi Minh Museum (Bao Tang Ho Chi Minh), 7 Le Loi. Tel: 054-822 152. Daily 7.34–11.30am and 2–5pm.
Museum of Royal Fine Arts, 3 Le Truc. Tel: 054-524 429. Tues–Sat 7am–5pm, admission fee.

Festivals

Many traditional and religious festivals take place in Vietnam, particularly in the north in and around Hanoi during *Tet*. Festivities last three days (officially), preceded, particularly in Ho Chi Minh City and Hanoi, by a week-long flower market. Dates, unless otherwise stated, fall in the first lunar month.
Mai Dong Festival Takes place from the 4th to 6th at the Mai Dong Temple in Hai Ba Trung District, Hanoi, is held in honour of Le Cham, the Trung Sisters' brave female general who fought against the Chinese in the first century.
Dong Da Festival Held on the 5th, in Hanoi's Dong Da District, commemorates King Trung Quang's victory at Dong Da and those who died in this battle against the Tsing in 1789.
An Duong Vuong Festival Occurs between the 6th and 16th, in the temple of the same name in Co Loa village near Hanoi. Held in memory of King Thuc An Duong Vuong, one of the founders of ancient Vietnam who built the Co Loa Citadel.
Le Phung Hieu Festival Held on the

7th, at the temple of the same name in Hoang Hoa district, Thanh Hoa Province.
Lim Festival On the 13th in the Lim village pagoda, Ha Bac Province. Features singing and a wide range of cultural and artistic activities.
Ha Loi Festival Held on the 15th at Ha Loi Temple in the Me Linh suburb of Hanoi. Commemorates the Trung Sisters.
Den Va Temple Festival Dedicated to Tan Vien, God of the Mountain, and held in the Ha Tay suburb of Hanoi on the 15th.
Ram Thang Gieng The most important Buddhist festival, takes place on the 15th.
Van Village Festival Celebrated in Hanoi's Viet Yen District from the 20th to the 22nd.
Lac Long Quan Festival From the 1st to 6th days of the third lunar month, at Binh Minh village, Ha Tay Province. Dedicated to Lac Long Quan, the quasi-legendary ancestor of the Vietnamese people. Features traditional music, elders dressed in traditional silk robes, fireworks displays and a stunning display of young ladies carrying altars laden with fruit and flowers through Binh Minh's narrow streets.
Huong Tich Festival Takes place throughout the spring in the spectacular Huong Son mountains west of Hanoi in Ha Tay Province. Can be visited at the same time as Lac Long Quan Festival.
The Buffalo Immolation Festival, Celebrated during spring in the Tay Nguyen Highlands.
Tay Pagoda Festival Held from the

Tet: Vietnam's New Year

Tet Nguyen Dan is the most important festival on the Vietnamese calendar. It takes place late January or early February, on the day of the full moon between the winter solstice and the spring equinox, and lasts three days. It is a time of hope, when relatives gather to celebrate new beginnings and to honour ancestral spirits.

Houses are given a good spring cleaning and decorated with

flowers. Parades and government sponsored fireworks displays occur in parks and over Hoan Kiem and West Lakes. Excellent celebratory cakes are for sale, and families hold feasts.

During the Tet holidays, the whole of the country closes down, and transportation and hotels get booked up well in advance for the weeks before and afterwards. Don't plan spontaneous travel.

5th to 7th day of the 3rd lunar month in Quoc Oai, Ha Tay Province, is dedicated to Tu Dao Hanh, a revered Buddhist monk and teacher. An excellent opportunity to see the traditional water puppet theatre in an historical and idyllic setting. Also features rowing contests and mountain climbing.

Den Festival Takes place between the 9th to 11th day of the third lunar month in the ancient capital of Hoa Lu in Ninh Binh Province. It commemorates King Dinh Bo Linh and General Le who fought against the Sung invaders.

Dau Pagoda Festival Celebrated on the 8th day of the 4th lunar month in Thuan Thanh, Ha Bac.

Easter More in the south.

12 April Anniversary of Vietnam's first King, Hung Vuong.

15 May Buddha's birth, enlightenment and death, celebrated in pagodas, temples and homes throughout the country.

July/August On the 15th day of the 7th lunar month offerings of food and gifts are made in homes and temples for the wandering souls of the dead.

September/October Mid-Autumn Festival on the day of the full moon in the 8th lunar month. Celebrated with sticky rice mooncakes filled with lotus seeds, salted duck egg yolks, peanuts and melon seeds. Brightly coloured lanterns depicting all manner of things – dragons, boats, butterflies – are carried by children in evening processions.

The Kiep Bac Temple Festival Held in Hai Hung Province on the 20th day of the 8th lunar month to commemorate the national hero Tran Hung Dao who wiped out the invading Mongol forces in the 13th century.

25 December Christmas.

Shopping

What to Buy

There is a wide variety of traditional Vietnamese handicrafts to choose from, including embroidery, silk paintings, lacquerware, pottery, mother-of-pearl inlay, ceramics, precious wood, jade, bamboo and wickerware, baskets, sculpture, wood, marble/bone carvings, jewellery, engraving, silk and brocade.

You may like to add a *non la*, the famous Vietnamese conical hat and an *ao dai*, the traditional costume worn by Vietnamese women, to your wardrobe. Green pith helmets, worn by soldiers during the war and by cyclo drivers and labourers today, are sold.

Strong laws and heavy taxation have discouraged the sale of antiquities and export is strictly controlled. Goods illegally exported can be confiscated at border crossings and the airports. Strict controls on the export of wood products is in force. A reputable dealer will obtain export papers and ship your purchase with little trouble. Copies of bronze Buddhas, old porcelain, wood statuettes and objects used by hill tribes and numerous cults are for sale in many shops in the old quarter.

HO CHI MINH CITY

Shops
Books/Newspapers
Bookazine, 28 Dong Khoi, Dist 1. Tel: 08-829 7455. Has large-format arts books and magazines.
Fahasa Bookshop, Xuan Thu, 185 Dong Khoi, tel: 08-822 4670, e-mail: fahasa-sg@hcm.vnn.vn. Books in English and French.

Crafts
Heritage, 53 Dong Khoi, Dist 1. Tel: 08-823 5834. Inexpensive reproductions and a certificate of non-authenticity.
Kim Phuong, 125 Le Thanh Ton, District 1, tel: 08-827 7091. One of three galleries with exceptional hand embroidery on silk and linen.
Nga Shop, 61 Le Thanh Ton, Dist. 1. Tel: 08-825 6289. Excellent lacquer products.

Fashion, Clothing and Tailors
Khai Silk, 107 Dong Khoi, Dist. 1. Tel: 08-829 1146, www.khaisilk corp.com. High quality silk, both ready made and made to measure.
Song, 76D Le Thanh Ton, Dist. 1. Tel: 08-824 6986. Readymade clothes in western sizes and embroidered linens.

Supermarkets
Diamond Plaza, 34 Le Duan, Dist. 1. Tel: 08-825 7750. Designer brands and a bowling alley.
Citimart, 21 Nguyen Thi Minh Khai. Shop here for necessities.

Shopping Areas
Binh Tay Market, Cho Lon's main marketplace located on Thap Muoi street has everything imaginable.
Le Thanh Ton Street. Several shops along this street sell embroidery and silk clothes in Western styles. A shop across from the Norfolk Hotel sells modern glass, ceramics,

Ho Chi Minh's Market

The city's central market is **Ben Thanh Market**, at the intersection of Ham Nghi, Le Loi, Tran Hung Dao and Le Thanh Ton Streets. Just about everything is for sale here, from fruits, vegetables, rice and meats to electronics, clothes, household goods, and flowers. Not for the squeamish, there is a fascinating fish/meat section, where you may catch a glimpse of live frogs hanging by the leg and other delicacies. There are also some small food stalls selling soup and rice dishes.

linens and wood items, all made in Vietnam. Near the New World Hotel a shop sells glass, ethnic fabrics and ceramics.

Dan Sinh Market, at the corner of Yersin and Nguyen Thai Binh streets. Once known as the American market, this place now only has a few stalls in the back selling paraphernalia related to the Vietnam War. In most of the other stalls, you will find housewares, tools, machinery, clothing and electronics.

Antiques

Ho Chi Minh City's main antique street is **Le Cong Kieu**. Beware of fakes.

Lucky, 309 Huynh Van Banh, Phu Nhuan District, tel: 08-845 9957, Wide range of antiques.

Oriental Home, 2A Le Duan, District 1, tel: 08-910 0194, fax: 08-910 3504. One of the better antique shops in town.

Art

Original art can be found in shops on Dong Khoi street. Copy painters flourish in the Pham Ngu Lao area and can produce portraits from photos. Below is just a sampling:

Apricot Gallery, 50–52 Mac Thi Buoi, District 1, tel: 08-822 7962. Another branch in Hanoi.

HCMC Fine Arts Association, 218A Pasteur, District 1, tel: 08-823 0025.

Particular Art Gallery, Level 3, Kim Do Business Centre, 123 Le Loi, District 1, tel: 08-821 3019. Works by famous Vietnamese artists.

Pho Hoa Art Gallery, 107 Dien Bien Phu Street, District 1, tel: 08-829 6720. Vietnamese contemporary fine arts.

XQ Hand Emroidered Painting, 81 Dong Khoi, District 1, tel: 08-822 2856. Authentic embroidered designs.

Dong Khoi Street

The area south of the Cathedral to the river, including Hai Ba Trung, Nguyen Hue, Dong Khoi and the side streets joining them, has everything from designer labels to ethnic knick knacks.

HANOI

Shops

Bookshops

Bookworm, 15A Ngo Van So. Tel: 04-943 7226, e-mail: bookworm@fpt.vn. This is the only English bookstore in Hanoi.

Sach Cu, 5 Bat Dan. A small private collection of old books, many in French.

The Gioi Publishers, 46 Tran Hung Dao. Tel: 04-825 3841. The national publisher for books about the culture and history of Vietnam, many in English.

Trang Tien Street, between the Opera House and Hoan Kiem Lake. Numerous bookshops with many English, French as well as Vietnamese titles.

Crafts

Chi Vang, 17 Trang Tien. Tel: 04-936 0027. Good quality embroidery available here.

Vietnamese Craft-Guild, 1A-3 To Tich. Tel: 04-828 9717. Crafts and some old ethnic articles.

Supermarkets

Intimex Supermarket, 22–32 Le Thai To, near Hoan Kiem Lake.

Trang Tien Plaza, on the corner of Trang Tien and Hang Bai streets.

Shopping Areas

Art

Art galleries are omnipresent but concentrated on Trang Tien Street between the Opera House and Hoan Kiem Lake.

Apricot Gallery, 40B Hang Bong, tel: 04-828 8965; www.apricot-

Hanoi's Markets

These sell all manner of foods and packaged goods. Some also sell electronics, household goods and clothing.

Cho Hang Da, at the corner of Dau Duong Thanh and Hang Dieu.

Cho Hom, at the corner of Tran Xuan Son and Pho Hue.

Cho 19–12 (or Cho Ma), 41 Hai Ba Trung.

artvietnam.com. Leading Vietnamese artists are represented here.

Hanoi Art Gallery, 36–38 Tran Tien, tel: 04-943 7192; www.hanoi-artgallery.com. This art gallery is the city's slickest art space.

Mai Hien–Anh Khanh, 99 Nguyen Thai Hoc, tel: 04-846 9614, fax: 04-823 0886. This well-known painting couple run their own gallery.

Nam Son, 41 Trang Tien, tel: 04-826 2993, fax: 04-825 9224, 893 3471. The best of the state-owned galleries in this neighbourhood.

Salon Natasha, 30 Hang Bong, tel: 04-826 1387. Showcases up-and-coming artists.

Antiques and Handicrafts

Several shops on the river side of Nghi Tam just north of the Sofitel Plaza Hotel sell old furniture, handicrafts, statues and ceramics. Beware of fake antiques. Excellent reproductions of temple figures and altars can be found in shops throughout the Old Quarter.

54 Traditions, 30 Hang Bun, tel: 04-718 2389. Artefacts of the 54 ethnic minorities, and antique beads and coins, designed as modern fashion jewellery.

Craft Link, 43 Van Mieu, tel: 04-843 7710. Very popular handicrafts shop with a wide range of items made by hill-tribe minorities.

Dong Phuong Orient House, 7 Xuan Dieu, tel: 04-716 0131.

Furniture Gallery, 8B Ta Hien, tel: 04-826 9769. Antique furniture and knick-knacks.

Vietnamese Craft Guild, 47A Ly Quoc Su/1-3 To Tich, tel: 04-828 9717.

Church Street

West of Hoan Kiem Lake is a shoppers mecca along Hang Trong, Nha Tho, Nha Chung and Au Trieu streets. Good quality crafts, clothes and propaganda art are found here.

Silk, Embroidery and Tailoring

There are many upmarket shops on Hang Bong and Hang Gai streets that will make clothes to your design with their stock of fabric or material brought from elsewhere.

Getting Acquainted

The Place

Situation From the isthmus of south Thailand to Singapore island.
Area Peninsular Malaysia and the states of Sabah and Sarawak cover 329,000 sq. km (127,000 sq. miles).
Capital Kuala Lumpur.
Population 26 million, comprising Malays, Chinese, Indians, Pakistanis and other indigenous groups. 21 million people live on the peninsula, with the rest in Sabah and Sarawak. Kuala Lumpur has around 1.5 million inhabitants.
Language Bahasa Malaysia (Malay).
Religion Mainly Muslim.
Time Zone 8 hours ahead of Greenwich Mean Time (GMT), so New York is 13 hours, Los Angeles 16 hours and London 8 hours behind, Australia 2 hours ahead.
Currency Ringgit (RM)
Weights and Measures Metric
Electricity 220–40V, 50 cycles, using three square-pin plugs.
International Dialling Code 60

Climate

Malaysia's weather is generally hot and sunny all year round, with temperatures averaging 32°C (90°F) during the day and 24°C (75°F) at night. Humidity is high at 80 percent. Temperatures in the highland areas, such as Cameron and Genting, are lower and much more tolerable.

The monsoon season of April/May brings heavy rain to the west coast of Peninsular Malaysia. The east coast of the peninsula and Sabah and Sarawak experience their monsoon season between November and February. The inter-monsoon periods can also be wet. Light showers come and go, helping to relieve the heat.

Thick haze has been recurrent from July to October, especially for the Klang Valley, Sabah and Sarawak, for some years. Most of the smoke and soot is blown in by the southwest monsoon from parts of Indonesia hit by forest fires, which have been worsened by the dry weather caused by the El Niño phenomenon.

Economy

Petroleum, natural gas, electronic goods, computer parts, automobiles, timber, palm oil, cocoa and rubber are the main exports. Malaysia's main trading partners are Japan, Singapore and the United States.

Government

Malaysia is the official name of the former British protectorates of Malaya, British North Borneo and Sarawak. Independent since 1957, the Malaysian government is regulated by the Parliament comprising the King (Yang di-Pertuan Agong) and two Houses: the House of Representatives and Senate. Executive functions are carried out by the Cabinet, led by the Prime Minister.

Business Hours

In an Islamic nation with a British colonial past, the definition of the working week varies. It runs from Monday to Friday in all states except Terengganu, Kelantan, Kedah and Perlis. These four states with a stronger Islamic tradition retain the traditional half-day on Thursday and businesses are closed on Friday, not Sunday.

The working day begins at 8am and ends at 5pm, with time off on Friday from noon to 2.30pm for Muslim prayers. Most private businesses stick to the nine-to-five routine. Shops start to close at 6pm, but large supermarkets, department stores and shopping malls are open 10am–10pm.

Fixed Public Holidays

1 January New Year's Day (except Johor, Kelantan, Terengganu, Kedah and Perlis)
21 January Birthday of the Sultan of Kedah (Kedah only)
1 February Federal Territory Day (Federal Territories of Kuala Lumpur, Putrajaya and Labuan only)
12 February Hari Hol Almarhum Sultan Ismail (Johor only)
5 March Ishak and Mikraj (Kedah and Negeri Sembilan only)
8 March Birthday of the Sultan of Selangor (Selangor only)
10 March Birthday of the Sultan of Terengganu (Terengganu only)
11 March Official Opening of the State Mosque, Shah Alam (Selangor only)
8 April Birthday of the Sultan of Johor (Johor only)
19 April Birthday of the Sultan of Perak (Perak only)
1 May Labour Day
7 May Hari Hol Pahang (Pahang)
29 May Dayak Day (Hari Gawai) (Sarawak only)
30 & 31 May Harvest Festival (Federal Territory of Labuan and Sabah only)
5 June Birthday of Yang di-Pertuan Agong (King)
14 June Birthday of the Yang di-Pertua Negeri Melaka (Malacca)
16 July Birthday of the Yang di-Pertua Negeri Pulau Pinang (Penang only)
16 July Birthday of the Yang di-Pertuan Besar of Negri Sembilan (Negeri Sembilan only)
31 July Birthday of the Sultan of Kelantan (Kelantan only)
23 August Birthday of the Rajah of Perlis (Perlis only)
31 August National Day
16 September Birthday of the Yang di-Pertua Negeri Sabah (Sabah only)
16 September Birthday of the Yang di-Pertua Negeri Sarawak (Sarawak only)
26 October Birthday of the Sultan of Pahang (Pahang only)
25 December Christmas Day

Planning the Trip

Visas & Passports

Passports must be valid for at least 6 months at the time of entry. Remember that Sabah and Sarawak are treated like separate countries, and you will have to go through customs and immigration with your passport again there, whether coming from Peninsular Malaysia or travelling between the two states.

A social single-entry visa valid for 3 months can be applied for at Malaysian diplomatic missions.

Citizens of all Commonwealth countries (except Bangladesh, India, Pakistan, Sri Lanka and Nigeria), ASEAN countries, the US, Switzerland, the Netherlands, San Marino and Liechtenstein do not need a visa. Citizens from some EU, South American and South African countries and Arab nationals do not need a visa for a visit not exceeding 3 months.

For updates, check the **Tourism Malaysia** website (www.tourism.gov.my) or the **Immigration Department** website (www.imi.gov.my).

Health

Travellers have little to worry about in a country where the health standards are ranked among the highest in Asia. Visitors are advised to take out private medical insurance before they leave, nonetheless, just in case of emergencies.

Water in cities is generally fine, but it is safest to drink it boiled. Bottled drinks are widely available. Avoid iced water from roadside stalls. Drink sufficiently to avoid dehydration; make sure you have more liquids than you would normally if you're coming from a cold country.

Money Matters

The ringgit (Malaysian dollar) is available in RM1, 5, 10, 20, 50, 100, 500 and 1,000 notes. There are 1, 5, 10, 20 50 sen and RM1 coins.

Most currencies can be exchanged for ringgit, but the popular ones are US dollars, British sterling pounds, Euro and Singapore dollars. Banks and licensed money changers offer better exchange rates than hotels and shops, where a service charge may be levied (usually 2–4 percent).

Credit cards are widely accepted in major cities. Note that some retailers add a 2–3 percent surcharge for the privilege of using plastic – so ask first before paying. Make sure that you have enough cash before you leave for smaller towns or remote areas.

What to Bring

There is very little need to worry about leaving something important behind when you visit Malaysia. Toiletries, medicines, clothes, photographic film, suntan lotion and straw hats are all readily available in most towns, and definitely in the large cities. In fact, the best advice is to take as little as possible so that you can travel lightly.

If you are planning to visit the hill stations, a light sweater would be a good idea for the cooler evenings. If you're embarking upon the Mount Kinabalu climb, a lightweight plastic raincoat is essential, as are a warm hat and gloves, but all these items can be found in the major cities.

Camping gear is often available for hire in national parks, but it is also in great demand; so it may be best to bring a lightweight tent with you. If you intend to go jungle trekking, the Taman Negara National Park issues a list of recommended contents for the average backpack: rucksack (lightweight and waterproof), sleeping bag (if climbing), cooking pots/utensils, Swiss Army knife or similar, plates/cutlery, can opener, *parang* (local knife for cutting wood etc.), notebook and pens, camera and film, 1 litre water container (minimum), spare set of clothes, soap, toothbrush, etc., repair kit, food – rice, noodles, canned foods, packet soups, dried fish, fresh vegetables, sweets/chocolate, fat, tea/coffee, powdered milk, sugar, rolled oats, fruits and nuts.

Sanitary products for women are also available in larger centres, but tampons are not easy to come by in small towns. Toilet paper is not widely available, so you may wish to bring your own.

What to Wear

Informal wear is most suitable and comfortable. However, since this is a predominantly Muslim and conservative country, observance of local customs is important. Men may wear T-shirts or cotton shirts with short sleeves, and open sandals. Women should not wear dresses, skirts or shorts that are

Tourist Offices Abroad

● **Australia (Sydney)**
Level 2, 171 Clarence Street
Sydney 2000, NSW
Tel: 02-9299 4441–3
e-mail: mtpb.sydney@tourism.gov.my
● **Canada (Vancouver)**
1590-1111 West Georgia Street
Tel: 604-689 8899
www.tourism-malaysia.ca
● **United Kingdom**
57 Trafalgar Square
London WC2N 5DU

Tel: 020-7930 7932
e-mail: mtpb.london@tourism.gov.my
● **United States (New York)**
120, East 56th Street, Suite 810
New York, NY 10022
Tel: 212-754 1114/5
www.visitmalaysia.com
(Los Angeles)
Suite 970, 9th Floor, 818 West 7th Street, Los Angeles, CA 90017
Tel: 213-689 9702
e-mail: mtpbla@tourism.gov.my

too short and should always have a bra on. Topless sunbathing is frowned upon. In cities, towns and villages, shorts are not a good idea – save them for the beach. Check the required attire before entering any house of worship.

For businessmen, a white shirt and tie are adequate for office calls – jackets are seldom required. For women a tailored dress or business suit is appropriate. In the evenings, only a few exclusive nightclubs and restaurants favour the traditional jacket and tie. Most hotels, restaurants, coffeehouses and discos accept casually elegant attire. However, jeans and sneakers are taboo at some restaurants and discos, so to avoid embarrassment, it is best to check the dress code of better establishments in advance.

Getting There

BY AIR

Malaysia is connected by about 41 airlines to international destinations. The **Kuala Lumpur International Airport**, or KLIA (tel: 03-8776 4386; www.klia.com.my), located in Sepang 70 km (43 miles) from the city centre, is the key gateway in and out of Malaysia.

The **Penang International Airport** is linked by direct international flights from several Asian cities, including Bangkok and Singapore, while the **Langkawi**, **Kuching** and **Kota Kinabalu** airports are served by direct international flights from Singapore.

Malaysia Airlines (MAS), the national carrier (tel: 03-7846 3000, toll-free within Malaysia 1300-883 000; www.malaysiaairlines.com), flies to over 100 international and domestic destinations.

Local budget airline **AirAsia** (24-hour call centre tel: 03-8775 4000, toll-free within Malaysia 1300-889 933; www.airasia.com) offers cheap fares online for both domestic and Asian destinations. A new budget long-haul airline, **AirAsia X**, is scheduled to commence flights from UK and China destinations to Kuala Lumpur from July 2007.

Malaysia Airlines flights depart from KLIA while AirAsia flights (both domestic and international) depart from the **Low Cost Carrier Terminal** (LCC-T; tel: 03-8777 8888; www.klia.com.my/LCCTerminal), located about 20 km (12 miles) from KLIA. Feeder buses running at 20-minute intervals link the two terminals.

There is an airport tax of RM40 for international flights, which is usually built into the airfare.

BY RAIL

Train services to and within Malaysia, operated by the **National Railways**, or KTMB (tel: 03-2267 1200; www.ktmb.com.my), are clean, cheap and reliable. Railroads link Kuala Lumpur with Thailand in the north; Singapore in the south; and the east coast of the peninsula. The rail terminal in Kuala Lumpur is **KL Sentral**.

If you are travelling from Bangkok to Kuala Lumpur, change trains in Hat Yai (southern Thailand) or Butterworth (northern Peninsular Malaysia). The express journey takes about 20 hours and costs RM150 (first class). A less travelled route is via the east coast through the Thai town of Sungai Kolok and the town of Rantau Panjang in Kelantan, from where you can take a bus to Kota Bharu, where there are other overland options to other cities.

The express journey from Singapore's Tanjong Pagar Railway Station to Kuala Lumpur takes 8 hours and costs RM70 (first class).

BY ROAD

From Thailand

The North-South Expressway ends in Bukit Kayu Hitam (Kedah), the main border crossing between Malaysia and Thailand. Other border crossings are at Padang Besar (Perlis) and Rantau Panjang (Kelantan). Buses and taxis serve these points.

Buses from Thailand travel along the peninsula's west coast from Hat Yai. The journey to Kuala Lumpur takes about 9 hours and costs RM35. Many buses from Hat Yai, Bangkok and Phuket also terminate in Penang, from where you can take a local express bus. The east coast route is via Sungai Kolok (Thailand) and Kota Bharu.

From Singapore

The peninsula is linked to Singapore by two causeways: the Johor–Singapore Causeway from Woodlands (Singapore) to Johor Bahru, and the Second Link from Tuas (Singapore) to Tanjung Kupang. From these two points, connect to the North-South Expressway, which runs along the west coast. Buses to Peninsular Malaysia depart from Beach Road (outside Golden Mile Complex), Lavender Street and Queen Street. The bus journey to Kuala Lumpur takes about 5–6 hours and costs RM30–80.

Puduraya is the main bus terminal for the cheaper bus services, while several of the pricier operators terminate at various places in the city. These include **Aeroline** (tel: 03-6258 8800, Singapore tel: 65-6733 7010; www.aeroline.com.my; terminates at Corus Hotel on Jalan Ampang and in Petaling Jaya); **Airebus** (tel: 03-2141 7110, Singapore tel: 65-6333 1433; www.airebus.com.my; terminates at Crowne Plaza Hotel in Jalan Sultan Ismail); **Plusliner** (tel: 03-2272 1586, Singapore tel: 65-6256 5755; www.plusliner.com; terminates at the Old Railway Station); and **Transnasional** (tel: 03-2161 1864/2070 3300, Singapore tel: 65-6294 7034; www.nadi.com.my/transportation_home.asp; terminates at the Malaysian Tourist Centre on Jalan Ampang).

Alternately, you can rent a car in either Thailand or Singapore and have complete freedom during your stay in Malaysia. The North-South highway makes travelling along Peninsula Malaysia's west coast a breeze – with trips from the Thai border to Singapore possible in about 10–12 hours. However, try to avoid border crossing on Friday afternoons or during public holidays as there can be bad congestion.

Practical Tips

Media

The main daily English-language newspapers are *The New Straits Times* and *The Star*. Business papers include *The Edge* and *Business Times*. The *Malay Mail* is an afternoon tabloid with a more chatty, local slant. Sabah and Sarawak have their own papers, including *The New Sabah Times*, *Sabah Daily News*, *Daily Express*, *Sarawak Tribune* and *Borneo Post*.

Postal Services

The Malaysian postal service (www.pos.com.my) is reliable, and there are post offices everywhere, generally open Mon–Fri 8am–5.30pm and Sat 8am–1pm.

International courier services include **DHL** (tcl: 1800-888 388), **Fedex** (tel: 1800-886 363) and **UPS** (Kuala Lumpur tel: 03-7784 2311).

Telecommunications

TELEPHONES

Most of the rooms in larger hotels have phones with International Direct Dialling (IDD) facility. To call overseas, dial 00 followed by the country code, area code and phone number. The country code for Malaysia is 60. To call a Malaysian fixed-line number from abroad, dial your international access code, followed by 60 and the local area code, omitting the initial 0, then the number you want.

Emergency Numbers

Call **999** for ambulance or police and **994** for fire or rescue.

To make a call to a number within a state, simply dial the number without the area code. For a call to another state, dial the area code with the initial 0 and the number you want.

PUBLIC PHONES

Calls from a public phone cost 30 sen per 3 minutes. These can also be used for calls to numbers in other states and for international calls (look out for phones marked "international"). Booths are either coin operated or use phone cards.

MOBILE PHONES

Mobile phones use the GSM network. If your mobile phone has a roaming facility, it will hook up to one of Malaysia's. Otherwise, prepaid local SIM cards, with which you get a local mobile number, are very affordable, starting at RM20 for registration and air-time.

INTERNET

Major hotels offer Internet access in their business centres and in the rooms for high fees. Cybercafés with broadband or WiFi Internet access

Tourist Information in Malaysia

Tourism Malaysia (www.tourism.gov.my) has offices throughout Malaysia.
Kuala Lumpur Head Office
24–27th & 30th Floor, Menara Dato' Onn, Putra World Trade Centre, 45 Jalan Tun Ismail.
Tel: 03-2615 8188
Malaysia Tourist Information Centre (MTC), 109 Jalan Ampang KL. Tel: 03-2164 3929
East Coast Region
5th Floor, Menara Yayasan Islam Terengganu, Jalan Sultan Omar, Kuala Terengganu.
Tel: 09-622 1893
Northern Region
Level 56, KOMTAR, Penang.

Embassies/Consulates

● **Australia**
6 Jalan Yap Kwan, Seng, KL
Tel: 03-2146 5555
● **Canada**
18 Floor, Menara Tan & Tan, Jalan Tun Razak, KL
Tel: 03-2178 2333
● **New Zealand**
Level 21 Menara IMC, Jalan Sultan Ismail, tel: 03-2078 2533
● **United Kingdom**
186 Jalan Ampang, 50450 KL
Tel: 03–2170 2200
● **United States**
376 Jalan Tun Razak, 50400 KL
Tel: 03-2168 5000

can be found in all the capitals and most towns and tourist areas.

Medical Treatment

All large towns have government polyclinics and private clinics. Travel and health insurance, as well as documents concerning allergies to certain drugs should also be carried.

Hospitals in the Kuala Lumpur area that have outpatient emergency services include:
Hospital Kuala Lumpur, Jalan Pahang, tel: 03-2615 555.
Gleneagles Intan Medical Centre, Jalan Ampang, tel: 03-4255 2786.

Tel: 04-264 3494
Southern Region
L3–26, Level 3, Johor Tourism, Information Centre, 2 Jalan Ayer Molek, Johor Bahru.
Tel: 07-222 3591
Sabah
Ground Floor, EON CMG Life Building, 1, Jalan Sagunting, Kota Kinabalu. Tel: 088-248 698
Sarawak
2nd Floor, Rugayah Building, Jalan Song Thian Cheok, Kuching.
Tel: 082-246 575
Sabah and Sarawak also operate independent tourism offices. Check www.sabahtourism.com and www.sarawaktourism.com.

Getting Around

On Arrival

Buses and public and private taxis and limousines operate from major airports in Malaysia. Many airports, including Penang, Kuching and Kota Kinabalu, have taxi desks where you purchase a coupon; the price is fixed. Kuala Lumpur's old railway station and the KL Sentral transport hub also use a coupon system. Tolls are paid by the passenger. Elsewhere, enquire about fares at the information desk.

By Air

Malaysia Airlines (tel: 03-7846 3000, toll-free within Malaysia 1300-883 000; www.malaysia airlines.com), runs an extensive network of airways over the entire nation. In Kuala Lumpur, all MAS domestic flights operate out of KLIA.

Below is a list of MAS offices:
Alor Star, Sultan Abdul Halim, Kedah, tel: 04-714 3202.
Johor Bahru, Suite 1.1, Level 1, Menara Pelangi, Jalan Kuning, Taman Pelangi, Johor, tel: 07-331 0036.
Kota Bharu, Mezzanine Floor, Kompleks Yakin, Jalan Gajah Mati, Kelantan, tel: 09-748 3477.
Kota Kinabalu, Departure Level, Kota Kinabalu International Airport, off Jalan Petagas, tel: 088-515 314.
Kuala Lumpur, Bangunan MAS, Jalan Sultan Ismail, tel: 03-746 3000.
Kuala Terengganu, No. 13, Jalan Sultan Omar, Terengganu, tel: 09-622 9279.
Kuantan, 7, Ground Floor, Wisma Persatuan Bolasepak Pahang, Jalan Gambut, Pahang, tel: 09-515 6030.
Kuching, Bangunan MAS, Lot 215, Jalan Song Thian Cheok, Sarawak, tel: 082-244 144.

Labuan, Level 2, Airport Terminal Building, Sabah, tel: 087-431 737.
Langkawi, Langkawi International Airport, Kedah, tel: 04 955 6332.
Miri, Lot 239, Beautiful Jade Centre, Sarawak, tel: 085-417 315.
Penang, 2nd Floor, Menara KWSP, 38 Jalan Sultan Ahmad Shah, Penang, tel: 04-217 6321.
Sandakan, Ground Floor, Block 31, Sabah Bldg., Jalan Pelabuhan, Sabah, tel: 089-273 970.
Sibu, 61 Jalan Tuanku Osman, Sarawak, tel: 084-321 055.
Tawau, 1st & 2nd Floors, TB 319 Block 38, Jalan Haji Sahabudin Fajar Complex, Sabah, tel: 089-761 293.

Air Asia (tel: 03-8775 4000; www.airasia.com) offers low-fare flights to most main destinations such as Penang, Langkawi, Kuching, Kota Kinabalu, Sandakan, Tawau and Kota Bharu, as well as flights between Kota Kinbabalu and Miri, Sibu, Bintulu and Kuching in Sarawak. The airline also offers a selection of holiday packages to most destinations. The airline operates out of the LCC-T at KLIA and from Terminal 2 at Kota Kinabalu International Airport. In Sarawak, AirAsia uses the same terminal as MAS.

Berjaya Air (tel: 03-2145 2828; www.berjaya-air.com) is the only airline to offer flights to Tioman, Redang and Pangkor islands. Using 48-seater Dash 7 aircrafts, Berjaya Air operates from the Sultan Abdul Aziz (Subang) Airport in Kuala Lumpur to the two islands. The airline also offers flights from Singapore to Redang and Tioman.

Fly Asian Express (tel: 03-8775 4000; www.flyasianxpress.com), popularly known as FAX, was established in mid-2006 to take over a number of internal routes previously handled by MAS in Sarawak and Sabah. Miri is the hub for most of these flights. The FAX website uses the same simple booking facilities as AirAsia.

By Rail

PENINSULAR MALAYSIA

Train services are operated by the **National Railways**, or **KTMB** (tel: 03-

2267 1200; www.ktmb.com.my). There are air-conditioned first- and second-class coaches and bunks on the night trains. Third-class coaches are fan-cooled. Express services stop only at major towns; the others stop everywhere.

The west coast rail line goes through Kuala Lumpur to Butterworth (Penang) and joins Thailand at Padang Besar, Kedah. The Ekspres Rakyat (ER) departs every morning from Singapore to Butterworth and vice versa. Ekspres Sinaran (XSP) is the other morning service and links Kuala Lumpur and Butterworth.

The night trains are the Ekspres Senandung Malam sleepers (ESM) servicing Kuala Lumpur–Singapore and Kuala Lumpur–Butterworth, and Ekspres Langkawi (EL) servicing Kuala Lumpur–Hat Yai.

The east coast line branches off at Gemas in Johor, heads through the central forests and emerges at Tumpat in Kelantan, near the border with Thailand. Only night trains, the Ekspres Timuran (XST) Singapore–Tumpat and Ekspres Wau (XW) Kuala Lumpur–Tumpat (via Gemas) do this route.

SABAH

The only public train in Borneo operates daily from the Tanjung Aru Station in Kota Kinabalu via Beaufort to Tenom in the interior; this is one of the world's greatest train journeys. North Borneo Railway (tel: 088-254 611) operates three tourist services between Tanjung Aru and Papar per week. Note, however, that at the

Railpass

For foreign tourists (except Singaporeans), KTMB offers a **Visit Malaysia Rail Pass** for travel over a period of 5, 10 or 15 days on KTMB services in Peninsular Malaysia (and Singapore). For information, contact KTMB (tel: 03-2263 1111; www.ktmb.com.my).

time of writing, the railway network in Sabah is being closed in phases for maintenance; it will likely fully reopen by 2008.

Public Transport

TAXI

Taxis remain one of the most popular and cheap means of transport. You can hail them by the roadside, hire them from authorised taxi stands, or book them by phone, in which case, mileage is calculated from the stand or garage from which the vehicle is hired.

Although most taxis are fitted with meters, not all drivers use them. Make sure that your driver is willing to use his meter, or negotiate a charge at the beginning of the journey.

There is a surcharge for a telephone booking and traffic jams, trips between midnight and 6am will have a 50 percent surcharge and there could be a small additional charge for more than two passengers.

From most airports and railway stations, taxi fares are fixed and you should prepay at the taxi counter. Reliable call taxi services in Kuala Lumpur can be booked with **Comfort Taxi** (tel: 03-2692 2525), **Public Cab** (tel: 03-6259 2020), **Supercab** (tel: 03-2095 3399), **Sunlight Radio Taxi** (tel: 03-9057 1111) and **Selangor Radio Taxi** (tel: 03-2693 6211).

BUS

Three types of buses operate in Malaysia: the non-air-conditioned buses that travel between the states, the non-air-conditioned buses that provide services within each state, and the air-conditioned express buses connecting major towns in Malaysia. Buses seldom adhere to the schedule but are frequent between 9am to 6pm. Buses within towns and cities usually charge fares according to distance covered.

Travelling by bus within Kuala

Water Transport

Around the peninsula, boats are the chief means of travel to the islands and in parts of the interiors.

Regular ferries service the islands of Pangkor (6.30am–7pm), Penang (6am–midnight) and Langkawi (8am–6pm). Boats out to islands on the east coast generally do not follow schedules, and in the monsoon season (November–February), services may stop altogether. Note that the sea can be choppy just before and after the monsoon period and services may be cancelled.

In the northeast, services begin at 8.30–9am and stop at 2–2.30pm. Other than during public and school holidays, it is generally fine to arrive on the Perhentian Islands (from Kuala Besut) and Kapas (from Marang) without having booked your accommodation, but it is safer to

Lumpur and to the surrounding areas of Petaling Jaya, Subang Jaya and Klang is definitely not for the faint-hearted. Published or posted timetables are a mystery to most, and listings of the stops or final destinations of each route are equally elusive, save for the signs carried on the front of each individual vehicle. However, for those determined to savour this fascinating grass-roots mode of transport within the capital and its environs, the experience is likened to an exhilarating roller-coaster ride, thanks to the drivers' daredevil attempts to meet their quotas, irrespective of traffic laws and other road users.

In Kuala Lumpur, north- and southbound services are found at the **Puduraya Bus Station** (tel: 03-2070 0145) on Jalan Pudu and the old railway station; coaches to the east coast and Tasik Kenyir depart from the **Putra Bus Station** (opposite the Putra World Trade Centre); and the interior destinations such as Kuala Lipis are serviced from **Pekeliling Bus**

pre-book accommodation and therefore boats at Redang and Tenggol (from Merang).

In the southeast, Mersing services the bulk of the Johor islands and Tioman, while Tanjung Leman is the staging point for the Sibu isles. Scheduled ferries depart Mersing only to Tioman (arrive at Mersing as early as possible) and Rawa (one service at midday). Tioman can also be accessed from Tanjong Gemok. The Tanjung Leman boats depart daily at 11am, 1.15pm and 4.30pm.

In the interior, Taman Negara is the only destination with scheduled boats (9am and 2pm). It is generally all right to arrive at Tasik Kenyir, Kenong and Tasik Cini without booking, but arrangements for Temenggor (for Belum) and Tasik Bera must be pre-booked.

Station (tel: 03-4042 7988) on Jalan Pekeliling. Some north-bound buses leave from **Duta Bus Station** (tel: 03-6203 3150) on Jalan Duta.

Private Transport

CAR RENTAL

Having your own transport gives you the freedom to explore places off the beaten track at your leisure. Peninsular Malaysia has an excellent network of trunk roads and a dual-carriageway on the west coast. Driving is also enjoyable in Sabah and Sarawk, but you need a sturdy vehicle or even a four-wheel drive, and plenty of time. Visitors need an international driving licence.

Malaysian drivers can be speed maniacs and bullies – the bigger the vehicle, the more so. Give way. In towns, motorcyclists can shoot out of nowhere or hog the road.

The principal car rental firms are listed here. Most have branches in the main towns throughout Malaysia including those in Sabah and Sarawak.

Cars are usually for rent on an unlimited mileage basis. Weekly rates are also available. Four-wheel drive is advisable in Sabah, Sarawak and the central regions of the Malay peninsula. The Automobile Association of Malaysia (AAM) is the national motoring organisation and has offices in most states – it has a prompt breakdown service, tel: 1800-880 808.

Kuala Lumpur
Avis Rent A Car, tel: 03-9222 2558; www.avis.com
Hertz Rent A Car, tel: 03-2148 6433; www.hertz.com
Pacific Rent A Car, tel: 03-2287 4118/9; www.iprac.com

Kuching
Mayflower Car Rental, tel: 082-410 110; www.mayflowercarrental.com.my
Pronto Car Rental, tel: 082-236 889

Kota Kinabalu
Padas Jaya Rent A Car, tel: 088-239 936
Kinabalu Rent A Car, tel: 088-232 602; www.kinabalurac.com.my

Security & Crime

Malaysia is an extremely safe place to visit. Lone female travellers will encounter few problems, and violent crime against either sex is very rare. Malaysia does not suffer from the theft problems of Indonesia and Thailand, but you should still exercise reasonable caution with your luggage and possessions. Topless bathing is not a good idea in Malaysia. Though not illegal, it will embarrass Malaysian families and sensibilities. And, as anywhere, it may attract unwanted attention from men.

Warning: Trafficking in illegal drugs can result in the death penalty, and many tourists have had holidays hastily curtailed by prison; a few have also been executed.

Where to Stay

Choosing a Hotel

Malaysia offers an abundance of accommodation choices. There are international brands, home-grown chains, resort-themed and boutique establishments, serviced apartments as well as simple resthouses and backpacker hostels. With plenty of choices around, accommodation options – even high-quality ones – remain remarkably affordable.

Always enquire about packages, which include a buffet or local breakfast with the room, and if you stay more than one night, you can try bargaining for better rates. Internet rates are usually lower than walk-in or call-in rates, so check out individual hotel homepages and the **Malaysian Association of Hotels** website (www.hotels.org.my).

All hotels are required to display net rates (including the 10 percent service tax, as well as 5 percent government tax).

Price Guide

A general guide for a standard double room, excluding taxes.
$$$$ = above US$100
$$$ = US$50–100
$$ = US$30–50
$ = under US$30

Hotel Listings

KUALA LUMPUR

JW Marriott
183 Jalan Bukit Bintang
Tel: 03-2715 9000
Fax: 03-2715 7013
www.marriott.com
Centrally located luxury hotel with

fabulous spa, and the well-known Shook! restaurant with four kitchens – Japanese, Italian, Chinese and grills. It's part of the Starhill Gallery complex; guests can use the Starhill's spa and health facilities, as well as charge their dining expenses at the mall's Feast Village to their rooms. **$$$$**
Mandarin Oriental
Kuala Lumpur City Centre
Tel: 03-2380 8888
Fax: 03-2380 8833
www.mandarinoriental.com
Set within the office/shopping complex featuring the world's tallest twin buildings, this hotel has 643 luxurious rooms and executive apartments, six restaurants featuring sumptuous buffets, a grill and bar, and a Cantonese restaurant specialising in seafood. Its Thalgo Marine Spa provides relaxing diversion. **$$$$**
The Regent of Kuala Lumpur
160 Jalan Bukit Bintang
Tel: 03-2141 8000
Fax: 03-2142 1441
www.regenthotels.com
One of KL's more elegant hotels situated in bustling Bukit Bintang and well-known for its service and opulence. Its 468 rooms are tastefully furnished and come with huge bathtubs and nature-based L'Occitane toiletries. Classical music welcomes you in the stylish lounge, while the gym has Roman baths. **$$$$**
Concorde Hotel
2 Jalan Sultan Ismail
Tel: 03-2144 2200
Fax: 03-2144 1628
www.concorde.net
Central, busy hotel close to nightlife and trendy eateries. It has 673 rooms, and a popular coffee shop and lounge attracting spill-over weekend crowds from the nearby Hard Rock Café. **$$$**
Federal Hotel
35 Jalan Bukit Bintang
Tel: 03-2148 9166
Fax: 03-2148 2877
www.fhihotels.com
Hotel shares the same age as Malaysia with a colourful history, situated right on Bukit Bintang. It has 450 rooms, a revolving lounge,

decent Chinese restaurant, full-window café that is great for people-watching, supper club showcasing golden oldies stars, and an 18-lane bowling alley. **$$$**

Hotel Maya
138 Jalan Ampang
Tel: 03-2711 8866
Fax: 03-2711 9966
www.hotelmaya.com.my
This home-grown boutique hotel has rustic timber flooring and floor-to-ceiling glass panels looking out to either the Twin Towers or kl Tower. Its guests-only Sky Lounge provides views of both. The food outlets are excellent; in particular, try the *sosaku* (creative) Japanese cuisine – which blends continental and Asian flavours. **$$$**

Le Meridien
2 Jalan Stesen Sentral
Tel: 03-2263 7888
Fax: 03-2263 7222
www.lemeridien.com
A swanky establishment with contemporary decor, Jim Thompson upholstery, luxurious marble-clad bathrooms, and a lovely landscaped pool area. Like the rooms, the restaurants have great views of the city. Located within the rail transport hub, so access to and from the airport or any other part of town is easy. **$$$**

Pacific Regency Hotel Apartments
Menara PanGlobal, Jalan Punchak, off Jalan P. Ramlee
Tel: 03-2332 7777
www.pacific-regency.com
This serviced apartment located opposite the KL Tower has studios and two-bedroom, family-style units, all with fully equipped kitchenettes and free wireless broadband access. The rooftop Luna Bar is one of the city's top hang-out places. **$$$**

Capitol Hotel
Jalan Bulan
Tel: 03-2143 7000
Fax: 03-2143 0000
www.capitol.com.my
This 240-room hotel is smack in the middle of Bukit Bintang, with no car park and a faceless lobby, but it has a one-stop service to answer all guests' needs; good restaurant and a café with gourmet sandwiches and coffee. **$$**

Where to Eat

What to Eat

All of Malaysia's medium-class hotels have decent eateries, the higher-class ones have good restaurants, while hotels at the very top of the range will probably have at least one Western outlet.

Hotels also usually offer high-tea at the weekend, and their coffee houses would have the usual buffet breakfast, lunch and sometimes dinner, to cater to value-for-money demand. Western fast-food chains such as McDonald's, KFC and A&W are everywhere, as are coffee-house chains like Coffee Bean, Starbucks and Gloria Jeans.

Otherwise, try the local fare, which is not only different according to where you are, but subdivide into regional varieties, too. The best often comes as hawker food, sold at street stalls or in coffeeshops; sometimes you can get authentic preparations in restaurants, but you miss out on the atmosphere of the roadside stalls. Restaurants charge a 10 percent government tax and 5 percent service tax.

Restaurant Price Guide

A general guide for dinner for two people, excluding beverages.
$$$ = above US$40
$$ = US$20–40
$ = under US$20

Restaurant Listings

KUALA LUMPUR

CT Rose
Jalan Datuk Abdul Razak
(opposite Sekolah Kebangsaan Kampung Baru)

Mobile tel: 016-997 8701
When the craving strikes, droves head for this biggest *nasi lemak* (coconut rice) stall in the city, complete with a stunning view of the Twin Towers. The *nasi lemak* is served with sambal (chilli paste) and a variety of sides, such as deep-fried anchovies, quail eggs and fried chicken. Open daily 6.30pm–5.30am. **$**

Frangipani
25 Changkat Bukit Bintang
Tel: 03-2144 3001
This chic French fine-dining outlet, with tables set artfully around a pool, offers a lovely intimate atmosphere. Must-haves are the tea-smoked salmon with coffee-flavoured mash, roasted duck confit with mustard cream, and its wicked signature dessert, chocolate ganache with candied almond meringue. Open Tues–Sun for dinner. **$$$–$$$$**

Hakka Restaurant
6 Jalan Kia Peng
Tel: 03-2143 1908
With a heritage of over 40 years and solid Hakka culinary traditions, this family-run restaurant is the best place for authentic Hakka food. Unmissable are the Hakka noodles with minced pork sauce, *mui choy kau yuk* (braised pork belly layered with preserved vegetables) and the unique stewed fish head with fermented red rice. Open daily for lunch and dinner. **$$**

Kedai Ayam Panggang Wong Ah Wah
1, 3, 5, 7 & 9 Jalan Alor, off Jalan Bukit Bintang
Tel: 03-2144 2462
Grilled chicken wings are the main draw, but equally lip-smacking are the grilled fish (such as stingray and mackerel), oyster omelette, and chilli-fried cockles. There's also satay from the stall in front. Open daily 5pm–3.45am, except alternate Mon. **$**

Little Penang Kafe
Lot F001 & F100, Mid Valley Megamall, Lingkaran Syed Putra
Tel: 03-2282 0215
Well regarded for its Penang-style noodles, from *char kway teow* (fried flat rice noodles) to the hot and sour

asam laksa with a spicy tamarind fish gravy, to Hokkien prawn noodles. Order the multi-coloured *ice kacang*, a sweet shaved ice treat. Another branch at Suria KLCC (tel: 03-2163 0215). Open daily for lunch and dinner. **$–$$**

Old China Café
11 Jalan Balai Polis
Tel: 03-2072 5915
Best time-trip café, where the historical ambience, old photos and memorabilia and marble-topped tables provide the perfect location for just as memorable Nyonya cuisine. Specialities include *laksa* (noodles in spicy gravy) and fish head in tamarind sauce. Try the delicious sago dessert called *gula melaka*. **$$**

Restoran Oversea
84-88 Jalan Imbi
Tel: 03-2144 9911
It's been around 30 years and has a loyal following for its Chinese cuisine with contemporary twists. Think butter-fried crab claws, black pepper lamb ribs and crispy cod with pork belly. The classic favourites are excellent too; try the steamed marbled goby, *chaa siu* (barbecued pork) and roast suckling pig. Open daily for lunch and dinner. **$$$**

Saravanaa Bhavan
1007 Selangor Mansion,
Jalan Masjid India
Tel: 03-2287 1228
Outstanding Indian vegetarian food. Have a banana leaf meal – rice served on a banana leaf with an assortment of sides, from pumpkin mash and chilli paneer (fried cottage cheese with chillies and onions), to cauliflower Manchuria and mushroom *roghan josh* (mushrooms cooked in yoghurt and spices). Open daily 8am–10.30pm. **$**

Still Waters
Hotel Maya, 138 Jalan Ampang
Tel: 03-2711 8866
Exquisite *sosaku* (creative) cuisine, combining Japanese and Western ingredients. There are delicately balanced dishes such as *den miso*-gratinated lamb, beef wasabi and pan-fried foie gras with daikon. For dessert, try the pandan chawan *mushi* (steamed egg custard with screwpine juice). Open daily for lunch and dinner. **$$$**

Culture

Museums

Malaysia has a host of museums. Most intriguing and most talked about is the **Sarawak Museum** (tel: 082-244 232) in Kuching, founded in 1888 by the second white Rajah, Sir Charles Brooke, and the great evolutionist Alfred Russel Wallace. Their foresight resulted in the finest collection of Borneo artistry, and the museum is visited annually by more than 10,000 people.

Other museums worth visiting include Kuala Lumpur's **National Museum** (tel: 03-2282 6255), with its life-sized displays of court and *kampung* life, the **Perak State Museum** (tel: 05-807 2057) in Taiping and the **Royal Abu Bakar Museum** (tel: 07-233 0555) in Johor Bahru.

Most are open 9am–6pm daily, except for Fridays when they are closed between noon–2.30pm. Admission is free or at a nominal fee. Tours are rare, and information is usually in English and Bahasa Malaysia. Permission to view archives not on display can be obtained by consulting the curator. For more information, call the **Department of Museums**, tel: 03-2282 6255; www.jmm.gov.my.

Art Galleries

Paintings on Malaysian art gallery walls mirror the traditional way of life, and the conflict with the new. Much can be gleaned about how young Malaysian artists envision the future. Batik painting is much favoured, combining an old art with contemporary scenes. But other media are equally popular, and range from watercolours of *kampung* scenes to abstract oil paintings to performance art.

The **National Art Gallery** is at 2 Jalan Temerloh, off Jalan Tun Razak. The Gallery houses more than 2,500 pieces of painting, sculpture and graphic artworks by local and foreign artists from the 1930s to the present time. It is open daily 10am–6pm, and admission is free. Tel: 03-4025 4990.

Besides the main public art galleries, there are many small galleries in towns, cities and artists' villages, where you can buy a painting from the artist himself. For more information, call **Tourism Malaysia**, tel: 03-2615 8188.

Festivals

It's difficult to say which is the most exciting spectacle – a blowpipe's bull's eye in the Borneo interior; a top that spins for 50 minutes under a makeshift canopy on Malaysia's east coast; an imperial howl at Penang's Chinese opera; or an Indian dancer with bells on her toes. In Malaysia, not only do all these occur, but several may be going on at the same time. The country has a public holiday nearly every month, not counting the market feasts, royal birthdays and religious processions that sprinkle calendar pages like confetti.

The Muslim calendar consists of 354 days in a year. The Chinese and Hindu calendars, unlike the Gregorian calendar, use the lunar month as their basic unit of calculation. Hence dates vary widely from year to year. These festivals and celebrations with variable dates probably include some of Malaysia's more exciting events. For immediate events, read the daily newspapers, *Vision KL* or *KLue* or look up www.tourism.gov.my.

Shopping

General

Shopping malls are found in every city and comprise a supermarket, department store (the big chains sell branded goods) and lots of little shops, including boutiques, shoe-stores, and stores selling watches, electrical goods, computers, mobile phones, music shops, bookshops and/or stationery/magazine stores, sometimes with money changers and tour agencies, cinemas and video-arcades. Some malls specialise in certain items. They usually have eateries, too, including hawker fare-type food courts, Western fast food chains, or restaurants.

KUALA LUMPUR

The main shopping area is around **Jalan Bukit Bintang** and Jalan Sultan Ismail. Here you'll find **Bukit Bintang Plaza** (BB Plaza), which is joined to **Sungei Wang Plaza**, well known for its electrical items and photographic equipment. The more upmarket **Lot 10** across the road from Sungei Wang Plaza has mid- to high-priced items and branded goods on the top floor. Down the road is the even more upmarket **Starhill Gallery**, with its international-brand boutiques. Next door at **KL Plaza** is the American Tower Records, Kuala Lumpur's largest music store. **Imbi Plaza** and **Low Yat Plaza** are the places for computer goods, including software and peripherals. **Berjaya Times Square** and **Mid Valley Megamall** are two massive integrated shopping cum entertainment centres.

Central Market on Jalan Hang Tuah is probably the best place for souvenirs, with its two levels offering Malaysiana and Asian hand-crafted goods. For more uniquely Malaysian gifts, check out the **Kuala Lumpur Craft Centre** (tel: 03-2162 7533), on Jalan Conlay, which has original artwork and quality handicrafts, as well as **Royal Selangor**'s visitor centre (tel: 03-4145 6122) on Jalan Usahawan 6 in Setapak Jaya, showcasing stylish pewter gifts and tableware.

KL's glitziest shopping malls are **Suria KLCC** at the base of the Petronas Twin Towers, which houses all the big chains as well as interesting boutique shops, international cuisine and cosy cafés as well as cinemas, and **Avenue K** sited opposite it.

Sogo Kuala Lumpur on Jalan Raja Laut has eight floors, a waterfall on the top floor, restaurants and offices while nearby **Maju Junction** is popular with office workers.

Down the road, **Pertama Complex** is good for shoes. **The Mall** on Jalan Putra opposite the Putra World Trade Centre is still popular for *haute couture* and specialist shops; there is a stuffy hawker centre on the forth floor and souvenir stalls.

Jalan Tuanku Abdul Rahman has small interesting shops selling Asianware such as Chinese embroidery and antiques. The **Globe Silk Store** along this road has affordable clothes and textiles. Lorong Tuanku Abdul Rahman is closed to traffic every Saturday 5–10pm and transformed into a *pasar malam* (night market) with bargain goods hawked in stalls.

Jewellery, Indian saris and comfy cotton *kurta*-pyjamas are found behind this road in Masjid India. The famous and crowded **Petaling Street** *pasar malam* comes to life 5–11pm every evening, with a variety of stalls offering textiles, clothes, leather goods, jewellery, and "designer watches".

MELAKA

Jalan Hang Jebat, formerly known as Jonker Street and once the place

Antiques and Curios in Kuching

Antiques, Iban textiles, handicrafts, and quality collectibles as well as pretty and interesting handcrafted souvenirs are readily available in Kuching.

Walking down the **Main Bazaar** can take all day for a shopping enthusiast. Old trading houses and shophouses have been converted and restored into galleries and shops selling a range of goods.

Look out for **Fabriko** (tel: 082-422 233), with Edric Ong's fine range of silk woven *pua* blankets, and scarves with authentic Iban motifs using natural dyes. **Nelson's Gallery** (tel: 082-411 066) offers an eclectic collection of tribal art and ceramics. Lucas Goh's **Atelier Gallery** (tel: 082-243 492) opposite the Chinese History Museum is also filled with fine textiles and collectibles, while **Arts of Asia**, in the Main Bazaar, has beautifully crafted wooden bowls, statues, and woodcarvings among its treasures.

At the **Sarawak Handicraft Centre** at the Sarawak Tourism Complex, watch crafts being fashioned by hand and buy the results.

Anggun Collection (tel: 082-422 495) on Jalan Satok is well worth a short taxi ride from downtown for its exclusive fabrics and ready-made garments with Sarawakian motifs.

Don't miss Kuching's **Sunday Market** which starts on Saturday afternoon. Held at Jalan Satok, the market is filled with Dayak vegetable sellers, Chinese and Malay stalls selling all manner of handicrafts and jungle products.

to shop in Melaka, has been a victim of money-driven urbanisation in recent years. Traditional craftsmen have been evicted and several historic shophouses have been demolished or else subject to sham restoration projects where only the facades are kept while the interiors been modified beyond recognition. Still, antique collectors and bargain-hunters will find what they want if they search hard enough. Authentic artefacts and relics, some over 300 years old, can be found along with a host of other more recent collectibles.

Amid shops selling traditional crafts are trendy modern and creative handicraft shops such as the **Orang Utan House** at No. 59, run by an artist whose humorous T-shirts and artwork make great souvenirs. **Wah Aik Shoemaker**, formerly at No. 92, has unfortunately been demolished and moved to No. 103 Jalan Kubu, outside the main conservation area. This shop is famous for its tiny shoes made for Chinese women with bound feet, an ancient Chinese tradition of beauty that has long since died out.

Handicraft stalls are at **Taman Merdeka**, and there is a *pasar malam* on Sunday at **Jalan Parameswara**.

The city's biggest shopping mall is the **Mahkota Parade** at Jalan Merdeka, which also has an Asian antique and handicraft centre.

PENANG

Georgetown's maze of little shops around **Jalan Penang** is great for antiques and curios, such as antique clocks, old bronze and brassware, chinaware, Dutch ceiling lamps, old phonographs and Chinese embroideries and porcelain and batik. **Saw Joo Aun** at 139 Jalan Pintai Tali has a large range of antique furniture.

Little India on Lebuh King and Lebuh Queen has brightly coloured saris and *kurta*, brassware and jewellery. Chulia Street has good second-hand bookshops.

Night Markets

Open-air *pasar malam* (night markets) are good to soak in the local atmosphere and find bargain-price items, including clothes (which you try on in the open), shoes, trinkets, CDs and DVDs (often pirated) and household items. You can usually buy fresh produce, including fruit, and delicious local street food and titbits. The traders are itinerant, so check locations in the local press or at your hotel.

Chowrasta Market specialises in all kinds of cotton, silk and other materials, as well as dried local foods such as nutmeg, preserved fruits and biscuits.

More bargain-price Chinese souvenirs are at the Kek Lok Si Temple in **Ayer Itam**. **Batu Ferringhi** and **Teluk Bahang** have brightly coloured, hand-painted batik sarongs and T-shirt souvenirs; the night market at the former sells fake but decent quality designer clothes and watches.

Modern shopping malls are at KOMTAR and **Gama** on Jalan Penang, the **Midlands Shopping Mall** on Jalan Kelawei, the **Gurney Plaza** at Gurney Drive, the **Island Plaza** at Tanjung Tokong, the suburban **Sunshine Square** in Bayan Baru and **Bukit Jambul Complex**, which also has an ice-skating rink.

JOHOR BAHRU

Johor Bahru is home to giant shopping malls, such as the 440-unit **Holiday Plaza** on Jalan Dato Suleiman. Another popular spot is the **Plaza Pelangi** in Taman Pelangi. The new **Johor Bahru Duty Free Complex** on Jalan Ibrahim Sultan (Stulang Laut) has 180 shops.

TERENGGANU

In Kuala Terengganu, the **Central Market** on Jalan Sultan Zainal Abidin is the place to go to for batik and local handicrafts. **Teratai Arts and Craft** (tel: 09-625 2157) on Jalan Bandar is a lovely gallery owned by renowned artist Chang Fee Ming. It showcases his depictions of local life as well as curios from all over Asia, including coconut-shell crafts and textiles.

Outside of town, the **Chendering** industrial estate offers handicrafts and batik. **Noor Arfa Batek House** (tel: 09-617 5700) here welcomes visitors to watch and even participate in batik production. There is an excellent showroom as well.

KELANTAN

Like Terengganu, Kota Bharu's **Central Market** has copious amounts of batik and foodstuffs. The ultimate handicraft heaven is the road to PCB (Pantai Cahaya Bulan), along which certain *kampung* are renowned for their particular handicraft. Contact Tourism Malaysia for more information.

KOTA KINABALU

Kota Kinabalu is more orientated towards adventure and relaxation than shopping. Several air-conditioned plazas have an array of shops selling locally made clothes and some international brands.

Some handicraft shops can be found in **Wisma Karamunsing** and **Wisma Merdeka** where **Borneo Books** has the best range of books on the country. **Borneo Trading Post** (tel: 088-232 655) at the Waterfront has quality handicrafts, jewellery, homewares and paintings from Borneo and Southeast Asia.

The **Handicraft Market** (popularly known as Filipino Market) offers an interesting excursion into the more colourful side of Kota Kinabalu – pearls (some genuine), Filipino handicrafts, basketware and shell crafts abound. Beware of pickpockets and snatch thieves.

Centrepoint is a new huge shopping complex, for both locals and tourists alike.

Nightlife

Pubs, discos and karaoke dens are how Malaysians party at night. The best nightlife is in the capital. Elsewhere, the action concentrates in hotel lounges and discos. Other than in Kuala Lumpur, people tend not to dress up, but shorts and sandals are definite no-nos.

Nightclubs/Discos

KUALA LUMPUR

Nightlife has tended to congregate in specific areas; the main ones are **Jalan Sultan Ismail/Jalan Ampang**, **Asian Heritage Row** around Jalan Doraisamy, **Bukit Bintang**, **Bangsar** and **Sri Hartamas**.

Clubs charge an entry fee from 10pm or 11pm, which includes one drink. Wednesday is ladies' night in most places, which means free drinks for women. Happy hour is usually 5.30–9pm, when drinks are at half price, which should be taken advantage of since alcohol is very expensive in Malaysia.

Some places enforce a dress code which, for men, stipulates at the minimum, a collared T-shirt, long trousers and covered shoes, while other places have a "no jeans, shorts and sandals" rule.

Almost all the larger hotels have bars featuring live music, which usually begins at around 10pm. Bands usually play broad-appeal, middle-of-the-road music.

Popular bars include the chic and classy **Alexis The Bar Upstairs** (29A Jalan Telawi 3, Bangsar Baru, tel: 03-2284 2881), playing acid jazz; **Luna Bar** (Pacific Regency Hotel Apartments, Jalan Punchak, tel: 03-2332 7777), a rooftop, outdoor lounge bar with a pool in the middle and views to die for; and **The Poppy**

Collection (18-1 Jalan P Ramlee, tel: 03-2141 8888) with such sexy bars as Passion, Bar Mandalay and the Havanita Cigar Lounge.

One of the best clubs in town is **Nouvo** (5 Jalan Sultan Ismail, tel: 03-2170 6666), featuring music mixed by local celebrity DJs and many international guest spinners. The Havana-style club **Qba** at the Westin Kuala Lumpur (Jalan Bukit Bintang, tel: 03-2731 8333) has a live Latin band. Cigars and boutique wines are the other attractions of this classy two-storey place. The **Zeta Bar** at the Hilton Kuala Lumpur (3 Jalan Stesen Sentral, tel: 03-2264 2501) is styled after the Hilton London's namesake nightclub; it's patronised by the who's who of Kuala Lumpur. **Zouk** (113 Jalan Ampang, tel: 03-2171 1997) is a long-standing favourite for its popular 1980s-inspired Wednesday Mambo Jambo nights at Velvet Underground, as well as for the Loft's ever changing line-up of local and international DJs.

PENANG

Most of the action in Georgetown tends to centre at **The Garage**. The popular **Gurney Drive** along the waterfront also has numerous bistro-type pubs that open till the early hours.

Cubar Club (75 Gurney Drive, tel: 04-227 9823) is a popular multiple-outlet nightspot with a wine bar, a lounge, a barbecue restaurant and karaoke rooms, plus a beer garden with wooden decks and fairy lights, where you can sip Italian wine and shoot pool. **Slippery Senoritas** (The Garage, tel: 04-263 6868) is a salsa club and Mexican restaurant where DJs spin a combination of R&B, house and current hits until 10pm when a live band takes over. **Soho Free House Pub** (50 Jalan Penang, tel: 04-263 3331) is a British tavern with a pool table, football on the telly and hearty pub grub.

The choices for dancing are slim, though **ChillOut Club** at The Gurney (Gurney Drive, tel: 04-370 7000) has four bars and clubs, each

playing a different style of music, including funk and R&B.

PULAU LANGKAWI

Nightlife concentrates in **Pantai Cenang** and **Pantai Tengah**. At **Beach Garden Bistro** (Pantai Cenang, tel: 04-955 1363), you can sip margaritas under the stars after a dinner of steaks and pizzas. **Chin Chin Bar** at Bon Ton Restaurant and Resort (Pantai Cenang, tel: 04-955 6787) has cocktails and wine to accompany quiet conversations. Liqueur-flavoured coffee is its signature.

KUCHING

Kuching's nightlife centres on a few areas, such as **Jalan Padungan** and **Jalan Bukit Mata Kuching**. There are also bars and nightlife outlets in the hotels and resorts.

Jambu Tapas Bar (32 Jalan Crookshank, tel: 082-235 292) is a popular place to hang out at, especially on Friday nights when there is live jazz from 8.30pm onwards. **Soho** (64 Jalan Padungan; tel: 082-247 069) is the chicest bar in Kuching, playing a mix of jazz, Latin and dance tunes. **Eagle's Nest** at Jalan Bukit Mata Kuching is another popular place for both pub grub and drinks at reasonable prices, as well as pool and darts.

KOTA KINABALU

A range of bars and pubs at **The Waterfront** offer drinks and entertainment both indoors and on the boardwalk. Here you can find the **Cock and Bull Bistro**, a popular pub with live music, plus a pool table and wide-screen TV broadcasting football. **Shenanigan's Fun Pub** at the Hyatt Regency Kinabalu (tel: 088-221 234) is a firm favourite for its creative drinks and live music. **Cocoon** (Jalan Tun Razak Segama; tel: 088-211 252), located opposite the Hyatt, entertains with live bands and DJ-spun R&B tunes.

Getting Acquainted

The Place

Situation The small state of Brunei is along the northwest coast of Borneo, bordering the South China Sea and Sarawak.
Area 5,770 sq. km (2,228 sq. miles), one of the smallest countries in the world.
Terrain Around 70 per cent of Brunei is rainforest.
Capital Bandar Seri Begawan.
Population 379,444, of whom around 67 percent are Malays and 15 percent Chinese. The rest are Indians and indigenous tribes. There are also round 250,000 expats in Brunei.
Language Malay, but most people also speak English.
Religion Islam is the official religion, but other faiths are also practised.
Time Zone The same as Singapore and Malaysia, 8 hours ahead of Greenwich Mean Time, so New York is 13 hours, Los Angeles 16 hours

Business Hours

The overlap of Muslim custom and modern business makes opening hours a bit complicated.
Government offices open 8am–12.15pm and 1.30–4.30pm Monday–Thursday, and Saturday. Closed on Friday and Sunday. During the Muslim fasting month of *Ramadan*, open 8am to 2pm.
Private offices follow 8am–5pm business hours weekdays.
Shops are usually open 9am–9pm. Some close at 10pm.
Banks 9am–3pm Monday to Friday, 9–11am on Saturday.

and London 8 hours behind, Australia 2 hours ahead.
Currency Brunei dollar (B$), tied to the Singapore dollar. Torn Singapore notes are not accepted at most places.
Weights and Measures Metric
Electricity 220–240V, using three square-pin plugs.
International Dialing Code 673

The People

The majority of Bruneians are Malay, with some similar customs and beliefs as the inhabitants of Malaysia. Brunei is strictly Muslim, so the state is more or less dry of alcohol, and sale of pork is limited to designated sections in supermarkets. As a form of respect for the majority Muslim Bruneians, eating places display "non-halal" signs to indicate that they do not cater to Muslims.

But although strictly Muslim, Brunei is hospitable to visitors and tolerates other religions. In deference to the country's beliefs, however, visitors should adhere to the following codes of conduct:
- Remove shoes before entering a mosque or private home.
- Never walk in front of someone at prayer nor touch the *Koran* in a mosque.
- Do not pound the right fist into the left palm.
- Avoid pointing or beckoning someone with your index finger. Use a clenched fist with your thumb sticking out instead.
- To call someone towards you, wave your entire hand with the palm facing down.
- Members of the opposite sex do not shake hands in Brunei, while men prefer a light handshake rather than the vigorous shake that is common in the West.

Climate

The climate is hot, humid and sunny all year round. The rainy season is in September to January. April to July is usually the driest period. Temperatures can range

Public Holidays

- **1 January** New Year's Day
- **January/February** Chinese New Year
- **23 February** National Day
- **31 May** Anniversary of the Royal Brunei Armed Forces
- **15 July** Sultan's birthday
- **25 December** Christmas Day

Various Muslim festivals, such as Ramadan and Prophet Mohammad's birthday, are celebrated as public holidays. They are subject to the lunar calender and thus change from year to year.

from as high as 32°C (90°F) in the day to 22°C (71°F) at night.

Government

Brunei is a monarchy, ruled by the Sultan. Democratic elections do not exist, however – the last was in the 1960s – the Sultan's brother and sister are also ministers. The judicial system, based on the British judiciary, is presided over by the Supreme Court and Magistrate's Court, with breaches of Islamic law tried by special courts (*Syariah*).

Economy

Although around three-quarters of the country's food has to be imported, Brunei is one of the richest nations in the world. Oil is its livelihood, with Brunei Shell Petroleum its largest employer and exporter. The Sultan of Brunei is stupendously wealthy, and all Bruneians have a high standard of living, with good wages, free healthcare, schooling and pensions and no income tax. Although plans are afoot for when the oil supply dries up – most notably tourism, manufacturing and beef production – the prospect of a Brunei without oil is still a long way off. That means prices may be high for the budget-conscious traveller.

Planning the Trip

Visas & Passports

US citizens can stay up to 90 days without a visa. Citizens of Belgium, Canada, Denmark, France, Indonesia, Italy, Japan, Liechtenstein, Luxembourg, Maldives, Netherlands, New Zealand, Norway, Oman, Philippines, Republic of Korea, Spain, Sweden, Switzerland and Thailand do not need a visa for a stay of up to 14 days.

British, German, the Netherlands, New Zealand, Singaporean and Malaysian passport holders can stay for 30 days without visas. Australians with confirmed tickets to a third country can apply for a transit visa valid for 72 hours on arrival. They can obtain a visa-on-arrival at the airport for visits not exceeding 30 days.

All visitors must have onward/return tickets and sufficient funds to support themselves while in Brunei.

Holders of other passports must have a valid visa. These are obtainable at Brunei embassies overseas. If there is no embassy in your country, try the nearest British diplomatic mission.

Customs

Duty-free allowances for Brunei (for those 17 or over) are 200 cigarettes, 50 cigars or 227 grams of tobacco, and 60ml of perfume. Foreigners are allowed to bring in two bottles of wine or spirits and six cans of beer for their own use. Narcotics, weapons and pornography are strictly forbidden. Drug trafficking carries the death penalty.

Health

Brunei is a safe country from a health and hygiene point of view. Standards of healthcare are good, but visitors are advised to drink bottled water and to take out private medical insurance.

Money Matters

The Brunei dollar is on par with the Singapore dollar. It comes in denominations of 1, 5, 10, 50, 100, 500, 1,000 and 10,000 dollar notes and 1, 5, 10, 20 and 50 cent coins. Credit cards are widely accepted.

What to Wear

Light cotton or summer clothes are ideal. Women should cover their head, knees and arms when entering a mosque. Men may be required suits and ties at some formal occasions.

Getting There

BY AIR

Brunei International Airport in Bandar Seri Begawan is well served by regional Asian airlines. Royal Brunei Airlines flies to over 20

Tourist Information Abroad

Tourist information on Brunei is limited. There are no tourist offices abroad, but you can obtain brochures from Brunei's diplomatic offices in your home country:
● **Australia**
10 Beale Crescent, Deakin, A.C.T 2600, Canberra
Tel: 02-6285 4500
● **Canada**
395 Laurier Avenue East, Ottawa, Ontario K1N 6R4
Tel: 613-234 5656
● **United Kingdom**
19/20 Belgrave Square, London SW1X 8PG
Tel: 0207-581 0521
● **United States**
3520 International Court NW,

Women Travellers

Brunei is a very safe country to travel around, even for the lone female visitor. Though Muslim, Bruneian women are less conservative than their counterparts elsewhere in Southeast Asia, and because there is such a substantial expatriate population, the men here are tolerant of Western ways. Pay heed to Muslim sensibilities, though, by dressing modestly in public places.

destinations. There is a B$12 airport tax (B$5 for flights to Singapore and Malaysia) payable on departure. Infants below two years of age are exempted.

BY SEA

Ferries travel daily between Bandar Seri Begawan and Labuan, a tax haven island off the southwest coast of Sabah, from where you can take another ferry to Kota Kinabalu in Sabah. The ferry service operates between 7am and 4pm and departs from the Serasa Terminal in Muara Town.

Washington DC 20008
Tel: 202-237 1838
Useful publications available from them on request include: *Brunei Darussalam in Profile* (facts and figures on the country), *Brunei Darussalam in Profile* and *Selamat Datang*.

If you intend an extended stay in the country, however, your best bet is to wait until you arrive and get hold of a copy of *Brunei Insider's Guide (BIG) Magazine*, an excellent free guide on Brunei published by Brunei Tourism (tel: 238 2822; www.tourism brunei.travel), which is available at the airport and hotels throughout the country.

Practical Tips

Media

Newspapers: Foreign magazines and newspapers are sold in Bandar Seri Begawan. English-language publications available daily are the *Brunei Times* and the *Borneo Bulletin*.

Television and radio: TV is a diet of Bruneian, Malaysian, Indonesian and international cable TV programmes. Some of Brunei's radio channels broadcast in English while some have programmes in English at specified times. Broadcasts are interspersed with the Muslim call to prayers five times daily.

Embassies

United Kingdom: 2.01 Level 2, Block D, Yayasan Sultan Haji Hassanal Bolkiah Complex, tel: 222 2231, 222 2131.
United States: 3rd floor, Teck Guan Plaza, Jalan Sultan. Bandar Seri Begawan, tel: 222 0384.

Tourist Information in Brunei

The Brunei Tourist Information Bureau has an office at the Government Rest House on Jalan Cator in Bandar Seri Begawan, open during normal business hours. *Explore Brunei* is the government's guide, with a good map of Bandar Seri Begawan.
● Brochures and information are also obtainable from the Tourism Development Division, Ministry of Industry & Primary Resources, Jalan Mentiri Besar, Bandar Seri Begawan 3910, Brunei Darussalam, tel: 238 2822; www.bruneitourism.travel.
● If you are staying for a while, the

best source of information is *Brunei Darussalam, A Guide*. Published by Brunei Shell, it is written for expats based in Brunei and has good suggestions for places to visit and day trips. It is available at bookstores and the Brunei Shell Marketing office PGGMB Building on Jalan Kianggeh.
● *Brunei Insider's Guide* (BIG) is a free quarterly magazine published by Brunei Tourism that provides a comprehensive listing of attractions and events in the country. The magazine is available in all hotel rooms in Brunei and at Brunei diplomatic offices abroad.

Telecommunications

There are plenty of public phones throughout the capital and most of them operate on calling cards such as Hello, Netkad and Payless. These cards, in B$5, B$10, B$20 and B$50 denominations, can be purchased at most stores. Prepaid calling cards for the two mobile telephone operators, DST and Bmobile, can be purchased from their respective outlets. You can send faxes from most Telbru offices or from hotels. Rates are very high.
International access codes:
AT&T: 800 1111; MCI: 800 011;
Sprint: 800 015.

Postal Services

Post offices are plentiful in all areas of Brunei. The main post office at the Old Airport, Berakas, opens 8am–4.30pm daily except Friday (8–11am and 2–4.30pm) and Sundays, when they are all closed.

Medical Treatment

Medical standards are high in Brunei and, unlike in the rest of Southeast Asia, there is no risk of malaria. RIPAS Hospital and Jerudong Park Medical Centre are comparable to the best in Asia, and there is a nationwide network of smaller hospitals and clinics.

Getting Around

On Arrival

Brunei International Airport is about 12 km (8 miles) from the centre of Bandar Seri Begawan. Normal travel time into the city is 15–20 minutes. Taxis cost B$25–35. Hotel transport is normally available if you provide the hotel with your flight number and arrival time.

Public Transport

The Brunei Bus Service charges a B$1 flat rate for any distance in one route. It starts at 6am and ends at 9pm. The buses run at intervals of 15–20 minutes.

TAXIS

Metered taxis cost B$3 for the first kilometre. Fares range from B$10 for a short trip in the city centre to more than B$100 for a journey from Bandar Seri Begawan to Kuala Belait.

Private Transport

CAR RENTAL

Car hire agencies at the airport and the major hotels charge B$100 per day for an economy-sized sedan. Cars with drivers cost B$360 a day (10 hours). Petrol is cheap in Brunei.

Water Transport

Between the Bandar Seri Begawan waterfront and Kampong Ayer, the standard fare for a boat trip is 50 cents. For charter journeys, the price is negotiable, ranging from B$15 to 20 per hour.

Where to Stay

Shopping

Culture

Choosing a Hotel

Hotels in Brunei are generally in the high-end bracket, and budget accommodation is almost non-existent. However, some top-end hotels are just slightly higher than the equivalent in Malaysia.

Price Guide

A general guide for a standard double room, excluding taxes.
$$$$ = above US$100
$$$ = US$50–100
$$ = US$30–50
$ = under US$30

BANDAR SERI BEGAWAN

The Empire Hotel and Country Club
Muara Tutong Highway
Kampong Jerudong
Tel: 241 8888
www.empire.com.bn
Located 15 minutes from Brunei International Airport and just outside Bandar Seri Begawan. This beachfront resort – with a Jack Nicklaus-designed championship golf course – overlooks the South China Sea. **$$$$**
Hotel Sheraton Utama Begawan
Jalan Tasek
Tel: 224 4272
www.sheraton.com/utama
Centrally located, and 9 km from Brunei International Airport, the hotel's facilities include newly refurbished rooms with cable television; gym and fitness centre; and a business centre. **$$$$**
Le Gallery Suite and Hotel
Mile 1, Jalan Tutong
Tel: 224 1128
Brunei's very own boutique hotel for design-conscious visitors. **$$**

What to Buy

Brunei specialities include textiles, baskets, brocade, silver and brass. For a one-stop shop for such souvenirs, Brunei Arts and Handicrafts Training Centre is a two-minute drive east of downtown Bandar Seri Begawan. Prices tend to be higher than elsewhere in Southeast Asia. Import tax on luxury goods has been abolished.

Where to Buy

Experience the open air local market alongside the Kianggeh River or the night market in Gadong. The following is a list of recommended department stores and supermarkets.
Hua Ho is one of the biggest chain of department stores in Brunei and has a number of branches throughout the capital.
First Emporium, Muhammad Yussof Complex, B.S.B.
Gadong Centrepoint, Gadong, B.S.B.
Kota Mutiara Dept Store, Darussalam Bldg, B.S.B.
Millimewah Dept Store, Darussalam Bldg, B.S.B.
Seria, Seria Plaza, Jln. Sultan Omar Ali, Seria.
Yayasan Sultan Haji Hassanal Bolkiah Complex, B.S.B.

Museums

Brunei Museum 6km from the centre of BSB, houses a collection of 15th-century Bruneian artefacts, with an interesting section on oil. Open 9.30am–5pm daily, except on religious public holidays and Friday when it opens 9–11.30am and 2.30–5pm. Buses run from the central station to the museum.
Malay Technology Museum, next door, sits on the riverbank and centres round the technologies and livelihood of the water villages of Brunei. Open 9.30am–5pm daily, except Tuesday (when it is closed) and Friday when it opens 9–11.30am and 2.30–5pm.
Brunei History Centre traces the history of the Sultan and his family. Open Monday to Thursday and Saturday 8am–12.15pm and 1.30–4.30pm. Admission is free.
Royal Regalia Building displays royal artefacts, silver and gold armoury, coronation crown, royal chariots and other ceremonial paraphernalia. Open 8.30am–5pm daily, except Friday 9–11.30am, 2.30–5pm.
Sultan Haji Hassanal Bolkiah Islamic Exhibition Gallery houses the king's personal collection of holy manuscripts and artefacts from the Islamic world.

Getting Acquainted

The Place

Situation Tip of the Malaysian peninsula on the Strait of Malacca.
Area 699 sq. km (267 sq. miles).
Population 4.48 million, of whom 75 percent are Chinese, 14 percent Malays, 9 percent Indians and the rest other ethnic groups.
Languages Malay, English, Tamil and Mandarin are official languages.
Religions Buddhism, with Taoist elements, is practised by the majority of Chinese. The Malay population is Muslim, and Indians Hindu, Muslim or Sikh. All Eurasians and significant numbers of Chinese and Indians are Christian.
Time zone 8 hours ahead of Greenwich Mean Time (GMT).
Currency Singapore dollars ($), divided into 100 cents.
Weights and measures Metric
Electricity 220–240 volts, using several plug configurations, including 3-prong square, 2-prong flat, and 2-prong round.
International dialing code 65 (no area codes).

The People

The customs, religions and languages of nearly every nation in the world have converged in Singapore at some time in history,

Singlish

It may sound like a machine-gun rattle, but it's actually English. Singaporeans blend words, disregard syntax and add "*lah*" to about everything.

although Buddhism and Taoism are the most commonly practised religions. Adjectives beginning with "multi" are commonplace on the Singapore scene, and a cosmopolitan tolerance is part of the city's character.

With everyday etiquette relaxed and straightforward, visitors behaving courteously stand little chance of unintentionally giving offense. Some ceremonies and special occasions, however, recall inherited traditions, and a familiarity with certain customs will set everyone at ease.

Climate

The average daily temperature is 27°C (81°F), often rising to around 31°C (88°F), and cooling only to around 24°C (75°F) at night. Humidity averages 84 percent.

The northeast monsoon blows from November to January, and the southwest from May to September, and wind speeds are light all year.

Spectacular thunderstorms occur frequently between the monsoons, in April to May and October to November. The average rainfall is 2,352mm (93 in) with the heaviest rains falling between November to January, and the least falling in July.

Economy

Singapore is one of the world's busiest container ports with some 140,000 ships cruising in its straits per year bringing with them around 450,000 tonnes of cargo. As Singapore lacks natural resources, finance and business services, manufacturing, commerce, transport and communications, and construction are the backbone of its thriving economy, which consistently has an inflation rate of around 1–1.5 percent. Major trading partners include the US, Malaysia, European Union, Hong Kong and Japan.

Per capita Gross National Income is over US$29,000. In 2006 Singapore's economy registered a growth of 8 percent. It has a strong tourism industry with 9.7 million visitor arrivals per year. The

government's aim is to improve the already efficient infrastructure and become the business hub of Asia Pacific, with first-class products and services.

Government

Singapore has a single-chamber parliamentary government, with general elections held every five years. The People's Action Party (PAP), in power since 1965, is led by Prime Minister Lee Hsien Loong. President S.R. Nathan is the Head of State.

Business Hours

Offices 9am–5pm
Banks 10am–3pm weekdays, 9.30–11am Saturday. Some also open 11am–4pm Sunday.
Shops 10am–9pm (most open on Sundays). Department stores usually open until 9.30pm. Many shops and F&B outlets in Orchard Road open until midnight on the last Friday of the month.

Public Holidays

- **1 January** New Year's Day
- **January/February*** Chinese New Year (two days)
- **March/April*** Good Friday
- **1 May** Labour Day
- **May*** Vesak Day
- **9 August** National Day
- **October/November*** Deepavali
- **25 December** Christmas Day

On the two days of Chinese New Year many restaurants and shops are closed. Bear in mind too that over Ramadan and the Chinese New Year accommodation and transport are usually booked.

* Variable dates depending on the Chinese, Muslim, Hindu or Christian calendars. Other public holidays with variable dates are **Hari Raya Puasa** and **Hari Raya Haji**. Check exact dates with the Singapore Tourism Board (tel: 1800-736 2000; www.visitsingapore.com).

Planning the Trip

Visas & Passports

Visitors need to satisfy the following requirements before they are allowed to enter:

- Passport valid for at least six months;
- Confirmed onward or return tickets;
- Sufficient funds to maintain themselves during their stay in Singapore;
- Visa, if applicable.

Citizens of British Commonwealth countries (except India and Pakistan), the UK, European Union, Canada and the US do not require visas. Such visitors will automatically be given a 30-day social visit pass when arriving at the airport, in the form of a stamp in their passports.

Check with a Singapore embassy or consulate if you need a visa for entry, the rules of which are regularly subject to change, or look up the **Singapore Immigration and Checkpoint Authority** (ICA) website at www.ica.gov.sg.

In addition, the visitor must hand in a completed disembarkation/embarkation card to the immigration officer. Upon immigration clearance, the disembarkation portion will be retained while the embarkation card returned to the visitor. When the visitor leaves Singapore, the embarkation portion must be handed to the immigration officer.

Visa Extensions: Your social visit pass can be extended by another 2–4 weeks by submitting the requisite form at the ICA's **Visitor Services Centre**, 4th Storey, ICA Building 10 Kallang Road, tel: 6391 6100. Forms may be downloaded directly from the ICA website at www.ica.gov.sg. Note: a local sponsor is required in order to apply for an extension of the social visit pass. The easier way to extend your stay is to leave the country, such as to Johor Bahru across the border in Malaysia, for a day and have your passport re-stamped on entry into Singapore.

Customs

The duty-free allowance per adult is 1 litre of spirits, 1 litre of wine or port and 1 litre of beer, stout or ale. No duty-free cigarettes are allowed into Singapore although they may be purchased on the way out.

Duty-free purchases can be made both upon arrival and departure except when returning to Singapore within 48 hours. This is to prevent Singaporeans from making a day trip out of the country to stock up on duty-free goods. In addition, visitors arriving from Malaysia are not allowed duty-free concessions.

The list of prohibited items includes drugs (the penalty for even small amounts can be death); firecrackers; obscene or seditious publications, video tapes and software; reproduction of copyright publications, video tapes or discs, records or cassettes; seditious and treasonable materials; endangered wildlife or their by-products; chewing tobacco and imitation tobacco products; and chewing gum other than for personal use.

A complete list of prohibited, restricted and dutiable goods is available from the airport's **Customs Duty Officer**, tel: 6542 7058 (Terminal 1), tel: 6546 4656 (Terminal 2), or check the **Singapore Customs** website at: www.customs.gov.sg.

Health

Singapore is as sparklingly clean as billed. Safe drinking water and strict government control of all food outlets make this a hygienic place to visit, but should the need arise, medical facilities are excellent. Most of their services are available to non-citizens but at substantially higher rates. For this reason, ensure that you have bought adequate travel insurance policy.

Vaccination against yellow fever is necessary if you are arriving from a country where the disease is endemic. Singapore is malaria-free although dengue fever, spread by daytime mosquitoes, occurs occasionally in the residential neighbourhoods. However, there is no cause for alarm as these are not areas usually frequented by tourists.

Money Matters

The Singapore dollar is divided into 100 cents. Notes are in $2, $5, $10, $20, $50, $100, $500 and $1,000 denominations, and there are $1 and 1, 5, 10, 20 and 50 cent coins. There are no restrictions on the amount and type of currency you can bring into Singapore.

Traveller's cheques are probably

Tourist Information Offices Abroad

The Singapore Tourism Board (www.visitsingapore.com) has offices in many countries.

● **Australia**
Level 11, AWA Building
47 York Street, Sydney
Tel: 02-9290 2888

● **New Zealand**
1340-C Glenbrook Road
RD1, Waiuku,
Auckland
Tel: 09-834 8641

● **United Kingdom**
Singapore Centre
Grand Buildings, 1–3 The Strand,
London WC2N 5HR
Tel: 020-7484 2710

● **United States**
1156 Avenue of the Americas,
Suite 702, New York, NY 10036
Tel: 212-302 4861
5670 Wilshire Boulevard #1550
Los Angeles, CA 90036
Tel: 323-677 0808

the best form of money to take, in US dollars or sterling. Banks and licensed moneychangers offer better exchange rates than hotels. Some shops will even accept traveller's cheques as cash. Major credit cards are widely accepted, and can be used to obtain cash at banks and ATMs.

What to Wear/Bring

Light summer clothes that are easy to move in are the most practical choice for a full day out in town. Men should wear a white shirt and tie, women a smart business suit, for office calls.

In the evening, only a few plush nightclubs and exclusive restaurants favour the traditional jacket and tie. Most hotels, restaurants, coffee houses and discos accept casually elegant attire. However, jeans, T-shirts, sneakers and shorts are taboo at some restaurants and discos. To avoid embarrassment, it is best to call to check an establishment's dress code in advance.

You really can travel light in Singapore, as shops are excellent and shopping is perhaps the national sport.

Getting There

BY AIR

Singapore Changi Airport is frequently rated the best in the world. The airport is so efficient that one can be in the taxi – after clearing immigration, retrieving bags and passing through customs – in 15 minutes after landing.

Over 80 airlines operate more than 4,000 flights a week to **Changi Airport**'s three terminals, **Terminal 1** (T1), **Terminal 2** (T2) and the **Budget Terminal**, which is aimed at budget travellers. Terminals 1 and 2 – which can handle over 5,000 passengers per hour during peak periods – are linked to each other by the Sky Train. Passengers can shuttle between the Budget Terminal and the main terminals by the BT Shuttle Service. The airport

has been conceived for maximum comfort and convenience, with a wide range of services and shops – in other words, it's a great airport to wait out a delayed flight.

Transit passengers who have a minimum of five hours' layover time before catching their connecting flight can book a two-hour **Free City Tour**. Bookings can be made at the Singapore Visitors Centre counters at T1 and T2, which open for registration from 8am to 4.25pm daily; six tours are available daily from 9am to 5pm on a first-come-first-served basis.

Free maps and guides to the city are available, including the free airport magazine, *Changi Express*, which details all the airport services. If you need help, look out for the Information and Customer Service counters scattered in the terminals or the 24-hour help phones, which will link you to the appropriate customer service officers.

For more information on airport services, contact **Customer Service** (tel: 6541 2267; www.changi airport.com.sg). For information on flight arrival and departure times, call 1800 542 4422.

Flying from UK and US

There are regular daily flights out of London and major European cities direct to Singapore. Flying time is between 12 to 13 hours. Many UK and Europe travellers heading to Australia and New Zealand often use Singapore as a transit point to break the long journey. From Singapore it is another 4½ hours to Perth, 7½ hours to Sydney and Melbourne, and 10 hours to Auckland.

A flight from Los Angeles or San Francisco which crosses the Pacific Ocean takes about 16–18 hours with a stop in Seoul, Taipei or Tokyo along the way. From New York, flight time is about 22 hours including transit time.

The national carrier **Singapore Airlines** (www.singaporeair.com) is based at Changi Airport and flies to some 99 destinations in 41 countries. It has non-stop flights from Los Angeles and New York to Singapore.

BY SEA

Arriving slowly by sea is a pleasant experience. Most visitors arrive at the **Singapore Cruise Centre** (tel: 6513 2200; www.singaporecruise. com) located at the HarbourFront Centre. The facility is also used by several regional cruise operators such as Star Cruises (www.star cruises.com) and by many large cruise liners stopping over on their long voyages from around the world.

Tanah Merah Ferry Terminal (tel: 6545 2048), located near the Changi Airport, handles boat traffic to the resorts on Indonesia's Bintan island as well as Tanjung Pinang, its capital, and to Nongsa, on neighbouring Batam island. Ferries to Malaysia's Sebana Cove also depart from here.

Changi Ferry Terminal (tel: 6214 8031), also near Changi Airport, handles regular ferry services to Tanjung Belungkor on Malaysia's east coast.

BY RAIL

Visitors can also enter and leave Singapore by rail through Malaysia. Five trains a day, all operated by **Keretapi Tanah Melayu Berhad** (KTMB) (tel: 6222 5165 in Singapore; www.ktmb.com.my), connect Singapore to Kuala Lumpur and other west coast and central Malaysian cities. A daily *International Express* Train connects Singapore to Thailand, as does the ultra-upscale **Eastern & Orient Express** (tel: 6392 3500 in Singapore, 800-524 2420 in the US; www.orient-express.com).

The E&O is the ultimate recreation of a bygone age of romantic Asian rail travel. Decked out in the E&O livery of cream and racing green, it carries a maximum of 132 passengers on the three-night, 50-hour trip from Bangkok through southern Thailand, Butterworth to Kuala Lumpur and Singapore.

The Tanjong Pagar Railway Station (tel: 6222 5165) is on Keppel Road, a 20-minute walk from the Tanjong Pagar MRT station.

BY ROAD

There are good roads down the west and east coasts of Peninsular Malaysia crossing either the Causeway at Woodlands or the Second Link in Tuas into Singapore. The Second Link is far less prone to the frequent congestion that the Woodlands checkpoint experiences.

Private air-conditioned buses run from Hatyai in Thailand and many towns in Malaysia to Singapore. The ride from Hatyai takes about 15 hours with stops for refreshments and arrives in Singapore at Golden Mile Complex along Beach Road. Call **Gunung Raya** (tel: 6533 9988; www.gunungraya.com) for bus tickets to Hatyai.

Hasry (tel: 6294 9306; www.hasryexpress.com) as well as Gunung Raya above have buses which connect Singapore to key Malaysian cities like Kuala Lumpur, Penang and Melaka. Buses arrive and leave from its Lavender Street office.

Other coach operators such as **Plusliner** (Kuala Lumpur tel: 03-2272 1586, Singapore tel: 6256 5755; www.plusliner.com), **Aeroline** (Kuala Lumpur tel: 03-6258 8800, Singapore tel: 6341 9338; www. aeroline.com.my) and **Airebus** (Kuala Lumpur tel: 03-2141 7110, Singapore tel: 1800-247 3287; www.airebus.com.my) offer the more luxurious and roomier 26-seater, executive-class coaches. These link Kuala Lumpur and other major Malaysian cities to Singapore.

Fines

Singapore is an extremely safe place, and violent crime and theft are rare. But to keep these high standards, the country imposes fines on just about every misdemeanour: from smoking in public places and dropping litter, to crossing a road other than at a pedestrian crossing to, believe it or not, failing to flush a toilet!

Practical Tips

Media

Newspapers and Magazines

The *Straits Times*, *Today* and *Business Times* are good English-language dailies, with the tabloid *New Paper* appearing in the afternoons. *The Edge Singapore* is a business and investment weekly. The *International Herald Tribune* is available on the day of publication. Some of the best sources of listings and information on events are magazines like *8 Days*, *I-S* and *Time Out Singapore*. American, British, Australian, European and Asian newspapers and magazines are available at newsstands hotel kiosks everywhere, and bookstores such as MPH, Times, Kinokuniya and Borders. These bookstores have extensive selections of international books and media.

Television and Radio

There are eight programme channels, the ones in English being Channel 5, Central and NewsAsia. Several radio stations feature English shows. Eight of the local radio stations broadcast in English. BBC World Service is on 88.9FM.

Postal Services

Singapore Post (tel: 1605; www. singpost.com) is very efficient and mailboxes can be found near every MRT station. An aerogramme or airmail postcard to anywhere costs just 50 cents. Letters weighing not more than 20 grams to North and South America, Europe, Africa and Middle East countries cost S$1.10 and to Australia and New Zealand. The fee for a registered item is S$2.20 (plus postage).

Apart from postal services,

Singapore Post provides other services such as parcel delivery, issuance of travellers' cheques, local and foreign money orders and bank drafts, philatelic sales, post-box mail collection, and a variety of other services.

Singapore Post's main branches are at **Change Alley**, 02-02 Hitachi Tower, 16 Collyer Quay, tel: 6538 6899 (Mon–Fri 8.30am–6.30pm, Sat 8.30am–1pm) and at **1 Killiney Road**, tel: 6734 7899 (Mon–Fri 8.30am–9pm, Sat 8.30am–4pm, Sun and public holidays 10am–4pm). The Singapore Post branch at the Departure Hall, **Changi Airport Terminal 2** (tel: 6542 7899) is open 8am–9.30pm daily. Most other branches are open Mon–Fri 8.30am–5pm (Wed until 8pm) and Sat 8.30am–1pm.

Courier Services

Singapore Post has a courier service called **Speedpost**, which services more than 200 countries at fairly reasonable rates. Call 1800-225 5777 or check www.speedpost.com.sg for more information and rates. International couriers in Singapore include DHL (tel: 1800-285 8888), **Fedex** (tel: 1800-743 2626) and UPS (tel: 1800-738 3388).

Telecommunications

TELEPHONES

Most hotels rooms have phones that allow you to make International Direct Dial (IDD) calls. Charges are reasonable.

Singapore's country code is 65. There are no area codes. To call overseas from Singapre, dial the international access code 001 followed by the country code, area code and local telephone number. Alternatively you can dial 013 or 019 for cheaper IDD rates, although the lines may be weaker.

PUBLIC PHONES

There are three types of public pay phones commonly found at

Useful Numbers

Fire/Ambulance 995
Police 999
International Operator 104
Local Directory Enquiries 100

shopping centres and mrt stations. Coin-operated pay phones for local calls (increasingly rare these days), card phones using phonecards for local and IDD calls, and credit card phones for local and IDD calls.

Phone cards can be used for both local and overseas calls. Local calls cost 10 cents for the first 3 minutes and 10 cents for every subsequent 3 minutes, up to a maximum of 9 minutes. Phone cards can be purchased from post offices and convenience stores.

MOBILE PHONES

Only users of GSM mobile phones with global roaming service can connect automatically with Singapore's networks. If you're planning to be in Singapore for any length of time, it's more economical to buy a local SIM card from one of the three service providers: Singtel (tel: 1626), M1 (tel: 1627) and Starhub (tel: 1633). All local mobile numbers begin with an 8 or 9.

INTERNET

To get online, head to an Internet café (try **Chills Café** at 39 Stamford Road, #01-07; daily 9am–midnight tel: 6883 1016; www.chillscafe.com.sg) or public libraries for cheap Internet access. Alternatively, sign up for **Wireless@SG**, a new system that provides free wireless connection at selected hot spots around Singapore. Visitors will need a mobile device with WiFi facility, and will have to register with one of the three service providers: iCELL Network (tel: 6773 4284; www.icellnetwork.com), QMax Communications (tel: 6796 0313; www.qmax.com.sg) and Singtel (tel: 1610; www.singtel.com). Check the

Infocomm Development Authority website www.ida.gov.sg for an updated list of hot spots.

Medical Treatment

Singapore has the best healthcare facilities in the region. Private clinics are abundant; the average cost per visit varies between S$30–55 for a general practitioner and S$100–150 for a first consultation by a specialist.

Government and private hospitals, found all over the island, include:
Singapore General Hospital, 7 Outram Road, tel: 6222 3322; www.sgh.com.sg
Mount Elizabeth Hospital, 3 Mount Elizabeth Road; tel: 6737 2666; www.mountelizabeth.com.sg
KK Women & Children's Hospital, 100 Bukit Timah Road; tel: 6293 4044; www.kkh.com.sg

Tourist Information

The Singapore Tourism Board (www.visitsingapore.com) runs a 24-hour tourist information hotline: 1800-736 2000. Visitor centres are at the following locations:
Singapore Changi Airport Transit Halls, Terminals 1 and 2 Arrival Halls and Transit Halls; **Junction of Cairnhill and Orchard Road;** Suntec

Embassies

Please call to confirm opening hours before visiting.
● **Australia**
25 Napier Road
Tel: 6836 4100
● **Canada**
1 George Street, #11-01
Tel: 6854 5900
● **New Zealand**
391A Orchard Road, #15-06, Ngee Ann City Tower A
Tel: 6235 9966
● **United Kingdom**
100 Tanglin Road
Tel: 6424 4200
● **United States**
27 Napier Road
Tel: 6476 9100

City Mall, #01-35; **Liang Court** Level 1; **Singapore Cruise Centre,** #01-31D, Arrival Hall, HarbourFront Centre; and **InnCrowd Backpackers' Hostel,** 73 Dunlop Street, Little India.

Tipping

Tipping is usually not practised in Singapore. It is not allowed at the Changi Airport and discouraged in many hotels and restaurants, where a 10 percent service charge is routinely added to bills on top of the Goods and Services Tax (GST) of 7 percent. Tour guides and drivers do appreciate tips (5 to 10 percent). Very small tips (S$1–2) can be paid to taxi drivers, porters and hotel housekeeping staff.

City Tours

Various private and group tours are offered by Singapore tour companies. These can be booked directly or through hotel tour desks. Use guides licensed and trained by the Singapore Tourism Board. There are city tours, river tours, as well as specialised tours focusing on food, farming, Chinese opera and feng shui (Chinese geomancy). Tour operators include **Holiday Tours** (tel: 6738 2622) and RMG **Tours** (tel: 6220 8772; www.rmgtours.com.sg

The zany **DUCKTours** (tel: 6338 6877; www.ducktours.com.sg) take you from land to river as they cover key tourist sights in their amphibious half-boat, half-truck vehicles. The same company also offers **HiPPOTours,** which are city sightseeing trips on open-top double-decker bus. Visitors can hop on and off at designated stops along the way. **Journeys** (tel: 6325 1631; www.singapore walks.com) offer the **Original Singapore Walks,** which take you to the more unusual places of interest, including fresh-produce markets, red-light districts, "haunted" nooks and graveyards.

Getting Around

Orientation

Singapore is an easy city to get around. The hardy walker can easily cover most areas of interest such as the Singapore River area, Chinatown, Civic District, Arab Street, Little India and the Orchard Road area on foot. These and all the outlying places of attractions can be reached easily with public transport (MRT and buses) or by taxi.

On Arrival

Changi Airport is linked to the city centre by the East Coast Parkway (ECP) and to the other parts of Singapore by the Pan-Island (PIE) and Tampines (TPE) expressways. There are five types of transport from the airport – taxi, car, bus, airport shuttle and MRT.

TAXI

At all three airport terminals, the taxi stands are situated on the same level as the arrival halls. A surcharge of S$3 (or S$5 from 5pm–midnight Fri–Sun) applies in addition to the fare shown on the taxi meter. There are two other surcharges which are added to the fare where applicable: for rides between midnight and 6am and ERP (Electronic Road Pricing) tolls. The taxi trip to the city centre takes about 20–30 minutes and costs around S$25, excluding the surcharges.

PRIVATE/RENTED CAR

If you are to be picked up by a private car at Terminal 1, take the inclined travelator in the Arrival Hall to the ground level, which leads to the Passenger Crescent where a private car pick-up point is located. At Terminal 2, the car pick-up point is on the same level as the Arrival Hall. Car rental counters are located at both terminals.

PUBLIC BUS

In the basements of Terminals 1 and 2 are public bus depots. Buses depart between 6am and midnight daily, and information on bus routes is available at the bus stands. Service No. 36 gets you direct into the city. You'll need the exact fare as no change is given on board. The bus stops closest to the Budget Terminal are a 15-minute walk away on Airport Boulevard. It is easier to take the BT Shuttle Service to Terminal 2 to transfer to the MRT service or to either terminal for the bus service to the city.

AIRPORT SHUTTLE

The comfortable **Maxicab** operates between the airport and major hotels in the city, with flexible alighting points within the CBD. Tickets at S$7 for adults and S$5 for children are available at the shuttle counters located at the terminals.

MRT

The MRT link to Changi Airport is located underground next to Terminal 2. A ride to the city centre takes about 30 minutes and costs S$1.50.

Public Transport

BUS AND MRT

Singapore's public transport system is fast, efficient, comprehensive, spotlessly maintained and cheap. An especially helpful source for all information about the use of buses and the MRT is the **TransitLink Guide** which is available at most bookstores and newsstands. This booklet gives complete details of all bus and MRT routes and contains a section on public transport services to major tourist spots. Or call one of the following:
SBS Transit, Tel: 1800-287 2727
SMRT Buses, Tel: 6482 3888
SMRT Corp, Tel: 1800-336 8900
TransitLink, Tel: 1800-767 4333
If you are going to be moving around a lot by public transport, it is convenient to buy a **TransitLink ez-link card**, which is a stored-value card for use on the MRT and buses. The ez-link card is available from all Transit Link offices at MRT stations and bus interchanges for S$15, of which S$5 is a non-refundable deposit. To use this card, tap it on the electronic readers located at MRT turnstiles or the entrances of buses. The electronic readers will automatically deduct the maximum fare. When exiting from MRT turnstiles and buses, tap the card again against the electronic reader and the unused portion of the fare is credited back to your card. You can top up the value of your card when it runs low.

TAXI

Taxis are plentiful. A string of surcharges apply to the fare: 50 percent extra from 11.30pm to 6am; for trips leaving the business district; during peak hours; during public holidays; for advance bookings; Electronic Road Pricing (ERP) fees; and trips from the airport. Most drivers speak or understand some English. To book a taxi, contact:
Comfort, Tel: 6552 1111
CityCab, Tel: 6552 2222
SMRT Taxi, Tel: 6555 8888

Private Transport

In a bid to tackle congestion and keep down pollution, the government severely restricts city traffic. Don't bother to drive as car rentals are prohibitively expensive and the Electronic Road Pricing (ERP) system is a hassle.

Where to Stay

Choosing a Hotel

In terms of accommodation, amenities and service standards, Singapore's upmarket hotels easily compare with the best in the world. Deluxe, first-class and business-orientated hotels all have conference and business facilities, in-room computer ports, cable television and in-room IDD phones. If you arrive without prior hotel reservations, the hotel reservation counters at the arrival halls of the Changi Airport Terminals 1 and 2 and the Budget Terminal can help with bookings. The counters are open 24 hours daily. Or simply call the hotel of your choice direct.

When making reservations directly – even from the airport – it is wise to ask for discounts or special rates. Rates are subject to 10 percent service charge and 7 percent GST (Goods and Service Tax).

Price Guide

A general guide for a standard double room, excluding taxes.

$$$$ = above US$150
$$$ = US$100–150
$$ = US$50–100
$ = under US$50

Hotel Listings

The Fullerton
1 Fullerton Square
Tel: 6733 8388
www.fullertonhotel.com
The city's former General Post Office, this restored landmark sits in the heart of the Civic District, along the Singapore River. Business travellers will appreciate its proximity to the financial district and its contemporary art deco interior filled with Philippe Starck fittings. Café, exquisite Chinese restaurant, trendy bar and exclusive fine-dining restaurant with stunning views. One Fullerton across the road entices with more waterfront dining options. $$$$

Grand Hyatt
10 Scotts Road
Tel: 6738 1234
singapore.grand.hyatt.com
A stone's throw from Orchard Road and its MRT station. Minimalist, almost stark decor, comfortable rooms and excellent service are its defining hallmarks. Restaurants serving Chinese, Italian, stylish mezza9 restaurant with elegant bar, coffee house, bar/club. Its free-form pool with lush gardens is a haven in this busy neck of the woods. $$$$

Raffles Hotel
1 Beach Road
Tel: 6337 1886
www.raffleshotel.com
The city's most famous and most expensive hotel, beautifully restored to its former grandeur with upmarket shopping annex, hotel museum and Victorian-style theatre. A total of 13 restaurants and bars offering Continental and American-style deli foods, innovative Asian and local cuisines and lots of old-world atmosphere. $$$$

Ritz-Carlton Millenia
7 Raffles Avenue
Tel: 6337 8888
www.ritzcarlton.com
Striking modern hotel, with US$5 million art collection and Singapore's biggest guest rooms (and stunning bathrooms with views to match). Located beside the Suntec conference centre. Restaurants serving New Asia cuisine, fine Cantonese, and a stylish café. The bar with a riveting glass sculpture as its talking point is perfect for after-dinner drinks. $$$$

Shangri-La's Rasa Sentosa Resort
101 Siloso Road, Sentosa
Tel: 6275 0100
www.shangri-la.com
Singapore's only beachfront hotel overlooks the South China Sea. It offers a fine buffet breakfast, free watersports equipment and has a good seafood restaurant. While it is not the most convenient place to stay for access to the city, it does have a free downtown shuttle service. $$$–$$$$

Hotel 1929
50 Keong Saik Road
Tel: 6347 1929
www.hotel1929.com
This boutique property combines a mix of old-world Singapore architecture and nouveau-chic style. No two rooms are designed the same way and many are embellished with unique furniture from the owner's private collection. Its Ember restaurant has won rave reviews for its chic ambience and creative fusion cuisine. $$$

Marriott
320 Orchard Road
Tel: 6735 5800
www.marriott.com
Pagoda-roofed hotel at the corner of Scotts and Orchard Roads. Opposite the MRT station and perfect for shopping and nightlife. Popular café-restaurant with outdoor seating, distinguished Chinese restaurant serving *dim sum*. The famous Tangs department store is just next door. $$$

Mandarin Singapore
333 Orchard Road
Tel: 6737 4411
www.mandarin-singapore.com
Serious shoppers would do well to stay here as all the major malls and boutiques (and two MRT stations) are within walking distance. Continental cuisines served in Singapore's highest revolving restaurant; International and Chinese food available in speciality restaurants; lounge, 24-hour Chatterbox coffee house is noted for its local speciality of Hainanese chicken rice. $$$

New Majestic Hotel
31–37 Bukit Pasoh Road
Tel: 6511 4700
www.newmajestichotel.com.
This hot boutique hotel oozes style and individuality from all corners, from the custom-designed rooms done up by some of Singapore's brightest young artists to its

acclaimed modern Chinese restaurant. **$$$**

Pan Pacific
7 Raffles Boulevard
Tel: 6336 8111
www.singapore.panpac.com
John Portman-designed hotel with grand atrium. Well located beside Suntec City, the island's biggest convention centre. Cantonese restaurant with grand views (from 37th floor), traditional-style Japanese restaurant, outdoor buffet dining, Italian and North Indian restaurant, bakery, coffee shop, lounge bar. **$$$**

The Scarlet
33 Erskine Road
Tel: 6511 3333
www.thescarlethotel.com
Located near Chinatown, this 84-room boutique hotel in an exquisitely restored prewar shophouse is luxurious and dramatic, with characterful ensuite rooms. **$$$**

Hotel Rendezvous
9 Bras Basah Road
Tel: 6336 0220
www.rendezvoushotels.com
Four-star hotel next door to the Singapore Art Museum and close to the Civic District. Its Rendezvous Restaurant is sure to delight diners with its famous spicy *Nasi Padang* (Indonesian-style rice and curries) The spacious Palong Lobby Bar is the ideal spot to relax after sight-seeing or a long business day. **$$**

Phoenix
277 Orchard Road
Tel: 6737 8666
www.hotelphoenixsingapore.com
Excellent value for its fantastic location on Orchard Road. Next door is the Somerset MRT station. All rooms have a personal multimedia computer with Internet access. **$$**

YMCA International House
1 Orchard Road
Tel: 6336 6000
www.ymca.org.sg
Situated in the colonial Civic District close to Dhoby Ghaut MRT station. There are conference facilities, a coffee house, rooftop swimming pool, fitness centre, squash and badminton courts. **$**

Where to Eat

What to Eat

Singaporeans love to eat and their preoccupation with culinary matters means that finding good food here – at the right price – presents no problem. Whether you fancy *haute cuisine*, ethnic foods, vegetarian or spicy local dishes, you are sure to find many great choices.

All hawker centres and food courts – which have an astounding variety of foods – are subject to regular government health and safety inspections, so you can be well assured of hygienic standards and fair selling practices.

Local favourites at these centres include Hainanese chicken rice, prawn noodles, fish ball noodles, satay, fish rice porridge, barbecued chicken wings and a wide range of barbecued seafood including lobster, prawns and fish.

The restaurant dining scene is equally exciting, with fine-dining French restaurants, simple bistro-style food and Italian fare, East-meets-West "fusion" cuisine as well as a slew of Asian restaurants.

Several areas are host to a variety of eateries. Among these locations are **Ngee Ann City** (Orchard Road), with at least three floors of restaurants; **Boat Quay**, **Clarke Quay** and **Empress Place Waterfront** with rows of restaurants (all are strung along the Singapore

Restaurant Price Guide

A general guide for dinner for two people, excluding beverages.
$$$$ = above US$80
$$$ = US$50–80
$$ = US$30–50
$ = under US$30

River); the all-weather **Far East Square**, **Robertson Walk** (off River Valley Road); **Marina Bay** at One Fullerton building; the ever popular **Holland Village**; and the city's latest dining hub, **Rochester Park**.

Restaurant Listings

Banana Leaf Apolo
54 Race Course Road, Little India
Tel: 6293 8682
Located within walking distance of the Little India MRT station, this is one of Singapore's most popular South Indian restaurants, famed for its fiery fish-head curry. Vegetarian dishes are also available. Meals are served on banana leaves. **$**

Blue Ginger
97 Tanjong Pagar Road
Tel: 6222 3928
A stylish modern restaurant in a converted shophouse offering time-honoured Peranakan cuisine. Very good food but small portions; try the fresh mackerel simmered in spicy tamarind, the beef *rendang* and the deep-fried eggplant. **$$**

Cherry Garden
5 Raffles Avenue
The Oriental Singapore
Tel: 6331 0538
Imaginative Hunan, Sichuan and Cantonese dishes served in a Chinese-style spring courtyard with timber ceiling. Signature dishes include camphor-smoked duck, lotus leaf-wrapped chicken and stir-fried chicken with red pepper and garlic. **$$$**

Coriander Leaf
#02-02 Clarke Quay,
3A River Valley Road
Tel: 6732 3354
This cutting-edge restaurant, helmed by chef Samia Ahad, dishes out innovative Mediterranean, Middle Eastern and Asian fare. If sufficiently enamoured of the food – most people are – sign up for the restaurant's cooking classes.
$$–$$$

East Coast Seafood Centre
1110 East Coast Parkway
A collection of informal, family-type restaurants that fill up on weekends. A good place to gorge on seafood prepared Singapore-style.

Cheap unless ordering Sri Lankan crabs. The restaurants here include **Red House** (tel: 6442 3112), **Long Beach** (tel: 6448 3636) and **Jumbo** (tel: 6442 3435). **$$**

Ember
Hotel 1929, 50 Keong Saik Road
Tel: 6347 1928
The Modern European cuisine here is delightfully robust yet reined, and sometimes comes with wonderful Asian accents. Everything is good, really, and you should definitely have the Maine lobster linguine in clam *jus* and slow-roasted lamb loin.

Equinox
68–72 Floors, Swissôtel The Stamford, 2 Stamford Road
Tel: 6431 5669
A complex of five restaurants and bars sits atop the hotel. Start with drinks at the New Asia Bar on the 71st level while taking in stunning city views out its floor-to-ceiling windows, then descend one level to swanky French-Cambodian restaurant Jaan, decorated with Murano crystal and shimmering Cambodian silk. **$$$**

Glutton's Bay
01-15 Esplanade Mall
Tel: 6336 7025
Dine on some of Singapore's best-loved street food under the moonlight. A popular spot with both locals and tourists, Glutton's Bay has 12 push-cart hawkers selling favourites like barbecued chicken wings, char kway teow (fried flat noodles with clams in dark sauce) and oyster omelette. Open daily for dinner only. **$**

Lei Garden
#01-24 CHIJMES, 30 Victoria Street
Tel: 6339 3822
One of Singapore's best Cantonese restaurants, Lei Garden is renowned for its *dim sum* lunches and fresh seafood dishes served in an exquisite formal setting. **$$$**

Les Amis
#02-16 Shaw Centre, 1 Scotts Road
Tel: 6733 2225
Very chic award-winning restaurant with great wine cellar. Modern French cuisine is exquisitely prepared with attention to freshness and simple, but pure flavours. **$$$$**

Lingzhi
#01-01 Far East Square
7–13 Amoy Street
Tel: 6538 2992
The vegetarian cuisine here is so good, some would gladly give up meat for life. The goodness of soy, mushrooms, nuts and vegetables is creatively employed in beautifully presented dishes. **$$$**

Rendezvous Restaurant
Hotel Rendezvous
9 Bras Basah Road
Tel: 6339 7508
Its history stretches six decades but the steamy corner coffee shop is now a comfortable air-conditoned restaurant located in Hotel Rendezvous. Still enduring are its fiery *nasi padang* favourites from fish to vegetable curries and *sambal* (spicy) seafood dishes. **$$**

Saint Pierre
#01-01 Central Mall
3 Magazine Road
Tel: 6438 0887
One of the top spots in Singapore for high-end French cuisine given a Japanese twist. The setting is stylish, and top favourites include the innovative foie gras dishes, black cod in miso sauce and desserts like Grandma Stroobant's flourless chocolate cake. **$$$**

The Rice Table
#02-09 International Building
360 Orchard Road
Tel: 6835 3783; also at
43 Cuppage Road
Tel: 6735 9117
One of the very few eateries in town serving the Dutch-Indonesian *rijsttafel*; the individual dishes making up the meal are also available à la carte. **$$**

Tepak Sireh Restoran
73 Sultan Gate, Kampong Glam
Tel: 6396 4373
This resplendent mustard-coloured building next to the Istana Kampong Gelam was originally built for Malay royalty. The restaurant's recipes, reportedly handed down through generations, live up to expectations. Only buffet-style meals; recommended are its beef *rendang*, squid curry and pandan tea. **$**

Culture

General

Once decried as a sterile cultural desert with no soul, Singapore has transformed itself over the last few years into a lively arts and entertainment city.

The performing arts scene is enlivened by such professional and amateur companies as Theatreworks (English-language theatre), Singapore Dance Theatre (ballet) and Singapore Lyric Theatre (opera), while the annual cultural calendar is headlined by the **Singapore Arts Festival** (www.singaporeartsfest.com) in June, which is well regarded for its line-up of innovative works from around the world.

The iconic **Esplanade – Theatres on the Bay** (tel: 6828 8222; www.esplanade.com) is Singapore's main performing arts centre, a landmark that many hope can rival the Sydney Opera House. Music, theatre, dance and outdoor performances are hosted in this large complex. This is also where the noted **Singapore Symphony Orchestra** performs regularly; check www.sso.org.sg for programme updates.

Buying Tickets

Tickets to performing arts events can be booked by phone, in person and online (and paid for in all cases by credit card) with **SISTIC** (tel: 6348 5555; www.sistic.com.sg) or **Ticketcharge** (tel: 6296 2929; www.ticketcharge.com.sg).

SISTIC outlets are located at 1 Temasek Avenue (Millenia Walk), 252 North Bridge Road (Raffles City Shopping Centre) and 435 Orchard Road (Wisma Atria). Ticketcharge outlets are located at 176 Orchard Road (Centrepoint) and 163 Tanglin Road (Tanglin Mall).

Art Galleries

The many art galleries in Singapore offer a whole gamut of choices – from rare European masterpieces to modern abstracts by young local artists. Most galleries offer worldwide delivery service.

Art-2 Gallery
#01-03 MICA Building
140 Hill Street
Tel: 6339 9371
www.art2.com.sg

Art Seasons Gallery
5 Gemmill Lane
Tel: 6221 1800
www.artseasons.com.sg
International contemporary art pieces reside in this three-storey gallery above a wine bar.

Artfolio
#02-25 Raffles Hotel Shopping Arcade, 328 North Bridge Road
Tel: 6334 4677
www.artfolio.com.sg
Contemporary Asian art, including works by prominent Malaysian-born artist Eng Tay.

Opera Gallery
#02-12H Ngee Ann City
391 Orchard Road
Tel: 6735 2618
www.operagallery.com
Showcasing paintings and sculptures of internationally renowned contemporary artists and 19th-century masters.

Soobin
#01-10 MICA Building
140 Hill Street
Tel: 6837 2777
Specialising in Southeast Asian and Chinese art.

Local Listings

The STB's *Official Guide to Singapore, Time Out Singapore* and *WHERE Singapore* are full of relevant information. *The Straits Times'* What's On section, *8 Days* magazine and the *IS* magazine are also excellent sources.

Shopping

General

Singapore's downtown is stuffed with air-conditioned malls, department stores and boutiques, and the ethnic neighbourhoods offer additional street markets and unique shops. Most shopping centres and shops are open from 10am to 9 or 9.30pm daily.

Prices for many goods in Singapore are equal to or higher than those in Western countries. One of the best times to shop is the **Great Singapore Sale** (www.greatsingaporesale.com.sg), which runs from the last week of May through June and July. There are good discounts on a wide range of goods during these eight weeks.

Tax-free shopping: Although a Goods and Services Tax (GST) of 7 percent is levied on most purchases, this can be refunded if you spend a minimum of S$100 at shops participating in the **Global Refund Scheme** (tel: 6225 6238; www.globalrefund.com) or the **Premier Tax Free Scheme** (tel: 1800-829 3733; www.premiertaxfree.com). At shops with the "Tax-Free Shopping" or "Premier Tax Free" sticker, fill in a voucher for your purchases. Before your departure, validate the voucher at the airport customs, then present it together with your purchased items at the Global Refund counter or Premier Tax Free Scheme counter for your refund.

Where to Buy

ANTIQUES AND HANDICRAFTS

Shoppers for Buddhist art and antiques should check out **Lopburi**

Arts & Antiques (#01-03/04, Tanglin Place, 91 Tanglin Road, tel: 6738 3834). Shipping and certificates of authenticity are provided. There is a cluster of antique shops at **Tanglin Shopping Centre** (19 Tanglin Road), including **Antiques of the Orient** (#02-40, tel: 6734 9351; www.aoto.com.sg), **Akemi Gallery** (#02-06, tel: 6735 6315), Hassan's Carpets (#01-12, tel: 6737 5626; www.hassans carpets.com), **Naga Arts & Antiques** (#01-49, tel: 6235 7084; www.nagaarts.com) and **Renee Hoy Fine Arts** (#01-44, tel: 6235 1596).

Dempsey Road (Tanglin Village), near the Botanic Gardens, is also filled with many tiny antique and Asian collectible shops. **Pagoda Street** and **Mosque Street** in Chinatown are also well known for their antique stores.

COMPUTERS

Funan DigitaLife Mall, 109 North Bridge Road and **Sim Lim Square**, 1 Rochor Canal Road, are two shopping centres packed with numerous computer stores.

FASHION AND CLOTHING

Orchard Road is Singapore's major downtown shopping strip. Among the largest shopping malls here are **Wisma Atria**, noted for its fashion boutiques; **Ngee Ann City**, with the Japanese department store **Takashimaya**; **Paragon**, with numerous luxury boutiques; and **Centrepoint**, a long-time favourite of Singaporeans. **Far East Plaza** and **The Heeren Shops** have trendy streetwear at low prices. Two popular home-grown emporiums are **Tangs** with well-loved fashion, beauty and household sections, and **Robinsons**, Singapore's oldest department store located at Centrepoint.

The **Civic District** is also dominated by malls good for fashion shopping. These include **Suntec City Mall**, **Raffles City** and and **Marina Square**.

Getting Acquainted

The Place

Situation Over a distance of around 5,280 km (3,200 miles), the 18,110 Indonesian islands (6,000 of which are inhabited) are dotted from the Asian mainland down into the Pacific Ocean.

Area Though the total area (sea and land) is about 2.5 times greater than Australia, the land area is just 2 million sq. km (770,000 sq. miles).

Population 220 million, rising by nearly 2 percent per year. Java is the most densely populated island, with almost 115 million inhabitants. Over 60 percent of Indonesians live on Java and Bali, although these islands account for only 7 percent of the nation's land mass.

Languages The national language is Bahasa Indonesia, similar to Malay, but most Indonesians also speak one of over 250 local languages. (Some estimate there are as many as 500 distinct languages.)

Religion 87 percent Muslim, with small numbers of Hindus, Buddhists, Christians and Confucians.

Time zones Indonesia's considerable spread covers three time zones. Java, Sumatra and West and Central Kalimantan are on Western Indonesia Standard Time, 7 hours ahead of GMT. Bali, Lombok, East and South Kalimantan, Sulawesi, Nusa Tenggara and West Timor are on Central Indonesian Standard Time, 8 hours ahead of GMT (the same time zone as Singapore and Hong Kong). Maluku and Papua (Irian Jaya) are on Eastern Indonesia Standard Time, GMT plus 9 hours.

Currency Rupiah (Rp or IDR)

Weights and Measures Metric

Electricity Mainly 220V using rounded two-pin plugs. Small hotels operate on 25-watt bulbs, so light can be quite dim at night. Power cuts are frequent in rural areas.

Climate

All of the archipelago's islands lie within the tropical zone, and the surrounding seas have a homogenising effect on temperatures and humidity. Consequently, local factors like topography, altitude and rainfall produce more variation in climate than latitude or season. Mean temperatures at sea level vary by only a few degrees throughout the region (25–28°C, or 77–82°F). In the mountains, however, the temperature decreases about 1°C (2°F) for every 200 metres (650 ft) of altitude, which makes for a cool, pleasant climate in upland towns like Java's Bandung or the hills north of Jogja and Bali's Ubud.

Much of the archipelago also lies within the equatorial ever-wet zone, where no month passes without several inches of rainfall. The northeast monsoon means that many western islands receive drenching precipitation for part of each day between November and April, and the tropical sun and the oceans combine to produce continuously high humidity (between 75–100 percent). The eastern islands, however, receive little rainfall throughout the year.

The southeast monsoon tends to counteract this generally high humidity by blowing hot, dry air up from over the Australian landmass between May and October.

Business Hours

Government offices 8am–3pm weekdays, except Friday when they close at 11.30am. On Saturdays, they are often open until around 2pm.

Business offices weekdays 8–9am until 4–5pm. Some companies work Saturday mornings as well. **Banks** 8am–3pm on weekdays.

Planning the Trip

Visas & Passports

All travellers must possess a passport valid for at least six months after arrival and tickets proving onward passage.

Visa regulations are constantly changing. At the time of writing, free 30-day visas are given to citizens of only 11 countries. Visas-on-arrival are given to 52 other countries (US$10 for a 3-day stay; US$25 for a 30-day stay). All others must apply to the Indonesian embassy or consulate

Public Holidays

Many public holidays are based on the lunar calendar and these dates are therefore variable (indicated by *)

January 1: New Year's Day
***January/February:** Chinese Lunar New Year
***February/March:** Hindu New Year or Seclusion Day (Nyepi) Birthday of the Prophet Muhammad
***March/April:** Good Friday
***April/May:** Ascension of Jesus Christ
***May/June:** Birth, Enlightenment and Death of Buddha (Waisak)
***July/August:** Ascension of Prophet Muhammad
August 17: National Independence Day
***September:** End of the Muslim fasting month
***November/December:** Muslim Day of Sacrifice
December 25: Christmas Day
***December/January:** Islamic New Year

in their home country for a visa before travelling.

A *surat jalan* (travel permit) is required for visits to certain destinations, such as Aceh.

Health

Yellow fever vaccinations are required if arriving within six days of leaving or passing through an infected area.

Determine if you will be travelling in a malaria-infected area (not all of Indonesia is). Use insect repellent and wear long pants and long-sleeved shirts around dawn and dusk. Sleep under a mosquito net in infected areas.

Dengue fever, carried by daytime mosquitoes, is far more prevalent in Indonesia than malaria is, especially during the rainy season (November–April). There is no prophylactic; take the precautions described above if travelling in an infected area.

Healthcare in Western-standard hospitals in large cities is good. However, in villages sanitation and health provisions are poor. Health insurance allowing air evacuation is recommended.

Indonesian tap water is undrinkable. Bottled water is widely available. Street food is risky. Avoid salads, ice and unpeeled fruit outside Western-standard hotels and restaurants.

Money Matters

Indonesia's national currency, the *rupiah*, comes in bank note denominations of 100,000, 50,000, 20,000, 10,000, 5,000, and 1,000. Coins come in 1,000, 500, 200, 100, and 50 rupiah.

Changing money: Bring only new notes (no coins), as practically no one will change dirty or marred bank notes. The best exchange rate is usually obtained at money-changers. Hotels usually offer a lower rate, and banks often offer even worse rates. It is advisable to change most currencies in the cities. Rupiah may be freely converted to foreign currencies

when leaving. Be sure to ask for small notes for taxis and tipping.

Traveller's cheques: Good at major hotels and banks in cities only.

Credit cards: MasterCard and Visa are accepted at most large hotels, restaurants and shops. American Express and Diner's Club cards are less prevalent. Adding 3–5 percent to the bill for credit card use is an accepted practice.

ATMS: These are ubiquitous in large towns and cities.

What to Wear/Bring

Light, loose clothing is the most practical. Shorts and scanty tops should be reserved for the beach, as Muslim Indonesians expect a high standard of modesty. Casual and smart-casual clothes are acceptable for nearly every occasion.

Essentials are insect repellant, sunblock, sunglasses and a sun hat. Also bring an adequate supply of prescription medicines and always hand carry them, as checked luggage can get lost or delayed.

Getting There

BY AIR

Most flights arrive either at Jakarta's **Sukarno-Hatta International Airport** or Bali's **Ngurah Rai Airport**. There are now international arrivals throughout the country.

Garuda Indonesia (www.garuda-indonesia.com) is the national carrier. The international departure tax must be paid in rupiah and averages about Rp 100,000.

BY SEA

Occasional luxury cruise liners stop in Bali. Check with a travel agent in your home country.

Batam and Bintan islands, part of the Riau archipelago, are serviced by high-speed ferries that connect to Singapore.

Practical Tips

Media

The Jakarta Post is the major English-language newspaper. In addition, most international newspapers – English-language and others – are available at the newsstands of large hotels and major airports. *Tempo* magazine, published in Indonesian and English, is a good source of political and business news. Several magazines list events and restaurants, such as *Jakarta/Java Kini*, *Hello Bali*, and *Bali and Beyond*, which are distributed free in large hotel rooms but can also be found at newsstands.

Television is available everywhere, even in the most remote locations. Larger towns and cities have cable TV, so in addition to Indonesian channels, they receive CNN, HBO, MTV and the like.

Postal Services

Regular airmail to Western countries takes 7–10 days, whereas express airmail delivers in as little as 3 days. Domestic mail is fast and generally reliable except to outer islands. Post offices are generally open Monday to Thursday 8am–2pm, Friday 8am–noon and Saturday 8am–1pm. The central post office in larger cities may stay open later.

International courier services like DHL (tel: 0800-133 3333), Fedex (0800-188 8800) and UPS (tel:

Emergency Numbers

- **Ambulance:** 118
- **Fire:** 113
- **Police:** 110

0807-187 7877) offer reliable overseas deliveries.

Telecommunications

TELEPHONES

Telephone services are rapidly being modernised and overhauled, particularly in urban areas. Don't be surprised to see telephone numbers with as few as six and as many as eight digits. As the phone system is brought into the 21st century, telephone numbers often change. Although every effort has been made to ensure that telephone and fax numbers in this guide are correct, if a number listed doesn't work, it has probably been upgraded – and changed.

Hotels offer international direct dialling (IDD) services, with the usual surcharges. International calls can also be made from public phone kiosks called *wartel*. Dial 001, 007, 008 or 017 for an international line, and 102 for international directory enquiries.

If calling Indonesia from overseas, dial the country code 62, followed by the area code (leaving out the zero), then the telephone number. When calling from one province to another in Indonesia, dial the area code with the zero in front of it.

MOBILE PHONES

Indonesia uses GSM 900 and 1800 networks. Coverage may be limited to main towns and cities, depending on the provider.

INTERNET

Public kiosks, called *warnet*, and cyber cafés provide Internet access, as do large hotels and resorts.

Medical Services

HOSPITALS AND CLINICS

International-standard medical facilities are available in large cities. However, some expatriates living in Indonesia prefer to fly to Singapore for medical treatment and carry medical insurance that also covers emergency airlift evacuation. The following hospitals and clinics, all open 24 hours, have English-speaking staff.

Jakarta
SOS Medika (AEA International Clinic)
Jalan Puri Sakti 10, Cipete, Jakarta
Tel: 021-750 6001

Yogyakarta (Jogja)
AMK (Asia Medika Klinik)
Jalan Abubakar Ali No. 3, Jogja
Tel: 0274-748 2100; 748 3100
Emergency tel: 081-328 107 779

Bali
BIMC
Jalan Bypass Ngurah Rai
No. 100X, Kuta
Tel: 0361-761 263

International SOS Bali
Jalan Bypass Ngurah Rai 505X, Kuta
Tel: 0361-710 505

Security & Crime

Indonesia is certainly safer, on the whole, than most Western cities. As with everywhere, watch out for pickpockets in crowded areas, thieves in cheap hotels, and the occasional scam artist. Take the usual precautions. Don't leave valuables unattended, and watch your purse, wallet and backpack in crowded areas. Report any theft immediately to the police or a security officer, as without a police report, new passports and travel documents can be difficult to obtain.

It is unusual for a young woman to travel alone in Indonesia, and solo females may have to put up with being pestered by gregarious Indonesian men. However, women will be quite safe as long as they dress and behave modestly.

Embassies

All foreign embassies are based in Jakarta, though many have

Trouble Spots

Although Indonesia is largely a safe country for travellers, contact your own ministry of foreign affairs to keep yourself informed of the current situation in trouble spots such as Poso (Central Sulawesi).

consulates in Bali. France, Italy and the Netherlands also have consulates in Jogja. The major embassies in Jakarta are:
Australia: Jalan H.R. Rasuna Said, Kav 15–16.
Tel: 021-2550 5555
UK: Jalan M.H. Thamrin 75, Menteng. Tel: 021-315 6264
Canada: Jalan Jend Sudirman Kav. 29 World Trade Center.
Tel: 021-2550 7800.
Germany: Jalan M.H. Thamrin No. 1. Tel: 021-390 1750.
Switzerland: Jalan H.R. Rasuna Said Kav X/32. Tel: 021-520 7451
The Netherlands: Jalan H.R. Rasuna Said Kav. S3.
Tel: 021-525 1515.
United States: Jalan Medan Merdeka Selatan 5, Jakarta Pusat.
Tel: 021-344 2211.

Tipping

Although tipping is not standard in Indonesia, small gratuities for good service are always welcome. Airport and hotel porterage is Rp 5,000 per bag. Tipping taxi drivers is not mandatory, but rounding up the fare to the nearest Rp 1,000 is standard. However, if you are travelling with a hired-car driver or a guide, a tip is a good idea.

Most hotels and some upscale restaurants add a 10 percent service charge to bills.

Take Heed!

Possession of narcotics is a serious crime in Indonesia. Prosecution can mean a long prison term – perhaps even death – and/or huge fines.

Getting Around

By Air

Indonesia's domestic airline industry is in a constant state of flux. Remote airports extend runways to accommodate larger aircraft, airports are upgraded, and new privately owned airlines are established.

In addition to **Garuda Indonesia** (www.garuda-indonesia.com), **Mandala Airlines** (www.mandalaair. com) and **Merpati Nusantara** (www.merpati.co.id), smaller airlines such as **Adam Air** (www.adamair. co.id), **Batavia Air** (www.batavia-air.co.id), **Lion Air** (www.lionair.co.id) and **Sriwijaya Air** (www.sriwijayaair-online.com) make travelling within Indonesia easier than before.

It is best to arrange all domestic flights once you are in Indonesia. Note that in remote areas, flights are not linked to computerised reservation systems, so you have to purchase tickets in the town itself rather than pre-book them from a larger city.

Reconfirm all domestic flights to make sure they are on schedule. Be sure to get a computer printout with a confirmation number.

Each airport sets its own departure tax, which averages Rp 30,000.

By Sea

PELNI (Pelayaran Nasional Indonesia), the state-owned shipping company, serves about 30 ports, with each ferry accommodating 1,000–1,500 passengers in four classes. As ferries are often dangerously overloaded, travel by sea is not recommended. However, intrepid travellers can check www.pelni.co.id for schedules.

In bad weather, the seas can be quite rough, particularly between Sumatra and Java, between Bali and Lombok, and around Komodo.

By Bus

Buses are the mainstay of local transport in Indonesia. Generally, there are three classes. Top are luxury, air-conditioned buses, called *ekekutif* (executive)-class buses, with TVs and toilets. They often travel from town to town during the night when roads are less congested. On Java and Bali, *ekekutif*-class air-conditioned mini-buses and vans travel during the day, for example from Jakarta to Bandung, to serve commuters and tourists.

Bottom-grade (and very cheap, called *ekonomi*) full-sized or mini buses transport locals from village to village. Most offer standard routes but stop everywhere, are packed and stuffy.

In between, *ekspres* (express) buses cover longer distances. Some are a little better than *ekonomi*, others are air-conditioned and can be booked ahead.

By Train

There is an adequate train service in Java, a more limited one in Sumatra, but it's virtually non-existent elsewhere.

In Java, the railway extends from the west (which connects with ferries to Sumatra) and to the east (which connects with ferries to Bali). Visitors usually ask for *ekekutif*-class seats, which is far more comfortable than *ekonomi* ones. However, for long trips (such as from Jakarta to Jogja), tickets on a domestic no-frills airline can be about the same price but the travel time is greatly reduced.

City/Town Transport

Be prepared for delays any time you travel in Indonesia, as roads are always crowded during the day.

Intercity Transport

City-to-city transport is arranged through local booking offices. The easiest way to obtain schedules and tickets is to ask your hotel for assistance.

TAXI

Taxis are ubiquitous in cities and the good ones are metered and air-conditioned. If a driver refuses to turn the meter on, get out and get another taxi. Not all drivers speak English, so having your destination and address written down could be helpful.

Taxis can also be hired for the day for touring or to go from one city to another. Some have rates by the hour or distance; others may want to negotiate the fare. Ask to see the rate schedule first before agreeing on a price.

RENTAL CAR

Self-driving in Indonesia is dangerous; roads can be narrow and are always overcrowded. Motorcycles weave in and out of traffic, men pushing carts suddenly appear, and dogs and chickens frequently stray onto the roads. If a collision occurs, you are responsible for all costs, which could be endless. In addition, you need an international driving license or tourist driving permit before hiring a car.

Bookings can be made at hotels or at the airport with either local or international car rental companies. If you do decide to self-drive, practise defensive driving diligently.

A better option is to hire a car with a driver. Negotiate better rates if you are booking a vehicle for a week or longer but note that you are responsible for the driver's food and lodging, and for the petrol.

You can ask for an English-speaking driver. If none is available, you can hire a guide for a nominal extra cost. Guides in Jakarta, Jogja and Bali speak several foreign

From the Airport

In Jakarta, Jogja and Bali, taxi service from the airport is coupon based and efficient. Avoid the touters and head to the clearly marked taxi desk for a ticket, then go directly to the taxi queue. Prices are fixed and taxis are air-conditioned. Drivers may or may not speak English, so it's a good idea to have your destination and address written down.

In Jakarta, DAMRI airport buses run from 3am to 10pm, servicing strategic stops in the city. The air-conditioned buses run every half hour between the city and the airport for a US$1.50 fare.

languages, so you can request the language you prefer. If you stop for a meal or snack, it is expected that you also treat the driver and guide. Tips for good service are always appreciated.

PUBLIC MINI-BUS/BUS

Navigating Jakarta is now easier than ever via its new busway, which comprise seven corridors of bus-only lanes connecting all points to downtown Jakarta. Buses are air-conditioned and clean.

Mini-buses (collectively known as *bemos* in Bali and *angkot* in Java) are inexpensive. Almost every bemo on the road in Bali may be hired by the trip or by the day. Just tell the driver where you want to go and then agree on a price. However, don't expect them to speak English.

MOTORCYCLE

Motorcycles are readily available for rent in Jogja and Bali. They are very cheap and a great way to get around. Note that Indonesia law requires that every driver and passenger wear a helmet.

Where to Stay

Choosing a Hotel

In large cities, local and international hotels range from one to five star. Bali's multitude of luxury resorts are often highly rated in worldwide surveys. In more remote places, however, expect only the most basic. During high season (August–September, December–January), prices are higher. The best prices for brand-name hotels are often found on the Internet.

Price Guide

A general guide for a standard double room, excluding taxes.
$$$$ = above US$150
$$$ = US$100–150
$$ = US$50–100
$ = under US$50

Hotel Listings

JAKARTA

Grand Hyatt Jakarta
Jalan Jend M.H. Thamrin
Tel: 021-390 1234
www.hyatt.com
One of Jakarta's best, this sophisticated hotel sits above the Plaza Indonesia mall. Excellent service. **$$$$**
Shangri-La
Jalan Jend. Sudirman Kav. 1
Tel: 021-570 7440
www.shangri-la.com
This 32-storey luxury hotel is centrally located. An excellent Chinese restaurant serves *dim sum* on Sundays, while the popular B.A.T.S. bar is on the first level. **$$$$**
The Dharmawangsa
Jalan Brawijaya Raya, No. 26

Tel: 021-725 8181
www.dharmawangsa.com
Intimate boutique-style hotel with only 100 rooms, a third of which are suites. A haven of understated luxury, with expensive artworks throughout. **$$$$**
Crowne Plaza Jakarta
Jalan Gatot Subroto
Tel: 021-526 8833
www.crowneplaza.com
A five-star hotel with an excellent Spanish restaurant, Plaza de Espuma. Includes a 24-hour café and 24-hour business centre. **$$$**
Gran Meliá Jakarta
Jalan Rasuna Said
Tel: 021-527 3747
www.granmelia.co.id
Part of the Spanish-run Melia Sol chain. An elegant 428-room hotel with beautiful landscaped gardens. Known for its good Sunday brunch. **$$$**
Arcadia
Jalan Wahid Hasyim No. 114
Tel: 021-230 0050
e-mail: arcadia@indosat.net.id
This small and interesting hotel of Art-Deco design is well located and has a good range of services. **$$**
Sofyan Cikini
Jalan Cikini Raya 79
Tel: 021-314 0695
Fax: 021-310 0432
www.sofyanhotel.com
A small, comfortable hotel that's a taxi ride away from the city centre. The staff is friendly and there is a good range of services. **$$**
Djody
Jalan Jaksa 35
Tel: 021-390 5976
Situated close to Medan Merdeka (Freedom Square) and the Gambir train station. There are several small restaurants within walking distance. The rooms are very basic, with fan or air-con but no hot water. **$**

YOGYAKARTA (JOGJA)

As Indonesia's second-largest tourist destination, Jogja offers a full range of accommodation from luxurious presidential suites to simple, inexpensive hotels. *Losmen* (guesthouses) are along **Jalan Prawirotaman** and in the **Pasar Kembang** area near the train station.

Amanjiwo Resort
Borobudur, Magelang
Tel: 0293-788 333
Fax: 0293-788 355
www.amanresorts.com
One hour north of Jogja, the Amanjiwo is surrounded by four volcanoes and overlooks Borobudur in the distance. This excellent resort promises to immerse guests in the elegance of Javanese culture. **$$$$**

Losari Coffee Plantation Resort & Spa
Desa Losari Grabag, Magelang
Tel: 0298-596 333
Fax: 0298-592 696
www.losaricoffeeplantation.com
A lovely boutique resort on 22 hectares (54 acres) of working coffee plantation in the highlands. Approximately 1½ hour's drive from Jogja, Solo or Semarang. Restored *joglo* villas, a spa, infinity-edge swimming pool and delicious food. **$$$$**

Hyatt Regency Yogyakarta
Jalan Palagan Tentara Pelajar, Jogja
Tel: 0274-869 123
Fax: 0274-869 588
www.hyatt.com
An idyllic resort with a spa, golf course, Camp Hyatt for kids, excellent restaurants and bars, tiered swimming pool and five-star pampering. **$$$**

Dusun Jogja Village Inn
Jalan Menukan 5, Jogja
Tel: 0274-373 031, 384 438
Fax: 0274-382 202
www.jvidusun.co.id
This small, tranquil boutique hotel offers a unique and artistic atmosphere where intimacy, comfort and style come together. Recently renovated rooms have terraces or balconies with views of the gardens. Saltwater swimming pool, restaurant, bar. **$$–$$$**

Puri Artha Hotel
Jalan Cendrawasih No. 36, Jogja
Tel: 0274-563 288
Fax: 0274-562 765
A simple, clean hotel near universities and language schools, so it is popular with foreign students. **$$**

BALI

Many visitors to Bali, particularly families, opt to stay in villas, which are privately owned investment properties that are fully furnished, usually with pools and are staffed with a housekeeper and a cook. Most are concentrated in Seminyak and Canggu, but they can also be found elsewhere on the island. Look for villas on the Internet, or if in Bali, pick up a copy of *Bali Advertiser* or one of the many real-estate brochures on villa rentals.

Sanur

Bali Hyatt
Jalan Danau Tamblingan, Sanur
Tel: 0361-281 234
Fax: 0361-387 693
www.hyatt.com
With 389 rooms overlooking the sea, each with private balcony. Pluses are two swimming pools, a Balinese spa and supervised camp for kids. **$$–$$$**

Puri Santrian
Jalan Danau Tamblingan, Sanur
Tel: 0361-288 009
Fax: 0361-287 101
www.santrian.com
Family owned and operated, specialising in the Balinese warmth and generosity of spirit. 55 garden-view rooms; 50 beach-view rooms and 21 bungalows. **$$–$$$**

Kuta and Legian

Hard Rock Beach Hotel
Jalan Pantai, Banjar Panee Mas, Kuta
Tel: 0361-761 869
Fax: 0361-761 868
www.hardrockhotels.net
Across the street from famed Kuta beach in the heart of Bali's entertainment and shopping district. Children's club, large pool and of course Hard Rock Café. **$$$$**

Poppies Cottages
Poppies Lane 1, Kuta
Tel: 0361-751 059
Fax: 0361-752 364
www.poppiesbali.com
Twenty well-designed cottages in beautiful gardens with pool only 300 metres (328 yards) from the beach. Very popular, so reservations are essential. **$$**

Seminyak and Petitenget

The Legian, Bali
Jalan Laksmana, Seminyak Beach
Tel: 0361-730 622
Fax: 0361-730 623
www.ghmhotels.com/thelegian
An upscale luxury-suite resort along a wide sandy beach. Its architecture combines Balinese design with modern minimalist touches. Daily free shuttle to Kuta. **$$$$**

Oberoi Bali
Jalan Laksmana, Seminyak Beach, Petitenget
Tel: 0361-730 361
www.oberoihotels.com
Located right on the beach, 74 rooms and villas have either a sea or garden view, some with private pool. The hotel's coral-rock verandas and villas are adaptations of classic Balinese palace designs. Has a spa with open-air massage pavilions. **$$$$**

Jimbaran and Bukit

Bvlgari Hotels & Resorts, Bali
Jalan Goa Lempeh, Banjar Dinas Kangin, Uluwatu (Bukit)
Tel: 0361-847 1000
Fax: 0361-847 1111
www.bulgarihotels.com
A tribute from the Italian jeweller to the world of luxury. Traditional Balinese style is blended with contemporary Italian design. Nestled between the cliff and the ocean near Uluwatu on the island's southernmost tip. **$$$$**

Four Seasons Resort Bali at Jimbaran Bay
Jimbaran
Tel: 0361-701 010
Fax: 0361-701 020
www.fourseasons.com
Built on a terraced hillside amid landscaped gardens, this award-winning resort has a spectacular view of the bay and Gunung Agung. An all-villa resort, each with its own plunge pool. **$$$$**

Karma Jimbaran Resort
Jalan Bukit Permai
Tel: 0361-708 848
www.karmaresorts.com
A complex of 23 ultra-luxurious private villas, with one to four bedrooms, all with private pools. Excellent restaurant called di Mare

on the grounds, with New York chef Raymond Saja at its helm. **$$$$**

Ritz-Carlton, Bali Resort & Spa
Jalan Karang Mas Sejahtera
Tel: 0361-702 222
Fax: 0361-701 555
www.ritz-carlton.com
This sprawling four-storey resort with club rooms and villas is perched on a bluff overlooking Jimbaran Bay. South East Asia's largest thalasso spa and 12 restaurants and lounges. **$$$$**

Nusa Dua and Benoa
The Balé
Jalan Raya Nusa Dua Selatan
Tel: 0361-775 111
Fax: 0361-775 222
www.thebale.com
A serene, luxurious retreat for relaxing and re-energising. Only 20 villas, each with private pool. Has a "no children" policy. Unique collection of health and well-being treatments. **$$$$**

Conrad Bali Resort & Spa
Jalan Pratama 168, Tanjung Benoa, Nusa Dua
Tel: 0361-778 788
Fax: 0361-773 888
www.conradhotels.com
Fronted by a white-sand beach, this has 298 rooms and suites overlooking the ocean, lagoons or gardens. Its spa emphasises water and plant-based aromatherapy treatments along with some from Indonesia. **$$$–$$$$**

The Laguna Resort & Spa
P.O. Box 77, Nusa Dua
Tel: 0361-771 327
Fax: 0361-771 326
www.luxurycollection.com/bali
Newly refurbished rooms and suites, all with private balconies and 24-hour butler service, Laguna Spa. Swimming lagoons, water sport activities by the beach and tennis courts. **$$$**

Ubud
Four Seasons Resort Sayan
Sayan
Tel: 0361-977 577
Fax: 0361-977 588
www.fourseasons.com
Award-winning resort overlooks the Ayung River on terraced rice slopes.

Many suites and villas have private plunge pools and outdoor showers. The decadent spa facilities promise a sublime experience. **$$$$**

Komaneka Resort at Monkey Forest
Jalan Monkey Forest
Tel: 0361-976 090
Fax: 0361-977 140
www.komaneka.com
Great central location, set back from main road; very quiet. Charming bungalows, rooms and suites, gardens, pool, restaurant, spa, art gallery and boutique. **$$$$**

Maya Ubud Resort & Spa
Jalan Gunung Sari, Peliatan
Tel: 0361-977 888
Fax: 0361-977 555
www.mayaubud.com
Just minutes by foot from Ubud, this is a spacious, stylish, luxurious resort set in 10 hectares (25 acres) of hillside garden stretching 780 meters (850 yards) along a peninsula high above two river valleys. **$$$$**

Uma Ubud
Jalan Raya Sanggingan, Banjar Lungisiakan, Kedewatan
Tel: 0361-972 448
Fax: 0361-972 449
www.uma.como.bz
A small resort away from mainstream Ubud. The focus is on holistic experiences, featuring nature, culture, yoga and Asian-inspired therapies devoted to the body and spiritual wellbeing. **$$$$**

Alam Indah
Nyuhkuning
Tel/Fax: 0361-974 629
www.alamindahbali.com
On the non-touristic side of the Monkey Forest there are three small hotels owned by the Café Wayan founders. The recently renovated **Alam Indah** overlooks a tranquil river valley; **Alam Jiwa** and the newly opened **Alam Shanti** have rice field panoramas. A fourth, **Kebun Indah** on Monkey Forest Road, suits those who like to be closer to the action. Each has a pool. **$$**

Where to Eat

What to Eat

The staple for the majority of Indonesians is rice. Coconut milk and hot chillies are popular ingredients in the local cuisine, and dishes can range from very spicy meat, fish and vegetables to those which can be quite sweet. Popular dishes are *nasi goreng* (fried rice), *satay* (grilled beef or chicken on skewers) and *gado gado* (boiled vegetables with peanut sauce).

Jakarta's eateries offer something for everyone: fine dining, practically any ethnic food imaginable, Western-style fast food, and very simple local fare from *warungs* (roadside food stalls). Thanks to its large student population, Jogja is known for *lesahan*, cheap, simple food served seated on floor mats. The city has simple eateries featuring dishes from throughout Indonesia. Bali offers a wide range of cuisines with prices to suit all budgets. The best restaurants and cafés are found in the major tourist centres: Ubud, Kuta/Legian/Seminyak and Sanur.

Restaurant Price Guide

A general guide for dinner for two people, excluding beverages.
$$$ = above US$25
$$ = US$10–25
$ = under US$10

Restaurant Listings
JAKARTA

Café Batavia
Jalan Pintu Besar Utara 14
Tel: 021-691 5531
A stylish restaurant housed in a

19th-century Dutch building in old Batavia area. Good Indonesian and international dishes. Open 24/7. **$$$**

Dragon City
Lippo Plaza Podium, Jalan Sudirman
Tel: 021-522 1933
This popular business-lunch meeting point serves Szechuan seafood delicacies. **$$**

Oasis
Jalan Raden Saleh No. 47
Tel: 021-315 0646
A landmark restaurant reminiscent of old-world colonial elegance. The specialty is *rijstafel*, served by waitresses in traditional dress, each carrying a separate dish. **$$$**

Sari Bundo
Jalan H. Juanda 27
Tel: 021-380 6909
One of the best places to try spicy-hot Padang food where several dishes are laid out. **$**

Sriwijaya
The Dharmawangsa,
Jalan Brawijaya No. 26
Tel: 021-725 8181
Very elegant restaurant located in the upmarket Dharmawangsa Hotel. The menu features a blend of European and Indonesian dishes like spiced coconut soup and coriander roasted lamb. **$$$**

YOGYAKARTA (JOGJA)

Gabah
Jalan Dewi Sartika 11-A
Tel: 0274-515 626
A modern restaurant in a tree-lined neighbourhood, located near Gadjah Mada University. Great food in a comfortable atmosphere. Open for lunch and dinner. **$$**

Gadjah Wong
Jalan Gejayan
Tel: 0274-588 294
Three dining areas, accompanied by Javanese, jazz or Western music. Remarkably good food in a friendly, upmarket setting surrounded by tropical gardens. Open for dinner. **$$**

Milas Vegetarian Café
Jalan Prawirotaman IV No. 1278
Serves freshly prepared Indonesian and Western vegetarian food, sans MSG. Milas also holds programmes

that support local artists, children and street youth. Open weekdays noon–9pm, Sat–Sun 10am–9pm. **$**

Via Via Café
Jalan Prawirotaman 24B
Tel: 0274-386 557
Popular with budget travellers, this café serves Indonesian and Western food. Offers excellent travel information and alternative tours. Open all day. **$**

BALI

Sanur

Café Batu Jimbar
Jalan Danau Tamblingan 75A
Tel: 0361-287 374
This café, popular with expats, serves fresh fruit juices, healthy salads and light dishes. There's a farmer's market every Sunday 10am–2pm, with organic produce and freshly baked goods. Next door is The Pantry, a one-stop shop for international foods with a small wine cellar. Open all day. **$–$$**

Massimo Il Ristorante
Jalan Danau Tambingan 206
Tel: 0361-288 942
www.balimassimo.com
Authentic southern Italian cuisine enjoyed amid a warm, relaxing atmosphere. Great pizzas, plus a kids' menu. **$**

Mezzanine Restaurant & Bar
Jalan Cemara 35
Tel: 0361-270 624
Western and Thai food, sushi and teppanyaki are served in a lovely open-air setting surrounded by water gardens. **$$$**

Kuta and Legian

hu'u
Jalan Petitenget, Kerobokan
Tel: 0361-736 443
www.huubali.com
Candle-lit haven and entertainment playground with a 14-metre (50-ft) lap pool and wooden lounge decks. Menu features high-end Western and Asian fare. Dinner 4–11pm, tapas 4pm–1.45am. **$$$**

The Living Room
Jalan Petitenget No. 2000XX, Kerobokan
Tel: 0361-735 735

Delicious Modern Asian fare. Garden seating amid fairy lights and inside in an open-sided pavilion that feels like an expensive home. Charming staff. **$$$**

Made's Warung 1
Jalan Pantai Kuta
Tel: 0361-755 297
Great food and meeting place that has been popular for over 30 years. Try the spare ribs, Thai salads and homemade ice cream and yoghurt. The roomier Made's Warung 2 is in Seminyak. **$$**

TJs Mexican Restaurant
Gang Poppies 1
Tel: 0361-751 093
Serves the best enchiladas, tacos, tostados, nachos and margaritas. Try the aubergine or tofu dip with chips – goes well with a cold beer. **$$**

Seminyak, Petitenget and Kerobokan

Kafé Warisan
Jalan Raya Kerobokan 38, Kerobokan
Tel: 0361-731 175
www.kafewarisan.com
Modern French–Mediterranean cuisine; sophisticated fine dining. Fine imported wines and cocktails. Open for lunch Mon–Sat and daily for dinner. Reservations essential. **$$$**

Ku dé Ta
Jalan Laksmana No. 9, Seminyak
Tel: 0361-736 969
www.kudeta.net
Trendy restaurant on the beach serving tasty fusion cuisine. A favourite with expats for Sunday brunch. **$$$**

La Lucciola
Jalan Laksmana, Temple Petitenget, Kerobokan
Tel: 0361-261 047
Excellent Mediterranean food served in a large, two-level thatched structure that overlooks the sea. Great for brunches and sunset cocktails. Open all day. Bookings advisable. **$$$**

Tratorria Cucina Italiana
Jalan Laksmana
Tel: 0361-737 082
Smallish restaurant with a lively atmosphere. Fantastic pastas, pizzas, salads, beef and seafood dishes. Reservations recommended. Open for dinner only. **$–$$**

Nusa Dua and Jimbaran

The majority of good cafés and restaurants in Nusa Dua and Jimbaran are in hotels. However, in **Jimbaran**, beachside dining under the stars is a favourite indulgence. Scores of *warung*-style cafes offer seafood.

Ubud

Ary's Warung
Jalan Raya Ubud
Tel: 0361-975 053
Contemporary Asian cuisine and vegetarian dishes in a stylish café in the middle of Ubud. Wine menu and cigar lounge. **$$$**

Café Wayan
Jalan Monkey Forest
Tel: 0361-975 447
www.alamindahbali.com
Ibu Wayan serves tasty local dishes and also Western specialties in an outdoor garden setting. A long-time favourite with Bali visitors. Ibu Wayan's family also owns: Laka-Leke Restaurant in Ubud, Café Wayan in the Bali Bird Park, and two cafés in Lombok. **$$**

Ibu Oka's Warung Babi Guling
Jalan Ubud Raya
Just in front of Ubud Tourist Information, Ibu Oka serves Bali's favourite dish, *babi guling* (roasted pig). Locals and tourists sit on the floor sharing low tables. Highly recommended. **$**

Naughty Nuri's
Jalan Raya Sanggingan
A road-side shack serving mouthwatering grilled ribs, fresh tuna (grilled or as sushi), the coldest beer in town and delectable martinis. About 20 minutes from Ubud's main street. **$–$$**

Warung Enak
Jalan Raya Pengosekan
Tel: 0361-972 911
www.warungenakbali.com
Sensational Indonesian dishes from all over the archipelago served in a Made Wijaya-designed building that combines a series of Balinese pavilions and garden courtyards. Try the 18-course *rijstaffel*. Guest pick-up from local hotels is available. **$–$$**

Shopping

What to Buy

JAKARTA

Handicrafts

Pasar Raya at Blok M is the best one-stop shop for the full gamut of Indonesian products. Good, but smaller, are **Sarinah** on Jalan Thamrin and **Keris Gallery** in Menteng. These stores stock everything from baskets, cane chairs and leather sandals to placemats, paintings, carvings, clothes, toys and batik.

At the **Jakarta Handicraft Centre**, Jalan Pekalongan No. 12A, there is a large collection of high-quality handicrafts. As most of the merchandise is manufactured for export, the wood has been treated for climatic changes.

Many of the antique and art shops along **Jalan Kebon Sirih Timur Dalam**, **Jalan Majapahit** and **Jalan Paletehan** (Kebayoran) also sell handicrafts.

Antiques

Although some copies are difficult to detect, there's a better chance of getting genuine articles at reputable dealers who offer refunds. **Darma Mulia Gallery**, Jalan Ciputat Raya No. 50B, tel: 021-749 2850, provides a free hotel pickup service for serious buyers. **Cony Art**, Jalan Melawai Raya No. 189E (near Blok M), tel: 021-720 2844, has two floors of antique ceramic collections, mainly from Sulawesi. **Johan Art Curio**, Jalan H. Agus Salim No. 59A, tel: 021-3193 6023, has a large collection of old Chinese porcelains and statues.

Other shops are scattered throughout the city, but especially on **Jalan Kebon Sirih Timur Dalam**,

where there are several tiny shops. **Djody** is especially well respected.

The so-called "antique" market on **Jalan Surabaya**, near Embassy Row (Jalan Diponegoro), has numerous stalls selling porcelain, puppets, tiles, brass and silver bric-a-brac. Most of it is new but has been made to look old, but it's still an interesting place to browse. **Jalan Ciputat Raya**, a little outside of town, is well worth a visit for those interested in larger pieces such as furniture.

Designer Goods

These days, Jakarta is best known for its astonishing array of designer goods: clothing, jewellery, watches, shoes, handbags, and home decor accessories. Jakarta's burgeoning shopping malls have them all, and they're scattered throughout the city. The best of the best are at **Senayan** (six upmarket malls in one area), **Kelapa Gading** and **Pondok Indah**.

Others

It's also fun to shop in **Kemang** where there are no malls. The main road, Jalan Kemang Raya, and many connecting streets are filled with small shops selling everything from English-language books to art, scattered amongst great cafés serving every kind of food imaginable.

YOGYAKARTA (JOGJA)

Batik

Jogja is renowned for its traditional batiks. If visiting villages, it's a good idea to bring a guide if you don't speak Indonesian. **Bima Sakti Batik Collective**, Giriloyo village, Bantul (near Kota Gede) is not a shop but a whole village of batik makers. **Imogiri** is home to hundreds of traditional batik makers. There are many small shops at the base of the royal cemetery and a new Batik Museum funded by the Netherland's Prince Claus.

Two other places showcase batik: **Museum of Batik and**

Embroidery (Jalan Dr Sutomo No. 13A, 2 km/1 mile north of the Keraton; Mon–Sat 8am–noon; entrance fee; tel: 0274-562 338) has a private collection of Javanese batik dating from the 1880s and embroidery. **Ullen Sentalu Batik Museum** (Jalan Boyong, Kaliurang; Tues–Sun 9am–4pm; entrance fee; tel: 0274-895 161; www.boulevard webart.com), displays Keraton batik fashions and historical Javanese art objects.

Some of the best batik studios in Jogja are: **Bixa Batik Studio** (Pengok PJKA GK 1/7/43F; tel: 0274-546 545), well known for its natural dyes; **Winotosastro Batik** (Jalan Tirtodipuran), which has some of the highest quality batiks in town; and **Brahma Tirta Sari** (Banguntapan, call for directions; tel: 0274-377 881; www.brahma tirtasari.org), which has traditional batik motifs in unique, colourful contemporary designs.

Batik Fashion Designers

Jogja is also home to some of Indonesia's most famous fashion designers, including: **Ardiyanto** (Jalan Magelang Km 5.8; tel: 0274-562 777), with many artefacts along with batik designs and home decor accessories for sale in a villa-style gallery; **Afif Syakur** (Jalan Padega Marta No. 37A, Pogung; tel: 0274-589 914), with many silk designs; and **Nita Azhar** (Jalan Pogung Baru 33D, Pogung), whose elegant designs are in silk.

Lurik

A much older traditional textile is experiencing a revival. *Lurik* features colourful combinations of stripes and squares in harmoniously balanced motifs, each with a symbolic meaning. The most prominent example of *lurik* is seen in the jackets worn by the palace guards at the Keraton. For more information about *lurik*, to visit the oldest workshop in Jogja that still weaves the ancient textile by hand, or for products featuring *lurik* designed for modern tastes, visit **LAWE**, Galeri Amri Yahya, Jalan Prof. Dr. Ki H. Amri Yahya No. 6,

Gampingan, Jogja, tel: 0274-717 8833, fax: 0274-555 968, www.houseoflawe.com.

Handicrafts and Furniture

Jogja's second-largest revenue earner is the export of locally made handicrafts and furniture. For a wide array of handicrafts in one location, visit **Titon Handicraft** (daily 8.30am–4.30pm) at Jalan Minggiran MJI/1627, Dukuh (Ring Road Selatan, on the road to Bantul), tel: 0274-378 476, 371 105. It is a showroom for export handicrafts and also has some furniture.

Pasar Seni Gabusan Bantul (Jalan Parangtritis Km 9.5, Bantul; tel: 0274-367 959, 788 2049) is a large, modern marketplace set up to display the works of craftsmen from the area, including pottery, batik, natural products, stone carvings, home furnishings and much more.

Visiting the villages where handicrafts are made gets visitors out of the city traffic and into the countryside with beautiful views. It also helps support the local craftsmen.

Leather

Manding, Bantul, 15 km (9 miles) south of Jogja. Leather shops on both sides of the main street, including jackets, shoes, wallets, bags, purses and home accessories.

Pottery

The best-known pottery village is **Kasongan, Bantul**, 10 km (6 miles) south of Jogja. About 1 km (½ mile) of shops line both sides of Jalan Raya Kasongan. Pottery is also made in **Pundong, Bantul**, about 8 km (5 miles) south of Jogja off Jalan Parangtritis and in **Pagerjurang hamlet, Melikan village, Klaten**, 43 km (27 miles) east of Jogja on the way to Solo. Expect to find vases, tableware and pots.

Silver and Gold

Kota Gede, south of Jogja, is best known for its silver shops, but also

produces gold jewellery. Local shoppers recommend the small shops located along both sides of Jalan Monodorakan, Kota Gede's main street. **Borobudur Silver** (Jalan Menteri Supeno 41, tel: 0274-374 238, 374 037; www.borobudur-silver.com) produces sophisticated silver jewellery and decorative items in addition to traditional designs seen in Kota Gede.

Wooden Handicrafts

The craftsmen in **Kerebet village, Pajangan, Bantul**, 15 km (9 miles) south of Jogja, **Pucung, Bantul**, and **Bobung Pathuk, Gunungkidul** produce wooden masks, small animal figures, sculptures and accessories, some with a natural varnish finish and others using a batik finish.

BALI

Bali is a great place to shop. Boutiques and roadside stalls are everywhere, with thousands of artisans, craftsmen, seamstresses and painters supplying the tourist trade.

Woodcarvings

Good woodcarvings can be found in the shops along the main roads in **Mas** (Ida Bagus Tilem's Gallery and Museum is well known).

Paintings

The artists' centre is **Ubud**, where there has been an explosion of new galleries featuring local and foreign artists. Visit **Neka Art Museum** on Jalan Raya Campuan for an outstanding array of Balinese art. Other galleries and museums in the area include: **Seniwati Gallery of Art by Women** (Jalan Sriwedari 2B, Ubud); **Antonio Blanco Renaissance Museum** (Jalan Campuan, Ubud); **Rudana Fine Art Gallery** (Jalan Cok Rai Pudak No. 44, Peliatan, Ubud; www.museum rudana.com; and **Agung Rai Museum of Arts (ARMA)** on Jalan Pengosekan, Peliatan, Ubud.

On **Monkey Forest Road** and **Jalan Hanumon** there are many shops with fine art as well as local whimsical art.

In Seminyak, there's a new art space focusing on international established and emerging artists: **Franklin Lee Gallery**, Jalan Laksmana No. 34A, Seminyak, www.franklin-lee.com.

Stone Carvings

For traditional sandstone carvings, stop at the workshops in **Batubulan**. **Wayan Cemul**, an Ubud stone carver with an international following, has a house full of his own creations.

Textiles

Gianyar is the home of the hand-loom industry, but **Blayu**, **Sideman**, **Mengwi**, **Batuan**, **Gelgel** and **Tenggangan** villages all produce their own style of weavings.

Fashion

Over the last few years, Bali has become home to international designers who formerly only had shops overseas. Now these designs can be found in their Bali stores. These include: **Biasa** (Jalan Raya Seminyak No. 36, Kuta; tel: 0361-730 308; www.biasabali.com), with casual women's wear; **Paul Ropp** from New York (Jalan Pengubengan No. 1X, Kerobokan; www.paulropp.com), with colourful, modern wear; and **Milo's**, in Kuta Square Block E1–1A, Kuta, which has unique designs, many with bright, colourful flowers.

Jewellery, Gems and Pearls

The centres for traditional metal working are **Celuk** and **Kamasan**, where silver jewellery and ornaments are on sale at reasonable prices.

Maru (Jalan Laksmana No. 7A, Seminyak; tel: 0361-734 102; www.marugallerbali.com), is a high-fashion jewellery shop.

Several foreign jewellery producers are based on the island and combine the skills of Balinese master smiths with international designs primarily for export. Two showrooms worth visiting are: **Treasures** (Ary's Warung on Ubud's main road, tel: 0361-976 697; www.dekco.com), specialising in 18–22 karat gold; and **Gemala** (Jalan Raya Pengosekan, Ubud; tel: 0361-976 084; www.gemalabali silver.com), offering hand-made silver and gold jewellery with semiprecious gems. If you wish to tour American designer **John Hardy**'s studio in Ubud, you may request an appointment online at www.johnhardy.com.

Antiques, Furniture and Reproductions

Be careful when buying antiques: there's no guarantee of the actual age of the items, which include intricately carved doors, ornate wedding beds, ceremonial daggers, colonial-style lamps, masks and textiles. Chinese ceramics and sculptures from many parts of Indonesia and China are also available to the discriminating buyer. The antique shops adjacent to Kerta Gosa in **Semarapura** house collections of rare Chinese porcelain pieces, with old Kamasan *wayang*-style paintings, antique jewellery and Balinese weavings. Prices are reasonable. On the main streets of **Singaraja** are a few of the best antique shops in Bali.

There are innumerable furniture shops in Kuta, Legian, Seminyak, Kerobokan and Sanur selling "antiques", reproductions and garden furniture. Simply hire a car, drive down the main "furniture roads" and stop at the shops on either side of the road. Overseas buyers say prices are so reasonable that even with the freight fees to get their purchases home, they still save money.

Ceramics

Jenggala Keramik in Jimbaran is a good source for tea sets, vases and dinnerware. It also runs an excellent café and ceramic-making classes. In Sanur, **Pesamuan Studio** has outlets at One World Gallery on Jalan Hanoman in Ubud, Made's Warung 2 on Jalan Raya Seminyak, and at its factory at Jalan Pungutan No. 25, Sanur.

Culture

General

In addition to traditional performing arts exhibition spaces, Indonesia's larger towns and cities have a surprisingly large number of alternative venues. Whether sponsored by foreign institutions or private establishments, their mission is cultural exchange. They offer art exhibitions, theatre, music, films, readings and other events by both local and international artists. Many offer free admission or charge only a small fee. Check for events and opening times upon arrival.

JAKARTA

For culture in any form, the first place to check is the **Ismail Marzuki Arts Centre** (Taman Ismail Marzuki, or TIM), Jalan Cikini Raya No. 73, tel: 021-3193 7325. Jakarta's foremost centre of cultural and performing arts, TIM hosts a variety of Indonesian performances, theatre productions, as well as visiting dance and music performances, art and films. It also has a planetarium.

Museum Wayang, Jalan Pintu Besar Utara No. 27, tel: 021-692 9560, has traditional *wayang kulit* shadow puppet shows every Sunday 10am (free). **Gedung Kesenian**, Jalan Gedung Kesenian, tel: 021-380 8283, is a restored Dutch *Schouwburg* playhouse and offers dance and musical performances. **Wayang Orang Bharata Purwa**, Jalan Kalilio No. 15, Pasar Senen, tel: 021-421 4937, puts on traditional Javanese performances of *wayang orang* (dance-drama) and *ketoprak* (folk drama).

Balal Sarbini (Sarbini Dome), Plaza Semanggi, tel: 021-2553 6341, is the city's first "opera house". Opened in 2004, it has top-notch acoustics, sound and lighting systems and a spacious stage. It is home to the Nusantara Symphony Orchestra, and is also used as a venue for art and cultural performances.

Other venues include: **Centre Cultural Francais**, Jalan Salemba Raya No. 25, tel: 021-390 8585, www.ccfjakarta.or.id; **Erasmus Huis**, Jalan H.R. Rasuna Said Kav S-3, Kuningan, tel: 021-524 1069; **Goeth Institut**, Jalan Sam Ratulangi No. 9–15, tel: 021-2355 0208, www.goethe.de; **Istituto Italiano di Cultura**, Jalan Hos Cokroaminoto 117, Menteng, tel: 021-392 7531/2, www.itacultjkt.or.id; **Komunitas Utan Kayu**, Jalan Utan Kayu 68 H, tel: 021-857 3388, www.utankayu.org.

YOGYAKARTA (JOGJA)

Gamelan
Javanese-Mataram-style gamelan compositions are played every Monday and Thursday 10am–noon at the Bangsai Sri Manganti *pendopo* (pavilion) at the **Keraton**.

Wayang Kulit
Wayang kulit (shadow puppet theatre) is truly the most influential Javanese art form, the one that has traditionally provided the Javanese with a framework through which to see the world and themselves. There is voluminous literature in Dutch and English on the subject. Traditional performances are always at night, beginning at 9pm and ending at dawn. However, they have been shortened for tourist enjoyment.

Venues for *wayang kulit* include: the Bangsai Sri Manganti *pendopo* (pavilion) at the **Keraton**, every Saturday 9.30am–1pm; **Sasana Hinggil**, South Palace Square (Alun Alun Selatan), every second Saturday of the month 9pm–5.30am; **Sono Budoyo Museum**,

Jalan Trikora No. 6, Sunday–Friday 11am–1pm.

Javanese Dance
The most wonderful time to experience Javanese dance is on a moonlit evening at **Prambanan**. The famous *Ramayana* epic is performed 7.30–9.30pm during the dry-season months May to October. During the rainy-season months (November to April), performances are held at **Trimurti Theatre Prambanan** every Tuesday and Thursday. Every Sunday at 1am, the **Keraton** offers court dances at the Bangsal Srimanganti *pendopo* (pavilion). Weekly performances of a classical court repertoire and *Ramayana* are also at the royal family compound **Dalem Pujokusuman** (Jalan Brigen Katamso), which houses the renowned Sasminta Mardawa Dance School. **Purawisata Open Theatre** (Jalan Brigjen Katamso) has nightly *Ramayana* performances 8–9.30pm. The introduction to the performance and characters is in English. Most hotels offer transport.

Performing Arts
The most innovative Javanese performing arts (dance, music, theatre and *wayang kulit*) performances are held at the **Performing Arts High School (SMKI)** on Jalan Bugisan, one of five government tertiary-level schools in the country, training the most promising young dancers from the Yogyakarta area. Another school is the **Indonesian Arts Institute (ISI)** on Jalan Parangtritis.

Other venues include: **Bentara Budaya**, Jalan Suroto Jogjakarta, tel: 0274-560 404; **Benteng Budaya** (Fort Vredeburg), Jalan Jend, Ahmad Yani No. 6, tel: 0274-586 934; **Kedai Kebun Forum & Resto**, Jalan Tirtodipuran No. 3, tel: 0274-376 114; **Taman Budaya Jogja**, Jalan Sriwedani No. 1, tel: 0274-523 512; 580 771; **Lembaga Indonesia Perancis (LIP)**, Jalan Sagan No. 3, tel: 0274-566 520; and **Via Via Café**, Jalan Prawirotaman 30, tel: 0274-386 557.

BALI

Beneath the exuberance of Balinese dance-dramas lies a learned set of motions presented in a highly stylised form. Each gesture has a name that describes its action; for example a sidestep may be named after the way a raven jumps. No play is complete without music; no dance without a story or meaning.

Balinese dances accompanied by gamelan orchestras are presented at major hotels all over the island and attending them is an excellent way to support the many dance schools, teachers and students who keep the dance tradition alive. Village performances – which the local people enjoy as much as the tourists do – help to support entire communities.

Bali's most famous dance is arguably the **kecak**, which gets its name from the rhythmic chanting of the chorus, scores of men and boys who encourage the main performers. The classical **legong** dance is performed by young girls wearing elaborate costumes and headdresses. In **wayang kulit** (shadow puppet theatre), two-dimensional puppets are carved from leather and jointed at the elbows and the knees. Most of the puppets are based on characters from epic Indian tales such as the *Ramayana* or the *Mahbharata*. Suspended at the centre of a white screen, a lamp illuminates and casts a shadow on the screen. The audience sits on the opposite side of the screen and is entertained by the shadows.

Dance venues and times change frequently. The best way to find them is to enquire at your hotel. Performance schedules for the villages near Ubud are available at the Tourist Information office, Jalan Raya Ubud (the main road), where you can also purchase tickets. For performances in outlying areas, the ticket price includes transport from the Tourist Information office.

Getting Acquainted

The Place

Situation 7,107 islands dotted in the China Sea to the west and Philippine Sea to the east.
Area 300,000 sq. km (116,000 sq. miles).
Population Just under 90 million people, 12 million of whom live in the greater Metro Manila area.
Languages Pilipino (derived from Tagalog) and English.
Religion The main religion is Christianity: 80 percent of all Filipinos are Roman Catholic, 11 percent Protestant/other Christian, 7 percent Muslim, 2 percent Buddhist/other.
Time zone 8 hours ahead of Greenwich Mean Time (GMT), so New York is 13 hours, Los Angeles 16 hours and London 8 hours behind, Australia 2 hours ahead. Sunrise and sunset are at about 6am and 6pm.
Currency Peso (P)
Weights and measures Metric
Electricity 120 vac 60 cycles
International Dialling Code 63

Business Hours

Offices Government/business hours are Monday–Friday 8am–5pm and workers break for lunch from noon–1pm. Some private offices are open on Saturdays 8am–noon.
Banks Monday–Friday 9am–3pm.
Small shops Monday–Saturday 9am or 10am–7pm.
Larger shops Most shopping centres, department stores and supermarkets are open 10am–7 or 8pm daily.

The People

Filipinos are basically of Malay stock, though there is evidence of Indian, Chinese, Spanish, Arab and North American stock. The population increases annually by about 1.6 million (over 2 percent). Attempts to implement family-planning programmes have met with strong opposition from the Catholic Church. Life expectancy averages 67 years, and the functional literacy rate is 84 percent.

Climate

A tropical country, much of the Philippines has a hot and dry climate from March to May. Generally, the southwest monsoon – and the typhoons it brings – predominates from June to October. The dry, cooler season during the northeast monsoon period lasts from November to February. Year-round temperatures range from 78°F (25°C) to 90°F (32°C); mean annual humidity is at 83 percent.

Rainfall varies with the region:
Type 1 has two seasons, dry November–May and wet June–October. Type 1 areas are found mainly in the western half of Luzon (including Manila), Palawan, Coron, Cuyo and the lower part of Antique, Iloilo and Negros.
Type 2 lacks a distinct dry season but has a pronounced maximum rain period December–February. Areas include eastern Bicol, eastern Mindanao, northern and eastern Samar and southern Leyte.
Type 3 areas, which do not have a pronounced maximum rain period but a short dry season of 1–3 (November–January) months, include central Luzon, Visayas and western Mindanao.
Type 4 sees even rainfall throughout the year and is found in the eastern coast of Luzon, Leyte and Bohol, and in central Mindanao.

Sitting in the typhoon belt, the Philippines has about 15 typhoons each year. High season is June–October, with the peak in July–September, coinciding with the height of the southwest monsoon.

"Whatever Happens"

The Philippine attitude of *Bahala na* (whatever happens) prevails outside Manila, so don't be surprised if shops don't stick to any particular schedule.

Economy

Following the Asian economic crisis of 1997, the Philippines has faced an uphill struggle towards becoming a newly industrialised country. When Gloria Arroyo, a trained economist, became President in 2001, her active courtship of foreign investment saw the country's GNP hovering around 5 percent by the end of 2006.

The agricultural sector employs more than 40 percent of the population and contributes 20 percent of GNP. The country is, however, moving away from agricultural and mineral exports, and has begun to diversify into higher-value manufactured goods. So while coconut oil and sugar remain major exports, the top-dollar earners now include electronics, apparel and clothing accessories, and computer-related products.

Government

The official name of the country is the Republic of the Philippines, but the most common name used in tourist promotions and by most Filipinos is the Philippine Islands.

A 1935 constitution, modelled on that of the United States, was suspended in 1972 by the then-President Ferdinand Marcos, when he declared martial law. A new constitution was ratified the following year, but over time Marcos meddled with the constitution until he had complete power and authority. After the February 1986 "People Power" uprising that ousted Marcos, the country reverted to a democratic form of government.

In a February 1987 plebiscite, the islands ratified a new constitution, providing for a democratic republican state and a presidential form of government. This paved the way for an elected bicameral legislative body. Following the experience of Marcos' two decades of rule, the president is now limited to a single six-year term. In 1998, Fidel Ramos, widely credited with bringing the Philippines back to fiscal and political sanity and stability, turned over the presidency to Joseph Estrada. Estrada was empeached in 2000 for bribery, betrayal of public trust and violation of the constitution, and ousted from his position in 2001. Gloria Macapagal Arroyo is now President.

For administrative purposes, the republic is divided into 17 regions, 79 provinces, 117 officially chartered cities, 1,506 municipalities and 41,993 *barangays*.

Public Holidays

January 1 New Year's Day. Fireworks and celebratory gunfire ring in the new year.
April/May Maundy Thursday, Good Friday. Flagellants in the streets, processions and *Cenaculos* (passion plays). In Pampanga and elsewhere, devout Catholics are voluntarily crucified.
April/May Easter Sunday Morning processions; family celebration.
April 9 Araw ng Kagitingan (Day of Valor/Bataan and Corregidor Day). Bravery of Filipino soldiers during World War II commemorated at Fort Santiago in Intramuros.
May 1 Labor Day. A tribute to the Philippine worker.
June 12 Independence Day – from Spain in 1898. Parades at Rizal Park in Manila.
October/November Eidal Fitr. Marks the end of Ramadan, the other dominant religion, Islam.
November 1 All Saints' Day. Most Filipinos travel home to visit ancestral tombs and spend the day with their family.
November 30 Bonifacio Day celebrates the birth of nationalist leader Andres Bonifacio.
December 25 Christmas Day.
December 30 Rizal Day. Wreath laying ceremony at National Hero's Monument in Rizal Park (Manila), in honor of the revered Jose Rizal.

Planning the Trip

Visas & Passports

All foreigners must have valid passports. Except tourists from countries with which the Philippines have no diplomatic relations and nationals from restricted countries, everyone may enter without visas and stay for 21 days, provided they hold onward or return tickets.

Visitors who wish to extend their stay to 59 days should contact the Bureau of Immigration and Deportation, Magallanes Drive, Intramuros, by Jones Bridge (Mon–Fri 8am–5pm).

Health

Yellow fever vaccination is necessary for those arriving from an infected area. There is a risk of malaria year-round in remoter areas below 600 metres. Some mosquitoes are resistant to drugs so seek advice on medication from a tropical institute in your country.

Drinking water is generally safe in Metro Manila, although it is wise to drink mineral or bottled water (readily available everywhere).

It is advisable to have medical insurance, as payment must usually be guaranteed before treatment, and health-care standards are poor compared with Western standards.

Money Matters

The Philippines' currency, the peso (P), is divided into 100 centavos. The US dollar, pound sterling, Swiss and French franc, Deutschmark, Canadian dollar, Italian lira, Australian dollar and Japanese yen are all easily convertible. Outside Manila, generally, the US dollar is

widely accepted after the peso.

Traveller's cheques can easily be cashed in Manila and, with a bit of work and fees, in the provinces. Major credit cards are widely accepted in Manila, though limited to major establishments in other cities. Avoid street money changers.

At the time of press, the exchange rate was US$1 to P50.

Tourist Information

● **Australia**
Philippine Department of Tourism, Level 1, Philippine Centre, 27–33 Wentworth Ave, Sydney
Tel: 02-9283 0711
Fax: 02-9283 0755
e-mail: ptsydney@ozemail.com.au
● **United States (New York)**
Philipine Center, 556 Fifth Avenue, New York, NY 10036
Tel: 212-575 7915
e-mail: pdotny@aol.com
● **United Kingdom**
Philippines Department of Tourism, 146 Cromwell Road, London SW7 4EF
Tel: 020-7835 1100
Fax: 020-7835 1926
infotourism@wowphilippines.co.uk

Getting There

BY AIR

More than 500 international flights arrive in Manila weekly. The **Ninoy Aquino International Airport** (NAIA), the Domestic Terminal and the Centennial Terminal are located 7 km (4 miles) from the city centre. International flights also arrive at airports in Cebu, Davao, Laoag, Subic and Clark.

What To Bring

Light and loose clothes are best, but pack a sweater even during the hottest months. There is no need to bring any equipment other than possibly a travel plug adaptor and photographic supplies. Medicines are available in major cities and film processing everywhere.

Practical Tips

Security

Travellers should be aware of lingering problems with both anti-government insurgents in some remote areas and Muslim separatists in Mindanao. The government has engaged in negotiations with both groups, and the situation has, for the most part, improved significantly.

Parts of Mindanao remain dubious areas for foreign travellers. Similarly, the remote islands of the Sulu archipelago can be dangerous; there have been several kidnappings of foreigners in Sulu and Basilan.

Before travelling in the countryside, check with your foreign ministry for updates on the situation.

Pickpocketing and theft are a real problem, particularly in crowded spots like bus and railway stations. Thieves work in gangs and are skilful, so carry money and essentials like your passport in a money belt round your waist. On no account leave luggage unattended.

Media

NEWSPAPERS AND MAGAZINES

The myriad daily newspapers in English include the *Manila Bulletin*, *Philippine Daily Inquirer*, *Manila Standard* and *Philippine Star*, most of which are available online. The *Fookien Times* is published in English and Chinese. Local free weekly newspapers published in English include *What's On & Expat* (www.whatson-expat.com.ph), and *Foreign Post* (www.theforeignpost. com). *Citiguide* is a bi-monthly, smaller-format newspaper listing events, dining, nightlife and shopping opportunities, available at newsstands, and restaurants.

A large selection of foreign publications is available: *Newsweek*, *Time*, *Far Eastern Economic Review*, *Asian Business*, *The Economist*, *Reader's Digest*, *Vogue*, *Yazhou Zhoukan*, *Asian Wall Street Journal* and *International Herald Tribune*. These are sold in major hotels, bookstores, supermarkets and at newsstands.

TELEVISION

Government-owned People's Television (Channel 4) broadcasts a variety of programs, including the latest national and foreign news, sports events, live coverage of government-sponsored events, variety shows, foreign shows, and soap operas.

Other independent stations include: Radio Philippine Network (RPN) channel 9; Greater Manila Area TV (GMA) channel 7; Intercontinental Broadcasting Network (IBC) channel 13; Alto Broadcasting System-Chronicle Broadcasting Network (ABS-CBN) channel 2, ABC channel 5, and Studio 23 channel 23. Most hotels have cable or satellite television, offering a cosmopolitan range of international news and programming. A tourism channel called Living Asia TV promotes domestic rediscovery of the Philippine islands, broadcasting airline arrivals and departures between programs.

RADIO

Most radio stations are privately owned, broadcasting a range of music, news, commercials and

Useful Links

An excellent website with links to all things Filipino is www.filipinolinks.com. For great information on restaurants, hotels and nightclubs, try www.clickthecity.com.

entertainment talk. Station 100.3 FM plays soft rock and love songs. 89.1 Wave FM plays R&B, lounge and house. 105.1 FM features easy listening hits while 107.5 FM plays alternative music to cater to young listeners.

Postal Services

Post offices are open Monday–Friday, 8am–5pm; 8am–noon on Saturdays. The **Philippine Postal Corporation** is at Lawton Plaza (Liwasang Bonifacio), Intramuros, Manila. Hotel desks provide the most convenient services for purchasing stamps and posting letters. At Ninoy Aquino International Airport, the post office is in the arrival area.

The Philippine mail system is slow and unreliable. Articles of value are often pilfered from the mail. It is fine for postcards but not much use for anything else. International courier services like **DHL** (tel: 1800-1888 0345), **Fedex** (1800-10 855 8484), **UPS** (tel: 1800-10 742 5877), and **TNT** (tel: 02-551 5632) offer inexpensive and reliable mail service within the Philippines, as well as speedy but costly overseas deliveries.

Post Offices in Manila

Manila Post Office Liwasang Bonifacio, Manila
Makati Post Office corner Gil Puyat Avenue (Buendia) and Ayala Ave
Pasay Post Office F.B. Harrison, Pasay
San Juan Central Post Office Pinaglabanan, San Juan

Telecommunications

Most of the larger Philippine hotels have IDD, telex, fax and internet facilities available to guests at a small charge.

The prefix "0" must be dialled for all calls made within the Philippines. When calling the Philippines from overseas, dial the international access code, followed by 63 and the phone number (without the preceding "0").

Public payphones require P2–3

Telephone Codes

International access code: 00
International operator: 108
Domestic operator: 109
Directory assistance: 114 or 187
Philippines country code: 63
City codes:

Manila	02
Angeles	045, 0455
Bacolod	034
Baguio	074
Batangas	043
Boracay	036
Cagayan de Oro	088, 08822
Cebu	032
Clark	045
Davao	082
General Santos City	083
Iloilo	033
Subic	047

or prepaid telephone cards. Some small shops also provide informal phone services.

MOBILE PHONES

The Philippines, which has always had notoriously bad telephone service, has embraced mobile phones wholeheartedly and they are now as reliable as, or in fact more reliable than, many land lines. Their reach is impressive – from the remote regions of Mindanao to the northern islands of Batanes.

Emergency Numbers

Police/Fire/Medical Emergency
117
Tourist Security (24 hrs)
02-524 1660, 524 1728
Tourist Information
02-524 2384, 525 2000
Police Headquarters (24 hours)
02-723 0401. Camp Crame,
EDSA, Metro Manila
Manila Police 02-523 3378
Makati Police 02-899 9014
Pasay City Police
02-831 8070
Quezon City Police
02-921 5267

Mobile phones in the Philippines use the GSM network. If your mobile phone has a roaming facility, it will automatically hook up to one of the country's networks. However, mobile phones from Korea, Japan, and the US sometimes have compatibility problems.

A simple and convenient solution is to buy a cheap (US$40 new, US$20 used) mobile phone upon arrival and use it with prepaid calling cards, available everywhere. It can be resold upon departure at small cellular shops for about half of its original purchase price if it is still in good condition. Mobile phone dealers are found throughout the city.

If compatibility is not an issue, you can also make calls on your cell phone with a prepaid local SIM card (around US$8), with which you get a local number.

Medical Treatment

As well as malaria, rabies is also prevalent in the Philippines. If bitten by any mammal, seek medical treatment immediately. Bilharzia (schistosomiasis) is another problem, so avoid swimming in fresh water. Pools that are chlorinated are safe.

Mercury Drug is one of the most widely-found pharmacies in Manila; some branches are open 24 hours.

Recently, foreigners have been travelling to Manila to undergo laser eye surgery, which is cheaper here than elsewhere. Standards for eye care clinics can be remarkably high, but choose carefully.

The most important Manila hospitals are located at:
Asian Hospital
Filinvest Corporate Center, Alabang,
Tel: 02-771 9000
Cardinal Santos Medical Center
Wilson Street, Greenhills San Juan
Tel: 02-727 0001 to 46
Makati Medical Center
2 Amorsolo corner de la Rosa
Streets, Makati City
Tel: 02-888 8999, 892 5544
Manila Doctor's Hospital
667 United Nations Avenue,
Ermita, Manila
Tel: 02-524 3011–77

Medical Center Manila
1122 General Luna Street, Ermita
Tel: 02-523 8131/65
Philippine General Hospital
Taft Avenue, Manila,
Tel: 02-521 8450
St Luke's Medical Center
279 Rodriguez Boulevard,
Quezon City
Tel: 02-723 0301, 723 0101
In Davao: **Davao Doctors Hospital**: General Malvar Street,
tel: 082-222 0850, local tel: 106.
In Cebu: **Chong Hua Hospital**:
Fuente Osmeña, tel: 032-253 9409. **Cebu Doctors Hospital**:
President Osmeña Boulevard,
tel: 032-255 5555.

Local Tourist Office

Metro Manila
• Department of Tourism (DOT), DOT Building, Room 207, T.M. Kalaw Street, Ermita, tel: 02-524 2345, 525 6114, fax: 524 8321; e-mail: ncr@tourism.gov.ph; www.wowphilippines.com.ph
• DOT, Ninoy Aquino International Airport branch, tel: 02-832 2964, fax: 832 1687.

Embassies in Manila

Australia: 23/F Tower 2, RCBC Plaza, 6819 Ayala Ave, Salceda Vil, Makati City,
tel: 02-757 8100.
Canada: 6/F Tower 2, RCBC Plaza, 6819 Ayala Ave, Salceda Vil, Makati City,
tel: 02-857 9000.
New Zealand: 23/F, BPI Buendia Centre, Sen. Gil Puyat Avenue (Buendia), Makati City, tel: 02-891 5358, fax: 891 5357.
United Kingdom: 17/F, L.V. Locsin Building, 6752 Ayala Avenue corner Makati Avenue, Makati City, tel: 02-816 7116, fax: 819 7206.
United States: 1201 Roxas Boulevard, Ermita, Manila, tel: 02-523 1001, fax: 522 4361.

Getting Around

General

Getting out of Manila by car can be a problem. Traffic is usually a tremendous snarl – this cannot be emphasized enough. It is often easier to fly out or to take a ferry.

If you have to travel by road, the bus is a perfectly good option, or private cars (or hired taxis). Be prepared for heavy traffic. Bring along something to read and drinking water. You won't be going anywhere fast.

Aside from light rail transport in Manila, the trains are not recommended for foreigners. They are painfully slow and extremely outdated.

By Air

Transportation around the archipelago normally originates in the country's hub, Manila. Cebu City is coming into its own as a regional hub for flights going around the Visayas and into Mindanao. Flying is quick and cheap, with domestic airlines spanning much of the archipelago. Domestic flight schedules are in constant flux; contact the airlines directly for the latest update. There is usually a nominal departure tax of around P50–200 at most airports.

Philippine Airlines, tel: 02-855 8888, www.philippineair.com

Air Philippines, tel: 02-855 9000, fax: 851 7922; www.airphils.com

Cebu Pacific, tel: 02-702 0888; www.cebupacificair.com

Asian Spirit, tel: 02-851 8888; e-mail: info@asianspirit.com; www.asianspirit.com

Laoag International Airlines, tel: 02-551 9729

Water Transport

Inter-island boat travel was once uncomfortable and not very safe. Thankfully transport companies have effectively addressed these issues in recent years. They now offer comfortable cabins and a range of travel options suited to all budgets. Travel may take a little longer, but this mode of transport is rewarding: some of the ports have hardly changed in decades. Seemingly half the local populace greets arriving boats at the wharf. Tickets on major sectors (e.g. Manila–Cebu) can be booked through travel agencies. Check websites for special discounts, package tours, new offerings and even e-ticket bookings.

Negros Navigation, Pier 2, North Harbor, Manila, tel: 02-245 5588; www.negrosnavigation.ph. Ports of call include Bacolod, Cagayan de Oro, Coron, Dipolog, Dumaguete, Dumaguit (Kalibo), Estancia, General Santos, Iligan, Iloilo, Manila, Ozamiz, Puerto Princesa, Roxas, Tagbilaran.

Sulpicio Lines, 415 San Fernando, Binondo, tel: 02-241 9701–04.

Pier 12, Manila, tel: 02-245 0616.

WG&A SuperFerry sails to Bacolod, Cagayan de Oro, Cebu, Coron, Cotabato, Davao, Dipolog, Dumaguete, Dumaguit, General Santos City, Iligan, Ozamis, Puerto Princesa, Surigao, Tagbilaran, Zamboanga. 12th Floor, Times Plaza, U.N. Avenue, Manila, tel: 02-528 7000, www.superferry.com.ph.

By Bus

The areas surrounding Manila and provincial capitals are relatively well serviced by a reasonably good network of roads. Potholes are a feature and traffic moves at a snail's pace – especially through cities. Dozens of bus companies operate services to the main tourist centers and fares are low: the 6.5-hour journey from Manila to Baguio costs P350 on air-conditioned buses. (The temperature in these buses tend to be very low; it is best to take a light jacket along.) Long-distance buses make frequent stops at rest stops along the way, which offer snacks and "comfort rooms" (toilets), usually requesting

At the Airport: Arrival and Departure

Arrival: Manila's **Ninoy Aquino International Airport** (NAIA) Terminal 1 services most international airlines, while flag carrier Philippine Airlines uses Terminal 2 (Centennial) for international and domestic flights.

After clearing customs and claiming baggage, rent a car or take a taxi. Rental cars in Manila come with a driver; traffic in this city should not be underestimated. If opting for a "coupon" taxi, pay a fixed rate to your destination at one of the counters inside, then head outside to wait for the next taxi. Cheaper street taxis can be found on the departure level. Most taxi-related crimes happen when travelers are coming from the airport with all their valuables, passport and luggage in tow. Saving the few dollars difference between a street taxi and coupon

taxi is not advised, but for those on a tight budget, regular taxis can be found by heading upstairs to the departure area, where taxis drop off passengers. Most Manila hotels offer free or inexpensive shuttles. Look for the people holding up small signs with the names of hotels.

Departure: It is easiest to reach the airport by private car or taxi. Give yourself plenty of time, especially during rush hour, typhoons and holidays.

Most airline counters open 3 hours prior to departure. Independent travelers should reconfirm their tickets 48–72 hours before departure; Philippines Airlines insists on reconfirmation.

The Manila airport departure tax is P550 (about US$11), payable in peso or US dollars.

a donation of P1 for their upkeep.
Baliwag Transit goes to Bulacan,
Nueva Ecija, Isabella, Cagayan Valley
and Pampanga, tel: 02-912 3343.
Batangas Laguna Tayabas Bus Co
(BLTB) goes to Batangas, Calamba,
Iriga, Legaspi, Lipa, Los Banos,
Lucena, Naga, Nasugbu, Ormoc,
Tacloban, Calatagan, Tagaytay and
Sta.Cruz, tel: 02-913 1525.
Dangwa Trans Co. goes to Baguio
and Tabuk (Kalinga), tel: 02-731
2879.
Farinas Transit goes to Angeles,
Vigan and Laoag, tel: 02-743 8582.
Maria de Leon Transit goes to
Angeles, San Fernando La Union,
Vigan and Laoag, tel: 02-731 4907.
Dominion Bus Lines goes to San
Fernando La Union, Vigan and
Laoag, tel: 02-741 4146.
Victory Liner offers routes to Baguio,
Bolinao, Cagayan Valley, Dagupan,
Dau (Angeles), Olongapo and
Tuguegarao, tel: 02-727 4688
(Cubao), www.victoryliner.com.

By Train

Train travel is slow and not
recommended. Manila's sole line
runs from Tutuban Station in Tondo
south to Legaspi City, and north to
San Fernando, La Union.

Car Rental

Cars may be rented without a
driver, but opting for a driver is
highly recommended in the
Philippines. Even if you know your
way around town and can run red
lights with the best of the jeepney
drivers, parking is a nightmare. If
you must drive, make sure you
have a valid foreign or
international driver's license.

Driving in the Philippines is very
different from the rest of the
world. Here, stopping at red lights
is optional, though a traffic
policeman directing traffic has to
be obeyed. However, a few
policemen, known as *buwayas*
("crocodiles") might pull a driver
over on a spurious charge and
then demand a bribe. It is better to
bargain down and pay the bribe

Public Transport

MANILA

Grouses of travel by public
transportation are slow city traffic,
and hot and crowded conditions in
the vehicles. In Metro Manila, non-
air-conditioned bus and jeepney
rates are P4 for the first 4 km
(2 miles) plus 50 centavos for
every kilometer thereafter. For air-
conditioned buses, the rate starts
at P8 for the first 4 km (2 miles).

The jeepney is the Philippines'
most colorful mode of transport,
originally constructed from
American jeeps left behind after
World War II. Routes are fixed.

Air-conditioned buses ply major
thoroughfares and the South and
North expressways. Air-conditioned
bus terminals are located in
Escolta, in Binondo, Manila, Ayala
Center (Makati) and in Cubao,
Quezon City.

Motorcycles with side cars,
called tricycles, may be available for
short trips on the smaller streets.

Manila's elevated rail system
consists of two Light Rail Transit
lines: LRT1 (yellow line) and LRT2
(purple line), and the Metro Rail
Transit line: MRT3 (blue line). The

than it is to threaten to report him,
which could escalate the situation.
Budget Car and Van Rental have
offices in NAIA, the Peninsula
Manila and Subic Bay. In Manila,
tel: 02-776 8118–20.
Hertz Rent-A-Car, Ninoy Aquino
International Airport: Arrival Area
Main Lobby, tel: 02-896 1505.
Makati City: G/F, El Rico Suites,
1048 Metropolitan Avenue, Makati
City, tel: 02-896 1505;
www.hertz.com.ph.
National Car Rental has offices in
Manila (NAIA, tel: 02-833 0648; 38
Timog Avenue, Quezon City, tel:
02-374 3151; 5032 P. Burgos St,
Makati City, tel: 02-818 8667) and
Baguio City (Room 213, Laperal
Building, Session Road, tel: 074-
442 6381); www.nationalcar.com

oldest and most crowded of the light
rail systems is the LRT1, which runs
along Taft and Rizal avenues
between Baclaran (near the airport)
and Monumento, providing access
to many of Manila's historical
attractions. The newest of Manila's
light rail systems, the LRT2, has 11
stops running east-west along Aurora
Avenue from Recto to M.A. Roxas in
Marakina, meeting the LRT1 by
Doroteo Jose Station, and the MRT3
at Cubao (Aurora) Station. Finally, the
MRT3 runs from Taft Avenue along
EDSA till North Avenue in Quezon City.
The final gap from North Avenue to
link with the LRT1 station in
Monumento is being constructed.

Tour Operators

For official tour operators and
guides registered with the
Department of Tourism (DOT), call
02-524 1703. Over 60 tour
operators are listed in the Directory
of Philippine Tour Operators, all of
whom are members of the Philippine
Tour Operators Association.
Banca Safaris operates boat tours
to some of the farthest corners of
the country such as Batanes,
Palawan and Mindanao. Tours are
organised by a team of top local
authors and photographers,
mobile tel: 0920-387 5837;
www.bancasafaris.com.
Freeport Service Corporation runs
tours to Subic Bay, – the former
military base itself – incorporating
jungle treks and the survival skills
of native Aeta people. 2/F, Building
H8211 Burgos Street, Causeway
Rd, Subic Bay Freeport Zone, tel:
(047) 252 2313 to 15, fax: 252
7710, e-mail: fsc@svisp.com
Tribal Adventure Tours leads trips
true to its name, from rafting on the
Chico River in the Cordillera to
climbing new routes up Mt
Pinatubo. Tel: 02-821 6706, 823
2725, www.tribaladventures.com.
Bataan Tours runs tours throughout
Bataan and to Corregidor island. De
Guzman Bldg, Saint Joseph Street,
Poblacion (near Max's), Balanga
City, Bataan. Mobile tel: 0917-697
7671, (047) 237 1877, e-mail:
bataantravel@hotmail.com.

Where to Stay

Choosing a Hotel

The Philippines offers a wide range of accommodation for every budget, from beach resorts and pensions to luxury hotels.

The capital city offers numerous deluxe hotels. "Tourist belt" hotels along Roxas Boulevard and in Malate–Ermita are convenient for conventions, while business travelers wind up in Makati or Ortigas. Most Manila hotels offer full business facilities.

Price Guide

A general guide for a standard double room, excluding taxes.

$$$$ = above US$150
$$$ = US$100–150
$$ = US$50–100
$ = under US$50

Hotel Listings

METRO MANILA

Ascott Makati
6F Glorietta 4, Ayala Center, Makati
Tel: 02-729 8888
www.the-ascott.com
Set in the heart of the Makati CBD, the Ascott Makati has huge rooms equipped with washing machines and dryers, furnished kitchens and entertainment centers. Full range of amenities, plus butler service. **$$$$**

EDSA Shangri-La Hotel
1 Garden Way, Ortigas Center
Tel: 02-633 8888
Fax: 02-631 1067
www.shangri-la.com
True Shangri-La style; close to ADB, Megamall. Tennis, fitness center, pool. Italian and Chinese dining, popular for business lunches. **$$$$**

Makati Shangri-La Hotel
Ayala Ave corner Makati Avenue
Tel: 02-813 8888
Fax: 02-813 5499
www.shangri-la.com
Among Manila's finest hotels. Outstanding service. Fine Japanese, Filipino, Chinese, French dining. Live jazz music. Tennis, gym, swimming pool. **$$$$**

Mandarin Oriental Manila
Makati Avenue corner Paseo de Roxas, Makati
Tel: 02-750 8888
Fax: 02-817 2472
www.mandarinoriental.com/manila
The Philippines' Best Business Hotel five years running. High class but warm service, with Wi-Fi, gym, pool and a luxurious spa. Excellent restaurants and a brand-new Martini Bar expansion. **$$$$**

Oakwood Premier
Ayala Center 6th Floor Glorietta 4, Ayala Center, Makati
Tel: 02-729 8888
Fax: 02-728 0000
www.oakwood.com
Luxury serviced apartment from the US corporate housing firm Oakwood. The rooms are huge and equipped with washing machines and dryers, kitchens and utensils, VCRs and a "home-like" atmosphere. **$$$$**

The Pan Pacific Manila
Adriatico corner Gen. Malvar Street, Malate
Tel: 02-536 0788
www.panpacific.com
Located close to the World Trade Center, this hotel has contemporary-style rooms with bay views; the top-floor Pacific Lounge provides the best city views. There is a fitness center, swimming pool and several restaurants in Adriatico Square. **$$$–$$$$**

Dusit Hotel
Nikko, Ayala Center, Makati
Tel: 02-867 3333
Fax: 02-867 3888
www.dusit.com
A stately hotel in the heart of Makati with large, recently renovated rooms. Full business services and landscaped gardens on the premises for peaceful wandering in the midst of the city. **$$$**

New World Renaissance Hotel
Esperanza Street corner Makati Avenue, Makati
Tel: 02-811 6888
Fax: 02-811 6777
www.renaissancehotels.com
Good value – four-star hotel with five-star perks. Large rooms in neutral tones. Fitness center. Continental, Chinese cuisines. **$$$**

Sofitel Philippine Plaza
CCP Complex, Roxas Boulevard Pasay City
Tel: 02-551 5555
Fax: 02-551 5610
www.sofitel-asia.com
With cozy rooms that overlook Manila Bay, Intramuros. Outdoor pool in tropical setting. Excellent gym, tennis, driving range. Several restaurants in garden setting. **$$$**

Bayview Park Hotel
1118 Roxas Boulevard corner UN Avenue, Malate
Tel: 02-526 1555
Fax: 02-522 3040
www.bayviewparkhotel-manila.com
Good value. Recently renovated business hotel dating from 1960s, opposite US Embassy. Higher rooms have delightful bay views. Gym, pool. Café, bars. **$$**

Manila Pavilion Hotel
United Nations Avenue corner Orosa Street, Ermita
Tel: 02-526 1212
Fax: 02-526 5566
www.manilapavilion.com.ph
Rooms overlook Rizal Park or Club Intramuros; earthy tones, attentive service, many repeat customers. Gym, pool, casino, restaurant. **$$**

Millennium Plaza Hotel Makati
Makati Avenue corner Eduque Street, Makati
Tel: 02-899 4718
Fax: 02-899 4747
www.millenniumplaza.com.ph
Business hotel. Rooms with kitchenettes available. Pool and restaurant. **$$**

New Horizon Hotel Mandaluyong
778 Boni Avenue, Mandaluyong
Tel: 02-532 3021
Fax: 02-532 3026
www.newhorizonhotel-manila.com
Located on EDSA, this hotel offers complimentary WiFi, a gym and a European-cuisine restaurant. **$$$**

Where to Eat

What to Eat

Filipino cuisine is an intriguing blend of Malay, Spanish and Chinese influences. Many visitors are surprised by its mildness after having experienced other more fiery Southeast Asian food such as Thailand's tongue-lashing curries.

Some typical Philippine dishes worth trying are chicken *tinola* and *pancit molo*, dumplings of pork, chicken and mushrooms cooked in a broth. *Adobo* is pork or chicken in small pieces, simmered in a light vinegar with garlic and spices. Seviche-like *kinilaw* is fish marinated in a garlic and chilli vinaigrette with raw onions.

A typical fiesta dish, *lechon* is suckling pig stuffed with tamarind leaves and roasted on an open spit over heated coals. *Sinanglay*, another festive dish, is fish or crab with hot pepper wrapped in Chinese cabbage, and cooked in coconut milk. Other Filipino favorites include egg-roll-like *lumpia*, a salad of heart-of-palm, pork and shrimp wrapped in a tissue paper-thin crepe and served with garlic and soy sauce, and *kare-kare*, a rich mixture of oxtail, knuckles and tripe, stewed with vegetables in peanut sauce and served with *bagoong*, a fish-based sauce.

Restaurant Listings

METRO MANILA

Casa Armas
J. Nakpil Street corner Bocobo, Malate
Tel: 02-523 5763
Wonderful Spanish food. *Bocarones* (marinated sardines with garlic), Spanish sausage, garlic shrimp and olives; *paella*, garlic chicken (order in advance) and unbelievable crab. Reservations recommended. **$$**

Casa Xocolat
B. Gonzales Street, off Katiupunan, by Ateneo University
Tel: 02-929 4186
A wonderful little place celebrating the Pinoy love for cacao and chocolate in its different forms, from churros to rich hot drinks to fondues. Focaccia sandwiches and other creative entrees are on the menu too. There's also WiFi Internet access and a pleasant patio. **$**

Gerry's Grill
25 branches around Manila and the country, including 20 Jupiter Street corner Antares Bel-Air, Makati
Tel: 02-897 9862
Very cheap Filipino food. The chargrilled (*inihaw*) squid and tuna belly, traditional *tanigue kinilaw* (marinated raw fish) and *kilawin puso ng saging* (marinated heart of banana) are recommended. For dessert, try the leche flan custard. Reservations recommended. **$**

Guava
1st Level, Piazza Serendra, Bonifacio Global City, Taguig
Tel: 02-856 0489
Try creative Filipino fusion dishes such as *kare-kare* with bagoong and *tsokolate* (peanut curry with fish paste and chocolate), *monggonisa* (chickpea sausage), and *Pinoy na foie gras* (local foie gras). **$$$**

Il Ponticello
2/F, Antel 2000, 121 Valero Street Makati
Tel: 02-887 7168, 887 4998
Trendy Italian eatery. Try Chef Romeo Garchitorena's *risotto del Boscaiolo* and *ai funghi Porcini con Gorgonzola*. Ponticello turns into a modern late-night bar. **$$**

Kashmir
816 Arnaiz Avenue (Pasay Road) Makati
Tel: 02-844 4924
524 Padre Faura Street, Ermita
Tel: 02-524 6851, 523 1521
Excellent curried mutton and kebabs, spicy or mild. Strictly vegetarian food available. **$$**

Lami Barbecue
TM Kalaw corner Parade Street, Luneta Park, Intramuros
Tel: 02-400 7440
Charcoal-roasted Cebuano food. Great location near waterfront. **$**

The Legend (Hong Kong) Seafood Restaurant
Boom na Boom Compound, CCP Complex, Roxas Blvd, Pasay City
Tel: 02-833 1188, 833 3388
Choose your fish or other seafood from the aquarium, Hong Kong style. Salt and pepper squid and fish lip soup are amongst the most popular here. There's a nice Hong Kong feel to the premises. **$**

Old Manila
Peninsula Manila, Ayala corner Makati Avenue
Tel: 02-810 3456
Has earned its place as among the finest of Manila's French restaurants. Certified Angus beef, plus exquisite delicacies from around the world. Sublime *foie gras*, and casserole of lobster with homemade egg linguine. Reservations recommended. **$$$**

Patio Guernica
1856 Jorge Bocobo Street Remedios Circle, Malate
Tel: 02-521 4415, 524 2267
An old Spanish church turned into a stylish Spanish restaurant. Cosy and romantic. **$$**

Seafood Market Restaurant
1190 Jorge Bocobo, Ermita
Tel: 02-524 5761, 524 5744
Pick and choose your own live seafood and vegetables, then tell the chef precisely how you like it, and voila! Delicious. **$$**

Seafood Wharf Restaurant
Army-Navy Club Compound, South Drive, Luneta Park
Tel: 02-536 3522
Choose your own fresh ingredients and let the chef get to work. Relax on the open-air deck overlooking Manila Bay, or take a quick dip in the pool before dinner. **$**

Restaurant Price Guide

A general guide for dinner for two people, excluding beverages.
$$$ = above US$50
$$ = US$20–50
$ = under US$20

Culture

Buying Tickets

For information about concerts, plays and other events, call **Ticketworld** at 02-891 1000. Tickets can be purchased over the phone with credit cards, then picked up by arrangement at one of their many outlets around the city, such as at National Bookstores or at Glorietta cinemas.

Aside from concerts and plays at the Cultural Center of the Philippines, Ticketworld handles Philippine Basketball Association (PBA) games at Ultra in Pasig City, and Pasay's Cuneta Astrodome.

DANCE

Ballet Philippines is the country's foremost company, followed by the **Philippine Ballet Theater**. The **Bayanihan National Dance Company** and **Ramon Obusan Folkloric Group** excel in cultural and folk dancing.

THEATRE AND CONCERTS

The following venues also host theatrical and musical performances:

GSIS Theater
GSIS Building, CCP Complex, Manila
Tel: 02-891 6161

Manila Metropolitan Theater
Liwasang Bonifacio, Manila

Philippine Ballet Theater
Ortigas Avenue, Pasig City
Tel: 02-631 2222 x 8201
Schedules plays and musicals year-round.

Tanghalang Pilipino
CCP Complex, Roxas Boulevard, Manila
Tel: 02-842 0137, 832 3704

William J. Shaw Theater
5/F, Shangri-La Plaza, EDSA corner Shaw Blvd, Mandaluyong
Tel: 02-633 4821 to 25
Performances by Repertory Philippines.

MUSIC

The Philippine Philharmonic Orchestra, **Philippine Madrigal Singers** and UST **Symphony Orchestra** perform regularly at the Cultural Center of the Philippines (CCP; www.culturalcenter.gov.ph), tel: 02-832 1125–39. Various open-air concerts are held in Rizal Park every Sunday at 5pm, and in Paco Park on Friday at 6pm.

Cultural Center of the Philippines (CCP)

The sprawling **Cultural Center of the Philippines** complex on Roxas Boulevard houses theaters, museums, a library, restaurants, galleries and exhibition rooms. Most of Manila's plays, ballets and concerts take place here. The building was constructed as the pride and joy of former first lady Imelda Marcos nearly 40 years ago. Tel: 02-832 1125–39; www.culturalcenter.gov.ph.

MOVIES

Movie-going is as popular as ever, and one of the best entertainment bargains in town. American films are the most popular, while Tagalog cinema is also a big deal for locals.

With the opening of **Mall of Asia**, the Philippines has its first IMAX movie theatre, with an 8-storey screen and bone-shaking sound. For tickets, call 02-556 IMAX.

For information about movies at the various **Robinsons Malls** around the country, check out www.robinsonmovieworld.com. For movies at **ShoeMart Malls**, call SM Dial-a-Movie at tel: 02-833 9999. For **Ayala Malls** movie tickets, check out www.sureseats.com.

Shopping

What to Buy

BASKETRY

Popular Philippine baskets are found everywhere. Made from natural rattan, *nipa*, bamboo, abaca and palm, the baskets come in a range of sizes and purposes, and are both functional and decorative.

HANDICRAFTS

Abaca hats, placemats, coasters, bamboo trays, shells, ceramic pots and *gewgaw* are ubiquitous in airport tourist shops, the **Makati** commercial center and **Ermita** tourist belt. Newer developments include lovely handmade paper, picture frames made from coconut husks and bamboo, and capiz-shell Christmas ornaments. Native woven pieces are always popular.

EMBROIDERY

The no-tie-required *barong Tagalog* is beloved by casual tourists and foreign expatriate businessmen. Ask the hotel concierge to suggest a tailor. Choose either the translucent pineapple fiber, *piña*, with the finest hand embroidery, or the cheaper *ramie* or cotton with machine-embroidery. For women, there are the embroidered *terno* dresses, with matching scarves, bags and handkerchiefs.

JEWELRY

Aside from pearls, the most typical Philippine jewelry is made of shell and silver. Mother-of-pearl is perhaps the most popular. Don't purchase items made from coral or tortoise shell, as supporting such unsustainable trade contributes to the degradation of the Philippine environment.

The best silver jewelry is found in **Baguio**, where the guild-like training of St Louis University has engendered fine craftsmanship.

You can also find wood and vine jewelry in the specialty shops of **Ermita** and **Makati**, as well as beadwork from the tribes, notably the necklaces, earrings and ornamental hair pieces of the T'boli, Mangyan and Ifugao people.

PEARLS

Quality pearls from Mindanao can be found in quantity at **Virra Mall** in Greenhills, **San Juan**, Metro Manila. Most of the strands are freshwater pearls in irregular shapes, exotically beautiful and selling for a song. Cultured pearls are available as well, with Mikimoto "seconds" finding many satisfied customers. South Sea black pearls, at bargain prices compared to the international market, are sold too.

FURNITURE

Beautiful wicker and rattan furniture is light enough to ship without spending large amounts of money. **Angeles City** is the shopper's best bet and offers made-to-order items.

BRASSWARE

To this day, Mindanao's craftsmen continue to manufacture gongs, jewel boxes, betel nut boxes, brass beds and cannon replicas. **Ermita**'s tourist belt area hawks a fair amount of brassware.

WOOD CARVING

Giant hardwood carvings of the mountain-dwelling Ifugao were among the first local items that the Americans brought home. What they missed were other, more fascinating items, such as carvings of the rice granary god (*bulol*) and the animal totems from Palawan that can now be found in the Ermita tourist belt. Visit the woodcarving village in **Baguio**, or make your way through the Central Cordillera, especially **Banaue**.

Where to Buy

HANDICRAFTS

Balikbayan Handicrafts
290–298 Palanca Street, Quiapo
Tel: 02-734 9040
3F Market! Market!
Fort Bonifacio, Taguig
Tel: 02-886 7798, 886 7813
Alabang Town Center Expansion
Tel: 02-842 1661, 842 5376
1010 Arnaiz, Makati
Tel: 02-893 0775 to 77
Kayumanggi Arts and Crafts
Ninoy Aquino Avenue, Parañaque
Tel: 02-820 6916

Shopping Malls in Manila

Shopping malls abound in Metro Manila, most offering daily air-conditioned comfort (10am–8pm) and reasonable prices for the foreign visitor. Near the airport, visit the **Duty Free Fiesta Mall** and **Duty Free Philippines**. Just north, in the Malate–Ermita tourist belt, are **Robinson's Place** and **Harrison Plaza**, on Mabini Street. North of the Pasig, check out the flea market-esque **Tutuban Center**, in the heart of **Divisoria market**, or **SM Shoemart Manila** (81 C Palanca Street, Quiapo).

Quezon City's shopping options range from **Araneta Center** – including **Ali Mall** and **SM Shoemart** – in Cubao to **Isetann Shopping Mall** (C.M. Recto corner Quezon Boulevard). South, in San Juan, the **Greenhills Shopping Center** stands along Ortigas Avenue, with pearls available at **Virra Mall**, and many restaurants nearby. In Mandaluyong City, Philippines' largest mall, **SM**

Silahis Center
744 General Luna Street, Intramuros
Tel: 02-527 2111
Also at LRI Plaza N. Garcia Street, Makati
Tel: 02-898 2125
Alabang Town Center
Tel: 02-842 1505
One-stop shopping for handicrafts.

ANTIQUES

Jo-Liza Antique Shop
664 Jose Abad Santos, Little Baguio, San Juan
Tel: 02-725 8303, 725 8151
MegaMall tel: 02-635 3013
Alabang tel: 02-807 2256
Grandma's Gallery
206 M. Paterno Street, San Juan
Tel: 02-724 4293, 723 3736
Call for appointment.
Goldcrest Village Square and **Glorietta 4**
Ayala Center, Makati. Several antiques vendors.

Megamall, is located on EDSA. Other area malls include the upscale **Shangri-La Plaza Mall**, **Rustan's** and **Crossings Department Store**.

In Makati, **Ayala Center** includes department stores such as **Landmark**, **SM Shoemart** (soon to be relocated to Fort Bonifacio) and **Rustan's**. **Greenbelt Shopping Complex** and **Makati Cinema Square** (with its indoor firing range) round out the list of regular malls, while the upscale boutiques of **6750 Ayala Avenue** carry internationally known brands.

The **SM Mall of Asia**, built in Pasay at the end of EDSA, is the largest mall in the country and sixth largest in the world.

Southwards, the residential community of Ayala Alabang in Muntinlupa City offers the **Ayala Town Center**, **Festival Mall** (Corporate Avenue corner Civic Drive, Alabang) and **SM Southmall**.

ART & PHOTO CREDITS

Picture Spreads

Maps Berndtson & Berndtson Productions

© 2007 Apa Publications GmbH & Co. Verlag KG (Singapore branch)

INSIGHT GUIDE SOUTHEAST ASIA

Cartographic Editor **Zoë Goodwin**
Production **Caroline Low**
Design Consultants
Klaus Geisler, Graham Mitchener
Picture Research **Hilary Genin**

Indonesia

a – f

g – k

l – r

Laos/Cambodia

Singapore

Thailand